11/3
071⁹
150-
PRCE
W9-CJD-030
05-

07724
STRAND PRICE
$ 5.00

Will H. Hays

WILL H. HAYS

THE MEMOIRS
OF
WILL H. HAYS

DOUBLEDAY & COMPANY, Inc.
Garden City, New York
1955

The Master, by Thomas Curtis Clark, used by permission of Mrs. Thomas Curtis Clark.

Library of Congress Catalog Card Number 55–8402

Copyright ©, 1955, by Doubleday & Company, Inc.
All Rights Reserved
Printed in the United States
at
The Country Life Press, Garden City, N.Y.
First Edition

Foreword

I T W A S because of the peculiar character of my professional life, dealing so largely with mass movements and popular forces—like those in national politics and in international motion pictures—that the publishers of this volume asked me to set down some of these experiences and observations, with my personal interpretation of some of the changes that have taken place. They seemed to feel that such a recital, telling a story that leads from Sullivan, Indiana, around the world and back, might shed light on some of the ways in which public opinion and public action may be directed into wholesome channels.

Perhaps the greatest lesson I have learned is that *it is possible to change public opinion, to marshal it behind constructive projects* like woman suffrage or clean movies. Two indispensable factors are a sound plan and a vigorous organization for winning the co-operation of right-thinking men and women. One of the surest, simplest policies is always to *seek points of agreement,* not points of difference. These convictions I have voiced over and over in such slogans as "Things don't happen—they are brought about"; and "Whatever ought to be done is doable."

I have no corner on such a philosophy of life. It has animated the whole vigorous pioneering spirit of millions of Americans. Perhaps it seemed to burn with unusual fervor in such sections as the Midwest "Valley of Democracy," where faith in our homes, our friends and neighbors, our state, our nation, and our God seemed as natural as the air we breathed.

Years ago I wrote a magazine article entitled "I Learned a Lot from the Folks Back Home." This book tries to tell the story—or many stories—of how I have seen this typically American philosophy of life at work. In a real sense, it is the story of thousands of men and women with whom it has been my privilege and joy to associate, through more than half a century, in projects that seemed to us worth while.

In the preparation of the book I have had the aid and advice of many good friends. For their valued counsel and assistance I thank Dirrelle E. Chaney, Wythe Williams, and Fred Niblo, Jr. For the actual marshaling and arrangement of the material, special thanks go to my "operations officer" in the enterprise, Ernest B. Chamberlain.

W. H. H.

CONTENTS

PART ONE...

... Youth

CHAPTER I

From Generation to Generation

PERSONALITIES, rather than events, form my earliest memories: my mother and father first of all, of course then Grandfather and Grandmother Cain—my mother's people—who lived nearby in a town generally regarded as the oldest settlement in that part of the United States, next to Vincennes.

I was born in Sullivan, Indiana, on November 5, 1879. That was sheer luck on my part, for the stork was flying fast that morning and I was almost born on the Evansville & Terre Haute Railroad. My mother had been visiting her family in Carlisle—ten miles south—and barely made the grade that early November day. I never did hear how she got home from the depot. All I know is that Dr. Hinkle presided at the ceremony. Dr. Hinkle—James R. was the rest of his name—was a family doctor out of the storybooks, who prefaced every examination from earache to broken bone with, "H'm, let me see your tongue!" My parents had such affection for the good doctor that they named my younger brother after him—Hinkle Cain Hays.

Ours was a neighborhood of real Hoosier homes. And they were Christian homes. That is the essence of the environment that shaped my boyhood. From such fountains flowed the influences that shaped the life of a nineteenth-century boy whose ties still bind him to an Indiana town. That was the conviction underlying the story Ray Long asked me to write for *Cosmopolitan* in 1926—"I Learned a Lot from the Folks Back Home." And that same conviction is the key to the longer life story which forms this book.

There are many ways in which one might try to define a religious home, but to me it is a thing of the spirit. Our home had the kind of spiritual "air conditioning" in which it was a joy to live. I never heard a harsh or angry word pass between my father and my mother. Father's way of life—his work in court and in his office, and all his efforts for the benefit of our town—seemed to me very good, even if a bit strenuous. And my mother was beloved by everyone. During those earliest years it probably never occurred to me that people might not be good; the people with whom I lived were! It also never occurred to me that the world might not be a good world—even a wonderful place; the part of it that I knew seemed so! This belief in people I owe to my home and to my neighbors.

Sunday was a day of rest. Work done on Sunday, Mother would say, brought no reward. Father was not so strict and would occasionally take us out late Sunday afternoons in summer—driving Frank, the bay horse —to eat a watermelon in the open country at the edge of town. A few church members criticized him, and Mother suffered some inner conflict about it.

But there was no sign of the repressions and inhibitions we hear so much about from Freudian critics of nineteenth-century American life. Though my home was religious, it was in no sense puritanical or severe. I can't remember ever being punished, though there must have been plenty of times when I could have been! My father—unlike my mother, who had the sweetest nature I have ever known—had quite a temper.

To both Father and Mother, the Christian life meant the Ten Commandments, self-discipline, faith in time of trouble, worship, the Bible, and the Golden Rule—all of which I am sure we might well practice more fully today.

My mother's character is indicated by the fact that not until I was fairly well grown did I discover that my two elder sisters were actually half sisters—Father's children by a previous marriage. My mother made no distinction between us that I could ever discern.

How well I remember my grandfather Cain and my quiet, capable grandmother. William Henry Cain, a teacher and preacher, was known and respected throughout the region. I remember him—with his gray hair and deftly trimmed gray beard—as a gentle and most benign person. Early ordained as a minister in the Methodist Church, he became an inspiring preacher. His wide culture and deep religious feeling transfused his sermons and the occasional poems he wrote. By the time I became conscious of his work, he was superintendent of schools in Carlisle and held in the highest esteem by the whole community.

My grandmother, Nancy Duncan Cain, was recognized as a woman of sterling character, simple of heart and retiring in manner, yet with great dignity and poise. To me, the marvel was her unlimited capacity for baking biscuits! And as I look back, it occurs to me that her apparent diffidence was deceptive. For there was no question as to who ran the household.

Her younger daughter, my aunt Sally Cain, was a character. She was a woman of exceptional energy and, occasionally, of explosive force. She had taught school since she was sixteen and she went right on until she was seventy. I remember that she had an effective piece of apparatus at school—a switch always standing in the corner of the room. "Spare the rod and spoil the child" was then still in fashion.

The Cains lived in a two-story house as austere as a monument, with no porch in front and no outbuildings except a smokehouse and one of those outer conveniences once described as "open plumbing, openly arrived at." The back yard was big enough for a few peach trees and plum trees, with scattered vegetable patches. The interior of the house, typical of the period, had a parlor with canonical horsehair upholstery on carved walnut frames, a Bible on the center table, and artificial flowers under a glass globe. Canonically, too, the room was kept shut all winter, and during the rest of the year the shades were generally drawn.

The frequent family expeditions to Carlisle were always exciting, since they began with a carriage ride to the depot and ended with a drive in a hack from the Carlisle station to the Cain home. My room was always the one on the second floor—the one that had the feather bed. That bed was a real experience! It was so soft and thick that when I was dropped in the middle of it I could hardly see over the sides. I remember it was always very cold at first, and then very warm—almost too warm, except in bitter weather.

The Cain house played a large part in my early boyhood, and I have preserved a substantial memento of it. In the back yard of our home in Sullivan there is a slab of brown sandstone—about four and a half feet long and eighteen inches wide—which had served as the single step leading to the front door of Grandfather's house. It now serves as a garden seat, supported by two blocks of hard white stone taken from the front steps of my father's house, where I was born. The feature about this stone step which made an indelible impression on me was the freak cone-shaped hole near one end—to a little boy quite inexplicable. Into this hole, I remember, I would put my finger, trying to figure out what in the world had made it so smooth. As a simple matter of fact, the hole had been made by the repeated dripping of water from a point in the roof; but it was much later that I learned the lines, "Little drops of water, Little grains of sand . . ."

Looking back, I believe that there were many such practical experiences in that slower-moving time that taught us lessons in patience and contemplation.

The house where I was born—near the center of Sullivan—was a one-story frame structure, two rooms wide and four rooms deep, with an extension containing the kitchen and the woodshed. It was not much to look at, but it had a big yard with a barn at the lower end and a horse pasture beyond. The house went through a colossal transformation while I was still very little. There wasn't enough room in it for all of us when Martha and Bertha—my half sisters—were at home with us. Father's income was growing a little, in spite of the hard times that gripped the country during most of the eighties—so an engineering project, unprecedented in Sullivan, was undertaken. The front part of the house was detached from the rest and moved back down the lot and around the barn—to become a very comfortable residence on Thompson Street, directly behind our home; there my grandparents and my aunt Sally lived after Grandfather Cain retired. Between the garden on our lot and their back yard there was a fence with a gate in it—but the gate was never closed! The new structure, built on what remained of our house, had a wide porch and such other "extravagances" as the taste of the day dictated. I liked it.

Our yard gave me plenty of room to kick up my heels, but it was only when I got old enough to handle a lawn mower that I realized how big it was. I didn't know there was so much grass in the whole country as I was expected to mow once a week! In addition to the yard itself there was a strip between the sidewalk and the curb eight feet wide—called, for some reason or other, "the lawn"—which I always mowed last, having learned by happy experience that when Father came home early from the office on Saturdays and found "the lawn" still shaggy he would mow it himself.

But the yard had compensations, including a couple of apple trees, a croquet set, a swing, and a hammock—all of which attracted the children of the neighborhood. In summer vacations, when we could not arrange a picnic anywhere else, we occasionally organized one in our own back yard.

To me, our street—West Washington Street—is one of the most beautiful residential streets in the world. The maple trees, gradually greening in spring with the slightest touch of color, deep green in summer, golden brown and rich red in the fall, are a picture. It is a street of homes and memories. Our family's livelihood was made possible by the work at one end of the street; our daily life centered in the homestead three blocks away; it ended on the edge of town, in Center Ridge Cemetery, where my father and mother, my sister Martha, my grandfather and grandmother Cain, and my aunt Sally are buried.

When I think of my father I remember him with a cigar in his mouth and a match behind his ear. He was a prodigious worker, busy every day and all day, frequently going back to his law office after supper; and he smoked as hard as he worked. I don't remember Mother ever objecting, and when I would see her brush the ashes from his coat and clean up the library table, it seemed to me that she really loved to see him enjoy anything the way he did his cigars.

But so far as I was concerned, she had other views. She make a deal with me when I was very young that if I would not smoke, chew, or drink until I was twenty-one she would give me a hundred dollars— quite a contract for the little lady to make. I made the bargain and kept it. But the day I was twenty-one I got a big trick cigar—much bigger than the ones Father smoked—and took it home; calling Mother, I sat down in Father's favorite chair in the corner of the library. I lit the cigar and took a couple of puffs, with Mother sitting there, not knowing what was going to happen. Then I put it out. Those two puffs were my first and last.

When I recall that Indiana was not ready for statehood until 1816 and that my grandfather was born in 1818, I realize that one has to go back only to the third and fourth generation to cover the whole history of our midwestern civilization. Feeling that this is a common heritage worth assaying as a background of my own story, I have been looking back into our Indiana history to see what light it might shed.

Our own family lines—in their origins and their successive migrations —were typical of many families who settled in what has been so often called "The Valley of Democracy." I like to recall that one of my Hoosier friends, the late Meredith Nicholson, gave that title to one of his books. And with justice! For I believe that the varied stocks and strains, cultures and faiths that settled the Middle West developed as co-operative, as honestly democratic a way of life as is to be found anywhere in the world.

If we Hoosiers are accused of provincialism, we don't apologize. We love to talk about our native state. We agree with the opinions voiced by Josiah Royce in his *Philosophy of Loyalty:*

We need . . . in this country, a new and wiser provincialism . . . the sort of provincialism which makes people want to idealize . . . their own province; to hold sacred its traditions, to honor its worthy dead. . . . Further centralization of power in the national government, without a constantly enriched and diversified provincial consciousness, can only increase the estrangement of our national spirit from its own life.

Most of us in America are content to look back two or three generations. Being a nation built by immigrants and settlers, we are chiefly interested in how our own family came to be what and where it is, and in how our fathers and grandfathers lived and worked. Perhaps this is especially true in the great stretches of our country that weren't even settled until the nineteenth century.

My mother's parents I of course knew well; Grandfather Cain lived until I entered college, and Grandmother six years longer. When I was a boy, the name Cain took on glamor because the family had come originally from the Isle of Man, lying in the middle of the Irish Sea. A look at the map seems to make this thirty-mile-long isle the focal point of the families to which I trace back. For records and traditions have them coming also from Scotland, from England, and from Ireland. And one of my mother's lines—the Voorhees family—from across the Channel in Holland. I am sure this is a typical American story, duplicated thousands of times.

That the Hays family of Indiana stems from sturdy Scotch-Irish emigrants—many of whom came early in the eighteenth century to Virginia through the port of Philadelphia—is evidenced by the census records of 1850 for Beaver County in southwestern Pennsylvania. My father was certainly Scotch-Irish in physical characteristics. Here is the first statement that my grandfather, Harrison Hays, was born in Virginia, May 22, 1818, and his wife, Elizabeth Rowles, in Ohio on July 7, 1824. Suggesting early pioneering by the clan, the 1790 census of Washington County, Pennsylvania (part of which formed the later Beaver County), shows both a John Hays and a William Hays living there.

Further listings in the 1850 census show four of the early children: James, six; John, five (my father); Margaret Ann, two; and Jacob, six months. At this time Harrison Hays (his given name is my middle name) was a farmer in Black Hawk, South Beaver Township, about seven miles north of the Ohio River and three miles east of the Ohio state line. And here he remained until about 1859, when—now with a family of eight children—he crossed over into Ohio, settling in Middletown Township of Columbiana County, in the farming district of Achor, near Negley, where he is buried. I prize the photographs of the stone shafts bearing his name. And, most of all, a photostat of pages in their big family Bible—starting with a record of their marriage on February 9, 1843, followed by the names and birth dates of their *twelve* children, from 1844 to 1865. All these births, plus two of the deaths—and several of the eleven marriages recorded on separate pages—are almost surely in Harrison's Spencerian handwriting. If so, there is indication that he was a man of some education. This seems to be borne out by the fact that at least three of five sons who grew to manhood went to college—two of them taking honors at Mount Union College, Alliance, Ohio, which fortunately was not over thirty-five miles from home.

From many historical records we know that Hays families, under several spellings, were well represented among early settlers here in America, both Catholic and Protestant, the first coming by the middle of the seventeenth century. Some had reached Pennsylvania from Ireland by 1728. They have spread into all of the forty-eight states. There is considerable evidence that the root family was originally French, and Huguenot, but that they settled and were naturalized in England and Ireland. In this country the name Hays frequently appears among the early settlers in New Jersey, from which whole bands of families moved out to the "Red Stone" country in southwestern Pennsylvania, where Grandfather lived. They loved to move along.

Similarly, the Rowles family was early found in New Jersey, Maryland, and Virginia, and later in Pennsylvania and Ohio—states growing rapidly during the middle of the nineteenth century.

Life in the Midwest in the 1850s was calculated to kill or cure. Not a few children died in infancy, but many of those who lived developed remarkable toughness of fiber and firmness of character. I saw it in my father. His youngest sister used to tell her son how the whole family walked to church—*six miles and back*—summer and winter, when he was a boy on the farm.

In my maternal line, as I have said, the Cains go back to the Isle of Man; the Duncans—the family of my mother's mother—to Scotland. My grandmother, Nancy Duncan Cain, born December 8, 1824, in Stark County, Ohio, was the daughter of John Mason Duncan and Catherine Voorhees, both of Pennsylvania. Here again we strike a family name— Voorhees—that goes through a great variety of spellings, many of them doubtless growing out of mere slips or personal preferences.

Grandfather Cain was the son of Robert Peak Cain, born in Massachusetts in 1784, who died January 13, 1854, in Illinois—the year after his son was ordained to the ministry. Robert had earlier lived in Albany, New York, and in Ohio. His wife—born also in Massachusetts, in 1799 —was Abigail Washburn. His father was Thomas Cain, believed to have been born about 1750 in England, who served in our Revolutionary War and died in Massachusetts. His wife, Elizabeth Peak, was also English.

One could hardly ask for a family tree with more varied or more hardy branches. The fruitage of such branches, multiplied by the millions, is the America we know. More particularly, perhaps, it is the America into which I was born in southern Indiana in 1879.

We Hoosiers are very conscious of our history. It is interwoven with the whole romance of the "Northwest Territory," opened to colonization by the Ordinance of 1787. The story is as full of Indians and hunters, log cabins and flatboats, itinerant preachers and judges, as a "Western" movie is of horses, cattle, and wide-open spaces. Vincennes, our neighbor to the south, has lived under four flags: Spanish, French, British, and American. The tides of empire swept over us, each living its memories.

During the latter half of the seventeenth century all of the country drained by the Mississippi and the Ohio rivers was added to the vast claims of the French Empire in the New World. In the effort to hold all of the country between the Mississippi and the Alleghenies against English aggression, the French established many posts to command rivers and outlets of trade.

The legends lingered. Whenever I went to Vincennes I was conscious that the fort—the site of the principal village of the Piankashaw Indians —dated from 1702. Sullivan County boys learned all that story young:

how the settlement, built up with the aid of French settlers from Canada who followed the lead of the daring pioneer, Sieur de Vincennes, became the first "European village" in Indiana—the land of the Indians! Jesuits, fur traders, British captains, colonial adventurers—all were part of this explosive frontier drama.

Until the close of the French occupation in 1763 the Vincennes region was part of the province of Louisiana. But with Wolfe's victory in Canada the English gained the upper hand, and the seat of government at Vincennes was nominally in London. By 1779, through the American Revolution and the conquests of George Rogers Clark, our territory became a part of Virginia, with our capital at Richmond. In 1784, after our lands had been ceded to the new federal government, the capital was in New York. In 1788 the practical administrative capital had been moved out to Marietta, the first settlement in Ohio; and in 1800, for the first time, it came within the limits of what was soon to become our state. You can see that we had experience with government very early! I suppose we shall never be able to get away from such cracks as: "While some are born writers, artists, and lawyers, and others work for a living, all Hoosiers are born politicians."

Undoubtedly the best-known chapter in our early history is that written by George Rogers Clark and his amazing little "army" which seized the territory for the new nation! He was the great defender of our earliest settlers. The hardships of his men and the brilliance of his campaigns have become legendary. He captured the posts of Kaskaskia and Vincennes in July of 1778, raising the American flag for the first time in Indiana. In 1783, by the Treaty of Paris, the territory became a part of the new American republic.

Special ordinances of 1785 and 1788 opened these lands—now embraced in Ohio, Indiana, Illinois, Michigan, and parts of other states—to the settlement of pioneer homemakers who formed the first big wave of continental expansion westward.

The first settlements in Sullivan County had been made near Vincennes, on lands obtained by a treaty made by the French with the Indians as early as 1742. By a land law of 1791, Congress made attractive provision for settlers: Four hundred acres of land were to be given to the head of any family living in the region in 1783, and one hundred acres to each man enrolled in the militia in 1790. These grants were known as "donations," "military donations," or "surveys."

In 1803 General William Henry Harrison—governor of the territory, and the first of the famous Harrisons to stand out in Indiana history—concluded a new treaty with the Indian tribes, which confirmed the earlier cession of 1742 and the "Old Indian Boundary" which ran across our county. The recorded settlements in Sullivan County date from this year of 1803, when James Ledgerwood pioneered in the vicinity of

Carlisle—the same Carlisle where my grandfather Cain lived when I was a little boy.

The big log-cabin home built by the Ledgerwoods, like those of other settlers, had literally to be their "castle"—a fort they could defend against Indian attacks. Made of the strongest timbers available, with a projecting upper story well provided with loopholes, such a "blockhouse" gave its defenders direct control of all approaches. Such a fort became a central gathering place for the entire neighborhood during times of danger. These pioneers were experts in the fine art of sticking together! Eleven families worked together in the construction of "Fort Haddon" in 1806.

Soon other things began to develop, for these settlers were people of culture and taste—and they didn't leave their "civilization" back East. The first Vincennes newspaper, which began publication in 1807, records the incorporation of the Wabash Baptist Church in that year.

The year of 1809 was even more significant. The first recorded political election—for representative of Knox County to the Territorial Legislature—was held, just twenty years after the establishment of the federal government. I like to recall that it was also in 1809, in similar backwoods surroundings and in a log cabin just like those in Indiana, that Abraham Lincoln was born. His father moved the family from Kentucky to Indiana in 1816, and then on to Illinois in 1830. Lincoln had a Hoosier boyhood.

Also in 1809 a new treaty with the Indian tribes extended the public domain to a point a dozen miles above Terre Haute, but the peaceful settlement of this region was delayed by Indian troubles stirred up by the War of 1812. General Harrison defeated the Indians in a decisive battle at Tippecanoe on the Wabash River—a pleasant meadow site I first enjoyed as a boy—which gave rise to the campaign slogan of 1840, "Tippecanoe and Tyler Too." Few slogans have been more prophetic, for Harrison died of pneumonia after only a month in the White House, and Tyler succeeded him.

These stories of pioneering and politics made a tremendous impression on me as a boy, because I knew Benjamin Harrison, General Harrison's grandson, and watched him play cards at our home in Sullivan. He was there in 1888, associated with Father on a famous lawsuit, just before his election as President of the United States. That made the early history of our State still more real.

By 1816 Congress felt that things in Indiana had "settled down" enough to admit us as a state. More land was under cultivation, the Swiss were growing grapes on the hill slopes along the Ohio, and a traveler of that day noted the "fine farms," the gristmills, and the "corn of uncommon luxuriance." The opening of one coal mine was reported, with the coal "showing near the surface"—a description sounding very natural to one raised in southern Indiana.

Sullivan County, like other early counties, proceeded to organize itself as rapidly as possible, with amusing concern over the location of the future county seat. A historian of Sullivan County states that there was "considerable speculative activity in the promotion of town sites which . . . would be in a position to bid for the privilege of becoming the county seat." This prospect stimulated the early growth of Carlisle, where the first sales of lots occurred in June of 1815. The organization of the county—in 1816—practically ended acquisition by claim; all available land was then put up at public sale.

One story about Carlisle always intrigued me: tradition maintained that court was often held in the open air under a big beech tree. As a little boy already planning to be a lawyer, I thought that would have been great fun. One of the commonest causes of suit was non-payment of taxes—small as they were. A gauge of prices is found in the fact that whiskey sold at seventy-five cents a gallon!

Something that puzzled me as a boy was that while we were strongly "Union" as a state—with members of the G.A.R. looked up to almost with reverence—so many of the ancestors of these veterans had originally come from the South. Apparently the majority of our earliest settlers came from Virginia and Kentucky, which is perfectly natural, since southern Indiana is straight west of Virginia. As a matter of record, Augusta County, Virginia, organized as early as 1745, originally embraced the present states of West Virginia, Kentucky, Ohio, Indiana, and Illinois. Early records also show a considerable number of Hays families who settled in Virginia—moving westward as the country grew.

Precisely the same thing happened in the case of other families, like the Haddons from Virginia. Captain Jesse Haddon, who made such an impression on me as a youngster, had led a company in the Civil War and never shed the picturesque look of the cavaliers. To his dying day he wore long, flowing hair, a wide-brimmed cowboy type of hat, and carried two huge "six-shooters"—by what permission, I never knew.

There were many other well-known families in our own region, with not a few picturesque names that reminded one of earlier origins: Baileys from Kentucky; Baslers from Switzerland; Bedfords from South Carolina; Corbins and Calverts from Virginia; DePauw, for whom the university was named; Estabrooks from Vermont; the Hokes, who were Pennsylvania Dutch, and on and on.

Perhaps best known of all, because a direct descendant was our family doctor, was the Hinkle family. The doctor used to tell me stories about Philip Hinkle, who came to Sullivan County from Kentucky in 1819. His father, Nathan Hinkle, a hero of the Revolutionary War, spent his last years in our county. Long afterward a monument was erected to him and to others buried in Sullivan County who had fought in the Revolution. It made a great impression on me that the old man had voted from the very beginning of our national government! "Doc" told how he had taken a keen interest in every election until he was a very old man, when he had to be assisted to the ballot box. When he died, in 1848, he lacked only half a year of being a hundred years old.

These pioneer settlers, turning their backs on comforts, must have been some of the hardiest and most self-sufficient stock ever developed anywhere, at any time! And as to variety and quality of ore—French, Swiss, Dutch, English, Irish, Scottish, German; Northerner and Southerner; Catholic, Protestant, and Jew; Episcopalian, Baptist, Presbyterian, Quaker—the "melting pot" had it all to work on in our neck of the woods. I doubt whether any better-balanced American alloy—hard, tough, yet flexible—was produced anywhere on the continent than in our "Valley of Democracy." As I once said to the Indiana D.A.R. meeting at French Lick: "In a sense, Indiana is the heart of America. We are descendants of courageous and liberty-loving people. Physical hardships to early Americans were far less onerous than the despotism that crushes men's souls."

The marvel of this pioneer spirit was well put by Thomas J. Wolfe, writing in 1909 of our Sullivan County history:

> With a knowledge of the conditions of a century ago—the limitations of travel, the meagreness of information about distant localities, and the practical absence of all the facilities which now make communication both easy and rapid—it seems nothing less than remarkable that men living in the Old World and the settled states of the East should assume the risks and hardships of an emigration to the interior of America—there to found homes and spread the civilization of an older order.

It is because I believe so strongly that purposes and experiences like those shared by my ancestors and my neighbors are active forces in my own inheritance that I have wished to make them a part of this story. These hard Hoosier pioneers, who feared God but nobody else, strikingly personified the theme of a modern documentary film based on the Freedom Train. In that film the creation of our America was epitomized in these simple words:

> Free men, starting from scratch,
> were building the kind of
> world they wanted.

CHAPTER 2

My Hoosier Tradition

PREDESTINED as I was—coming from a staunch Presbyterian family—to start with a Hoosier heritage and to be vitally interested in politics all my life, I seem to have chosen a fortunate time to be born. There being little left of 1879 except Thanksgiving and Christmas, the new year threw us squarely into one of the hottest political fights of the generation.

During those two years, by intense state-wide activity on the part of a zealous committee, the Republican party elected the complete Republican state ticket and sent General Benjamin Harrison to the United States Senate.

After the nomination of James A. Garfield and Chester A. Arthur by the Republican National Convention in June, the Indiana organization "determined that the effort to redeem the state from the Democratic misrule in 1880 should be made." It is also recorded that "the national committee saw that the election of Garfield and Arthur depended on Republican success in Indiana, established headquarters for the West at the Denison House in Indianapolis, and cordially and unreservedly co-operated throughout the campaign with Chairman New and the State Central Committee. Speakers without number were put on the stump to second the masterful work of Governor Porter." As a result, Indiana returned a good majority in November for Garfield and Arthur.

Years later I was proud to learn that my father had been secretary of the Sullivan County organization in that campaign. I also like to think that the campaign of 1880 must have revived the enthusiasm that had been aroused by the Abe Lincoln Rally held in Sullivan in 1860. The picturesque feature of that earlier event was a team of twenty-one head of oxen drawing a huge flat wagon on which a group of rail splitters were at work!

Reading the files of the Sullivan *Union* for 1880, when the official census gave Sullivan a population of 2,166, I found several minor events of significance in one way or another. One item read: "Dr. Crowder's boys raised a 75-foot Garfield-and-Arthur Pole." This custom of pole-raising was one of the big features of a political campaign. That same year appears to have brought the first electric lights to Sullivan when the W. W. Coles Circus illuminated its tents by this novel method.

Two events I think are worth mentioning: the first is a dispatch which appeared in the Sullivan *Union* of January 7, 1880:

Petersburg, Va., Dec. 30: One hundred and seventeen colored emigrants from Goldsboro, N.C., arrived this morning en route for Indianapolis, via Washington. The emigrants, consisting of men, women and children, are under charge of the General Passenger Agent of the Baltimore & Ohio Railroad. Several hundred others are to follow.

Apparently this was the first of many such parties, and it formed the nucleus of the thousands of Negroes in Indianapolis, who frequently proved to be an uncertain factor in subsequent elections.

Perhaps the most exciting local incident was a genuine explosion. Captain W. T. Crawford, one of our best citizens, was manufacturing what he called a "Hyperian Illuminator," using kerosene and some other ingredients which he claimed would make the fluid non-explosive. Apparently he was wrong. His young son, Webster, punched a hole in the tank containing the mixture and touched a match to it. The tank exploded, wrecked the blacksmith shop adjoining, and knocked out every tooth in Webster's head. This story was told to a lot of boys growing up in Sullivan as a warning against trying to bite off more than they could chew.

But neither young Webster nor any of us starting to grow up in the eighties could by any stretch of the imagination have pictured the wonders that were to come "in our time": the endlessly increasing marvels of electricity; the omnipresent auto, at which a neighbor, Jerry Lockwood, had tried his hand in 1877—putting together a cumbersome contraption weighing fifty-five hundred pounds, powered by a steam engine, which broke down in the streets of Sullivan and had to be hauled away by four horses; the "safety" bicycle, which was soon to be the companion of all of us; the motion picture, on which feeble experiments were just getting under way—later resulting in a world-wide art industry destined to absorb my attention through twenty-five years; the radio and the airplane—as yet unknown.

In our lifetime we have seen the population of our nation more than double, its industry and activities pyramid, its relations with the world encircle the whole globe. We could not know it then, but we were born at a wonderful time.

It's a hard thing to draw an exact line between what I actually remember and what I was told but heard so often that it now seems real. As I have already said, I certainly remember a good deal about our first home and the things in the yard; my velocipede; my visits to Grandmother Cain's—and her biscuits and feather bed; our bay horse, Frank;

Sunday school and watermelons! But with remarkable clearness, at least five pictures stand out in my mind—each one connected with something that developed into a lifelong interest or conviction.

My first "speech" in public seems to have been made when I was four, on a program arranged by our Sunday school. I have never been able to forget the words:

> Full four years have rolled away
> Since these little eyes beheld the day,
> These little feet have learned to walk,
> This little tongue has learned to talk,
> And this little speech I've learned to say,
> Now, Ladies and Gentlemen, I bid you good day.

I doubt whether that first speech changed any votes, but perhaps it didn't have to.

The second clear memory is of the presidential campaign of 1884, when I was five. I saw James G. Blaine, the Republican candidate, when he came through our town on a speaking tour during his campaign against Grover Cleveland. Tradition has it that he was introduced by one of our local worthies as "the peer, if not the equal, of any citizen in America." At the age of five I was interested only in my uncle Jeff's success in keeping me up on his shoulder, above the heads of the crowd milling around the rear platform of the special train.

The third picture is of a very wet and very dark thunderstorm that broke suddenly one late afternoon when I was starting to lead the cow home from pasture. This daily chore I was doing for a neighbor—at a salary that may have been twenty-five cents a week. The rain came in such torrents that I didn't know what to do. But the cow did! She lay down, with her head calmly facing the storm, to "sit it out." Not wanting to leave her, I lay down beside her, getting what protection I could from the rain, waiting and shivering. After what seemed a long time to those waiting for me at home, they came looking for me.

From this incident my aunt Sally drew quite a text on the value of seeing a job through. Years later, when I resigned from the Cabinet as Postmaster General—to head the Motion Picture Producers and Distributors of America—she proclaimed with disapproval that it was the first time I had not "stuck with the cow."

Fourth, I see a little desk my father gave me that same year—I think—of which I became uncommonly proud. That desk can now be found in the attic of my Sullivan home. Inside it there is an imposing-looking volume which I believe is *Hubbell's Legal Directory*; it should properly be considered the first book I acquired for my law library. On the front of the desk still appears the sign I painted there—"Judge Willie Hays."

The last picture is one I saw nearly every afternoon. I still remember

sharply the thrill of seeing Father come home from his law office while
it was still daylight. The children playing outside would run to greet
him, hanging onto his arms and his hands and even his coattails—professional men wore Prince Alberts to business in those days—until he
got to the house. He belonged to them all somehow, and they belonged
to him. That was Father; and that, too, was Sullivan, and a thousand
towns like it in our America of those remote eighties.

The way I was brought up I could not have imagined a town without churches any more than I could have imagined one without homes
and schools, without horses and wagons and stores. My father was a
"pillar of the church." And Captain Crawford, the Sunday-school
superintendent, was to my young eyes almost as imposing as the minister. To me, they were very great figures; there was authority in their
very presence.

Captain Crawford was one of the real personages of our town. For
years he made our Sunday school a force in the community. He was
tall and straight as an arrow, with snow-white hair and ruddy complexion. He had a mustache but no beard. He had been a captain in the
Civil War at an early age; he kept his military bearing and maintained
the right to be regarded as a captain in any situation for which he was
responsible. He was highly respected. His principal business was looking
after the procurement of pensions and their collection for the veterans
or their families. He frequently interjected in his Sunday-school talks
something about the Civil War.

He was always a leader in the fights for temperance in our community.
When I have thought about my own feeling on the subject, I have
wondered whether Captain Crawford's continual rubbing it in was not
a causative factor in my own abstinence.

When I went to church I am sure I did not appreciate that we were
worshiping in one of the historical landmarks of Sullivan: that our little
building had been put up in 1861 through the sacrifices of a small group
of Presbyterians who had founded the organization in 1857 with only
sixteen members. The initial cost of the building had been only seventeen hundred dollars! But we worshiped in that sturdy edifice, with its
heavy oak timbers and solid framework, until 1907. The picture of that
church—roughly seventy-five by forty feet, with its parsonage on the
same lot—is as vivid to me as the Empire State Building in New York
or the Capitol in Washington.

In the semi-centennial year of 1907 a committee, of which Father was
a member, was appointed to raise the sum of fifteen thousand dollars
for a new and larger church—"modern in every respect." A newspaper
story in 1908 announced: "The building will be built of Bedford stone
and brick. The basement will be fitted for a dining room, storeroom, and
lavatories." And all at fifteen thousand dollars! Just twenty years later—

at the General Assembly of the Presbyterian Church held that year in San Francisco—I had the honor of announcing, as chairman of the Laymen's Committee, the completion of a national pension fund of fifteen million dollars!

My family, on both sides, was closely connected with the early development of schools in Sullivan County. During the early seventies Grandfather Cain, Aunt Sally, and my father taught in Ascension Seminary, our strongest independent school. One of Father's students was Mary Cain, eventually to become my mother. And the whole story is interesting to me because it parallels so much of the educational development of our country.

Some glimpses into the quaint school life of the day came to me when I ran across a little book used as an account and memorandum book by Grandfather Cain or Aunt Sally—or both. It is a small, well-preserved, leather-bound volume put out by "Field, Leiter & Co." in Chicago in 1871 as their spring catalogue. A line cut shows an imposing six-story building, now long known as Marshall Field's, at the same corner— State and Washington streets. The blank "Memorandum" pages had been used for various notations, such as definitions of rare words used in the classroom; a description of the sphenoid bone; a sermon outline on the theme "Put on Christ"; a table of measures; spelling of difficult words, and so on.

One of the most interesting pages gives a list of subjects which apparently formed a part of the curriculum: "Reading, Physiology, Orthography, Penmanship, Analyses, History, Arithmetic, Physical Geography."

The following entries would seem to be Grandfather's:

Mother's dress . . .	$1.92½
Trimmings	.20
Thread	.07½
	$2.20

Similar figures for Mary's dress were $1.92½; also, "My shirts, $1.00; Bosoms, $.65—total, $1.65."

Another entry: "Tuition due for Spring term" from various pupils ran from $1.50 to $3.00—or $6.00 at the most. And finally: "Amount earned 1st month—$45.00."

Until after the Civil War the educational facilities in Indiana were very limited, except in the cities and larger towns. One early attempt to conduct "county seminaries" was short-lived. Sullivan's lasted from 1843 to 1851. The income from the portion of the taxes which in those earlier days could legally be devoted to schools was almost nil. As a result, many small private schools took root wherever a teacher of exceptional faith and courage or a group of parents with a strong cultural background could accomplish this.

Such a situation developed in our county in 1861. In that year William T. Crawford—the same Captain Crawford who years later was my Sunday-school idol—then scarcely twenty-one years old, wholly on his own initiative opened a private school which he conducted in a small two-room cottage in Farmersburg. The little school grew so fast that he had to build a two-story building at his own expense. His methods of teaching were new and so far ahead of those practiced at the time in Sullivan County as to attract students immediately. The second term he had to divide his pupils into forenoon and afternoon groups.

But young Crawford soon enlisted, commanded Company H of the 85th Indiana, and did not return until 1865. Without delay he reopened his school, at once saw it grow, and secured two teachers to assist him. The school was now given the name of Ascension Seminary. It soon added a department for the training of teachers—something badly needed. From all accounts, including the testimony of my own father, Professor Crawford had that rare gift—the ability to impart his enthusiasm to others. The seminary was actually the pioneer normal school of Indiana, and its work inspired the erection of the State Normal School at Terre Haute. Those were the days when rural "district schools," held only a few months in the winter, were hard put to find teachers.

Professor Crawford's seminary had another remarkable influence. Between 1865 and 1872, when the enrollment of both boarding and day pupils had risen to the hundreds and more room was urgently needed, an interesting solution was found. The new Central School building at Sullivan being near completion, the school trustees persuaded Professor Crawford to take the superintendency of the town's graded schools and transfer Ascension Seminary to the upper floors of the new building. Here it went on for several years, giving their chief training to many of the men and women who became our leading citizens and who maintained a lifelong loyalty to their early teacher.

It wasn't too hard for a boy growing up in southwestern Indiana in the eighties to dream that he could hear the echoes of the settlers' axes and flails, the gunfire that preserved the Union, and the voice of the Great Emancipator. Lincoln has always been real to me. I saw men every Memorial Day in their blue uniforms and visored caps and with medals on their breasts; men whom I knew as our good neighbors; men who had fought under Lincoln only fourteen years before I was born. And the great reunions of the Grand Army of the Republic—held at the fairgrounds in midsummer, with the Carlisle Band and Mordecai Dix's fife and drum corps—were magnets which drew us irresistibly. And did I not hear the stories of the fifteen battles in which Company H, made up almost entirely of Sullivan County men, distinguished itself? Could anything arouse a stronger patriotism in little boys just beginning to learn of their country's past?

The signs of the pioneer struggle for survival in a new country were still all about us. As Mark Sullivan, who was born in 1874, says in his panoramic history, *Our Times*, he saw in his youth "many of the oldest ways of life" which were "still common": the corncrib; the ancient lantern with a candle inside; candle molds; early coal-oil lamps; the simplest farm tools, such as the flail, the treadmill, and the hand "cradle" for sowing wheat, oats, and rye. I can bear the same testimony and add plenty of items to the list.

All these things imprinted on my mind a respect for resourcefulness, for skill and adaptability, and for sheer hard work—a respect from which I have never been able to escape. For example, one of the most honored men in the Wabash Valley was the annual champion cornhusker. I remember one such champion "shucked" and delivered 231 bushels within ten hours. The merchants of our region were only too glad to put up prizes for such contests.

Among the familiar Hoosier customs were community picnics and celebrations. I can remember them as far back as I can remember anything. They seem to be peculiar to Indiana. Occasionally they are still held there in all their ancient glory. On the Fourth of July a great all-day picnic, with a prodigious lunch and moving oratory, was a fixture. So were the "old settlers' picnics," at a number of which I was later to make some of my earliest speeches. In all my experience these gatherings still set the high-water mark for warm group friendliness on a big scale. We didn't talk so much about democracy then—we didn't need to, it was all around us.

Special features, such as "old fiddlers' contests," added color and rhythm to those happy days. All these get-togethers helped to keep alive among our people a kind of neighborly hospitality that sometimes called out quite unexpected expressions from visitors.

Other traditions and sentimental associations clung to our woods and fields and streams. Paul Dresser, who once lived in Sullivan, made "The Banks of the Wabash" known to all America. To us who lived there, the river was bound up with our lives in many ways. There were romance and beauty in the very name. To the youngsters, there was spooky mystery in the stories of Civil War deserters who had hidden out for months along the river. And we loved to hear the tales of a band of desperadoes, headed by Paul Lindsay, who occupied an island in the Wabash just above Merom. This band committed robberies and even murders, and for years terrorized that part of Sullivan County as well as Crawford County in Illinois. Lindsay himself was shot to death about 1873 by a posse of our Sullivan County citizens who went to his island home to capture him. His body was never found and was believed to have been sunk in the river. Here were all the makings of a modern movie thriller!

Each spring we were intrigued by the arrival from all sections of the country of mussel-diggers and pearl-diggers. As the Merom newspaper put it: "In a short time the banks of the Wabash will be places of business instead of idle spots in which to sit and enjoy the warm rays of the sun."

One other phase of the river's life left an even deeper impression, because it so often struck home. Too many times the Wabash, swollen by spring freshets, would break through its levees at one point or another in our county. How well I remember the hurry-up calls and the hasty gathering of men with their teams, because Father was so often on a committee charged with the care and repair of the levees. Sometimes the county commissioners were involved, and occasionally the courts had to be invoked if a farmer refused to sell earth needed to make repairs. At other times the January thaws would bring on floods that would break through and damage thousands of acres. These emergencies and the awful power of water running wild loomed mighty big to me. Yes— "The River" was a real part of my life.

In a fairly recent historical sketch—I can't rceall whether it was in a film or on the radio—someone was asked: "What do you think Lincoln would counsel if he were to step into the midst of our present U.N. proceedings?"

"Patience," was the simple answer. *"Patience."*

If I have learned something about patience, I believe it was partly because I saw how long it took for things to develop from simple beginnings. Our Hoosier tradition was full of such instances. We could still see the landmarks of some of these early projects and we heard stories about them. Our county seat had moved three times before it finally settled in Sullivan. All our older friends could tell about the first railroad train that came through our town in 1854. The first coal mining in the county began in 1866. The first jail in Sullivan was built of logs—its site was still pointed out to us. The first public school was also a log structure. The first postmaster of Sullivan—Sanders M. Howard, appointed in 1842—is said to have served the community from his hat, passing out the mail to people as he met them on the streets, just as Lincoln did a few years later when he was a postmaster in Illinois. And yet, as Postmaster General in 1921, I was to head a department employing more than 325,000 people, the largest distributing organization in the world. Where could you find a better object lesson in slow, steady growth?

And men knew *quality* in those quieter days, especially when so much manufacturing was the work of master craftsmen whose pride lay in what they themselves could produce with their own hands. I remember Father saying that the best custom-made buggy cost between $150 and $200—and that in the days when $50 a month was a good salary. It still is in certain countries!

In 1882 our Sullivan Fire Department was organized, but it took two

or three experiments and a disastrous fire, wiping out half the west side
of the square, to arouse the town sufficiently to secure an adequate fire
engine.

In recent years I ran across a surprising description of railroading on
one of the minor lines in 1884 given by Charles Ackerman, who had
been a brakeman and line repairman on the old Indiana & Illinois Southern, now a part of the Illinois Central system. He told how he was
getting $45 a month for his services and was able to build a three-room
house at Switz City at a cost of $400. (No cipher is omitted at the end
of that last amount!) The house, he told us, "had two porches, a bow
window, and was completely furnished inside and out." Much of his
trading was done at a company store, on "orders" which took the place
of cash payments most of the time. "There were times when the company was six months behind on the pay roll."

But that wasn't all! Conditions of roadbed, bridges, and equipment
were so primitive that, as Ackerman said:

> We would leave home on our trip, never knowing when we would return.
> Many was the time when we would be out for a whole week on account of
> washouts and high water. . . . On one occasion we left Sullivan on a trip to
> Switz City and got into the ditch and lost all our train but the engine. . . .
> I have seen the passengers raise their umbrellas to keep the rain from them on
> some of the coaches we used at that time.

And all this when I was already five years old! I wonder how such accounts would sound to my fellow directors of the C.&E.I. Railroad today!

In other fields too—like law and politics—I have seen similar changes
from the more primitive and picturesque to the modern and allegedly
"efficient." Certainly the most picturesque politician in our county was
one of the commissioners, Louis O. Turnbull. A newspaper dispatch
from Vincennes described the phenomenon:

> That whiskers are a mark of wisdom is the thought uppermost in the minds
> of the officers at the courthouse whenever the trio of county commissioners
> from Sullivan happens to Knox on business. They are well known as the
> "Whiskered Commissioners," and are well deserving of their name. The two
> junior members of the board both wear beards of only ordinary length and
> show that, measured by the standard of county commissioners, they are only
> of ordinary quality.
> But the third member, Louis O. Turnbull, is proud of the fact that he
> wears the longest beard of any man in Sullivan County, a beard which per-
> haps cannot be equaled in the state. His beard, when allowed to hang down,
> reaches far below his knees. His skill in the art of hairdressing makes it un-
> noticeable, however, as in public he always wears the beard inside his shirt.

Going back a generation or more, stories of the old "circuit-riding
lawyers" made an indelible picture in my mind. According to the recol-

lection of an early settler, reprinted in our Sullivan *Union,* it was a rugged chapter:

> Our early lawyers considered the whole state as one vast circuit, which they traveled on horseback, sometimes alone and sometimes in squads.
>
> Their long rides on horseback, along blind paths and dimly defined roads, crossing unbridged streams, sleeping in the open air as they frequently had to do, and leading colts and driving steers home, taken on fees, fully developed their physical and intellectual energies and gave them a vigor and self-reliance possessed by few of the modern students.

Just one more "flashback" from the memory of another member of the original Hinkle family, who in 1904 recalled some of the flavor of the early Indiana days—and I like to believe that some of the tough fiber developed in those settlers lives on in the Hoosier tradition. He wrote:

> Talk about hard times! The younger generation can have no conception of what was endured by those pioneers of the West in those days. What little surplus could then be produced had no market in reach in which to sell anything for money. To raise the small amount required for taxes then was the study of the farmer for months before becoming due, and when the pittance was got together a horseback rider from the locality of Pleasantville to Merom, then the county seat, made a trip of more than 40 miles on horseback, over roads little better than cow paths to pay a tax of 75 cents up to $2.

In this chapter I have tried to jot down some of the early impressions —pictures of pioneering courage and resourcefulness, of the bonds that brought neighbors together for common purposes which they believed were for the good of all, of the early progress toward a fuller civilization —that I now realize must have entered into my blood, and into my mind and heart.

CHAPTER 3

From Six to Sixteen

M Y boyhood was very happy and very busy, even without auto, movie, or radio. There was little to prevent the Home, the Church, and the School from operating on me effectively. But beyond such influences, as I look back, there was scarcely a year from 1885 to 1896 when something novel was not happening. Those were anything but dull days.

I often wonder whether we youngsters drew quite so sharp a line between work and play as boys and girls do now. Certainly there were games, and there were such things as chores, but both going to school and leading the cow to pasture were fun! Probably I knew that riding my pony involved currying her and cleaning out her stall, though I admit to having persuaded my sisters to relieve me at this latter task more than once. Whether a declamation or a spell-down would be classified as work or play is beyond me. We managed to make a contest of nearly everything.

From first grade through high school I had all my work in the same Central School Building to which my grandfather, my father, and my aunt Sallie had come as teachers in 1872, when Captain Crawford's Ascension Seminary was affiliated with our public school system. Father had been co-principal until he resigned, to devote himself to the practice of law.

About my first years of school I have one painfully clear picture. Being smaller and lighter than the other boys in the class, and not well equipped by nature for fisticuffs, I remember only too well how I would often go home the back way to avoid running into a bunch of boys who liked to fight and who thought I was a good target. More than once the boy who came to my rescue was the one colored boy in my room. His name was Licey Bosley, and he was a pretty tough bird with his fists, but a mighty good friend and protector.

My mother told me that Aunt Millie and Andy Bosley, Licey's mother and father, had been slaves near Nicholasville, Kentucky, prior to the Emancipation Proclamation. After Andy was set free, he served as a Union soldier to the end of the war. At its conclusion the Bosleys, with another Negro family from Kentucky, settled in Sullivan and engaged in the manufacture of brick. The story made quite an impression on me. Aunt Millie and Uncle Andy lived on as respected members of our community until the outbreak of World War I.

Another memory is connected with the town of Carlisle and with Grandfather Cain, for whom I had a respect bordering on reverence. Long since, I have found out that many people felt the same way about him. This time, when I was nine years old, Grandfather had arranged for me to come over and give a declamation at some evening event. The following day he reported to my mother that Willie had made a "very successful appearance" but that he was somewhat concerned over the boy's nervous reaction the day following, and he hoped my mother would watch my health very carefully. That must have been the first of many such expressions of concern over my health, which actually was always better than my frail appearance would indicate.

In those days the teachers in our Sullivan schools were people of standing in the community and had an important relationship to the families of their pupils. Frequently a teacher would be at our house for supper, and my two sisters and I would always be at the table. Although I had thought of a teacher as a pretty severe character, I changed my mind after Nan Wood told the following story at our table one night.

It seems that one of her new pupils, a little boy, had held up his hand and said, "Miss Wood, may I go to the privy?" This was a little too much for the teacher, who replied:

"Charlie, now wait a minute—you don't want to say it like that. Let's see what one would say." Addressing the whole class, she asked, "Children, under circumstances like that, what do you say in your house?"

One little boy was recognized and answered, "Miss Wood, in our house we say, 'May we go to Miss Jones's?' "

Another little boy said, "Miss Wood, we say, 'May we go out?' "

And then a little girl volunteered, "Why, Miss Wood, at our house we say, 'May we be excused?'—And oh, Miss Wood, don't you know, coming to school this morning, I saw the biggest dog excusing himself on our rosebush!"

That caused such laughter on the part of everyone, including Father, that thereafter I greatly admired Miss Wood and changed my opinion of teachers.

One historic celebration, which came during my last year in grammar school, impressed us all. Columbus Day in 1892 was a red-letter day because it marked the four hundredth anniversary of the discovery of America. Everything else was put aside and the schools united in a big affair. It was a great lesson in patriotism and in the recognition of a Providence that had reserved this land for our new nation.

The principles of "confidence and co-operation," which many years later I made the basis of my first appeal to the leaders of the motion picture industry, I seem to have begun practicing very early, in partnership with my chum and next-door neighbor, Davey Goodman. He and I engaged successively in at least three commercial projects. In all of them we had lots of fun and some profit.

A lemonade stand was our first venture. It usually stood between the two cedar trees in our front yard, close enough to the sidewalk to make it difficult for passers-by to escape our insistence. At one cent a glass this was about as painless and polite a form of holdup as two small boys could perpetrate. But it was only a tune-up for our more businesslike ventures.

For the life of me I can't remember how the sign painting started, but it lasted two or three years. The signs were painted on barns and fences in the neighborhood of Sullivan whenever we could talk farmers into the advantage of letting us advertise in nice bright colors the clothing that could be bought at Sol Goodman's store. Davey's father was the principal clothier in town and a lifelong friend of our family. At times this selling and painting campaign made school look like an avocation. The barns and fences near the old swimming hole in Buck Creek were painted almost solid!

The third job—printing—was a bit more professional. It was really a concession. Davey and I, with the unspoiled enthusiasm of our years, persuaded the officials of the county fair to give us the right to produce and sell the programs for the afternoon races and other daily events. Each day of the fair we had to ride out in the morning on our bicycles, get the entries for that afternoon, and ride back as fast as we could to get the lists to the printer. The entries went in the center of a four-page program already set up, which gave general information about the exhibits, an index showing in which building each exhibit was to be found, and advertisements of the local firms, the latter given to us as much because of our fathers as because of our persistence.

One day, riding pell-mell back to the fairgrounds with our racing sheets, my front wheel hit a big dog running across the road, and I took a header. When I came to in Dr. Hinkle's office, my only concern was what had happened to the programs.

One other occasional job was in quite a different category. I won my spurs as an organ pumper at our little Presbyterian church. In those days organs had no electric motor. A long handle, like that on an old-fashioned pump, had to be moved up and down hard enough and often enough to keep up good air pressure, indicated by a little gauge. Dwight McTir, the not too decorous son of the minister, was chief organ pumper and I—a little younger and small then, as always—was not quite up to steady labor at this distinguished job. But, being ambitious to qualify, I did my turn and still have in my possession a little membership card in the esteemed Guild of Organ Pumpers.

As I have said, we got a lot of play out of our work. Riding our bicycles was always fun, even when doing errands. I did a good deal of horseback riding, too, forming a habit kept up all my life. We had a good many picnics, and the very difficulty of getting over to the Wabash River, ten miles away, made it all the more an outing. Like most small-town boys, we swam and fished a lot and many boys did a good deal of hunting, for there was still plenty of game in season. There were neighborhood games, like hare-and-hounds, that have now been practically forgotten. And in school we were beginning to put on little plays about the same time George N. Cohan was making his first professional stage appearance.

But whatever we did here and there, life for a Sullivan boy in the eighties and nineties centered in his home to a degree impossible for a boy today to imagine. I learned things from Father and Mother that I could have learned nowhere else. One was the lesson of meeting people of all sorts and of learning something from them all.

Since Father's law practice took him all over the state, we had a good many visitors in our home. Often a visiting judge would come to the house in the evening to discuss some matter of legal interpretation with Father, whose opinion was held in high regard. Home and business never seemed far apart. Our house was only three blocks west of the square. This square—with Father's office on the northwest corner of Washington and State, where he had established it some years before I was born—was almost as much the center of our family life as it was of the town's. My habit of dropping in at his office started early.

Thinking of distinguished visitors whom I met as a boy, the two men who stand out are Robert Todd Lincoln, whom I believe I saw twice— once, I know, on our front porch—and Benjamin Harrison, whom I saw many times in 1888, the year he was elected President. That summer he spent several weeks in Sullivan as an attorney associated with Father and others in the prolonged trial of the most important case ever heard in our city. It concerned the will of a man named Wise; the testament was contested at great length but finally affirmed.

Mr. Harrison was the most distinguished man I had ever met. Father had explained—and I may have heard it in school, too—that he was the grandson of General William Henry Harrison of Virginia, first territorial governor of Indiana and conqueror of the Indians at Tippecanoe; and that his great-grandfather, Benjamin Harrison, had been one of the signers of the Declaration of Independence. That couldn't help leaving an impression: it brought our nation's history close to home.

One of my clearest recollections of President Harrison is of his desire to find me a pony. He and Father had talked it over, and he made the effort when he went back to Indianapolis to spend Sunday. When this failed, Father took up the search. I'll never forget the day when he first told me he had found at Bloomfield—the county seat of Greene County, where he practiced law a good deal because it was in our circuit—an Indian pony that he thought would be just right. One evening a little later, after he had been talking with Mother, he called me into their bedroom and told me Daisy was arriving the next day. That had me puzzled. But after keeping me in suspense long enough, Father told me that Daisy was the new pony. To get her over from Bloomfield, twenty-five miles away on the narrow-gauge railroad, seemed to us quite a project.

Just the year before Daisy arrived something happened—though no one could have been prophetic enough to see it—that was to play the leading role through more than a quarter century of my life. Edison took the first steps toward the motion picture. By 1887 he was working on the possibility of combining his new phonograph with small animated pictures. This dream was not fully realized until 1926, when I found myself literally the mouthpiece of an announcement that shook the cinema world with the force of a revolution: the talking motion picture had arrived!

Maxims were a real factor in the education of a nineteenth-century boy. Some were handed down orally. Many we memorized as we painstakingly wrote them over and over in our copybooks. But I was unusually fortunate. Just after my twelfth birthday Father gave me a "code" of rules for living which I know fixed some principles in my mind for keeps. He had clipped those rules from a magazine and had numbered them in the margin. He pasted the clipping on the flyleaf of my Bible, with a notation at the top:

A Code: Presented by his father to Master Willie Hays, Feb. 26, 1892, with a belief that it will be observed. Affectionately,

John T. Hays

That word "belief" got me: I was going to do my best to live up to Father's expectation. The two rules which he underlined in ink and which have been literally followed are these: *Drink no kind of intoxicating liquors,* and *Never speak evil of anyone.* Inside the Bible is another inscription:

To my dear nephew as a token of *love* from his Aunt Sally. "The fear of the Lord is the beginning of wisdom."

The complete code, which I still think deserves consideration, reads as follows:

1. Keep good company or none. Never be idle. If you cannot be usefully employed, attend to the cultivation of your mind.
2. Always speak truth. Make few promises. Live up to your engagements.
3. Keep your own secrets, if you have any.

4. When you speak to a person, look him in the face.
5. Good company and good conversation are the very sinews of virtue.
6. Good character is above all things else.
7. Your character cannot be essentially injured, except by your own acts.
8. If anyone speaks evil of you, let your life be such that no one will believe him.
9. *Drink no kind of intoxicating liquors.*
10. Ever live within your income.
11. When you retire to bed, think what you have been doing during the day.
12. Make no haste to be rich if you prosper.
13. Small and steady gains give competency with tranquillity of mind.
14. Never play at any game of chance.
15. Avoid temptation through fear you may not withstand it.
16. Earn money before you spend it.
17. Never run into debt unless you see plainly a way to get out again.
18. Never borrow if you can possibly avoid it.
19. *Never speak evil of anyone.* Be just before you are generous.
20. Keep yourself innocent if you would be happy.
21. Save when you are young to spend when you are old.
Read over the above maxims at least once a week.

As I grew up I came to appreciate better the special qualities of my home town. To me these qualities seemed right and good. Sullivan was and is a typical midwestern town—warm and human. When the time came to make a decision it was there that I brought up my own son, Bill, in a friendly community where he would instinctively believe in America and her people. He believes in both.

In 1890, Sullivan numbered less than twenty-two hundred. In a small town it is hard to pretend. The mental picture of unassuming families working hard for a living, knowing each other as equals and treating each other with consideration—often with genuine affection—never entirely fades. The scriptural truth that "no man liveth unto himself" can become a lasting reminder to a boy fortunate enough to grow up in such surroundings.

Our town, like the typical town of New England, was built around a square, or village green, called Coffman Park. This square was the center of village life. There one found the county courthouse, the stores, and the theatre. Nearby were the churches and the Central School Building. In the center stood the bandstand, where folks gathered on Friday nights to listen to concerts by the town band. The young people came to dance on the broad sidewalk nearby—it must have been one hundred feet long and fifteen feet wide—and it was considered entirely proper to ask any girl to dance, whether she was in your own "crowd" or not. This mixing of groups was welcomed by everyone. There was a fine spirit, almost like that of a state fair, but the dancing was never disorderly. It gave everyone a chance to circulate freely and helped to kill inhibitions.

These were the golden days of the "road show." Probably the most memorable event celebrated at Dear's Opera House during my boyhood was the appearance in 1890 of the great actress Modjeska. Seats were sold by subscription, and enough funds had been raised to bring the famous artist to our little town. Madame Modjeska was a personal friend of her compatriot, Dionesi Chranicki, a Civil War veteran who conducted a boardinghouse in Sullivan, and they had a touching reunion in Modjeska's private car. The story gave us youngsters quite a thrill, though few of us saw the play.

But the weekly importance of the square was as a gathering place for the county on Saturdays. Sullivan was the center of a rich farming area, and the farmers of the surrounding country made a ritual of this weekly trip, to do their buying, get the news and gossip, and talk politics. Although there was a hitching rack around all four sides of the square, there were days other than Saturdays when the rack was full. We already had a "parking problem"!

The hitching rack is also remembered as one of the civic problems to which the Woman's Club gave its attention. It was probably when I was in high school that they made so much fuss about it that the rack had to be removed. The hitching space certainly did get muddy whenever there was the slightest rain, and it doubtless was a good deal of a mess. It was this same Woman's Club, affiliated with the State and General Federations, that persistently agitated to get the first paved streets.

Sullivan was reasonably progressive, and various town improvements came along in due course. We had plumbing in my boyhood home—our own well and cistern—but at first no adequate public water supply. This poor supply, coupled with inadequate fire-fighting equipment, accounted for too many exciting fires. In those early days a fire at night, with the terrifying clanging of the town's fire bell, was a great horror to me. But still I wanted to go and was sometimes allowed to.

The installation of the first telephones in Sullivan was a great event. At first they were very clumsy affairs; ours was attached to the dining-room wall at the height of an average adult. I remember the first long-distance call. It was from the attorney of the long-distance telephone company, who said he was calling from Harrisburg, Pennsylvania. Father had warned us about the call, and when it came through, supper stopped dead. After the business was concluded Father held me up so I could talk to the attorney, who, in turn, put his "little boy" on so that we two could exchange greetings. People who more lately have called me "Telephone Bill" will see how early the habit was acquired.

I could almost write the story of my boyhood in terms of transportation, beginning with the broomstick that had a shoestring through a hole at one end for a bridle, and the hobbyhorse of diminutive stature but loud colors that followed. The velocipede was the exciting next step, and I had to be photographed beside it in kilt and sealskin cap. I can still see this funny little picture standing on a table in Mother's bedroom, beside a picture of me at six months. I was her first child, and I know she loved me with complete devotion, as I did her.

I have already told how Father bought me an Indian pony named Daisy. It was on that pony that I learned to ride, apparently without too much trouble. But I did have one accident which taught me a lesson. One year when my grandparents came to spend Christmas with us I undertook to act as outrider for the horse-drawn bus bringing them from the station to our house—a considerable adventure. After they had gotten out and gone into the house, the saddle slipped and Daisy dragged me from the front of the house to the barn gate. That may have spoiled my Christmas, but it did teach me that the saddle girth should always be tight—a lesson which I have found to have value in other areas of life also.

Daisy and I made drama on another occasion. Father and Mother were away and Aunt Sally was taking care of my baby brother, Hinkle. When he developed a stomach-ache she gave him a dose of iodine, thinking it was Brunker's Balsam, a pet family remedy. Horrified when she discovered what she had done, she yelled for me to go for the doctor, quick! I was out in the yard on Daisy's back and was off like the hero chasing the villain in the last reel of a Western. The faithful Daisy made the race of her life. Dr. Hinkle's office being right on the public square, on the ground floor, just one step up from the street, we were in his reception room—both Daisy and I—before we stopped.

How old I was when the pony became "kid stuff," I don't remember, but I do know how intensely the dream of a bicycle began to develop. Boys of today can scarcely imagine how large a bicycle loomed in our minds. And for any but a wealthy family it was a major investment: the $150 that a Columbia bicycle cost would probably be the equivalent of at least $750 today. But more than that, the bicycle was a great social institution. As Mark Sullivan puts it in the first volume of *Our Times*, "The Nineties was the day of the bicycle." As a matter of historic fact, Sullivan points out that the "safety bicycle"—so called because there wasn't the danger of taking a "header" that existed with the old high-wheeler—wasn't developed until 1889, when I was ten years old, with pneumatic tires following soon after that.

The vogue of the new machine was tremendous. It probably did more than any one thing to reduce the length and number of skirts and petticoats; it made communities conscious of the condition of their roads and sidewalks; it started an exciting era of racing, both road races and those on dirt tracks. Special uniforms or costumes were developed. Clubs

sprang up—ours was called the Ledgerwood Bicycle Club, with its usual
gathering place Mart Farley's shop. It was the ambition of every healthy
male to do his first "century"—ride a hundred miles in a day—as soon as
he could, and run up a good score of them, just as a novice golfer today
tries to "break a hundred."

One of my Sullivan chums, Dirrelle Chaney, whose father had a place
in Washington in the nineties, rode there from Sullivan in a week over
ordinary dirt and gravel roads—a distance of seven hundred miles—making two hundred miles on one of those days! I had no such physical
stamina as that, but I enjoyed the freedom my Columbia gave me to get
around the country and learn more about people and farming.

The bicycle didn't displace the horse as the automobile has succeeded
in doing. The sharp aroma of the livery stable, the clanging anvil of the
blacksmith shop, and the good leathery smell of the harness shop still
spelled excitement to a youngster. In our own barn we had Frank, the
bay horse, and later Doc; either one was well able to pull our two-seated
carriage and, later, the "surrey with the fringe on top" that has latterly
become famous in song.

I seem to have been fascinated by railroads always, and there was an
unusual amount of interesting history connected with railroading in our
part of the state. Many of these things were real to me because my father
was at various times counsel for most of the lines; he talked to me about
lawsuits and claims, always had passes, and took me on many of his trips.

The old Indiana & Illinois Southern, which ran east and west through
Sullivan, was significant even in my youth. Backed by important Chicago interests, it was tied up in some mysterious way with financial
powers that political speakers loved to assail but that were beyond the
understanding of any of us boys at Sullivan. It was during this period
that there was some conflict between E. H. Harriman and Stuyvesant
Fish, and I know that Father was the attorney for, and had the confidence of, both of them. In fact, the property in question was put in his
name while the road was changing hands.

The picturesque and primitive about these early railroads appealed to
me. The old "narrow gauge" passing east and west through our town
was built only four years before I was born. According to the stories, it
was a "jerk-water" road if there ever was one! Our local newspaper later
dug up some amazing reminiscences. One old-timer wrote, "Those who
had the misfortune to be passengers on one of its trains never forgot the
occasion." Among its nicknames the road was dubbed *The Tri-Weekly*
(or, perhaps, "weakly") and *The Streak of Rust*.

A further quotation from the Sullivan *Union* reminiscences may well
show how far we have come since those days:

One story about the narrow gauge is to the effect that a damage suit was
filed against the old company. The plaintiff claimed damages on account of a

train leaving five minutes ahead of time, causing him to miss an engagement and lose big money—but the Defendant proved the train was 23 hours and 55 minutes late.

Discarded box cars were used as depots along the entire road, and one old-time agent—formerly stationed at Linton, we believe—has written a book on *Twenty Years in a Box Car*. The trains were ridiculed by people along the road, who claimed that the train went east one week and back west the next.

Strangely enough, we Indiana high school boys were in at the birth of another of the great American achievments—the automobile. Historians tell us that "in nearly every village and town in America, *especially in the Middle West,* the local mechanical genius devoted his whole being to this new device. . . . In many respects this was the American spirit at its best—a feverish ferment of intellectual curiosity, mechanical ingenuity, and cleverness of adaptation."

An Indiana boy could certainly not be blamed for taking pride in the fact that on July 4, 1894, Elwood Haynes of Kokomo gave his newly developed auto a successful road test and eventually was known as the "father of the automobile in America." The new contraptions certainly stimulated American humor and gave us all something to joke about. One of the earliest cracks was the alleged comment of an astonished Chinese: "No pushee, no pullee; but, allee samee, go like hellee."

Again I am driven to the conclusion that I chose a fortunate time to grow up. When the great World's Columbian Exposition opened—delayed a year in its purpose of marking the four hundredth anniversary of the discovery of America by Columbus—I was "thirteen going on fourteen." I had a big bump of curiosity which Father had done a great deal to stimulate. He helped me to understand what we saw at Chicago. I couldn't possibly overestimate what the whole experience meant to me and to millions of others. The extravagant words with which Mark Sullivan has described the event seem to me justified when he writes:

The World's Fair at Chicago in 1893 was one of the most far-reaching stimulants to men's imaginations America has ever seen. It was the largest, the most generally attended and, in practically every respect, the best of the many America has had. *The mood it evoked in the average American was one of awed exhilaration.*

The fair made Americans conscious of having traditions and stimulated us to travel as never before. As Mark Sullivan has pointed out, it "caused nearly every person of the twelve millions who visited the Fair to go home with his soul enriched, his mind expanded and more flexible." What an experience for a boy about to enter high school that fall! Nothing ever gave my mind such a boost.

One special experience, out of the ordinary, I now know gave me a definite point of view. Father and I attended several sessions of the

World's Parliament of Religions. This was one of a series of international congresses covering every phase of economic, scientific, philosophical, and religious thought, which became one of the most important features of the exposition's program. As the name implied, it really was a conference of representatives of all the leading religions, gathered from the four corners of the earth. I don't know of any conference that has equaled it for breadth and mutual tolerance. It was conducted in such a spirit of mutual respect for one another's experiences and traditions as to impress even a thirteen-year-old boy.

Looking back to this parliament, I can see another truth illustrated: one gains more from any experience for which he is at least partially "conditioned." I was conditioned for it because Father was a firm believer in the universality of religion and practiced it. I have already mentioned that our next-door neighbors were Jews, and Davey Goodman my closest chum. I am sure Father had found, as I did later, that among small-town folks there can develop a religious tolerance that amounts almost to a religion, and that belief in the brotherhood of man and the fatherhood of God is a natural result.

I am sure that my lifelong interest in interfaith and interracial movements stems not only from the faith of my own family but from the Chicago experience of 1893. Time and again, consciously or unconsciously, I have pleaded and worked for "The Parliament of Man, the Federation of the World." I believe it is both a necessary and a possible goal.

Our Sullivan High School in the mid-nineties offered a three-year course only, but several of us in the Class of 1896 were able to get into college that fall. Of the nineteen members of the class, I think six or seven took college courses of one type or another. For that day, this was not a bad record. Our classmate, Frank Aydelotte, destined to make an outstanding record as an educator, both as president of Swarthmore and as director of graduate studies at Princeton, went to Indiana University and a few years later became one of the first group of Rhodes scholars. Other members of the class went to Wabash, DePauw, and elsewhere.

We were not a bad crowd, our Class of 1896, but I must admit that many of us could think up all kinds of things that a teacher would wish had never been concocted. One was an instrument inappropriately called the "tuba." This was nothing more than the keyboard out of a little three-by-two-by-six music box. This steel scale was thicker at the side that was not the keyboard, so that when it lay on the floor and one foot of a diligent student held down the solid side, his other foot could run up and down the scale gently, but audibly. I never did find out how this instrument got into our high school room, but its use was something of which no high school group should have been guilty, even though some were majoring in music.

When the tuba was on the floor and the immediate operator was playing it, Professor McNabb might be standing at the very desk of the
operator without recognizing him as the guilty party.

"What is that noise?" he would ask. "Do you know what is making
that noise?" The guilty pupil would deny any knowledge of it.

I have never understood just what there was about the acoustics of
the room that made it so hard to find out where the sound of that in-
fernal thing came from. It is true that Professor McNabb did not hear
too well and that he had a kind of nervous trouble which, when he was
intent, caused him to nod his head repeatedly. During the days when the
tuba was in operation the vigor of his nodding almost broke his neck!
There were breathless seconds when he came pretty close to the current
culprit, but when things got too hot for the operator his foot would
quietly push the instrument to the boy in front or behind, and the
recipient would take over and carry on the music.

Some of the class finally became ashamed of themselves, realizing that
it was wrecking Professor McNabb—and also, I guess, because we began
to be afraid. We had a way of getting cold feet when we really got close
to a showdown.

Out of school we had plenty of legitimate fun of our own manufacture. As one of our best commentators has noted, "the American of
the Nineties had the capacity for being entertained by sheer fun, which
is an expression of high spirits and wholesome relation to life." Almost
all the young people of Sullivan knew each other, and it was easy to
organize a dance, a picnic, or an informal tennis tournament. And there
were always our bicycles—still a bit of a thrill to all of us—so we got a
real kick out of our bicycle club and its meetings and tours.

I never sang in the church choir; none of the boys did. We were allowed to participate with the girls in Sunday school and in the Christmas Eve celebrations held at the church, and to distribute the little
mosquito-netting bags containing an orange and some varicolored candy.
On those occasions the boys could go along with the singing, but otherwise they were of no consequence in the music of the church. This
would have made no difference anyway so far as I was concerned. To
remember the words, I claim considerable ability; to carry a tune, none
whatever.

However, I early became interested in the choir. There was a girl in
it, a little older than myself, but a classmate. Her name was Grace
Nicoson: she was the stepdaughter of the Sunday-school superintendent, Captain Crawford, and was very pretty. As I was aspiring to a
better acquaintance, luck played into my hands in the best Horatio
Alger tradition.

We used to have Sunday-school picnics on the banks of the Wabash
near a little town called Merom—a long nine-mile horse-and-buggy ride

from Sullivan. There was a sand bar where picnickers who wanted to swim or wade could go—all under the eyes of a few oldsters who were chaperons, policemen, and lifeguards combined. At this particular picnic I was watching my favorite damsel from the river's edge when I saw that she had gone beyond her depth and heard her scream for help. I could not swim and I did not actually do anything that entitled me to any credit, but because I had had my eyes on her anyway, I reached her first as she was struggling in the water and got hold of her hand while I was still not over my depth. As she was struggling hard toward the bank, my help was just enough to make me look like a real lifesaver. The incident was much talked about and I think an item even got into the Sullivan paper. In any event, it gave me the chance to take shameless credit, just for the sake of fluttering around the particular young lady.

In another direction, our little high school gave us exceptional opportunities: we had a lot of "oratoricals" and debating. This was my dish. I had already met a good many lawyers and politicians in our home or over at the courthouse, and I could not imagine anything better than to become a good speaker. Public speaking had a tremendous vogue in those days. Without any benefit of public-address systems, radio, or publicity, a man had to be able to get up in front of an audience, hold it, and make his point stick.

I went out for every speaking activity in sight, and fairly early in high school won the Demarest Medal given each year for a speech on temperance. We had our interscholastic debates too. One of my boyhood friends in Sullivan recently wrote me recalling one of those events. It seems that Bob White—now publisher of the Sullivan *Union*—John Denny, and I composed a team that debated against Farmersburg High School. My friend wrote me that "Bob says he was pretty jittery but that Will Hays was cool and collected." I think it only seemed that way to him. At any rate, we three drove the several miles to the schoolhouse in White's buggy and were all afternoon getting there because of muddy roads. Bob thinks this was in March of 1894, and he is sure we won. At the schoolhouse there was a big crowd, all of whom reached the place in buggies. Afterward we were given a wonderful supper—such as a bighearted Hoosier housewife knew how to prepare—at the home of Milton Mitchell. It was quite a day.

Outside of school events we had public speaking under the aegis of our local chapter of the Lincoln League, which was quite a force in our country. This gave us more opportunities for oration and debate. Since the subjects were often of a distinctly patriotic character, this must have helped to groove still deeper certain paths in my thinking and my feeling about our country.

Earlier, on my eleventh birthday, my reading had been given a definite stimulus by a very practical device. As a present, Father gave me a sturdy ledger, in which he had written the request that I enter in it the name of every book I read and a brief review noting the impression it had made. That record was faithfully kept until I was through college. Perhaps it helped me to cultivate some degree of observation in my reading. Since popularity in the mid-nineties was shifting somewhat from English authors to American authors, including our young Indiana group—Ade, Nicholson, Tarkington, McCutcheon, and others—I probably became increasingly interested in American literature and history.

This taste was stimulated by my interest in public questions, for which discussions by Father should receive much of the credit. In turn, these questions became the subject of debates and orations. We noticed, for instance, the inauguration of rural free delivery in 1896 and waited for it to come to Sullivan. Such events as strikes—we had one at the Sullivan County mines in 1893—set us all to thinking, because labor and capital had worked together so well in our vicinity.

This coal strike created quite a sensation in our town. Father was hung in effigy by a few hotheads because of his connection with getting coal cars shipped. It seems that local action had to take place before the state would intervene: the coal cars had to be moved. When one of our town characters—Captain Bill Lucas, a deputy sheriff—was summoned to court to be sworn in, he refused to come and sent word that he would "take two men and move the cars, but he wouldn't bluff." He had fought under General Custer and was admired for his character and courage. These miners were friends of the Sullivan citizens, and friends don't like to shoot at friends. Like Lucas, they didn't want to have trouble. And they didn't have it.

Our Commencement Day, May 29, 1896, is as clear in my mind as if it were May of this year. It felt like a great occasion, and it was. Every member of the class had to speak, and we were not afraid to tackle the biggest subjects we could find. Bob White discussed the Monroe Doctrine; Destine Denny, "Women's Success"; Will DeVoe, "Good Citizenship"; one of the girls, "A Pessimistic View of Modern Society." Frank Aydelotte and John Denny debated the question: "Resolved, that the United States Government immediately tender its support to the interference by Russia in the Armenian affair." I could not get away from the theme of "The World's Parliament of Religions."

The words "hanging around" rarely have for their object anything as austere as a courthouse, at least for a little boy. To me it was natural because I went so often with Father, and the other men there were our friends and neighbors.

In boyhood my life's ambition was, still is, and always will be, to be a real lawyer. As a youngster, I was fascinated by law cases. They used to say I was like the cat in the courthouse—always in the way. I would hang around there after school and on Saturdays, and climb up on the flat-topped post by the jury box, where I could see and hear what was going on. Probably some of the court jargon stuck in my mind and became a part of my way of expressing things, so that when I was admitted to the Bar, only a few months out of college, the whole business seemed at least natural.

In those early days in Sullivan before telephones were common, local attorneys were summoned by the court bailiff in a novel manner: he simply opened a courthouse window and shouted the name of the lawyer three times. The lawyer nearly always heard his name called, but if he didn't some passer-by would tell him.

The Sullivan courts heard a variety of cases that must have added something to my stock of general knowledge as I grew up. There were suits connected with receiverships, wills, rights of way, personal damages, trusteeships, workmen's compensation, requisitioning of earth to be used on the levees, property rights, insurance companies, election frauds, mining, mergers, and murders. Quite an education for a boy in knee pants! And quite a chance to study life and people and rights and motives. In those days, in a county court they usually got down to essentials, even in legal terms. This boyhood predilection paid good dividends when I became a lawyer myself.

The very summer we graduated from high school I was introduced to politics with a bang. The outstanding political experience of my life was not the 1916 election in Indiana; it was not the 1918 election; it was not the Republican National Convention in 1920, when I was chairman; it was not the moment when we knew that the majority of 1920 had reached seven million—nor was it when I saw the elected candidates inaugurated as President and Vice-President of the United States. No! It was when, at the age of sixteen, my father took me to the 1896 convention in St. Louis at which McKinley was nominated.

The first evening, as we went into the dining room of the Planters Hotel, we stopped at the table where General Lew Wallace and Colonel Richard W. Thompson, delegates-at-large from Indiana, were dining. I remember Colonel Thompson introducing me to General Wallace and saying that I was going to Wabash College at Crawfordsville that fall. Wallace looked me over and said to Father, "You had better put him on a farm for a couple of years." Colonel Thompson was a great figure in our section of Indiana and a power in the nation. Through his influence I got close to all that went on in the convention, soaking it up like a sponge.

After we got home Father gathered up all the newspaper clippings covering the convention, put them in an envelope, sealed it, and endorsed on the outside: "For Willie Hays, with the hope that he will take a citizen's interest in politics." I found that envelope in a drawer in my desk the first year I was chairman of the Republican National Committee. Father had certainly started something. From that day to this—and I have been pretty close to it many times—the choosing of the right man to be our President has seemed to me about the greatest single responsibility of the American people.

To complete my first lesson in national politics Bryan, the Democratic nominee for the presidency, came to our town on his campaign tour that fall. At that time and for years afterward Sullivan County was overwhelmingly Democratic. The keen interest in politics and the intense partisanship and rivalry resulted in some picturesque forms of demonstrations. In our county big glee clubs were organized by both parties, with the palm awarded in 1896 to the Republican clubs, both for size and quality. The Sullivan Republican Glee Club, composed of both young men and women and coached by a professional singing teacher, traveled around to the rallies in style. A huge wagon body extending out over the wheels, with a roof, curtains, flags, and bunting, was further decorated with a string of "full dinner pails," the slogan of the McKinley campaign. The wagon had a small organ, placed directly behind the driver's seat; chairs and benches were arranged to accommodate the forty or more singers. Henry Barnard drove the six horses that pulled the huge affair, which must have looked like a moving stage. Our club once traveled across the Wabash to Robinson, Illinois, twenty-two miles away, to sing at a big rally there. Some of the townships had mule teams of as many as twenty mules pulling their glee clubs.

At all the chief meetings there would be excellent speakers, big crowds, the raising of a campaign pole seventy-five to one hundred feet high, and a picnic dinner along with the raising. But a party pole had to be well guarded lest the opposing side cut it down in the dead of night.

The Bryan meeting of 1896 was the biggest ever held in Sullivan. It was estimated that a crowd of forty thousand heard the "Boy Orator of the Platte" that day, and the Democrats outdid themselves. Things were so arranged that eight out-township processions hit the Hamilton Township at the same time, coming from different directions. As the newspaper account put it, "Each township had its glee club and band, or fife-and-drum corps, and when all joined together in parading the streets of Sullivan, the occasion was one that will never be equaled."

That fall, at seventeen, with the echoes of the Republican National Convention still ringing in my ears and the excitement of the McKinley-Bryan campaign raging, I surely must have done a lot of thinking about politics.

CHAPTER 4

Wabash College, 1896–1900

O U R class went to college in the "Gay Nineties"—whether we knew it or not. Perhaps we did have an inkling of it. The mood of those days was so different that I cannot help asking myself what part this spirit of the nineties played in my four years at Wabash and what it may have contributed to my permanent make-up.

If styles of attitude in any generation influence young people most of all—as in the "Jazz Era" following World War I—what were the styles of the nineties? Some characterizations and examples mentioned by Mark Sullivan in *The Turn of the Century* may help to depict the mood of those years. We boys in college were sure to be influenced by the current mood, for it was in the very air we breathed.

The term "gay" was well deserved—and in the best sense, not the worst. As Sullivan notes: "There was plenty of enjoyment in the Nineties, both high-spirited and the quieter sort that went with a more leisurely way of life." In college we called the high-spirited sort "monkey business," and we had plenty of that. Sullivan holds that in humor "the America of the Nineties was so rich—both in productivity by writers and appreciation by the public—that one is tempted to say no other decade equalled it." George Ade was one of our home-bred boys who helped it along. One of the many phrases he coined which have become part of our common vernacular is "the cold grey dawn of the morning after."

Finley Peter Dunne, then in his prime as a Chicago newspaper political columnist, is another example. His role was something like that of Will Rogers, but his pen was the only instrument he needed to rope the public. In politics the nineties were a period of deep, often angry, feeling—a situation ideal for "Mr. Dooley's" comments. These comments were so penetrating that Theodore Roosevelt was deferential to him, appreciating his influence for good, and so funny that everybody had to smile. His definition of the two major political parties was simple: Republicans—"we commind"; Democrats—"we denounce an' deplores."

Of our Indiana Senator Beveridge's oratory, Mr. Dooley wrote: "Ye could waltz to it." But of the acrimoniousness of politics during the nineties, he said: "If ye ar-re a tired la-ad an' wan without much fight in ye, livin' in this counthry is like thryin' to read th' Lives iv the Saints at a meetin' iv th' Clanna-Gael." Looking at America, Mr. Dooley saw the "crownin' wurruk iv our civilization—th' cash raygister."

As a fellow commentator put it: "Most useful of all, Mr. Dooley supplied the softening solvent of humor to the American atmosphere in times of acute controversy." We need such men! Mr. Dooley was so popular that cartoons were drawn and songs were written about him. The chorus of the best-known song ran like this:

> Oh, Mister Dooley, Oh, Mister Dooley,
> The Greatest Man this country ever knew.
> Both diplomatic and democratic
> Oh, Mr. Dooley—ooley—ooley—iley—oo.

One of our college parodies substituted for the last two lines the profound couplet:

> He warmed his nightie on anthracitie,
> Oh Mr. Dooley—ooley—ooley—iley—oo.

In another field often taken as a good index of the public mind, the nineties have been called the flowering time of the American drama. The best plays went on the road far and wide. It is recorded of Julia Marlowe that "she burst on the students of Harvard College like each one's personal dream." At the same time minstrel shows were extremely popular, and Uncle Tom's Cabin, with Eliza and the bloodhounds, was still playing across the country.

As for music, Mark Sullivan notes four characteristic phenomena. Our indigenous Negro melodies had not yet been jostled by ragtime and other variations. Classical music had been tremendously stimulated by the performances at the World's Fair, and fine symphony orchestras were fast developing. Paul Dresser, the Hoosier composer of "On the Banks of the Wabash," had something of the Stephen Foster spirit. And John Philip Sousa, the "March King," not only wrote the most typical music the country had produced, but with "The Washington Post March" moved America's feet to a new dance beat. The "two-step" swept the country. We were all keen to learn it! All these things contributed to the mood of the nineties.

On the domestic side, the nineties still witnessed plenty of independence and many of the home industries that had been so common in pioneer days; but changes were coming steadily, even in the small towns and on the farms. Butchering on individual Indiana farms was fading out as packing houses came in; the burning of wood for fuel was going out as the use of coal increased.

But plenty of farmers' wives in Indiana were still almost independent of canneries; preserving was a household rite that followed the seasons, from strawberry time through raspberries to blackberries, and on to peaches and pears. On the farms, and even in the villages, as Sullivan recalls, "a kind of pride caused wife and husband as well to seek to produce and preserve as much of their food as possible—*a workmanlike individualism* destined to be overcome by the ease of railroad transportation, by the cheapness of quantity production in factories, by refrigerator cars and by cold-storage warehouses." It's my guess that nine tenths of my Wabash classmates saw plenty of this "workmanlike individualism" as they were growing up. I know I did, and I have always tried to practice its spirit, if not its form.

Anyone who grew up in the nineties remembers them as a time of simple and inexpensive living—and a period of hearty, even boastful, Americanism. It was a picturesque and colorful time. Augustus Thomas caught its spirit when he wrote: "Life itself had a gentle pace, social intercourse a more genial temperament. Friends, meeting, stopped to exchange a word; men in groups told stories, laughed—*the time of peace, wherein we trusted.*"

To me, that picture is absolutely true. It was a healthful climate in which to live. As college boys, it agreed with us. It nurtured sentiment, the love of beauty, belief in people, and faith in the future.

If the nineties were a time of inexpensive living, major expenditures like a college education were something to be reckoned with. It was a family joke that I went to college in my freshman year on the long-distance telephone company. Though my parents were sure they were going to send me to college, they were not at all sure how they were going to swing the expense. It happened that Father had been defending a damage suit for the telephone company, and the check covering his fee arrived just at the critical moment. I remember the general rejoicing and Mother's assurance that, once more, the grace of God had been operating.

I started off to college as the McKinley-Bryan campaign was getting under way. Being busy getting started, I do not remember much about that campaign, but I do remember that the Republican orators were emphatically declaring that the future of the nation was at stake. I probably took for granted that these spellbinders were right, for I had been brought up a Republican. But at that moment I was less concerned with that problem than with the very personal question of how I was ever going to get along so far away from home as Crawfordsville. Homesickness was an honest fact.

If my homesickness was real, it didn't last long. Through a boy whom I met on the train on the way to Crawfordsville I secured a room in Mrs. Lee's rooming house at 209 East Pike, where I lived happily all the four years. The fact that Mrs. Lee had two daughters, Jessie and Autumn, who were going to dances just when I was beginning to feel an interest in such matters probably had something to do with the pleasure with which I returned to Mrs. Lee's each September.

The question of which fraternity I should join bothered me for a while, as I had good friends among both the Phi Psis and the Phi Delts. It was Benjamin Harrison who decided it for me. Harrison was a Phi Delt, and what was good enough for a former president of the United States was good enough for me. I survived the initiation and took considerable part in the affairs of the fraternity, both at college and afterward.

If I might have felt that my home town had missed me as much as I missed it since leaving, I must have been quite taken aback when Christmas vacation came. It never occurred to me that any of my old friends would fail to recognize that I was returning from my first term at Wabash. But while I was walking up the street, carrying my suitcase, Mart Farley, the blacksmith, called out: "Hi, Willie! Going someplace?"

In college, as in high school, I was an average student—no more and no less. But Wabash has always held high standards, and we had to work. I got along pretty well with the professors, because the first year I worked very hard and established a reputation. I hadn't planned it that way just to make the subsequent years easier, but that was the way it worked out, and it proved a first-rate plan. That first year I suppose I was really scared that I would fail, not having learned to study too well in high school. Moreover, since I was taking the classical course, I had to pack two years' work in Greek into one. That furnished one of the horrible trials of my college life. If it had not been for dear old Professor Zwingli McLean, I don't think I would have made it. Fortunately Zwing was a kind man.

There were several professors at Wabash who had an influence on me —including Dr. Bodine in geology and Dr. Emery in chemistry. I got along splendidly with Dr. Tubby Tuttle, who was the professor of history and political economy. American history probably was my favorite subject, and American leaders my favorite heroes. They helped form my philosophy of life and of politics. The comment on the Declaration of Independence made by Jefferson illustrates what I mean: "All its authority rests on the harmonizing sentiments of the day, whether expressed in letters, printed essays, or the elementary books of public right, as Aristotle, Cicero, Locke, Sidney, etc." The conception that "harmonizing sentiments" of many people give proper authority early became for me one of the central principles of political action.

There was one man there with whom I didn't get along so well. He was Professor Studley, who taught mathematics; he was as exact and cold as a multiplication table. To him, things either *were* or they *weren't*. To make it worse, he was the freshman class adviser. Each class had a member of the faculty as its own particular shepherd, and the authorities in their wisdom had chosen this "tough bird" to shepherd the freshmen. It was no shepherding. He was as stern as Zwingli McLean was kindly, but I do not doubt that he did us a lot of good—as a cold shower does on occasion.

One incident in his class in higher algebra I can never forget. He would give us little cards on which a problem was written and send us to the blackboard; with the card in our left hand and a piece of chalk in our right, we would work out the problem on the board. This particular time I had a problem which was a good deal of a poser. I read it several times and then stood motionless at the board—so long that it attracted the attention of the good professor.

"William, what is delaying you?" he asked.

"Professor," I said, "I can't understand what this means."

"Read it!" he said with emphasis.

I read it: " 'What is the probability of drawing an ace, king, queen, jack, and ten of the same suit in five draws in a pack of cards?' "

"What is it that you do not understand about that question, William?" Professor Studley asked.

Then I made a mistake when I replied: "I do not understand, Professor Studley, what you mean by the 'same suit' in a 'pack of cards.' "

From one Amalby Faley—called "Fig"—in the back row came a raucous snort, loud enough to upset the whole class, and Professor Studley, in the loudest voice I ever heard him use, cried, "William, you may go!" It took me several days to get back into the class.

I used to say at the time, I remember, that I wanted someday to be a trustee of Wabash College just so I could fire Studley. But he beat me to it. By the time I became a trustee he had gone to his reward.

My athletic activities at college were negligible, though I did play some tennis. All those years I weighed 110 pounds, so I couldn't throw my weight around very much. In fact, the story went the rounds of the campus that "one day when Will Hays was throwing the sixteen-pound hammer he forgot to let go for the heave and followed the hammer through the air."

Social life at Wabash was by no means complicated, nor limited to one's own fraternity. A number of my best friends were in other fraternities or in none. The total college enrollment at that time was not more than two hundred, and I probably knew by name or by sight nearly every man on the campus—and quite a number of families in the town of Crawfordsville, often referred to as "the Athens of the West."

Wabash was, and still is, a college for men, but the town was blessed with many charming and beautiful girls. I should know—I married two of them, though not at the same time. Fraternity parties were always fun and the Panhellenic dances in the spring something to remember. They were the high spots of our social year.

My fraternity seems to have served another purpose too, as a proving ground for embryo politicians. Naturally we practiced class politics within the college, but we also tried our hand at intercollegiate affairs in the State Oratorical Association. Apparently we developed some nefarious schemes by which a Phi Delt was elected as his college's representative in every case where we had a chapter. The result was the election of a complete Phi Delta Theta slate of officers in the state association. However, I must hasten to say that this never affected the decision of the judges when it came to the contest itself.

Four years at Wabash only strengthened my ties with home and my appreciation of all that my parents stood for. I think I wrote pretty regularly, and I am sure they did. Father had a way of putting excellent advice in his letters and making it seem an encouraging suggestion, never a command. In a letter of October 6, 1896, in which I find "I rejoice over that two pounds you have gained," there occurred two bits of wisdom by which I have tried to profit:

Am glad you have made up your mind as to your fraternity, and would advise you to act at once, if you are satisfied, as that is the best rule of life. When you have duly considered any proposition on which you are required to act, act with decision and pass it, understanding always that you expect to abide by the decision without regret. . . .

Be slow in forming intimate lines of friendship. After you get accustomed so that you are no longer lonely, it is the wisest of maxims to be retired, and have few very intimate chums.

The right policy is to be friendly to everyone, and not too intimate with any. This gives you independence not obtainable in any other manner. This is especially so as to your lady friends.

Fortunately I was spared the uncertainty and delay many boys experience in choosing a profession. The example of Father as a lawyer was always in the back of my mind. Never was there any question but that I, too, was to be a lawyer.

This early choice enabled me to make at least a "pre-professional" course out of the four years at Wabash, although the curriculum was only that of a liberal arts college. There was no law course or law degree. But both in the courses I elected and in my extracurricular interests, I am sure I was choosing then what seemed likely to help my preparation for legal practice and for the field we now call "human relations." I went in pretty heavily for oratoricals and debating and, in fact, for any type of public speaking. Every summer I read law in Father's office—a common custom in those days, in place of law school.

This looking ahead to law and politics probably drew my interest particularly to public questions; certainly the history-making events of 1896 to 1900 gave us plenty of incentive. Provincialism was giving way to nationalism, and nationalism to internationalism. America was definitely

becoming involved in world affairs, which we tried our best to understand. How many of these events later had direct bearing on my life in
politics and in motion pictures (especially as a world industry), it would
be hard to say.

A glance at those events shows what sharp new images were flashed
on the minds of students during those four years; they were a liberal
education in themselves. In 1896, Mark Hanna became national chairman of the Republican party and gave it new vitality. Gold was discovered in the Klondike. Idaho granted full suffrage to women—a precursor
of their victory in 1920, for which the National Committee had worked
hard. In 1897 a non-partisan monetary convention, representing twenty-
six states and sixty-four cities, met at Indianapolis and approved the gold
standard then in effect. In May of that year an International Postal
Union Conference met in Washington and signed a universal agreement on June 15. On June 19, Japan formally protested against the
annexation of Hawaii by the United States. How much more meaning
that has for us now!

The year 1898 carried us out into the main stream of world events.
On New Year's Day the creation of Greater New York City was inaugurated with fitting ceremony and with the announcement of a
population of 3,438,899—less than half its present population! On February 15 the U.S.S. *Maine* was blown up in Havana Harbor. When war
against Spain was declared there was a tremendous outburst of patriotic
excitement on the Wabash campus. As I have often said in Hoosier
speeches, "In this country you can put down a drill most anyplace and
patriotism will spout out like a geyser." On May 1, Dewey sank the
Spanish fleet in Manila Bay. On August 14 the Spanish-American War
was over and we were given Puerto Rico and Guam. On December 10
the peace treaty was signed and Spain ceded the Philippines to the
United States for twenty million dollars.

In January of 1899 the American flag was raised over Wake Island—
a name so much better known today. In July the United States signed
the Hague Peace Convention. In September, Admiral Dewey started
home from the Philippines to an abortive presidential candidacy.

And what a thrill my chum Max Puett and I had in the fall of our
senior year, when it was arranged that we could make our first trip to
New York, at the time of the Dewey home-coming celebration, to get
our first view of the city where I have spent so much of my life during
the last three decades. I shall never forget this first glimpse into the
bigger world.

In 1900 the first treaty concerning the Panama Canal was signed on
February 5. On April 30 an act was passed making Hawaii a territory
of the United States. On June 19, McKinley was renominated—this time
with Theodore Roosevelt as running mate, supposedly "sidetracked" into

the vice-presidency. On November 1 the U. S. Census Bureau announced a population of 76,304,799 and located the mythical "center of population" near Columbus, Indiana, eighty-five miles east of my home. We were really in the center of things!

My four years at college, I suspect, were not greatly different from those experienced by thousands of other lively youngsters in the Gay Nineties. It was a happy and carefree time that I like to think back upon. There was a sense of real friendship among the forty-odd young men who had spent those years together as we came up to Commencement Day in June of 1900. Wabash was a liberal arts college; it was also a Christian college. It had been founded in 1832, when Crawfordsville was nothing but a pioneer settlement in the wilderness, by nine circuit-riding Presbyterian ministers who were concerned over the lack of educational facilities. Their religious conviction, which furnished the stimulus for the founding, gave a permanent spirit to the life of the college.

Wabash helped us to build a personal view of life in which God and man, art and science, the individual and society, all found their place. I believe I voiced the faith and hope of the whole class when, in my commencement oration on "The Zeitgeist"—the spirit of the times—I made the fatherhood of God and the brotherhood of man my basic theme and closed with Tennyson's memorable words from *Locksley Hall*:

> *Till the war drum throbbed no longer,*
> *and the battle flags were furled,*
> *In the Parliament of Man,*
> *the Federation of the World.*

To a degree hard for many to realize today, this was the faith and sincere hope of my generation. *It is still my faith and hope.*

I cannot close this chapter without once more trying to picture what the opening of the twentieth century meant to us. It was the great turning point of our whole generation. We were projected into a new world with an emotional and spiritual lift that we may never see again.

It is plain historical fact, increasingly evident as we have passed the middle of this century, that 1900 did mark an amazing number of changes in our national life. Since changes were a vital part of our education and training, and the new conditions they brought became main factors in the world in which we were to work, perhaps they deserve notice here. This is especially true in my case, because I graduated from college, became precinct committeeman of the Republican party, began the practice of law, was admitted to the Bar, and cast my first vote for

President—all within the twelve months of 1900. The pattern was definitely set.

Because of long-time personal acquaintance with Mark Sullivan and the conviction that his estimate of the first quarter of this century closely parallels my own, I have glanced again at his volume, *The Turn of the Century*, to compare notes on some of the changes that seem to have had direct relationship to my own experience. In many cases that relationship will become evident only as I retrace my life through its successive periods.

First, to mention certain favorable characteristics of latter nineteenth-century life, in some of which change gradually began to appear. The old-time school had been tied closely to the community and to the home; the teachers were often a number of able and ambitious young men on the way to one of the other "learned professions." The spirit of religion and patriotism was strong in the schools. Even geographies were equally confident of the superiority of America and the Christian religion. Schools also put great emphasis on elocution, because public life was the most prized career. Of this I saw a great deal in Indiana.

Other aspects of life reveal inherited values that were beginning to be lost. In 1900 the principal mediums of culture were home, religion, schools, and reading. "About the turn of the century new mediums arose and old ones changed in their relative influence. . . . There was added a new and potent source of manners and points of view—the Motion Picture." We were entering into a new world; for many people "it was difficult to carry into this faster, richer, more luxurious world the simple faith in God and man."

In the realm of politics, only four western states had woman suffrage; this change was slow in coming. Americans were troubled over "expansion" and "imperialism." Warnings were issued about the "beginning of the importation of various literary missionaries from Russia." The Republicans had adopted a slogan, "All we need to do is to stand pat," but Theodore Roosevelt reversed that trend.

As symbolic of the "ferment" at work, Edwin Markham's poem *The Man with the Hoe* seemed to be taken as the average man's symbol for the political and economic mood of the time. And Jacob Gould Schurman gloomily described the American spirit of his day in the words, "A waning Christianity and a waxing Mammonism are the twin spectres of our age."

However, the majority of the phenomena noted seem to indicate progress or development—or at least hopeful change—in one field or another. With several of these developments I was to have personal contact. On the political side, "front-porch campaigns" came into style. The G.A.R. was still an influential force. John Hay completed negotiations, in January of 1900, for the "Open Door" in China. The United

States, after the Boxer Rebellion, gave back part of her share of the Chinese indemnity, to be used chiefly to send Chinese to the United States as students—a classic example of international friendship. Dr. Lyman Abbott and Theodore Roosevelt, with whom I was to have much to do, participated in these negotiations.

Roosevelt's rise, evolution, and influence were symbolic of the new forces at work. He was "energetically, intelligently busy. His exuberant vitality . . . gave a lift of the spirits to millions of average men. . . . He brought in a stream of fresh, pure, bracing air," according to Mark Sullivan. Under him there was progress in industrial arbitration, a field which I was to find of the greatest importance in the motion picture industry. A dozen important changes in government—legislative, political, judicial—took place, many of them giving more direct action to the voters and firmer basis for my belief in the grass-roots type of political thought and action.

On the personal, or cultural, side there was enrichment in many directions, much of it doubtless stemming from the World's Fair. In 1900, novels of rural life and novels based on American history enjoyed great popularity, and the dramatized novel began to have a vogue which has continued to grow, encouraged further by the motion picture.

Attempting to sum up, Mark Sullivan writes: "It was a period characterized by an immense elevation that came to America as a whole, accompanied by an immense enrichment of the individual American." This took place particularly, as he points out, in the outward reach of the senses: radio, telescope, microscope, motion picture; in the quantity of power brought to our service; in our knowledge of the universe; in our leisure.

In comparison with this material advancement, Sullivan comments: "Whether man was spiritually enriched also; what use he made of his increased years on the earth, his increased leisure; the energies released by machinery from the need of getting a livelihood—the whole question of the spiritual experiences of man during this period is one about which it is not possible to speak so broadly or so confidently."

During the telling of this story I know that I shall have a number of experiences to relate which will reflect at least my own conclusions and convictions on these vital questions.

CHAPTER 5

Going to Work

I SAID the last good-bys to my classmates at the close of our Wabash commencement in June of 1900 and suddenly realized that my student days were over and that a desk in Father's law office was waiting. The commencement admonition—"this day is not the end, it is only the beginning"—needed no underlining. For me it was literally true, and it was with genuine anticipation that I boarded the train for Sullivan.

In my case there was no "cold, cold world" waiting for me outside the warm and friendly college walls. I was going home. There was no intricate problem of adjustment. I was simply going to continue reading law as I had been doing summers and vacations, and I was going to commence practice as soon as the court approved.

Since I was working among people I had known all my life, there could hardly have been a more natural or comfortable way to start. When I see the uncertainties so many young men face today I am most grateful for the friendly field in which my lot was cast. I wanted to be a lawyer above all else, and the opportunity was waiting. I believe opportunities still wait if the desire and determination are strong enough.

Father had had to travel a longer road. Born in 1845 and living on the farm until sixteen, he had attended the Iron City Commercial College at Pittsburgh, and then the high school at Lisbon, Ohio. Finally, ready for college, he entered Mount Union at Alliance, Ohio, meeting all his own expenses by hours of work on the outside. He had been graduated from Mount Union in 1869, taking the highest honors in natural science and mathematics. He taught school from graduation up to 1874, chiefly in Ascension Seminary in Sullivan County. He had read law in the office of Sewell Coulson and was admitted to the Bar in 1875, having purchased an interest in the firm of Buff & Buff—a partnership which he dissolved in 1878.

In that same year, having been elected prosecuting attorney for the Fourteenth Judicial District, and feeling enthusiastic about Indiana and confident of its growing opportunities, he suggested to his brother, Harrison Jefferson Hays—Uncle Jeff to us—that he leave Ohio and join him in the practice of law at Sullivan. That first association of Hays & Hays lasted until 1892. From that year until 1900, Father conducted

an independent practice and, as this practice was gradually reaching out
into a considerable portion of Indiana, I have no doubt that he looked
forward to the day when his eldest son would be ready to join him.
And so Hays & Hays again became a reality in 1900 and was given
further family reinforcement when my younger brother, Hinkle, joined
us in 1912. Later our sons became junior members of the firm.

By 1900 the name of John T. Hays of Sullivan had become known
in the legal affairs of many of our Indiana railroads, coal companies,
and other corporations. Also, Father had many successful criminal and
civil suits to his credit. Certain kinds of businesses, such as the securing
of liquor licenses, our office would not handle. But it served the community and the county in an infinite variety of ways. It was an ideal
place for me to learn law.

During the summer of 1900 that was my job—to learn as much law
as I could, as fast as I could, by reading, by observation in court and
out, by doing preliminary work on inquiries and cases, and through
discussions with Father. His training as a teacher, as well as his knowledge and experience as a lawyer, was my good fortune. I don't think
I could have had better legal training in any office than I had in my
own father's. He knew the law and had profound respect for it. And
it is hard to see how I could have found in any law school of that day
a training process more concrete, more varied, or more practical. There
were no recitation periods or term marks, but there were case studies
galore, the consulting of sources *ad infinitum,* daily discussion with
counsel, and real trials—not mock ones. It was a stimulating summer.
Whether it gave me any vacation or not, I have truly forgotten; but that
did not seem important in comparison with a job to which I had been
looking forward so long.

The other side of my coming back home to "settle"—as we used to
think of it when settling had more finality than it does now—was that
I could pick up all my old associations. They included church and
Sunday school, where I was soon teaching a class of boys; regular tennis
playing, with an occasional town tournament; making a talk here and
there; and getting better acquainted with the practical problems of farming.

With the perspective—at the time of writing this—of almost fifty years
since college, I want to try to appraise the training and equipment with
which I started to work. This training must have given me a very definite
bent, because nearly everything I have done since 1900 seems in principle, at least, to be related to the ideals and the type of action acquired
as a boy and as a young man.

Both heredity and environment conspired to set a definite pattern that
became an integral part of me. That is why I have tried to analyze
them. That analysis shows that a sense of individual responsibility, a

friendly attitude toward other people that I have often tried to express
in the words "live and help live," and an unwavering faith in the reality
of God—all were a consistent part of my Christian, Hoosier heritage. My
family believed that the Golden Rule was a workable principle. So did
many of our fellow citizens. And I have always found that this attitude
of good will brought more understanding and better co-operation than
any other attitude. Unless you know how people *feel* about things, it is
pretty hard to get them to *do* anything about them.

From my father I am certain that I learned most in the way of a
working philosophy of life. This included, as I have already said, a code
of practical "rules" pasted on the flyleaf of my Bible. As I try to list the
broader principles of living in which Father set a pattern—as much by
act as by word—there are nearly a dozen that seem worth noting:

To consider the profession of law as an essential public service; to respect
the dignity of the bench; to be patient with juries.

Father viewed the bench with something akin to reverence. In his
opinion the judge was a figure to be treated with profound regard. I had
plenty of chance to observe that the judges on their part similarly held
him in deep respect and esteem—a feeling shared by the Bar of the
entire state. As to juries, Father was philosophical. "Will, don't ever
guess what a jury will do," he said to me once. "You may lose confidence in your own judgment."

To be willing to start work early and quit late.

Father himself was a terrific worker, often spending the whole evening
at the office—in addition to a full day. In my early days as Postmaster
General they had some fun over the fact that the janitor was the only
man who beat me to the department. This doesn't mean that life in
Sullivan was "all work and no play." As in college, there continued to
be plenty of extracurricular activities—tennis, parties, lodge meetings,
and so on.

To get along with people and to value the fraternal spirit.

Father was democratic in the best sense of the word; he put the
brotherhood of man into daily practice. He liked and respected other
people and drew the same reaction from them. He never considered it
any great problem for townsmen to get together on matters of common
interest. And he considered that fraternal orders occupied an important
place in life. It was early that I became a "joiner"—as was he.

*To do whatever is possible to bring things about, rather than to "trust to
luck."*

A delightful expression of this principle is found in the letter of
1878 in which Father asked Uncle Jeff to move out to Indiana and go

into partnership with him. In referring to the growing practice and prospects which justified the expansion, Father wrote: "I give Providence the Glory; but I did the engineering." That sounds a little like the famous phrase allegedly coined by a chaplain in the heat of a Pacific battle: "Praise the Lord, and pass the ammunition." On the other hand, while recognizing that "the best-laid plans of mice and men" sometimes go astray, Father was equally clear that difficulties and mistakes were often of our own making and that it was precious little use to blame them on someone or something else.

To finish the job.

This was so ingrained in me that once, when I was suddenly asked to write on a slip of paper the thing that I most wanted, I simply wrote the four words: "To finish the job." Whenever I have felt that I had the privilege of being connected with something of value and had any responsibility for it, I have never wanted to give it up.

To enlist the service of others in projects for the common good.

Father could always get along with people and was eager to work with them. He was easily the most proficient person I ever saw in getting people to do things. In a little while he was able to influence any group into which he entered, and always by a kindness and a subtle persuasion which brought everyone into step toward the desired end. If I have had any one goal above others in the projects with which I have been connected—civic, political, industrial, or philanthropic—it has been to get people together for common action which they considered good.

To think of capital and labor always as co-workers.

Personally, I have never thought of anyone as working *for* me, but always as working *with* me. It was natural enough to acquire this viewpoint when one grew up in a small town where the most respected worker in the church, the grand master of the lodge, and the leader in charity work were, respectively, carpenter, coal miner, and brick mason —actual instances, these. The New Testament tells us that Joseph was a carpenter. In surroundings where one man is regarded as better than another only when he behaves himself better, one gets well grounded in the opinion that *fundamental rights are equally sacred and sacredly equal.* In Sullivan, labor and capital also knew that in the shifting prosperity of the community all went up or down together.

To believe in the possibilities of arbitration.

When I was a boy there occurred a local strike which had causes warranting a real protest but which was unfavorably affected by action that was thoroughly un-American. Honest laborers who were neighbors and friends suffered, as well as the whole community. I remember my father's influence in the settlement of that dispute. As I have said, he was the attorney for the railroad and the coal mines, but he had the confidence of the men as well. I know they left it to him to work it out—both the men who had the investments and the workers who met him as equals and who knew him as a friend. It was a successful and fair arbitration.

To take a citizen's interest in politics.

This, Father expressed the hope that I would do—shortly after the Republican National Convention of 1896, which we attended together. I grew up taking for granted that active participation in politics is a civic duty. Hoosiers pretty well agreed that it was every man's business to help run the country, though often disagreeing violently on how to do it.

To go slow in issuing ultimatums.

Father told me that he himself had learned this lesson from an experience early in his schoolteaching days. He had found it necessary to discipline one of the "bad boys" who had run more than one teacher out of school. With some heat—for Father had a temper—he told the boy that if he did not do so-and-so he would be expelled. In telling the story in later years, Father always pointed out two things: first, that it wasn't good for the boy to threaten such a showdown; and second, that it could have turned out badly for him because the boy's father was head of the school board. Father was no compromiser, but he knew that in human relations ultimatums were poor strategy, for both sides!

Many things I must have learned quite as much from Father's example as from his advice. In everything connected with our Presbyterian church I followed in his footsteps as naturally as water runs downhill. I recognized the responsibility of laymen. When he died in 1919—to run ahead of my story—I was elected an elder to succeed him. Some years later, when I was living away from Sullivan most of the time, I was elected honorary elder, and my brother carried on the family connection as active elder. Father was a great man in the true, essential qualities, and I know now that his influence spread out more widely in the community and in the state than I could possibly have known at the time.

Nor do I forget the influence of our home and of other homes that seemed almost like my own. I acquired a faith in the American family as a sort of common denominator of American life. I saw such families tread the paths of romance as naturally as their own village streets. I saw them hold fast and help perpetuate in our country the sacredness of life and the value of individual goodness. And I even have records to prove that this is not merely a later reflection. In a talk to miners not long after 1900—down in their mine—I said: "It is to the ideals of the home that we must go back. It is the source of our right impulses. It is there that we learn patience and diplomacy."

It seems clear to me that my faith in folks and in their goodness was a natural product of our own home life. And I believe that ours was a Christian home, typical of millions of homes of that day. It would have been difficult ever to escape from such an influence, even if I had wished to. I might properly quote the Good Book: "The lines are fallen to me in pleasant places; yea, I have a goodly heritage."

At the risk of repeating and because educators are giving so much attention to the subject these days, I want to emphasize that to me there was no gap between college and work, no chasm to be bridged between education and life. And from the very first, life included not merely the practice of my profession, but participation in politics and in other community activities. This was a duty which Theodore Roosevelt, whom I consistently admired, had been vigorously practicing and urging for years. Back in 1894, in an article in *The Atlantic Monthly,* he had written:

A heavy moral obligation rests upon the man of means and upon the man of education to do their full duty to their country. . . . Their education . . . certainly ought to make them feel that they should stand foremost in the honorable effort to serve the whole public by doing their duty as Americans in the body politic.

He was even more specific when he expressed the idea that the man with an education is "in honor bound to do his full duty as a citizen by *helping his fellow citizens to the extent of his power in the exercise of the rights of self-government."* To me, as to many young men of my generation, Theodore Roosevelt brilliantly personified the ideals of active citizenship, and he undoubtedly influenced my lifelong attitude toward politics to an unusual degree. Later, and up to the time of his death in 1919, it was my good fortune to talk with him frequently on matters of politics and citizenship. I felt about him the same way as did so many others. Certainly no man ever gave me such inspiration, the feeling of such an intense desire to do my part, as did Theodore Roosevelt.

The ideals of Lincoln also were a definite factor in my political philosophy. I referred to him constantly in my early speeches, or made him the central theme. I have always had his picture on the wall near my desk. His supreme achievement of holding the nation together made a tremendous impression on me. I revered the spirit so well expressed in Thomas Curtis Clark's sonnet *The Master*, written in memory of Lincoln:

> *We need him now—his rugged faith that held*
> *Fast to the rock of Truth through all the days*
> *Of Moil and strife, the sleepless nights; upheld*
> *By very God was he—that God who stays*
> *All hero-souls who will but trust in Him,*
> *And trusting, labor as if God were not.*
> *His eyes beheld the stars, clouds could not dim*
> *Their glory; but his task was not forgot.*
>
> *To keep his people one; to hold them true*
> *To that fair dream their fathers willed to them—*
> *Freedom for all; to spur them; to renew*
> *Their hopes in bitter days; strife to condemn.*
> *Such was his task, and well his work was done—*
> *Who willed us greater tasks, when set his sun.*

That first year out of college gave me working experience with a number of practical ideals having mainly to do with some sort of organized group, or group activity. One intimate and non-political group which eight of us organized had business as its impetus. We called it the "Red Ravens." It was a sort of private mutual-benefit and fraternal association. We paid fairly substantial dues and held the accumulated moneys in a mutual trust fund. We put most of our money into a building, which we owned for a number of years. The organization lasted for more than forty years. And it meant a real profit in association as well as in cash.

Another was the local Republican party. There I began at the first step as a precinct chairman—a job at which I started my work by ringing doorbells—even before my twenty-first birthday. Sullivan County was a Democratic stronghold, and it was an uphill task to rebuild a Republican organization.

As to direct political action, several of us figured that we would have to do something pretty concrete to make any headway against the well-organized Democrats. The group of older men who ran local Democratic affairs was customarily known as "the Ring." This Ring determined the nominations, which was equivalent to election. They were fine people, some of them being rather elderly contractors and others being county officials. We young fellows, only about half a dozen to begin with, became the nucleus of a group which we called "the Syndicate." We didn't have much weight in the elections at first, but we kept organized —and grew.

In our work we got moral support from some of the fine old boys who had been Republicans way back before the Civil War—notably three stalwarts who had been captains in the Union Army and bore their titles proudly. One of them, Captain Haddon, who wore his hair hanging down to his shoulders like Buffalo Bill, used to invite me down to old settlers' meetings in Haddon Township while I was still in college; and the year I graduated, Captain Springer invited me to the Decoration Day observance in the little church in Gill Township, where the richest farms were located. They wanted me to get into politics, and they knew as well as we know it today that "politics is people."

One day in Chicago, about this time, another veteran gave me an object lesson in patriotism that I have never forgotten. The occasion was a G.A.R. parade down Michigan Avenue. An aged fellow, with his clothes dirty and ragged, shuffled up to the curb beside me. He looked like a real down-and-outer, but there was a G.A.R. button on the lapel of his dirty coat. When the flag came by, this wreck of a man, half crippled, pulled himself up to his full height and saluted, for the moment glorified and lifted quite out of himself by the surge of patriotism in his heart. I have never forgotten the expression on his face.

As soon as I got into Republican party activities I discovered that some of my strongest personal convictions were important political issues too. Among these were woman suffrage, prohibition, and direct action on the part of the whole electorate. The first and the last issues were and are, of course, related.

My intense interest in suffrage was undoubtedly connected with my aunt Sally—a strong, independent, clearheaded person, if I ever knew one. A particular incident had to do with sidewalks. An ambitious, thrifty woman—if she had been a man she would probably have been the head of a savings bank—Aunt Sally taught school for fifty years and had saved her money. She owned four houses and some lots on our street. A formal petition, signed by a certain number of property owners who were legal voters, was necessary in order to determine the kind of material to be used in the new sidewalks. No one except Aunt Sallie owned more than one lot, but when she signed the petition along with the men her name was stricken off because she was not a legal voter. As a woman, she could do nothing but *own and pay*. I have heard plenty of explosions, but none like Aunt Sally's that day.

One other lesson—and a good working principle it has often proved to be—I learned from one of our most picturesque Sullivan citizens, Cap Lucas, the old Indian fighter who had served under Custer but, fortunately for him, not at Little Big Horn. Being fond of horses, Cap ran a livery stable, and a mighty good one. In his stable he had a particularly fine span of black horses, which he would rent out only to his most reliable customers. Even to them he would give a last word of caution as they drove away—*"Go easy with the whip!"* This is equally good advice for those holding political office under a constitution like ours.

I have already mentioned that from 1892 to 1900 Father had been conducting an independent law practice, but that as soon as I was out of college the firm again became Hays & Hays. I cannot have been of much help to Father those first six months that I had my desk in his office. What I didn't know about the law was almost perfectly represented by the contents of the rows of lawbooks lining the walls. However, I was working at it.

But learning law was not my only responsibility. Father warmly encouraged my going into politics, just as he himself had done back in 1880, when the Republicans in our state had won a real victory.

In Indiana, men interested in politics expected to begin at the bottom, at the "grass roots." At first, for us young fellows, there may have been more footwork than headwork, but we knew what we were aiming at. We wanted to know every single one of our possible constituents; we wanted to know what they thought about public matters, and we wanted to get the facts to them all. I never for a moment doubted that the most complete self-government was the best. To me, politics was not an academic matter; it was the active participation of my friends and neighbors in the governing of their own town and their own state. At first I knew as little about politics as about law; but I practiced—and practiced steadily.

I was also encouraged to join the local Masonic lodge, which took all that politics left of my evenings and any spare time I could find during the day. In the course of the following few years I became a member of nearly all the fraternal orders in our vicinity. They were active and vigorous organizations. They gave me inspiration, understanding, and a host of friendships.

Father put me on another job which I carried on for years and greatly enjoyed. He was president of the West Jacksonville Coal Mining & Transport Company, which had purchased the mineral rights on about ten thousand acres around Star City in one corner of our county, in addition to about four thousand acres which it had to purchase in fee simple. Father was responsible for the farming of the four-thousand-acre tract, and as soon as I went into his office he put me in charge of it. I knew little about farming, but experience came fast and it was not long before I could gauge pretty accurately how many tons there were in a haystack and make a fair deal with Ned Crowder, the hay buyer.

What I liked about the job was that it took me out into the country, and I was glad when Father bought a farm of his own. Every country lawyer in Indiana seems to have the ambition to own a farm. Wendell Willkie, I recall, owned at least two. Father's farm consisted of two quarter sections of land, 320 acres, in the good Wabash River bottom, and I remember well how pleased he was with it, having accomplished what he had so long wanted to do.

One other activity I carried on pretty steadily, according to the records. For a young fellow I made an unconscionable number of speeches. They were made on all sorts of occasions—at old settlers' picnics, at churches, at lodges, at Labor Day and Fourth of July celebrations, and so on. These talks were carefully written out and, in many cases, given from memory. Years later, my generous and painstaking secretary, Julia Kelly of Indianapolis, who was with me from State Council of Defense days through the motion picture period, typed all these speeches delivered from 1900 to 1918 and had them beautifully bound into two souvenir volumes. A record of a younger man's beliefs, their ever-recurring note is a complete faith in America and American folk, and the conviction that, working together, there is no limit to what they can accomplish. I still hold to that credo.

It would be hard to plan a bigger birthday than I celebrated on November 5, 1900, when I was twenty-one. There was a party, and Mother fulfilled her promise and paid me one hundred dollars for not smoking or drinking up to that moment. As it so happens, I never have since.

The age of twenty-one being the minimum for admission to the Bar, that momentous ceremony was also brought to pass on my birthday. Having taken the oath required by law, my admittance to the practice of law at the Sullivan Bar by Judge William W. Moffett was one of the proudest moments of my life. For several months I had been allowed to practice occasionally, by courtesy and sufferance of the judge. But now I really belonged! Father had not lost any time bringing it about.

But even admission to the Bar did not quite complete my day. Fate and the calendar made it election eve, and the next day I had the privilege of voting for the first time. Having helped to elect McKinley and Theodore Roosevelt, I went to bed that night a lawyer, a voter, a grateful son, and a very happy young man.

There was one other happy and unexpected milestone in that earliest Sullivan period. It deserves a place of honor among the many splendid chapters that could have been written by young men like myself under the now-famous title, *Life with Father*.

This incident took place on New Year's Day in 1902, when I had been working alongside Father in his law office for only a year and a half. After dinner on that day he asked me to walk up to the office with him. When we arrived there the rooms were cold and we kept our overcoats on for a while as we sat down at our desks and looked over the mail.

Pretty soon Father got up and went over to a typewriter—a thing he seldom did. He started slowly poking out something with one finger.

When I offered to type whatever it was, he said no. After he finished he took the sheet over to his desk, sat down, read it carefully, and signed it. He then folded the sheet of paper, put it in an envelope, and addressed it. After doing all this carefully he got up, put on his overcoat and overshoes, and started toward the door. Stopping at my desk, he handed me the envelope and said, "I'm going on down home, and you come when you get ready. Read this, and sign it if you want to."

When I opened the envelope I was amazed to see a document which gave me a one-third interest in the firm. But there was just one catch in it. That was that I should put in as many hours as he did—and he was a prodigious worker. However, a saving clause read: "Time spent in the study and practice of *Masonry* will be considered time spent in the office." That clause was a great tribute to what he had found, and believed I would find, in the Masonic Order.

No young man entering upon the fuller practice of his profession could have failed to be moved by the welcome to such partnership—from such a father.

PART TWO...

...Law and Local Politics

CHAPTER 6

"Willie—Master in Politics"

THIS story has reached a point where I feel like calling on
the reader to help me appraise my Indiana experiences. As a man looks
back to his youth it is always interesting to see which features of his
environment seem to have been most decisive and formative. Part One
tried to sketch the obvious influences that surrounded me in Sullivan:
home, neighbors, church, school, region. These continued to operate
while I was learning my trade as a lawyer and trying my hand at politics,
as well as at farming, Masonry, and many other interests.

In attempting to find the factors that motivated me in the first decade
after college, let us think for a moment of this same period in the life
of the country—the ten or a dozen years before World War I. They
were the last days of the sometimes maligned "horse-and-buggy" era.

In my home Frank, the family horse, and my earliest automobiles
overlapped for several years. The era of the horse was slowly passing,
though we did not realize it at the time, and the automobile was halt-
ingly moving toward the commanding position it holds today. It was
still the day of moderate speeds—far from anything supersonic. It was
still the day of world peace, a peace that most of us took for granted.
We honestly believed that war as a world factor was a thing of the past.

It was still the day of the quiet, patient, and laborious cultivation of
field and farm which had built Indiana and the whole Middle West.
But industry was growing fast. Almost all my friends were interested
in one way or another in things outside the town community—in crops,
cattle, timber, coal, manufacturing, transportation, and so on.

We were not so isolated from metropolitan or cultural advantages
as one might suppose. We were avid readers of city newspapers, which
came regularly into our homes. Even small towns like Sullivan were
visited by first-class road shows to an extent hard for the present generation to believe. As for political speechmakers in those days before radio
and television, they were always on the road. Those were days of hot
political debate, from the country-store circle on up. Old-fashioned
oratory, on plenty of occasions other than political campaigns, was in
full bloom.

Political activities were legion, especially in Indiana. Things never died down from one campaign to the next. It was one round of committees, caucuses, conventions, elections, victories, defeats—and then the whole thing over again. Campaigns were brought home to us by such means as young people of today have never seen. Some of these things I have already referred to—huge touring glee clubs, 75-foot flagpoles, torchlight parades, thousands of people driving in to the county seat by horse and wagon from all over to hear the presidential candidate. The voluntary activity and hard work that went into these campaigns were unbelievable. In trying to account for the intensity of my early interest in politics, all these things have to be remembered.

I kept in as close touch with my father and mother as I possibly could until 1919, the year in which they both died. Many weeks I went back to Sullivan—from wherever I was—at the cost of what many people would consider extraordinary time, effort, and expense, just to be with my family, teach my Sunday-school class, and go to church on Sunday. Nor was I alone in this habit. I knew of a brick manufacturer in Ohio who for an amazing number of years never missed Sunday school, wherever he might be. This conscientious and habitual devotion to church may well have been one of the definite factors in the spiritual life of the Middle West, with its strong New England traditions.

The social life of our community was a real and active thing, although simple in its forms. We had civic pride and worked together for the improvement of the appearance and services of our town. I gradually assumed certain business interests, particularly connected with farming and later with banking and other concerns, often in co-operation with Father. My profession of law, into which I had entered so naturally and so completely, was absorbing, as any lawyer knows.

As all these interests were real and constant, it is still a question how my attention to politics was aroused so early, how it was stimulated so constantly, and how it gradually assumed what seems to have been a controlling interest in my life. As I tell this story I hope that the reasons will become clear.

Perhaps we have here a fair example of the adage, "As the twig is bent, so grows the tree." The experience of 1896, when Father and I attended the Republican National Convention in St. Louis and saw McKinley nominated, looks like the most decisive single event in my life. That experience was crystallized for me in the envelope of clippings covering the convention that Father gave me.

Father's hope that I would take a citizen's interest in politics had apparently become a reality. An impression of the tremendous importance of national politics to the whole life of the country had probably been quietly at work in my mind ever since that convention. When

I got through college and settled in Sullivan I found myself at once, even before my twenty-first birthday, chairman of my precinct. From that day until 1922 I was never to be without direct participation in the political life of my town, county, state, or nation.

This absorption in political activity is perhaps easier to explain today than it was to account for at the time. The strangest thing about it is probably the fact that I never held any elective political office except a three-year term as city attorney of Sullivan. My activity from precinct committeeman right up to national chairman was a volunteer service, a labor of love. In those days no salary was attached to any of these chairmanships, no matter how much work was entailed. I probably went "up the ladder" because others recognized my willingness to work. To borrow an analogy from athletics, I "maintained my amateur standing"; I never became a "professional." I loved political organization and I threw myself into it with delight, but I never accepted money for doing so and I never considered myself a professional "politician."

This attitude was in line with my deepest personal convictions: faith in God, in folks, in the nation, and in the Republican party. My belief in the ability of men to work together toward common goals made me a "joiner." This is one of the basic elements in political activity, which is the getting together of *people*. I was also terrifically proud of America and of the record we had made in self-government and in advancing the cause of freedom. The speeches that I made as a young man reflect this emotional element. And I believed then, as I do now, that the morality and the responsibility of the individual citizen are the bulwarks of any government founded on liberty, enlightened by law.

Going one step farther, I early held the belief that as long as a man puts himself wholeheartedly into his convictions it is possible for him to accomplish almost anything he undertakes. I felt this especially because Americans were free to work out their own destiny unhampered by outside limitations or compulsions. Thus, as I try to analyze it now, my belief in individual responsibility, interdependence, and potential accomplishment was the basic thread which ran through the thinking that supported my political activity.

The final conviction which kept me active was my belief in the Republican party. It must be remembered that when I came onto the political scene in 1900 the country had known only two outstanding Democratic presidents—Andrew Jackson and Grover Cleveland. It was natural that I should relate the nation's progress to the Republican administrations. Our party, dramatically conceived when the national foundations trembled, had heralded its own birth by saving the very life of our nation. As I remember putting it in one of those youthful speeches of mine: "It cared for us and, under its wise guidance, we grew from that weakened cohesion to this nation which has no equal; whose shores are the steppingstones to freedom, whose laws are the offspring of justice, and whose flag is an inspiration to men of all climes."

Convictions alone might have left me only a sideline political amateur who never gets into the game but only looks at it from the bleachers. This was never what I wanted. From the first I welcomed all the *experience* that came my way and accepted every opportunity. For instance, from 1902 to 1906 I spoke on twenty-nine occasions, seven of them strictly political. As to political action, I served one term as precinct committeeman and two terms as county chairman, until I was appointed state chairman of the Speakers Bureau in 1906. During that same four-year period I found myself a member of the Rules Committee of the Second District Convention; in 1904, of the Executive Committee of the Indiana Lincoln League; of the State Executive Committee; and chairman of the Fairbanks train in 1906. During that period I attended many district and county conventions, Governor Hanly's inauguration in 1904, and the State Convention that same year. For a young man in his middle twenties this looks like enough activity to interfere considerably with his own business, but Father and I both believed that it *was* part of my business. It certainly was the school of hard knocks, and it was a thorough grounding in the principles of political education, organization, and action from the ground up.

In all honesty I must admit that during this period I did campaign for one political office, prosecuting attorney, losing in a confirmed Democratic stronghold by fifty-three votes. It was nearly always the custom for some young Republican lawyer to run for this office, although he was rarely elected. It was considered a good chance for a young man to put himself before the people—especially before the older Republican voters—so that he might thereby increase his acquaintance. The year I ran for prosecutor I went around and talked to a lot of folks. I spent nothing on campaign literature except for printing some small cards which I gave out during talks to farmers and others. I learned a lesson in that campaign which was important for the rest of my life. I have always believed that in politics one must go to the people to find out what they are thinking, talking about, and hoping for. It was a part of what we now call *political education*—but it was no one-way street. With neither radio nor television, this education of the people had to be carried on largely by word of mouth and, in my case at least, at the expense of a lot of footwork.

Politics in Indiana was considered a trade to which a young man had to be apprenticed, as truly as a cobbler or a silverworker in the Middle Ages. There was no royal road to political prominence. To use the more common metaphor, it was a slow climb up a ladder of many rungs. In my case it took eighteen years. And because it may have some bearing on the practice of politics in America, now as then, let me try to retrace the steps.

In January of 1902 I was re-elected a precinct committeeman and also elected a delegate to the District Convention. I was only twenty-two years old. We young Republicans in Sullivan were pegging away, but the opposition was still too strong for us. Even a proposition to incorporate Sullivan as a city was defeated, as it was in two more elections. It was 1910 before Sullivan's first *city* administration existed, and that was Republican.

To show how repeated efforts are often necessary to gain elective office, John C. Chaney of Sullivan, one of Father's close friends, was nominated for Congress in 1902. He was already recognized as a leader and was prominent as a speaker or presiding officer at meetings and conventions of all sorts, but he was defeated in the fall elections by almost eight hundred votes. However, he won in 1904.

I remember October of 1902 as being a month full of meetings, the coming of political trains, and an immense amount of just plain talking to voters. Perhaps I remember best a meeting in nearby Linton, where Mark Hanna, the chairman of the Republican National Committee, climaxed a magnificent sweep through Indiana. It was estimated that in two days he had spoken to at least ninety thousand people. One of the prized photographs on my study wall shows Mark Hanna on a raised plank platform addressing the big Linton crowd. Although we lost in Sullivan County, in November Indiana went Republican by twenty-five thousand and the party obtained control of Congress. Theodore Roosevelt had been serving as President since the death of McKinley the previous autumn.

One of the humorous events in connection with this election was the offer made by thirteen young Democrats of our county to nine of us Republicans that if John Chaney was defeated for Congress by more than a thousand votes we would give them a dance. The Democratic boys lost the wager by 210 votes and, as a result, they gave *us* a very delightful dance at Sherman Hall the week after the election. We had a good time but had to admit that if we aimed to win any *local* elections greater effort was obviously needed. We kept plugging ahead.

The year 1903, being an off one, was comparatively quiet, but we were already looking ahead toward the 1904 campaign. To show how hard it was to keep politics submerged, I remember William Jennings Bryan's visit to Sullivan that year and his address at the Methodist Church. Father was on the reception committee, and Bryan's talk was supposed to be wholly non-partisan, but he managed to get in his ideas on the silver question and the tariff just the same.

For me, 1904 opened with election on January 11 to my first term as county chairman. Since it was a presidential election year, we all knew there was even more to be done for national interests than for local candidates. We wasted little time getting organized after the County Convention had been held, aiming to help the Republican snowball start down the mountainside well in advance of the State Convention in April. Frank Hanly, Republican candidate for governor, visited Sullivan; and I, perhaps overconfidently, reported to our state chairman that Sullivan County Republicans meant to give the Democrats a campaign that would be a revelation to them. We certainly tried to speed it up.

Our county Democrats responded in kind. They had a vigorous chairman, Abe Frakes, who had worked up a first-class roster of voters. They knew their people. But at their County Convention difficulty developed between the supporters of Alton B. Parker, the eventual presidential candidate, and William Randolph Hearst. Fourteen Hearst delegates were eventually elected against six for Parker, but the presiding officer declared that a motion to adjourn had carried before the Hearst faction could introduce a resolution endorsing their candidate. Indiana politics was quite a horse race even in the earlier stages.

To show how organization percolated down into the minor units, I remember that in May the convention in our Curry Township was attended by 285 Republicans. The size of that meeting was considerably enhanced by the presence of Perly Hayworth, who was commonly referred to as Sullivan's "biggest" Republican. He weighed 345 pounds —quite as much as William Howard Taft at his "mostest."

June of 1904 brought the National Convention in Chicago, with the nomination of Theodore Roosevelt and Indiana's Charles W. Fairbanks. We were all enthusiastic, and my contacts with national figures began to grow. Elihu Root delivered the keynote address, and Harry S. New, of whom we were proud, was elected national committeeman from Indiana. There was one notable figure missing—Mark Hanna. His death in Washington the previous February had been a great loss to the national Republican organization. He had been a consummate organizer; and though many thought him arbitrary, he contributed much to the concept of thoroughly marshaling party forces behind a well-thought-out program. He will go down in history as one of the great national chairmen. With his memory I have a strangely personal tie: the carved walnut, red leather upholstered armchair in which he sat time and again as chairman of the National Committee when it met at the Union League Club in New York has stood for many years in my office.

Let me turn for a moment to Theodore Roosevelt, though later I shall want to discuss him more fully when my personal story crosses his. Up to 1904, to me he was chiefly a name, though a great name, as to all my generation. I had deep admiration, respect, and affection for him. Like other young men, I felt the strength of his character. I believed in his fixed purpose to bring about greater social justice. He was so honest in his mental processes that even his enemies had to respect him. He set for me an ideal and a pattern of public service better than any other man in political life. After my father, he was my greatest inspiration. Of that I am sure. My feeling toward him has never changed.

With the enthusiasm of the National Convention running through my veins, I went back to Sullivan and called the County Convention to order. In September we opened county headquarters in the rear room of a building where Goodman had his clothing store. This headquarters may have seemed a very modest place, but it was open every day, with someone on duty at all times to handle the questions and requests of all visitors.

The fall months were again filled with campaigning. Successively there came to Sullivan the Democratic presidential candidate, Alton B. Parker, who strangely suggested in a coal-mining district that the laborer was worth no more than a dollar a day; J. Frank Hanly, our candidate for governor; William Jennings Bryan, stumping for the Democratic ticket; Charles W. Fairbanks, our own vice-presidential candidate; and our Hoosier Senator Albert J. Beveridge, one of the most eloquent orators America has ever heard. Despite all this activity and anything we could do, Sullivan County again went Democratic. But we were beginning to make a dent in the local situation.

Following these efforts I got a real boost: both Chaney and Fairbanks wrote me cordial letters in appreciation of our efforts in Sullivan. These gestures were not only unexpected but extremely encouraging.

Every year the Sullivan *Union* published a series of wisecracks about what various citizens would most like for Christmas; it was a form of community ribbing. That year they proposed that what Will Hays would rather receive than anything else would be Abe Frakes's poll of the county—and perhaps they were not far wrong. I had learned how important it was to know every family in your bailiwick.

Nineteen-five brought the inauguration of Theodore Roosevelt as President in his own right and Frank Hanly as our Indiana governor. I was sent to Indianapolis for Hanly's inauguration, and this, I know, made a lasting impression on me.

The rest of the year was reasonably quiet. We soon began to talk about renominating our fellow townsman, John Chaney, for Congress, which we did. He had worked hard, made a good record, and had never been discouraged by his losing fight on several occasions before his election, cheerfully giving his own time and his own money when he knew there was no chance of winning. After defeat he simply got ready for the next race—until he finally won. In my mind he still remains as a perfect example of a conscientious public servant. In Congress he represented all of his constituents faithfully, being keenly interested in the Invalid Pension Committee and the other interests of the old soldiers of his district.

It will probably come as a surprise to most readers that Mr. Chaney's was the first "billion-dollar Congress." Hard as it is to believe, this was the first Congress which passed annual appropriation bills, for the entire government, surpassing one billion dollars.

Another local political feature of this period was Republican County Headquarters' plea for a "clean election." It was sent to the central committees of the Democratic, Prohibition, and Socialist parties of our county, urging all of us to refrain from corrupt election practices in any way, shape, or manner. This proposal was an outgrowth of the observations of our little Sullivan "Syndicate," to which I have referred; we realized that at the time our town seemed to have a well-organized Democratic clique which was pretty much running things—through the ballot, to be sure. That appeared to include ballot-burning, ballot-stuffing, and ballot-fixing! The Prohibitionists and the Socialists heartily joined in the effort to safeguard the polls, and a system of watchers was organized effectively.

And now I come to the next step, which led to operations on the state level and indirectly on the national level. Our state chairman and later governor, James P. Goodrich—another of my political idols and mentors —appointed me head of the State Speakers Bureau in 1906. This was a complete surprise. Apparently the impression had gotten around that there was an organizer down in Sullivan County who was not afraid to work hard and give considerable time. From my point of view it was a real opportunity to tackle a job of organizing a hundred and one speakers and co-ordinating their appearances with the activities of ninety-two countries and thirteen districts. I tackled this job with enthusiasm, although it took me away from home and necessitated the setting up of a Speakers Bureau headquarters in Indianapolis. Since it also led to my responsibility for the campaign train of Fairbanks, it was an introduction to campaigning on the national level.

Since these early lessons in politics stand out so clearly in my own mind—the first experience of each sort naturally being the sharpest—let me try to set down some of the principles that early seemed to me basic in this field. These were about ten in number, and I offer them with the thought that they may be of some value to young men and women who want to take part in self-government but have had no experience in practical politics:

1. Since *"politics is people,"* you have to like people and be happy in working with them.

2. Be convinced that *participation in self-government* is a moral duty of a good citizen and give it a place of corresponding value.

3. Be ready for *hard work,* unremunerated and, in large measure, unrecognized—at least on the lower rungs of the ladder.

4. Be ready and willing to *begin at the bottom* and conscious that political activity, to be sound and reliable, must also start at the bottom—namely, at the grass roots.

5. Accept the fact—like any other good teacher or leader—that *patience, perseverance,* and *repetition* will be necessary.

6. See that the *"office"*—wherever it is—is *always open.*

7. Know that *a solid organization,* built up step by step, with someone responsible for each unit, is necessary for good results.

8. *Get people together* as often as necessary in committee meetings, dinners, rallies, and conventions. Only by such means can enthusiasm and group action be fully developed.

9. Put *enthusiasm, energy,* and *confidence* into every activity—remembering that the members of the group take the cue from the leader.

10. Never lose sight of the *dignity of self-government,* and have confidence that people will participate if they can be brought to realize that they are actively helping to care for and to guide their own community and their country.

It would be utterly impossible to estimate what proportion of my time during these early years was actually given to politics. In fact, it would be difficult to know where to draw the line. Much of what I did in various activities certainly had a bearing on my work as county chairman. There seemed to be half a dozen major interests: law, business, church, civic affairs, fraternal and social groups, and, more closely, personal relationships.

I have always said that my one ambition in life was to be a real lawyer. I certainly "played" at being one as early as the age of six. Obviously Father's example was always strong and I went into his office and into partnership with him just as naturally as thousands of other sons have entered their fathers' businesses.

On the other hand, circumstances and other interests appear from the first to have drawn me in other directions so often as to make complete absorption in law impossible. It was not that I didn't take my cases seriously; perhaps it was more a case of physical circumstances of my own creation which kept me from devoting greater time to my profession. Whether or not I would have accomplished more by sticking only to the law is a purely academic question. Apparently we are prisoners of our own personal limitations and of our own peculiar predilections. Trying to be honest, I must record the fact that various other activities and objectives seemed to me just as important as cases at law.

My early years in practice were probably much like those of other young attorneys living in country towns in the Middle West. Our work had to do primarily with the special activities of the region. Father's reputation was so well established that we were called in as counsel in a large proportion of the important cases. The volume of business handled by Hays & Hays gradually but steadily increased. We moved to larger offices in 1925 and finally, in 1948, opened a branch office in Indianapolis, since our work had become to so large a degree state-wide.

Our cases fell largely into the general classification of coal mines, railroads, water, personal-damage suits, wills and estate litigation. We also handled matters such as the incorporation of a township. Personally, I was given a number of trusteeships which led increasingly into the field of business.

If the reader knows that much of Sullivan County was coal-mining territory, he will at once understand the prevalence of these cases in our office. In October 1902 it was reported: "There is hardly a foot of coal land in the county that is not under option, and many farmers are reaping a harvest of money by selling the coal that underlies their land for $40 to $50 an acre." This was not far below the value of the land for farming. The matter of coal I mention by way of explaining why mines and railroads were so large a part of our business.

There were scores of important suits that we handled, but after this lapse of time few would be of interest to the reader. A number were damage suits arising out of accident or death resulting to miners. One case I recall had twenty-one witnesses, including expert medical witnesses. The suit was brought for $25,000 damages, but it was settled for $3,000. Looking back, I am amazed by the extremely moderate sums for which many of these cases were settled—some, involving unquestioned injuries, for as little as $50 or $100. One must wonder when he reads current newspaper reports today of judgments reaching $100,000 or more. Is it that human life and earning power are so much more highly valued; or that our whole scale of living, from an earlier point of view, is inflated; or that one is suing an allegedly wealthy corportion which can "afford to pay," instead of a small community business or unit of government like a county; or is it a combination of these and possibly other reasons?

When I recall the nature of some of the decisions in damage suits I cannot help wondering about the shift in sentiment from that day to this. In 1903 a suit was brought on account of the death of Hickman Rich and his wife, killed in 1901 by a passenger train at Pittman's Crossing, two miles north of Sullivan. The decision of the court held that the complain of the plaintiff, the deceased man's brother, was invalid because it did not show that Rich had taken sufficient precaution.

A humorous damage case was brought by a young woman named Earline Sinclair, who had been severely hazed in December 1903 by Cass Township school children, first for refusing to stand treat to them (perhaps it was just before Christmas), and second because she had a framed picture of Theodore Roosevelt on her schoolroom wall. The

$10,000 damage suit was finally decided the following year with an award of $200. This was a rather expensive ducking.

From earliest days our firm were the attorneys for several of the railroads that ran through our state. In cases like the Chicago & Eastern Illinois Railroad we had been general counsel for Indiana for many years. More than once in those early days we had to do with the reorganization or the sale of small roads which were absorbed in larger systems. One case was the Indiana & Illinois Southern—the narrow-gauge road that ran east and west through Sullivan. The moving spirit of that road, Perry H. Blue, lived in our town; he was a close friend of our family and from early youth stood out in my mind as quite a figure. I remember that when his little railroad was converted into a broadgauge and joined to a larger system it seemed to me a tremendous enterprise—something like joining the east and west divisions of the Union Pacific. During my early practice Father, as trustee, sold this Indiana division of the old I. & I.S. at public sale to the Illinois Central for $268,714.24.

But even law has its bizarre aspects. One such case was that of Brocksmith *v.* Bostock-Ferrari Amusement Company. Otto Brocksmith sued the amusement company because one of their bears frightened his horse, which ran away—Brocksmith's kneecap being broken in the ensuing accident. This had taken place during an Elks carnival at Vincennes in 1902. The case was venued to the Sullivan Circuit Court; after two days the jury returned a verdict awarding the plaintiff a judgment for $750. He had asked for $2,000, although it was claimed that the injury would cripple him permanently.

Although Sullivan was by no means in dry country, water was the cause of much litigation. Drainage ditches, levees, water supply—all manner of such cases came into our office. One important one had to do with the contract for constructing a twelve-mile levee to protect nearly ten thousand acres of land from inundation by the Wabash. Another, when I was city attorney, was concerned with terms connected with installing a new water system for the town. Though I am getting ahead of my story a little, this matter sent me—at the request of the mayor—out to Denver to attend a national irrigation conference, which proved quite an eye-opener.

Many of these legal cases were bound up with political or government action, and this made them doubly interesting. I found, as others have, that law and politics make a good combination. Politics and law are constantly reacting on each other. Both are *of, by,* and *for the people,* and each can provide relief from any deprivation for which either might be responsible.

During the years 1902 to 1906 I found myself increasingly interested in business, though on no scale comparable to politics or law. Quite naturally I was drawn gradually into several enterprises with which Father was already connected. One was a coal company—a subsidiary of United States Steel—of which he was secretary. Another was a traction company which aimed to build a line from Sullivan to Linton through the coal belt. A third was banking, since Father was already connected with the Citizens Trust Company of Sullivan, organized in 1903. A fourth involved the natural resources of our county, especially gas and oil. Oil was first found near our town late in 1904, and a local company was organized immediately, with my father as one of the directors. They struck oil at nine hundred feet, some ten miles from home.

Although these business interests were not at first strictly mine, my heart was in them: I worked at them, and they formed the foundation of my own later concerns. Here again, quite obviously, I learned much from Father.

I have already mentioned that both my parents were active in everything connected with our Presbyterian church. I hope I followed their example here too. My first responsibility—and one that I carried a great many years—was my Sunday-school class of boys, even including my younger brother at one period. This class involved a lot besides a Sunday-morning session. We had picnics and fishing trips in the summer and, during the winter, parties and stunts of various sorts. I know I enjoyed this association and it proved a strong home-town tie.

These first years of law practice and politics might almost be considered a postgraduate education carried on in my own community by what is now called the "case method." Of my various instructors, Father was certainly the chief. I think it must also have been a pretty good introduction to personal participation in all sorts of community projects. Certainly I became convinced that when people in a town really want some civic improvement they can *get together and bring it to pass,* as long as it is within reason. This faith became a cornerstone of my practical creed. Much later, in the motion picture industry, I found it equally applicable on the national level if one could marshal the sentiment of strong representative groups. National politics was to prove but an extension of the same principle, with the citizens as voters.

Our particular Sullivan project during the first decade of this century was the library. At that time public libraries were almost unknown in small communities. Many people have forgotten that it was Andrew Carnegie's epic-making vision and generosity which brought almost three thousand public libraries into being early in this century. In 1903 we received a letter from the Carnegie Foundation stating that Mr. Carnegie would donate ten thousand dollars for a library building as soon as the Town Council agreed to appropriate a thousand dollars a year for its maintenance. Here again it was Father who offered the resolution providing the financial maintenance through a special tax levy.

We were all delighted when the library was dedicated in 1905; it was an occasion for a real community celebration.

Another line of activity that we seemed to carry on pretty steadily was speechmaking. Often Father and I would both be off in different directions delivering speeches on the same day. My own specialties seemed to be Memorial Day and Labor Day addresses and also talks at old settlers' meetings—of which our county had many—and gatherings of the G.A.R. The text of most of these speeches I have kept. As I look them over today I find that my feeling about our country has changed very little. No one was afraid to be enthusiastically patriotic in those days.

Hoosiers are congenital joiners, and I followed the habit. Neither socially nor otherwise could I ever have been accused of being an "isolationist." Fraternal orders in the Middle West were extremely active bodies, perhaps especially so in the smaller towns where there are fewer public functions. Interest in my college fraternity, Phi Delta Theta, probably started me in this direction, and I have never lost contact with the organization. As early as 1902 I attended the national convention in New York and soon after was elected president of Epsilon Province, our own midwestern region—an office which I held for eight years. In 1911 I went to Washington to attend another national meeting of the fraternity. Ultimately I was to become national president.

My membership in the Masonic Order perhaps became a closer association, since it was more vitally connected with the men with whom I was daily living and working. My entrance into the order took place before I was twenty-one and under delightful circumstances. The members of the Sullivan lodge elected me without my father's knowledge. Then, as a particular compliment, they asked him to administer the Third Degree, which he did without any knowledge that I was the candidate. This gave him great pleasure. Only four years later, in company with Fred Bays and Dirrelle Chaney, I received the Thirty-second Degree in Indianapolis and joined the Shriners. At the same time I was elected president of my Scottish Rite class of 124 novitiates and was asked to give the address at the class banquet.

These fraternal organizations continued to be an important part of my daily life: Phi Delta Theta, Panhellenic, and the Masonic Order. To these I added the Elks, after the Terre Haute chapter had instituted our Sullivan chapter in 1905. Sullivan Elks took an active part in local charity. I particularly remember one Christmas when Captain Bill Lucas and myself decided that we would make it a real Christmas by distributing toys to the children, instead of merely giving out baskets of food.

Among the speeches I delivered during these early years were a number of Elks memorial addresses, both at Sullivan and at other lodges in

our region. In August 1906 I had an opportunity to attend the annual
Elks meeting at Denver. Later, when vacationing in Colorado, I occasionally had opportunity to get to these annual meetings.

It is undoubtedly true that my close associations in these various
fraternal organizations were another contributing cause of my growing
interest in politics.

No young fellow in my town was too busy to get in a little relaxation
—at home, on a tennis court, or taking an occasional vacation. These
memories are very clear in my mind, especially the tennis. In 1902
Dirrelle Chaney and I lost in the finals of the town tournament to
Frank and Will Aydelotte. Frank, who went to high school with me,
was already an instructor in English at Indiana University. Three years
later he was our Indiana Rhodes Scholar at Oxford, and after 1918 the
American secretary of the Rhodes Trustees. Sullivan was always proud
of Frank, following him through his long presidency of Swarthmore
College and his years as director of the Institute of Advanced Study at
Princeton.

The year 1902 was also the year of my engagement and marriage to
Helen Louise Thomas of Crawfordsville, whom I had first known during my college days at Wabash. Father built us a cottage on West
Washington Street, and there we took up residence in December. Those
were the days when even young families spent many evenings at home. I
think my reputation at the card table was considerably higher than that
on the tennis court—a bit of early training that made me welcome
canasta in later years and emerge as a pretty fair hand at poker. We did
quite a little entertaining at home and occasionally had weekend guests.

My first two ventures with automobiles were both connected with
Max Puett, with whom I had a long friendship which continued out to
my California days. It was from him I bought a Toledo "steamer" when
he graduated to a gasoline car in 1903. I certainly spent the better part
of the next few weeks learning how to "steam up" and drive the contraption. I also remember with terrible clearness the first real tour I took
in it, which was to Crawfordsville. We got ready with great care because
it was going to take the better part of the next day. When we finally
got steam up and the bags were in the car we got as far as the front gate
when something happened to the gaskets in the boiler. Steam filled the
whole front yard—and we got no farther. However, when the car was
again working, I discovered that its speed was limited only by the nerve
of the driver, as anyone who has owned one of these early steamers can
confirm.

Vacations meant more to us in those days than they do today, probably because we had so few of them; it was before the day when the
family automobile could whisk one all around the country. Under the
circumstances, however, I did quite a bit of moving about in business

and in politics, and also on vacations. In 1906 we started going to Colorado, a practice which continued for a number of years and which became a very important chapter in our family life.

These early days were certainly not lacking in activity: the Syndicate in politics; railroads and coal-mine cases at law; banks and early gas and coal interests in business; church and Sunday school, and miscellaneous speeches; fraternity and lodges; and always personal contacts. People—*always people*—were the chief ingredients of my Sullivan days. I loved those years and I know that they entered deeply into all that came after.

Whatever I had done in politics from 1900 to 1906, far from discouraging me or diminishing my interest, only led me to increase my efforts. Looking ahead another six years, I find my experience up to 1912 was probably the best possible preparation for the emergency—I might truly say the catastrophe—that struck the Republican party when Colonel Roosevelt left it to set up the Bull Moose organization. Certainly in those twelve years I learned as much from our failures as from our successes. If the Republicans in Indiana had enjoyed smooth sailing up to 1912 I am sure we would have been totally unprepared for what that year brought and for the difficult job of reuniting Progressives with Republicans that absorbed us from 1914 to 1918.

As to my own Indiana activities, I remained as chairman of the Speakers Bureau through the middle of 1910, when I declined reappointment because of my election as chairman of the Second Indiana District the preceding February. Re-elected in 1912, I remained district chairman until chosen state chairman of the Republican Central Committee on Lincoln's Birthday, 1914. During these same years I also filled the one elective political office which I was ever to hold—that of city attorney in the first administration of the newly formed city government of Sullivan. In this position my annual salary was four hundred dollars. I doubt whether that pay "corrupted" me.

In the six-year span—1907 through 1912—there were several events which turned out to be significant both to me and to the political fortunes of the country. It is also interesting to note that from year to year Indiana rarely lacked one or more representatives in the high councils of the nation. We were not out on the shore; we were close to the center of national currents. For instance, in 1908 Harry New was the Republican national chairman—a fact that increased my sense of nearness to national activities.

That year was one of intense activity. This was my second campaign as chairman of the Speakers Bureau and my first national campaign in that capacity. At the end of March I left Sullivan for Indianapolis, where I again tackled the job of co-ordinating our state-wide speaking program.

When Republicans gathered at Chicago for the National Convention on June 16, 1908, William Howard Taft was nominated for President, with Roosevelt's warm endorsement. When Hoosier Harry New, as national chairman, called the convention to order I could not have known that I myself would be standing in his shoes at the very same spot just twelve years later. *Politics is not carried on by prophets, though something of a prophetic sense is a wonderful asset when founded on true insight.* One other interesting Hoosier touch was George Ade's appointment as a member of the Notification Committee. As we shall see, this led directly to the holding of the notification ceremony on Ade's own farm in Indiana.

The autumn campaign was full of excitement, as usual. Taft addressed at least six thousand people when his special train stopped at Sullivan. I remember he was so hoarse that Senator Hemenway had to take over until the train pulled out. Our neighbor, John Chaney, introduced Taft, with the aid of two bands and a glee club. Taft spent only three days in Indiana, but his crowds were enormous. In nearby Terre Haute he addressed between thirty and forty thousand people. In those days our citizens traveled many miles to hear a presidential candidate.

One bit of local excitement bobbed up during this campaign. Congressman Chaney's secretary—a fine young man—was a Democrat. The Sullivan *Times* did not like the idea of a Republican having a Democratic secretary. They took an obvious poke at the young man in their editorial columns; he came back fast and took an actual poke at the city editor—which gave him both satisfaction and a considerable fine.

As expected, the campaign culminated in the election of Taft, who carried Indiana by nearly eleven thousand votes. In spite of this, we lost eleven of thirteen congressmen, and the entire Sullivan County Democratic ticket was re-elected. Even at that, we could not have known the full meaning of the disappointment we were to experience in the great rift of 1912.

Almost before we know it, the new elections of 1910 were upon us. In the preceding off year I had been able to give more time to mending my own fences—to taking care of my law practice and my business and personal interests in Sullivan. This alternation between concentration on profession and politics went on year after year; it was necessary and it proved to be not such a bad plan.

For me, February 1, 1910, was another milestone on the political path. At our Second District Convention at Vincennes the delegates, by acclamation, named me district chairman. More than any preceding step, this was both an honor and a responsibility. I felt obliged to resign the Speakers Bureau job after my election as district chairman, because I could neither do two jobs at once nor be in two places at the same time.

I was interested in doing one job and doing it as well as I could. And I knew that the work of thoroughly organizing our district for the next election would be all I could handle well.

However, I had not entirely cut loose from state activities, because at the State Convention in April I was named secretary of the convention. These details I mention because it now seems clear that, in the vernacular, I had a perfect "course of sprouts" step by step in the practical field of political organization.

The above observation also applies to questions of public policy which were taking shape in Indiana as political issues: prohibition and woman suffrage. Here again I had a direct personal acquaintance with the workings of the suffrage idea. A Sullivan woman—Mrs. Antoinette D. Leach, our only woman lawyer—was a vigorous fighter for woman suffrage. She worked hard to induce our women to take an active part in politics. She was the first president of the Sullivan County Woman's Suffrage Association, and the first woman to be chairman of the County Democratic Committee. As if to underscore her position, Mrs. Leach announced her independent candidacy for state representative from Sullivan County. Also in 1910, although defeated, she soon had Representative Headrick of our county introduce into the legislature a bill calling for equal suffrage. I was wholly sympathetic to the movement and as national chairman had the opportunity to help secure the ratification of the amendment in August 1920.

To show the constant boiling over of the political cauldron and the high caliber of the men on the political scene, let me mention two meetings. In October our Senator Albert J. Beveridge spoke at Shelburn, at the invitation of the coal miners, and a big gathering from all over the county gave him a rousing ovation. At least four thousand persons attended the meeting in the ball park, many delegations coming with brass bands or fife-and-drum corps. Following on Beveridge's heels came Gifford Pinchot and half a dozen others. All this activity was to me a continuous lesson in unified action and perpetual—almost backbreaking —effort. It was daily dinned into me by actual circumstances that convincing people is both difficult and necessary.

One thing that added to our work was the gerrymandering done in Indiana by the Democrats. During this period many counties which were predominantly Republican were shifted to districts which were strongly Democratic, so that their vote would not visibly affect Democratic majorities. At least eight of our thirteen districts were so rearranged. This procedure was legal and not hitherto unknown, being within the rights of the legislature. For us, it simply made the going harder.

In 1911, probably for the first time, there began to be some talk about the possibility of my being the next state chairman. This was the beginning of a quiet little boom which put me into that office in 1914. My lifelong friend, John G. Bryson, had a part in that boom.

The year 1912 was a crucial one. Knowing its importance, I shifted my attention very heavily to politics. The first months were spent on improving and strengthening the organization itself; anyone who has been in politics knows what that means. As to detail, it involved an enormous number of personal conferences with leaders of every geographical division and subdivision of the district, which at that time included seven counties. It also meant holding committee meetings and conventions in the different townships and counties. It meant, too, instruction of leaders in issues and campaign methods. We had to make sure that our Republican leaders in every voting unit had the best possible lists of their voters, the best plans of procedure, and the best ways of passing the information on to the voters. The final goal was getting the people to the polls. Knowing what we were up against, we worked hard.

It is important at this point to notice that our district delegates in January of 1912 passed a resolution strongly endorsing the administration of President Taft. Of course this was the thing to do. No one could anticipate the tragic split between Taft and Roosevelt that was to take place before we cast our votes in November.

At the end of February, after my election as state vice-chairman, a business trip to New York resulted in one of the most important things that ever happened to me: Colonel Roosevelt had just thrown his hat into the ring. He had made a speech in Columbus which drew a great deal of attention and some sharp criticism because he had advocated, among other changes, the recall of judicial decisions.

I aready had an appointment to see him in New York in his office at *Outlook Magazine*. When I met him he asked me what I thought of his recommendation about judicial decisions, and I told him I thought it was "anarchy." As I recall, he said, "Well, it isn't quite as bad as that, is it, Will?" Before I left he introduced me to Frank Knox and two of the colonel's strongest supporters. By far the most important outcome of this conference was that he asked me if I would consider the national chairmanship of the new Progressive party, if and when it should take complete form. The rumblings were already going on. It was perfectly clear in my mind that my place was in the Republican organization, and I so told the colonel. I never regretted the decision. It was certainly unusual that he should even have broached the subject to a thirty-two-year-old Hoosier district chairman.

Our Indiana State Convention in March was a fair preview of what was to happen at the National Convention in June. The Taft forces came out on top with a majority of 105. As delegates-at-large to the national convention they elected Charles W. Fairbanks, Harry S. New,

James E. Watson, and James D. Oliver. At our following District Convention the delegates were not instructed, but the Roosevelt ticket was defeated by forty votes. Remember, it had been only a couple of months since our district had passed a resolution endorsing the Taft administration.

When the National Committee met in Chicago and began on June 6 to review the cases of contested delegates—just as happened in the Republican National Convention of 1952—the contests were decided overwhelmingly in favor of Taft, although popular sentiment for Roosevelt had been steadily gaining momentum. The whole story is a familiar one to political historians and has been retold many times. On June 22, Taft and Sherman were again nominated to head the Republican ticket. Of all the Roosevelt delegates, only 107 cast votes for the colonel and 344 responded: "Present but not voting." The latter action had been requested by the colonel himself, who withdrew his own nomination a few hours before the balloting began.

Shortly after the nomination the Roosevelt men dramatically walked out of the Coliseum and over to Orchestra Hall, where Colonel Roosevelt instantly became the standard-bearer of the new Progressive party.

My memories of that convention, like my feelings at the time, are mixed. As events of 1920 were to prove, the fact that President Taft's name was placed in nomination by a fellow Ohioan, Warren G. Harding, was more significant than I could have known then. The chief impression, I fear, was one of uproar and of a critical discord which was a sad thing to witness. I felt this deeply, for I admired and loved T.R. until his dying day, but I sensed that this party split would be vastly damaging to the Republican organization, at least temporarily. I know I went back home realizing what the task ahead of us was bound to be. The nomination of Wilson and Indiana's Governor Marshall on July 2 made it no easier.

The new Progressive party, which had chosen the designation "Bull Moose," began organizing in our county the last of August, as it did pretty well throughout the state. The general sentiment of the Republican organization, however, was that we continue to commend, endorse, and work for the continuance of the Taft administration.

The weeks flew by. We worked doubly hard to counteract whatever effects a third party might have. No amount of effort could suffice. November came, and it was a dreary month. For the Democrats it was "cherry-blossom time" in Washington. Wilson and Marshall had clearly triumphed. Democratic sentiment had brought almost state-wide victory in Indiana, where we lost the governorship and the state legislature as well as the administration in my home community. We had been badly beaten after apparently gaining ground in the previous years. We ran a poor third. It was heartbreaking. Somewhere along the line there had been a big mistake. For the next six years it was like driving through a cornfield with a cultivator pulled by a horse and a zebra. It proved to be no easy job to get the zebra to behave like the horse, though the harmony was gradually brought about. Whatever I had learned about politics and people and issues and conciliation and co-operation in the sixteen years since 1896 had to be brought into full play. This had been my graduate course in politics. It remained to be proved how much I had profited by it. That is a story of the next half dozen years.

It is a good philosophy to believe that whatever we do is useful preparation for something else in the future. Certainly it has worked so in my case, perhaps to an unusual degree. Nearly everything that I have done seems to have fallen into a pattern. Much has had to do with some form of organization, either in the effort to bring certain events to pass, as in an election, or to affect certain public policies and attitudes, as in the motion picture industry.

As later events turned out, the years 1907 to 1912 were perhaps more important to me as political education than in any other way. But some other events and interests of those years deserve mention.

As to purely personal interests, the most important were our new home, into which we moved in 1909, and our first trip abroad that same year. The third was my renewed interest in Wabash College because my younger brother Hinkle was there from 1908 to 1912 and followed closely the same path that I had taken—bringing him, too, after graduation, via much public speaking, to join Father and me in the law office.

As to my trip abroad, two experiences stand out most clearly. The first had to do with a British lawsuit. Just as we were boarding the *Oceanic* in New York I picked up a newspaper and read the front-page headlines that an Indian student, while passing down a reception line, had shot and killed the Viceroy of India with a gun concealed partly by a handkerchief and partly by his sleeve. I was amazed when I arrived in London eight days later to find that the man had been indicted, arraigned, and on trial for eight days. The following day he was convicted and, being a fanatic, made no explanation for his action. To me, it was a striking example of speedy English justice.

The other experience was a visit to Hyde Park, where I mingled with a crowd of perhaps twenty-five thousand people who were milling about and demonstrating against some action by the government. The protest was apparently led by labor, and the kinds of things that were said from the soapbox might have caused headlines even in Union Square. I talked with many among the crowd and quickly came to the conclusion that this free assembly was a good demonstration of the advantage of "letting off steam." I rather think that this notable example of free speech had a subconscious influence on my later attitude as Postmaster General when I lifted the ban on certain newspapers accused of radicalism.

The most interesting single conversation that day was with a splendid "bobby" with whom I developed quite a friendship. Immediately spotting me as an American, he told me that he had a brother who owned a farm in North Dakota—a fact which made him extremely interested in the United States. He asked questions like a lawyer, and we had a good time together. From his brother he had received extravagant praise of conditions and opportunities in America. At the moment we were standing where we could see Westminster Abbey and, pointing to that magnificent landmark, I said, "Anyway, *there's* something we don't have in America." Instantly he replied, "No, not yet."

During these years, as I found a little more capital, my business interests increased. My situation was typical of young men in the smaller communities, all of which were steadily growing and doing things on a modest domestic basis. What we now classify as "small business" was the thing with which I was reared. It was all about us. I had some interest in the Sullivan banks; our little circle of Red Ravens bought the Thomas Dunn Building in 1908; three of us owned a warehouse which was destroyed by fire in June of 1910; I bought the Goodman Building in 1911. These local interests, as well as a circle of lifelong friends, have been among the reasons that I have always kept Sullivan as my home and my legal residence, however much time I may have spent in New York and California.

All my other interests were subordinate to law, which was my only true profession. During these years, as I was getting into my thirties, cases became more numerous, more interesting, more complicated, and more lucrative. A new field—that of water—began to claim more attention. During that decade the country was in a period of rapid growth. As city attorney I had responsibility for seeing that all the steps in the installation of our city water supply were correctly taken, with adequate protection for the future.

This new field of water litigation was concerned particularly with drainage and levees. Father's purchase in 1903 of a farm in the Wabash River Valley was the first thing to interest us in the development of these bottom lands. This was a real pioneer project. The building of a ditch or a levee, however, frequently entailed lawsuits because some people wanted it and others did not. When it was a case of buying earth to build the levees, a fair price had to be arrived at. I was involved in many such cases.

The necessity of watching the levees was a constant anxiety to the civil authorities, for at certain seasons there was always the danger of their breaking and flooding thousands of acres of rich farmland. Like the Ohio into which it emptied, our Wabash River and its tributaries occasionally broke their banks. This had happened so often in Gill Township that the committee decided that concrete abutments would have to be placed along two miles of the levee. The contractor's price for this job was only thirteen thousand dollars. Money went a long way in those days.

As I look back on those suits, I realize that they gave me a constant education in conciliation. In each one of them, either at law or by some method of arbitration, we had to arrive at the best possible decision, often with many persons ranged on both sides. I have always been glad that this kind of experience came to me so early. And I hope it was a lesson that I have never forgotten.

In 1911 we had to do with the taking over of the E. & T.H. and the Evansville Belt Railroad by the C. & E.I. A little later we handled the purchase of a group of coal mines by the C. & E.I. Railroad, a procedure which was perfectly legal at that time. Growing railroads tried to make sure of an adequate supply of coal, then their sole fuel. I consummated a similar sale in New York on the trip when I met Colonel Roosevelt, in connection with the incorporation of the coal company. I was one of the incorporating trustees. And so at different times I sat on both sides of the table, first representing the public and then a corporation. These cases gave me a series of lessons—some of them tough ones —in trusteeship and various types of responsibility. Since this responsibility was often to friends and neighbors rather than to some impersonal corporation, I am sure that it gave me a different viewpoint.

The most interesting personal cases were more often with wills and crimes. Two of them stand out most distinctly. The first involved the will of Captain Jesse Haddon, descendant of one of our earliest pioneers, a picturesque old man who had died in 1906, leaving the bulk of his estate to indigent orphans of Haddon Township. The will was instantly contested by one Frank Crawford, who won a decision after a seven-day fight and stood to inherit the bulk of the estate. The next thing we knew, Mrs. Flora Haddon, who claimed to be Captain Haddon's surviving wife, paid the costs of that trial, took a new trial, and secured a change of venue to Knox County. As soon as Frank Crawford heard of this he hurried over from Hawaii with the intent of proving himself a legitimate son of the captain, and the chief, if not the only, heir. In his earlier suit he had alleged that the defendant, Mrs. Flora Haddon, was not in fact a wife. However, the woman had a small daughter who was likewise a party to the defense. When Frank Crawford arrived in Sullivan and saw this little girl for the first time he immediately loved her like a sister and instructed his attorneys to leave no stone unturned to prove that the defendant had been lawfully married to Captain

Haddon, in spite of the fact that such a finding would give him only one third of the estate instead of all of it.

The story behind Frank Crawford was that he had been deposited on the doorstep of a Polly Crawford of Danville and had been raised by her under her name, although she had told him at the time of her death in 1895 that he was not her son. His real mother was Mary Caroline Wortman, a blue-eyed girl of Oaktown, who in her youth had been the belle of the neighborhood and had interested, among others, Captain Haddon, who later married her after the birth of her son. Mary Wortman had died in 1899.

Mrs. Flora Haddon, the second wife and defendant in this suit, claimed that she and Captain Haddon had been married in Indianapolis on February 1, 1901, by Bluford Hillman, a Negro minister. It was Flora Haddon's daughter, of course, who caused Frank Crawford to change his mind about the will.

When the case was decided in 1909 the jury also found for the plaintiff, Frank Crawford, who came into one third of Captain Haddon's estate and had his name changed legally to Frank Haddon, the case having established that Mary Caroline Wortman had been a legal wife. The verdict provided for the setting aside of the will made in 1876 —long before Captain Haddon had married his second wife, Flora. This case was remarkable, not so much from the legal angles as from a study of human nature at work on human nature. It could be called an instance of "all's well that ends well."

Then there was the Carter murder case, the most exciting case that Sullivan had seen in many a day. As briefly as I can tell it, this was the story:

On the afternoon of the Bryan Rally—October 22, 1906—the Orrs and the Carters were at Leach's Saloon, where Joe and Bob Orr allegedly got into a quarrel with James Carter, father of Ray and Elmis (Nick) Carter. A number of men had gathered at the saloon to watch a boxing match between Nick Carter and a Negro boy. Bob Orr was said to have made some slighting remark about the fight which allegedly touched off James Carter. Nick, his son, stepped into the argument and was said to have cut Joe Orr with a knife, whereupon Joe knocked him down.

Then another man standing there shoved all the participants in the fight out into the rear yard of the saloon and locked the door. This left Bob and Joe Orr out in the yard with the three Carters. Again, it was alleged, Nick Carter went after Joe Orr with a knife. Orr knocked him down and James Carter then struck Orr on the head with a cane, in turn knocking him down. When Nick got up it was reported that he seized a paving brick and delivered a terrific blow to Joe Orr's head while he was still prostrate. The Carters then departed and Orr's wound was treated, but he was so badly injured that he suffered paralysis and died a few days later.

Joe Orr had lived in Sullivan most of his life; he was by profession a printer, and until his death had been the foreman of the Sullivan *Union*. W. P. Stratton and I were retained to represent the State of Indiana. At the end of a four-day trial and twelve hours of deliberation by the jury, Carter was found guilty of murder in the second degree, with his sentence subsequently fixed at life imprisonment.

Several interesting comments could be made on this case. Perhaps one is that violent personal fights were not uncommon in those days. Roy, the oldest son of Joe Orr, was later killed in a fight at Shelburn; William, who was an excellent linotype operator, met his death in a fight at Evansville; and Len Orr, a powerful man and a brother of Joe, died in December of 1908 as the result of a shovel blow to his head, the culmination of a dispute over a well which was being dug at his home.

Another strange postscript to the story was the parole of Nick Carter, which I, having argued for his conviction, sought for him some years later, agreeing to be responsible for him.

One other best-remembered case concerned a shipment of lemons, claimed to have spoiled en route. But that was only half the story. The more memorable half concerned the reception Los Angeles gave the United States Navy on its round-the-world cruise.

I can hardly disclaim responsibility for bringing these two events together. Our office had been retained by a California bank to recover the value of a draft which had not been honored by the Indiana merchant who had received the lemons. It appeared to me that my time could be spared better than that of some of the older members of the firm; and if I took California depositions when the fleet was in, that would be clear gain. So it worked out!

I left Sullivan on April 13, 1908, the day before the fleet was scheduled to arrive off San Diego, and reached Los Angeles on the sixteenth, in the midst of all the excitement. Southern California was agog, impatiently awaiting the arrival of the sixteen battleships which had been going through target practice in Mexican waters.

All through the day and night the streets were packed. Never before or since have I shared a more intense outpouring of patriotism. Through a whole week, in mounting crescendo, the display of fervor continued. This was six years before the outbreak of World War I, and firsthand experience with our Navy was a new thing to most people. We had not become too familiar with the sinews of war nor gone stale on celebrating the might of our military forces. Patriotism was an exuberant, unspoiled feeling.

Well do I remember that succession of events: a great banquet on Monday night; auto day on Tuesday; military parade, Wednesday; auto tour, Thursday—and so on. All through every day the sailors had the "freedom of the city." I had a wonderful time mingling with them on the streets, in restaurants, at ceremonies, and anywhere I happened to be. They were a fine lot of men and boys. Everybody was proud of them and wanted to do something for them. Repeatedly I saw newsboys give sailors newspapers and refuse payment. I saw streetcar conductors refuse fares. In restaurants the sailors were treated as if each one were an admiral. The flag flew everywhere—and in everyone's heart. I was proud that Theodore Roosevelt had made this magnificent demonstration to the world.

One amusing, seriocomic incident I happened to witness. Some sailors had entered a restuarant and, in their opinion, had been overcharged. The owner made the mistake of not listening to their protest. However, the sailors paid and went out. But it was only a matter of minutes until they were back with a lot of their buddies. Building a human pyramid on each other's shoulders, they pulled down all the flags decorating the front of the building. Then they started through the restaurant like a Sherman tank and cleaned it up. Nobody made any attempt to stop them, not even the Los Angeles police. Only a little while later, while I was still in the neighborhood, I saw an ambitious citizen selling little pieces of broken china, carried around on a tray, as happy souvenirs of the occasion.

It took me three days to take the depositions about the shipment of lemons. The receiver's charge had been that they had spoiled because they were imperfectly iced. My experience with the witnesses was wholly pleasant and satisfactory. Everybody still seemed to be in good humor.

I returned to Sullivan early in May and the case quickly went to trial. It resulted in a verdict for fifteen hundred dollars—a larger amount than we had expected, very nearly the whole claim put in by the California bank. The claim was appealed but stood up in the courts, so the story ended happily.

That whole trip to California has remained vivid in my mind—partly, of course, because it was my first visit, but also because of my subsequent visits and prolonged stays there. On my second trip, ten years later, I went as chairman of the Republican National Committee and as pleader for Liberty Bond sales. Four years after that my third trip was taken to initiate the Motion Picture Association's program in the studios of Hollywood. California remains a very bright spot to me to this day.

Among all these early legal experiences I cannot forget the repeated efforts to boom Father for a judgeship. The suggestion was first made in the newspapers in 1910; it came up again and again for half a dozen years. But he would never give it any consideration. He was adamant against accepting any position on the bench where there was a possibility that he would be serving as judge when one of his own sons came up to argue a case before him. This kind of integrity, wholly ingrained in John T. Hays, was recognized by all his colleagues. This experience also was doubtless woven into my esteem for the law, which held my attention, however often interrupted, and remained my North Star through all these years.

CHAPTER 7

Eventually the Republican Party

N O W I must try to tell the story of the rebirth of the Republican party in Indiana after it had run a poor third in the elections of 1912 owing to the sudden appearance of the Bull Moose. Following that catastrophe, the political condition of the party was like that of a man who has just been in a serious automobile accident. Convalescence and resourceful therapies became the "order of the day" for several years. Because I was so close to these events, many of them become a necessary part of my story.

In telling of this resurgence as I witnessed it, I shall try to touch only the most effective factors. Perhaps the first of those was a special State Advisory Committee appointed by the state chairman, Fred Sims, to have full charge of affairs during 1913 and 1914. This was a recognition of the need of enlisting all the counsel and co-operation we could find. I was a member of this committee. The second step was the sending out in April 1913 of letters to all Republicans in the State, giving them encouragement as a result of elections in Chicago, St. Louis, and other cities where the Bull Moosers had run third. This seemed like a significant shift.

The Bull Moose factor was the third and most constant element in our calculations for the next half dozen years. Although the assimilation of Progressives will receive attention later, it had its roots in the activities of 1913 and was a corollary of a positive program of Republican party organization for victory in 1914, 1916, and 1918.

The fourth factor—and the keynote of any success in popular politics —was *intensified organization*. Much of this story has to do with various phases of such activity. There is no doubt that we Hoosiers like to get together. Marking the Republican rebirth, I can recall a continuous stream of meetings, banquets, conventions, and that characteristic get-together which we called a "love feast." Into these meetings we poured an almost religious fervor.

One of the most inspiring and influential meetings, especially in its after-results, was the banquet of the Republican Editorial Association, attended by three hundred men. This association was always a powerful ally. We all felt it important that editors have the fullest possible knowledge of the policies the organization intended to follow, and that they be encouraged to help us inform the public. At this particular banquet it was decided that only experienced newsmen should be assigned to cover publicity functions connected with the party. To assure better consensus of opinion, an advisory committee of one editor from each congressional district was appointed. This publicity activity represented but one unit in an over-all state-wide organization.

For me, of course, the next milestone was my election on Lincoln's Birthday in 1914 as the new state chairman. This office had been mentioned frequently, though I had tried to keep away from any discussions. I succeeded Fred Sims, who had been vigorous in an effort to inject new spirit into our party.

In taking over the reins of the state organization it seemed only proper to make some statement of my political creed and principles. I had always been convinced of the necessity of strong, active political parties as practical instruments of government. I never considered them as opportunities for personal aggrandizement, but rather as a means by which thinking men may promulgate and practice principles for the care of their own country, for the control of the influences surrounding the place they call home. It seemed to me then, and it seems to me now, that any man who thinks of politics otherwise is unaware of the privileges and responsibilities of his citizenship.

Feeling the urgency of immediate action, we opened headquarters on the day following my election and held a meeting of the new State Committee that same day. What proved to be one of the most important announcements was that of the selection of the new state secretary, L. W. Henley. "Jack" Henley was at the time managing editor of the Terre Haute *Star*, then a Bull Moose paper. With this background, there was significance in his acceptance of a position with the Republican State Committee. It was a good augury. In fact, Jack's enthusiastic services to the party were a big factor in our progress during the next few years, and I cannot omit paying him a hearty tribute for the part he played.

As to some features of the headquarters program, I want to emphasize first that our new policy was to *maintain an open office the year round*. The custom for years had been to maintain active headquarters only through a campaign. But from then on, committee officers were to push the work practically every day in the year.

Among our early headquarters activities were the preparation of the *Year Book*, which was a party handbook; conferences with local leaders; and the setting up of the State Advisory Committee. We pushed everything as rapidly as possible. The handbook we wanted ready by April

15, in advance of the State Convention. This was an innovation, since customarily it was not published until late summer. Getting it out early had a double purpose: it stimulated the early completion of county organizations, and by reporting all these signs of activity it was open evidence that Republicans were out in earnest. All this helped to revive the old-time fighting spirit which had always been a mark of any active political party.

Week in and week out meetings of all sorts were held throughout the ninety-two counties. There was jubilation when the Eleventh Congressional District "love feast" piled up an attendance of six hundred guests. When a little later, just before the State Convention, almost fifteen hundred people in the Ninth District turned up for their banquet there was no place big enough to handle them; the overflow from the Masonic Temple went to the Methodist church, to the Colter Hotel, and to several restaurants. People sensed that the size of that gathering was clear evidence of renewed vigor.

Our regular state-wide Republican organization was well augmented by other groups working in close co-operation with us. As an example, the Lincoln League actually radiated out through the whole state and parallcled us right down through every district organization. These friends were always ready to step in and help. In the same way the Marion Club at Indianapolis was a big help whenever anything was going on in the capital. For the State Convention they came up with a hundred-member reception committee. They even had a group within a group called the "G.O.P.," into which many of the Republican leaders were initiated. This was another bond stimulating unity among the leaders.

Everything in 1914 looked toward the State Convention. The story seems to break down into four divisions: *preparation, organization, innovation,* and *description.* Much of the preparation had been going on quietly for months. Its essence was complete organization, from the grass roots up. Its fruit was a big, enthusiastic, efficient convention. Nor were the trappings omitted—the Hotel Severin alone bought four hundred flags for the occasion.

Undoubtedly what most people remember about our elephant march was the elephant himself. He was the biggest detail of our preparation, and the biggest innovation. By negotiation with the Cincinnati Zoological Gardens we had secured "one large elephant with saddle" for the opening of the convention. Naturally we defrayed all the costs—transportation, feed, and caretaker's expenses. We brought that behemoth to Indianapolis as a symbol of a G.O.P. alive—and on the march! On the day of the convention the elephant headed a procession of Republicans marching from the Hotel Severin to Tomlinson Hall, to the victorious beat of drums and the stirring blare of bugles. That huge animal came into the hall to the consternation of everybody, but he said more than anyone on the platform!

It is unnecessary to go into details of the convention except as they may illustrate earlier political methods with which many current voters are not familiar. Again there was much work behind the scenes, as in the careful compiling of a list of declared candidates for state offices: seven for attorney general; six for auditor; five for United States senator; three for state treasurer; three for state geologist; and several for the other state offices. The selection of a temporary chairman was left to me, but most other details were taken care of by the various committees which had been set up under the state organization. These all did their work well.

Probably the most important committee, with the help of many advisers, was that which assembled material for the platform. Hundreds of recommendations and suggestions were boiled down and arranged for ready consideration. Since they represented the sentiment of many interested voters, they were a big help to the final Platform Committee. I later used the same plan on a much larger scale in preparation for the work of the Platform Committee at the National Convention of 1920. The inclusion of planks on the Panama Canal tolls and the Mexican situation indicates that it was already our practice in Indiana to draw up a platform which would harmonize on major foreign issues with that of the Republican National Committee. Probably this feature, as well as our effort to give every Republican a chance to express his opinion if he cared to, was also new.

The most frequently mentioned innovation was the "school" for county chairman and precinct committeemen. This school met in the assembly room of the Hotel Severin early on April 22, the first day of the convention. The "teachers" included a past national chairman—Harry S. New—three former state chairmen, and George F. McCullough of New York. Announcements had gone out to county chairmen and thirty-three hundred precinct committeemen. The response was such that the hotel's assembly room could barely hold the crowd. This turned out to be first-rate campaign education.

Tomlinson Hall, with a capacity of four thousand, could hold only part of the crowd that tried to get into sessions of the State Convention. It seemed as if there were enough brass bands to fill the hall. But each band led its own delegation from every section of the state. They took turns playing patriotic airs, and at the opening session the 1,423 delegates cheered and yelled for an hour.

The convention floor had been laid out to resemble a map of Indiana, and the delegates from the various districts were seated in their actual position on the state map. This in itself resulted in a note of sectional pride and rivalry. When the delegates packed up and started back home one could feel that they carried with them a feeling of success for the November elections.

Unquestionably there was a sharp contrast between the spirit of the 1912 campaign and that of 1914. We now began to feel the definite weakening of the Progressive movement which had so relentlessly split the earlier Republican vote. Evidences on the national scene were not hard to find. In Chicago, during the mayoralty campaign of 1913, Republicans had cast two and a half times as many votes as Progressives. In St. Louis the Progressive party cast less than five thousand votes and the Republicans overwhelmingly elected their mayor. This was encouraging to us. Similar evidence was beginning to come in from districts in our own state.

By the end of June local and county conventions were being held regularly, and so effectively as to indicate genuine Republican revival. The most encouraging thing was that in some cases half the delegates were ex-Progressives.

As I think back over these matters I can see at least two reasons for going into some detail here. First, apparently it was my work in Indiana as state chairman which led to my election as national chairman. Second, many inquiries have come to me through the years as to the merit of various methods in political campaigns. So this may be as good a point as any at which to anlayze the processes of state political organization, particularly anything that might be called an Indiana innovation.

While in 1914 we recognized that our first job was to rebuild confidence within the party members themselves, some new projects were at once undertaken. One of the most important was the Young Men's Republican Movement, first announced in September. Our aim was to have first voters become actively identified with the regular Republican organization. Our state-wide setup included a chairman for each county and three lieutenants for each township. The membership reached about ten thousand. The enthusiasm and sincerity of these young voters infected party ranks all up and down the line.

One interesting observation about political campaigns is that extra activity on your own part serves to make the other side work all the harder. This was proved by an editorial which appeared at the end of June reporting that the Democratic chairman had called his State Committee together and warned them that the Republicans could win if the Democrats did not get busy. They also decided to base their campaign more on national than on state issues, which in the circumstances was probably wise. They were that much stronger in Indiana because our former governor, Tom Marshall, was then Vice-President. They really did not have too much to worry about, because they continued to win interim elections—as in Sullivan, Terre Haute, and Indianapolis. On

January 1, 1914, my own town was taken over by a Democratic city ad-ministration—a thing that was a bit hard for me to swallow.

At the same time evidences of bad and careless government, and even allegations of corrupt registration and election practices on the part of the Democratic state administration, were coming to light. In particular, the 1913 state legislature was accused of passing laws when members were incognito or incommunicado. The Marion County Grand Jury returned thirty-four indictments on December 4, 1914, against thirteen members and employees of the previous legislature. Apparently two bills had become laws unbeknown to the members of both the Assembly and the Senate—a revelation that caused considerable concern. According to the testimony, the bills were signed by the Speaker of the House, the President of the Senate, and the governor; no one else was any the wiser. A clerk had allegedly sent word in one instance that one of the bills had passed the House and was transmitted to the Senate, and vice versa as regards the announcement made to the House.

Obviously these accusations laid the Democratic party open to effec-tive Republican attack. As in some national campaigns, this was unques-tionably a factor in our favor, and it made us even more careful to conduct our own campaign on a clean-cut platform.

The use of time from the close of the State Convention in April to the opening of the active 1914 campaign can be summed up in two words—*organization* and *conferences*. But it was by no means all work. In particular, the Marion Club did its best through hearty social affairs to contribute to the labors of the workers an atmosphere of good-fellow-ship and relaxation.

The State Committee, being determined on a vigorous and systematic campaign, set to work to put the policy into action in every possible way. For example, it was decided to have each member of the State Com-mittee, which included all district chairmen, spend one solid week of the campaign at state headquarters familiarizing himself with all that was going on and assisting Secretary Henley and myself in carrying out whatever ideas the members of the State Committee themselves had agreed upon. This week spent at headquarters was also definitely an innovation. It was well called a "no-loose-tooth-in-the-rake" move. An-other thing we tried to be certain of was the carrying out of the plank which promised the *right of individual participation, free from dicta-tion by party management*. We never forgot this pledge, and I believe we did carry it out.

The next important matter was that of campaign speakers. In May we felt a serious lack of able men to send to district and county con-ventions called for June and July. Something had to be done quickly. A trip to Washington seemed called for. I went there in June and persuaded a number of legislators that the complexion of the next Congress would certainly depend in part on their co-operation in giving Indiana some of their time. I must have called on fifteen or twenty congressmen and senators. Several responded generously. Among them were Senator Borah of Idaho, Senators Townsend and Smith of Michigan, Congressman Humphrey of Washington, and Senator Cummins of Iowa. As the conventions approached, our larder of oratorical talent was well supplied.

We developed a bit of technique in the holding of state conferences in July that proved an excellent two-way street. Through them the State Central Committee acquired an accurate picture of political conditions on the local level, while district and county workers were able to carry back home new ideas for more effective work, and to acquire a yardstick for judging their own results. These meetings again gave opportunity for state-wide workers to participate in the management of party affairs. High-flown oratory was by-passed in favor of getting down to business. We were gratified by the response of county chairmen; they not only came themselves but in many cases brought with them their vice-chairmen, secretaries, and prominent party workers. I remember how, at the second of these conferences, two men who had been members of the same legislature twenty years before saw each other again for the first time. "Let's get together" was a living thing!

Another useful move that came out of these conferences was our decision to send out twelve crews of practical organizers to make trips over the whole state early in September. Each crew, consisting of five to seven men, went into a particular congressional district. The nucleus of the group consisted of the congressional candidate and the district chairman, who explained "organization" to county and township workers who had not attended the conferences in Indianapolis. Here again our state organization had a fine opportunity to sense the political atmosphere in its native habitat just before the campaign began. The attendance at these meetings was beyond our fondest expectations.

Meetings and conferences were supplemented by a steady stream of communications. These went out to county chairmen and precinct committeemen always once a week, usually twice a week, and often three times a week, from July right up to Election Day. They contained material of all sorts: requests for information, requests for help to the Lincoln League or the Young Men's Movement, suggestions on the registration of voters, campaign publicity, and inquiries as to local estimates of votes. Few specific instructions were sent, and then only in regard to procedural details about registration or voting. It will be no surprise to those familiar with campaign work to hear that the brief, intensive work of the campaign itself did not compare in effort with the continuous spadework done from the closing of the State Convention in April to the opening of the active campaign in the third week in September.

Senator Borah of Idaho and Hugh T. Miller, Republican nominee for U.S. senator from Indiana, officially opened the active campaign before a jam-packed crowd in Tomlinson Hall. This year was probably not out of the ordinary, but the campaign certainly did contain all the typical ingredients. Speeches were made up and down and back and forth across the state. Countless stickers were attached to letters, reading, WE ARE ON OUR WAY—REPUBLICAN VICTORY NOW. A million seals passed through the mail bearing the picture of an elephant with his trunk and one front foot raised high—ready to move. A banner on his back bore the letters "G.O.P.," and at the bottom of the sticker was the motto: *Better Government; Lower Taxes.* Early in October big five-by-eight-foot posters appeared bearing the picture of our senatorial candidate, the slogan, EVENTUALLY WHY NOT NOW?—and some succinct statements of party policy. Our State Committee had obtained permission from the Pillsbury Flour people to parody their slogan, which was aimed especially at reuniting Progressives with Republicans.

Another innovation was the holding of "prosperity processionals" in many counties. These were great parades which caterpillared all over the county, starting from the county seat. Headquarters supplied a speaker who addressed crowds at every stopping place, and the county organization would see that a band headed up the procession of vehicles. Because of all these activities, the level of enthusiasm kept rising.

The results of the election were not, to say the least, entirely as we had hoped. Hugh Miller lost the senatorial election to Benjamin F. Shively, Democrat; Oscar Bland lost in the Second District congressional race to William A. Cullop; and most of our state ticket was defeated. On the other hand, some impression was made on local levels, where results began to show up first. Fundamental changes were quietly going on at the grass roots—the source of all important shifts of sentiment. More encouragement came from the fact that the Progressives, as a voting quantity, were being virtually eliminated. The average Republican gain per county was 820 votes; the average Progressive loss, 579; and the average net Democratic loss, 104. The total Republican gain in Indiana was approximately 13,000—greater than the combined Democratic and Progressive losses. We could take courage from the fact that we seemed to be on the right track. The Republican party was being revivified; the Democrats had to work harder and worry more to hold their state control; and we had gained a lot of knowledge and experience which we could put to good use in 1916. After our election defeat of November 5, Republican State Headquarters opened up as usual next morning.

About this time it was first suggested that I run for senator in 1916—a suggestion repeatedly made during the following two years. Also at this time I was appointed a member of the Advisory Council of the National Republican Congressional Committee. Letters of congratulation coming to me from party leaders outside Indiana were particularly gratifying. Senator Borah, who had helped us so vigorously, wrote me in part:

The Republicans of Indiana, with you as their leader, made a magnificent fight. You did vastly more than I thought you could do when you started your campaign, and you did more than the Republicans over the country thought you could do.

You are right in assuming that you have laid the foundation for success in 1916.

When the campaign was all over and autumn had rolled by we sent Christmas greetings to every worker: county and district chairmen, editors, executive and advisory committees, members of the Lincoln League, district chairmen of the Young Men's Movement, county captains, and party leaders generally. I voiced my own gratitude for all their assistance during the campaign and of course wished them the happiness of the Christmas season and the best of everything for the New Year.

We did not take the passing of the election as an excuse for closing headquarters or diminishing our efforts. We continued to supply speakers wherever they were requested, as well as to offer general advice. We continued to receive suggestions and to be on the lookout for information that would strengthen the next campaign. Thus we remained a clearinghouse for local units and a central point to which the national organization could turn for information on the political climate obtaining in Indiana.

To maintain the sinews of war—in other words, a healthy budget—we set up a Committee of One Hundred, composed of active Republicans in sympathy with the idea and able to contribute one hundred dollars apiece.

Because state headquarters remained open, workers continued to gather there for political shop talk. Often among these were elected members of the executive or legislative branches of the state government. For our state organization this proved an invaluable contact with current problems of practical politics. We had constant experience with the expressed needs of the voting public and with the obstacles encountered in efforts to effect desired measures into law. So real was our contact with these forces that we were editorially accused of lobbying, a charge completely denied and later publicly retracted by the newspaper making it. All we were trying to do was to keep ourselves and our clientele in constant touch with state-wide political developments. And we never lost sight of the fact that we were preparing for 1916. One lesson which came out of 1914 was the value of good publicity. Throughout 1915 we co-operated with a permanent party publicity agency on a national scale. It was significant that a Hoosier ex-president of our Republican Editorial Association was spearheading the work in Chicago. Among others, Senators Root, Borah, Lodge, Cummins, and Weeks had interested themselves in such a movement in Washington. Through the Indiana editors, I believe we contributed considerable strength to the National Republican Publicity Association, founded shortly under the leadership of former Senator Jonathan Bourne, Jr.

These years increasingly confirmed in my mind the fact that, in any final analysis, the country is controlled by public opinion. Much of my later work in the motion picture industry was based on this thesis. In those days the supreme agency in forming this opinion was the press of the nation. We realized that without its aid no cause could advance, and that against it no idea could long survive. Its conscientious free-dom, I early saw, was as vital for the preservation of our American institutions as is clean air to the preservation of life. We strove to keep the press an open avenue for the securing and dissemination of ideas.

In this effort the Indiana Republican Editorial Association was a tremendous help, as an important arm of the state organization. Some-times the association sponsored activities of its own, and it always supported any party undertaking. Through the press the whole con-stituency could be kept in touch with our activities wherever firsthand contact was impossible. From our side we often turned to the editors to find out what folks were thinking.

My contacts with newspapermen have been so many and so close that it would be impossible for me to overrate their influence. How often have I seen editorials arouse, shape, and consolidate public opinion. On the other hand, editorials were often written as the expression of widespread opinion already formed, but inarticulate until someone took the responsibility of giving it voice. A good newspaperman finds him-self in a unique position: simultaneously he is often first and last.

Our continuing project was the reorganization of the party, which we worked on intensively, particularly through the spring, summer, and fall of 1915. Two particular reasons for our extra effort were, first, the new Indiana primary law which caused certain changes in political procedure, and second, the fact that the gradual healing of the Bull Moose breach called for changes in the Republican party constitution. The interpretation of the new primary law became a bothersome issue and quite too complicated to warrant more than mention at this late date. In principle we welcomed it inasmuch as it gave more play to the individual's participation in party affairs. One practical result was that it made candidates campaign once for the primary and then again for election, a double duty that sometimes proved onerous. But at least it threw the responsibility for nomination on the voter.

Since the law sometimes made it technically difficult for a former Progressive to affiliate with the Republican party, such cases began to get into the courts. The legal provision was that a voter, in order to affiliate with the party, must have supported and voted for a majority of the said party's candidates in the preceding election. This apparently difficult obstacle was considerably reduced by the ruling that only party members might challenge others wishing to vote with that party at a primary—and we were only too glad to welcome Progressives back into the fold. We tried to keep county and local workers informed of this interpretation so the first primary might register all possible gains.

Our ties with the national organization were brought closer by considerable correspondence between National Chairman Charles D. Hilles and myself concerning Indiana conditions in 1915. I was already able to report that Progressive strength had been reduced to 25 per cent of its 1914 vote. Within our state we kept busy, and we were greatly encouraged by support from out-of-state leaders, some as far away as Nevada.

It was helpful during the off year of 1915 to receive so much enthusiastic support from various political and social clubs, which really became an important segment of our Republican forces. Large luncheons were held, addressed by national speakers. The strong Columbia Club put on a membership drive that netted two thousand new members. The McKinley and Harrison clubs were similarly active. Several of those with their headquarters in Indianapolis had branches, or local clubs, affiliated with them. All staged sizable affairs, which stimulated the interest of voters and influenced the trend of political thought in many communities. Where no organized group already existed, local Republicans were quick to set up their own clubs. I attended many such meetings all over the state, getting acquainted with thousands of workers and voters. Now as little as possible did I let business interfere with pleasure—pleasure of this sort! But when it came to meeting actual obligations of our law firm, these of course had to come first. Frankly, at this late date, it is a little hard to see how I covered as much of Indiana as I did.

One other interesting development of the club idea, and of the emphasis on arousing the interest of first voters, was seen in the organization of the Young Republicans at Wabash College, my alma mater, in December of 1915. As a matter of fact, there was an effective Republican League of Clubs, a national organization which encouraged the formation and activities of groups of all sorts. Apparently the Young Men's Movement was the particular contribution of Indiana to political club activity. The importance of these political clubs should never be overlooked. They were to the state organization what a Coca-Cola machine is to an office; for "the pause that refreshes" is an integral part of political success.

Another of our characteristic Hoosier social functions turned to the advantage of party politics was the so-called "love feast." Of the twenty or more held during 1915, let me say a word about one held in April and addressed by Senator Harding of Ohio. For this banquet meeting five hundred enthusiastic party workers flocked to Vincennes. Aspirants for almost every state office appeared. Every candidate in the Second District was there. Quite appropriately, we met in Harmonie Hall, amply decorated in red, white, and blue. Vincennes supplied a good orchestra and a band.

On this, as on other similar occasions, as state chairman I asserted that there was just one rule the Republican party in Indiana was going to have; namely, that *the rights of the individual members of the party should be and remain equally sacred and sacredly equal.* That seemed to me sound politics. Further, I constantly preached that *successful politics is a matter of assimilation, not elimination.* The aim is always to find common ground on which the largest possible number of citizens may unite for their mutual welfare.

It was at this Vincennes banquet that, in the midst of an interrupted and overlong introduction of Senator Harding, one of the workers seated a little way down the room was getting restless, and he whispered in a voice that could be heard easily at the head table, "Well, the son-of-a-bitch looks like a senator, don't he?" Half a dozen years later, when I was Postmaster General and Harding was President, I was calling on him early one morning while he was dressing. As he pulled his shirt over his head he burst out laughing. "Bill Hays, do you remember that Tom Nugent who said, 'The son-of-a-bitch looks like a senator, don't he?' " Then he laughed again. Some incidents stick in the memory forever.

One of the best proofs of this 1915 activity was that the Democrats were not too happy about it. They seemed to worry about the number of our meetings, the enthusiasm, and the degree of political awareness that was being awakened throughout the state. When their State Committee met in August they decided on an aggressive campaign, to begin early in September and to continue until the 1916 election, more than a year away. Vice-President Marshall was brought back to the state to address an audience of ten thousand at Danville early in September, and other events were scheduled with big-name speakers. Thus the Democrats felt compelled to pursue activity that they had neither anticipated nor prepared for.

As 1916 arrived we had the satisfaction of knowing that we had worked hard to be ready. Three and four Republican meetings were taking place each week. There was no dearth of candidates striving for places on the Republican ticket, and we could look forward with mounting hope. At the same time new factors entered the political scene, both of which seemed to catch on quickly: one was the Fairbanks-for-President boom and the other the Hays-for-senator boom, and each deserves mention.

I mention the Hays-for-senator boom first because it was of less consequence. Newspaper editors were probably responsible for first suggesting that the state chairman be considered as a senatorial candidate in 1916. These expressions seemed to be motivated by the amount of news created by our Republican state activities.

The first proposals came soon after the close of the 1914 election, in connection with the fact that Senator Kern's term would expire in 1916. I had never declared myself a candidate, nor did I ever have any comment to offer, except that I appreciated it. I was thoroughly committed to the state chairmanship.

The situation was further complicated in the middle of March 1916 by the sudden death of Senator Benjamin F. Shively. Since this created two senatorial vacancies to be filled, speculation grew. Again approached on the matter, I asked for a few days to consider it. The more I thought about it, the clearer it seemed that the 1916 job as state chairman was my job—one I wanted to finish, and my particular opportunity for service. And so on March 18 I announced that I definitely would not seek the nomination for the late Senator Shively's seat. I also felt that leaving the chairmanship would doubtless conduce to political boat-rocking which might upset our earnest desire to put forward our own favorite son, Charles W. Fairbanks, for the presidential nomination that autumn.

The problem of senatorial nominations brought about a rather bitter fight between Harry New and James Watson. The latter felt hurt by the inconclusive outcome of the primary vote and even intended to go into the State Convention and try to upset it. Fortunately the matter was satisfactorily settled in the convention, which agreed that New should be the candidate for the long term and Watson for the short term. In this connection, perhaps it is again worth pointing out that I as chairman and the other members of the State Committee held strictly aloof from these contests, to avoid becoming identified with any group backing a particular man, the respective merits of the candidates not being our business. As I said again and again, our job was "to elect and not select." We could ill afford any favoritism.

The Fairbanks-for-President boom was a project of much more importance. It claimed our major attention for several months—right up to the National Convention. Fairbanks had been Vice-President under

Theodore Roosevelt from 1905 to 1909; he had an untarnished reputation and had not faded from national notice while out of office.

Feeling confident that he was a thoroughly legitimate candidate, in the spring of 1915 we began to collect evidences of favoring sentiment both inside Indiana and in other sections of the country. Convinced of the sincerity of large segments of public opinion, a group of ardent supporters launched a definite presidential boom after consulting Mr. Fairbanks. By July the movement was definitely organized by both letter and personal appeal for specific activity on the part of his friends. In reporting to National Chairman Hilles, I announced that Indiana was strong for Fairbanks. Prominent out-of-state Republicans kept on adding their approval.

At a big meeting in December, Mr. Fairbanks expressed his attitude with utmost sincerity and good faith. He said at one point, in acknowledging the honor that was being paid him:

"I would be more embarrassed if I did not realize that it is chiefly due to the fact that I stand for that party and those policies in which we have a mutual interest and a common faith. . . . We have always held the public good to be superior to public place. We have always stood for that which we have believed was in the best interest of the state and the nation."

I know that these were not merely words spoken on a political occasion but a true statement of our candidate's innermost feeling. The loyalty of his fellow citizens was amply proven by the big primary vote of 176,000 which he received in the spring of 1916. When the die was cast and the boom turned into a campaign, it became a prominent part of our state activity.

As far as the State Convention of 1916 is concerned, I need mention only features that were new or different from those of 1914. The primary was the chief one. It had made us a lot of extra work, being really a small-scale election, and it created new problems.

One innovation was a meeting of all candidates for places on the state ticket. They had been invited for a definite purpose—to pledge themselves, collectively and individually, to support the ticket at the November election regardless of whether or not they won the nominations in the State Convention. We again impressed upon them that the State Committee was not taking part in anyone's contest. I told them I assumed that each was working for the success of the party over and above individual preferment. Our job was to referee for these men. The idea of calling them together to tell them just that was more appreciated than I could have anticipated in advance.

Fresh indication that the breach was healing was seen in the fact that an ex-Progressive, Horace C. Stillwell, was made permanent chairman, much to everyone's satisfaction.

Another interesting factor was that the platform, though brief, declared our position on almost all chief issues of the day, including important national questions. Later we were delighted to find that this platform, drawn in April, harmonized with the national platform of June wherever the same subject was covered. This was by no means an accident, for we had made it our business to integrate state politics with national wherever possible.

Our election of delegates to the National Convention was marked by a smoothness unusual to find in the midst of such keen competition. At the close of the convention the entire State Committee marched over to the home of Mr. Fairbanks and pledged its undivided support. My election that same day as chairman of the state delegation to the National Convention, on the proposal of James A. Hemenway, was both unexpected and flattering, such action usually being taken later in the convention city.

As June of 1916 approached, our eyes were focused intently on Chicago, where the National Convention was to be held. We opened Fairbanks headquarters in the Congress Hotel the last week in May, providing a reception committee of thirteen women and twenty-seven men—an indication of expected activity. The big Indiana political clubs were ready to participate at full strength, with well over two thousand loyal Hoosiers. On June 2, fifty-one Republicans still working on the home front received wires from me requesting their presence in Chicago to aid on the battle line. With few exceptions they came, to help make the Fairbanks boom a success.

The large majority of boosters arrived on the fifth, bringing the Indianapolis Military Band and a group of whoopsters from the Marion Club, all wearing gold badges reading FAIRBANKS. The Marion Marching Club of Indianapolis, which had made a great impression in 1888 at the nomination of Benjamin Harrison, was now rejuvenated for Fairbanks. The big, noisy Indiana parades stopped traffic and generally disrupted Michigan Avenue on June 6, when the blast of a cannon announcing the start of the parade caused near panic among the horses of the mounted police. Going down the avenue playing "On the Banks of the Wabash," and finally in concerts at the Grand Pacific, Great Northern, and Congress hotels, our band and crowd were probably the noisiest contingent at the convention.

The fact that I had been elected chairman of the Indiana delegation gave me another responsibility through the convention. Though we Hoosiers were trying to get a "favorite son" nominated, uppermost in our mind was the success of the party in the national election. I made a statement at the time, and used a phrase now familiar to all: "The only way to get a *new deal* in the international and domestic affairs at Washington is by the restoration of the Republican party to power, instead of by merely the election of a Republican president." This question took on special significance because of our belief, based on pre-election estimates, that the government would remain Democratic if Indiana were lost.

Our confidence in Fairbanks had been confirmed when Bull Moosers and Republicans at home agreed on him without a shade of difference in their enthusiasm. We naturally felt that if we had found a candidate so successful in healing the political breach in Indiana, his appeal would bring about the same effect elsewhere. Certainly confidence and enthusiasm pervaded Fairbanks' headquarters. We felt we had something so good that we wanted everybody else to share it.

Any familiarity with national conventions proves that this feeling is shared by many states. There were almost a score of reasonably strong prospects for the nomination, and ten names were put before the convention. It is simple history now that Charles Evans Hughes was nominated on the third ballot, with Fairbanks named as his vice-presidential running mate. Though he was not completely pleased, the vice-presidential nomination was a real honor for Fairbanks, for the party, and for Indiana. It had been spontaneous and would have been impossible to stop. Here, once more, in accepting, Fairbanks was motivated by a sense of loyalty to the party.

Judged by developments in 1920, it was significant that Senator Harding was made both temporary and permanent chairman of the convention. His popularity on this occasion was certainly a definite factor in his nomination four years later, when I was serving as national chairman.

An unsuccessful attempt was made by the Progressive party, simultaneously in Chicago, to get together with us on a nominee. A strong joint committee was appointed to seek a presidential candidate on whom we could both agree, but no agreement was found. It was reported that Colonel Roosevelt made that peace parley possible, though it was unsuccessful. When the colonel refused to run, the Progressive ticket ceased to exist. As far as our action was concerned, the Progressives were apparently not too pleased with the nomination of Charles Evans Hughes.

One unusual aspect of the Indiana delegation to the Republican convention was that it had been Fred Sims's humorous idea to increase it to thirty-one members—the thirty-first delegate being Will H. Hays, Jr., then six months old. As to this "mascot delegate," one newspaper report stated: "The youngster was not present to express his appreciation of the most unusual distinction ever accorded an Indiana Republican who had not been a regularly elected delegate to the National Convention." Continuing the by-play, the Sullivan Elks later had a little fun when they put Bill, Jr., into a great big loving cup and presented him to me.

Since 1916 was a presidential election year, that campaign, in a sense, overshadowed our own. Although our state candidates overworked themselves trying to reach our ninety-two counties, it was still more important for us to focus attention on the presidential race. Already there was a shortage of lithographs of Justice Hughes, and we rushed a demand for another 100,000 and for literature of any description to satisfy our huge mailing list. We needed a lot of material for our list containing 250,000 Democrats, "amenable to reason," 7,000 traveling men, 25,000 first voters, nearly 39,000 members of precinct executive committees, 75,000 farmers, and 100,000 other Republicans.

One of our publicity innovations—the brain child of Fred Beetson, later associated with me in the Motion Picture Association—was poster advertising in streetcars all over the state. We got exclusive control of the use of this method of publicizing political activities for the duration of the campaign. The advertisements were patriotic in character rather than partisan, and the cards were changed every two weeks from July through October. Bearing large flags, they made an impression with such messages as: *Exercise your sovereign right of citizenship—help govern yourself. If you interest yourself sufficiently in the politics of the country the right principles will be practiced and able, conscientious candidates elected.*

As to meetings and speakers, I began exerting myself to have Justice Hughes include our state on his first trip West. Because Indiana was recognized as strategic in the 1916 vote, we also needed all we could get of T.R., Taft, Weeks, Sherman, Root, Lodge, and Longworth. With the political shift indicated by the vast number of newspapers swinging over to the Republican standard, we wanted to capitalize on every possible change of sentiment.

I first tried to get Hughes for the week of August 28, to speak at the Tractor Exhibition at Indianapolis. This is held on a three-hundred-acre plot west of the city and draws at least seventy-five thousand farmers. Though this plan was impossible, we were happy when he gave us three days in late September, touching seventeen cities. Our state office had carefully worked out details for these appearances, and we were gratified by the response. It also proved of some consequence that Theodore Roosevelt endorsed the candidate so vigorously.

On Hughes's second visit to Chicago something interesting happened—or almost happened. Three of us from Indiana had reserved-seat tickets to the big Hughes meeting on September 12, when he opened his campaign. With tickets in hand we found our way to one of the front rows and I led the way to our seats. As I reached them I found my seat occupied by the coat and hat of a man in his shirt sleeves. Getting a little hot when he did not immediately remove them, I threw them down in his lap in no very kindly gesture. The man next to him looked up and shouted, "Why, hello, Bill Hays." It was James J. Davis, later Secretary of Labor in the Harding Cabinet and one of my very good friends. I said in surprise, "Hello, Jimmy." A moment later he said, indicating the man of the hat-and-coat incident, "Bill, meet Bat Nelson." Was my face red! Here was I—at 110 pounds, a less than bantamweight lawyer-politico—figuratively throwing down the gauntlet to one of America's most highly touted professional fighters.

To get back to the Indiana situation, we found increasing good feeling throughout the state and a definite Democrats-for-Hughes movement springing up. Farmers, industrialists, doctors, educators, and professional men in other walks of life were flocking to his standard. We learned that this was also becoming true nationally, as in the case of Colonel George Harvey, who had been a strong Wilson Democrat.

Things really began to move at the end of August: on the thirty-first we opened the campaign in Indianapolis, when the big meeting at Tomlinson Hall was marked by the greatest representation of national leaders that had come to Indiana in years. Senator Sherman made the chief address, and the note of victory which he struck seemed to be genuinely echoed by the delegates.

The Fairbanks notification, held on his own beautiful lawn the next day, was the scene of one of those incidents that turn out to be prophetic —in this case prophetic of my long motion picture associations that began in 1922. In reporting the meeting, the Indianapolis *Star* made much of "the indefatigable motion picture men who flooded the grounds with equipment and provided additional entertainment for a public whose eyes and ears were unaccustomed to the technique of movie-making."

Our campaign at once moved into high gear. Apparently our house was in much better order than expected by out-of-state party officials who came to confer with us. The numerous comments made on the thoroughness of our state-wide organization revealed to us a surprise that was almost offensive. What did they expect of politically minded Hoosiers!

Signs of Republican harmony continued to multiply. Theodore Roosevelt was all over the lot, and in some of his speeches he fairly burned up the Wilson preparedness program. He thoroughly enjoyed exposing what were to him inexcusable inconsistencies in the defense policy.

It is interesting to recall that almost at this same time President Wilson himself arrived in Indiana for a speaking tour—our state being just as important to the Democrats—and I attended a luncheon in his honor at the Claypool Hotel. This sort of social interchange was not unusual. We had even invited Tom Taggart, Indiana's leading Democrat, to our convention, although the pressure of other business compelled him to decline. Once the active campaign was opened, life seemed to be one endless series of meetings. This was the time of harvest for which local workers had long been preparing. Because of headquarters responsibilities, it was possible for me to address only an occasional meeting; we were a *working* organization. But I tried my best to get to meetings planned by the Young Men's Republican Clubs.

Possibly our extensive use of traveling men as "preachers" of political doctrine was a bit novel. They had an organization almost three thousand strong, greatly augmented during the campaign, and they carried the word into every corner of the state.

Another innovation was our wide use of motion pictures, urging citizens to study the issues, register, and vote. Since these movies were shown in our Indiana commercial theaters, we owed a debt of thanks to the theater owners themselves for originating this idea. We had our own man making movies at important events, and these pictures proved useful.

It is no wonder that we were kept busy, for we attempted to organize every practicable group and carried our activities into every sphere. We tried to be ready for everything all the time, and the committee's secretary, Jack Henley, who never left his post, had seventeen sub-groups in his setup.

Speakers Bureau	Foreign Voters Bureau
Press Bureau	Wet and Dry Bureau
Young Men's Movement	Negro Bureau
Labor Bureau	Women's Bureau
Traveling Men's Bureau	Finance Committee
Republican Clubs Bureau	Dissatisfied Democrats
Soldiers Bureau	Legislative Bureau
Organizers Bureau	Publicity Department
Mailing List and Literature Bureau	

And this setup was the mainspring for thousands of letters and quantities of literature pouring out into the state. Most of all, it was the place where we tried to solve the special problems that kept pouring in on us. These problems came often through the direct contacts that I maintained with county chairmen and precinct committeemen, for there is no substitute for person-to-person discussion. I can guarantee that there was no busier telephone in the state of Indiana than mine!

During that year Indiana was especially in the limelight because the fact that both vice-presidential candidates—Marshall and Fairbanks— were Hoosiers put a little extra emphasis into everything that was done.

Special interest was shown in our gubernatorial race because the Democratic candidate, John A. N. Adair, had been continually absent from the state for ten years prior to 1916; knowing so little about local conditions, he was in no position to answer the many charges of inadequate state government hurled at him by our Republican candidate. Two months before the election Adair admitted that it was useless for him to try to answer the Goodrich accusations. This was the amazing situation which caused the Democrats to concentrate on national issues, where they felt their position was stronger. They had the great advantage of being in while we were still out. We tried to be particularly careful not to make any slip-ups in our own plans and arguments. At least complacency had no chance to defeat us.

And so it was that on November 8 we could herald the victory of two United States senators, nine out of thirteen congressmen, the entire state ticket, and the majority in both branches of the state legislature. Goodrich's plurality was 12,771; New's over Senator Kern, 11,501; and Watson's over Taggart, 9,616. And, so far as Indiana was concerned, Hughes carried our state by 7,294. In the national vote, out of a total of twenty-nine states, the Republicans elected sixteen senators against the Democrats' fourteen. In a total of thirty-six states we elected twenty governors to fourteen for the Democrats and one for the Prohibitionists. How Hughes lost the nation—the far-western states having cast the die that sealed his defeat—I shall mention again in my story of the Progressive element in Republican politics.

Organization is a hard thing to describe. Too often we take it for granted. In other cases we labor over some details that do not count. Judged by the comments of many out-of-state visitors—including newspapermen, who are trained observers—our Indiana Republican organization of 1916 was about as thorough a piece of work as seen up to that time. One commentator called it "the most complete and workable of any in the Union." Certainly the editorial comment and congratulations that came to me as state chairman were gratifying. Equally strong words of commendation came from national figures like Nicholas Murray Butler, Senator Theodore Burton and James A. Garfield, both of Ohio, and National Chairman Willcox. One of our Democratic rivals, S. F. Peabody, wrote: "My respects to the man who 'skinned' us out of Indiana. I would not so heartily congratulate you if we had not been able to get along without Indiana."

Personally, I felt that the most important thing to be done next was for the state Republican administration to carry out pre-election promises and basic Republican policy as fully as possible. Governor Goodrich completely agreed, and we worked closely to this end. In January the Republican members of the Indiana House met with me at the Hotel Severin to discuss how best we could square our performance with our promises. Particular issues were state-wide prohibition, limited suffrage for women, and the Constitutional Convention enactments.

The inauguration of Governor Goodrich had just taken place, and that was a great day for all of us. How well I remember passing through the crowds that jammed the corridors of the State House—in company with the governor and his wife—as we made our way to a platform erected for the ceremony. Charles W. Fairbanks was prominent in the group. Governor Goodrich's address clearly reflected the spirit which had rebuilt the party and the political climate pervading the new state administration. Among other things, he said:

"Responsibility to the people and faithfulness to public trust is the best answer which can be made to those who insist that democracy is a failure; it is the surest safeguard of our free institutions.

"I believe in the good sense and honesty of the people and am certainly desirous of an administration of public affairs conducted in the interest of the state as a whole and not for any special interest. This they ought to have; they should not be satisfied with anything less."

One of the major questions—the building of a new state constitution —brought out a quip by an editorial writer that I have never forgotten. He said that the state constitution might last longer than either party, and for that reason there had better be no politics in the proceedings.

The next and most bothersome practical question was the filling of state appointive offices. Every practical politician knows what this means. Rightly used, appointments to office are a necessary means of carrying out governmental administration, which by vote of the people has been entrusted to the party in power. Unworthily used, these offices become a source of selfish partisan politics, and even of maladministration and corruption. In Indiana we had been out of office for eight years, and for every executive position to be filled I think there must have been ten applicants, each feeling himself better qualified than the previous one. Filling these appointments was a difficult thing; this is one of the heaviest responsibilities borne by an elected official. When one considers how carefully a man is screened for a responsible place in a business or professional organization, where at best his "public accountability" is not comparable to that of a public servant, he better realizes this problem. Whenever an appointment is to be made, the pressures exerted are enough to wear a man down if he is really conscientious, as Governor Goodrich certainly was. Party members, Democrats, labor groups, ex-Progressives, faithful public servants—one group or another could not help being offended by every choice made.

Actually it was John McCardle and the governor who had most to do with appointments. In no sense did they come within my sphere, though plenty of people asked me to use my influence. As state chairman, I was not a public official. To make my position perfectly clear, let me say that I had never been paid any salary as chairman, not even traveling expenses. I certainly could not do more than the job entailed, although any responsibility involved in the office was taken care of to the best of my ability. When the election was won I certainly did not have time to sit around in Indianapolis advising on matters where my opinion might perhaps have been appreciated but by no means required. The State Committee had been assembled to elect, not select, and we hewed to this line both before and after the election. I had my own law practice to get back to as fast as possible.

I have no doubt that the task that devolved on Governor Goodrich, and the pressure of trying to satisfy so many folks who had waited eight years for a Republican administration, was one cause of his serious illness in the fall of 1917. To pay such a price is a bit of political irony.

As to local results, we elected a Republican mayor in Sullivan, as also happened at Terre Haute and half a dozen other cities. These municipal elections of November 1917 were probably the most important single activity during the year.

Meanwhile our participation in the war was beginning to create political problems as well as personal ones. There were rumors that the Wilson administration was appointing men of conscription age to civil-service jobs and sending them across the country as public relations agents; even that the Democrats were running their own party newspaper at public expense. General objections to Wilson's assumption of so much power were being heard more and more frequently in 1917. The country was not used to it, and many people were startled by some of his ideas that at the time seemed quite radical. The war bureaus offered further cause for public concern, and Congress gasped at the expenditure of public funds.

So it was that 1917 was an increasingly busy year for me, a Republican year for Indiana, and a war year for all America. Much of this activity I shared as chairman of the State Council of Defense, which will form another chapter in this story. Our Republican state government in Indiana worked with complete loyalty and devotion with a Democratic national government toward the common goal of victory.

All this time, from 1912 to 1918—from age thirty-three to thirty-nine —I was what one might call a struggling young lawyer. My struggle, however, was not one for clients but for time. Each year the pressure seemed to increase: the busier I was in politics, the busier our law practice would be. But, like most other men who find themselves in this position, I would not give up either and simply kept redistributing my time so as best to accommodate both these major interests. Looking back, I wonder whether we were not able in those simpler days to save considerable time that today goes into the hopper of complex modern living.

During these years our business expanded, our office was moved, and the community helped us celebrate the fortieth anniversary of Father's law practice. He had been in the same office in the same little town, working with the same friends, for four full decades. On February 27, 1915, Father and I gave the Bar Association a banquet in my home, with more than thirty lawyers present. Warm addresses were made by several who had known my father most of his life—known him as lawyer, citizen, churchman, and head of a family. It was a moving occasion. Perhaps I remember it with more feeling than anything that has happened during my whole career in the law.

Most of the important cases that came into our office during these years had to do, as usual, with railroads, mines, and the purchase of land for growing enterprises. The Grasselli Chemical Company of Cleveland, a leader in its field, asked us at this time to secure for them a tract of land near Terre Haute on which they erected a plant—notable for those days—which became one of the major industries of our region. The C. & E.I. Railroad continued to be our client, as it is today, and likewise the Monon. Then the Illinois Central appointed us their attorneys for the whole state of Indiana. In an earlier contact with this railroad I had gone to Chicago to see whether their shops, which were being moved from Palestine, Illinois, might not come to Sullivan. Bloomfield and Linton were also bidding for them because they employed two hundred men and would be a definite contribution to the prosperity of any small city.

An interesting case in which politics and law were merged was a suit which we filed in the U. S. District Court asking on behalf of the Illinois Central Railroad for an injunction against the operation of the Adamson Act. It was this act against which I had asked Nicholas Murray Butler to speak during the campaign. Now, as attorneys for the Illinois Central, which opened the fight in Indiana, we were testing the matter at law. Our participation in this controversy may have brought me to the attention of the Monon Railroad people, for in June of 1916 they asked me to be their general counsel. It would have meant a full-time job and would have involved my going to Chicago for good; it would have cut off not only my private practice but the whole work of the state chairmanship. All these factors weighed so heavily that I guess I barely considered accepting the position.

As things developed, our firm found itself involved in many purchases of land—especially coal land. In one important case the Miami Coal Company asked us to purchase for them something like two thousand acres just north of Terre Haute. James and John Connery, owners of the company, became very close friends of mine and have continued so through all the years.

One of the most personal happenings of this period was my father's sale of his farm over in the Wabash Valley section. We were really a bit disappointed, for we knew he had derived a great deal of pleasure from it. Later, when we came to administer his estate, we found in an envelope the government bonds in which he had invested the proceeds from that sale. He had written on that envelope:

This is the money received from the Gill Township farm. I put it in Government Bonds in this manner because I believe my boys can do better with these bonds and the coupons thereon than in running a farm.

Perhaps that is what you might call a left-handed compliment. As a matter of fact, both my brother Hinkle and I long before had purchased farms of our own and have held onto them, thus continuing one of the customs of a true country lawyer.

The three men in the Hays family—Father, Hinkle, and myself—continued to fill a pretty continuous string of speaking engagements here and there. When I had to be off to Indianapolis, Chicago, or New York during those years, Father and my brother obligingly responded to the invitations to me. Before the days of broadcasting, an unbelievable number of local speeches had to be given throughout the whole country. This was a major activity, a trademark, of the era. Even businessmen practiced oratory more than they did golf. Yet what was civic was also social, what was business was usually civic, and what had to do with the church could often be at the same time both social and civic. In a sense, though in no narrow one, all these activities bore on politics, since *politics is people*. These subdivisions of my life do not really indicate different functions; they indicate different and shifting emphases. In Sullivan, and in the Indiana of that day, life was more unified than it is today. We did not think of "watertight compartments" in which to keep our different interests. Life—our own, that of our friends and of our communities—was all one.

However, I still would make a distinction between public life and the more strictly private life, which in my case became rarer and rarer. I did manage to sneak off occasionally to Colorado during the summer, or perhaps down to the South Carolina mountains, and "sneak" is pretty close to the proper word. When you knew people all over the state, with hundreds of whom you were carrying on all sorts of projects, the possibilities of being able to keep your whereabouts a secret were almost nil. And so it was that, while I loved all my work and welcomed the opportunities to do some alleged services, I often longed for the day when, like my father and my mother, I could take off for Florida or northern Michigan and be as carefree as a deer in the closed season.

In my own life the big event of this period was the birth of Bill, Jr., in December of 1915, to which I have already referred. From then on there were two "men" in my immediate family, bound together in a relationship which has always been wonderfully close and satisfying.

Just one more glance ahead. A "boom" is a peculiar political phenomenon. While it is a special characteristic of politics, a boom is no stranger to one concerned with this field than lightning is to a student of meteorology, and booms occur in political campaigns about as often as lightning occurs with rainstorms. Thus it is that I simply record the fact that, one time or another, I seem to have been boomed for almost every office known in the United States. Some of these booms were just so many words. It seems there was always someone who thought I should be doing something else, that I would allegedly make a good governor, a good congressman, a good senator, even a good president. I am not saying anything about the judgment involved in these proposals, but hasten to point out, first, there is plenty of difference between being boomed for an office and holding it, and second, my range of activities always seemed to be more diverse than would have been encompassed by any single office.

How far this spreading of activities was due to my own inherent nature and how much to various sets of circumstances, I shall never know.

CHAPTER 8

Indiana State Council of Defense

W E now know how greatly World War I altered the course of civilization. It was a time of beginnings and endings. Not only did it change the course of nations, but it automatically sent millions of individuals down new paths. It was so with me. When we joined the conflict on April 6, 1917, my instant reaction was a desire to get into it. I tried for acceptance in every branch of service, but not one would have me. My 110 pounds at age thirty-eight would not meet even the lowest of minimum requirements. I thought that perhaps I could learn to pilot an airplane, but the authorities disagreed with me. Even with Senator New's help I found no way to overcome the obstacles.

Only three days after the House had concurred in the declaration of war, I had made what seemed the most logical and substantial offer of service within my power: the offer to raise a regiment. It was a bona fide one, conveyed in a letter to Governor Goodrich. The idea sprang out of the Young Men's Movement in Indiana, which, though Republican in origin, was dedicated to the good of the nation rather than merely to that of partisan politics. In my offer as state chairman I was speaking not only for a great body of eager young men but for their assured financial support. My letter to the governor named the eleven men who had "authorized me to offer this to you as a possible service in the country's cause and as an expression of our confidence in you." These men had promised to stand the entire cost of equipment.

Though this offer did not fit into the nation's official mobilization plans, it fairly represents the response that marked the year 1917. Perhaps never before or since have we felt such a spontaneous surge of patriotic fervor as in that second week of April. In Sullivan, as in cities, towns, and villages across the country, people were drawn together to voice their feeling, to endorse the action of Congress and the President, to pledge their common effort, and to ask God's blessing on the cause.

While I met with no success in getting into military service, I found that a great civilian branch of service was coming into being, in which I was to spend the first half of the war period. For me, as for many others, there then came some of the busiest and most stimulating months of my life.

All this started on May 21, 1917, when Governor Goodrich determined just where and how I was to serve. Out of the blue he announced my appointment as chairman of the State Council of Defense. This job, like that of Republican state chairman, was of course strictly gratuitous, but I was so glad to have something I could get my teeth into that I snatched the opportunity. Our state at once felt itself a part of the organized national effort.

The Council of National Defense had been brought into being in 1916, when it first was realized what might lie ahead, and it served, in effect, as the civilian branch of the War Department. That is the simplest way to think of it. By 1917, when the war started, it was occupying five floors of the Munsey Building in Washington—a modest organization compared with what we were to witness during World War II. And as soon as war was declared, the state councils of defense were set up from coast to coast on authority of the respective state legislatures.

In 1917 our people had not yet had any experience with "total war"—with all its controls, allocations, rationing, and so on. The business of the country, like the lives of its citizens, still had a freedom and spontaneity that we took for granted. Now, suddenly, the Council of National Defense made plans and exercised nationwide guidance covering the major features of our economy or, as it was called in directives, "the civilian war effort."

Young people of today may be surprised to learn that from the first the scope included many natural resources and basic products: coal, lumber, oil, hides, rubber, wool, aluminum, brass, copper, cement, lead, mica, nickel, steel, zinc, alloys, pig tin, scrap iron, and wire rope. It covered a wide range of manufactured goods, including optical glass, canned goods, gauges and dies, cotton goods, knit goods, woolen manufactures, shoes and leather, mattresses and pillows, alcohol, chemicals, and tubular products. Almost all transportation became its business: locomotives, railroads, car services; shipping and priorities, inland waterways; automotive transport; military transportation; freight tariffs and passenger tariffs; and even storage facilities. The production and transportation of military goods and supplies of course were paramount.

It was early seen that any effective control over needed supplies for some allocation of *man power*—a phrase which took on new meaning in 1917. This meant "mobilization" of strengths and skills in many areas: labor, wages, and hours; women in industry and in defense work; mediation and conciliation; vocational education; dentistry, medicine, and surgery; and even publicity. As the war effort widened, there were increasing calls for many specialized skills and services.

As added strains were put on our whole domestic economy and, in particular, on the resources of communities near military camps, new problems arose, such as general medicine, hygiene and sanitation, public health hospitals, schools and recreation. Over everything hovered the mounting questions of food, prices, housing, and the over-all cost of living.

I mention all these things because most of them, as emergency problems on a national scale, were then new to us. Some needs, to say nothing of equitable solutions, developed only gradually. As soon as they were clearly in sight, a new request or directive—in those days I think there were more of the former than the latter—would go out to the state councils. It was soon obvious that Washington could not *solve* these problems; at best it could only suggest general policies which, to be effective, had to be carried out at the *state and local level.* In some cases the national council, weighted down by its responsibilities, seemed to forget the fact that grass must grow from the roots up.

The Advisory Commission of the national council included some of our finest and ablest leaders: Daniel Willard, president of the B. & O. Railroad; Howard E. Coffin, vice-president of the Hudson Motor Car Company; Julius Rosenwald, the philanthropist and also president of Sears, Roebuck & Company; Bernard M. Baruch, banker, to whom the country continues to look for wisdom on great issues; Dr. Hollis Godfrey, president of Drexel Institute; Samuel Gompers, president of the American Federation of Labor, who will perhaps go down in history as the truest pioneer and statesman of the labor cause; and Dr. Franklin Martin, director general of the American College of Surgeons. Rarely has a sounder or wiser group of men been found to guide citizen action.

Under their counsel, state headquarters rapidly sprang into being. In Indiana we were settled in the State House in quarters which sufficed until late October. As we expanded it seemed best, being a state agency, to stay right there, and we simply put up temporary partitions. Success was going to depend on the efficiency of our organization, not on the appearance of our offices.

Freedom of speech is generously employed in Indiana, or we could never have produced so many writers and politicians. So from some quarters quite a cry went up over the fact that I was at the same time chairman of the Republican State Committee and of the Council of Defense. Several newspapers called Governor Goodrich biased, and one asked for "some big, brawny, progressive man who can appreciate the importance of the position." What "brawn" had to do with it, I wouldn't know. Some persisted in seeing all our early undertakings as having a political slant. In the circumstances, this early opposition sometimes seared a bit.

On the other side of the shield, there were equally strong approval and support. Professor James A. Woodburn of Indiana University, the president of the League of American Citizenship, wrote:

> You will know how to mobilize our patriotic forces. You should have an effective organization behind you in every county. . . . You are the man to carry this movement forward with great efficiency and vigor. We are under great obligations to you for past services.

I hoped this was true, but certainly his endorsement helped. And when an editorial noted the fact that the Democratic state chairman was holding a salaried position with the federal government, whereas the Republican chairman was donating his efforts, the skies cleared a bit more.

The personnel of the state council was like a blue-ribbon jury. In their respective fields they were the best that could be found, and certainly inspired confidence. All nineteen appointments were made by the governor. I cannot omit naming some of them: Senator Tom Taggart, Indiana's leading Democrat, universally respected and one of my staunchest supporters throughout; Frank Dailey, a former district attorney; H. R. Kurrie, president of the Monon Railroad; Arthur W. Brady, president of the Union Traction Company; Charles W. Fairbanks; Mrs. Anne Studebaker Carlisle; Charles Fox, state head of the AFL; and Indiana's beloved humorist, George Ade. These appointees, chosen from all over the state, represented all political parties.

We made as little to-do as possible about financing. The work was originally financed by bank loans as needed, but expenses were pared to the bone. One good friend lent us his expert accountant to simplify our procedures and help us in determining costs. We borrowed no more than needed and spent no more than we had. Not one of us, I imagine, had ever heard of "deficit financing."

Our first efforts were aimed at three central goals:

1. the state-wide recruiting of volunteers to give their time and talent to the work entrusted to the state council;
2. marshaling public support; and
3. co-ordinating all participating agencies of every sort.

The relationship between state and national agents was worked out in a satisfactory manner, the two being well integrated. The relation was definitely a two-way street; each supplied the other with needed information and each made specific requests of the other. The over-all policies naturally came from the national council, but they quite as frequently sought advice and help from us. One instance was a Committee on Scientific Research; we were able to set up a group, under the president of an Indiana polytechnic institute, to which technical problems could be referred as they arose. The national council was fully appreciative of our efforts, as was also Secretary of War Newton D. Baker, who wrote us at the time: ". . . The work of the Indiana Council has been particularly gratifying. More power to you."

Our work was facilitated by the setting up in Chicago of a regional headquarters of the national council, which made it easier for Indiana and other midwestern states to get quick action. Soon relationships between neighboring states expanded so that each of us helped the other. It was another splendid case of "Let's get together."

Co-operation took still another form when the national council encouraged state representatives to visit each other's headquarters and compare notes on the most effective ways of reaching common objectives. Governor Harding of Iowa and six members of his Council of Defense came to Indiana early in 1918. From our state the party went on to Ohio to study that state's labor exchanges, and Indiana's Nat Squibb accompanied them. While they were with us the head of each department in the Indiana council described to them the chief aspects of his work.

I found that the work of developing our state defense organization was not unlike my responsibility as state Republican chairman, though with wider objectives. The task of getting into every county and community and there forming a little group to take responsibility was the same. The motive power—the safety of the nation rather than the success of a political party—was the thing that enabled us to do the bigger job. The forms the job took were legion. We used similar techniques of organization—especially state conferences, county sub-committees, and traveling teams of advisers. Incidentally, it would have been hard to find better preparation for my next assignment—that of national chairman of the Republican party—which, unknown to me, was just around the corner.

In July and again in December we had two of the most effective state conferences I have ever witnessed, with every county represented. In July the central theme was mobilization, the fullest possible mobilization of all our resources. We asked the county representatives to set up their own headquarters and to make arrangements to be financially as self-sufficient as possible. We urged them to get behind food and fuel conservation, the co-ordination of all social and industrial activities, and the promotion of whatever local activities they thought calculated to make the war effort most successful. We emphasized the value of Red Cross work, the Boys' Working Reserve, Four-Minute Men to address people wherever they gathered together, and the need for effective publicity.

By December the war had become much more real, and our conference that month reflected our heightened effort. As if to highlight the intense feeling, we overcame considerable difficulties in order to bring Sousa's band from the Great Lakes Naval Training Station. They came, 312 strong, and we met their expenses of four thousand dollars through contributions by fifty-nine firms, associations, and individuals. Under the personal direction of John Philip Sousa, the March King, they made a tremendous impression on the two thousand men and women assembled. When they played "The Stars and Stripes Forever," "Over There," and "America," it was an experience to remember. And we felt close to the heart of America when a wire just received from President Wilson was read: "Pray extend my warmest greetings to the conference and express to them my confidence that it will redound to the benefit of the whole nation."

The program was loaded with speakers of national authority and personal prestige. Among them were Dr. Ray Lyman Wilbur, Senator Albert Beveridge, George Creel, Meredith Nicholson, Dr. Henry Van Dyke, Lieutenant Paul Perigord of the French Army, and Father John Cavanaugh, president of the University of Notre Dame. Lieutenant Perigord was in reality a French priest who had gone into the trenches when the fighting started and already held three citations for bravery. The national council was sending him around the country to help folks realize what the war was like, and he was certainly effective. Medill McCormick, who spoke especially to newspapermen, also was able to tell us what was really going on, because he had been on the Allied war front for two months. The second day of the December conference was less dramatic, but full of business.

We held nearly a score of sectional meetings all over Indiana. Groups responsible for food conservation, fuel conservation, Women's Division, Medical Division, and so on, had their own definite problems to help each other solve. At the meeting of the publicity division our most illustrious guest speaker was George Creel. Preceding his address to the Indiana editors a few of us had gathered for dinner at the home of W. C. Bobbs, the publisher. I remember Meredith Nicholson being there. Creel really "knocked 'em dead," and it was a tremendous honor to have him with us. Later he wrote: "I wanted to get in contact with the men of your State Council of Defense, for we have a feeling in Washington that the Hoosier State, more than any other state in the Union, has got the meaning of what we want to do and what we have done." It was Creel, too, who told me personally that Indiana's organization was far and away the best in the country. All this I quickly passed on to the other members of the state council.

Though the December conference was more effective than we could have expected, we did not rest on our laurels. There were continual follow-up meetings, mostly in the counties, but in some instances of state-wide bearing.

By February I could tell our folks that Indiana had given more than four times the required number of men for the Army—standing *first* in the nation—and that it had oversubscribed the Liberty Loan, the

Y.M.C.A. and Red Cross drives. I like to think that all these things taken together meant that we had gotten into the war effort to the best of our ability.

Organization should always be for the purpose of accomplishing something that needs to be done, not merely for the sake of putting up a show or keeping the wheels going round. In the work of defense our job was primarily *mobilization*—the very word up to that time had probably never been in common usage. Since then its use has become only too well known. Our task was primarily the mobilization of the civilian economy in three major fields: man power, production, and transportation.

Naturally the most important aspect of mobilization was that of man power, especially in regard to conscription, civilian registration and labor allocation, vocational training, school children, professional people, specific civilian defense workers, and the Home Guard. The country quickly learned how much "fighting" had to be done on the home front, and realized the small percentage of men who actually saw front-line fighting.

The supervision of conscription was placed in the hands of 276 men— three men forming a board in each county—appointed by Governor Goodrich. The sheriff, county clerk, and one citizen originally made up these boards. The citizen was later required to be a doctor, and still later a board of lawyers was added to help men interpret their conscription status. The response of these board members was typical of the spirit of the hour: 271 attended the first meeting at Indianapolis two days after their appointments, the five absentees being prevented by illness.

Military registration was the first event that fixed the fact of the war in everybody's consciousness. This occurred on June 5 and included men from age twenty-one to thirty. In our own county 2,446 registered. When on July 20 the first names were pulled out in the lottery at Washington, the very first number drawn was 258—a coal miner from our neighboring village of Hymera. On September 23, Sullivan County sent off its first ninety-one men. The day before, the city gave a big dinner marked by a roll call of the draftees. On Sunday morning six thousand persons marched four abreast down Main Street to the Illinois Central Station, where they saw these ninety-one recruits leave for Camp Taylor in Louisville.

For those ineligible for military service another form of mobilization was called for in the National Public Service Reserve movement. The national director wanted every man and woman in the state to be catalogued, with a statement as to whether or not each would be ready to respond to a specific call for his services. As things developed, this matter of labor allocation was one of the most difficult questions we had to handle.

The policy of replacing men with women was not nearly so well established in World War I as it became later. There was still some pressure from labor unions. Since they felt they were fighting an uphill battle against the industrial exploitation of women and children, our council had to consider this atmosphere in any plans it made. The actual need for women's labor and their thorough willingness to help were the factors that finally decided the policy. Such labor problems were handled by county committees consisting of a representative of industry, one of labor, and one interested citizen. Each committee co-operated with the Y.W.C.A., the Associated Charities, and the juvenile courts, as well as with a representative of the Indiana Manufacturers Association, to assure the physical and moral well-being of women engaged in factory war work.

To say that Indiana did not have labor problems would be to distort the truth. To mention only one, complaints kept coming to us of discrimination against union labor, and some of these cases were not easy to solve. In this connection it is interesting to remember that Samuel Gompers himself, then president of the American Federation of Labor, came out to Indiana in January of 1918 to attend a meeting of the United Mine Workers and sat in on a state council meeting at our special invitation. When he mentioned the fact that three quarters of a million persons had unionized since the beginning of the war, he was pointing out both a trend and a factor in our problem.

One of the earliest special requests was that we try to supply ten thousand shipbuilders. This was a request which could not be handled in a hurry, but we did our best to recruit capable material for the East Coast shipyards.

Before long we were receiving calls which could be filled only by finding applicants and training them. The case I remember best was a call for trained telegraphers, of which the Army Signal Corps asked us to produce nine hundred as quickly as possible. This was immediately referred to the council's educational section. The following week Professor Collicott reported that the response of educational institutions was excellent. Within a short time centers in a dozen cities had made arrangements to open classes. By January of 1918, 679 students were studying telegraphy in eleven Indiana schools. To help meet the quota, we encouraged a friendly rivalry among different sections of the state, such as had sprung up with good results in meeting a Liberty Loan quota, and we had full assistance from local newspapers in spreading the call.

One of the first, and largest, groups organized for the war effort was the school system of the state. This was done through Horace Ellis, state superintendent of public instruction and a member of our council. In June we had advised the ninety-two county superintendents that thirty-seven speakers would go through the state explaining the part that school children and educators could play in the war effort. The most concrete project in this field was the Boys' Working Reserve, proposed early in July. One week was set aside for the registration of boys from sixteen to twenty-one years of age. My own county, with a quota of 530, enrolled 588 in this wholly voluntary, non-military youth program. Every county but two had set up machinery for the Boys' Working Reserve prior to the enrollment week named by the governor. Most of the actual work done by these boys was agricultural. This became so valuable that the state superintendent directed high school principals to release these boys from school attendance to help harvest perishable crops in September of 1917. Many workers of draft age were thus replaced. Again, when it was proposed that fallen timber be used instead of coal, it was felt that the Boys' Working Reserve could be used to survey county timberland for this purpose. As a matter of fact, this boys' project caught on so well that in northern Indiana what was tantamount to a Girls' Working Reserve was also organized.

Another development of the schoolwork, of which our council was most proud, was the publication of a special handbook. After much discussion and more work a volume of 152 pages, entitled *Indiana's War Service Textbook for High Schools,* was published in February 1918. This book covered everything that the council wanted school children to know about the war effort and what they might do to aid it.

There were various groups which had to be brought into the defense picture in order to complete the circuit of state-wide mobilization. Among these were bankers, ministers, doctors, businessmen, Red Cross workers, and Home Guardsmen—all of whom were important to the successful prosecution of the war.

The banker's role in the war effort was threefold: we had to turn to the banks for the actual financing of council activities; for the handling of funds in connection with Liberty Loan drives and War Fund solicitations; and, lastly, for loans to assure the prosecution of work on the home front when essential to the success of the war effort. If the banks had been unwilling to co-operate, if their response had been halfhearted or, for any reason, funds had not been forthcoming, our Defense Council project would, at best, have been anemic. The willing dollar was our lifeblood—and the banks were the heart of our success.

In connection with Liberty Loan drives, the bankers wrote a brilliant chapter. Early in the war George Ade, chairman of the council's publicity committee, made it his special interest to popularize Liberty Loan Bonds as a form of investment and to persuade bankers to redouble their efforts in getting this idea over to their depositors. We devised all sorts of means—such as a series of Thrift Weeks—to assure success, and we made a special effort to use county chairmen and state committeemen of both political parties as helpers in putting over the urgency of the drives. I wanted to be sure that every reservoir of finance, large or small, would be reached. On the other hand, our council had responsibility for protecting Indiana's citizens from dishonest, fraudulent, or needless drives. And we did our best to bring about consolidation and centralization of appeals wherever possible.

The clergy was another source of guidance to which we turned in matters affecting the moral well-being not only of men in the service but also of our citizens. Under Dr. Albert B. Storms we organized a committee on religious, moral, and social forces. Among other things, we turned to the churches to back up the war-born drive of the national Young Men's Christian Association for thirty-five million dollars. This large sum was needed because General Pershing had asked the Y.M.C.A. authorities to assume major responsibilities—canteen, recreation, athletics, music, education—at every Army installation here and abroad. These possible commitments called for the expenditure of large sums of money for personnel, transportation, supplies, and services of every sort. The clergy, properly informed, were most helpful in making this appeal clear to their people.

One of the last functions of the council in which I participated was a patriotic meeting on Lincoln's Birthday—sponsored by the Men's Club of the Meridian Street Methodist Episcopal Church. Mayor Charles Jewett, Eugene Pulliam, and I were there to speak to this group about bringing Christian principles and thinking into the whole social fabric. As it happened, it was during this meeting that a messenger brought a telegram informing me that I had just been elected chairman of the Republican National Committee. We probably did not comprehend then as fully as we do now that we were facing a whole new set of problems in trying to maintain the social structure under war pressures. Here the clergy had a big responsibility. The tasks that today are so often handed over to a psychiatrist were still pretty much in their hands. Their role in the war effort was larger than most of us realized. The adjustment to new environments, to the loss of loved ones, to hardships caused by the war, to life under unnatural circumstances, all brought such a flow of problems to ministers and priests as had never faced them before.

The doctors, obviously, had heavy responsibilities. The medical section of the state council, under Dr. Emerson, did yeoman service. Almost at once Dr. Emerson urged the establishment of a Medical Board at Indianapolis, which was shortly convened, by orders of the War Department, to examine applicants for the Medical Reserve Corps of the Army. Filling the quota of Army doctors was one of the toughest mobilization problems we faced. It was so serious that the government was contemplating the drafting of physicians up to fifty-five years of age.

By dint of effort, however, and by nationwide response, the government presently had ceased to be in serious straits for physicians.

Dr. Emerson acted as a daily liaison between the Army and local doctors, concerning himself with everything medical touching upon the war effort; and the state-wide organization behind him made his efforts doubly effective. The notable fact that Indiana ranked second in the nation in supplying pharmaceuticals was primarily due to the supply house of Eli Lilly, the largest Indiana firm engaged in this work and one of the oldest and most reputable in the country. The work of the medical section is a good example of what we were aiming at—*complete mobilization*. They helped iron out problems incidental to examinations of medical and dental students; they devised ways to meet the quota of nurses; they assured the Army a steady flow of medical supplies; they kept the public informed of health problems and how best to meet them; and they encouraged preparation for post-war medical emergencies that were bound to develop.

As to the businessmen, the multitude of tasks that I saw devolving upon them suggested to me that their energies might be channeled more effectively if they operated through their fraternal associations. To work out such a plan, the heads of twenty-five to thirty fraternal organizations, representing at least half a million in membership, met with me in September. And so we set up a new section called the Council on Fraternal Organizations, with Knights of Columbus, Odd Fellows, Masons, Knights of Pythias, and Red Men represented through the state heads of their respective orders.

Another group loosely associated with the Council of Defense was the American Red Cross. Petitions for new Red Cross chapters began to come in almost immediately after the declaration of war. The Red Cross was one of the first organizations to sponsor a big drive for funds, because by experience they were already equipped to carry on work affiliated with the Army. I well remember how William Fortune, head of the Red Cross in Indiana, appeared before our council at one of our first meetings to appeal for our assistance in the state-wide campaign. Because we had representatives everywhere, we were able to offer much help, both in the organization of new chapters and in stimulation of the drive.

One of the clearest memories many women have of World War I is the number of socks they knitted. It was announced very early that we needed four thousand pairs by September 1 for the Indiana regiment. This work was carried on by the county councils, which were given definite quotas. The first quota was met almost a month ahead of time. Really, there was no end to the socks that were needed for the thousands of men continually tramping in the cold mud.

The Home Guard was another state organization with which we co-operated. This unit was needed to replace men called into active service. It was soon decided to call this the Liberty Guard and to seek enrollments of men between the ages of eighteen and forty-five. Our governor declared that this force was needed to curb treason, provide flood and fire protection, and to ensure public safety—as in guarding railroad bridges—with much responsibility thrown on the guardsmen themselves. Thus it was that the State of Indiana mobilized its man power. As I remember it, there were many cases where a man would be engaged in war work under two, three, or even four different classifications. He could not help it—nor did he try—for in Indiana we mobilized our man power for total war. Almost literally, not a man, woman, or child was without a direct stake in the effort.

Foodstuffs for animals as well as for humans were just about half the production problem in 1917, as in 1941. They certainly were by far the most important item in our production program.

We thought of production as the second step in mobilization, man power being the first. Although the word "mobilize" originally meant to most of us simply putting armed forces into readiness for active service, it came to mean much more during total war: it meant to organize and adapt industry and any form of production for fullest service to the nation. Certainly in the work of the state council the mobilization of food resources was the most interesting, most widespread and continuous part of our work. For this, there were many reasons.

First, it was tied in with the National Food Administration under that great American public servant, Herbert Hoover, whom I first came to know well in this relationship rather than in politics. That friendship has continued right down to the present day, I am happy and proud to say.

Second, the food program enlisted women more fully than did any other part of our activity. And our food projects well illustrated the state-wide scope of our council and its ability to touch every family through thousands of representatives. Although at times it made special calls on the clergy, the universities, the schools, the women, and the farmers, in the last analysis it depended on everyone.

Last, since it did touch everyone and involved real pressures and sacrifices, the food problem was plagued by black markets and hoarding, as we had never known them. At the same time it became an avenue of insidious propaganda and of dangerous rumors—many apparently of enemy origin—aiming especially to discourage and frighten women, on threat of personal injury, from signing pledge cards in the food conservation program.

Herbert Hoover's connection with this whole project deserves a word of comment. As we all know, his humanitarian services in the field of relief wrote a brilliant chapter in our national history. In June of 1917 the President announced Mr. Hoover's appointment as Food Commissioner. This was recognized as both a great honor and a tremendous responsibility, and there was hearty approval of the Chief Executive's choice. It was soon justified by the wisdom and thoroughness of the survey of supply and demand which Mr. Hoover made in July, and by the clearness of the recommended program which he considered essential to the successful prosecution of the war. This national program, which we in Indiana did our best to put into practice, included half a dozen chief planks: the reduction of waste; curtailing the consumption of staples; substitution of vegetables and other perishable foods, wherever possible, for staples; the consumption of food where it was produced; home canning of fruits and vegetables; and, finally, the substitution of other cereals for wheat. Every one of these recommendations received hearty support, especially from women, who could best understand what they meant.

Almost at once Mr. Hoover began calling the state food administrators down to Washington for conference. Our Dr. Harry E. Barnard would bring the result of these meetings back to our council meetings, so we could set the wheels in motion. He was soon able to report that the first steps were being carried out in considerable measure. By August, free curb markets had been set up in seventeen communities; and 173 Indiana towns and villages were then carrying on intensive campaigns against food waste.

The next phase of our battle was one of the most important. The National Food Administration had originated what was known as a Hoover Food Pledge Card, to be signed by homemakers. The purpose was to enroll every housewife in the drive to conserve food in the home. We considered this so important that a complete enrollment organization was established, with the machinery maintained through October, when a final and more intense campaign was conducted. By that time ugly rumors and foreign propaganda had been pretty successfully met and housewives were no longer troubled by it. Late in September, Indiana ranked fifth among the states in the number of women enrolled in the Hoover program. After our final intensive drive we ranked third!

Another popular device employed was a widely heralded Conservation Week set for the last week of October. On the first day, designated as Conservation Sunday, the subject was the sole topic of sermons throughout the state. The fact that clergymen were the first to urge the Hoover food program gave the drive a fine impetus. On the following Tuesday the famous program of meatless Tuesdays and Fridays was inaugurated. Throughout the whole week wheatless meals were encouraged, with emphasis on the substitution of corn bread. On Wednesday the county councils sponsored general rallies to popularize the program and announce what had been accomplished. On Thursday merchants put special window displays in their stores to stimulate the purchase of substitute foods. Friday was given over to impressing school children with the need for strict food conservation. Saturday was a day of special enrollment for women. And the concluding Sunday was dedicated as a day of prayer for those engaged in the fighting. It was at the end of this week that Indiana had moved up from fifth to third place in the nation.

International needs soon intensified our appeal. Belgium, France, and Italy were desperate; hence, still greater production at home was needed. Soon we were called upon for a 70 per cent reduction in wheat consumption, and our people did their best to respond.

Another dramatic phase of our program was the urgent request for ten million bushels of seed corn. Part of this was needed because much seed corn—some varieties had taken fifteen years to develop—was lost in the severe December weather, in Wisconsin and Michigan especially. An emergency call went out. The week of February 4 was set to survey the whole state, with the county councils putting on the personal pressure. In no other way could these needs have been met except through this long line of voluntary workers on the local level. Long ago I learned that *no national or state program is worth much unless it is voluntarily undertaken by citizens in their own communities.* That lesson apparently needs constant relearning in each generation.

Several of our emergency problems concerned livestock—cattle, pigs, and sheep. High prices for feed and a good beef market early brought calls for relief. There was a great temptation to slaughter milch cows for beef, and the council did its best to persuade farmers for patriotic reasons not to yield to this temptation. Within the year we were able to help reverse this trend, and found that farmers were importing milch cows rather than destroying their own.

Cattle, however, did not concern Indiana as much as hogs. The first help came when banks agreed to make loans with a minimum of difficulty to farmers who wished to undertake raising livestock, particularly hogs. The program was stimulated by conferences held late in October at Purdue University—of which our state agricultural college is a department—when the particular topic of discussion was the ratio between the price of pork and that of feed. This phase of our effort was pointed up by the release of statistics showing that 125,000 tons of pork monthly were required to feed the armed forces and our Allies, and that only 80,000 tons were then being shipped. Indiana was urged to increase her pork production by 20 per cent. Leading hog breeders who had been conferring at Purdue were at once sent out through the state under the direction of Professor G. I. Christie to talk and urge hog-raising.

In another move to ease the pork shortage and to prevent skyrocketing prices, as well as to increase wool production, the idea of raising sheep was vigorously pushed in October. William H. Dye, a prominent ex-Progressive, became intensely interested in this possibility and repeatedly urged it on our council. In precisely the same direction George Perkins, ex-financial mainspring of the Progressive party, and then in charge of Mayor Mitchell's Food Supply Committee in New York City, had likewise interested himself in sheep-raising possibilities in New York State. He had already purchased sixteen thousand sheep in the West and had them distributed in New York State. We found that two Hoosiers were already in the West purchasing sheep and that banks were gladly making loans. After full discussion it was decided that thirty thousand ewes should be added to the Indiana flocks. It took a lot of work, under the supervision of a five-man committee—three of them members of our state council—but with the help of county councils in distributing sheep and encouraging their raising, the task was accomplished. One tragic aspect of this problem was that during 1917 it was known that nine thousand sheep had been killed by stray dogs. Sheriffs, marshals, policemen, and constables were therefore "not discouraged" from impounding or killing stray or dangerous dogs.

The problem of the dairymen was an important part of our food problem in two directions: milk and beef. As I have said, high prices for feed and a good beef market sorely tempted them to slaughter their valuable herds of milch cows. One type of solution was finally suggested. Nat Squibb, a council member, conferred with Food Administrator Hoover and Congressman Cox about the possibilities of making alcohol from soft corn. Hoover gave the plan his immediate support, and three weeks later, at its January 9 meeting, the council embodied this plan in a bill. The idea was to retrieve as much food value as possible from this spoiled corn. It was already known that the residue from its distillation would provide both a good and an inexpensive feed for cows. With Hoover's full support, the bill carried provision for a twenty-million-dollar appropriation for government purchase of the alcohol manufactured.

At the same time the price of bran was fixed at 38 per cent of that of wheat, a measure which reduced stock feed by as much as ten to fifteen dollars a ton. In still another direction assistance came to the dairymen through the efforts of state veterinarians, who offered their help to the farmer in the control and elimination of diseases which annually struck the herds. We always were concerned about tuberculosis, hoof-and-mouth disease, and undulant fever. Through these special efforts millions of dollars in meat and dairy products were saved.

A danger, almost unbelievable to us then, loomed in the form of rumors of sabotage in connection with livestock, particularly by stockyard fires. Hoover was sufficiently concerned by reports to warn the state councils by wire to inform stockyards and grain elevators of the hazard.

Whatever the problem, the new idea or the quota to be met, the State Council of Defense was so fully organized that there was some place to take it. Even the Food Committee alone was divided into six departments. There was always an organization to consider such problems as cash-and-carry food buying, to assure sufficient stocks of fertilizers, to secure drain tiles for fields, to equalize prices so that production would be assured. The sincerity of these men and women who gave time and talent to the solution of the endless food problems as well illustrated by the offer of Dr. R. C. Julien, who volunteered to go to Europe to study intensive farming. Such men were devoted, sincere experts in their various fields.

As was to be expected, women were invaluable to this whole project. The tremendous growth of canning clubs was an illustration: women by the thousands preserved more food than they had the previous year. To get the fullest enrollment of women in the food conservation program, a state-wide drive was made with responsible chairmen for townships, precincts, and even blocks. Out in the country the blocks were a mile square! Complete coverage assured that not a woman in the state was missed. At least ten thousand women canvassed the state for the August 15 registration. Although the women's role in the food program was doubtless their most important contribution to the success of World War I, it was by no means their only one, as we all know.

In other directions the Indiana League for Women's Service, for example, encouraged the idea of women making shirts for soldiers, and various other projects. As the war progressed, the women's work was more thoroughly organized, and in October a regular Women's Section was added to the state council. By that time women available for all sorts of work had been catalogued and programs in which they were interested had been sufficiently tried out to prove their practicability. Thus it was possible for Mrs. Anne Studebaker Carlisle to set up almost a dozen divisions. Enrollment and Women's Service was under the direction of Julia Landers; Food Production under Hortense Tapp Moore; Home Economics, Mary Matthews of Purdue; Child Welfare, Mrs. Albion Fellows Bacon; Women in Industry, Mabel Maney; Health and Recreation, Mrs. George G. Hitt; Food Conservation, Mrs. Carl J. Fischer; Liberty Loans, Mrs. Fred McCullough; Red Cross and Allied Relief, Mrs. James W. Fesler; existing social-service agencies, Vida Newson; and Educational Program, Catherine Merrill Graydon. To carry on this work the women had their own headquarters in the State House, with an office staff to assist in keeping data correct and available. They mailed out great numbers of information folders and kept track of something like fifty thousand women who had voluntarily registered to help in various capacities.

We should not lose sight of the fact that at the same time our Indiana women—especially the Woman's Franchise League—continually urged the council to endorse the then pending Nineteenth Amendment, guaranteeing equal suffrage. They presented their case strongly in December, the committee representing 230 active chapters. To show how seriously we considered the matter, we referred it to the council's policy committee, of which Charles W. Fairbanks was chairman. In due course his committee recommended our endorsing woman suffrage, not as a war measure but "as a matter of sheer right and common justice." This action became most significant when not long afterward, as Republican national chairman, I helped to secure the requisite number of state ratifications to convert the amendment into law. Thus again, one chapter of my activity led into another.

After food, the next most important production problem was that of fuel. In the Indiana of 1917 that practically meant coal—much of it soft coal. Our main questions were these: state or federal control, inflation, transportation and distribution, and strikes. All of these gave us plenty of thought.

Inflation came first, as it did all along the line. To protect our people, some remedy must be found. What should we counsel our citizens to do —put in coal at high prices, or wait for some sort of price control?

The second problem, which necessarily followed, was this: could Indiana provide a remedy, or could relief be secured only through action by the federal government? This question remained open for a long time. As early as our June meeting Will Irwin proposed a resolution, quickly adopted, that Congress confer on the President the power to fix the price of coal and to regulate distribution. Indiana's relations with Washington were such as to make us believe that action on Irwin's proposal was both necessary and advisable. But as things worked out, relief for Indiana was so delayed that we were much disposed to try state control. We at once set up a strong coal committee to study the problem continuously.

At about this time or before, I had consulted George F. Porter, assistant to the director of the national council. He realized that the problem was national and soon called together a group of operators, who met in Washington and agreed on what they considered fair prices. This decision did not carry through into effective action, but in the interim the national council requested the states not to fix prices. So things went on until August, with no relief in sight.

Another practical factor lay in trouble between labor and management, which further aggravated a bad situation. Critical strikes resulted. One of the most serious occurred in the Clinton district, where the

Public Service Commission had directed a railroad to supply adequate transportation facilities for the miners. When this was not furnished by the specified date, four thousand miners walked out, with a resulting daily loss of eighteen thousand tons of coal. In another strike, involving a plea for wage adjustment, the loss was fifteen thousand tons a day. The council at once appointed a small committee to investigate this latter strike, which came at a time when Indiana was already experiencing a shortage of nearly four million tons as a result of the war. Because of transportation difficulties our out-of-state supply was cut off. The council suggested all means of alleviating the fuel shortage that it could devise. One was a request to merchants to turn out their store lights at nine o'clock on week nights and at nine-thirty on Saturdays. This helped a little. Another move, already mentioned, was to gather as much fallen timber as possible to replace coal. In August a group of thirteen states, meeting in Chicago to seek common relief, brought enough pressure to bear on Washington to hasten federal action. This group recommended drastic regulations by state and federal governments covering production, transportation, distribution, and price control. It emphasized the need of thorough investigation to determine equitable prices. Most of all, it urged immediate governmental action, yet with the utmost possible co-ordination with state action.

Since this problem of state-federal control has become so much more vital since 1917, it is interesting to recall something that happened at this August meeting. After considerable discussion a vote was taken to determine those who preferred federal action to that of the states. The vote was exactly five to five. Our Indiana group was particularly in favor of federal control because after the President had signed the Lever Bill on August 10, representatives of the Federal Trade Commission came to Indianapolis to consult with Governor Goodrich. He had submitted data on which the Lever Bill was based, he had been encouraging the Chief Executive to take action, and the close relationship between the two led us to believe that federal action was now the wise course. Beyond that, we already had pretty definite knowledge that it was coming.

These issues that I have sketched illustrate the dual problem our council continually faced: adoption of practicable goals, and harmonious agreement on the best means of reaching them. Our Hoosier folks had their hearts in the right place, but there were plenty of differences of opinion as to how needed measures could be accomplished. This was especially true for those in industry, where practicable difficulties were more numerous than in other fields of war activity. Getting unanimous endorsement on important national programs constituted a major victory for the administration and no small commentary on the co-operative spirit of the state councils of defense.

Our third general sphere of activity under mobilization was transportation, and it was primarily a problem of priorities. Among many problems, there were four that were continuous: alleviating the refrigerator- and coal-car shortage, allocating open-top cars for coal transportation, securing better train service for miners, and deciding whether or not public projects should be pursued during wartime.

The suggestion was made that an injunction be issued to put a stop to public works for two months. As a quasi-legislative governing agency, the state council found itself in a difficult position. We frequently suggested, and sometimes requested, definite remedial legislation. In this case we passed a resolution recommending to the railroad committee of the national council the consideration of a general order to all railroads to cease furnishing cars for the transportation of material for public road and street building and other work of similar character until the demand for coal cars was met. Washington soon issued an order prohibiting anywhere the use of open-top cars after November 1 for anything except the shipment of coal. Thus our Indiana action had national results.

The question of furnishing proper transportation for miners resulted in an invitation to them by Charles Fox, state head of the AFL and also a member of the Defense Council, to present their case. Their request for better facilities had already been approved by the Public Service Commission. It was pointed out to them that the railroad involved was in the hands of a receiver and that new equipment was out of the question. However, improvement was possible in the matter of train schedules to bring men into the mining area on time, and this we were able to accomplish.

A larger question, apparently affecting many people and much work already in progress, involved the relative importance of public projects in wartime. If there had been no car shortages the question might not have arisen. As it was, it became quite an issue. We wrote to the national council to ascertain its over-all policy on public construction. The answer, which came from the War Department, was a request to decrease public works. We then forwarded copies of this letter to all municipal and county councils. Further word soon came in a letter from the Secretary of War, calling for the suppression of all public projects for the duration. We were quite aware that in certain cases Secretary Baker's request was being ignored; hence this subject came before the council again in December 1917, when a resolution was adopted calling for the complete suspension of all public works, the council feeling that the work was not as essential as a steady supply of coal.

The passage of this resolution and the reactions to it well illustrate the function of both the council and public opinion. Our action was a matter of carefully considered opinion and advice, not one of law. When it was announced in the Indianapolis *Star*, a wave of objections quickly followed. The secretary of the Chamber of Commerce of Indiana strongly voiced this opposition. The city administration, various groups of residents living in affected areas, and no less than nineteen Indianapolis organizations told the council in no uncertain terms that they did not understand the resolution. A track-elevation project was already under way in Indianapolis, and these groups, expecting to share the benefits, did not wish to see it stopped. They passed many counter-resolutions requesting the state council to reconsider its position. Yielding to this wave of opinion, the council set January 2, 1918, for a hearing. But as far as we were concerned, we still felt bound to honor Secretary Baker's request.

After announcement of the hearing, meetings were held all over the city to sound out public opinion. The situation was clear: these folks who were protesting saw the track elevation at close range—it touched them directly and was for their benefit and that of their families. The council, conscious of its public responsibility to the entire state, saw the project as part of a whole: one part of a tremendous effort, and apparently not in harmony with the rest of that effort. The war was not being won in either Indianapolis or Indiana. If such public works were not discouraged throughout the whole country, the national war effort would be jeopardized. *A vital principle was involved.* Even though the council was hopelessly outnumbered and put under tremendous pressure to reverse its position, we refused to do so, although we pointed out to the citizens involved that our action carried no legal force. We made it clear that we would not attempt to get any official sanction without informing the citizens that such action was pending, so that they might be heard along with the council. Following the hearing, a full transcript of proceedings was sent to all interested parties for further consideration.

This question was taken over on the national level when William G. McAdoo took charge of the railroads. All the papers were mailed to him with a letter which Mayor Jewett of Indianapolis and two others helped me write. It was then believed that A. H. Smith, assistant to Mr. McAdoo and also president of the New York Central Railroad, would be given responsibility for considering and deciding this and similar questions. It so happened that the New York Central was the road then engaged in the Indianapolis track elevation. The city went on agitating for a continuation of the work, and a representative arrived to discuss the situation. McAdoo's representative also came to the city to inspect the progress of the work. This was during the month of February 1918, just about the time I resigned to accept the Republican National Committee chairmanship. By then the coal situation had eased somewhat —we had a fuel director with considerable authority. By the time final decisions were reached and the work resumed and completed, the war was over. I am pretty sure that sort of thing happened in many fields in 1918. But the track-elevation project still stands in my mind as an excellent illustration of a typical American problem: the placing of local interests or group interests over and against the national interest, which is often so hard for the individual to see.

Our general question of public relations, as I look at it, had to do primarily with two phases: information and morale. As to morale, that concerned "the strangers within our gates"—soldiers and recruits quartered in Indiana—our own boys who were on the way into the war, and our civilian population.

Our responsibility for soldier morale looked in two directions: toward providing the wholesome and eliminating the unwholesome. Right in our midst, on the outskirts of Indianapolis, we had one of the large training centers, Fort Benjamin Harrison, into which, in the early months of the war, poured many thousands of recruits from a large surrounding territory. Our council at once saw the big job of furnishing as much good, happy American entertainment and recreation as possible. To this end we co-operated especially with the War Recreational-Social Bureau and also with the Y.M.C.A. and Red Cross. This co-operation was similar to that worked out by the USO in World War II.

The less happy side of this unprecedented situation was the growth of opportunities for unwholesome entertainment, including the organized vice which has been an age-long accompaniment of war. For a while the situation was reportedly so bad that there were rumors that Fort Benjamin Harrison might be transferred to other territory. Forces for good buckled down in an effort to clean up the city. Our state council had an active committee on public morals which did effective work, resorting to appeals to the police in cases where necessary. I know that conditions were considerably improved.

By natural instinct our people were particularly drawn toward the welfare of the Indiana boys whom we knew, as they became part of our growing Army here and abroad. This care and aid took many forms. One of the first was a mammoth demonstration in August, when thousands of Hoosiers gathered in Indianapolis to give the 1st Indiana Field Artillery Regiment, commanded by Colonel Robert H. Tyndall, a rousing send-off. We encouraged events of this sort all over the state. Other projects included a Comfort Fund, which aimed to provide two dollars per soldier to furnish incidental conveniences; we organized correspondence committees to see that personal letters went to boys in the service; we sent to recruits their own home-town papers and other similar and personal reminders that the folks back home were thinking of them.

One of the more public projects was the raising of $125,000 as Indiana's share in the big War Library Fund which supplied such a stream of magazines and books to the camps here and abroad. The council also co-operated with the Y.M.C.A. in furnishing and distributing tobacco to our soldiers at the front.

By December of 1917 our council was already considering a suggestion of Major McWhirter that some provision be made for the return of veterans after the war was over. The plan suggested was to raise a fund—actually a Governor's Staff Fund—to take care of disabled veterans until either the state legislature or Congress made appropriations to cover the situation.

As I think of our efforts to build up civilian morale, I believe they were chiefly directed toward a simple, obvious objective: giving people the truth. We believed that facts were the best antidote for the malicious rumors which enemies of various sorts were spreading. This proved to be true. The council realized that the burden of war rested on the whole people. We wanted to remind them continuously that our cause was wholly right and that, deservedly, we would be victorious. It is hard now to realize how new to our people this whole war experience was and how stunned they were to find the world in such dreadful, destructive conflict. Some of the first war pictures brought back from the front were more shocking than we can realize today.

Strangely, one of the most interesting questions developing during these months was that of motion pictures. Technically this came under George Ade's publicity bureau. For a while we received frenzied protests against the adverse effects of some pictures. Movies were then relatively new, especially as a form of world-wide communication, and some producers and exhibitors were more interested in making money than in responsibility to give the public accurate information. Further, the whole method of war in Europe was new, even to the generals of the line. It is no wonder that our people were profoundly shocked by the nature of these battle scenes and of other strange revelations coming from abroad. Many were frightened and resentful over what our sons were facing. But within a few weeks some of our council members began to see that these films had a tremendous educational value, especially if selected with care and distributed with purpose and some proper introduction. The committee set out to do just this.

George Ade himself was tremendously interested in studying the possibilities. He personally selected seven specially prepared war films on such subjects as torpedoes, Red Cross work, submarines, and so on, all of which could go on one program. The council authorized their exhibition. These particular films, prepared with the help of the national council's Committee on Public Information, revealed how we were preparing for war and how war was being carried on across the sea. Considering my later years of association with motion pictures, I must confess that although these films seemed to me useful I probably did not realize their influence as fully as I did four years later, when my whole attention was turned to them. They must have made some impression, however, for one of my first acts after assuming the presidency of the Motion Picture Producers and Distributors Association was to invite the co-operation of the National Educational Association.

In 1917 and 1918 public opinion lacked today's most flexible medium —the radio. Public speakers were employed to a tremendous degree. They were by all means our most effective way of getting a personal message to the people. We conducted a speakers bureau along the same lines I had followed with the State Republican Committee. Rallies were held all over Indiana for various special purposes. Our theme was a plea for complete support and participation, especially in the September activity drive. We sent men into every corner of the state to give the fullest possible information. Americans want to know what is going on. And our efforts to inform them paid off in public confidence.

There were two or three happenings in Indiana that gave us a feeling of closeness to the war. Many will remember that it was a Hoosier who fired the first shot into the German trenches. Again, it was a boy from Evansville—James B. Gresham—who was the first to die in France. That nation asked that his body remain in France as a special symbol of our willing help. Indiana had other "firsts" also. We were first with the number of volunteer fighting men, the first state over the top in Red Cross membership, in Red Cross drives, in Liberty Loan subscriptions, and in the Y.M.C.A. fund. These facts made morale, and morale made these facts.

One of our less pleasant experiences was the discovery that we needed to be on guard against disloyalty, both in speech and in act. An instinctive consciousness among our people quickly expressed itself in committees of protection. These volunteer groups assumed the task of routing out disloyal speech and, when such seemed treasonable, of taking measures to bring legal pressure to bear. Supporting these efforts, the council did not apologize for its statement in September that since a state of war did exist the time for argument over the basic issues was closed. We felt that any who deliberately hindered the war effort in any way, who sought an inconclusive peace, or who discouraged full effort on the part of every citizen, should be denounced.

The Indiana Patriotic League was an asset in this fight against expressions of disloyalty. The league carried on its education and its appeals widely and made great use of individual initiative in its campaign. That such efforts were necessary I had already seen in connection with wild rumors about food conservation.

Day in and day out the local newspapers were our constant support. In bulk, they were certainly our most important medium of information. Early in our efforts I addressed a message to the editors, assuring them as to our dependence upon them and how fully we appreciated the importance of their part in the work the council was trying to do for the whole state. Through the newspapers, George Ade's publicity bureau worked magnificently. The minute he took the job of publicity chairman he threw himself into the effort—reporting the formation of a committee of fifteen newsmen by the time of our second meeting. This committee handled splendidly the business of getting weekly bulletins to all the county councils. It did wonderfully effective work in the form of editorials written by such authors as Booth Tarkington, Meredith Nicholson, Gene Stratton Porter, and others, which presented the main issues in persuasive form. There is no question that the absolutely non-partisan character of these articles was convincing. In spite of this, from time to time there were some attacks on me and on the council—apparently made on partisan grounds. But I like to recall that some of my worst assailants later became some of my best friends. I also like to remember the wonderful loyalty of Tom Taggart, our number-one Democrat, who did more to silence complaints and alleged criticism by Democratic papers than any other man.

Many times since 1918 I have had occasion to think of Theodore Roosevelt and his almost violently pro-American attitude. Any hyphenated or lukewarm Americanism, the colonel detested. The consciousness of his attitude probably contributed to the clearness with which I saw our council functioning in Indiana. There was also, perhaps, another bond between us in the fact that neither of us was able to get into military service. The administration's uncompromising refusal to listen to T.R.'s pleas really broke his heart. He was a fighter, in war and in peace, and it almost killed him to have to sit still.

The last item in this story of the State Council of Defense is, of course, my resignation. Like other events in my life, this seemed to be decided for me by circumstances over which I had no control. Election to the chairmanship of the Republican National Committee catapulted me into a larger sphere of activity, but one which in no wise seemed to differ in spirit, at least to me. In my letter of resignation to Governor Goodrich, I expressed this conviction. Among other things, I said:

In this new work I shall measure my action, first, as to how best to win the war. I know we agree that there is but one side to the question of the war, and that on that side, supporting the war in the fullest measure to its victorious conclusion, shall stand every political party entitled to any consideration whatever. If, by any chance, my arm may be a little stronger or my voice reach a little further, just that much stronger and that much further will my efforts be extended in support of the country's cause in this war.

Governor Goodrich's letter accepting my resignation showed that he fully sympathized with this view. He and I completely agreed that it was the business of the Republican party, as it was the business of every loyal citizen, to win the war as completely and as quickly as we possibly could.

The reader may already have gathered that Governor James P. Goodrich was one of my political ideals. He was a man of complete unselfishness and devotion to the service of our people. It was because of my great admiration for him that I so deeply appreciated his commendation of the council's work when he wrote:

You have made Indiana the model State Council in the nation, and brought great credit to our commonwealth, and I am certain that the record which Indiana is making and intends to make in support of our common country against the enemy is due in great proportion to the splendid efforts of yourself and the Indiana State Council of Defense.

Perhaps it would seem that my change of titles which took place in mid-February 1918 would signal a difference of emphasis and direction in my life, but in reality it did not. As Republican chairman, my first sweep through the country was on a Liberty Loan tour. That was my message and my purpose.

I do not think that I ever really left anything behind. I carried with me whatever convictions I had formed during the war and either fitted them into a new pattern or expanded them to fit the larger task. Republican politics for me suddenly became national. Whatever patriotic purposes I had formed reached out into the broader field. What had been nourished in the soil of Indiana was now put at the service of the country.

CHAPTER 9

Shooting the Bull Moose

T H E story of the Progressive party is one of the strangest tales in American politics. Though it was the culmination of an intense political faith which had taken various forms under various leaders, it came into being in a matter of hours. At its birth it was the projection of Theodore Roosevelt. As it looks now, its short life proves at least two things: first, that no party in America should be built around an individual, and second, that we are essentially a two-party country. That has always seemed natural to me; and our political history seems to prove that the country as a whole considers that on major political questions there are usually only two sides, not three or four.

From my own viewpoint and that of my own story, the Progressive party was tremendously important. For the Republican party it posed a problem with which my activities were so closely bound up that it might be called the determining element in my political experience.

This problem brought into sharp relief my deepest political convictions; it did much to develop them and undoubtedly led me to the chairmanship of the Republican National Committee. To trace this story, it will be necessary to go back a few years in national events.

The break between Taft and Roosevelt, which finally led to the birth of the third party, can be traced back to 1908, when Taft followed Colonel Roosevelt as President. Much of this story is well known. Both men have so sure a place in history that it is no disparagement of their qualities to observe that the marked differences between the two—when circumstances drew them into certain situations—inevitably brought about a clash.

It was in February of 1912 that Roosevelt made a speech in Columbus, Ohio, which practically advocated a recall of judges and a review of judicial decisions, with neither of which I could possibly agree. As I have mentioned, the matter became a personal one when later that month, by appointment, I met the colonel in New York. When I told him how strongly I disagreed with his recent declarations, he said: "That's all right, but I want you to be chairman of a third party." This I felt entirely unable to do, and told him so. From the standpoint of our own state and of my interest in Republican success, I was extremely anxious that there be no such split as he seemed to forecast.

As we all know, the break which resulted in the actual formation of the third party came during the Republican National Convention in Chicago in June 1912. The two issues involved were, of course, Taft and Roosevelt. The idea had been growing rapidly for several days that an injustice was being done to those favoring the colonel by the so-called "steamroller" tactics of the National Committee. The fact that Taft was nominated on the first ballot by no means indicated the harmony that one would expect. The men who were fighting for both the leading candidates knew no bounds of loyalty to either. But, sitting through that convention, I went through some bitter hours as I realized what was happening. I had known since January that we were in for a fight when Ed Lee, chairman of the Indiana State Republican Central Committee, came out for Roosevelt. I was chairman of the Second District Convention, which had endorsed Taft's administration and renomination. Furthermore, I had been elected vice-chairman of the State Committee when Fred Sims was elected chairman to succeed Lee. The minute Roosevelt threw his hat in the ring we knew that the National Convention was headed for a bitter contest.

Both as district chairman and state vice-chairman, my own position was clear: unless I resigned these two offices I could take no side in the matter of candidates, for I fully agreed with the state organization that its function was to elect the party nominees and not to nominate men for office. We were working for party success and not promoting a particular personality, whether for road supervisor or President, no matter who it might be. We were well aware that all our strength would be needed to put any nominee in office, even under the normal competition of the two-party system. We hesitated even to think of the weakening that a third party would cause.

At our State Convention in March 1912 the Taft forces had a strong majority. In my own Second District, delegates named to the National Convention were not instructed, but the fact that the Roosevelt ticket was defeated proved the current Taft sentiment.

And so things went until the eve of the Chicago convention. Then the air was filled with bitter disputes over rival Taft or Roosevelt delegations which sought to be seated. Practically every contest was decided in favor of Taft, so that his nomination was all but fore-ordained. The complete lack of harmony in the convention was tragically evidenced by the fact that after announcement of the decisive vote, 344 deeply disappointed Roosevelt supporters bolted the convention in the Coliseum, proceeded to Orchestra Hall, formed the Progressive party, and nominated Theodore Roosevelt as their standard-bearer. In the light of the facts, there can be no question that these supporters felt that a great injustice had been done to the colonel and that they had been deprived of their rightful share in the deliberations of the convention.

Thus on June 22 was born a Sacred Cow, which soon turned out to be a Bull Moose. What was destined to be a White Elephant bemoaned the turn of events, for the Elephant was doubtless wise enough to know that the Donkey would win the race in November. What had happened nationally soon reached down into states, districts, counties, townships, and precincts. Certainly the most important thing to note—and this was admitted by leading Progressives—was that this was a movement from the top down and not a well-nourished grass-roots affair coming up out of the national soil.

That was the factor which wrote the death notice of the third party much earlier than it would have been written had it sprung from the people. But it is also only fair to note that the men who launched the Progressive party honestly felt that the Republican National Committee had assumed arbitrary power, exercised so unjustly as to create the impression of denying free representative government. Judged by the price the party paid, a greater mistake could hardly have been made.

It was a striking thing, but perhaps not a healthy sign, that the evolution—the rise and fall, if we wish to call it such—of the Bull Moose party occurred so rapidly. If we look carefully we might discover four phases: organization, internal disintegration, Republican assimilation, and a final "shadow" showing. As one looks back, there was probably too little time and too little basis for a permanent party.

From still another point of view the Progressives sought to be an entirely independent party. Their leaders took a definite position against rejoining the Republican party from which they had broken off. They sought to capitalize on their "progressive" principles; but these were gradually taken over by one of the old-line parties. Eventually, as we now know, the Democrats under Franklin Roosevelt and Harry Truman went far beyond any "progressivism" ever imagined by the Bull Moose.

Launched with a running start under Colonel Roosevelt, the party made haste to organize for the success of their standard-bearer in November. In Indiana the situation was alarming. Their state leader, Ed Lee, was an able politician and a sincere worker, who until the preceding January had been Republican state chairman. The new party organization reached our county in August, and in September the "Moosers" of our Second District held their first convention. Time was short, but unusual progress was made.

In October the Bull Moose almost had its rider shot off its back when a demented crank fired at the colonel in Milwaukee. But he was not seriously wounded, and the campaign went on galloping apace toward November. I believe the majority of seasoned political workers frankly expected the election of Woodrow Wilson, with the opposing voters split in two. In Indiana a Democrat became governor and carried with him a Democratic legislature. In my own county Democrats elected the entire ticket. Since this was the nadir of our Republican fortunes, I want to record the Indiana vote: the Democrats polled 281,890 for Wilson; the Progressives 162,007 for T.R.; the Republicans 151,267 for Taft. It was a new and disheartening experience to find our party running a poor third in such a momentous race.

One of the most important results of the 1912 election was that the Progressives of Indiana, fired up by their good showing, were encouraged to think they could win in 1914. There was no question about the determination and militancy of their party organization early in 1914, just before my election as state chairman. In at least ten enthusiastic district conventions held in January, Progressive sentiment against any fusion with the Republicans showed up clearly. The influence of leaders like Hiram Johnson of California and our own Albert J. Beveridge was strong. Loyalties were intense.

The Progressives in our state had the leadership of an able team: Beveridge, the orator; Lee, the organizer; and Toner, the strategist—all knowing how to put on a good show and keep sentiment up to high pitch. And they developed some strong appeals to the voters, one of which was their use of women speakers like Mrs. Medill McCormick. Another was the passage of strong resolutions, in almost every district convention, favoring the enactment of initiative, referendum, and recall. Experience shows that such tactics attract attention more than they win votes.

In some instances the new party seemed to offer a method of circumventing local party machines; the appeal of strong personalities occasionally overleaped party machinery. A striking instance was the case of Benjamin Shively, who had been a Democratic senator from the Eleventh District. In 1914 he announced his intention of seeking the Progressive nomination for representative from that district and was named their candidate in April. However, he ultimately ran on the Democratic ticket and was re-elected U.S. senator in November. I think this could justly be called an illustration of the unstable foundations and position of the Bull Moose party.

Their State Convention in Indianapolis in April 1914, with Progressive opinion well shaped, was the high-water mark of their strength in Indiana. Teddy Roosevelt's picture looked out over a mass of faithful followers. When the convention was called to order in Tomlinson Hall on the nineteenth, Beveridge was unanimously nominated for senator amid much high-flown oratory, singing, and cheering. The platform endorsed a long list of progressive reforms. Cold judgment might have said that it was too far ahead of the times to win wide support. It seemed to reflect the Progressive idea of current evils or needed reforms in almost every area of human activity. But the convention carried through its work to a logical conclusion, nominating a full state ticket and electing Edward Toner as the new state chairman to succeed Ed Lee, who honestly wanted to turn back to private life.

Although their campaign was carried through with vigor and the strong support of national speakers, the ticket ran third in the November election. The results must have been as disappointing as they had been in 1912 to equally earnest Republicans. Democratic victories swept the nation as the Progressives slipped none too happily into third place. In Indiana the swing back to the Republican party started from the bottom up, with the winning of county, city, and township offices. It is worth noting that we elected 427 township trustees, the Democrats 549, and Progressives only 37. Whether or not we sensed it at the time, this election marked the beginning of the real recession of the Progressive party.

A significant thing happened in Indiana in June of 1915. Party determination to organize for 1916 cost the Bull Moose its state chairman, Ed Toner, who now felt the battle could be carried on better under the Republican banner. Jackson Boyd succeeded him. Party leaders sought every opportunity to stir up new enthusiasm, and big names still drew. When Boyd resigned in December, Lee returned to head the state organization and pushed vigorous plans for 1916. Many counties went ahead organizing and naming tickets for the campaign and delegates to the 1916 convention, despite a thinning of the ranks.

After the State Convention in July, which was really carried through by a relatively small group of "ardent, uncompromising idealists," as current accounts called them, disaffection in the party ranks was increasingly pronounced. They went into the state campaign with a full ticket, but the November vote—4,000 as against 162,007 in 1912—told the story. The party, if not the principles, had succumbed to Republican victory. While we had been welcoming and encouraging assimilation, it had been ruled out as a policy by the Bull Moose, and its opposite— disintegration—had inevitably been going on.

Some of the Colonel's ardent supporters of 1912 had soon begun leaving the ranks. In March of 1913, Senator Kenyon of Iowa returned to the Republican fold, offering hope to us that others would follow suit. By early 1914 we were getting hundreds of encouraging letters from ex-Progressives all over the state. Commenting on the tone of this mail, I wrote Jack Henley somewhat optimistically: "This indicates a general movement among the Progressives to return to the old Party and again vote the ticket. I believe nearly all of them will be in line when election day comes." At that moment such a forecast may have had an element of blind faith, but things that encouraged us went right on happening.

Conversely, the Progressives were having their troubles. The difficulty of getting men to run on their ticket started in April 1914. Press support began wobbling with the failure of such newspapers as the *Progressive-Democrat* in May and of *The Citizen* and the Linton *Record* in June. Beyond that, the lukewarm reception given to the colonel in October indicated a sad loss of popularity for the ex-President and a fatal loss for the Bull Moose cause.

Simultaneously, encouraging things were happening to us. In July a hundred Progressives marched into the Hotel Severin headquarters and met with me in conference; they announced their purpose to take a vigorous part in the Republican campaign. This was a dramatic thing. When certain newspapers questioned what was behind it, these men signed a statement declaring that their action was *sponte sua* and totally without influence from headquarters. A similar spontaneous visitation took place in September, when fifty of the leading Negroes of Indiana—all active Progressive workers in 1912—notified me that they were back in the "old" party and assured me that 90 per cent of their people would be voting Republican in November. This delegation represented the best Negro citizenship of the state and included lawyers, ministers, physicians, and one bank president.

A more subtle indication of trends could be discerned in the increasing numbers of Progressives who could be spotted attending Republican organization meetings all over the state. They were not nagged or dragged; they came of their own free will.

These signs of growth were not sufficient to win us the elections in 1914, but they did put us second instead of third. And that election had a striking aftermath: many local officials who had been elected as Progressives publicly announced themselves as Republicans *following their election!* In other cases, active workers who had stuck with the Bull Moose through the election wrote letters informing our state headquarters that they were with us once more. One of the most important of these was Horace Stillwell, who said that he, for one, meant to pursue his principles from within the Republican party.

Our welcome to all these returned workers was sincere, and we assured them of absolutely equal voice in all councils. This policy—the heart of our Republican organization program—contributed to our growing strength right up to the 1916 elections, when the Bull Moose party faded from the picture. The return to the older party was brought about by the thinking of individual voters and by their leadership, and it was certainly aided by Republican removal of all causes of complaint as to party management. As a matter of fact, the Indiana Progressive organization itself had been guilty of the same dictatorial practices that it had so sharply criticized in the National Republican Convention of 1912.

In a new party, springing into existence under such dramatic circumstances, differences of opinion among the leaders were doubtless unavoidable. But they certainly worked to the party's evident disadvantage. Dissensions as to policy were so sharp that resignations of good men like Ed Toner followed. Such resignations, the difficulty of filling tickets, failures of the Bull Moose press, dwindling attendance at party meetings, and the growing belief that the Bull Moose was losing its effectiveness as a practical instrument for pursuing progressive principles—all these factors indicated the disintegration of the party from within.

The crowning blows to their cause came in June of 1916. At the Progressive National Convention in Chicago, George W. Perkins started talking amalgamation with the Republicans. On June 26, when Theodore Roosevelt dropped out, the heart of the Bull Moose stopped beating. The colonel transferred his energies to the cause of Charles Evans Hughes. The party in Indiana suffered a similar collapse. Nowhere in the nation had the Progressives grown strongly from the bottom up. I fear that too often the grass roots had been stepped on instead of cultivated!

After the stunning defeat of November 1912, it had been months before we Republicans could decide what manner of wild beast this Bull Moose and his fellows might turn out to be and how we might get them into the same corral with the mild old Elephant. On our Indiana ranch, at least, we made that our main business for the next four years, with results already noted. Since the peaceful recapture of these strays and bringing them back home was my main interest then, perhaps it deserves a little further telling.

The first call for the roundup came in 1913 from our state chairman, Fred Sims. The next friendly gesture came from Governor Goodrich, who showed a willingness to meet the Moose halfway on questions where there was a difference. Then in February of 1914 a really striking call came from the comptroller of New York City and also a prominent national ex-Progressive, William A. Prendergast. Addressing the annual Indiana Republican Editorial Association banquet, he said:

"The honest-minded Progressive . . . cannot help realizing that the net result of his efforts thus far has been to bring about Democratic victories with no consequent gain to the interests of the country."

Here we have this man who had placed Theodore Roosevelt in nomination in 1912 admitting to the world that the new party had not worked out as he had hoped. The fact that this wise and honest man had, within less than two years, reached the conclusion he did—to return to the G.O.P.—undoubtedly caused many other Progressives to reconsider. When this same man addressed our State Convention in April, urgently appealing all Hoosier Progressives to "come home" again, his words had a stirring effect, I well remember.

This shift in the currents of party sentiment, sharply stimulated in February of 1914, synchronized with my election as state chairman and the reorganization of the State Committee. It was both our business and our privilege to stimulate chain reactions set in motion by the original Prendergast impulse. This we did in various ways. Get-together efforts started quickly when a joint committee of Progressives and Republicans met in Indianapolis under the auspices of the "Republican Union." In their report they recognized the necessity of a strong opposition party and the fact that the Republican Party, rather than the Progressive, was better equipped to serve the interests of the country as a whole. E. E. Heller, Progressive chairman of the committee, significantly expressed the belief that the purpose of their party had been fulfilled, since "the Republicans are coming to us and propose to give us representation." He maintained that such was all the Progressives were asking for. This sort of thing—men sitting at conference tables and honestly seeking for unity—was tremendously encouraging. Here again it was "Let's get together." But someone had to take the initiative.

We encouraged other forms of amalgamation too. Our open invitations to attend Republican meetings and participate in the proceedings were accepted by many Progressives. In the convention of the Seventh District at least half those attending were ex-Bull Moosers. That spring almost every district convention passed resolutions favoring unity and extended what was tantamount to a formal invitation to Progressives to return, not as prodigal sons, but as active party members ready to work for good government. To show just how far this process had gone, my nomination for re-election to the Second District chairmanship was seconded by a leading Bull Mooser from each county.

By this time some of the older heads, led by our national committeeman, James P. Goodrich, who was soon to be governor—seeing that the time was ripe for a genuine reorganization of the Republican party in Indiana—put it up to some of us younger men to help tackle the job. On Lincoln's Birthday in 1914 the State Committee met, named me as chairman, and then proceeded with the election of new district chairmen. I knew we had a job to do. By the time of the State Convention in April, definite policies had been formulated. To begin with, we decided to hammer on the belief that the best way for citizens to keep watch over a democracy is to have two, not three, political parties, both strong and virile. On the other hand, we sought to convince voters of the integrity of our profession that the rights of all individual members to participate in the party's affairs should be and should remain *equally sacred and sacredly equal.*

I want to pause long enough here to pay tribute to the great Booker

T. Washington for coining that phrase, which I used so often in political organizing. I found it in one of his writings during the course of research at Wabash on my Master's thesis in 1904 on "The Negro Question." That phrase made an indelible impression on my thinking. Among the campaign slogans we developed were: *Fight the Democrats This year, Not the Progressives;* and later, *Eventually the Republican Party—Why Not Now?*

In a frank appeal for unity we sent out 8,000 letters in June to Bull Moose county chairmen, precinct committeemen, and active party workers, emphasizing their right to full voice in party affairs. The letters were actually received by 7,919 persons, and many replied that they had already reaffiliated with their local Republican organization.

The personal attitude of rank-and-file Republicans was helpful, expressing genuine welcome to men who had voted for Roosevelt in 1912. Facing a situation like that, made much clearer between 1933 and 1953, we took the attitude that it was more than a mere matter of saving a political party; we made it a question of saving our institutions, convinced that without a strong two-party system the possibility of a minority group controlling the country had become a reality. I wonder now if we could even have guessed how real that possibility was.

With our State Committee, assimilation was not merely an announced policy, it became the keynote of a continuous program. The desire for unity was reiterated throughout the state until it became a *fait accompli,* with the constant appointment of ex-Progressives to Republican committees, from the precinct up to the state organization level. These included many Bull Moose leaders, some of whom by 1915 were telling hundreds of voters that the real usefulness of the third party was gone. Such men as Ed Toner and Horace Stillwell were our strongest allies, our Exhibit A. It was these two who went to Chicago in May of 1916 to lay the groundwork for unity on a national scale. This Hoosier spirit had been illustrated again when in October of 1915, at the Ninth Indiana District Republican "love feast," there hung on the walls pictures of Roosevelt and Beveridge, although these two men did not rejoin the party until after June the following year.

It was an interesting side light on political tides that after our successful 1916 election in Indiana an earnest plea was made to our state legislature for the passage of progressive legislation. Many measures for which the Progressives had been working became law. This leads one to observe that it would be hard indeed to measure the influence of Theodore Roosevelt on succeeding developments in this nation.

If results in Indiana were gratifying in 1916, they were not so pleasing in the Far West, where the Bull Moose still cast a heavy shadow that gradually faded as it reached eastward. Hughes had been defeated, with the results in California by far the most disappointing. Wherever the responsibility may be put, it is plain fact to recall that Progressives, headed by Governor Hiram Johnson, and organization Republicans failed to get together. There were mistakes on both sides. As one confidant expressed it to me following the election: "The truth is that neither faction desired, or worked wholeheartedly for, unity and combined effort, and Governor Hughes was sacrificed between their respective ambitions and mutual antipathies and the desire of each to punish the other."

Surely, when the governor of a state refused to shake hands with a presidential candidate, a radical change in attitude was called for. The situation suggested to some outside observers that the Golden State needed a Hoosier treatment.

While we were still dressing Bull Moose wounds in Indiana and administering the remedies we had promised before election, a situation developed in New York that now seems to have been prophetic of the national chairmanship, still two years away. Apparently some impression had been created in national circles that Indiana had found how to harmonize the Progressive situation in 1916. George W. Perkins was of course one of the most prominent ex-Progressives who had gone along with us in that 1916 campaign. Now I began to be called to New York to talk with Colonel Roosevelt, Perkins, National Chairman Willcox, and others, and to offer any practical suggestions I could for national success in the 1918 elections, based on our Indiana experience. To me, this was a wonderful opportunity.

In the working out of organization plans and program by the Republican National Committee, some sharp differences of opinion arose. Perkins and others felt that the Executive Committee was planning in such a way as to hold party control among a small group—a most unwise impression to create at such a time. In talking with them I found the same dangerous idea that Progressives were not being equally consulted —apparently a nationwide reaction. As Hugh Miller suggested, "The regulars must recognize that Progressives and ex-Progressives are made up like human beings and are almost as numerous." I knew how important it was to create the impression as well as the fact of party unity, and I was constantly in touch with any men, several of them Midwesterners, who might be able to help the good cause along.

I cannot leave this period without saying one more word about the central figure in it all—Theodore Roosevelt. There was never any doubt about his patriotism or his sincerity. He now threw himself wholeheartedly into every effort calculated to encourage the rehabilitation of the party. He talked to people, saw prominent party leaders, sounding them out with the purpose of increasing their advocacy of active party unity. For example, he saw to it that I made the acquaintance of Senator Frelinghuysen of New Jersey, a man sympathetic to our objectives.

Senator Kenyon was just as active. Another stalwart was Senator Miles Poindexter, who believed that if "a free opportunity is given the masses of the party to participate in party government," the restoration of the two-party system would become a living reality.

That this creed, which I had always held, was daily gaining followers both in the East and the West was a happy augury for my national task.

PART THREE...

...*National Politics* 1918–1922

CHAPTER 10

Chosen National Chairman

IN the basement of an Indianapolis church on the night of February 13, 1918, a win-the-war drive was in full swing. As chairman of the State Council of Defense, I was one of the speakers on the platform.

Then, as always in those days, my slogan was "Win the War Now—Everything Else Is Chores," and at this time of war crisis, partisan politics was definitely of minor importance. So we were whooping things up and the room was crowded.

I was on my feet making one of several speeches that I got off during the evening rally. It was up to me as the council chairman to keep things moving at high tempo. I remember that during my talk I saw a young man coming down a crowded aisle, heading for the platform. He was from the local office of the Associated Press, and in his hand was a sheet of telegraph flimsy, the carbon copy of a dispatch that had come in from AP headquarters. He tried to give it to me while I was speaking, but it slipped through my fingers and fluttered to the floor beside the table. I gave it no further attention, because from the corner of my eye I could see the chairman of the meeting retrieving it. It was open copy and he glanced over it. As soon as I sat down, he jumped to his feet, shouting that he had an important news announcement. He explained that it emanated from St. Louis, and proceeded to wave the flimsy above his head. The crowd quieted as he read the brief dispatch, which stated that Will Hays of Indiana had just been elected chairman of the Republican National Committee, then in session at the Missouri metropolis. That was the way I received the news of my new job, which was to occupy almost all of my waking moments for the next few years.

It was natural for the crowd to greet lustily this announcement that one of its own Hoosiers had been called to this important post, and at once it became necessary for me to make another speech. The surprise and gratitude that I registered were real. I did not want the purpose of the meeting—the war drive—to get away from us. So I thought it well to try some humor, and I told a story about a cartoon showing a long freight train of the Chicago & Eastern Illinois Railroad rumbling across open country with a small dog running behind and yelping furiously at the caboose. The caption read: "Let him have it once; let's see what he'll do with it."

The audience caught on, and I was happy to explain that I felt myself to be a somewhat inconspicuous person to tackle the big job of defeating the Democrats in a national election, but also that I appreciated the chance to see what I could do with it. Then we got along with the rally, which turned out to be a great success, aided possibly by this news.

This story illustrates in a measure the reaction in the various parts of the country to the qualifications of the new national chairman. Naturally I was accepted enthusiastically in Indiana, where I was not only a native but had made good as state chairman by electing a Republican governor, both United States senators, and all the Hoosier congressmen.

My record was of course the basic reason for my election to the national post. But even so, some of the old-timers wagged their heads and wondered. This was true in the East, especially in New York. However, a verbal flashlight photograph of myself, sent out from Albany, caught the imagination of party leaders everywhere and helped me considerably. It happened at the State House, in the private office of Governor Whitman, where a number of the state party leaders, including Lieutenant Governor Shannon, met during the morning following my election. Sitting in at the powwow was Bill Orr, now and for many years an executive of Metro-Goldwyn-Mayer but at that time the private secretary of Governor Whitman. I had met Orr several times when in the East, and we had talked politics. At this gathering on the fourteenth of February at Albany, it soon appeared that "this young fellow Hays" was a chief topic of conversation, and "What is he like?" was the blunt demand made by the lieutenant governor, who had never seen me. "I'll tell you," Bill Orr replied. "He's the Billy Sunday of the Republican party, and God knows we damned well need an evangelist."

I had never considered myself an evangelist, but perhaps Bill Orr was right, particularly about what the party then required. Whatever success I achieved as the national chairman, and however my record may stand in the historical archives of the party, I shall always raise my hat to Billy Sunday as a star performer in both baseball and religion. Perhaps he was fortunate never to have entered the devious path of politics.

When I was summoned to assume the organization leadership of the Republican party this nation was going through a momentous period in its history. World War I was approaching its climax. Secretary of War Baker was boldly defending his conduct of the War Department and the training of hundreds of thousands of American youths for battle. The first big engagement of American arms was still ahead. In Washington the woman's suffrage amendment had passed the House, although not the Senate, and forecast a still greater change in American life.

In the Republican arena the acrimony of the Bull Moose campaign and its subsequent mischief were happily being dissipated. Only a month after my taking over the reins, at an accidental meeting in a Chicago hotel, the former Republican presidents, Theodore Roosevelt and William Howard Taft, shook hands and thus welded their broken friendship. This made my task far easier, despite the fact that Woodrow Wilson still remained supreme in the hearts of millions of his countrymen. Wilson had proved his great powers with the spoken word at home and abroad. His speeches had raised the flagging spirits of the Allies and undermined the morale of the enemy.

An epoch-making suggestion came from a representative in Russia of the Committee of Public Information. This was to have Wilson boil his ideas down into short, snappy paragraphs. The famous "Fourteen Points" was the result. The President was so pleased by this idea that he then gave out supplementary and overlapping terms, the whole becoming a complete set of plans for peace, including a constitution for a new world order—the League of Nations.

In the Republican and independent press, editorial reaction to the choice of chairman was generally favorable and expressed the belief that harmony would be restored between the various factions in the party. Reconciliation with the Progressives was further emphasized by a telegram I received from Theodore Roosevelt in which he said: "Your election means more to the country and the Republican party than anything else at this time could have meant." That word heartened me more than any other I received. Some years later I came across a typical comment of Colonel Roosevelt's made at that time. He said: "Hays is a trump. He is all right. He may make mistakes, but he won't make many. The party seems to be united on him and that's something well worth while. Now we've got to back him up. With Hays at work and on the job, I think we'll get results. For one thing, there's only one party now. Most of the Progressives have come back. Most of the others will follow. Those that won't return would sooner or later have quit even the Progressive party—they're just natural-born mavericks who won't stay long in any herd, and won't stay branded. Hays will, I am sure, weld the party firmly together. The day of factions is gone. But we have all got to help him."

I resigned as chairman of the Indiana State Council of Defense and shortly after left on my first trip East. The next few weeks were a constant round of dinners and conferences with prominent Republicans and political leaders in New York and Washington. This was the quickest way to get acquainted with the leading workers. The first of these was a dinner at the Union League Club, where I met four former national chairmen: William R. Willcox, Charles D. Hilles, Frank H. Hitchcock, and Victor Rosewater.

Willcox later gave a lunch for me at which for the first time I met Colonel William Boyce Thompson. I already knew that he had helped materially in the Hughes campaign. He had much to do with George W. Perkins. When I had concluded my speech he came up to talk with me. He was most cordial, and I remember just how he looked, with his bald head, and his cigar with the white paper holder and reinforced mouthpiece which he always used. He said to me that he had been taking a little interest lately in politics, that he liked what I had said, and that while he probably couldn't do much to help me in the organization that I had outlined, nevertheless there might be something in his own line that he could do, if the time came when I thought he could do anything of that nature I should call upon him. This came to pass very soon thereafter.

After a trip to the Coast in late March and April 1918 to open the third Liberty Loan drive—of which I shall speak a little later—I went down to Washington to report my conclusions to Senator Reed Smoot, chairman of the Republican Senatorial Committee, and Congressman Simeon D. Fess, chairman of our congressional committee. I told them that I thought we could carry the Congress, both Senate and House, in the fall elections. At the moment they did not agree, saying that they did not have any money to conduct a campaign and that the Congress was so overwhelmingly Democratic they did not think it possible to win. I realized that the National Committee had never functioned too successfully in an off year, but I was young and enthusiastic—and, apparently, overoptimistic. So I told the gentlemen that at least I believed we could carry the Congress if we worked hard enough, in spite of the war.

Senator Smoot and Congressman Fess then agreed that the National Committee could go ahead and take charge of the campaign, with the senatorial and congressional committees helping, but that it was up to me to find the money.

I went directly from the conference in Washington to New York and saw William Boyce Thompson. I told him why I was there and what I had seen and heard on the trip. I gave him the same reasons I had given to Smoot and Fess as to why we should try to win the Congress and at once begin organizing the Republican party nationally in a vigorous way. I told Colonel Thompson frankly that I was calling upon him, as he had told me to do when I considered the moment had arrived when he could render a real service to our cause. I gave him the opinion of Smoot and Fess as to the improbability of success; but Thompson was a gambler, a really successful gambler. He bet hard when he believed in anything, and he said, "How much will it take?"

I told him that I had put the same question to Smoot and Fess, and it was their suggestion that we would need an immediate assurance of $300,000. Just as quickly as the words were spoken he said, "Go ahead. Tell Senator Smoot you have the money. I will underwrite the $300,000. I will get two or three others, but I will be responsible for the whole."

That night I telephoned Senator Smoot, and I think that was the number-one reason for his long-time appreciation of my work. He was always most friendly to me. After we carried the country and later elected the President, he went to bat hard to get me appointed to a job which he proposed to create by act of Congress. The job was to direct the planning and execution of a complete reorganization of the government. I had some little trouble and embarrassment in getting Smoot off that track nearly three years later.

During the campaigns of '18 and '20 and frequently in '19, I would go out to Colonel Thompson's house. I remember during the '18 campaign, when it was rather new to me and I was under much pressure, that Colonel Thompson would frequently pick me up at headquarters as he motored from downtown in the late afternoon, and drive me out to his lovely place at Yonkers. He was a thoroughbred, but homespun and simple, and as direct in performance when he wanted anything as twenty lions organized for the same purpose.

While in New York, I announced an "open door" policy for the conduct of the national headquarters, saying, in part: "My policy, as far as I have been able to map it, will be one of assimilation and not of elimination. . . . I want all Republicans to feel at liberty to confer and advise with me, no matter what position they took in 1912. We reconciled the differences between the two factions in Indiana by adopting a conciliatory policy and I believe that with the assistance of men who think better government can be provided by the Republican party than by the Democrats I shall be able to apply and expand it to meet national conditions. There will be no 'casting up.' If personal ambitions are subordinated to the welfare of the country I am confident of succeeding. I am not concerned with individual or personal ambitions. It is not the province of the national committee to control nominations, but to elect candidates. Handling of the office of national chairman in any other way is a prostitution of the office which we shall never have so long as I am chairman."

Following the "open door" policy to the limit, I instituted a system of open conferences. At party headquarters I had a huge room capable of holding about seventy-five persons standing, for there were no chairs and the only furniture was a big table at one end. Sitting on the edge of the table, I received all comers and listened to their business. It worked, and much time was saved, for only rarely, in the case of the most important conferences, was the privacy of an inner office really necessary.

Before leaving New York on my first nationwide trip I called on Theodore Roosevelt, who was ill in Roosevelt Hospital, and on Charles Evans Hughes at his Broadway office. Colonel Roosevelt, who had lost the hearing in his left ear in the course of his vigorous boxing, left the hospital shortly after to open the Republican campaign in Maine with a great speech at Portland on March 28.

I returned to Sullivan early in March to arrange my personal affairs before plunging into the campaign preliminaries. We reorganized the law firm of Hays & Hays, retaining the same name but consolidating it with the firm of Buff & Stratton. Hays & Hays previously had consisted of John T. Hays, Will H. Hays, and Hinkle C. Hays. The new members taken in were Alonzo C. Owens, George W. Buff, and W. Paul Stratton.

After attending a meeting in Indianapolis of leaders of both political parties, held to further the third Liberty Loan drive, I went to Chicago to confer with Republican and Progressive leaders, including Harold L. Ickes—then a good Republican—Medill McCormick, and others.

Beginning in March, I spent much time in New York, Washington, Indiana, and Chicago planning for a huge Republican assembly either in Chicago or St. Louis to plan the election of a Republican Congress in the coming autumn.

It was my custom to dictate a summary of my appointments and activities during each day. These were days that took no heed of working hours. I was busy from early morning until late at night and took little notice of holidays. As an illustration, I insert a page, taken at random, from this diary.

Saturday, March 2nd, 1918

Got up at 6:45 and went to breakfast at Daniel G. Reid's residence, Fifth Avenue at about 59th Street, with A. T. Hert and George W. Perkins. A full discussion of the general situation and assurances on the part of Reid that he would help in every way—that he would have a dinner for me soon with about thirty men, and to call on him at any time for anything. Preferred headquarters New York, Washington and Chicago. Wanted same program as did Perkins. Met William Barnes at 8:45 at the Union League Club and talked with him for quarter hour. He was very practical, but inclined to stay out of the Whitman fight. Rushed to Roosevelt hospital to see T.R. Discussed Maine speech. Thence by car to 96 Broadway to see Charles E. Hughes who wants to help and says he will not be candidate. Back at Union League Club and met newspapermen. At 10:50 met Governor Milliken of Maine, who came to club to discuss Maine situation. Invited me to attend the Maine convention about the 28th. Says he aided in getting conference at Washington on the matter of the Maine platform. Eleven o'clock, Newton W. Gilbert. 11:15 Senator Hemenway. Go in car to H. C. Frick's residence, 70th and Fifth Avenue. Frick very cordial. Takes us all over his house, shows us 25 million dollars worth of art—no sign of guest register. Great interest and confidence in situation, and very much interested in war. Back to Judge Gary's at 12:40 and Gary takes us over his house. Shows us a lot of art, fine rugs etc. Beautiful. Puts no limit on what he wants to do and what he thinks of me. (Fooled.) At one o'clock some 15 steel men come in—Presidents of the steel companies of America, Midvale and Bethlehem—also President of the steel trust of Canada—all lunch with Gary. They were very pleasant and assured me unanimous support. Back to Union League Club at two o'clock. See William L. Ward for thirty minutes. He says he wants to give me benefit of his experience in every way possible. See Calder, Glynn, Gleason, also chairmen and secretaries of five boroughs comprising New York City. At 3:00 go to the St. Regis Hotel for half hour with Governor Whitman who offers assistance in every way possible, etc. etc. Ran into Perkins and Hert by accident, just as leaving, and talked with them for a moment. Perkins told me how to take care of situation that may arise in his absence. Telephone John McGrath. Back to hotel to see Dr. Rumeley, owner of the Evening Mail. He has "ideas"—goes to station with me, where meet newspapermen. Take six o'clock train.

It strikes me, on looking over the many pages of this diary, that I—and possibly the Republican party—had no union rules to govern either my activity or my ease.

CHAPTER 11

The Task of Organizing

THE constitutional amendment granting women the right of suffrage was now a national issue, and hence one to be thoroughly considered in respect to Republican policy. Personally, I favored the suffrage amendment both as a matter of justice and as good political strategy, and so stated in an interview in the New York *Times* on my second trip East. I hoped that at least two of the nine Republican senators then opposing the amendment would vote for it and thus ensure its passage. Of the forty-three Republican senators, thirty-four favored the amendment; of fifty-three Democratic senators, only twenty-eight were for it.

The first political skirmish at the polls after I became chairman came at a by-election in Wisconsin caused by the death of Senator Paul O. Husting, Democrat. The special election was set for April 2, 1918, and the winning candidates at the primaries were Congressman Irvine L. Lenroot for the Republicans and Joseph E. Davies for the Democrats.

The campaign was short but hot. Davies (the same Davies of later *Mission to Moscow* fame) had the open support of President Wilson, who loudly called on the voters of Wisconsin to elect him, and the Democratic campaign was conducted directly from Washington. Joseph P. Tumulty, secretary to the President, was in direct touch at all stages with the Democratic National Committee headquarters in Chicago, which later were transferred to Milwaukee.

I sent Harry Hogan into Wisconsin, and he opened headquarters in Milwaukee in conjunction with State Chairman George A. West and immediately began organizing for the special election. Following out my "open door" policy, the Republican books were cleared of past records and the party doors were opened wide to everybody who wanted to vote for a Republican. Close acquaintance with Harry Hogan had made me sure he could do the kind of job that was needed. As a very good friend over many years I want to pay him tribute as one of the finest political organizers I have ever known. A leading alumnus of Notre Dame, most active in their affairs, and a resident of Fort Wayne, he and I were brought up in the same hard-working school of Indiana politics. He was

THE TASK OF ORGANIZING

active in the Twelfth District, as I was in the Second, and we saw eye to eye on methods and goals. He knew how to marshal public opinion, as his splendid work in Wisconsin, and later in a unique motion picture legislative campaign in Massachusetts, so clearly proved.

This election was without precedent. The issue was absolutely new, being a referendum on the war, and the first ever held in this country. Vice-President Marshall, speaking for Davies at Madison, made an unfortunate statement on which our organization was quick to capitalize. Saying, "Wisconsin has a bad reputation in the eyes of the rest of the country," he expressed the opinion that the test of loyalty in this election was the casting of a Democratic ballot. The Republican state House of Representatives passed a resolution condemning this statement, and our organization had the speech translated into several foreign languages for distribution among various voting groups.

We brought the campaign to a close with a big rally in the Milwaukee Auditorium on the night of April 1. When the returns were in the next day, Lenroot was elected by a plurality of 11,669 over Davies and about 50,000 over Victor Berger, the Socialist candidate. It was generally agreed in Wisconsin that President Wilson's letter on behalf of Davies, in which he tried to make his support a test of loyalty to the national cause, and the bitter attack on the Republicans by Vice-President Marshall contributed decisively to the Republican success.

Commenting on the result, the Chicago *Tribune* said: "It was the first test of the new deal policy that Mr. Hays announced after his election as national chairman at St. Louis, and he got real results in Wisconsin. . . . In this respect the Wisconsin election was a showdown between the two rival national chairmen. Republicans of Wisconsin who have clawed at each other's throats for more than a dozen years went to the polls for the first time in a decade and voted as Republicans, for the Republican direct primary nominee. That was the Hays idea and the Hays practical principle, and it elected Lenroot."

Immediately after the Wisconsin fight I started on a three-week tour of the western states that took me to the Pacific coast. On this trip I passed thirteen nights in sleeping cars and made thirty-nine speeches. These public meetings were all in the interest of the third Liberty Loan. My private meetings were with Republican leaders.

Just as my first trip to California had involved both a task connected with the law practice in Sullivan and the arrival of the fleet during its trip around the world, so this second trip had also a dual interest and purpose. Not only was it to stimulate the sale of war bonds and to promote party harmony but also to further in every way I could a nonpartisan participation in the war on the thesis of my slogan, "Win the War Now—Everything Else Is Chores."

It was never suggested that there was anything inconsistent in the pursuit of these dual objectives. The Republican party had made an earnest effort to become the "war party," and from the time of my election as chairman until the war was over, the major purpose of all Republican activities was to further the purpose of the war. This doubtless won us much support.

The prime objective of this tour, being a natural one—to aid in the sale of war bonds—was received with acclaim by all Republicans and, indeed, by most Democrats. There was at no time any criticism that vigorous participation in the bond campaign could be misconstrued as any improper projection of politics into the situation. Bond organizations recognized no political division; the workers were Democrats and Republicans alike, and neither resented the position of the other, because neither offended the other in this bond activity by practicing partisan politics.

At Oakland things moved swiftly. I was met by Raymond Benjamin and Percy V. Long, chairmen, respectively, of the Republican and Progressive state committees of California, and by William H. Crocker, Republican national committeeman. After crossing the bay to the St. Francis Hotel, and immediately on arrival there, I was greeted by Mrs. Joe T. Akin and her daughter of Sullivan, Indiana, friends of our family for as long as I can remember. They had heard of my arrival and simply came to call. This was of no political significance, yet it was typical of experiences all over the country which were good food for the spirit.

Upstairs in the apartment were three newspapermen, and from that time on, until I left California on the way to Phoenix, I received uniform courtesy on the part of the California press. I talked with Benjamin and Long until two o'clock that morning and on Saturday, the thirteenth, saw many callers.

During this San Francisco visit I recalled the fear felt in advance by many, that the whole trip to the Coast was ill advised. Senator Murray Crane was especially worried, as was Senator Penrose. It was emphasized that California was a political cemetery for most political visitors. This objection I had overridden, partly because of ingrained faith, and partly because of my experiences in the Indiana campaigns of 1915, '16, and '17. I felt certain we would be guilty of a definite error if we did not try, and I was determined to make the trip.

The heart of the potential worry was California, and especially southern California. The presidential election debacle of 1916 hit hardest in California, when the late returns for Wilson over Hughes came in so dramatically and reversed the report of the previous midnight. No group was more shocked than we in Indiana. I had forgotten none of that and well knew that anything could happen in California. I had done my share of whistling in the dark as I planned the trip, when approaching California, and especially now as I was about to enter Los Angeles.

The results on the way out had been encouraging, and in San Francisco really cheering, but the local men there and those up from Los Angeles warned about "the South," and it was a solemn session that Benjamin, Al McCabe, Crocker, and I held that midnight. We arrived in Los Angeles on Monday morning, April 15, and the committee which met us consisted of former Lieutenant Governor A. J. Wallace and Marshall Stimson, both Progressives; Frank P. Flint, Republican and former U.S. senator; and Mrs. Richardson, chairman of the Los Angeles County Republican Committee.

On the way to the Hotel Alexandria, and after we arrived there, I got the latest and fullest exposition on the troubles with "the old-line Republicans," as of that morning. It was part of the plan that the Progressives should have the first chance to talk with me, and that they did, thoroughly, with Senator Flint and Mrs. Richardson fully cooperating.

At eleven o'clock a conference with a group of old-line Republicans had been planned by Mr. Crocker, who had written asking them to meet me. Among them was Harry Chandler, owner and editor of the Los Angeles *Times,* who came in the afternoon and stayed an hour. He was a most able citizen and his aid to me in politics, and later in motion pictures, placed me personally under great obligation to him.

All day, separately and in groups, I explained to these men what I believed to be the national political situation and the vital importance of a united Republican party, not only for the future of the party itself but also for the welfare of the country. I believed this, and I gave all I had in the presentation of this thesis. By the evening I felt that possibly we had made some progress, but certainly not enough to warrant the item in the paper next morning: "Before the chairman was in Los Angeles two hours, he had an agreement with the warring factions." It was not that easy, nor was I sure of the progress until a careful review had been made, after I had left, and word came back of the day-after reactions. Then I felt sure that no harm had been done and possibly some good.

While the emphasis had been upon politics in the advance notices of my visit, my participation in the Liberty Loan drive was a big part of my activities. Although of a different nature here than in some other places, notably Salt Lake City, where I formally opened the third Liberty Loan drive in the Tabernacle, much attention was given by the Los Angeles organization of the party to the bond effort.

Senator Flint and I attended a banquet where some four hundred Liberty Loan workers were holding a rally, each team of ten at a table. As their number was called the spokesman would rise and announce the amount raised by that team. Down the line, probably about the seventh table, Stoddard Jess was called to report for the team soliciting bankers. It was obvious that a big report was expected. When a very large sum was announced, the applause was tumultuous. The bankers had again done their part. Farther down the line came the table of the motion picture team. This interested me somewhat, although at the time I had no relation with motion pictures except occasionally to see one. But I could see that the audience was eager to hear this report. When it came, it far exceeded the amount announced for the bankers. The crowd tore the roof off. No one could help being impressed with what the motion picture industry had done. I was reminded of this many times in the years after, as I saw how motion picture people responded to every war appeal. It was that same night that I heard of the gift of $105,000 from William S. Hart, who later became one of my best friends.

Following the meeting it was suggested that I work again with the Liberty Loan folks, and a speech was planned for Wednesday noon at the Universal studio. This pleased me very much because I wanted to have more to do with the group, and I had the natural desire of every visitor to see what the inside of a big studio looked like.

With Mr. and Mrs. George Dinwiddie we picked up my old Indiana friends, Max and Madge Puett, at their home that day and went to Universal City. First we were taken to a set where a company was making a picture called *The Lion's Claw*. There I met Max Rosselli, Mae Murray, and many others. Max Rosselli staged a fight with four lions, as part of the action in the film. I remember two incidents that impressed me, in addition to meeting Mae Murray. Part of the entertainment for visitors was the taking of pictures in the lions' cage. Visitors were invited to enter the cage with the trainer and two or three lions and sit on chairs. The trainer and the lions were marshaled in the near background, framing our foolhardiness. I remember that both Mrs. Dinwiddie and Mrs. Puett were insistent that their husbands should not enter, and of course the ladies didn't, so it turned out that I was the only one in the picture.

The other incident with the lions was more realistic. The jungle set where the fight was to take place was all fenced in and about one hundred feet square. It was covered with the usual jungle equipment of underbrush, trees, and bushes and had two paths about four feet wide connecting the four corners diagonally. At the junction of the paths was an open circular space to which the sun could penetrate. The plan was to have two or three lions come down the paths to this open space, where the fight with the actor, Max Rosselli, was to be staged.

We were placed in the angle of the two paths with the cameraman and hidden in the underbrush. There was a great deal of build-up as this proceeded, and I remember very well that before the lions entered at the rear I was wishing that I was somewhere else, especially as there were apertures in the jungle through which our friends outside could watch us.

About the time the lions were released, I decided it might be just as well if I got out, and I started up the path toward the rear gate—too late. There was a lion coming down toward the point of the triangle, so I got back behind the cameraman. This was the only comedy element in that sequence. The lions came, they met and had their fight with Rosselli, and were herded out. No herding was necessary on my part.

Just before noon we went to the stand prepared for the bond meeting. The area was filled with cowboys on horses and cowboys afoot, Indians, clowns, troubadours, ballerinas, jockeys, thugs and ministers, priests and gamblers—in fact, all the actors and extras on the Universal lot, together with the mechanics, electricians, carpenters, and musicians—and all who could carried six-guns. It looked like a cross between a carnival and a massacre. But it was a splendid Liberty Loan meeting, concluding with the taking of subscriptions in the same generous manner as at the banquet. At the conclusion one of the most delightful incidents of the entire trip occurred when a little boy of five, clad in khaki, made an inspiring little speech.

I took away from Universal the choicest recollections. There for the first time I met Carl Laemmle, who later became so helpful in all my motion picture efforts. It would have taken a complete faith in Aladdin's lamp for me to have believed that before long I would be repeatedly going to that same studio on projects connected with the motion picture industry. Never, on those later visits, did I fail to find the same kindness and sympathetic reception.

National Committee headquarters were opened in New York and Washington on my return from this western trip. New York headquarters were formally inaugurated on May 3 in the Knox Building at the southwest corner of Fortieth Street and Fifth Avenue, where we had leased the entire third floor for three years.

On these early trips to New York in the first days of my chairmanship I made many valuable acquaintances. Soon after my introduction to Colonel Thompson, I first met Henry Clay Frick and Andrew W. Mellon.

I remember very well when Colonel George Harvey took me up to Mr. Frick's Fifth Avenue house to lunch with Frick and Mellon. Harvey was close to these men, had told me much about them, and especially thought that I should meet Mellon, who was in New York on business and was having a conference with Frick that morning when we arrived. It was a quiet lunch with quiet men. Compared to Frick and Mellon,

Harvey was a loudy. Both men, of course, were very impressive, and I was fully conscious of their great personal success in many fields.

On this particular day I listened—not an easy thing to do, since they were not prone to provide all the conversation—as they expressed an interest in ideas which I offered on the organization of the Republican party, its usefulness, and the need for two political parties, both strong and virile. They asked pointed questions about the moves in that direction, both in the Indiana campaign and as planned for the national effort. Mellon left first, then Harvey left, and Mr. Frick asked me to stay longer. He indicated why he had asked me to remain: to show me his art collection. He then told me that he intended eventually giving this art to the city—"provided it is here," he said, "when the time comes." I asked what he meant by that, whether he expected an invasion from Germany. No, he said, but he feared riots in New York City that might destroy things of beauty such as his art gallery.

I saw little of Mr. Frick thereafter. Mellon, however, I saw often. During the later campaign of 1920, I became deeply impressed with his wisdom. During that period I frequently left the National Committee headquarters, even at the busiest times, and motored for five hours to Mellon's home in Southampton, where I would place before him the picture of the political situation. I remember how Senator Weeks and others at headquarters wondered why I discussed such matters with him, since he had had no experience whatever in politics. But I found that he could take a set of facts and so marshal and analyze them that anyone could understand them better. His judgment gave me powerful support.

I went to Indianapolis the day before the Republican State Convention on May 29, 1918, and discussed the national planks in the state platform with Governor Goodrich, Senators New and Watson, Chairman Wasmuth, and others before presenting the draft to the committee on resolutions. I was made chairman of the Platform Committee, and my national planks were adopted in toto. In brief, they were:

An arraignment of the party in power for practicing petty partisanship.

A demand that all patriots, regardless of party affiliations, support the government.

A demand that every possible efficient instrument be used in winning the war, whether it be men or material, and that inefficiency wherever found should be replaced by efficiency.

A declaration that such criticism as was indulged in should be directed against those evils which were hindering the war program.

An insistence on peace with victory as distinguished from a peace by a bargaining compromise which would violate American rights.

A declaration in favor of a sane preparation now for the solution of the great and complex problems to be considered after the war.

A pledge of a forward-looking program for labor, the farmer, and business, and a reaffirmation of belief in the protective tariff and a declaration in favor of "the rehabilitation of a privately owned but government-aided merchant marine."

A strong declaration for woman suffrage.

Republican papers throughout the country, and some Democratic papers, praised the platform. The Philadelphia *Inquirer* said: "It is positive, it is courageous, and it is expressed in words that can be understood by all."

An amusing personal incident of the Indianapolis convention was printed in the St. Louis *Times* shortly after. It read:

Will H. Hays, the new chairman of the Republican National Committee, is extremely youthful in appearance. He is also quite democratic in habits, if not in politics. As Chairman of the Indiana Republican State Committee, he mingled freely with the crowds in hotel lobbies and on the streets. He is an inveterate newspaper reader, and usually carries from five to ten newspapers under his arm. A pompous politician jurist from a southern county arrived in Indianapolis at the hotel in which the Republican headquarters was located to get a line on what was doing in party matters. He was in the lobby when Hays came rushing through with the usual bunch of newspapers under his arm.

"Here, sonny," the pompous one called out, "give me a paper." Hays stopped, never batted an eye, handed the judge a paper, pocketed the nickel and proceeded to his office on an upper floor. Half an hour later, when the judge dropped in to have a chat with the chairman and found Hays at the desk, his dignity was completely submerged in his embarrassment.

A more complete exposition of my platform views appeared in an article which I wrote for the August issue of the *Forum* magazine. It was widely quoted throughout the country by newspapers of all political complexions and was credited with having had much to do with the results of the 1918 campaign, and in view of national and world trends since that year, it may be of interest to note two or three statements in that expanded platform:

A proper and just restriction of the present socialistic tendency in our government, to the end that while we fight to make certain forever the right of free government throughout the world we shall not forget that we have a Republic to preserve in North America.

Every thinking man and woman has noted the socialistic tendencies of the present government.

The Republican party from its inception has stood against undue federalization of industries and activities. We always have and still shall endeavor to find the middle ground so well defined as between "The anarchy of un-

regulated individualism and the deadening formalism of inefficient and widespread state ownership."

We will stand ever vigilant against any violation of American rights,
interests and honor.

So far as strictly party business was concerned, I considered my most
important task as national chairman to be the reconstruction of the party
as a strong national organization after the disastrous split in the 1912
campaign. My conviction that this was possible was based both on our
experience in Indiana and on my observation of the healing process going on steadily in many sections of the nation. To this end, much of my
time in the succeeding months was devoted to harmony meetings and
conferences aimed at drawing the discordant elements into an effective
working accord. During this period I traveled thousands of miles, addressed many meetings, and talked with hundreds of individuals of all
shades of Republican conviction, from the most conservative "stand-
patters" to the most ardent Bull Moosers.

The personal reconciliation between Theodore Roosevelt and William
Howard Taft gave added impetus to these efforts. The colonel was especially active. By his writings, his speeches, and his personal contacts he
was re-establishing himself as a constructive force in this rebuilding of
the party. He was always a fighter for what he thought was right, and
here was something into which he could throw himself with his old
zeal.

CHAPTER 12

The 1918 Fall Elections

O N E of the truisms of politics is that words publicly uttered by a spokesman of one party are often interpreted quite differently by his opponents. Their application and emphasis may easily be twisted quite out of their original context. The most conspicuous case I encountered in 1918 was connected with Joseph P. Tumulty, secretary to President Wilson. Although at this distance it is worth no long recital, it does illustrate a certain situation with which American voters must always deal. His communications went to great length.

On the day following the successful Maine elections, Secretary Tumulty, presumably at the instigation of the President, launched an attack upon me, based on the Labor Day speech I had made before a meeting of state chairmen in Chicago. He addressed a telegram to me in Indianapolis while I was in Washington, reading:

ON THURSDAY, SEPTEMBER 5, 1918, THE TOPEKA CAPITAL, PUBLISHED AT TOPEKA, KANSAS, QUOTES YOU AS HAVING MADE THE FOLLOWING STATEMENT TO THE THIRTY-ONE STATE REPUBLICAN CHAIRMEN WHO MET WITH YOU IN CHICAGO ON SEPTEMBER 2: "THE DEMOCRATIC LEADERS AT WASHINGTON WOULD NOT STOP AT ANYTHING THAT THEY BELIEVED WOULD ENSURE THE RE-ELECTION OF A DEMOCRATIC CONGRESS THIS FALL AND A DEMOCRATIC PRESIDENT TWO YEARS HENCE. THEY WOULD EVEN END THE WAR WITH ANY KIND OF COMPROMISE IF THAT WOULD ENSURE THE CONTINUANCE OF THE DEMOCRATIC PARTY IN POWER." I SHALL BE OBLIGED IF YOU WILL LET ME KNOW IF THIS IS A CORRECT STATEMENT OF YOUR REMARKS.

I replied to this on September 11, after a copy had been forwarded to me at my Washington hotel. My letter read, in part, as follows:

I have your telegram. On September 2 in Chicago I attended a meeting of the Association of Republican State Chairmen, called by its President and attended by fifteen of such chairmen.

At that meeting I made remarks referring in a general way to the length to which the Democratic leaders are going in their efforts to control the Senate and House and also as to the irrevocable stand of the Republican party for a vigorous prosecution of the war and against an inconclusive peace.

I did not use the words quoted in your telegram. What I said then, which I now reaffirm and which I shall continue to declare, was substantially as follows:

First, as to the means resorted to by certain Democratic leaders to get votes I said:

"In the special election in Wisconsin, the Democratic machine leaders published advertisements, undenied by them, addressed to the soldiers at Camp Grant, as follows:

" 'To the Wisconsin soldiers at Camp Grant:

" 'Tuesday, April 2:

" 'You are entitled to vote for United States senator from Wisconsin to succeed Senator Paul O. Husting.

" 'President Wilson, your commander in chief, desires all loyal Americans to vote for Joseph E. Davies for United States senator.

" 'Davies' election means joy at Washington and gloom at Berlin.

" 'Davies' defeat means gloom at Washington and joy at Berlin.'

"I regard this as an infamous prostitution of all patriotic proprieties and the grossest violation of the plainest civil duty worthy of the severest condemnation of all Americans. In this crisis when all patriots are striving to bring to the aid of the country's cause every resource in men and material, when thousands of Republican and Democratic boys are dying side by side, and when both political parties are loyal, such conduct is immeasurably reprehensible.

"From such actions it is evident, and I regret to say it, that these Democratic leaders will go to any lengths to carry the Senate and the House. Such unpatriotic efforts to use the war for partisan purposes must fail. Such inevitable failure was indicated by the Wisconsin result. It was further shown in the Michigan primary and will be conclusively proved in the Maine election next week. The American people will not tolerate it. This is the war of no political party. This is the people's war, and we demand that the war be kept out of partisan politics and that partisanship be kept out of the war. And what we ask from the party in power, we irrevocably pledge for ourselves."

Though Mr. Tumulty came back on September 12 with a very long letter, quoting from speeches by other Republicans which he considered partisan appeals, I made no further reply beyond the following statement to the press:

I think I have adequately answered Mr. Tumulty's reply to my retort as to his inquiry about Democratic leaders resorting to any expedient to maintain control of the government and Congress. I judge that the Washington administration must have been hard hit by the result of the Maine election. Perhaps that was one reason why Mr. Tumulty insisted on my being smoked out. I am satisfied with the situation if he is. We shall go right on doing our best to elect a win-the-war-peace-with-victory Republican Congress, and we expect to complete the job.

Our organization was all out to win the war as quickly as possible, and we coined the slogan, mentioned before, that soon was heard throughout the nation—a line stamped upon thousands of envelopes before being dropped into the mails: "Win the War Now—Everything Else Is Chores." During the recent war I revived this line for use on all my personal mail.

As national chairman, I naturally had little patience with the man who was too busy to take part in politics, which, after all, is the proper means of expressing satisfaction or dissatisfaction. "Abraham Lincoln did not think himself too good for politics," I told them, at the same time insisting on a constructive Republican program on the ground that no party can be of national service that merely waits for its rival's mistakes. This was the policy of the Republican party throughout almost the entire campaign.

During the month of August 1918, when the reports from Europe indicated that Germany might soon collapse, the President, in his absorption in war problems, made the statement: "Politics is adjourned." In this I could not see entirely eye to eye with Mr. Wilson, and so merely repeated my previous stand: "There must be no politics in war." The American people quite obviously agreed with this statement, as evidenced a little later by their decision, emphatically registered at the polls.

Most of September 1918 was devoted to speechmaking trips about the country, including a quick trip to Kansas and Missouri. At Louisville I addressed a meeting of a thousand political leaders from several states and went on to the Michigan State Convention at Grand Rapids. Before leaving on the western trip, I issued from New York a directive to all Republican party workers, reading, in part:

. . . There is no geography, political or physical, in the patriotism of this country. Democrats and Republicans alike love their flag and are ready to die for it. We continually insist for all parties that the war be kept out of partisan politics and that partisanship be kept out of the war.

Just as in Congress the Republicans led the fight that made possible the passage of the great war measures, so now the party membership and the organization has an immediate, definite war task in the accomplishment of which it can fully function. I repeat, let there be no contest in this country as to anything that touches the war except that contest—who best can serve, who most can give. . . .

Wherever Republicans are together, by two or two thousand, it shall be a "win the war" meeting. Just as the Republican Party's every action at all times has been and shall be determined solely by how we can contribute most to the war's success, so now our every thought and action shall be determined entirely by how we can make certain the quick subscription of the Fourth Liberty Loan. . . .

On the same day that I issued this appeal to Republicans to devote all their energies to the fourth Liberty Loan, the Democratic National Committee also issued a directive to their party workers. In part, it read:

You realize a Republican Congress means a divided authority. Do you want the President to be blocked in this great world enterprise by any such obstruction? Don't you realize that any such division of authority or any such hampering means a lessening of our war efficiency? The election of a Republican Congress in November would be viewed as a defeat for President Wilson by our allies, and particularly by our enemies. It would be viewed in Germany as a proof of their unwarranted claim that our country is not behind our war President. It would be a source of comfort and elation to the Kaiser and his cohorts.

This document was signed by the Democratic national chairman, Vance C. McCormick, and by W. D. Jamieson, assistant treasurer of the committee. Both directives were widely publicized, and many newspapers commented on the marked contrast between the two.

Not until September, at a meeting in Chicago, did I mention in a general way the lengths to which the Democratic leaders were going in their efforts to maintain control of Congress, citing in particular a special election in Wisconsin.

Later, another situation arose that was even more flagrant in so far as the phrase "playing politics in wartime" could be applied to the Democrats. Upon the insistence of Woodrow Wilson, the name of the late Henry Ford, who was an out-and-out Democrat, was entered for United States senator in the Republican primary against Truman H. Newberry, then a commander in the Navy. Ford, an acknowledged pacifist, had the entire Democratic state backing, with the added blessing of the President of the United States and commander in chief of its armed forces. This seemed to me to be a prostitution of patriotic proprieties, and I so stated in a later speech at the Chicago State Convention.

Quite unconscious of the storm even then in the making behind the apparent political truce, I made a speech at Grand Rapids, Michigan, on September 26, 1918, still insisting that we must show the enemy a united nation politically. "No Geography in Politics" was the title, and the situation and timing were so exactly duplicated in World War II that the text might also have been repeated. In part, it read:

This is no time for little things. All the organized diabolical forces of a scientifically trained brutality are at the throat of this country. And we appeal to all patriots, whatever their politics, to aid in every way possible in these efforts to keep partisanship out of the war management and all war activities. In the name of every American mother of those boys, I appeal for the support of the country's cause by all men and women without thought of party.

On the day this address was delivered, Woodrow Wilson already was considering the partisan appeal that he actually made a few days before the election, demanding the return of a Democratic Congress.

Reports of great Republican gains began rolling in to headquarters from all parts of the country within a few days of the publication of the Wilson letter and the Republican counterblasts. Colonel Roosevelt and William Howard Taft met on October 31 at the Union League Club in New York, where they prepared and issued a joint statement. While they were writing, Taft said: "This seems like old times, doesn't it, Theodore?" Colonel Roosevelt chuckled and replied: "Indeed it does, Will."

In their statement the two former presidents urged all Americans who were Americans first to vote for a Republican Congress; they deprecated extending the unified uncontrolled leadership of a commander in chief to the making of a permanent treaty of peace or to the framing of those measures of reconstruction which must seriously affect the happiness and prosperity of the American people for a century; they called attention to the leadership of Republican members of Congress as contrasted with the failure of Democratic congressional members to co-operate with the administration.

On October 25, 1918, President Wilson released his fateful letter demanding the return of a Democratic Congress.

Proof of the President's state of mind is found in the diary of his chief adviser, Colonel Edward M. House, which under the terms of the author's will now reposes in a vault at Yale University. This and other important papers were not to be published until twenty-five years after the author's death.

In 1936 the ailing Colonel House, in a letter to Charles Seymour, president of Yale, permitted Wythe Williams to inspect the diary and to make notes therefrom. Excerpts later appeared in Mr. Williams' book, *Dusk of Empire,* in a chapter on the League of Nations, approved by Colonel House prior to publication. From this the present author has drawn certain quotations which substantiate the fact of Woodrow Wilson's greatest political blunder. These supplement copious quotations from the diary which Colonel House had previously incorporated in his own published memoirs. On September 24, 1918, appears the following important entry:

The President spoke of politics in general, and expressed an earnest desire that a Democratic Congress should be elected. He said he intended making a speech or writing a letter about two weeks before the election, asking the people to return a Democratic House. I did not express my opinion of this.

A fact later remarked upon by intimates of Wilson and House should be noted: whenever the colonel advised with the President, his silence invariably expressed dissent. It might have been more fortunate for Mr. Wilson had House opened up at this time, but apparently nothing more was said about the proposed letter, and the President's wise counselor was on the Atlantic when the appeal was issued. It was dated October 25 and was addressed to "My fellow countrymen!" In view of the events that followed almost immediately, also in the light of the present trend of world affairs, it is worth repeating here. It shows how easy it is to change the course of history. The letter reads:

The congressional elections are at hand. They occur in the most critical period our country has ever faced or is likely to face in our time. If you have approved of my leadership and wish me to continue to be your unembarrassed spokesman in affairs at home and abroad, I earnestly beg that you will express yourselves unmistakably to that effect by returning a Democratic majority to both the Senate and the House of Representatives.

I am your servant and will accept your judgment without comment but my power to administer the great trust assigned to me by the Constitution would be seriously impaired should your judgment be adverse and I must frankly tell you so because many critical issues depend upon your verdict. No scruple of taste must in grim times like these be allowed to stand in the way of speaking the plain truth.

I have no thought of suggesting that any political party is paramount in matters of patriotism. I feel too keenly the sacrifices which have been made in this war by all our citizens irrespective of party affiliations, to harbor such an ideal. I mean only that the difficulties and delicacies of our present tasks are of a sort that make it imperatively necessary that the nation should give its undivided support to the government under a unified leadership and that a Republican congress would divide the leadership.

The leaders of the minority in the present Congress have unquestionably been pro-war, but they have been anti-administration.

At almost every turn since we entered the war they sought to take the choice of policy and the conduct of the war out of my hands and put it under the control of instrumentalities of their own choosing. This is no time either for divided counsel or for divided leadership. Unity of command is as necessary now in civil actions as it is upon the field of battle. If the control of the house and senate should be taken away from the party now in power, an opposing majority could assume control of legislation and oblige all action to be taken amid contest and obstruction.

The return of a Republican majority to either house of Congress would, moreover, certainly be interpreted on the other side of the water as repudiation of my leadership. Spokesmen of the Republican party are urging you to elect a Republican congress in order to back up and support the President, but even if they should in this war impose upon some credulous voters on this side of the water, they should impose on no one on the other side. It is well understood there as well as here, that the Republican leaders desire not so much to support the president as to control him. The peoples of the allied countries with whom we are associated against Germany are quite familiar with the significance of elections. They would find it very difficult to believe that the voters of the United States had chosen to support their President by electing to the Congress a majority collected by those who are not in fact in sympathy with the attitude and action of the administration.

I need not tell you, my fellow countrymen, that I am asking your support not for my own sake, or the sake of a political party, but for the sake of a nation itself, in order that its inward unity of purpose may be evident to all the world. In ordinary times I would not feel at liberty to make such an appeal to you. In ordinary times divided counsels can be endured without permanent hurt to the country. But these are not ordinary times. If in these critical days it is your wish to sustain me with undivided minds, I beg that you will say so in a way which it will not be possible to misunderstand either here at home or among our associates on the other side of the sea. I submit my difficulties and my hopes to you.

(Signed) WOODROW WILSON

On the same date Colonel House received the report in mid-ocean and again wrote in his diary:

I have been greatly disturbed by the President's appeal for a Democratic Congress. All he says is true, but it is a political error to appeal for a partisan Congress. If he had asked the voters to support members of Congress and the Senate who had supported the American war aims regardless of party, he would be in a safe position. In this way he would avoid personal feeling and would win, no matter which party controlled Congress, provided those selected had been loyal to our war aims. Here, again, the President has taken a great gamble. If it turns out well, he will be acclaimed a bold and forceful leader; if it turns out badly, an opposite view will be taken.

It seems to me a needless venture and had I been at home I should have counseled against it. He mentioned, the last time I was in Washington, that he thought of making an appeal. I made no reply, which always indicates to him my disapproval. As a matter of fact, we were so absorbed with the German notes that I brushed the question aside and gave it but little attention. I am sorry now that I did not discuss it with him to a finish.

Up to that moment it was generally believed that the Democrats had a better than even chance to carry the 1918 election. The Wilson letter was applauded by most of the party members, who assured themselves that it meant the continuance of a Democratic Senate and House.

As Republican chairman, I naturally did not share these views. I knew that the national resentment was mounting against Wilson for his earlier methods favoring the Democrats in Wisconsin and Michigan, and more especially for general domestic maladministration.

After the letter was published, our Republicans momentarily appeared dazed. Even the leaders, Senator Knox, Senator Lodge, and others, did not at once rise to the political opportunity that had been offered.

For thirty-six hours the Republican counterattack was held back. Then in my official role I attempted to jolt the party out of its trance and speed it into action. My timing turned out to be fortunate, for by then the President's appeal had percolated the mass voter mind. My broadsides brought only feeble replies from the national Democratic organization and overnight gained thousands of votes for the Republicans. The initial attempt on my part in rebuttal to the Wilson letter was brief. It read:

A more ungracious, more unjust, more wanton, more mendacious accusation never was made by the most reckless stump orator, much less by a President of the United States for partisan purposes. It is an insult not only to every loyal Republican in Congress, but to every loyal Republican in the land. It fully merits the resentment which rightfully and surely will find expression at the polls.

In the week that followed prior to the election, our attack continued, and without mincing words. Pronouncements were made over my signature of what many had thought but few had said openly, considering that these were war times and unity was necessary. The President himself remained silent, possibly realizing the stupendous blunder he had made. Republicans everywhere were aroused to an extent that sent them to the polls the following Tuesday to prove that they were free-born Americans, quite capable of action without specific instructions from the White House.

It appeared that all my earlier optimism for a Republican victory was about to be justified on the night of November 4, when I left for Sullivan to cast my ballot on the following morning. That night I issued the following forecast from headquarters in the Knox Building:

Last minute reports from every contested state confirm our advices of yesterday that the Republicans will carry both the Senate and the House. To equal the Democratic vote in the Senate the Republicans need to gain only four votes. We will gain at least seven. To equal the Democratic vote in the House the Republicans need to gain only five votes. We will gain at least 26.

When the final count was in, the vote gave the Republicans a majority of two in the Senate and thirty-four in the House. Woodrow Wilson doubtless lost his commanding prestige throughout the nation. Theodore Roosevelt, in a victory statement issued on November 7, paid me high honor and credit for my contributions to the result. Colonel Roosevelt said:

The result of the election is really extraordinary, inasmuch as the entire pro-German and pacifist vote was behind the Wilson Democratic ticket. . . . I regard the result as much more a victory for straight Americanism than Republicanism. . . . The American people have reflected deep honor upon themselves, and while we owe much to the various leaders, we owe more to Mr. Will H. Hays, the Chairman of the Republican National Committee, who has shown not only extreme practicable efficiency but the high purpose to serve the Republican party by making that party render conspicuous service to the nation.

The results of the election in Indiana were particularly gratifying to me, for not only did the Republicans elect the entire delegation to Congress, but they increased the Republican plurality by thirty-five thousand over 1916.

CHAPTER 13

The Roots of the Treaty

I T was high drama that the elections of November 5, 1918, with the war still a central issue, should have been followed only six days later by the Armistice. Overnight the whole situation changed. Had the events of the two days, November 5 and 11, been reversed, Wilson probably would still have had a popular majority vote behind him. As it was, it is certain that from nightfall of November 5, 1918, his fortunes began their inevitable decline.

In the years that followed, it was occasionally inferred that the man most responsible for the political overthrow of the twenty-eighth President of the United States was myself, but I decline the charge. As chairman of the Republican National Committee, it was my job to give battle to the opposing party.

The real reason for the Democratic defeat in 1918 and the subsequent waning of Wilsonian power was Woodrow Wilson himself. History has recorded him as a superior man—a statesman of foresight and high ideals, and a vigorous leader. But as a politician he was a blunderer, unwilling to heed excellent party advice. Had it not been for Colonel House, who was also a superior man, but with an uncanny political flair, he might never have become President. *Politics, so often maligned, remains essential to successful statecraft.* When Mr. Wilson finally disregarded the sage political advice of his great counselor, he foundered. And Will H. Hays had nothing to do with that.

The Armistice celebration naturally caused the election result to fade momentarily in the minds of everybody, including Wilson and his aides. They who never should have overlooked it even for a second, especially in view of their already laid plans for incorporating the League of Nations as part of the peace terms, went about their business almost as though the election had not happened.

Mr. Wilson, of course, still held the executive powers of the presidency, even though the legislative authority would soon be beyond his control, with the seating of the incoming Congress. While the full meaning of the American election was not generally understood by the European public, the leaders on the other side, notably Georges Clemenceau of France and Lloyd George of England—both schooled in the political chicanery that had dominated European chancelleries since the days of Talleyrand and Metternich—were fully advised and smugly satisfied. They well knew that in case they could not have their way with the President he still was accountable for his acts to the United States Senate. They of course did not know that American resentment was increasing also over what then, as again later, was considered the maladministration of our domestic affairs. Charges were constantly made, almost in the same language as was heard during World War II, concerning the waste, bungling, and general inefficiency exhibited in the name of the government as applied to home affairs.

Wilson under these conditions then made a second great mistake that aided two years later in ousting the Democrats from the government and electing Warren G. Harding to the presidency, meanwhile helping to defeat our acceptance of the Treaty of Versailles and keeping America from participation in the League of Nations.

This error was basically on the composition of the American delegation to negotiate peace, including Wilson himself as its chief.

A pre-convention agreement was reached between the Great Powers that each should be represented by five delegates. It was taken for granted that three of the Americans would be Democrats—the President, Secretary of State Lansing, and Colonel House. The hope generally expressed was that the two remaining delegates would be outstanding members of the Republican party.

Prior to the Armistice, Wilson discussed the matter with House, who had urged the choice of Elihu Root or ex-President Taft, or both. Wilson was not enthusiastic and kept delaying the matter. His final selection of General Bliss and former Ambassador Henry White showed either a complete misunderstanding or disregard of party politics. This was dangerous at a time when the election had gone so badly against him. Henry White, the sole Republican, was especially unpopular with our party leaders. His European diplomatic experience had been wide, but he kept up no party affiliations. In this selection Wilson was asking for trouble in advance.

The make-up of the American delegation was actually unpopular with leaders of Wilson's own party as well, including members of his Cabinet, as evidenced by their writings then and later. Attorney General Gregory also suggested Root and Taft, along with Governor McCall of Massachusetts and former President Eliot of Harvard.

President Wilson was determined to head the American peace delegation. Concerning his personal appearance and participation in the treaty-making, two outstanding and opposing opinions were presented. The first was shared by his own advisers and was prepared at the request of Colonel House. It was in the form of a memorandum written by

Frank Cobb, brilliant editorial writer of the New York *World*. It was dated Paris, November 5, 1918, the election day when the Democrats lost their control of Congress. The date is indicative that Wilson considered his personal role at Paris as paramount and quite apart from the fact that the majority of American voters might hold an opposite opinion. Mr. Cobb said, in part:

The moment Wilson sits at the council table with these Prime Ministers and Foreign Secretaries, he has lost all the power that comes from distance and detachment. Instead of remaining the great arbiter of human freedom, he becomes merely a negotiator dealing with other negotiators. He is simply one vote in a peace conference, bound either to abide by the will of the majority, or disrupt its proceedings under circumstances which, having come to a climax in secret, can never be clearly explained to the public. Any public protest to which the President gave utterance would thus be only the complaint of a thwarted and disappointed negotiator.

The second opinion, but of entirely different tenor, was presented by the twenty-seventh President of the United States, William Howard Taft, one month later. Mr. Taft said, among other things:

The advantages of his going seem clear. His presence in the conference will stamp upon it a democratic character in the eyes of all but the wild bolsheviki.

This will be a real aid in allaying the unrest among the peoples of the Allies. The conference between Mr. Wilson, Lloyd George, M. Clemenceau and Sr. Orlando must be useful to the world. In these four men we shall have the men of real power in the four great nations.

However different the situation might have been had Wilson taken the advice of counselors in his own party, he decided that the trip to Paris was necessary, come what may. Accompanied by Mrs. Wilson and a retinue of public officials and experts—financial, economic, and military—he sailed on the S.S. *George Washington* and arrived at Brest on Friday, December 13, which he considered a lucky date.

The special train arrived at the Gare du Bois de Boulogne, Paris, in a rare winter sunshine of early morning. The platform was covered with the red plush carpet reserved for visiting royalty. With mounted escort of the Garde Républicaine, brilliantly helmeted and plumed, the President of the United States rode down the Avenue des Champs Elysées in triumph. A million Frenchmen shouted welcome to one they looked upon as the new savior of mankind.

The drama of peacemaking was played out in Paris during the following six and a half months, while the rest of the world watched.

The treaty of peace that officially ended World War I was signed at the Palace of Versailles in the bright afternoon of June 28, 1919. The thrill of joy that accompanied the scratching of pens as the delegates bent over the table in the historic Hall of Mirrors vibrated around the world. That the parchment attested by the representatives of governments might be *a treaty without peace* was then unthinkable.

Momentarily the world dwelt in the glow of optimism. "Autocracy is dead—long live Democracy." This designation of belief in a better world was the theme song, as expressed to Woodrow Wilson by his greatest counselor, Colonel Edward M. House. And yet a note of cynicism—an indication of the speck in the cloudless sky—appeared in the dispatch from one American correspondent to his newspaper that evening:

Outside the palace was the imposing spectacle of tens of thousands of persons lining the great boulevard leading to Paris. Upon the Grand stairway were *chasseurs* in brilliant uniforms. Cavalry, with pennons flying, surrounded the great park. The magnificent fountains were playing for the first time since the war began. Airplanes droned overhead and cannon thundered. Making of peace was in full panoply of war. Imperial Rome did no more in her hour of triumph when the victim was dragged literally at the chariot wheel of the conqueror.

The document known as the Versailles Treaty—including the Covenant of the League of Nations—which was considerably buffeted and abused in the making, has since received more criticism than possibly any similar pact in previous history. It is charged today with being a main contributory to World War II, in that through it Europe remained involved in problems and promises that were impossible to solve, enforce, or fulfill.

In the closing months of World War II the hope was frequently (and piously) expressed that the mistakes made after the earlier conflict would not be repeated when the Allies of World War II came to face their beaten enemies at what is still called the council table of peace. So far, the mechanics of peacemaking following the late war have had only superficial resemblance to those dignified plenary sessions at Versailles.

Perhaps the difference in present-day procedure is due to the brighter light of modern publicity, which has dramatized the "walkouts" of the latter meetings in contrast to the threats of similar action at Versailles. President Wilson did order steam up on the liner *George Washington* to return him to America at one stage in the Paris conference, and Premier Orlando once prepared to return to Italy, but no action resulted from either gesture.

In so far as this nation was concerned, its properly authorized representative, President Wilson, signed the treaty. Its ratification by the Senate was another matter. There the document became such a storm center of attack and counterattack that it was literally torn apart and subjected to microscopic scrutiny. All later attempts to patch it together failed, until finally, instead of receiving the legislative blessing that would have made it, including the League of Nations, part and parcel of the American scheme of living, it was destined to run its course without the signature of Uncle Sam.

During this six-month period, from my fixed position on this side of the Atlantic, I made it an important part of my job to analyze the steps in the drafting of the Treaty of Versailles as they developed. The progressive story, however, was not always quickly available to a non-governmental and thereby an unofficial individual. I was the politcial strategist for the party that now held legislative control of the government, but that was still outside the limits of executive power, and as the Republican national chairman I charged myself with the responsibility of keeping the general public informed so far as possible concerning the daily progress at Paris, especially the factors that might affect the welfare of the United States. It was imperative that American opinion and judgment be based on all the facts we could get. The reaction on the temperature and pulse of our public that followed the official communiqués on the peacemaking was charted in every way possible. Nothing seemed more important for the national future. Therefore, it seems to me important now to present some of the highlights in the great drama then unfolding in the French capital up to the time that the President presented the treaty to the Senate of the United States and pleaded for its adoption. It is a story of many facets.

Theodore Roosevelt, in a strong attack on Wilson in November 1918, said:

Our Allies and our enemies and Mr. Wilson himself should all understand that Mr. Wilson had no authority whatever to speak for the American people at this time. His leadership has been emphatically repudiated by them. . . . If he acts in good faith to the American people . . . he will say frankly that his personal leadership has been repudiated, and that he now has merely the divided official leadership which he shares with the Senate.

The Armistice had come with a suddenness that caught people and governments unaware, although expert committees had long been at work in England, France, and the United States trying to formulate the various aims of the warring nations. But first it was necessary to dispel the dangerously disquieting atmosphere that prevailed. Therefore, while it was necessary to conclude some sort of peace at the earliest moment, the question of a breathing time in which passions might cool immediately came up for consideration.

Responsibility for the delay, before anything was accomplished, has been placed at the door of Wilson. He was determined to head the American delegation, but he first wanted to address Congress in December. Even on Armistice Day he sent the following cable to House:

WILL IT NOT BE WISE AND NECESSARY TO POSTPONE THE PEACE CONFERENCE UNTIL THERE ARE GOVERNMENTS IN GERMANY AND AUSTRIA-HUNGARY WHICH CAN ENTER INTO BINDING AGREEMENTS?

House was all for immediate action. On November 18 he wrote in his diary:

> I am trying to frighten those who are endeavoring to postpone the Conference. I am telling them that people soon will begin to murmur.

Almost a decade later, April 9, 1928, House wrote in his diary a detailed memorandum, retracing the arguments for a preliminary peace, to be followed by a necessary breathing spell before drafting the final treaty. Among other things, he wrote:

> The years that have been passed since June 1919, when the Treaty of Versailles was laid upon the table for signature, leave me with an unchanged mind regarding the desirability of making a quick preliminary peace as soon after the Armistice as was possible. Never were there more compelling reasons for following this procedure. The intensity of war, and the dislocation of regular human activities, made it vital to bring about something approaching normal conditions at once. A fixed sum should have been made for reparations—a just sum, and one possible to pay.
> Boundaries might have been drawn with a broad sweep, with provision for later adjustments. A general but specific commitment regarding an Association of Nations for the maintenance of peace should have been made; and then adjournment. A permanent peace could have been made at leisure.
> In all probability, the United States would have ratified both Treaties, for such a commitment would have all but insured ratification of the second. President Wilson would not have continued in Paris after the preliminary peace was made.

I did my best to help keep the treaty-making out of politics. But I was bitterly disappointed when it gradually became evident that, through his own acts and attitude, real success was becoming impossible for Woodrow Wilson.

It seemed to me then, and it has remained my opinion throughout the years, that no matter how high the pinnacle on which our twenty-eighth President will be placed in history, his springs of action were not only the result of political ignorance, but were in bad faith.

Wilson knew that he was getting sound and honest advice, and he ignored it. He knew that the stakes in play were for the betterment not only of the United States but of the whole world. This was disregarded. Therefore, I repeat my opinion that he acted selfishly and falsely, not only to the duty that rested upon him, but to his own conscience.

Perhaps it is more charitable to say, however, that in the make-up and mood of the Senate he found himself in a very difficult situation. For the arena of major combat and of final decision was the Senate of the United States. The two gladiatorial headquarters were the meeting room of the Senate Foreign Relations Committee and the home of the President, the White House, at 1600 Pennsylvania Avenue, Washington.

The fight over the Treaty of Versailles that finally centered in the United States is the story of a tragedy. It is a story that demands retelling now, when the world is in a far more evil condition than then, and on a much vaster scale.

Actually, although unconsciously, the American lines, for and against peace terms, were forming before the war was over, or even before the end was in sight. Early in 1918 a situation developed which had tragic consequences so far as it concerned the parchment later to be signed at Versailles.

It was "Gumshoe Bill" Stone, Democratic senator from Missouri, seconded by Senator James Hamilton Lewis, Democrat from Illinois, who on January 22, 1918, made the first congressional speech of political significance after America entered the war, and who thereby touched off a blaze that resulted in trouble. Apparently with partisan misunderstanding Stone directly charged that the Republicans were pursuing a studied effort to make politics out of the war. This was in exact reverse of the proved fact that the Republican effort then was not to *make* politics out of the war but to *take* politics out of the war.

Senator Harry New, our Indiana Republican, at once met the challenge. Stone had gone so far as to include in his attack the position taken by myself, then chairman of the Indiana Council of Defense and also Republican state chairman. That was a bad error. The Indiana Defense Council already had received the open approval of Secretary of War Newton Baker and had been cited in Congress as an example for the nation to follow in non-partisan conduct.

The debate continued for several days and aroused great interest throughout the nation. The charge made by the Democrats was refuted by another strong voice in the Senate in the following language:

"Nothing during the war has been so profoundly gratifying to me as the fact that since last April (when the United States entered the war) there have been no political lines drawn in the Congress of the United States. Until today, no political speeches have been made, no political motives expressed. Both branches have labored together with the common desire to prosecute the war to the quickest possible conclusion."

The speaker was Henry Cabot Lodge of Massachusetts, later to become chairman of the Senate Foreign Relations Committee and archopponent of Woodrow Wilson in the final Senate battle for a compromise, which resulted in the rejection of the Treaty of Versailles. A little later, on February 9, Senator Lodge began to lose patience and lashed out at the Democrats with the statement that "the conduct of the war is still virtually a one-party affair."

As the reader will recall, the Indiana Republican Committee had named me state chairman in 1914. The declaration of war on April 6,

1917, found me still in that position, and there I remained after my appointment as head of the State Council of Defense. We at once put the entire Republican organization into detailed war work and success-fully joined forces with Tom Taggart, a great Democrat, to keep the war entirely bi-partisan so far as Indiana was concerned.

CHAPTER 14

The League Runs into Trouble

CONFLICT of opinion, as well as emotion, is character-
istic of man. Politics is people. Therefore, politics is with us always. It
lines up for and against, on this or that project or personality, or both.
In the popular sense, it decides upon the majority that governs democracies. The United States has been fortunate in having only two major
political parties. Never has it been necessary to apply the formula of
political coalition to determine the balance of power.

The Third French Republic usually had a dozen or more parties
represented in the great semicircular hall of the Palais Bourbon known
as the Chamber of Deputies. This made for disorder. No single party
ever held a voting majority, and coalition was a matter of necessity. This
has little to do with the conference at Versailles except to show that, in
spite of the number of political parties, war-weary France was glad to
accept the treaty. Bad as it was, it at least held the outward appearance
of peace.

In the United States, with only two important political parties, the
fate of the treaty was a different story. Both the Republicans and Democrats were strong and vigorous. As Republican national chairman—our
party now holding the majority in Congress—I felt that we had succeeded in keeping politics from anything that touched upon the war, so
far as we were concerned. I hoped that we could carry this policy into
the program of peacemaking, for the treaty in its final form, no less than
the military victory, should be the paramount concern of every American, regardless of political affiliation.

The nation as a whole then appeared ready to follow this policy. Thus
the picture stood as of December 14, 1918, when President Wilson, immediately after his arrival in Paris, issued the statement that the creation of the League was the foremost task of the Peace Conference. He
was still both our Chief of State and Chief of Government; he was our
helmsman and wielder of executive power. His prestige abroad was
practically undimmed. The Republican congressional majority was not
so impressive but that with tact and wisdom the President might have
handled it, especially in view of the attitude then taken by the Re-

publican leadership both within and without the halls of Congress. *If there ever was a time when compromise was necessary, it would seem to be then.* But to Woodrow Wilson the idea of compromise apparently never entered into the order of the day. He was frequently reminded that Anglo-Saxon civilization had been built on compromise, but he stood stubbornly on the dogma that one could get nothing worth while in this life without fighting for it. It was therefore quite natural that the Republicans in the Senate should rally to give him battle.

The final reason why the Treaty of Versailles was not ratified by the United States Senate was largely the clash, not of ideas or ideals, but of temperaments. Throughout the long and bitter Senate debate an inflexible stubbornness was exhibited, first by Woodrow Wilson and also, toward the end, by Senator Lodge, then chairman of the Foreign Relations Committee and leader of the opposition. He thus became listed in the group of "Irreconcilables"—many of them for different reasons—which included Senator Reed of Missouri, Hiram Johnson, the redoubtable Borah, and Senator Knox, who felt so deeply that the treaty and the League provisions contained portions which were so bad that the whole might better be abandoned.

I paid Knox a visit after he had spent days in his own back room studying the Versailles Treaty and had come out with a great blast against it. I had respect for Knox's judgment and regarded him as a very great lawyer. I had followed his speeches and knew his general attitude toward the treaty. He was a 100 per cent American. He approached everything as a lawyer representing his country, and his first question was always how a given proposal would affect the interests of his client, the United States of America. He had been Attorney General of the United States, and the government had actually been his principal client for a long time. When I learned that he was opposed to the ratification of the treaty, with or without reservations, I was deeply concerned.

I told him I knew he was against the treaty but that I thought we had enough votes to pass it with reservations; that we would get a large majority of Republicans; that I thought that the Democrats who wanted international co-operation would vote for ratification with the amendments suggested by Elihu Root. But I said to him that, as firmly as I believed in the objective, I would be greatly concerned if he were to say to me that ratification of the treaty with these amendments would bring really serious harm.

His answer was immediate: "I cannot say to you that the ratification of this treaty with the reservations will mean quick and immediate harm to the Republic. I do say that this treaty with Germany as proposed, and the League, and even the reservations, will not prevent this.

"Young man," he said, "I will not be here. You will be here and I say to you that in twenty years, as certainly as we are in this room, there will be another war compared to which this war we have just been through will be like a Sunday-school picnic."

When I asked, "Upon what do you base so exact a conclusion?" he replied, "Because this treaty is so unilateral. Germany cannot carry it out. You cannot enslave a sovereign people."

"Well," I asked, "Senator, why do you not say that to the public?"

"Because no one would believe it," he answered.

Four days after the President's initial declaration concerning the importance of the League, Senator Knox asked the postponement of any action. This followed an earlier resolution he had introduced to the effect "that any project for any general League of Nations should be postponed for separate consideration, not alone by the victorious belligerents, but by all the nations."

The Pennsylvania senator thus was in favor of a "cooling-off" period, following the close of hostilities, along the lines so frequently discussed after the late war. He may even have been responsible for the introduction of that now classic phrase into our modern diplomatic vocabulary.

The Republican disinclination to accept any League without first subjecting it to careful scrutiny had been discussed at earlier conferences among party chiefs. It has been reported that as early as October 13 I "inspired" Theodore Roosevelt to issue an attack upon Wilson and his leadership. In answer to this I can only say that T.R. made many such attacks. He required no stimulant.

It is a matter of record that Roosevelt and Lodge held conferences in New York early in December, when they agreed that if the President obtained a League along the lines explained to the nation throughout the war years, it should be attacked by reservations.

One month later, on January 6, 1919, the great voice of Theodore Roosevelt was stilled forever. His last written word, found on his bedside table after death—a memo concerning myself as national chairman—showed that in his final hours he was still thinking of the future of the Republican party. The note, scribbled in pencil on a small pad, read:

Hays—see him; he must go to Washington for 10 days; see Senate and House; prevent split on domestic policies.

Roosevelt's insistence that harmony prevail on domestic issues then before Congress undoubtedly was based on his conviction that a struggle on the subject of foreign policy was inevitable. He doubtless felt that Republican interests might be better served if political differences were taken up one at a time.

Even then the signs indicated the full return of the Republicans to power in 1920. They had brilliant leadership inside and outside Congress. Their two ex-presidents, Roosevelt and Taft, had kept in full stride with the times. Despite the fact that the military victory had taken place during the regime of the Democrats, the public in general considered that the nation was due for a change. The fact that the war had ended and that the paramount interest of the hour was the manner of American participation in world peace perhaps made it easier for party lines to be drawn.

Undoubtedly the strongest and most dramatic personality of the Republican party, or of his generation, was Theodore Roosevelt. Had he lived, in all probability he would have been the candidate at the convention of 1920, and in that event Mr. Wilson, the twenty-eighth President of the United States, would have been followed by the twenty-sixth in the presidential line.

Theodore Roosevelt was in essence a truly great man, with the natural defects common to greatness. He became deeply embittered over Wilson's refusal to assign him to active military service in France. The argument that an ex-president of the Republic as a line officer might attract too much attention meant nothing to him. He had no desire whatever to make personal political capital out of the war. His one desire was to fight again for his country and to give his life if necessary. He never got over the disappointment when his offer to raise a division was turned down, and he never forgave Woodrow Wilson. As a matter of fact, his judgment may at times have been blurred, so acute became his dislike of the then occupant of the White House.

The final note by Colonel Roosevelt—his instructions concerning me —may indeed have been written primarily with the idea of bolstering Republican strength against the peace treaty, then in process of manufacture, and especially against the Covenant of the League, which was the all-in-all to Wilson. However, domestic issues were then having their day in Congress, and public feeling was aroused. Great care was necessary to preserve the national harmony until the even more important questions of foreign policy were made clear.

Roosevelt did not actually condemn the League, but he did not expect too much of it. Only a few days before his death he wrote an editorial for the Kansas City *Star*, which was published on January 13. One sentence reads: "For the moment the point as to which we are foggy is the League of Nations." Referring to a definition of the League purposes as outlined by ex-President Taft, the colonel said:

This enables us to say that we heartily agree in principle with this theory, and can without doubt come to an agreement on details.

But his practical viewpoint showed clearly in the words:

We all of us earnestly desire such a League, only we wish to be sure that it will help and not hinder the cause of world peace and justice.

This certainly was far better treatment of the League idea than that which came the following day from Senator Borah, who utterly condemned it by saying: "We have come in contact with two evil forces from the Old World—Prussianism and Internationalism."

In an address delivered at City Hall, New York, September 6, 1918, at the anniversary exercises of the birth of Lafayette and the Battle of the Marne, Roosevelt's opinion upon internationalism, as then expressed, was so clear that it bears repeating today. He said:

"It is sometimes announced that part of the peace agreement must be a League of Nations which will avert all wars for the future and will put a stop to the need of this nation preparing its own strength for its own defense. Many of the adherents of this idea grandiloquently assert that they intend to supplant nationalism by internationalism.

"In deciding upon proposals of this nature it behooves our people to remember that competitive rhetoric is a poor substitute for the habit of resolutely looking facts in the face. Patriotism stands in national matters as love of family does in private life. Nationalism corresponds to the love a man bears for his wife and children. Internationalism corresponds to the feeling he has for his neighbors generally. The sound nationalist is the only type of really helpful internationalist, precisely as in private relations it is the man who is most devoted to his own wife and children who is apt in the long run to be the most satisfactory neighbor.

"To substitute internationalism for nationalism means to do away with patriotism, and is as vicious and as profoundly demoralizing as to put promiscuous devotion to all other persons in the place of a steadfast devotion to a man's own family. Either effort means the atrophy of robust morality. The man who loves other countries as much as his own stands on a level with the man who loves other women as much as he loves his own wife. One is as worthless a creature as the other. The professional pacifist and the professional internationalist are equally undesirable citizens. The American pacifist has in the actual fact shown himself to be the tool and ally of the German militarist. The professional internationalist is a man who under pretense of diffuse attachment for everybody hides the fact that in reality he is incapable of doing his duty by anybody.

"We Americans should abhor all wrongdoing to other nations. We ought always to act fairly and generously by other nations, but we must remember that our first duty is to be loyal and patriotic citizens of our own nation, of America. These two facts should always be in our minds in dealing with any proposal for a League of Nations. By all means let us be loyal to great ideals. But let us remember that unless we show common sense in action, loyalty in speech will amount to considerably less than nothing."

Roosevelt forecast that the League "will prove entirely unworkable if the effort is made to unload upon it, in the name of internationalism, duties which in the present state of the world will be efficiently performed by the free nations only if they perform them as national duties." In the September 6 address he counseled:

"Test the proposed future League of Nations so far as concerns proposals to disarm, and to trust to anything except our own strength for our defense, *by what the nations are actually doing* at the present time. . . . During the last year Russia, under the dominion of the Bolshevists, has betrayed her allies."

And this was spoken in 1918!

On February 15, 1919, Wilson sailed back to America, triumphant and confident, with the League Covenant in his pocket, to confront his opponents in the Senate.

The Republican attack had already begun. The leaders, in addition to Senators Knox, Lodge, and Borah, were Senators Poindexter, Reed, Brandegee, and Cummins. The only Republican who then vocally defended the League was Senator McCumber of North Dakota. (The arguments ran all the way from the Monroe Doctrine to a comparison of civil-service employees in Constantinople and Washington.) Before leaving France, Wilson had extended a dinner invitation to the members of the Senate Foreign Relations Committee and the House Foreign Affairs Committee, requesting "that I be permitted to go over with you, article by article, the Constitution reported, before this part of the work is made the subject of debate in Congress."

Thus the Senate was prevented from talking. But meanwhile Wilson planned to return by way of Boston and to speak there on foreign policy. This plan was originally proposed by Secretary of War Baker, to demonstrate to Senator Lodge that Massachusetts opinion was strongly behind the League. Baker later changed his mind on the wisdom of the Boston speech and cabled Wilson that he should dock at New York and leave at once for Washington, "where your first public utterance should be to Congress." This advice, as in other important situations, was disregarded.

The President's request for senatorial silence at once aroused the resentment of his congressional opponents. Senators Borah and Fall declined Wilson's invitation to the White House dinner. Senator Lodge, while accepting, was furious at Wilson. He wrote to Henry White, saying:

As a gentleman and a man of honor, I have accepted the President's invitation here, and therefore complied with the President's request not to discuss the treaty. The President, however, does not seem to look at it in the same way, and is going to land in Boston, my home city, and address a great mass-meeting which is all arranged for while I am reduced to silence because I wish to observe what I think is required of an honorable man.

The White House dinner failed to check the widening personal breach between the President and the Republican leaders. Senator Lodge wrote of the occasion: "He was not able to answer questions. . . .

The President's performance under Brandegee's very keen and able cross-examination was anything but good. . . . We went away as wise as we came."

In the Senate, bitterness over President Wilson's personal participation in the Paris conference went so far as to bring forth a resolution by Senator Sherman which, in effect, would have made Wilson ineligible to retain the presidency. It was based on the clause in the Constitution providing for the inability of the President to discharge the duties of his office. Senator Sherman argued that with Villa on the rampage in Mexico and the Industrial Workers of the World fomenting disorders in the West, the duty of the President was to remain at home to give Congress information on the state of the Union.

On the fourth of March the President sent a cablegram to Colonel House in Paris, of which the following is a paraphrase:

YOUR PLAN ABOUT THE LEAGUE OF NATIONS FUNCTIONING AT ONCE DISTURBS ME A LITTLE BECAUSE I FEAR THAT SOME ADVANTAGE WOULD BE GIVEN TO THE CRITICS ON THIS SIDE OF THE WATER IF THEY THOUGHT WE WERE TRYING IN THAT WAY TO FORESTALL ACTION BY THE SENATE AND COMMIT THE COUNTRY IN SOME PRACTICAL WAY FROM WHICH IT WOULD BE IMPOSSIBLE TO WITHDRAW.

On this same date a round robin, signed two days earlier by Henry Cabot Lodge and thirty-seven other senators, was presented to the Senate, recommending the rejection of the League of Nations. On that day Senator Lodge became chairman of the Foreign Relations Committee and Congress adjourned. That night President Wilson spoke in the Metropolitan Opera House in New York and for the first time received the open support of ex-President Taft for the League Covenant.

But it was already evident that the chance of fully imposing the American point of view, even at Paris, had passed. On March 3, Colonel House wrote in his diary:

It is now evident that the peace will not be such a peace as I had hoped, or one which this terrible upheaval should have brought about. There are many reasons why it will not be one. . . .

The American delegation are not in a position to act freely. The elections of last November in the United States have been a deterrent to free action by our delegates. The British elections and the vote of confidence Clemenceau received in the French Chamber of Deputies, put the finishing touches to a situation already bad. If the President should exert his influence among the liberals and laboring classes, he might possibly overthrow the Governments in Great Britain, France and Italy; but if he did, he would still have to reckon with our own people and he might bring the whole world into chaos. The overthrow of governments might not end there, and it would be a grave responsibility for any man to take at this time.

I dislike to have forced upon us such a peace as we are facing. We will get something out of it in the way of a League of Nations, but even that is an imperfect instrument. . . .

On March 14, President Wilson landed again at Brest. Meanwhile Colonel House, during the President's absence, had laid himself open to criticism by accepting what appeared to be a compromise. Ray Stannard Baker, who made the return trip with Mr. Wilson, said: "The colonel would make peace quickly by giving the greedy ones all they want."

A comparison of the French demands with the suggested compromise, however, does not bear out this remark.

Henry Wickham Steed, editor of the *London Times,* declared:

No man at the Peace Conference was more opposed than Colonel House to the idea of giving the greedy ones all they wanted.

But no man knew better that mere obstinacy in defending abstract ideas without considering where compromise was practically expedient and harmless could only end by bringing Wilson into collision with facts and by discrediting him while spoiling the peace.

Another argument for compromise lay in the fact that President Wilson's position was far weaker in March than it had been in January. His visit to the United States had revealed the strength of the senatorial opposition. The Republicans in Congress, already antagonized by the personnel of the Peace Commission, were now making a constitutional issue of what they termed the President's disregard of senatorial prerogative. He had failed to placate the Senate Foreign Relations Committee, and public opinion manifestly was becoming more divided on the League of Nations. It was already clear that the President could not carry the Covenant through the Senate without clarification and amendment.

Thus Wilson returned to Paris in the position of being compelled to ask of the Peace Conference the favor of inserting into the Covenant clauses of peculiar interest to the United States.

House met the President at Brest and returned with him to Paris aboard a special train. Of this he says in his diary:

I had ample opportunity to go over the entire situation with the President and to get his story of his trip to the United States. He said "My dinner to the Senate Foreign Relations Committee was a failure so far as getting together was concerned." He spoke with considerable bitterness of the manner in which he was treated by some of the Senators. . . . However, I said to the President that the dinner was a success from my viewpoint, which was that it checked criticism as to his supposed dictatorship and refusal to consult the Senate about foreign affairs. He admitted this. I said that it also had a good effect upon the people, even if it had failed to mollify the Senators themselves.

The President comes back very militant and determined to put the League of Nations into the Peace Treaty.

However, it was not clear that the revision of the Covenant, largely designed to meet the objections of the United States Senate, could never be carried through, nor the amended Covenant passed, without the hearty support of the other principal Powers. Signor Orlando stood firmly behind Wilson upon every occasion. Lord Robert Cecil brought his personal influence and his debating power to aid in the passing of the Monroe Doctrine amendment. The Japanese yielded their own special amendment at the same time they supported that of Wilson. The objections of the French delegates, which might have spelled ruin for the American program, were finally swept aside by the French Prime Minister himself. But it would have been surprising, indeed, if after accepting the special American demands on the League of Nations the other principal Powers had not expected, and finally exacted, concessions that touched their own special interests.

In a speech on May 31, 1919, induced by the demurring of Serbia and Romania to certain features of the League Covenant, Wilson made this statement:

"If the world should be troubled again, if the conditions which we all regard as fundamental are challenged, the guaranties which will be given to you will pledge that the United States will send its army and fleet across the ocean."

But three months later, when the President left the White House to take his campaign for the League to the people, in his opening speech at Columbus, Ohio, on September 4 he said: "When this treaty is accepted, men in khaki will not have to cross the seas again."

On June 29, the day following the signing of the Versailles Treaty, President Wilson embarked upon the *George Washington* at Brest. His nerves were worn and his physique shaken, but his spirits were high. If he guessed anything of the struggle that lay before him in the United States, he concealed his suspicion and apparently could not foresee the tragedy of disappointment. The feeling of those who accompanied him on the boat was that the Senate must and would ratify the treaty; that the country would enter enthusiastically upon the venture of the League of Nations. That was what they wished.

The public overseas also still appeared to believe that Wilson could carry out his promises, even after the failure to live up to the Fourteen Points, which had been accepted by Germany as a contract. But four months earlier, thirty-eight senators had signed the round robin declaring against the League—the beginning of the organized fight that defeated the treaty. Elihu Root had also come forth with his firm stand, not against the League, but for it only with sound reservations. Therefore, in presuming that he still could make everything work by setting up the League of Nations as drafted, Woodrow Wilson was compromising with his own intelligence. On the same day that the treaty was signed, Colonel House wrote in his diary:

> My last conversation with the President yesterday was not reassuring. I urged him to meet the Senate in a conciliatory spirit; if he treated them with the same consideration he had used with his foreign colleagues here, all would be well.

The Peace Conference had opened informally in Paris on January 12, 1919. Peace was signed at Versailles on June 28 by the treaty plenipotentiaries of Germany and the Allied Powers. President Wilson presented the treaty to the Senate in July and in the same month it was ratified by the National Assembly of Germany.

By the end of October it was ratified by the governments of Great Britain, Italy, France, and Japan. It was defeated in the United States Senate on November 19.

There lies a vital phase of our story.

CHAPTER 15

Elihu Root Interprets the League

TODAY the whole world-wide question of internation co-operation for keeping the peace is such a burning issue that any light which can be thrown upon it by earlier attempts might be welcome. Since many of the League of Nations problems were similar to those of today's U.N.—including the leading role of our own nation—it has seemed to me that Elihu Root's study of that earlier plan might have bearing today. It is closely related to this autobiographical story because it was an integral part of the Republican party's campaign activity, and of what we considered our obligation to the public.

Throughout the treaty-making at Versailles, the great majority of Americans were much of one mind regarding the necessity of a peace treaty, with or without reservations already under consideration by the Senate leaders, as the day-by-day events at Versailles were reported by the press correspondents.

On July 10, when Wilson presented the results of Versailles to the Senate, the ordinary man probably considered the differences between the treaty and the reservations relatively small. His understanding of the subject, however, needed considerable clarification. In order to remedy this, and long before the treaty came into being, we made an endeavor to get before the public the best possible interpretation of the initial draft of the Covenant of the League of Nations. This was part of the Republican plan to keep the peacemaking as far as possible out of politics. The plan to capitalize Mr. Root's judgment was originated by Henry L. Stimson and myself.

On March 18, 1919, Mr. Stimson called on me while on the way to keep an appointment with his uncle, Elihu Root, in whose firm he had learned the practice of law. He told me that he thought the time had come for Mr. Root to get into action concerning the treaty. I had just returned from a trip throughout the West, sounding out public opinion, which I believed had reached the point of accepting some league, but not this League.

Meanwhile Senator Lodge and Root had exchanged letters on the general theme of the Versailles conference. The senator's letter indicated grave danger of entangling this nation in an agreement which it would not live up to when it came to the test, "and that would wreck any League." Lodge wanted a long talk with Root and hoped he would analyze the problem "as you alone can, and show the public what ought to be done to accomplish as much as can practically be accomplished by a union of the nations to promote general peace and disarmament." This quotation alone indicates that the Massachusetts senator always believed that a league of the right kind was a paramount necessity. It nullifies the repeated charge that his personal antagonism to Wilson completely warped his thinking upon this issue.

Henry Cabot Lodge of Massachusetts fully lived up to the proud tradition of his heritage. In matters concerning the Senate Foreign Relations Committee, of which he was chairman, he was justifiably sensitive about having anyone consulted over his head. But he could not resent consultations with Elihu Root, because Root was too big a man. His attitude was acknowledgment that Root was the man able to express the wisest viewpoint on the League problem.

When Mr. Stimson called on me, I urged the use of his persuasive powers on his uncle, Mr. Root. He did so on that same day, and at length. Mr. Root told him that he wanted the President to bring back a good league, but did not want the nation to accept a league that was not good enough. Stimson suggested that Root cable Colonel House or Henry White, setting forth his views.

The next day, when Mr. Stimson and I called together on Mr. Root, I insisted that he was the one man who could speak with full warranty on the needed amendments. He was our choice for the task, and it was indeed a task. Undoubtedly his was the greatest legal mind in America. He was co-author of the Hague Covenant and one of the outstanding international jurists of the age. As a public servant he had been United States senator from New York, Secretary of War, and Secretary of State in the Cabinet of President Theodore Roosevelt. At this meeting I promised that his views would reach ten million readers of five thousand newspapers and that copies would be mailed personally to a million individuals.

Mr. Root immediately said that if we thought he could help he would do so. It was agreed that I should write a formal letter requesting this exposition of his views, and I did so.

Mr. Root's reply was dated March 29, only five days later; but eight days elapsed before it was made public. Meanwhile it was studied and discussed in detail by myself and the author and finally was cabled *in extenso* to Henry White at Paris, to receive his approval as a member of the American peace delegation. It was in the form of a letter addressed to me as national chairman; actually it was a legal brief of about seven thousand words with an addendum covering six suggested amendments.

Mr. Root went carefully over every phase of the Covenant, citing the important changes he considered necessary, and insisting that under our Constitution a discussion in the Senate was a national duty. It remains to this day one of the great American documents in the science of law, and yet was written in a manner that anyone could understand.

In considering the matter of changes, Mr. Root first cited that Mr. Taft, who had joined the President in general advocacy of the treaty, had declared that it ought to be amended, in terms almost as strong as former Secretary of State Knox, and was thereby in full accord with himself. He mentioned the fact that Senator Lodge and President Lowell of Harvard, in a great debate at Boston, had both said the agreement needed amending. He further quoted Lord Robert Cecil to the same effect:

We now present to the Conference and to the world the result of our work. We do not present it as something that is final, but only as the result of an honest effort to be discussed and examined, not only by this Conference but by the public opinion of the world.

Mr. Root next showed why the Senate should consider the proposed Covenant. Treaties were ordinarily negotiated by ambassadors, ministers, or delegates, whose work could be supervised and corrected by the President and Secretary of State, who were able, from their different viewpoints, to see things the actual negotiators overlooked. In this case, since the President himself was negotiating the treaty in Paris, no one remained in Washington to supervise the negotiations; no one had authority to give the negotiators the benefit of independent official judgment unless the Senate performed that function.

For more than half a century the American government had been urging upon the world the arbitration of all questions upon which controversies between nations depend. Presidents Grant, Arthur, Harrison, Cleveland, McKinley, Roosevelt, and Taft in their messages to Congress had strongly approved the establishment of a recognized system of arbitration. Nations had begun to make treaties of arbitration, of which hundreds were already in force. The United States made some thirty treaties with most of the principal countries in the world, agreeing absolutely to arbitrate questions arising under international law. Strong opinion had developed in favor of establishing an international court of full-time judges.

Mr. Root pointed out that, after the Great War began, the American "League to Enforce Peace," at the head of which were Mr. Taft and Dr. Lowell, made the first plank in its platform that "all justiciable questions arising between the signatory powers not settled by negotiations shall—subject to the limitation of treaties—be submitted to a judicial tribunal for hearing and judgment."

The other class of disputes which give rise to war consists of clashes between conflicting national policies as distinguished from claims of legal right. They do not depend upon law or treaty, but upon one nation or ruler undertaking to do something that another wishes to prevent. Such questions are a part of international politics. They are similar to the questions of which our courts say: "This is a political question, not a judicial question, and we have no concern with it." The question whether Russia should help Serbia when Austria invaded Serbia in July 1914 is an illustration. Our own Monroe Doctrine is another; that is not an assertion of any legal right, but a declaration that certain acts will be regarded as dangerous to the peace and safety of the United States, and therefore unfriendly.

Such questions were continually arising in Europe. The way European nations had been in the habit of dealing with them was to bring about a conference of the nations involved, to find some way of reconciling their differences or of convincing the parties to the dispute that it would not be safe for them to break the peace.

In 1905, when the German Emperor's challenge to the French policy on Morocco had made war seem probable, the Algeciras Conference, brought about chiefly by the influence of President Theodore Roosevelt, resulted in preventing war. Similarly, in the last week of July 1914, Sir Edward Grey tried to bring about a conference for the purpose of averting the World War, but Germany refused to attend. She refused because she meant to bring on a war and knew that if she attended a conference this would become practically impossible.

The weak point about this practice of international conferences was that they had been left solely to the initiative of the individual nations; nobody had a right to call them and nobody was bound to attend.

The essential thing about the League of Nations plan was that it made an international conference on political questions compulsory in times of danger and practically impossible for any nation to avoid.

After this summing up, which consisted of about half his letter to me, the jurist went on to what he considered defects in the tentative plan.

He suggested that the Covenant give effectiveness to the judicial settlement of international disputes upon questions of right, by making the *arbitration compulsory* under the system established by the Hague Conference or before the proposed Court of Arbitral Justice. He wanted the term "justiciable questions" to be carefully defined so as to exclude all questions of policy. He argued that if that were done all references to arbitration in the document would have force and effect instead of being mere idle form.

His second suggested change in the Covenant provided for a general conference, followed by regular conferences at stated intervals, to agree upon and state in authentic form the rules of *international law,* so that the development of law might continue.

In his addenda Mr. Root included the drafts of two suggested amendments designed to accomplish these changes.

He said further that there never had been a time when the wisdom of the Monroe Doctrine for the preservation of peace and safety of the United States was more evident. Mr. Root noted that certain facile writers had pronounced the Doctrine obsolete and useless, but he knew of no experienced and responsible American statesman who had ever taken that view.

He declared along the same lines with regard to *immigration and emigration.* The nations of Europe are nations from which emigrants go. The United States is a nation to which immigrants come. Europe and America are bound to look at questions of immigration and emigration under the influence of different interests, friendly but opposing. Therefore, he believed that all these purely American questions should be excepted from the jurisdiction of the League's Executive Council.

Next Mr. Root took up the all-important Article X of the Covenant, declared by President Wilson to be the heart thereof, which contained the undertaking "To respect and preserve as against external aggression the territorial integrity and existing political independence of all members of the League." Considering this article as part of a perpetual league for the preservation of peace, Mr. Root's first impression was that it should be stricken out entirely. If perpetual, it would attempt to preserve unchanged for all time the distribution of power and territory made in accordance with the views and exigencies of the Allies at that particular juncture. Change and growth being the law of life, no generation can impose its will in regard to the growth of nations and the distribution of power upon succeeding generations.

Mr. Root's final opinion, however, was that Article X must be considered with reference to the particular situation then existing in Europe. The Allied nations in their Council must determine the lines of reconstruction. Their determinations must be enforced. Doubtless they would make mistakes, but there must be decisions. Under these conditions, the United States could not quit. It must go on to the performance of its duty, and the immediate aspect of Article X was an agreement to do that. Therefore, Mr. Root asked that the article be amended so that it should hold for a limited time and thereafter any member might withdraw from it.

The limitation of armaments was the next matter taken up. The Covenant provided that national armaments be reduced to the lowest point consistent with national safety and that the Executive Council formulate plans for a general agreement as to the amount of these reductions. It also provided for a permanent commission to advise the League on the execution of these provisions; otherwise one nation, suspecting another of secret preparations, would prepare to protect itself in the same way, so that the whole scheme of limitation would be destroyed. The only way to prevent that sort of thing was by giving the permanent commission the power of inspection and verification. Mr. Root argued that every country should assent to this, just as every trustee and treasurer is willing to have an audit of his accounts; and he annexed such an amendment.

Mr. Root concluded his brief by a declaration that the entire instrument known as the Covenant of the League was not conclusive or final. It necessarily left much to be determined later. These uncertainties, he said, were not matters for criticism but of necessity arising from the situation.

What to him seemed more important was the fact that no one knew when or upon what terms the Central and Eastern Powers were to be admitted to League membership. Therefore, the whole agreement was tentative. It could not really be a league of peace for a number of years to come. Rather, it could temporarily be only an alliance of approximately half the active world against or for the control of the other half. This is significant in reference to post-World War II conditions. Under these circumstances, it would be unwise to give finality to the agreement and make the specific obligations of its members irrevocable. Provision should be made for its revision in a calmer atmosphere, when the world was less subject to exciting and disturbing causes.

The last amendment submitted by Mr. Root was to the effect that the Executive Council call a general conference of League members not less than five nor more than ten years after the signing of the Covenant, for the *revision* thereof; at that time or at any time thereafter, on one year's notice, any member might withdraw.

The last paragraph was inserted in response to a suggestion made by me. It read:

If the amendments which I have suggested are made, I think it be the clear duty of the United States to enter the agreement. In that case it would be the duty of Congress to establish by law the offices of representatives of the United States in the body of Delegates and the Executive Council, just as the offices of Ambassadors and Ministers are already provided by law, and the new offices would be filled by appointments of the President, with the advice and consent of the Senate, under Article II, section 2, of the Constitution of the United States.

As "the titular head of the party organization," I did not participate directly in a struggle that was solely the job of the United States Senate. But it was my duty to assemble available facts in order that the general public, with complete understanding, might be able to give expression to its feelings in a way that the Upper House of Congress would plainly understand.

The fact that Elihu Root was a Republican and had held high office in Republican administrations was not the point. His response to my appeal was an act of patriotism, not a manifestation of political party interests. Not a single word written or uttered by Mr. Root on this subject was political, either in tone or intent.

George Harvey, later to become our Ambassador at the Court of St. James's, but then editor of *Harvey's Weekly* and one of the most violent of Wilson's opponents, was enthusiastic over the Root letter. He told Stimson that it would unite both wings of the party, the radicals and conservatives. The letter was generally regarded as the finest example of Mr. Root's power in the clear and concise expression of logically developed thought. It was a pity that his reasons and arguments were not fully available in Paris, along with the text of his amendments. For example, the comments by Joseph Tumulty, Wilson's secretary, showed that he analyzed them by themselves, without their accompanying exposition, and that he failed to appreciate the purpose of many of them.

Naturally I was delighted with the letter and the way it was received. It was having just the effect we had hoped for. President Lowell of Harvard, then a pro-League leader of the Taft school of thought, considered it admirable. In a letter to Mr. Root he expressed some criticism of both Wilson's egotism and the Senate's behavior. Root replied that "in judging my old comrades of the Senate, do not forget that they really had no time to consider the subject in the closing days of the short session, and they were boiling over with a perfectly natural rage because of Wilson's refusal to consult them and his practical denial of their right to discuss the subject at all. The offensively arrogant way in which the subject was presented here produced a very disagreeable effect upon me and it took considerable time for me to get into the right frame of mind for a dispassionate consideration of the League document."

One point omitted from the Root letter was privately expounded by the author to both Mr. Stimson and myself. This was his belief that the ostensible object of procedure in the League Council was "bunk" and "camouflage" because of the requirement for "unanimous decision" —a converse form of expression of the "veto" power in the United Nations of today, identical in meaning and equally dangerous. Mr. Root argued that any important nations could buy sufficient votes from the small states to prevent a unanimous vote and that therefore none of the great things put up to the Council would be well accomplished. But he was in favor of the Council, believing that its very existence, together with its regular procedure in calling conferences, might prove more and more important and that it might finally become some sort of safeguard of peace.

While the Root proposals, as well as those presented by Taft and Charles Evans Hughes, received some consideration and partial adoption by the conference of Versailles, they evoked no great enthusiasm, largely because of the attitude taken by our own peace delegation.

Almost three months after Mr. Root replied to my letter—June 19, 1919—he wrote to Senator Lodge. The big issues remained, and Root had bent his efforts toward finding a solution. This second important contribution to the public record, at once given to the press, was, like his letter to me, designed to do two things: to set forth a sound, constructive policy on the merits of the League issue, and to present that policy in such a way as to unite the two wings of the Republican party. By now Mr. Root had had time for reflection concerning the performance rendered by the peacemakers at Versailles, and his views were slightly modified. The letter was prepared at the request of Senator Lodge, who specifically asked an opinion as to the amendments proposed in the March letter addressed to me.

Mr. Root, in his reply, referred approvingly to my earlier invitation, and his letter to me remained the basis and substance of his further judgment. The jurist then declared that the various amendments that were subsequently incorporated in the Covenant by the members of the conference, while dealing to some extent with the subjects of his own proposed amendments, were very inadequate and unsatisfactory.

He also stated definitely that he preferred to see the peace terms and the League of Nations separate, as had been proposed in a resolution offered by Senator Knox, so that the Covenant could be considered by the people of the country without coercion from the necessities of a speedy peace.

It was pointed out clearly that nothing had been done to provide for the re-establishment and strengthening of a system of arbitration or judicial decision upon questions of legal right; that nothing had been done toward providing for the revision or development of international law. In these respects the principles maintained by the United States without variation for half a century were still ignored, and we were left with a program in which the hope of the world for future peace rested on a government of men, not of laws, following the dictates of expediency and not of right.

Nothing had been done to limit the vast and incalculable obligation which Article X of the Covenant undertook to impose upon each member of the League to preserve against aggression the territorial integrity and political independence of all members of the League all over the world.

The clause which had been inserted regarding the Monroe Doctrine was erroneous in its description of the Doctrine and ambiguous in meaning. Other purely American questions, as, for example, those relating to immigration, were protected only by a clause apparently empowering the Council to determine whether such questions were solely within the domestic jurisdiction of the United States.

On the other hand, Mr. Root thought that the Covenant still contained a great deal of high value which the world ought not to lose. The arrangement to make conferences of the Powers automatic where there was danger of war; provisions for joint action; the agreement for delay in case of serious disputes, with opportunity to bring the public opinion of the world to bear on the disputes and to induce cool and deliberate judgment; the recognition of racial and popular rights to the freedom of local self-government; and the plan, indispensable in some form, for setting up governments in the vast regions deprived by the war of the autocratic rule which had maintained order—all these ought not to be lost. European conditions required prompt action. Industry had not revived. The revival required raw materials. Credit was necessary. For this there had to be security for the fruits of enterprise, and for this there had to be peace.

Satan meanwhile was finding evil work for idle hands to do in Europe, evil work that affected the whole world, including the United States.

Under these circumstances, what ought to have been done? Mr. Root was clear on the point that, if the Covenant had to be considered with the peace terms included, the Senate should include in its resolution of consent to the ratification an expression of such reservations and understandings as would cure the defects which he had pointed out. He did not believe that anything could be done then about the system of arbitration and the development of international law.

He then suggested to Senator Lodge to put into the resolution of consent a reservation refusing to agree to Article X.

The jurist was very definite in his personal opinion as apart from the legal aspect on the much-debated Article X. He declared himself, in part, as follows:

. . . If it is necessary for the security of Western Europe that we agree to go to the support of, say, France if attacked, let us do that particular thing plainly, so every man and woman will understand the honorable obligation we are assuming. I am in favor of that. But let us not wrap such a purpose in a vague universal obligation under the impression that it really does not mean that anything is likely to happen.

Article X confronts us with consequences very similar to those which Washington had in mind when he advised us to keep out of the quarrels of Europe. By following this policy, the United States attained the position of disinterestedness which enables her to promote peace mightily. She is free from suspicion; she is not an object of distrust; her friendship is valued; her word is potent. We can be of more value to the peace of the world by keeping out of the petty quarrels that arise than by binding ourselves to take part in them. Just so far as it is necessary to modify this settled historic American policy in order to put into effect a practical plan for a League of Nations to preserve peace we ought to go and we ought not to go one step farther. If the step proposed by Article X is not necessary for such a plan then we ought not to take it.

In the same manner that the exchange of letters between Mr. Root and myself was made known, this letter from Root to Lodge was given general publicity. I had it printed in pamphlet form and gave it wide circulation. It had no stamp of political party headquarters. It was distributed with no other thought than as a public service to all the voters of America.

Early in July, I sent to Mr. Root a canvass of the Senate, made by Lodge, which indicated that all the forty-nine Republican senators would line up in favor of his last two reservations dealing with withdrawal, the Monroe Doctrine, and domestic questions. In spite of the optimistic nature of Lodge's report on the effect of Mr. Root's letter, the matter was by no means settled. Taft still was opposing any reservations, and my own position probably was interpreted by the public as "sitting on the fence," for I was trying to draw all elements of the party together. Various individual senators kept finding new difficulties and proposing new amendments. By the seventeenth of July I was able to inform Mr. Root confidentially that Taft had come around to the idea of reservations and had proposed the text of five.

CHAPTER 16

Final Rounds of the Treaty Fight

IN the Senate discussion of July 17, 1919, LeBaron Colt, Republican of Rhode Island, presented the League case clearly and concisely. He also alluded to public opinion at this time being critical of the President's methods at the Versailles conference.

Senator Colt felt that America could not divorce the League from the peace treaty and he called on members of the Senate to consider dispassionately the entire subject of American participation. He said, in part:

"Many believe that the President should have remained at home and should have consulted the Senate, and also should have ascertained the public sentiment before negotiating a treaty which, to their minds, is subversive of our traditional policy and binds America to a new world order.

"But not to try the experiment of a family of nations would leave the world in the same condition of international anarchy as it was before this war—a world divided into jealous and competing national units. . . ."

In the Senate debate on the League on July 21, 1919, Senator Pomerene, Democrat of Ohio, made an important speech in which he piously expressed the hope that the discussion be conducted along nonpartisan lines. While he repeatedly insisted that the preservation of world peace was so all-important that it must not become a party issue, he managed to make his discourse highly partisan.

He referred to the letter which I had written to Elihu Root on March 24, 1919, asking his views on the League. He also took exception to the manner in which I had signed the letter. Apparently it would have been agreeable to Pomerene if I had signed merely "Will Hays," or "Will Hays, American." But the letter had been signed "Will Hays, Chairman," and he declared that this meant "Chairman of the Republican National Committee." Senator Pomerene took further exception to the fact that Mr. Root had not addressed his reply to "Will Hays, American Citizen," but to "Hon. Will H. Hays, Chairman, Republican National Committee."

The senator also brought into his attack the press announcements that, as chairman of the Republican National Committee, I would come to Washington to confer with the Republican senatorial group as to what their attitude should be with respect to the League of Nations, to harmonize their differences and adopt plans. Apparently he thought it unusual that a party chairman should confer with the members of his party in his official capacity. This, again, was presented by Senator Pomerene in the form of a question as to whether my efforts were being made in the interest of an American peace or of a Republican program. The entire speech of the Ohio senator filled many pages of the *Congressional Record.*

However, Senator Pomerene reached the height of his argument that the debate be conducted along non-partisan lines when he complained bitterly that, as chairman, on March 22, 1919, I had issued a circular letter calling attention to the fact that I wanted as many speeches made as possible in the following eighteen months, and stated that while these speeches would not be under "direct Republican auspices" I had urged the speakers to use Republican material wherever consistent with proprieties.

Throughout his speech it was evident that the Ohio senator had not taken into account that the feeling within the Republican party was widespread and that the defeat of the Democratic party in the election the following year already was indicated. Nevertheless, Mr. Pomerene concluded his remarks with the unctuous admonition, "We entered this war to fight together, win together and, in my humble judgment, to keep the peace together."

In the second speech made by Senator Pomerene on that day, after attacks on Senators Knox and Lodge, he said that Article X should be amended so that it should hold "a limited time and that thereafter any member may withdraw from it." This was the exact language previously used by Mr. Root.

A little later on, Senator Pat Harrison declared that he had read with approval and appreciation the utterances of ex-President Taft, Mr. Wickersham, and "a host of other loyal and patriotic American leaders, including Representative Mann, the Republican leader in the House." He wound up his share in the debate by again referring to the position taken by myself, saying:

"Mr. Hays came down here the other day. He finally talked to the senators of the opposition and gave out an interview. In it he set forth your party's position but he does not agree with the distinguished senators from Idaho and Washington that the Republican party should come out against any League of Nations. But on the contrary he is in favor of the League with certain reservations. He says, 'These reservations must safeguard the sovereignty of the United States in every particular.' "

He insisted that the treaty had provided against every danger mentioned in my interview, and he decided that the interview itself was "Republican camouflage," intended to create in the minds of the people the impression that the Republican party was standing for national sovereignty, the regulation of its domestic affairs, and the continuation of the Monroe Doctrine.

The distinguished senator made no suggestion that the Republican party should adopt any other attitude.

In another interview, in Chicago, on September 7, 1919, I said that the question of ratification with reservations had already been reported as settled and only waited the word from President Wilson that would stop a Democratic filibuster. According to the New York *Times* the following morning, I had declared that it was for the President to determine when the test should be made; that he could expedite the treaty vote and that a quick decision was certain if he would accept the reservations.

The full text of my statement read:

I agree with President Wilson that the Treaty will be ratified and that the ratification will be accompanied by reservations absolutely safeguarding the full independence and freedom of action of this republic. That is the simple fact which the President may as well recognize first as last. At present he is only pounding against a stone wall of patriotism which has already become impregnable and is daily increasing in width, strength and height.

The Committee reservations constitute the irreducible minimum of the requirements of a substantial majority of Senators who cannot be coerced or cajoled into violating their oaths of office to hold America first. There is no partisanship in their position.

True, every Republican Senator without exception stands with the Committee, but because he is an American—not because he is a Republican. I sincerely believe, further, that an actual majority of the Democratic Senators feel the same way, and evidences multiply daily that when the time comes a considerable number will vote the same way.

It is for the President to determine when the test shall be made. The Treaty will be reported out this week and a vote can be had as soon as it can be reached under the rules, unless it is delayed by Senators acting under the direction of the President himself. It is simply now up to the Administration to decide whether it will or will not accept at once these essential guarantees of American independence which will unquestionably be promptly accepted by the other nations. It is imperative that this matter be settled right. It ought, by all means, to be settled promptly. The full responsibility for delay will rest upon the President, and him alone.

Wilson was adamant then, however, and he remained adamant. Months later—on November 24—House wrote him as follows:

A great many people—Democrats, Progressives and Republicans—have talked with me about ratification of the Treaty and they are all pretty much of one mind regarding the necessity for its passage with or without reservations. To the ordinary man, the distance between the Treaty and the reservations is slight . . . today there are millions of helpless people throughout the world who look to you and you only . . .

House had been left behind when Wilson set out on his homeward journey. His job was to work in Paris and London to further the fortunes of the League and lessen the forces of international distrust, while the President was fighting for the League in his tour of the western states.

During the Peace Conference the League had been regarded generally as primarily the protégé of President Wilson; but as the summer of 1919 progressed, signs became apparent that the European statesmen saw in the League an opportunity both for the execution of the treaties and for the handling of problems left unsolved at Paris. Evidently it was taken for granted that the Covenant would be ratified by the Senate and that the United States would assume a leading role in the inauguration of the League, as it had in the drafting of the Covenant.

On September 12, 1919, Colonel House sent the following cablegram to the President from London:

I HAVE RECEIVED A LETTER FROM CLEMENCEAU. IT INDICATES A GROWING ENTHUSIASM FOR THE LEAGUE. I THINK THERE IS NOW A GENERAL AGREEMENT THAT THE MEETING OF THE ASSEMBLY SHOULD BE HELD IN WASHINGTON JUST AS SOON AFTER THE SENATE RATIFIES THE TREATY AS POSSIBLE. I THINK, TOO, THAT ONLY A MERE PRO FORMA MEETING OF THE COUNCIL TO PUT IN EFFECT THAT CLAUSE OF THE TREATY RELATING TO THE SAAR VALLEY SHOULD BE HELD IN WASHINGTON. . . .

President Wilson started on his western tour on September 3 and delivered more than thirty speeches. What might have been the result if his physical powers had proved capable of bearing the strain after the long struggle in Paris, none can say. But on September 25 he collapsed and was hurried back to the capital. The forces battling for the Covenant had lost their leader.

The President should have realized by then that the country no longer was following his leadership. The Senate debates and public discussions throughout the nation during 1919 had changed public opinion, which at the time the treaty was first presented to the Senate certainly was favorable to a speedy conclusion of peace and membership in some form of international league.

By a curious coincidence and mischance, Colonel House also fell ill at the moment when he took ship for the United States. Warned by cable of the President's breakdown, he planned to return to Washington, where he hoped to testify before the Senate Foreign Relations Committee in its hearings on the treaty. He at least realized the imminent danger that the Senate would refuse to ratify the treaty, including the Covenant, unless extensive reservations were introduced. But his condition became worse during the voyage, and he left the ship in a state of almost complete collapse. At the moment when the cause to which both had devoted themselves was being weighed in the scales of fortune, Wilson and House lay ill, one in Washington, the other in New York.

Meanwhile, the vote in the Senate over the treaty ratification was coming up. Wilson's breakdown isolated him in the White House, and none of his advisers were permitted to enter the sickroom.

The unfortunate guardianship which surrounded President Wilson during his last months in office was the subject of careful study in an article by Charles M. Thomas, instructor in history at Ohio State University and former close friend of Secretary of War Newton D. Baker. The article brought forth the innumerable inconsistencies in information given out at the White House during the President's illness, and developed the idea that had the Vice-President been vested with the powers of the President at that period of the debate on the League, passage and ratification of the Covenant with reservations might well have followed. In part, the article reads:

The President's desperate struggle to secure the ratification of the Versailles Treaty may furnish an explanation of why his guardians concealed his true condition. They may have been motivated by a desire to preserve unweakened the principles for which he had fought. Vice-President Marshall was known to be in favor of the ratification of the Treaty with mild reservations and the immediate entry of the United States into the League of Nations. President Wilson demanded ratification with no reservations. The members of his household assumed the responsibility of concealing his condition from a Congress in which there were many members who would have welcomed a constitutional transference of the duties of the President to the Vice-President. *The attitude of the President's guardians is understandable but it led them into expedients of questionable propriety and ultimately resulted in a situation which excluded the United States from the League of Nations and ruined the most cherished hopes of Woodrow Wilson. . . .* [The italics are mine. W.H.H.]

Coming now into the final rounds of the treaty fight in the Senate, the Democratic forces battling for ratification lacked effective leadership. No one guided the fortunes of the Covenant; no one negotiated a compromise with the Republicans in the Senate. The President himself, from the isolation of his sickroom, was unable to judge the necessity for compromise if the defeat of the treaty and Covenant were to be avoided.

The main contest in the Senate extended over a period of two months. Many public commitments for definite compromise were made by

Senator Lodge; although he undoubtedly became firmer, narrower, and tougher in his fight for reservations, he remained more moderate than such essential bitter-enders as Reed, Borah, Brandegee, Watson, and others, who were out to scuttle the treaty at any cost. Jim Reed, for his part, sold the entire state of Missouri against the League, even down to the voters on the gravel roads.

Although the German delegates had the text of the treaty in April 1919, the U. S. Senate, the British House of Commons, and the French Chamber of Deputies, despite their repeated demands, were unable to obtain copies. The first copy, a photostat of the original, bearing the mark of the German Government printing office, was spirited out of Berlin by Wythe Williams and appeared *in extenso* in the *London Times*. At the same time another copy was passed to the American correspondent Frazier Hunt, who brought it to the United States by boat on June 9. Meanwhile the Senate had continued its endeavors to pierce the veil of secrecy which spread over the proceedings at Versailles and developed a feeling that Wilson sought in secret to bind the American people to new and strange policies. This increased after the Senate committee examined scores of witnesses, among them the President, as to what went on in France. The committee's sessions were public, being an application of Wilson's by then repudiated profession of "open covenants openly arrived at." It was the resulting publicity that caused Wilson to take his trip across the nation.

Democratic strategy in the Senate was led by Senator Hitchcock, and although the Democrats were the minority party, his position was far from being hopeless. Certain handicaps, however, Senator Hitchcock could not overcome. He was no match for the shrewd Lodge as a parliamentarian. Probably his hands were tied by orders from the President; he appeared to have no settled plan on how to obtain the necessary majority for acceptable reservations, and he offered his reservations far too late. It remains something of a mystery why he did not form a working majority from the mild reservationists of both parties who were unwilling to go as far as Lodge desired but who wanted something stronger than Hitchcock apparently was willing to do.

As chairman of the National Republican Committee, I issued on July 16, 1919, from New York, the following statement on the League of Nations Covenant:

The situation respecting the League Covenant is simply this: There must be *effective reservations*. These reservations must safeguard the sovereignty of the United States in every particular; must guarantee the Monroe Doctrine beyond the shadow of a doubt; must either eliminate Article X entirely or so modify it that our own Congress shall be morally as well as legally free after a specific period to decide when and where and to what extent our soldiers shall be employed; must retain our full control of immigration, tariff and all other purely domestic policies; and must provide full right to withdraw from the League at any time without hindrance or conditions of any kind, upon giving suitable notice.

It is up to the Administration to decide whether it will or will not accept these essential guarantees of American independence, which would unquestionably be promptly accepted by the other nations.

President Wilson, following his physical breakdown, allowed no opportunity to pass without letting the nation understand that, in his opinion, the Democratic party was the sole protagonist of the peace. He refused to consider the Lodge resolution, which included strong reservations. Thus urged by their leader, the Democratic followers of the President voted with the bitter-enders on November 19, 1919, when the decisive vote was taken.

On that date, in one of the most historic sessions ever recorded, the members of the United States Senate of the Sixty-sixth Congress commenced the final debate on the question of this nation's joining the League of Nations. The Senate convened at noon and did not call for final adjournment until eleven o'clock that night.

Ninety-three senators were present when Senator Lodge of Massachusetts presented his resolution of fourteen reservations to the Covenant. It was a great debate, with practically all of the "pros" and "cons" of the treaty developed by able orators on both sides. Particularly noteworthy were the reasons given by several strong Wilsonian Democrats for their advocacy of the reservations.

One of the strong arguments against the reservations had been that they would not be accepted by the other Powers. Senator Edge of New Jersey answered this argument very succinctly, saying:

"I have no fear of our Allies refusing to acquiesce in our reservations if they are presented to them. We only protect our own destiny and in no way deny them a similar privilege. If they made such reservations the League would function just the same without giving up individuality, sovereignty and independence."

Senator Harding of Ohio, who in the following summer was to begin the campaign which elevated him to the presidency, made his position clear. He said:

"I have not liked this Treaty. I think as originally negotiated it is the most colossal blunder of all time; but, recognizing the aspirations of our people and the people of the world to do something toward international co-operation for the promotion and preservation of peace, I have wished to make it possible to accept this Covenant. I could, however, no more vote to ratify this treaty without reservations which make sure America's independence of action and the preservation of our traditions than I could participate in a knowing betrayal of this Republic. . . . If the ratification is made with the reservations which have been adopted, then remains the skeleton of a

League on which the United States can, if it deems it prudent, proceed in deliberation and calm reflection toward the building of an international relationship which shall be effective in the future.

"The trouble with the whole League of Nations Covenant is that it was hastily negotiated to be made the foundation of a treaty of peace, when there ought to have been treaty of peace negotiations with a League of Nations created in the deliberate aftermath."

The strongest statement to be made by a Democrat in favor of the ratification with reservations came from Senator Walsh of Massachusetts:

"I feel it my duty and in the interest of America to vote for the ratification of this treaty with the reservations which have been offered and I believe if we do that we will make the League of Nations more popular in America, we will get behind it a public sentiment that will give it life and vitality, which it needs; give it support, for without the public sentiment of America behind this League it is a failure from the start. Without these reservations it has the sting of death."

My personal recollections of this momentous day are those of a backstage spectator who spent most of the time with Senator Lodge in his inner office. Senator Curtis of Kansas kept moving back and forth to the Senate floor, reporting what was going on. After President Wilson said that the Senate must pass the League plan "without the dotting of an 'i' or the crossing of a 't,'" several Democratic bitter-enders, like Jim Reed, then went out to beat the League at any cost.

As the hour of decision drew near I went out into the Senate gallery and watched the vote. Several senators apologized as they voted. With the final plea of their leader still ringing in their ears, the Democratic faithful could do little else than vote as the President had demanded: against the treaty and Covenant with the fourteen reservations.

And so the Treaty of Versailles, by a vote of fifty-five to thirty-nine, failed to obtain the necessary two thirds needed for ratification. Had the Wilsonian Democrats disregarded the President's wishes and voted for ratification with the Lodge reservations, the treaty would have been passed by a vote of eighty-one to thirteen. When the decision was rendered there was a deathly silence. Someone made the formal recommendation that they notify the President. Senator Penrose, sitting in the front row, said in a loud voice: "He knows it already."

The Republican group then came up to Senator Lodge's office for the "wake." Lodge said: "We did the best we could" and, reaching into the lower left-hand drawer of his desk, pulled out a photograph of himself. Before handing it to me, he autographed it and wrote the date, "November 19, 1919."

That was the end.

Five years later, in an address at Lincoln, Nebraska, Senator Hitchcock, the minority leader and spokesman for the President, in describing the final vote on the treaty, said:

"I have often wondered whether I made a mistake in the final vote. Had I voted 'yes' it is quite probable that several Democrats would have joined me and ratification would have been authorized. Whether Wilson would have perfected ratification or pigeonholed the treaty no one could tell. He certainly would not have done so at once because his convictions were strong that the people would vindicate him at the next election. However, the popular verdict in November 1920 was against it. He remained President until March 4 and without hope of vindication he still might have taken the treaty from its pigeonhole, Lodge reservations and all, and filed it with France to perfect ratification. That would have changed history—probably for the better."

The aftermath of the treaty fight dragged along through the year that followed, until the election of Warren Harding—in November 1920—registered the final verdict of the American electorate, dooming all American participation in the League of Nations.

Several months after the Senate vote—in the spring of 1920—after consulting senators of both parties, Senator Hitchcock sought reconsideration of the vote of rejection, with the view of obtaining a compromise on reservations. He found that President Wilson was more receptive to his suggestions and that Lodge also agreed to informal conferences. But of these meetings with Wilson, Senator Hitchcock wrote:

I visited him from time to time in his sick room and sought to persuade him to compromise on reservations. In some cases he yielded but generally his attitude was expressed by this conversation which I now recall:

"Mr. President," I said, "it might be wise to compromise with Lodge on this point."

"Let Lodge compromise," he replied.

"Well, of course," I added, "he must compromise also but we might well hold out the olive branch."

"Let Lodge hold out the olive branch," he concluded, and that ended it for he was too ill to argue with.

Compromise was urged upon the President by leading advocates of the League during the winter and following spring. Colonel House, out of the struggle because of illness, was convinced, after long talks with Lord Grey, that the Allies would accept the Lodge reservations if, through them alone, the United States could be brought into the League. After all, the success of the League would not depend upon this phrase or that, but upon the spirit of the member nations. Five days after the historic Senate vote House wrote the President, in part, as follows:

Much depends upon your decision in regard to the Treaty. Its failure would be a disaster not less to civilization than to you.

My suggestion is this: Do not mention the Treaty in your message to Congress, but return it to the Senate as soon as it convenes. In the meantime, send for Senator Hitchcock and tell him that you have fulfilled your every obligation to your colleagues in Paris by rejecting all offers to alter the document, and you now turn the Treaty over to the Senate for such action as it may deem wise to take.

I would advise him to ask the Democratic Senators to vote for the Treaty with such reservations as the majority may formulate, and let the matter then rest with the other signatories of the Treaty. I would say to Senator Hitchcock that if the Allied and Associated Powers are willing to accept the reservations which the Senate sees fit to make, you will abide by the result.

The Allies may not take the Treaty with the Lodge reservations as they now stand and this will be your vindication. But even if they should take them with slight modifications, your conscience will be clear. After agreement is reached, it can easily be shown that the Covenant in its practical workings in the future will not be seriously hampered and that time would give us a workable machine.

Three days later, November 27, 1919, House again wrote the President in similar vein. No record exists that President Wilson ever replied to either of these letters.

Confirmation of Colonel House's implication that the Allies would prove amenable to the idea of the treaty with reservations is found in a statement by Viscount Grey on February 3, 1920, to the effect that the Lodge reservations would be acceptable to Great Britain. A few days later Lloyd George acquiesced in this statement. "If the outcome of the long controversy in the Senate has been to offer co-operation in the League of Nations it would be the greatest mistake to refuse that co-operation because conditions are attached to it." Wilson was greatly angered by the publication of this opinion.

In March 1920, Senator Lodge made a motion to bring the League before the Senate again. President Wilson remained silent, but Senator Hitchcock rushed back to Washington to be present. In a letter to Senator Hitchcock the President reaffirmed his determined unwillingness to accept the reservations, especially any changes in Article X of the Covenant.

Ratification was again defeated on March 20, lacking the necessary two thirds by seven votes. The final vote was forty-nine for ratification, thirty-five against. Had the Democrats who voted against ratification (twenty-three in number) voted for it, the treaty would have been ratified by a vote of seventy-two to twelve.

After the Senate failed to adopt the ratification resolution on March 20, Senator Lodge secured the adoption of a resolution formally acknowledging the rejection of the treaty and sending the document back to the President. Wilson refused to act.

The House of Representatives took the first real step to make peace. On April 9, 1920, by a vote of 242 to 150, it adopted a resolution declaring the war with Germany at an end. On May 23 the Senate, by a vote of 43 to 38, adopted a peace resolution by Senator Knox as a substitute for the House measure, and the House accepted the revised version by a vote of 228 to 139. President Wilson vetoed it, and on the vote to override, the resolution was lost.

The Wilson administration had kept on the government payrolls a great army of war employees, under the cover of various war emergency laws. Under these measures an autocratic supervision of the people's private life and a governmental participation in American industry had been maintained. On June 3 the House, by a vote of 324 to 3, terminated these wartime laws, except the Trading with the Enemy Act, the various Liberty and Victory Bond statutes, and the passport law. The Senate concurred unanimously, thus demonstrating how both Republicans and Democrats were in accord in their determination that these laws should no longer hamper industry or afford an excuse for the administration's meddling. Wilson killed this repeal resolution by a pocket veto, holding it until June 5, the date that Congress adjourned, thus automatically invalidating the measure. The Democratic National Convention at San Francisco endorsed the President's stand and condemned the Republican Senate for its action.

From that time on, the treaty fight became merged with the oncoming presidential election campaign of 1920. In June the Republicans nominated Warren G. Harding for President and Governor Calvin Coolidge of Massachusetts for Vice-President, while the Democratic convention at San Francisco chose James M. Cox, governor of Ohio, and Franklin D. Roosevelt, then Assistant Secretary of the Navy.

The President made a final political gesture on October 3, 1920, in a letter addressed to the voters, asking for an endorsement of the League of Nations at the November election. He wrote:

You have been grossly misled with regard to the treaty and particularly with regard to the proposed character of the League of Nations, by those who have assumed the serious responsibility of opposing it. Those who drew the Covenant of the League of Nations would have been amazed and indignant at the things that are now being said about this great and sincere document.

The Democrats continued to keep the issue before the voters, and on October 6, when the campaign was warming up, Mr. George White, chairman of the Democratic National Committee, addressed a letter to me, as his opposite number on the Republican committee:

DEAR MR. HAYS:

In the interest of truth which the righteous certainly have no reason to fear, I venture to ask you to do all in your power to acquaint the voters with the text of the Covenant of the League of Nations. By some circumstance of which I am not advised, it was not printed in the Republican textbook.

The Democratic textbook contains this text and the committee has furnished it to all the newspapers which desire to use it.

Will you, in the interest of truth, use your influence and unite with me —or if you prefer, act separately and urge all newspapers to print the text of the Covenant in full within the next few days? There are so many more Republican than Democratic papers in the United States, that your request would secure the wide publicity which is desirable.

To this letter I replied on the following day, as follows:

My dear Mr. White:

Your letter is received suggesting that I join with you in an effort to acquaint the voters with the text of the Covenant of the League of Nations.

To acquaint the voters of the country with the truth about the Wilson League of Nations has been the earnest effort of the Republican organization ever since the Administration took over the cables which kept the country from knowing anything about the development of the Covenant. We will, of course, do anything further possible, with you or separately, as we are doing, to that end.

May I further suggest, likewise in the interest of truth, that we make an effort in some way to ascertain and advise the country just what the President promised Europe that this country would do, which may not be in the text of the Covenant. Won't you help us find out just what this was and let us give that to the country also? Governor Cox has promised to make good these pledges whatever they may be.

Further, and likewise in the interest of truth, I trust you will help acquaint the country with the substance of the Senate reservations voted for by over twenty-three Democrats. It seems these reservations have not been published in the Democratic textbook.

We have published a pamphlet of 64 pages devoted exclusively to the League of Nations, but will be glad to join with you, if you desire, not only in urging the newspapers to publish the text of the Covenant and the Senate reservations, but in issuing a pamphlet by the two Committees including both the text of the Covenant and the text of the Senate reservations.

I note that the President in his statement on Monday said, "There is nothing in the Covenant which in the least interferes with or impairs the right of Congress to declare war or not declare war according to its own independent judgment." Mr. Bryan, in his speech on Jackson Day, said "If we do not intend to impair the right of Congress to decide the question of peace or war when the time for action arises, how can we insist upon a moral obligation to go to war which can have no force or value except as it does impair the independence of Congress."

It certainly is the duty of all to help clarify the situation.

CHAPTER 17

A Treaty without Peace

A S evidence that we considered the question still alive, on October 15, 1920, thirty-one leading Republicans issued a public statement in favor of the League of Nations in the form in which it had been endorsed by the League to Enforce Peace. It was given to the press on the evening of that day by its chairman, Jacob Gould Schurman, president of Cornell University, operating from the University Club, New York.

The newspapers front-paged it the following morning with the intimation that it had been drawn up by Elihu Root, following a meeting in my office with Mr. Schurman, Paul D. Cravath, and George Wickersham.

This statement in letter form, I may now say, was planned with more labor and executed with more finesse than was then recognized, and despite the immediate fulminations of Mr. Cox, the Democratic candidate, and many supporting newspapers, it had the effect of turning thousands of votes to Senator Harding.

The League of Nations was definitely in politics in the 1920 campaign. Those of us who wanted to keep it out had been unsuccessful. Therefore, I wanted the situation clarified, as George White, the Democratic national chairman, had suggested. It was necessary to obtain some definite expression of what I believed to be the opinion of the majority. Also, I was not unmindful of the political aspect of the situation, and to have the declaration issued on October 15 by a group of able and unselfish men was calculated to assure vast numbers that a group of great influence in the Republican party was for international co-operation, and that the matter was not going to be dropped.

The initial declaration of the thirty-one signers was that they were "advocates of international action to promote peace." Their considered opinion was that instead of enacting "promises negotiated by President Wilson" they favored "an agreement which modifies some of those provisions, which are objectionable to a great number of people." Concerning Article X, they concurred with Hiram Johnson, Borah, and other extremists in the belief that it practically bound the United States to go to war for any League member.

The statement was not signed by William Howard Taft, a great pro-Leaguer, but by his brother, Henry W. Taft. The list of names included seventeen college presidents and executives. Among the signers, including Dr. Schurman, Wickersham, Cravath, and Taft, were the following: Lyman Abbot; Nicholas Murray Butler, president of Columbia University; Robert S. Brookings, president of Washington College, St. Louis; Charles W. Dabney, president of the University of Cincinnati; Frank Goodman, president of Johns Hopkins; Charles Evans Hughes; Herbert Hoover; President Lowell of Harvard; John Grier Hibben, president of Princeton; Alex C. Humphreys, president of Stevens Institute of Technology; Ernest M. Hopkins, president of Dartmouth; John H. MacCracken, President of Lafayette College; William Lawrence, Bishop of Massachusetts; Samuel G. Mather of Cleveland; George A. Plimpton, president of the Board of Trustees of Amherst; Henry S. Pritchett of the Carnegie Foundation; Charles A. Richmond, president of Union College; Henry L. Stimson; Isaac M. Ullman of New Haven; William Allen White; W. W. Willoughby, professor of political science, Johns Hopkins; and Ray Lyman Wilbur, president of Leland Stanford University.

As was to be expected, the letter was violently attacked editorially, especially by the New York *Times,* then a strong supporter of Governor Cox.

Three days later the *Times* published an opposition document signed by 120 former Republicans, but did not give it the front page, possibly because the signers were of considerably less weight than the thirty-one leading Republicans who had issued the earlier statement. It did contain the name of Ray Stannard Baker, who had accompanied Wilson to Paris, and of several college executives. It should be noted that, in the previous March, Mr. Baker, as a member of the League of Free Nations Association, had joined in an appeal to Wilson to compromise on the reservations and so permit ratification.

A few days before the election—on October 20—Elihu Root delivered a speech under the auspices of the National Republican Club of New York, in which he strongly expressed his conviction:

"It is my purpose to speak this evening of the League of Nations. I think a large majority of the American people earnestly wish for an organization among civilized nations through which the nations shall co-operate to prevent future wars and that the United States shall do her full share in that organization. I certainly desire this very strongly."

Charles Evans Hughes, the Republican candidate for the presidency in 1916, likewise entered the lists against Governor Cox in support of Senator Harding and of a modified League. In a number of campaign speeches Mr. Hughes in general supported the position taken by Mr.

Root. He stressed the point that since Cox and the Wilsonian Democrats insisted that Article X was the backbone of the whole treaty the Republicans were entirely justified in their critical examination of that document.

Mr. Hughes made a masterly analysis of the main points at issue and showed clearly that the accepted American viewpoint on international affairs, including even our firmly established Monroe Doctrine, was by no means represented in the draft of the League Covenant adopted in Paris.

This story of a great tragedy has been presented without analysis of the political conflicts between nations that went on at Paris or the conniving of European leaders against Wilson's incorporation of the League of Nations into the Treaty of Versailles. Its purpose has been to show, with some use of documentary evidence, the American reaction toward the treaty both in the making and in completed form, when, from the hands of the President, it passed for final review and judgment to the Senate of the United States.

During the long Senate debate and after the formal rejection of the treaty, the general feeling was that the final decision was due largely to personal animosity between Woodrow Wilson and certain Republican senators, notably Henry Cabot Lodge of Massachusetts, and that therefore it was a duel of temperaments that decided the future of this nation at that time.

Much can be found to sustain this thesis, but it is far from telling the whole story. Recognition of human weaknesses forces the conclusion that blame must be attached to both sides, that President Wilson was adamant when he should have shown at least the spirit of conciliation, and that Senator Lodge became more irreconcilable as time went on.

However, as I believe the foregoing evidence has shown, this rugged senator, as chairman of the Senate Foreign Relations Committee, not only was charged with a mission he considered a patriotic duty, but was a leader of a political party that was becoming steadily stronger and more positive in its demands for treaty reservations that required thoughtful consideration by the Senate and the people. That the voters clearly considered the Republican cause just, was proved at the polls in November 1920.

It is significant, going back several years prior to 1918, to find evidence that Senator Lodge then was far from being "irreconcilable." On June 9, 1915, he made a speech on the necessity of inviting the nations of the world into a league. He declared that such a league was neither impracticable nor utopian. On May 27 of the following year Lodge and

Wilson spoke at the same meeting of the League to Enforce Peace, at the Willard Hotel in Washington. On that occasion Lodge said:

"I do not believe that when Washington warned us against entangling alliances he meant for one moment that we should not join with other civilized nations of the world if a method could be found to diminish war and encourage peace."

And President Wilson said:

"The United States is willing to become a partner in any feasible association of nations formed in order to realize these objectives and make them secure against violation."

Both these men were replying to a speech made a few days earlier by Wilson's former Secretary of State, William Jennings Bryan, who objected to the League idea on the general thesis that it would involve the United States in entangling alliances with Europe and was incompatible with the Monroe Doctrine.

Certainly it would seem that the Democratic President and the Republican senator were of the same mind, at least while on that same platform. A significant summing up of Lodge can be found in a recent letter written by his grandson, then junior senator from Massachusetts, later appointed our delegate to United Nations:

No interpretation of Senator Lodge's attitude at the time of the League of Nations debate is necessary, since he has himself stated, for all time, what that attitude was. As he has said, he gave the League with reservations his genuine support and was surprised when President Wilson drew away enough Democrats to prevent its ratification on that basis.

Many efforts have been made to analyze tactical errors made by President Wilson that may have contributed to the rejection of the treaty. One such attempt was made in an article by Walter Lippmann, who wrote in substance that, first, Wilson sought to replace a strong wartime coalition, which he had been chiefly responsible for dissolving, with an entirely new organization—the League of Nations—it now appearing that the better course would have been to maintain the coalition so far as the peace settlement with Germany was concerned and then to develop gradually an international society for the promotion of good relations. Second, Wilson formulated an elaborate platform of principles which he demanded that the other nations accept, even threatening the non-co-operation of the United States unless they did accept. Third, he endeavored to commit this nation and all other nations to the use of military power, not for the specific object of enforcing a peace treaty, but as a world guarantee forevermore. His attempt to combine his code of principles with the general guarantee of force at once opened up the prospect of unlimited intervention and entanglement.

Woodrow Wilson, as President and Commander in Chief, in a war that then was considered victorious, certainly occupied a much stronger position than any other individual. While his party had lost the majority in Congress, the public still accepted him as a commanding personality, a man of high ideals and culture, charming manners, and a courage that later proved so great that he was willing to wreck his health in combat for what he believed to be right.

Nevertheless, as noted earlier, Mr. Wilson actually lost his fight for the American entry into the League long before that fight began, when he wrote the open letter to the voters in October 1918 asking the return of a Democratic Congress, even before the Armistice and when the League was not yet in the minds of mankind. After the voters reacted to that appeal, the President found that he had placed a chip on the shoulders of the majority members of Congress.

He made a further step in losing the struggle when he decided to be the first President to quit the territory of the United States during his term of office, and he lost it also through what, under different conditions, might have been considered minor flaws in his character.

Coupled with his idealism was his certainty that, above all, he was right. It was necessary at times for his closest advisers to cajole, humor, and also to admonish him. A striking illustration of this phase of Wilson's character was given to me at that time. After the day of great rejoicing, in June 1919, when with solemn ceremony the Treaty of Versailles was signed and sealed, the President departed for America. At that very moment he almost provoked an international incident that would seriously have strained American relations with France. President Poincaré had arranged a farewell state dinner at the Elysée Palace, which Wilson had declined to attend. The inner-circle ambassadors, Wallace and Jusserand, as well as Admiral Grayson, were unable to budge him. Then Colonel House appeared and told the President that this was an open affront to France. Wilson made excuses, saying that the time was too short, with the special train leaving at nine o'clock. It was pointed out that the French train would await French orders. Wilson then said that his wife did not wish to meet Madame Poincaré. Next he said that the food would choke him. House then pointed out that Poincaré represented the French nation, that Wilson had been a guest of France for the past six months, and that therefore he should go to the dinner and choke. Wilson weakened, went, and ate the dinner.

Linked with his courage was a stubbornness that too often seemed to blind him both to facts and to the honest advice of his friends. Had Woodrow Wilson listened not only to Colonel House but to many wise counselors who were with him heart and soul, he would have remained in Washington, whence it now appears that he could have dictated his own terms of peace, with the United States taking organized leadership in the post-war world.

The presidential election of 1920 was far from being exclusively a solemn referendum on the League of Nations. The issues were confused and entwined with many pressing domestic questions. The Democratic candidates, Cox and Roosevelt, supported the League wholeheartedly. Senator Harding wanted binding reservations and Coolidge was friendly. The issue was further confused by the fact that Cox was supported by such bitter-end opponents of the League as Senator Jim Reed, while the Republican candidate was endorsed by such stout proponents of the League as William Howard Taft.

President Wilson's speeches had struck the keynote for the arguments of the League supporters. They were filled with high moralities and the sense that the role of the United States was to be that of a *deus ex machina*, arbitrating the fate of the world from some Olympian height. To many of us they held little of realism or comprehension of the fact that we, too, were a part of the world order and that it was to our own self-interest to settle world disputes peacefully.

This view of American participation appears—fantastically prophetic of today's situation—to have been held in common by both Lodge and Wilson. In the Senate debate Lodge said: "If the United States enters any League of Nations it does so for the benefit of the world at large and not for its own benefit." And Wilson almost paralleled this when he said: "If America were at this junction to fail the world, what would come of it?"—apparently not concerned about what would happen to America, but only to the rest of the world.

In the influencing of public opinion, the most active of the pro-League groups was the League to Enforce Peace, organized in 1915. It had able leaders; William Howard Taft was president and A. Lawrence Lowell, president of Harvard University, chairman of the Executive Committee. Both were Republicans and both did a great deal to develop non-partisan public support for the League. Although originally it stood foursquare for the treaty as written, the League to Enforce Peace gradually veered from that position. Early in the summer of 1919, Mr. Taft was willing to accept reservations, and before the final vote in November, the Executive Committee asked for the passage of the treaty with the Lodge reservations, a complete reversal from the stand taken at the beginning of the fight.

A rival organization during the Senate fight was the League for the Preservation of American Independence, organized in the spring of 1919. It was the mouthpiece of the "irreconcilables," and its purpose was to defeat the League by amendments, reservations, or straight-out vote.

Church and religious groups seem to have been almost unanimously in favor of the League. It was endorsed by the Federal Council of Churches of Christ in America, the General Assembly of the Presbyterian Church, the United Brethren in Christ Board of Bishops, the Gideons, Disciples of Christ, Church Peace Union, National Society of Christian Endeavor, Religious Education Association, Northern Baptist Convention, the Evangelical Lutheran Church in America, and many other state and regional groups.

Some of the staunchest backers of the League to Enforce Peace were business and professional leaders. The league was endorsed by the American Bar Association, the Associated Advertising Clubs of the World, the United States Chamber of Commerce, the National Economic League, the National Retail Dry Goods Association, the American Manufacturers Export Association, the National Association of Builders Exchange, the National Association of Merchant Tailors, and many others. It was supported by most of organized Labor. Farmers' groups likewise were strongly in favor of the League idea. Women's civic groups generally supported it.

The attitude of returning servicemen, however, was not clearly crystallized. Petitions from newly formed American Legion posts were sent to Congress from time to time, but never enough to clarify the position of the veterans as a group.

Many racial groups, particularly the Irish, were opposed to the League.

A majority of the newspapers supported the League editorially in varying degrees. Many Republican and independent papers were favorable, and according to the *Congressional Record,* sixty-six Republican and fifty-six independent papers backed the League, while 95 per cent of the Democratic press was favorable.

During the period of uneasy and unreal peace that separated the two world wars, Winston Churchill delivered one of his poetic prophecies, warning of things to come. The world did not hang upon his words then as it came to do later. In fact, his words were hardly heeded. Mr. Churchill thus wrote in 1929, referring to the peacemaking at Versailles:

It is a tale that is told, from which we may draw the knowledge and comprehension needed for the future. The disproportion between the quarrels of nations and the suffering which fighting out those quarrels involves; the poor and barren prizes which reward sublime endeavor on the battlefield; the fleeting triumphs of war; slow rebuilding; the awful risks so hardily run; the doom missed by a hair's breadth, by the spin of a coin, by the accident of an accident—all this should make the preventing of another great war the main preoccupation of mankind.

In reviewing the crucial peacemaking events of a generation ago, where I occupied a ringside seat, I have been constantly impressed by

the parallels with events of our present day. After World War II came
to America, I made it my business to contribute all that I possibly could
in order to make certain that the mistakes of that earlier period be
avoided and that this time we find a formula for true unity. The evil
roots of those mistakes, deeply embedded in the hearts of men, are hard
to kill; those who lived through the tragedy of 1918–20 are better aware
of this than others, simply because they saw it happen. In my position
as national chairman of the Republican party more than a quarter century ago, during the critical period when victory was clinched and a
peace program formulated, I was only too well aware of the misunderstandings and the confusions that developed. I saw high-minded leaders
—able, earnest, and deeply patriotic—let small disagreements divert them
from great goals. I saw great statesmen, aiming at the same objectives
and agreed on fundamental principles, permit differences of method to
separate them beyond reconciliation.

A conspiracy of circumstances rather than a conspiracy of men brought
defeat. Neither side in that struggle had a monopoly on patriotism.
Starting from a base of general agreement as to the main purpose, *statesmen failed to concentrate upon areas of agreement.* Instead, *they were
impelled by the very earnestness of their beliefs to take a stand on the
margins of discord.* Hearts hardened in the process of struggle. Somehow, through a tragedy of errors, slogans took the place of reasoned
judgment. Differences of honest conviction crumbled into prejudices of
partisan emotion, while then, as now, the majority of the American
people certainly favored some machinery to head off new wars.

In the lives of nations, as in those of individuals, the errors of one
generation are inevitably visited upon another. Men and countries today
are haunted by the disturbing feeling that but for the mistakes made
after the first victory there might have been no need to win a second.

We must now make sure that another generation, composed of our
sons and grandsons, shall have no cause for a similar rebuke. Fortunately, this time there is a conscious, systematic, and determined
attempt by most men to preserve for the purposes of peace the unity
among nations that was forged under the pressure of war. But there
must also be unity of purpose within America itself. Both during and
after World War II the American people rose above the divisions and
temptations of party politics. We now know that we cannot have effective participation by our country in a world organization unless it is
rooted in non-partisan, all-American soil.

This determination to prevent another war must remain on a level
of patriotism above all recrimination. Statesmanship must always take
precedence over partisanship. In the present peacemaking, this has been
to the everlasting credit of many leaders in both our great political

parties. Factional differences were ruled out at every stage of our national preparation preceding the conference at San Francisco.

Such a spirit of unity is the more remarkable when we consider that a presidential election campaign, with its natural emphasis on party differences and party ambitions, had intervened. National unity which can survive that crucial test should survive the strains on unity which may lie ahead on the road to world organization.

I have had some share in the present-day effort to turn the hopes of peace into a functioning reality, and I know that unremitting vigilance is essential to safeguard our unity of purpose.

When I resigned as Postmaster General, I abandoned politics officially. But I remained a staunch Republican, and I still played the game of politics, not behind the scenes—because I make no secrecy of my actions —but unofficially.

During World War II, as soon as it was certain that Germany and Japan could not win and that the United States would emerge as the strongest of the earth's nations, it became clear to me that again, as in 1918, the conduct of American foreign policy was the greatest world problem. Therefore, I considered it a duty—even for one like myself long out of office—to try to do something about it.

Prior to the campaign of 1944, when Governor Thomas E. Dewey of New York opposed the re-election of President Roosevelt for a fourth term, I decided to put in my oar to harmonize both major political parties on one major goal. Whatever the domestic issues involved, and however bitter, it seemed to me a tragedy if international post-war organization to effect lasting peace were made a gauge of partisan warfare.

The bosses in the Kremlin started their campaign of refusal to co-operate with the Allies long before the war ended, while the United States was still going all out in extending aid to them. Early in 1943 it should have been clear to those in command in Washington, as it was to Admiral Standley, our Ambassador in Moscow, that we might expect plenty of trouble from Russia in the years ahead, especially when that nation disapproved the four-power declaration made at Moscow, of which she was one of the signers, and more particularly in the common effort to improve the status of China. I felt certain that a situation was arising, even before the end of the war, that was similar to that of December 1918, when President Wilson arrived at Paris to negotiate world peace. It was evident that active and practical world leadership was the destiny of this nation, in partnership with her Allies to whatever extent possible. This presented a problem so vast that it had to have the stamp of *complete national approval*. The failure of the great effort to restore a lasting peace at the end of World War II was a tragic story that had to be restudied. That it should not happen again must be the resolve of every American. The Republican delegates soon to assemble in a national convention faced a supreme privilege and duty.

Some time before the opening of the San Francisco Conference, I had my first meeting with Secretary of State Cordell Hull, in which we attempted to work out a clear bi-partisan basis for international relations, particularly to prevent the whole subject from becoming a political party issue. Together we agreed upon certain fundamental points to be put in each party's platform. These points were brief:

All rational people agree that world peace must be preserved in the future.

To preserve world peace requires co-operation of all nations, especially the large nations.

The co-operation of no nation is more essential than that of the United States.

It is manifest that to be effective and permanent the co-operation of the United States must rest on a non-partisan basis.

In those fateful situations the two great political parties have no greater duty or responsibility than to go on record and set an example at this time, through an absolutely non-partisan appeal to this and all future generations, to preserve and practice this non-partisan policy.

I went to Indianapolis on my way to our State Convention with a view to making Indiana the springboard for publicizing the proposed bi-partisan platform to be adopted at the approaching gathering. I immediately visited my old friend, Eugene Pulliam, editor of the Indianapolis *Star*. I called up Secretary of State Hull from Mr. Pulliam's desk and we had a lengthy conversation outlining the various points that were deemed necessary. This was the Friday preceding Labor Day in 1943. I then called up our national chairman, Harrison Spangler, at Mackinac, hoping to stiffen his position on our non-partisan foreign policy, on which the Republican conference there was about to adopt a definite policy.

One of the handicaps under which the American delegation at San Francisco labored was the uncertainty, occasioned by the sudden death of President Roosevelt, concerning just what international commitments had been made by the United States. This was brought home to me in a later conversation with Secretary Hull at Washington. Mr. Hull then told me frankly of his chief difficulty: "I do not know what has been promised." This was after Teheran.

Our delegation at San Francisco was neither Democratic nor Republican. It was American. The purposes at stake represented a challenge to the core of reason and tolerance in the American character. The meeting itself was not a peace conference, as was that earlier one of 1919. It was free from the burden of drafting detailed and specific peace terms between victor and vanquished. Its concern was simply to set up machinery for building a world of co-operative action in the maintenance of a secure peace and in the promotion of development and progress—all practically impossible unless the organization is endowed with the authority and power to use force if necessary to prevent war, threat of war, and preparation for war. This conference at San Francisco was a most important step, since its objective was to draft the actual charter for the United Nations Organization, to be then submitted to the member countries.

From my experience after Versailles, I knew the dangers of quarrels inherent in any undertaking as vast and complex as the machinery for world peace. Those of us who had sought earnestly and even desperately a quarter of a century ago to find a middle ground of agreement had failed. The temper of that period, unfortunately, was one of extremes, in which counsels of moderation and compromise proved ineffective. The blood, sweat, and tears of the second and infinitely more frightful world war had, it was hoped, generated a new spirit.

Thus far in the peacemaking following World War II, we have generally escaped the perils of internal disunity which wrecked our earlier effort. But this happy condition applies only to our domestic situation. On the international plane the disunity among nations is, unhappily, only too apparent. The world has been split into two camps! The old quarrels and misunderstandings of partisan politics that once plagued our domestic scene now are transferred to the field of international relations in the far more dangerous forms of ancient racial grudges and manufactured hatreds.

Senator Arthur Vandenberg, in a conversation with me following the Foreign Ministers' Conference in New York, made a prophetic statement, borne out by much that has happened since. He said: "We will have to go along without Russia, and I am ready to do it." This is the hard and bitter, but apparently the only, choice we can make—and particularly bitter after the bright hopes of international co-operation that flourished in the closing months of the war. But there is the handwriting on the wall, a wall the Western world now knows as the "Iron Curtain."

A similar thought was expressed by John Foster Dulles in giving me some of his impressions of Russia's rulers following the London Conference of Foreign Ministers. He said: "These men are themselves atheists. Stark and sinister realists; atheists politically and personally."

Those of us who hold the highest interests of the Republic at heart cannot help feeling deeply depressed over the growing schism between East and West, and the ruthless means constantly employed to widen that schism. The fact that we are now the most powerful nation on earth has brought no solution.

Georges Clemenceau, Father of Victory in World War I, loved France better than anything else on earth, just as I love my country. He knew that his country was weakened by war to such an extent that she must have powerful friends. He felt that a new war, with France involved, was probable. He realized that he was too old again to take the helm. When an American newspaper correspondent once suggested that he might again emerge from retirement to win the next conflict, a world of philosophy was in his reply: *"What does one really gain by winning a war?"*

From November 11, 1918, the Old World looked to the United States politically, as it had looked militarily. The war was won only to the extent of an armistice and an opportunity to make peace. The American Expeditionary Force—two million men on the soil of France—secured this opportunity.

In World War II the actual force of American arms contributed more than all else to victory on all battle fronts. Again we have been given the opportunity to make peace, the opportunity that eluded us after the first global conflict.

The peacemaking after World War I now looks to have been a failure. International retrogression, as traced throughout the following years, and the present instability of the entire world seem to offer conclusive evidence that the treaty signed at Versailles was indeed a treaty without peace.

What have we learned?

CHAPTER 18

1919—Endings and Beginnings

T H E story of peacemaking efforts and the League has been told at length because of its critical importance both then and now. For I believe the lesson is one by which we can still profit. But domestic affairs, party organization, and personal matters of deep interest were not to be forgotten.

The off-year congressional election of 1918 marked a turning point in my work as chairman. I was naturally elated at the success we had won at the polls, but I knew that hard work lay ahead. Until then the Republican purpose was to win the war as speedily as possible, but six days after the election the war was won, and the primary Republican purpose became the winning of the peace. Of the long and bitter fight to that end, in the Senate and in the press, I have treated in the preceding chapters.

Simultaneously with that struggle, but on the domestic scene, many pressing problems in the field of internal politics presented themselves, in which, as chairman, I was vitally concerned. Almost immediately after the election, trouble developed in Congress over Republican organizational matters, and I hurriedly went to Washington to lend a hand. Senator Boise Penrose was an aspirant for chairman of the Senate Finance Committee, but Progressive Republican senators, led by Senator Borah, had united to prevent his election. The Progressives had declared that rather than let that happen they would permit the Democrats to retain control of the Senate organization. The ten senators opposed to Penrose were Borah of Idaho, Cummins and Kenyon of Iowa, Johnson of California, Gronna of North Dakota, Lenroot and La Follette of Wisconsin, Norris of Nebraska, McNary of Oregon, and Capper of Kansas. Their protest against Penrose was sent to me by Senator Borah.

I called on many Republican members of Congress by noon after my arrival. As to who should become Speaker and who should be made chairmen of committees, I had nothing to say. But I impressed upon them all that the party had a responsibility of unity to the country. I was well satisfied with what I had heard that day and so told the press. As this was my first visit to Washington since the election, I was showered with congratulations on the overwhelming success of the campaign. Dozens of senators and congressmen called upon me at national headquarters to talk about the encouraging results.

The ironing out of local differences and difficulties, necessary if the party was to function effectively as a national instrument, also occupied much of my time and necessitated considerable traveling about. I made frequent trips out of our Washington and New York headquarters and conferred with many party leaders around the country.

About this time I was developing a project to establish "listening posts," or branch headquarters, of the National Committee in various strategic areas throughout the country. The purpose was to keep closer touch between the national organization and the rank and file of the party. The first of these listening posts was set up in San Francisco after conferences in New York with West Coast leaders. A national headquarters of the Women's National Executive Committee, also, was established in Washington with Mrs. Medill McCormick in charge. The women's committee, which I had appointed the previous September, acted in co-operation with the National Committee in planning how to obtain the fullest participation of Republican women in the party's affairs.

Permanent headquarters of the Republican National Committee were established in Chicago in the Congress Hotel Annex on January 1, 1919, and a meeting of the National Committee in Chicago was called for January 10. This meeting was clouded by the tragedy that struck in the first week of the new year—the death of Theodore Roosevelt.

Colonel Roosevelt was to have delivered an address on Americanism at the New York Hippodrome on the night of January 5, but was ill and canceled the engagement. In a message he sent to the meeting, delivered by his son, Captain Archibald Roosevelt, one paragraph read:

In the first place, we should insist that, if the immigrant who comes here does, in good faith, become an American and assimilates himself to us, he shall be treated on an exact equality with everyone else, for it is an outrage to discriminate against any such men because of creed or birthplace or origin. But this is predicated upon the man's becoming, in very fact, an American and nothing but an American.

Next morning the headlines shocked the nation with the news of Theodore Roosevelt's sudden death in his sleep at his Oyster Bay home. I was en route to Sullivan at the time because my son was seriously ill with pneumonia, and I received the news when the train stopped at Muncie, Indiana. It was a great shock to me and I said to the reporters: "The strongest character in the world has died. No one can take Theodore Roosevelt's place."

When the train reached Indianapolis, I was met by Governor Goodrich and Jack Henley. As they discussed the advisability of canceling the

meeting of the National Committee, called for January 10 in Chicago,
I told them:

"I am thinking of what Colonel Roosevelt would have counseled—from
my knowledge of his actions at other times, when grief lay upon his own
heart—and I believe he would not wish this done on his account. I am sure
his advice would be to 'carry on.'

"I had a luncheon appointment with him on the day when the report first
came of the death of his son Quentin in France. I presumed our meeting
would be called off, but it went right on. Colonel Roosevelt was busy in
work that he believed essential to the country, and he would not permit even
so poignant a personal grief to interfere with his tasks.

"A few days later the news of Quentin's death was confirmed. I had an
engagement to spend that Sunday with the colonel and his family at Oyster
Bay. I hesitated for a while, but finally decided to go ahead. I found that
he would have had it so. He bore this great grief stoically, as a warrior,
although I have no doubt that it was this sorrow that hastened his end.

"In recent months I have seen and talked to Colonel Roosevelt frequently.
I have been deeply impressed by the thought that his heart was on fire for
his country. I think that he was lifted entirely above the thought of self and
that his personal ambitions in the face of the present crisis in our national
history were completely subordinated to his devotion to America."

We decided to go ahead with the meeting.

Arriving at Sullivan, I found my mother, wife, and son all ill, although not seriously. No nurses were to be found in Sullivan, so I went
on to Chicago and sent a nurse back from there.

All social affairs in connection with the committee meeting were canceled, including a big dinner at the Hamilton Club, on account of
Colonel Roosevelt's death, and the entire meeting was held under the
pall of his passing. But it was perhaps the most impressive National
Committee session ever held between presidential elections. Precedents
all along the line were broken. Being unable to locate a clergyman when
the morning session began, I offered the opening prayer myself, asking
for divine guidance for the National Committee and for the leaders of
the Republican party all over the country.

During my formal report to the committee, I tried to pay my tribute,
and suggest a memorial, saying:

"It is difficult to discuss the death of Theodore Roosevelt. The ideals for
which he spent his life shall not fail. The banner that he carried shall not
trail for a moment. The lesson of his patriotism shall not be forgotten. I suggest for your consideration the idea that this committee sponsor a movement
for the development of a permanent memorial to this distinguished man.
Just what the nature of this shall be, or the extent to which it might be
carried, is a matter for thought, but it cannot be of a nature too substantial
or of an extent too great, adequately to measure the merit of the deceased.
I suggest that Colonel William Boyce Thompson be directed, as chairman

of a special committee, to give thought to this matter, with a view to proceeding as may be deemed best, under the auspices of the Republican National Committee, to develop and execute the idea."

The committee ratified this suggestion and also, by resolution, recommended that Sunday, January 19, be observed throughout the nation as Roosevelt Memorial Day.

Early in April I arranged to return to Sullivan for a long weekend. My young son was recovering from his attack of pneumonia and my father had written suggesting that I come a day earlier than usual as he had some things he wanted to talk over with me. Accordingly, I arrived on Friday morning, April 4. We had a consultation with some of his clients at the office that day, and in the evening I accompanied him to a meeting of the Sullivan Library Board, of which he was president.

Mother was "waiting up" for us when we returned, as she frequently did. Often she would peel apples for Father, and there would be a big dish of them, peeled and quartered, on the library table. Father's leather chair—it had a handle on the side to let it go back a couple of notches, and a footrest to pull out—stood in the corner, with a bookcase at the left and a light behind. Mother's chair was not a permanent fixture like Father's, but it usually stood at the end of the table.

That night the three of us talked for a while and then Mother went upstairs, Father and I talking on until quite late. We were both feeling happy over an experience that afternoon. For a long time Mother had been suggesting to Father that he ought to have a physical examination. Her anxiety did not grow out of any particular illness, for he had had remarkable health. He was sixty-five, I think, before he ever had a doctor, except for some bronchial trouble when he was a young man. This had grown out of a neglected cold and excessive work when he was in college, drilling oil wells at night and taking a business course on the side.

Father was a rugged man and took pride in the fact that when he felt under the weather he would breathe deeply, walk uptown rapidly, and "lick it." He was not a Christian Scientist, but he did put a great deal of faith in the belief that "folks could prevail upon themselves that they were not sick by just insisting on it."

After our talk in the office that afternoon I had said to him, "Let's both go and have a physical examination." Father thought that I had been working too hard, but we both felt well. Anyway, we went over to Dr. Crowder's office on the east side of the square.

What we were concerned about, in Father's case, was the possibility of high blood pressure. This worry grew out of the death of a close friend, a lawyer in Terre Haute, who had recently suffered a stroke. After the doctor had taken Father's blood pressure and found it to be approximately 130 over 80—which he said was very good indeed—Father suggested that he check his machine by borrowing another from the doctor across the hall and taking it again. This Dr. Crowder did, and Father asked him to write the result on his letterhead for him to take home to show Mother. That was the cause for our rejoicing that evening.

I went home to our house across the street quite late, feeling very grateful. We were all well, everything was going well at the office, I was doing what needed to be done as chairman, and Father, especially, was most happy.

Next morning I went to the office to continue the consultations of the day before. Father did not hurry down that Saturday morning, and when he got there, my sister Martha noticed that he did not seem well. He told her that he did not feel quite right and that on the way downtown he had felt dizzy and had stopped to lean against a light pole. He assured me, however, that it was nothing.

I had dinner with him again that night and he went to bed early. At four o'clock Sunday morning Martha hurried across the street in great distress. I heard her rapping loudly on the door, and when I went down to let her in I saw that something was wrong. She quickly told me that Father was very sick; that he had gone into the bathroom and had fallen; Mother, hearing the noise, had gone in and found him on the floor. She had called Martha, and they had gotten him to bed and called the doctor. I went over immediately; the doctor, who was already there, told me Father had had a stroke. He couldn't move his left arm or leg, and his speech was seriously impaired.

After a few hours Father became a little better and the doctor was hopeful that he might recover. He wanted very much to talk, and I am sure that he was thinking very clearly, because he would nod his head in answer to questions, and when I got pencil and paper he would write the answers with his right hand, though with some difficulty. I remember his writing, "I cannot say what I want to say." That I never will forget, for his eyes were full at the time and he realized there was real trouble.

His condition became progressively worse until Wednesday morning, when he sank into a coma; he died at noon on Thursday. I was at his bedside most of the time; he would recognize me and smile; in the early part of that period he would occasionally write a note. I felt it, the moment he died.

The funeral was held Sunday, April 13, from the home, conducted by the pastor of our Presbyterian church, the Reverend W. E. Gray. The honorary pallbearers were John C. Chaney, representing the Presbyterian church; Judge William H. Bridwell, the Sullivan Bar Association; Patrick McEnery, the Masonic fraternity; W. D. Hutchison, the Knights of Pythias; Judge D. W. Henry of Terre Haute; and Judge A. D. Thomas of Crawfordsville. Memorials were presented by the bar associations of Sullivan, Vigo, Clay, Greene and Knox counties; Governor Goodrich headed a large party of state officials who came from Indianapolis.

Mother had not been well for a long time, and I am quite sure her condition added to Father's worry, although he tried to conceal it. Several months previous to his death Mother had been taken to the Mayo Clinic at Rochester, Minnesota, for the removal of a growth that had long given them concern. I went with them. Mother was a little woman weighing just a hundred pounds, but it was a hundred pounds of pure soul and heroic heart. Father and I were in the glass-enclosed waiting room of the hospital when Mother was wheeled by to the operating room. We waved to her and she was as cheerful as she had ever been in her life. We waited a long time—much longer than expected—before we were met by the doctor, who was smiling and told us that everything was all right. We went home rejoicing.

Just before Thanksgiving of 1918, when Mother was able to be brought home, apparently recovered, Mr. W. J. Jackson, president of the C. & E.I. Railroad, wrote Father that he was sending his private car up to Rochester to bring her home safely, so that she would not have to change at Chicago. Father was to go up and come back with her. He had been the attorney for the C. & E.I. and its predecessor, the E. & T.H., in Sullivan for many years. It was typical of Mr. Jackson and of the way in which those Chicago railroad men regarded Father.

Mother was well for some months after the operation, but trouble came back in the same area. By the time of Father's death it had developed into a multicellular cancer, and she was fatally ill. I am quite sure that Father had realized that. She did not appear to be as ill as she really was, but after Father's death she became rapidly worse. As she was weak from shock, grief, and illness, we were worried about how she would stand the immediate ordeal of the funeral. We had arranged to have the doctor nearby, and a nurse was there to take care of her if she collapsed, as we feared she might.

At the exact hour of the funeral she seemed especially strong. We stood—my sisters, my brother, Mother, and I—by father's casket. When the others had gone, and just before the casket was closed, we knelt at Father's side. I was on one side of Mother and my brother Hinkle was on the other, holding her arms and ready to help her up. After a moment she rose vigorously. We had been fearful that she would faint, but she almost jumped up, and in a voice of inspiration said: "Come, children. Go with Mother." She turned and led the way out of the door with all her old-time vigor, out to the driveway and to the conveyance which was to take us to the cemetery. I have never seen such courage. There was no doubt in Mother's mind where Father had gone. She had the most consummate faith, as did he.

Mother continued to grow worse and weakened rapidly. On Decoration Day I was to be at Oklahoma City to make a Memorial Day speech. The plan was to go to St. Louis a couple of days before, there to be met by a delegation from Oklahoma headed by James McGraw, the Republican national committeeman.

McGraw had a fight on his hands for re-election, but I could not directly participate in the contest. I could, however, go down to his state and make some speeches, and it was decided I would do that over Decoration Day. It involved going to Muskogee for a speech first, then over to Tulsa for a night meeting, and at midnight taking a train for Oklahoma City. This schedule was carried out; I left New York to reach Terre Haute on an early morning train and motored down to Sullivan, going at once to Mother's bedroom. She was confined to her bed, really very ill, but she was cheerful, full of spirit, and apparently happy. But I was worried about her and thought that I ought not to go on, as I felt that she was probably putting up a cheerful front to relieve me. When I suggested that I stay, she reminded me of the time when Theodore Roosevelt went with me to the convention at Saratoga the day after he had the word that Quentin had been killed. She told me that I must not under any circumstances stay there with her, that she was all right, and that I must go through with my program.

So I did go to St. Louis, met the committee, and went on to Muskogee. At eight o'clock in the morning, when I got off the train with Mr. McGraw, his man met us with a telegram for me. I read it in the station and put it in my pocket without saying anything about its contents until we finished the morning meeting. It was from home, stating that Mother had died the night before at eight o'clock, the evening after the morning visit I had had with her.

Under these circumstances I had my hands pretty full. The meeting in the morning was successful; no one there knew anything about my trouble. When we got on the next train and I was in the drawing room with Jim McGraw, I handed him the telegram. He was a fine person, full of sympathy, and insisted that we call off the Tulsa meeting. I recalled the Theodore Roosevelt incident and told him what Mother had said. We decided to go on with the meeting, but we canceled the dinner to be given at the country club by Mr. McGraw and Eugene Crawley, formerly of Sullivan. Instead, we went to one of their homes for a quiet dinner and then to the Opera House, where five thousand people had assembled for a Republican mass meeting.

I did not know it before we went, but the evening paper in Tulsa carried an item that my mother had died the night before, so that many in the audience knew the situation. It was a significant meeting and I am sure that there was great sympathy among many.

At midnight we went on to Oklahoma City and had an afternoon memorial meeting there, a patriotic affair with no politics in it. Mr. McGraw had been busy carrying out a promise to get me a plane by which I figured to get back to Sullivan without delaying the funeral. Jim McGraw at first demurred; yes, he could get a plane, but he didn't think he should; they weren't safe, and so on. We thrashed that out and he said he would get it. The time came to go in the late afternoon of that Decoration Day. But McGraw had deliberately caused the plane to be put out of commission so it could not be run; I took the late afternoon train for home, arriving at an hour which caused only a brief delay in the funeral. Those days are stamped ineffaceably in my memory.

For many months before the Republican National Convention was due to open, I had been working on an idea that I felt to be of paramount importance to the party's success in the next national election. It was a plan for long-range study and preparation of the party platform. Too often in the past this most important feature had been neglected until the last moment, the result being a haphazard, hastily conceived program. This time I was resolved that things should be different, with a platform soundly planned and solidly constructed. I wanted an extraordinary committee created to carry on the work. This special platform committee as first created consisted of twelve National Committee members and twelve non-committee members; later it developed into a heterogeneous committee of 171. The group was not to supplant the Platform Committee of the convention, but was to anticipate their work and submit full recommendations, thus avoiding much of the jam of work that usually piles up in the last few days.

This plan I broached at a meeting of the Natoial Committee held in Washington in December 1919, at which the convention date was set for June 1920 in Chicago. The committee approved my suggestion, together with other recommendations, including a resolution urging all Republican states to hasten ratification of the suffrage amendment.

The announcement of the Committee of 171 created a mild sensation in Washington political circles, where it was taken as something altogether new in the way of campaign machinery. A couple of paragraphs from an article by Harold Phelps Stokes, Washington political commentator, will indicate the general reaction to the plan announced:

The unexpectedly large net that the Republican chairman threw over the Republican leaders of the country has drawn in fish of every scale. They may prove to be mere political window dressing but that doesn't seem to be what Mr. Hays has in mind. "This committee will itself be a working body," he says in his statement. Nobody who reads over the list can accuse the committee of being packed or hand-picked. . . .

The only common denominator these 171 miscellaneous Republican frac-tions have to sit upon is their antipathy for the present Democratic administration. If they can pull through from that point to complete agreement on constructive policy for their party, it will be something of a triumph. . . .

I met with the congressional members of the committee in Washington early in February, shortly after my return from a transcontinental tour, and passed on to them the observations I had made as to what the people were expecting from the Republicans, and some suggestions as to how the committee might proceed in the work of formulating recommendations for the platform. The general conference largely covered methods of committee procedure, but in individual talks with members I stressed the importance of expediting matters with a view to building up a good party record as quickly as possible. As to the committee itself, I believed we had inaugurated a plan which, if followed conscientiously, the country quite generally approved. "If a platform is merely a stall," I told them, "forty-eight hours is enough to spend over it, but if it is a real promise it ought to have long and thoughtful consideration, as this plan proposes."

On my tour I had found people everywhere, regardless of past affiliations, seeking Republican success because they seemed to believe it would encourage such policies as an honest, efficient, and economical business administration; a plan for the reduction of taxes; the repeal of taxes which kill initiative; and the spreading of the war debt over a large number of years. Also, back in that earlier day, I found the desire that is echoed today for better relations between capital and labor, with justice to both, as well as to the most important public.

The size and scope of the task undertaken by the committee are shown by a partial list of topics selected for study and research. It included tariff, international trade and credits, merchant marine, industrial relations and problems of labor and capital, regulation of industry and commerce, railroads, agriculture, farm tenantry and country life, high cost of living, conservation and waterways, currency and banking, taxation, national economy, retrenchment and budget, immigration, limitation of federal and state control, education, public health, public works, military and naval policy, pensions, war-risk insurance and soldier legislation, review of the Democratic administration, insular possessions, law and order and the administration of justice, social problems, and postal reform.

THEODORE ROOSEVELT

Hays—see him; he must go to Washington for 10 days; see Senate and House; prevent split on domestic policies.

These, the last written words of Theodore Roosevelt, scrawled on a memo pad on his bedside table during the night of his passing, are the dynamic words of a man of action. They carry on with the thought expressed to his sister a few days before his death:

> I have kept the promise that I made to myself when I was 21. That promise was to live my life up to the hilt until I was 60, and I have kept that promise.

And this, indeed, he did.

Theodore Roosevelt was my friend. This friendship, of short duration as years are counted, was of a completeness and intensity that do not reckon time and that brought the profoundest appreciation, which shall continue while life lasts. The more intimate our relations became, the deeper grew my regard, for the better one knew him the greater became one's appreciation. And I never left him that I did not consciously marvel yet again at the man.

We measure men by comparison. A man is great or small as he rises above or sinks below the level of the generation to which he belongs. When he is gone, we can estimate his size by the space left vacant. By either of these standards, what a man was this man! He was powerful in influence because men believed in him; he moved among his fellows daily with the most unexampled virility, giving and taking. No higher tribute can be paid.

I affirm that to love truth for truth's sake is the principal part of human perfection in this world. That, above all other things, Theodore Roosevelt did. He was honest in act, honest in word, honest in thought. The crime of sham was not his. He was himself with no pretense. He recognized the perfidy of pretense and the wickedness of make-believe, and he abhorred them with the wholesome hate they merit. What he thought, he said; and what he said, he believed. Honest himself, he attributed honesty to everyone with whom he came in contact. To him, every man was innocent until twice proven guilty. Then again, he would stand in faith, always giving another chance. But when convinced of the guilt of man or thing, he would see to its eradication with unerring judgment, fearless dispatch, and satisfying completeness approached by no one else.

"Never hit unless you have to—but when you hit, end it."

Mark Sullivan, in his monumental history, *Our Times,* said:

> It was one of Theodore Roosevelt's definite contributions to his time that he, being a Harvard man and of inherited wealth, showed to others of his class ways to spend their lives with satisfaction to themselves and advantage to their country.

I have heard the story that when Roosevelt decided very early to take part in politics his family was not immediately in sympathy with that form of public service; he was told by them that he would find no one at the meetings he proposed attending but "grooms, liquor dealers, and low politicians."

"Well," Roosevelt replied, "if that is so, then they belong to the governing class, and you don't, and I mean, if I can, to be of the governing class." And he was of the governing class from that moment until he died. He first governed himself, and at no time did he fail to apply to his own personal life, to his thoughts, and to his actions, the same code he applied to others. Weak physically, he made himself strong. Whenever wrong, he made himself right. With an entire absence of any false pride, he would consult his friends, urge suggestions, and freely adopt them. He is said to have had from his earliest youth this characteristic of absorbing good from everyone and everything with which he came in contact. He had it to the fullest in the wisdom of his maturity. He would discuss himself in as frank a manner as he would discuss his opponents.

His career as a member of the legislature, as Civil Service Commissioner, police commissioner, Assistant Secretary of the Navy, colonel of Rough Riders, governor of New York, Vice-President and President of the United States, as author, historian, naturalist, hunter, sportsman, husband, father, citizen, carried through it all as the one controlling motif a consistent determination to do what he thought was right. It mattered not one whit how that course affected him or anyone else or anything, if he thought it was right, he did it—and he did it to the hilt.

What a condemnation is his entire experience to those smug individuals who are either "too busy" or "too good" to interest themselves in public affairs, who sit with their hands folded, taking no part in governmental problems, expecting everything to be right, while they share no part of the burden in the effort to make them so.

It is passing strange indeed that men have to be urged to exercise the first privilege of sovereign citizenship—the right to help govern themselves. Yet such is the fact, and it is because of that fact that most governmental evils develop. Government functions through individuals; these individuals are elected through the processes of practical politics, a sequence which cannot be avoided; it is the best possible way. We can have better government only if we interest ourselves in public affairs, in the selection of those to whom this government is entrusted, in having thought and voice in its operation, and in making our country's affairs our own business.

The lesson of the patriotism of Theodore Roosevelt, which will live forever, is his monument. This patriotism was not the kind that is born of extremities; it was not that fire, splendid as it is, which burns in the souls of men only when their country is in danger.

His patriotism was not the patriotism stirred only by martial music— it was the patriotism of good citizenship, at the fireside, the plow, the mart, in low places and in high places, in season and out of season; it was the patriotism which caused him to make his country's welfare his own business and to interest himself continuously in the practical politics of his community. He always believed and acted the patriotism of peace as well as of war, and it moved the man to measure his every act from earliest manhood to the date of his death by how, in his good judgment, he could do the most for his country's welfare. This is the only patriotism which, in the last analysis, is worth while. It was this patriotism which made Theodore Roosevelt begin his fight for better government and in the prosaic time of peace make almost heroic his fight for little children, for social betterment, for economic justice, for the rights of labor, for the rights of capital, for the rights of Right, wherever that fight was needed.

We are wont to think of this man, with his outdoor mind and his two fists, as a man's man. He was that. He was that above all other things. Yet his chivalry would have graced any court. In this, too, there was no pretense. He was true to his manhood. His own mother, wife, sister, and daughters had made all womanhood sacred to him. He loved his home and recognized it as the one and only glimpse of heaven on earth afforded man—and he acted accordingly.

His great fight for preparedness and Americanism in this country against professional pacifism and parlor Socialism was not the development of his later years only. Back in 1897, when he was Assistant Secretary of the Navy, he cried for naval preparedness for the Spanish-American War, which he believed inevitable. He overhauled the Navy. He got, and spent for target practice, great appropriations for ammunition. And again, in 1914, 1915, and 1916, like a voice in the wilderness, he cried out, "Prepare, prepare, prepare."

By some he was called impetuous; yet when McKinley died he made the statement, "I promise to take over and continue to completion, so far as it lies within my abilities to do so, the policies of the great President who now lies dead." He was called warlike by some—yet he championed the cause of international arbitration of world differences of opinions and claims, both in and out of office practiced what he preached by submitting the Pious Fund case, and kept the great part of the world peaceful during his regime. He was for peace when peace was right, but if to win right for right's sake war was necessary, then he was for war or for whatever else was needed; and, above all, he was for America eternally, and there he was the severest partisan.

And how this soldier thought the thoughts, sensed the wants, and sympathized with the needs of the soldiers, and how full was his proper appreciation of them! Unable to go himself, always his heart was with his four boys and their comrades in World War I, and our entire Army was to him as were his four boys. He would say to me: "They say food will win the war, Liberty bonds will win the war, thrift stamps will win the war. They won't. They will all help win the war. But the war will be won by the fighting men at the fighting front and in no other way."

I was with Theodore Roosevelt on the morning he received word of Quentin's death. I was with him the next day at Saratoga when, with his heart literally crushed, he interpolated in a speech he was reading, saying:

"The finest, the bravest, the best of our young men have sprung eagerly forward to face death for the sake of a high ideal; and thereby they have brought home to us the great truth that life consists of more than easygoing pleasure, and more than hard, conscienceless, brutal striving after purely material success; that while we must rightly care for the body and the things of the body, yet that such care leads nowhere unless we also have thought for our own souls and the souls of our brothers. When these gallant boys, on the golden crest of life, gladly face death for the sake of an ideal, shall not we who stay behind, who have not been found worthy of the grand adventure, shall we not in our turn try to shape our lives so as to make in this country the ideal which in our hearts we acknowledge, and in the actual workaday business of our world, come a little nearer together, and make this country a better place to live in for these men, and for the women who sent these men to battle, and for the children who are to come after them?"

That fateful day of September 14, 1901, when Theodore Roosevelt in Buffalo took over the reins of office from the dead hands of William McKinley, had marked the beginning of a new era in American life, upon which his powerful personality put the imprint of his name—the Roosevelt Era. True, he was catapulted into power through an accident, but he made of the presidency such a political potency as has been wielded by few Americans. His sudden rise came at what he felt to be the nadir of his political career. As presiding officer of the Senate, he had had no outlet for his boundless energy. He felt he had been sidetracked —shelved—in the full power of his manhood. So discouraged with politics had he become that he began the study of law, as he said, "to equip myself for a new career."

Roosevelt had emerged from the Spanish-American War as the strongest potential leader among Republican politicians. His popularity was enormous and was needed by such Republican leaders as Senator Platt, who wanted him as governor of New York. Accordingly, he was elected, but soon showed his independence of thought. His tilts with Senator Platt became famous and, as Mark Sullivan said, "Platt now fully realized that he had a bear by the tail, a most energetic, impulsive, rampant bear."

Roosevelt's defiance of Platt had made his popularity nationwide, but he was reluctant to accept the nomination to the vice-presidency, which was being pressed upon him by followers throughout the country. He finally yielded to Senator Lodge's argument: "Theodore, the way to break a precedent is to make one."

It was Roosevelt who carried the brunt of the 1900 presidential campaign, stumping the country while President McKinley remained on the front porch at Canton, when the two were victorious with a vote of 292 to 155 for Bryan. The Platt-Hanna type of Republican leadership undoubtedly was gratified by the success of the strategy of "kicking upstairs" the troublesome Roosevelt. That was in the era of "vested interests," when "stand pat" had become the slogan of the "Old Guard." Their satisfaction was rudely blasted when an assassin's bullet laid President McKinley low. "That damned cowboy is now in the White House," Mark Hanna is reported to have said bitterly when he heard the news.

Others felt differently. "He brought in a stream of fresh, pure bracing air from the mountains to clear up the fetid atmosphere of the national capital," said Harry Thurston Peck. Roosevelt's first three months in the White House wrought a spectacular change in American thought. The "Roosevelt Era" was well on its way.

"The infectiousness of his exuberant vitality, high spirits, enormous capacity for work, tirelessness, his forthrightness, his many striking qualities gave a lift of the spirit to millions of average men, stimulating them to higher use of their own powers, and giving them a new zest for life," said Mark Sullivan. He rattled the dry bones of precedent and saw more people in his first three months of office than any other president before him. "Everybody must be my friend now," he told newspapermen. And to Southerners: "I am going to be President of the United States and not of any section."

Much of the economic liberalism enjoyed by this country today stems from those first few months of the first Roosevelt administration. Inspired by one of his fundamental traits, the instinct to respond to challenge, he attacked the legal immunities enjoyed by the holding companies, long a target for popular anger as being "above the law." He enunciated his "Square Deal" policy and inaugurated the famous "trust-busting" suits by seriously applying the long-dormant Sherman Anti-Trust Act of 1890. This bad news was brought to J. P. Morgan at his dinner table, and the financier immediately departed for Washington. Wall Street was demoralized by the news, for big-business legal talent had long believed the holding companies too safely entrenched to be attacked.

Although armed with not a shred of the legal authority such as the Chief Executive holds today, Theodore Roosevelt successfully settled the great coal strike of 1902 and established the principle of arbitration and the paramount rights of the public in labor disputes affecting the national welfare. This was one of his most outstanding achievements—

his demonstration that no group is more powerful than the government. Out of all this grew the Department of Commerce and Labor, the law for which President Roosevelt signed in 1903, making it the ninth Cabinet office, and which since has divided into two separate departments.

The climax of Roosevelt's crusade for economic reform came in the great railroad rate fight, and his victory brought new hope to thousands of small businessmen and their customers—the common people—all over the country. The practice of the great rail carriers of returning large and discriminatory rebates to large volume shippers at the expense of the little men had held the small businessman in chains for many years. The anti-rebate law was forced through a reluctant Congress by the sheer strength and resourcefulness of President Roosevelt; it brought into play every weapon in his armament. The parliamentary conflict lasted for many months, but Roosevelt won and the railroads were compelled to submit to government regulation.

This principle of governmental supervision in the public interest Roosevelt extended into other fields, notably the meat-packing industry. Exposed by Upton Sinclair in his book, *The Jungle,* this industry had become a national scandal until cleaned up by the federal meat inspection law which Roosevelt also forced upon Congress. From this battle he gained great personal political prestige after several congressional opponents of the law were roundly defeated at the polls.

Spectacular, theatrical—and controversial still—was the historic achievement of the Roosevelt administration in the construction of the Panama Canal. The President's own forthright admission—"I took Panama"—is still quoted as the basis for charges of imperialistic aggression on the part of this country. Yet few today would honestly say that the end did not justify the means. The picture civilization would present today if the Panama Canal had never been built is almost impossible to imagine. Certainly its lack might well have sealed the fate of this nation in the late war, and certainly the prosperity and general welfare of the people from whom the canal site was "seized" has been immeasurably uplifted.

In another issue which has grown into blazing importance today— racial discrimination—Roosevelt was an early crusader. That he was too early is the chief reason it can be recorded as one of his few defeats. One of his great ambitions on assuming the presidency was "to see the South back in full communion with the rest of the nation." He set out not only to include southern Democrats in his appointments but to consider fairly the Negroes.

His appointments heartened the South, but on October 18, 1901, he gave the most talked-about luncheon ever eaten in the White House, and his whole policy toward the South encountered a devastating counterattack. He had the great Negro educator, Booker T. Washington, as his guest, and it proved disastrous. The news spread like wildfire and was insanely misinterpreted. Southern editors and politicians were quick to recognize the weapon chance had given them to defeat the spread of Republicanism and the two-party system in the South and they grasped it eagerly. "By the Booker T. Washington incident the Negro became securely the reason for the South remaining as solidly Democratic as at any time since the Civil War," wrote Mark Sullivan.

Roosevelt personally made every effort to repair the damage, and in 1904 he received more southern votes than any previous Republican candidate, even breaking the Solid South by his sensational victory in Missouri.

The rise of Theodore Roosevelt in the estimation of his fellow men can best be appreciated by a review of the various adjectives and epithets applied to him. In the beginning he was called a "young squirt," a "weakling," a "punkin-lily," a "goo-goo," a "Jane Dandy," a "dude," and was accused of the "insufferable conceit" of "banging his hair," and uttering his *r*'s in a manner regarded as effeminate in the West.

But he remained in politics to find himself being called "strenuous," a "fighter with two-ounce gloves," "fire-eater," "Rough Rider," and finally plain "Teddy" and, by the highest authorities, the "outstanding American of his day."

CHAPTER 19

National Republican Convention of 1920

THE seventeenth Republican National Convention opened on June 8 with every gallery and corner of the huge Coliseum packed with humanity—fourteen thousand men and women. Bands blared and flags waved and all the traditional trappings of the big quadrennial G.O.P. get-together were present, except a candidate with enough delegates to assure his nomination.

Until the last possible moment that morning I had been in consultation with party leaders, trying to get agreement on the selection of a permanent chairman. It was eleven-thirty—more than a half hour late—when I stepped out on the platform and gaveled the convention to order. In the hush that followed, Bishop Charles E. Woodcock of Louisville offered the opening prayer, and the preliminaries were under way. Then I returned to the platform to give my report to the party:

"The Republican party has met in this free and open convention to accept from the people a mandate for the government of the United States. As chairman of the National Committee, I report progress. By next November the majority of the party should be at least three million. In spirit I report more than progress: I report fulfillment. The great party of this Union has become a union. It shall continue so. There will be no bolt from this convention."

I then announced that Henry Cabot Lodge had been selected by the committee to act as temporary chairman, and at exactly noon Senator Lodge mounted the platform and began his keynote address.

The first two days of the convention in the sweltering heat of Chicago's summer were occupied with the political maneuvering that is the important background of every such gathering—often more important than the actual business transacted on the floor. Developments of the second day indicated that Senator Boise Penrose and other eastern leaders were working to bring about the nomination of Senator Knox, while a mighty struggle was brewing between the Wood and Lowden forces as to which should have the advantage in the first ballot, it being conceded that two thirds of the delegates were for one or the other.

The tentative draft of our national platform had been given its finishing touches in Washington on June 2. No mention was made of prohibition, but a plank urging the speedy ratification of the suffrage amendment was recommended; no decision was reached on the soldier bonus or the League of Nations planks. The Resolutions Committee was swamped with applications for hearings by individuals and groups anxious to get their views converted into platform planks. Wets and drys, suffragists and anti-suffragists, economists, Irish sympathizers, League of Nations advocates and opponents, labor leaders and employers, all were heard. After two days and nights of this, all the planks were fashioned except those on the League of Nations and on labor. The subcommittee of thirteen appointed to draft the League of Nations plank adjourned at one o'clock on the morning of June 10, after an all-day session in which no agreement had been reached. The members were completely at sea and facing threats of a bolt by the Johnson-Borah group of irreconcilables. On the final day of discussion, however, a draft that I had obtained previously from Mr. Root was accepted. In the entire process, the difference between the original Root document and the final plank was negligible.

Mr. Root had been president of the Hague Tribunal prior to the World War, which caused its doors to be closed. During the Chicago convention he was at The Hague, on the invitation of the League of Nations, to help organize an international court and take down the shutters of the Hague Tribunal. The spirit of our party platform tended to revive and expand the Tribunal, somewhat to the exclusion of the League, which preferred to create a court within itself as the superstate, and throw the previous legal machinery into the scrap heap.

Unanimous agreement on the entire platform, including the treaty plank, was reached on June 10; and the announcement, made to the convention by Senator McCormick, was received with cheers. The treaty plank agreed upon by the Resolutions Committee endorsed the principle of the League of Nations, or international court, without specific mention of the League. It likewise denounced the League of Nations as proposed by President Wilson as un-American and dangerous to the sovereignty and safety of the country. It justified the opposition of the Republicans in the Senate to this League, whether that opposition was voiced against the whole treaty or in the form of reservations intended to safeguard American interests. This blanket clause, denouncing the Wilson treaty and the League plan, was so worded as to take within its language every Republican in the Senate, irreconcilable or reservationist.

The Coliseum was like an oven when late on the third day Senator Watson and the members of the Resolutions Committee brought their complete report to the floor of the convention. The reading of the platform was punctuated with wild cheering, and a mention of Theodore Roosevelt in connection with the conservation plank brought the delegates to their feet. After a Kansas delegate had seconded the motion, the platform was adopted unanimously.

Ten hours of sweltering heat and torrid oratory filled the fourth day of the convention, but at its close the delegates found themselves deadlocked. It was the day of the nominating speeches, and as the roll of the states was called, speaker after speaker responded with all the tricks of oratory known to politics. The wild demonstrations at the end of each prolonged the intervals, for it is against the ground rules of a convention for a speaker to name his man until the last possible moment. Leonard Wood's name was the first placed in nomination, and the demonstration following lasted for more than half an hour. Lowden's name was next proposed, and his demonstration exceeded Wood's.

The big applause for Hiram Johnson, whose name followed Lowden's, came from the galleries rather than the delegates. After this the other names placed in nomination were those of Coolidge, Pritchard, Dr. Nicholas Murray Butler, Herbert Hoover, Warren Harding, Governor Sproul of Pennsylvania, Senator Poindexter, and Senator Sutherland. With the exception of the demonstration for Harding, which was quite spontaneous, the cheering for each succeeding name became briefer and more perfunctory; when the final nomination was reached, the delegates were so fed up with seven hours of oratory that the fifteen-minute speech could not be heard ten feet from the speakers' platform over the hubbub of protesting delegates.

When the speechmaking finally subsided, it was easy for Senator Lodge to get order. A hush fell over the great hall as the chairman rapped his gavel and announced that the next business of the convention was a roll call for the nomination of a candidate for President of the United States.

Four ballots were taken in the next two hours, with the strength of the leaders in these opening rounds conforming closely to pre-convention estimates. Wood led on the first ballot, as expected, with 287½ votes; Lowden had 201, and Johnson 133½. Harding trailed well back in the field with 65½ votes. In the succeeding ballots the leaders all picked up delegates as the courtesy votes for various favorite sons began to fall off, but their relative strength remained practically unchanged.

The wearied convention was ready to adjourn after the fourth ballot, for it was evident that no candidate could command a majority. Wood's total had risen to 314½, Lowden to 289, and Johnson to 140½, while Harding had dropped to 61½. The convention clearly was deadlocked; only some drastic action or a political miracle could save the party from infinite harm. An extraordinary gathering of high-ranking Republicans in an all-night session not only accomplished the miracle but incidentally added a new phrase to the American lexicon of politics—the "smoke-filled room." The author of the phrase remains unknown to this day, but according to my memory it was coined by a reporter for a Democratic newspaper, who used it in his dispatches sent from the press gallery. Room 404 in the Blackstone Hotel will long remain famous in American political history. It was the reception room of Colonel George Harvey's apartment. Here, at two forty-five Saturday morning, Harding was informed that he was the compromise choice of a dozen party leaders for the nomination.

Friday night the convention hall had witnessed chaos and confusion; Saturday night was the deadline; otherwise the future of the Republican party was endangered. Harvey, who came to the convention at the invitation of many party leaders, was the central figure in the negotiations. That night the most prominent men of the party found their way to his suite, but not by request or previous understanding. The ensuing conference was not "set up." It was elastic, constantly changing in personnel. The participants were drawn there by the sheer magnetism of the crisis. The phrase "smoke-filled room" was a bogey used then, and since, to convey the entirely false impression that the choice of the presidential nominee was the result of chicanery, carried out behind the smoke screen of the cigar, for the mutual benefit of conniving politicians. Actually the accomplishment of that night was one of downright common sense and mutual give-and-take. In my opinion, that phrase, "smoke-filled room," might well be dropped from the future reporting of conventions, of whatever political party.

Senator Frank B. Brandegee of Connecticut acted as a sort of unofficial chairman of the gathering. Others present included Senators Lodge, Medill McCormick of Illinois, Smoot of Utah, Jim Watson of Indiana, James W. Wadsworth, Jr., of New York, William Calder of New York, Curtis of Kansas, and A. T. Hert of Kentucky and Joseph B. Kealing of Indiana, members of the National Republican Committee.

Lodge wanted Wood. McCormick and Watson wanted Lowden, and so on. Everyone wanted his man, but all knew the danger if the convention continued into the following week. Compromise—not with principles, but among men—was the obvious and seemingly inevitable answer.

Personally, although I had the adjoining suite, I was not present in the room that became famous for its aroma of tobacco. I stood absolutely pat on my determination that my job as national chairman was *to elect, not to select*. In Indiana a man doesn't bid at his own auction.

Although Harding's nomination was practically certain after that famous night of June 11, the senator himself did not feel sufficiently sure of the outcome to relinquish the idea of being a candidate to succeed himself for his Senate seat. Accordingly he wired his friends in

Ohio shortly before midnight, when the time for filing petitions expired, to enter his name in that race. At the same time he emphasized that he had not withdrawn from the presidential nomination contest.

The final day's session of the convention opened in a broiling temperature that kept mounting as the hall filled. The tone of the convention had subtly changed. After the turmoil and excitement of the previous day it was much calmer, for all the delegates were weary.

The leader seesawed through the first three ballots of the morning session. Then the time came to try out Harding, and the Ohio delegation was up on chairs, roaring and yelling. From all parts of the hall came shouts of "Harding." The break started on this ballot, with Harding picking up 28½ votes. New York and California leaders wanted a recess, but Harding backers objected. "No recess until we get Harding," they screamed. When the question was put, both sides voted so lustily that the chair was in doubt. Senator Lodge hesitated and stroked his beard. Up on the platform heads were together, arms around shoulders, with Smoot, McCormick, Warren Neyland, Watson, and others looking like a college glee club about to sound off. The group dissolved and Lodge announced: "The convention is adjourned until four o'clock."

The Harding parade marched into the hall when the afternoon session opened, with the delegates bearing banners reading: "The Republicans Need Ohio," and "Harding Means Ohio." It was a welcome diversion to the weary, jaded spectators in the galleries, munching hot dogs and drinking lemonade, and brought them out of their seats for the first time since the convention opened. The demonstration lasted until 4:50 P.M., when Senator Lodge gaveled the meeting to order and called for the ninth ballot.

The march to Harding was under way, and in this ballot he took the lead for the first time, with 374½ votes against Wood's 249 and Lowden's 121½, and the rest of the field trailing. On this ballot I had the honor of receiving a single vote, cast by a delegate from Oklahoma.

The situation was tense when the chair ordered: "The tenth ballot will now be taken." As the roll call progressed, Harding began to pick up votes all along the line. Michigan's vote put the Ohio senator over. He gained twenty-four there, giving him ten above the required majority of 493. From then on it was a procession, as state after state fell into line, many delegations "reconsidering" their vote and climbing on the band wagon. Before the roll call was completed, Senator Frelinghuysen of New Jersey moved the nomination of Harding be declared unanimous, and the only "noes" came from the Wisconsin delegation. The final tabulation gave Harding 674½, Wood 157½, and the rest trailing.

Chairman Lodge's voice had become so worn that he turned over the gavel to Frank B. Willis of Ohio, who announced that the next order of business would be the selection of a candidate for Vice-President. The names placed in nomination were Irvine Lenroot of Wisconsin, Governor Henry J. Allen of Kansas, Governor Calvin Coolidge of Massachusetts, Henry W. Anderson of Virginia, Senator A. J. Gronna of North Dakota, Judge J. C. Pritchard of North Carolina, and Senator Hiram Johnson of California.

The balloting turned into a Coolidge parade, and his final vote was the same as Harding's, 674½, with Lenroot the runner-up.

CHAPTER 20

"Back to Normalcy" and Woman Suffrage

I T is the lot of some workers in the political vineyards for their names sooner or later to be mentioned as possibilities for the presidency, no matter how far that idea may be removed from their own personal ambitions or the political probabilities. As far back as March of 1919 the New York *Tribune*, in a discussion of presidential possibilities by Geoffrey Parsons, had brought my name into the picture, saying:

> There is one other possible Republican candidate, in a class by himself. That is Chairman Will Hays of the Republican National Committee. His name bobs up in unexpected quarters. There is no widespread movement for him for the simple reason that no one knows whether Mr. Hays wants to be named in 1920. There is a very strong feeling in Indiana that Mr. Hays is Presidential size. There is also a strong feeling that the logical course for him is to serve as Governor before aspiring higher. He can have the nomination for Governor of Indiana in 1920 for the asking. He is now only 39 years old. There is plenty of time in 1924 and 1928. . . .

Considerable pressure was being brought to bear at this time to induce me to make the race for the governorship, as it had earlier been to run for senator, much against my own inclinations, for my whole desire was to remain as chairman of the National Committee and follow through with that job. In the Cincinnati *Enquirer* of March 22, 1919, Robert G. Tucker wrote of this "Hays boom":

> The way the stage is set, he can land the nomination merely by consenting to accept—which is a thing no one else has been able to do in the past 30 or 40 years. The situation is not without its complexities for Hays and his friends who would like to see him continue at the head of the National Committee through 1920. . . . But now comes the test for Hays. He is being assured—and the pressure will be increased—that for the good of the party, he must accept the nomination for Governor.

Other newspapers continued speculating in a similar vein, and the talk persisted until August 15, when I made a definite statement at Brookville, Indiana, eliminating myself from the gubernatorial contest. Previously I had consulted with many party leaders, asking their advice on the matter. Most of the Indiana leaders were strongly in favor of my entering for the governorship, but outside the state it was the feeling that I should stay on the job as chairman of the National Committee. This was my conviction too. In declining I took the ground that I could not be 100 per cent efficient either as a candidate for governor or as national chairman if I tried to make the race and manage the national campaign at the same time.

Presidential speculations on my name, however, kept bobbing up from time to time right up to the final days of the 1920 convention. During the days of the convention itself a number of newspapers and many of my friends persisted in listing me as among the dark horses, in spite of my declarations that such talk was distasteful to me.

Writing in the Chicago *Herald and Examiner* of June 9, Samuel G. Blythe said:

Will Hays, the vivacious chairman of the National Committee, had his triumphant quarter of an hour at the convention yesterday and was cheered more than any other feature of the session. This caused considerable satisfaction in certain quarters not entirely dissociated with Kentucky, Indiana and other contiguous states for the reason that, if this convention gets into a jam, it is the plan of statesmen from the quarters indicated to propose Mr. Hays as the logical canthook to break the jam.

In fact, while it may not in truth be said that Mr. Hays is a dark horse, because he is darker than that, being practically invisible at present, there may arise a contingency wherein it will be good politics for some Indianan with a loud voice to rise and ask, "What's the matter with Will Hays?" in the expectation that at least 493 delegates will respond, "He's all right!" and hurry from the convention hall to catch the first train home.

The Casper (Wyo.) *Tribune*, which had its representative at the convention, carried an editorial under the heading "Hays for President," which read, in part, as follows. However exaggerated the praise, it does reflect recognition of a revitalized Republican party.

There seems to have come to the delegates at Chicago a spontaneous idea that Will H. Hays, chairman of the National Republican Committee, ought to be the convention nominee for the presidency. In early, pre-convention days, similar suggestions were frequently made, but were met with discouragement from the chairman. . . .

There is no man in public life today who has a clearer conception of the Republican party's doctrine affecting good government. No man has been inspired to a higher sense of public duty to the people by a contemplation of the party's history and record. No public man in the country is more free from political and other influences that destroy independent action.

Mr. Hays can be pointed to as one of the best examples of pure American, with wholesome and plain American ideals. He thinks and acts in terms of the whole people, not in terms of special groups.

Due to his efforts alone the Republican national organization has been made forceful and strong; has been made to stand for the same high principles of conduct that the party teaches. He has brought the teachings into practice. Mr. Hays has done another thing: he has given politics a respectability it has not enjoyed of late years. He has brought about a working interest in the party on the part of its best members. For the first time in many years the Republicans are conducting the affairs of the party, instead of the bosses. Mr. Hays has restored the party to them. . . .

In directing the 1920 campaign that resulted in the election of Warren G. Harding as twenty-ninth President of the United States, I sensed that the nation was yearning, with a veritable homesickness, for a trustworthy period of peace. This was symbolized by Harding's slogan, "Back to normalcy," which won him wide support.

In 1920 we had not only the wounds to heal inside the Republican party, but the task of finding a fundamental standard of national existence which would restore our lost balance. Things were very different from the life we had known in 1914!

The United States, at the close of World War I, had become the world's richest and most powerful nation. Looking back, it can fairly be said that we did not know how to use our power. We may still have been insufficiently worldly-wise, for we did not properly exert our new strength. We were a suddenly overgrown, awkward giant among the older and possibly wiser world powers. The war had visibly lessened Britain's pre-eminence, and we could have stepped into her place. We might then have done something to halt new concepts of government that were taking place, notably in Russia, which have since run counter to every pattern of society that the modern world has ever experienced. Russia even then was planning to take over the position that Britain had lost, and thus gain the leapedship of the world.

Meanwhile the wealth of the world had been broken down. Trade routes were partially paralyzed and markets spoiled. Currencies were unstable. New national setups and boundary adjustments were causing local revolutions. Everywhere the ancient moral concepts had been undermined. Onto this stage stepped a new presidential candidate who was in himself a reassuring voice in a perplexed hour.

Warren G. Harding had risen to comfortable affluence as the publisher of a small newspaper in Marion, Ohio. He had become friendly with Harry Daugherty, then a restless, ambitious lawyer in Columbus, whose practice, according to Mark Sullivan's *Our Times,* was "less law than lobbying—in the borderland where law overlaps into politics."

In appearance Harding always gave the impression of physical grace and virility. He could have worn with ease the toga of the Roman. His resonant voice indicated friendliness and good nature. He was courtesy itself, and he possessed true kindness of heart.

Undoubtedly Harry Daugherty was most instrumental in inspiring the political ambition of Harding. He was persistent, audacious, and resourceful, while Harding was easygoing and placid. They made an excellent team and finally became so powerful in local politics that Harding became governor and later United States senator representing the Buckeye State. He might have been content to remain in the Senate, where he appeared to be completely happy, had it not been for the prodding of Daugherty. Even so, he evidently considered that his chances for the nomination were slim.

Accidental events help to make politics fascinating. Early in 1920, when the report came that the Ohio delegation would support General Leonard Wood, Daugherty instantly became vocal on the subject of Harding as a favorite son. "I found him sunning himself like a turtle on a log," said Daugherty, "so I pushed him into the water and persuaded him to campaign out beyond Ohio."

But even during the convention, Harding remained aloof and far from cheerful. Daugherty, his now acknowledged partner in the game of politics, was a veritable dynamo. His personal glee club, brought from Columbus, serenaded all delegations, with the idea of keeping the struggle as serene as possible, preparing for the moment when Wood and Lowden would kill each other off. Earlier he had done considerable gumshoeing around the country, whispering the name of Harding as the second choice. We have seen how the senator became the winner.

The "front-porch campaign" at Marion, after the custom set by William McKinley at his home in Canton, was Harding's idea. I favored it emphatically, for I felt that the candidate's natural dignity and hominess made him ideal for this form of vote-getting. And so telegraph wires were strung and a swarm of newspapermen descended upon Marion to tell the Harding story to the nation. It was an appealing story centered in the atmosphere of a charming small town. The place itself made a favorable impression on people. For details of the candidate's ancestry and boyhood, the newspapermen searched the countryside. In the galaxy of alluring place names were Blooming Grove, Whetstone Creek, Caanan Township, Corsica, and Caledonia, where old neighbors waxed enthusiastic in their demonstrations for Warren Harding, who had published their local newspaper, the Marion *Star,* for thirty-six years. Harding knew them all, and they all knew him. It had been a long, slow progress toward financial stability, during which Harding's outstanding traits of kindliness and good nature were part of the code that governed his daily publication of the news.

That code read: "Never heedlessly hurt the feelings of anybody. Be decent; be fair; be generous. I want this paper to be so conducted that it can go into any home without destroying the innocence of any child." At the start of his newspaper career Harding himself carried to the bank in a tin pail the pennies brought in by the delivery boys. His unpretentiousness did not change as he gradually became the town's leading citizen.

As a candidate for the presidency, Harding viewed his big task modestly. He would have been happier had the role not been assigned him. I, for one, always considered him a much abler man than he considered himself, and at times I wondered whether his calm and sometimes apparent disinterestedness might not be a handicap on Election Day.

On the other side of the contest, the pious pilgrimage undertaken by Governor Cox, the Democratic candidate, to the sickroom of Woodrow Wilson almost immediately after the Democratic convention undoubtedly placed the Wilson tag on the nominee and did not help his campaign. The people of America were disillusioned with the aftermath of war and were not enthusiastic about a man considered to be Wilson's protégé.

As to the League, many important Republicans—Root, Taft, Hughes, Wickersham, and others—continued to believe that America should adhere to the League. Therefore, the job of successfully straddling the issue became a necessity imposed upon the Republican candidate. To aid Republican unity, a formula was worked out, with the aid of George Harvey, known as the "Association of Nations." It was announced by Harding when delegations from Minnesota and Indiana visited Marion.

I planned to raise a campaign fund that would keep the party free from obligation to any private interests or any rich men. So far as the Republicans were concerned, I was determined, in every possible way, to clean up politics. All preliminary expenses of the National Committee and the cost of the convention had been paid for with individual contributions, mostly between fifty cents and $125, and we still had money in the bank. The remarkable fact was that 80 per cent of this sum was given by persons who never before had paid a dollar to the Republican cause, much coming from border states and some even from southern states. Early in August I sent out a call for one-dollar contributions to raise a total of two million dollars. Details were worked out between myself and Vice-Chairman William Boyce Thompson.

At the close of the Chicago convention I had had luncheon with a friendly political enemy. I told him my plans for the drive and my decision to limit contributions to a thousand dollars. My Democratic friend asked how much I expected to get, and I told him two million dollars. I emphasized that when persons voluntarily contributed to a cause—even if only a dollar—they were apt to work for it; that the amount of money raised by the one-dollar drive was not as important as the new friends that could be made for the party and the volunteer workers developed in every county and district.

When my friend asked what I would do if the thousand-dollar top-limit plan did not yield the funds actually needed for legitimate expenses, I instantly told him that I would then raise the limit to five thousand dollars, providing full publicity, so that people would know where every dollar came from. The gentleman, who apparently had not taken me seriously at first, finally became so impressed that he asked whether I would object to his borrowing the idea and putting it up to the Democratic National Convention.

"Not in the least," I replied. "I shall be pleased. If your party takes up the plan, we can clean up politics in this country. We don't hurt you, you don't hurt us, and the country is immeasurably better off."

The suffrage amendment had been passed by Congress on June 5, 1919, and immediately posed a question for Republican party policy. The ratification of the amendment then was up to the states, and the problem became one of local action, yet the question remained: Should the national party favor, oppose, or remain neutral?

Since pro- and anti-suffrage groups were found in both the major political parties, the simpler course would have been to remain neutral and run no risks of a breach in the hard-won party harmony which was emerging from the debris of the 1912 debacle. Convinced as I was of the justice of the women's cause, however, I felt that if the Republican party was to continue as a forward-looking party of progress, it could follow no other course than to endorse the principle of votes for women and actively urge ratification in all Republican states. Time and the now generally accepted fact of equal suffrage among free peoples have fully justified this course.

Long before the passage of the amendment by Congress I had been bombarded by partisans of both camps, but I declared my position early, and consistently urged both the passage of the amendment and its ratification. In my capacity of national chairman, I believed that the Republican party would be the chief beneficiary of the women's vote in case the amendment was ratified in time for them to participate in the 1920 election. Accordingly I prepared plans for incorporating women's activities into the organizational machinery of the national party.

At a luncheon in the Severin Hotel, Indianapolis, the first steps were taken toward organizing Republican women in Indiana. A week later a state-wide organization was formed for the participation of women in the 1920 election under the state legislative act of 1919 permitting women to vote for presidential electors.

Full participation of women was urged by me at a conference of Republican leaders in the Wardman Park Inn in Washington on May 22, 1919. The conference, called by the Republican Women's National Executive Committee, of which Mrs. Medill McCormick was chairman, was attended by women delegates from practically every state, together with many state chairmen and members of the National Committee. My suggestion for complete amalgamation, intended to check any tendency toward the formation of a separate women's party, received the complete approval of the women present.

Following the Washington meeting I issued an explanatory statement in which I said:

The Republican women in this country are a part of the party membership. In many states this has long been so. They come into this party activity not as women but as voters. . . . They are not to be separated or segregated at all, but assimilated and amalgamated, with the full consideration due every working member of the party in the rights of their full citizenship. There is to be no separate women's organization created within the party except and only in those cases where such an arrangement is needed temporarily. . . .

To further this policy, a series of regional conferences of men and women leaders was planned for early 1920. Miss Mary Garrett Hay of the Women's National Executive Committee and myself attended all these meetings, the first of which opened in the Congress Hotel, Chicago, January 5, 1920. Men and women organizational workers, including national committeemen, state chairmen, and members of the Women's Advisory Committees from the Middle West and beyond the Mississippi, were present.

Similar regional meetings were scheduled for Denver and San Francisco. En route I stopped at Des Moines for an all-day Republican jubilee staged in the Hotel Fort Des Moines and spoke at a luncheon given by the State Committee to the women delegates, who represented every congressional district in the state.

I arrived in Denver for the meeting there on January 8, and after a one-day stop-over at Salt Lake City, we moved on to San Francisco. There we were met by Mrs. Josephine Corliss Preston, a member of the Republican National Executive Committee from the State of Washington, accompanied by three women state chairmen: Mrs. Lou Davenport of Oregon, Miss Margaret Roberts of Idaho, and Mrs. J. H. Mendenhall of Washington. Mrs. Preston outlined a women's program adopted in her state, calling for the creation of a new Cabinet position—a secretary of education; also country-life development, education in rural communities, the building of rural high schools, Americanization of foreigners, equal pay for equal service, and a "bigger thrift program—the saving of time, talent, and health as well as of money."

More than eight hundred people participated in the sessions of the San Francisco conference, taking up suggestions for the national platform and discussing means and methods of organization. Out of these meetings came concrete suggestions for the platform committee of the National Convention:

National and state legislation for the regulation of child labor; the establishment of not more than an 8-hour day, a 44-hour week, and a weekly day of rest for women in industry.

The establishment of the Women's Bureau of the U. S. Department of Labor on a permanent statutory basis.

The establishment of a national employment service, with adequate provision for departments for women in national offices and in all local offices.

Appointment of both men and women as mediators in the conciliation service of the Department of Labor and as members of any wage adjustment boards or mediation boards appointed in the federal government to deal with industries employing women.

Equal pay for equal service.

Direct citizenship for women, not already citizens, through marriage, as a qualification for the vote.

Naturalization for married women to be made possible.

Compulsory education in every state for all children between 6 and 16, 36 weeks of each year, and that we favor such changes in our educational system as will provide for thorough education in citizenship of all our youth.

Full support to secure a federal department of education whose secretary shall be a member of the President's Cabinet. [This was accomplished in 1953—with the appointment of Mrs. Oveta Culp Hobby.]

A pledge of national minimum-wage legislation for women.

Additional conferences of the same sort were also held at Reno and Los Angeles, and at the end of this transcontinental tour our party was in agreement that the drift of opinion was decidedly favorable to the Republican party. While still in the West, I was gratified to learn that Indiana had ratified the suffrage amendment; Governor Goodrich had called a special session of the legislature, which acted on January 16, 1920.

While at the Denver meeting the governors of Wyoming and New Mexico had announced that they would call special sessions for the same purpose, and the only setback was the refusal of Governor Hart to summon the Washington legislature.

Meanwhile the anti-suffrage forces continued active and on February 12 launched another attack directed against me as national chairman. At the same time copies of an open letter were issued to members of the state and national committees, asking the "removal of Will Hays as a menace to Republican success in 1920." Political campaign managers, in the nature of things, become targets for both friends and foes, and I received my full share of unfavorable criticism during the suffrage contest.

As the date for the National Convention drew near, with the amendment still unratified by the required number of states, I designated

Captain Victor Heintz to assist the leaders of Republican women at the 1920 National Convention in drafting their plans for participation by the suffragists in party affairs. Nevertheless, on the opening day, 150 women marched to the Coliseum from the headquarters of the National Women's party and took picket stations close to the front wall of the big auditorium. They carried the party colors, purple, gold, and white, and a number of yellow banners questioning the Republican party on its stand toward suffrage. The pickets stood in a silent line, maintaining their practice of peaceful picketing, to remind the party that women still were awaiting the ballot. Mrs. Anna Kendall, a woman of eighty-two, carried the famous slogan which had appeared at every picketing the women had ever held. It read: "How long must women wait for liberty?"

Connecticut was a Republican state which I was eager to have ratify. On August 7 I received a delegation of Connecticut suffragists and promised them to send a message to Governor Holcomb—which I did— stating my reasons for calling a special session of the legislature. The women begged me to do this to answer an argument of Connecticut anti-suffragists that the governor had never been asked to call a special session.

"I've asked him a dozen times already," I told them. "I will do everything in my power that is consistent with the proprieties to bring about the ratification by the thirty-sixth state right away. I'll urge, beg, plead, explain, and argue. I cannot force." I then gave them a written statement, ending with the following paragraph, which I urged the women to spread broadcast over Connecticut:

Democracy in the United States is really nothing but a sham unless election day gives all Americans a chance to express their political opinions. Casting the vote is the only way to express their opinion effectively. To hold American women bound by the results of an election, to train them in schools and colleges to think for themselves as well as a man, to accord them freedom of utterance as a Constitutional right, and then attempt to deny them the opportunity to stand up and be counted on election day is a governmental blunder of the first magnitude.

In accordance with this policy and with the cordial approval of the presidential candidate, Senator Harding, I sent an appeal also to the Republican members of the Tennessee legislature. At Republican national headquarters it was decided to concentrate on Tennessee in order to make universal suffrage a reality as soon as possible. In addition to my appeal to the Republican members of the legislature, Mrs. Christine Bradley South was sent out from national headquarters to aid the women of Tennessee in their fight.

The suffrage amendment to the Constitution of the United States became a part of that document on August 26, 1920, when the state legislature made Tennessee the thirty-sixth state to ratify. Harriet Taylor Upton, vice-chairman of the Republican Executive Committee, wired me from Nashville, where she and others had been laboring with state legislators:

> REPUBLICANS, HOLDING THE BALANCE OF POWER, TODAY MADE RATIFICATION POSSIBLE IN TENNESSEE. REPUBLICAN LEGISLATORS REFUSED TO LISTEN TO FALSE ARGUMENTS, TO BE FRIGHTENED BY THREATS, OR TO ACCEPT SEDUCTIVE OFFERS. THEY STOOD BY THE NATIONAL PLATFORM FOR THE PARTY'S SAKE AND NATIONAL JUSTICE. TENNESSEE REPUBLICANS ARE A CREDIT TO THE COUNTRY AND NO ONE CAN KNOW TO WHAT EXTENT UNLESS THAT PERSON BE ON THE GROUND. I AM PROUD OF THEM. THE REPUBLICAN PARTY, HAVING FURNISHED TWENTY-NINE OF THE THIRTY-FIVE STATES, NOW MAKES POSSIBLE THE THIRTY-SIXTH.

Leaders and workers of both political parties at once began to widen the campaign to include women voters. Both parties claimed credit for the addition of women to the electorate, but the Republican party was on record as having done far more to bring about suffrage.

Republican national headquarters issued a statement giving the facts about the suffrage amendment, showing that twenty-nine Republican states and seven Democratic states ratified it, while seven Democratic states and only one Republican state rejected the amendment. Two Republican and two Democratic states failed to ratify.

Mrs. Carrie Chapman Catt declared the neutrality of the League of Women Voters on the partisan issue in a statement on September 17. She also addressed a letter to me, thanking me for my personal services and those of the Republican party in obtaining ratification.

Of the 36 states which ratified, 28 called special sessions for that purpose. Of these special sessions, 18 were called by Republican governors and 10 by Democratic governors. Of the legislatures ratifying, 27 were Republican, 7 Democratic, and 2 non-partisan. The total legislative vote for ratification in 36 states was 2,545 Republican, 1,211 Democratic, 323 non-partisan, and 47 Socialist and Independent.

That tells the story.

CHAPTER 21

The 1920 Campaign

O N June 21 plans were drawn up in Washington for an executive committee which, for the first time in the party's history, was not to be composed solely of National Committee members. Seven were to be women. I was to serve as chairman, while the vice-chairman was to be a woman, as was also the assistant secretary.

Senator Harding and I were agreed that most of the nominee's campaign utterances should be made from his front porch at Marion, Ohio —in fact, that we should "out-McKinley McKinley." The other members of the conference agreed that this was both the statesmanlike and dignified way to handle the campaign. It would not interfere with Senator Harding's frequent discussion of the issues and would provide him opportunity to give careful thought to detailed addresses, which could then be widely circulated. Republican organizations in all parts of the country would plan pilgrimages to Marion after the fashion of those to the Canton front porch in 1896.

Governor Coolidge came to Washington on June 30 to meet Senator Harding, and the conference developed into a sort of dress rehearsal of their campaign relationship. It began with a waffle-and-chipped-beef breakfast at Senator Harding's home, after which the candidates met the press. At this interview Harding emphasized his broad conception of the vice-presidential role in government as well as in the campaign. After breakfast the candidates and Mrs. Harding posed on the lawn for motion picture cameramen. Senator Harding searched the grass for four-leaf clovers and actually found one, which he pinned to Governor Coolidge's lapel. This little scene emphasized the great physical difference between the two men. Senator Harding was exceptionally broad-shouldered, well over six feet in height, with gray hair. Coolidge was of much slighter build, about five feet nine inches tall, and had light, sandy-colored hair.

Definite campaign planning was put off until after the Democrats had named their men, but two encouraging events marked this waiting period: assurance by General Wood, the principal contender for the nomination, that he would wholeheartedly support the Harding-Coolidge ticket; and a meeting of Progressive leaders and former followers of the late Theodore Roosevelt, where a similar pledge was unanimously given.

When on July 6 the Democratic convention nominated James M. Cox for President and Franklin D. Roosevelt for Vice-President, we at Republican headquarters were taken somewhat by surprise, for we had geared our campaign plans to the expectation that Secretary McAdoo would be our opponent. However, we were not disconcerted, for it had been determined in advance that the Democratic platform and policies, rather than the personality of the candidates, would be the main target for our attack.

At noon of notification day, July 22, a luncheon was held at White Oaks Farm, near Marion, for distinguished party leaders, and at two o'clock the notification ceremonies got under way in Garfield Park, Marion. As national chairman, I presided. The preliminaries were few and inspiringly simple: the Columbus Republican Glee Club sang the National Anthem, and an invocation was pronounced by the Right Reverend Bishop William F. Oldham. I then introduced Senator Lodge, who delivered the notification speech. After Senator Harding had given his splendid, genuinely humble acceptance address the audience sang "America" and the benediction was given by the Reverend Joseph Denning.

This almost spiritual occasion climaxed one of the most intensive periods of activity in my whole life, and I was deeply moved by it.

I went on to attend a meeting of the Indiana Republican editors, held at Turkey Run on July 30. They were gathered there to inaugurate a campaign in Indiana to elect a brother editor President of the United States. Senator Medill McCormick was the principal speaker, and a message from Senator Harding was read. I spoke but five minutes. I had to make a hurried departure to catch a train for New York, which involved an auto ride to Indianapolis that is still vivid in my memory.

A humorous account of that ride was written by W. H. Blodgett for the Indianapolis *News*, in which he said:

The vehicle that started Mr. Hays on the first lap of his 978-mile journey was the big touring car of George Fosdick of Crawfordsville, famous the country over for his ability to get speed out of his machine and remain on the road, and also for the ardor of his silk shirts. It was near 3 o'clock, and Mr. Hays' train was to leave the Union Station at Indianapolis, 78 miles away, at exactly 5:45 o'clock, central time.

"Of course, George," remarked the amiable and brilliant George B. Lockwood, who occupied the front seat with Mr. Fosdick, "there is no call for any classic or endurance runs, and the speed record is up about where it ought to be. You understand, George," and Mr. Lockwood grew confidential, "that it would be very embarrassing to the Republican party to have its national chairman scattered along the public highway just as the campaign is about to open."

"I never have scattered anyone along the highway yet," shouted Mr. Fosdick above the roar of the muffler, as he stepped on the gas. The car darted forward like a greyhound from the leash. Mr. Hays catapulted against the top, swerved a little to the right and settled down with a sigh of resignation.

"Comin', Bill?" shouted Fosdick back over his shoulder. "I'm staying with you, George," shrieked the national chairman. "I rode in an airplane down in Oklahoma to make time but if you had been there I would not have needed the plane.

"Indiana has the best corn crop anywhere," yelled Mr. Hays, casting a furtive glance at the speedometer registering forty-five, then sixty-five, then seventy-two. "Do you know, George, that these great fields of waving corn are to me symbolic of the real American life—the broad leaves—Meredith Nicholson wrote some clever stuff about corn, but he wrote about corn in general—he should have written about Indiana corn—Meredith is capable of that sort of thing."

"Yep," came the answer of Mr. Fosdick—this time over his left shoulder. Mr. Fosdick can throw his voice over either shoulder with equal agility. It is a wonderful gift of his.

Ponderous trucks, agile roadsters and jumping "Lizzies" got in the clear as the huge touring car flew through the great clouds of dust. Mr. Fosdick was doing a jig on the accelerator. He "had 'er in high" and looking over the top. Mr. Lockwood's cherubic countenance had taken on a dull grey that assumed the hue of ashes when Mr. Fosdick calmly fired one end of a cigarette, leaving one hand on the steering wheel. The national chairman was like a boy. He whistled and he sang. He whistles very well, but he is a very punk singer. A horse sprang through a broken-down pasture fence and tried to marathon with Mr. Fosdick. It was a fine-looking horse but its efforts were futile.

"That horse reminds me of the Democratic party," shouted Mr. Hays at Mr. Lockwood. "Gets out in the road, does a lot of kicking up and swashing around, but doesn't win the race." But Mr. Lockwood was too intent holding what little hair he has left to the top of his head, to be interested in any of Mr. Hays' similes, metaphors or comparisons.

At last Indianapolis. Curving and twisting through the great crowds emerging from the ball game at Washington Park, Mr. Fosdick drove his car safely to the Union Station with twenty minutes to the good.

"George," remarked Mr. Hays, showing none of the tremors that seemed to have centered in Mr. Lockwood's frame, "now that we are here I desire to say that I have only two ambitions in life—one is to win this election, and the other is to go back to Sullivan County, sit in front of a big fireplace, spit in the fire—and think of this ride."

After some trips for conferences with leaders representing New England, the Middle West, and the North Atlantic states, I felt more optimistic than ever. Reports indicated that the western states, which had been for Wilson in 1916, would be safely in the Republican column. The great interest and heavy voting in all the Republican primaries gave further evidence of an unmistakable trend. Even some of the Democratic primaries, notably in Georgia—where Tom Watson, anti-administration and anti-League Democrat, was nominated for the Senate —showed dissatisfaction widespread. By this time I was ready to make predictions that the landslide would exceed even that of 1904.

The Maine election, coming up on September 13, was recognized as of unusual importance, being the first opportunity for the expression of public opinion on Wilson's demand for "a great and solemn referendum" on the League Covenant. The resulting plurality of nearly seventy thousand rolled up by the Republicans, the greatest plurality ever recorded in Maine's history, was unusually gratifying because the campaign had been waged solely on the issue of the Wilson record and the League of Nations. A Republican governor was swept into office together with all four Republican candidates for Congress; all thirty-one Republican State senators were elected, and only eleven Democrats were returned to the House in a membership of 151. It was this election that gave rise to the quip, used later in the campaign, when Castle Hill, a town in Maine, voted 100 Republican to only one Democratic: "The postmaster apparently stood firm."

The Republican party officially opened its national speaking campaign on Constitution Day, September 17, with approximately five thousand speakers spreading over the country for an oratorical drive lasting until Election Day. The first addresses dealt mainly with the League of Nations, women's position in politics, the meaning of Constitution Day, and the necessity for everyone to "get out and vote." We planned that Republican doctrines would be discussed in every election district in the country, with a special group of speakers selected for college and university towns.

After speaking at the Chicago Constitution Day rally I returned to the New York headquarters, where I announced the formation of an advisory campaign committee of forty—twenty-four men and sixteen women. The group represented all shades of Republican opinion and typified the party's new-found unity. Included were Charles Evans Hughes, William Howard Taft, Herbert Hoover, Albert J. Beveridge, Governor Frank Lowden, Senator Miles Poindexter, and Henry C. Wallace.

Senator Harding's speaking dates, the only deviation from the front-porch campaign plan, had been scheduled for the month of October; and on the fifth I went to Marion for a long conference with the nominee and Harry Daugherty. Senator Harding was to leave the next day on a swing through the West which would take him to Des Moines, Omaha, Kansas City, and Oklahoma City. This trip was to be followed by two others, into the eastern and political border states, so that the nominee was to be almost continuously away from Marion until the last week in October.

In the course of our conversation we reviewed the general political outlook, which I reported as highly satisfactory, and discussed details of the campaign program, including the proposed eastern trip. I told Mr. Harding that the Democrats were preparing to concentrate on the League issue because they had failed to make headway on any of the others, and that President Wilson had assumed active leadership of his party for the final month of the campaign. The senator expressed his willingness to face that situation.

In mid-October I again went to Chicago to meet leaders from twenty western states for a final checkup on the political situation in their territories. I had been in touch with most of them by telephone and telegraph, and what I had learned convinced me that Republican senators would replace Democratic incumbents in California, Colorado, Idaho, South Dakota, and Missouri, where there were stiff contests. This was my last trip West before the election, and when I returned to New York I remained there for the final verdict of the people. I had previously registered to vote in Sullivan by mail, under the absentee voter law of Indiana.

As the 1920 presidential race came down to the wire on November 1, I felt completely confident of victory. From all the information available at headquarters, 368 electoral votes appeared certain for the Republican column, with a good chance of running the number above 400. After a long telephone talk with Senator Harding that afternoon at his home in Marion, I went to the theatre that night with a free mind. The play was the first performance of *The Half-Moon,* at the Liberty Theatre; among the first-night celebrities present were Georges Carpentier, Charlie Chaplin, Billie Burke, and Florenz Ziegfeld.

With arrangements made to run telegraph wires into Republican headquarters at 19 West Forty-fourth Street, partitions had been removed on the entire third floor to provide accommodations for the public. I received the returns on the fourth floor, where only members of the Executive Committee were present, but from there the returns were immediately relayed to the third floor, which was jammed with men and women prominent in Republican ranks.

When the returns began to indicate a vote of landslide proportions for our candidate, I issued a statement about ten o'clock characterizing the results as an indication "of an extraordinary agreement on the part of the people." At 11 P.M. I received a telegram from Senator Harding: "My gratitude along with congratulations on your capable and successful management of a great campaign."

With a few states still in doubt, the New York *Times* headlines for the early editions of November 3 read: HARDING WINS: HUGE MA-

JORITIES; BIG REPUBLICAN GAINS IN CONGRESS. Democratic Chairman George White conceded Harding's victory quite early.

The final figures showed a total of 404 electoral votes for Harding and Coolidge, with 127 for Cox and Roosevelt. The Republicans broke into the Solid South by carrying Maryland, Missouri, Oklahoma, and Tennessee. In the popular vote, the lead won by Harding and Coolidge was approximately six million. As a result of the election, the Senate had 54 Republicans and 42 Democrats; the House 274 Republicans, 158 Democrats, 2 Independents, and 1 Prohibitionist. The nation had sharply reversed itself politically, and after eight years of Democratic government under Woodrow Wilson, the Republican party was solidly in office.

As chairman I was naturally anxious to get some word from the candidate the day after election and, sure enough, the telephone call came through. Harding said: "How would you like to come over to Marion next Friday? I know that Friday is your birthday and you know that Tuesday, the second, was mine. It might be some fun to have the visit together on your birthday."

Arriving in Marion from New York on the morning of November 5 and rushing up the steps of the famous front porch two at a time, I met Harding just coming out of the door.

"Hello there, Bill." He grinned.

"Howdy, Mr. President." I grinned back at him.

"That's the first time I ever called you Bill," he said. "But a president-elect can get away with a lot of things, you know." We walked together from the house over to the headquarters building next door, with Harding's arm around my shoulders.

That was a memorable day. It included going to his printing shop and meeting all the boys, watching them set type and noting Harding's friendly, easy relations with them. We had breakfast, lunch, and dinner at his house, and some of the things he said that day later became quite significant. He spent the whole day with me and with his cronies. We had a fine, heart-warming visit. Before I left he called me into his study, picked out a photograph, and signed this inscription:

To my valued friend Will H. Hays—with grateful appreciation of the rarest and best services one American can render another, accompanied by birthday greetings for November 5th from one who celebrates November 2nd, in the spirit marked by the intervening days in November 1920. Gratefully and sincerely. . . .

My friends in Sullivan had planned a big home-coming celebration for November 9. After my visit with the President-elect at Marion I went to Indianapolis, where I was met by a delegation of friends who accompanied me home on a special interurban trolley car on the afternoon of the ninth. Streets and homes were decorated with flags, and a brass band met us at the square, playing "Back Home Again in Indiana." The children, dismissed from school, lined the curbs for the procession around Court House Square to the front lawn and porch of my home, where the ceremony was staged.

C. H. Stratton, one of my boyhood pals, acted as chairman, and welcome-home speeches were made by John C. Chaney, ex-representative from the Second District, and Charles D. Hunt, Democratic lawyer. Telegrams of congratulation were read from Harding and Coolidge, from Senators Watson and New, from Governor Goodrich and Governor-elect McCray.

In trying to tell my friends and neighbors what the election meant to me, I said:

"A non-partisan meeting like this is fitting because the overwhelming victory was far more than any mere partisan success. It was an expression from great majorities of their confidence in candidates and a program which they believed made for the best things for America at home and abroad. The splendid men elected are now the representatives of all the people and the confidence of the electorate has been rightly bestowed."

At the close of the meeting some of the crowd attempted to hoist me onto their shoulders and carry me around, but this so frightened my young son Bill, then only five, that he started to cry. When I posed for the motion picture cameras afterward, holding him in my arms, the tears were still in his eyes.

On the lighter side of the election aftermath was a story carried by Chicago newspapers:

"Eddie the Immune" Jackson, Chicago's pickpocket plenipotentiary, told the underworld how he was pinched by Secret Service men just as he was about to shake hands with President-elect Harding, in St. Louis.

"I was all set for a bumper trip when I was spotted," Eddie told the boys in Butch Carroll's. "We had made two stops on the way to St. Louis and I was getting in touch fine shaking hands with the crowds. I was taken for Chairman Will Hays several times.

"Let me tell you a funny one about Hays. Just before the election I was busy with a plant trailing both candidates. We were both active one day down in Marion. There was a large reception on with Senator Harding as the big card. I was working a worried member of the reception committee when I spotted my pal crowding Will Hays. I had to pass up my pickin's to signal my stall to lay off, I wouldn't stand for any rough stuff being pulled on Bill Hays."

During the post-election jubilation period I attended several dinners that stand out in my memory.

The Gridiron Club dinner in Washington was the thirty-fifth annual affair of that famous newspaper club and was made the occasion for a hilarious post-mortem on the presidential election, a chance for the politicians to see themselves as others saw them during the campaign. One of the skits was a front-porch meeting in Marion, set to music, with a cast representing Senator Harding, Harry Daugherty, ex-Senator Weeks, Al Jolson, W. J. Bryan, and "Slush Fund Rumor." Mr. Daugherty stalked the front porch in the role of Ko-Ko, the Lord High Executioner, and there was a rumpus when "Slush Fund Rumor" invaded the Harding lawn. During the skit a character representing myself sang plaintively to the Republican candidate a parody on "Then You'll Remember Me," entitled "So Please Remember Me." In another episode a crystal gazer, reading the political future, saw President Harding sending the League of Nations to the Alien Property Custodian. Mark Anthony Hitchcock delivered an oration over the body of the League Covenant, explaining that he came to bury the Covenant, not to praise it. Chief among the guests was our Hoosier Vice-President Marshall, to whom the club presented a large silver gridiron. A similar token was sent to the White House as a gift to President Wilson, who was unable to attend.

On December 18 I was a guest speaker at the Lotos Club dinner in New York to George Ade, along with Chester S. Lord, Franklin P. Adams, John Palmer Ganit, Julian Street, and Melville E. Stone. The company present was gathered to do honor to Indiana's great writer, a grand fellow and one of my close friends. Deviating from the line followed by the other speakers, who addressed their remarks to Mr. Ade as an author, I declared that George Ade could be elected governor of Indiana any time he would give the word, and that he probably was the most popular man in his native state. In the course of his response to the members of the club, the humorist quipped: "Perhaps you have heard of Will Hays. He is the ninety-pound Hoosier heavyweight. You may not know that during the war Will Hays and I kept the Germans out of Indiana. In fact, it may not be generally known in New York that Indiana was involved in the war at all."

The annual banquet of the Indiana Society, in Chicago, held January 15, 1921, was another unforgettable occasion. It developed into something of a "ribbing contest," in homely Hoosier fashion, and I was the principal victim. Fred Landis of Logansport presented my name for "President of the United States" and was, in return, elected Vice-President. Mr. Landis then said: "This society had trouble in securing a guest of honor for tonight. They came to see me about it. So I suggested Will Hays. But the committee said, 'What if this senatorial investigating committee lands on him? We won't want a guest of honor who may throw us down by being arrested in the middle of the soup course.' Then I said, 'Don't worry; they may get some of them, but they'll never get

Bill.' I had faith in him, faith in his integrity, and faith in his marvelous interference. He had been successful in Indiana politics for twenty years and never had been caught at it. And then I knew he had too fine a conception of the moral obligation of a church elder to let anybody get the goods on him. But the committee said, 'Just to play safe, let's put the dinner off until January.' Then the investigating committee adjourned. But Bill was ready for them. He came through with a deficit. Nobody knows how he ever managed it, but he could prove it by the books."

President-elect Harding had gone to Point Isabel, Texas, preparatory to starting a vacation trip to the Panama Canal, and had invited me to be a member of his party, but the many post-election details involved in winding up the National Committee's affairs prevented me from accepting. One of these was finances.

The heavy speculation that always precedes the inauguration of a new president chiefly revolves around the make-up of his Cabinet. In Harding's case, the newspaper surmises ran to many columns. Most of these "guess lists" included the name of Will H. Hays, and it was generally understood that I would go into the Cabinet either as Postmaster General or Attorney General.

The question of a Secretary of the Treasury first came to my attention through a telephone call from Senator Philander C. Knox, who said he wanted to see me. During our visit he said that Andrew W. Mellon ought to be the Secretary of the Treasury. This was a bold suggestion. To me, however, it was a most appealing one. The politics involved, good or bad, did not worry me. I thought it good politics to appoint to any job the best man who could be found to do that job, and that was the argument I used for the appointment of Mr. Mellon. There were, of course, those who raised the objection that he was very rich, but no one could question his capacity and particular fitness.

Senator Knox suggested that I go with him to Marion and discuss it with the President-elect. I agreed. He wanted to leave at once because he thought the time was ripe and that something might be developing. I had had no close relationship with Mr. Harding on the matter of his appointments, but I was delighted to accompany Senator Knox on this mission. I remember the morning we arrived in Marion and went to Harding's house for breakfast. Senator Knox had made the appointment, and when we had settled down, he at once stated the purpose of our visit. Harding's immediate reaction was sympathetic. He reviewed Mr. Mellon's capabilities, which had been well stated by Senator Knox. He asked my opinion, especially as to the political effects of such an appointment. As I recollect it, he then said that he had "considered appointing" General Dawes and had "gone rather far in that direction." However, he added that the Mellon suggestion was most appealing, especially in view of Senator Knox's strong presentation. While General Dawes's appointment would have been very good, indeed, Knox's arguments won out, and Harding subsequently appointed Mellon to the Treasury post. The wisdom of that appointment was soon proved by Secretary Mellon's notable performance in the office. It has always been a great satisfaction to me that I was able to make some contribution, however small, toward bringing it about.

No final decision was reached by Mr. Harding regarding the members of his official family until late in February. I went to St. Augustine for a final conference with him on February 15, and we discussed not only the Cabinet but many other problems of the new administration. It had been decided late in January that in any case I should continue as national chairman for several months following the inauguration, and that at the meeting scheduled for March 3 no resignations of any officers of the national organization would be presented.

It was the unanimous desire of the committee members not to change officers at the beginning of the administration. They wanted the new leaders to have a voice in any plans for reorganizing party machinery. It was expected that Mr. Harding would have much to say about the selection of a new chairman, and it was felt that his task would be easier if he were free of party affairs during the change-over of administrations.

On February 22, 1921, Washington's Birthday, the President-elect announced that his Cabinet would be:

Charles Evans Hughes	Secretary of State
Andrew W. Mellon	Secretary of the Treasury
John W. Weeks	Secretary of War
Harry M. Daugherty	Attorney General
Will H. Hays	Postmaster General
Edwin Denby	Secretary of the Navy
Albert B. Fall	Secretary of the Interior
Henry Wallace	Secretary of Agriculture
Herbert Hoover	Secretary of Commerce
James J. Davis	Secretary of Labor

The seamy side of politics is a matter that can rarely be avoided in a true narration of almost any American political fight, and the Harding campaign had rather more than its share. Mud-slinging and malicious canards have been political weapons in all ages among all nations, though in latter years the responsible leadership of all our American parties has made every effort to eliminate them. Fortunately, these disgraceful and disgusting features usually defeat their own ends.

At Republican headquarters we had been aware of a false propaganda campaign directed against Senator Harding, beginning almost immediately after his nomination. The lies originated in Ohio and hinted at Negro blood in Harding's ancestry. We paid little attention until the stories began to gain circulation outside Ohio, disseminated through underground channels hard to trace. On October 29 and on the following day the Cincinnati *Times-Star* exploded the lie, attributing it to the "underground section of the Democratic campaign," and tracing Harding's white ancestry.

One of the bitterest controversies of the 1920 presidential race centered around the campaign funds and expenditures of both parties. Charges and countercharges, culminating in a Senate committee investigation, filled the news columns throughout the latter half of that summer. A little retelling may have some recent as well as historic interest.

In mid-August the Democratic candidates, Governor Cox and Franklin D. Roosevelt, brought charges that the Republican campaign fund would exceed $30,000,000, and that such a sum "could not be honestly expended." In the course of their campaign speeches they further asserted that certain interests were banded together to buy the presidency, and that millions had already been contributed to the Republican war chest with sinister intent.

Replying to these charges in a speech at Augusta, Maine, on August 21, I said, in part:

"Mr. Roosevelt gave as the authority for his accusation 'an item' he had 'read in a newspaper.' Mr. Cox submitted no evidence whatever. Both these men knew that the Republican National Committee had adopted a plan which I announced more than a year ago for financing our campaign by a method of decentralized giving, securing small contributions from a great many, with a limit of one thousand dollars as a maximum for any contribution; that Mr. Harding had publicly approved the plan and that the committee had readopted it after he was nominated.

"Knowing all this, Mr. Roosevelt asserted that our campaign fund would reach the colossal sum of $30,000,000 and Mr. Cox declared, apparently of his own knowledge, that millions have already 'gone into the Republican treasury' from 'certain interests banded together to buy the presidency. . . .' That, I submit, is a serious charge. If it could be substantiated no punishment of those found guilty could be too severe. It cannot be, of course, for the quite simple reason that it is not true. . . .

"Nothing has been, and, of course, nothing will be, concealed. By reason of the enlarged electorate and the greatly increased cost of all things, we figure that there will be required a total of about $3,000,000, an average of about ten cents per voter. . . . The larger part of the total amount we hope and have reason to believe we shall be able to raise under the plan of limited subscriptions, which thus far has proved successful. . . ."

Mr. Cox, apparently not satisfied with my reply, continued to reiterate his charges. Such an attitude on the part of the opposition was not altogether displeasing to Republican headquarters. If Democratic strategy was to be one of misstatement and exaggeration, we felt that the reaction from such tactics would do more to injure their prospects than anything else they might do or say.

The Senate sub-committee investigating campaign expenditures, sitting in Chicago, then took a hand. Senator Kenyon, the chairman, sent a message to Governor Cox, requesting him to submit any information he might have to substantiate his charges that the Republican party had raised or was raising a $15,000,000 fund, and that a "capitalistic ring" had control of the party and was "trying to buy and control the presidency." Senator Kenyon's wire read in part:

I THINK NO ONE WHO HAS FOLLOWED THE WORK OF THIS SUB-COMMITTEE COULD CLAIM THAT IT WAS ACTUATED BY ANY PARTISAN MOTIVES. WE ARE ANXIOUS TO DO THE FULL WORK PLACED UPON US BY THE SENATE RESOLUTION. . . . I DO NOT KNOW THAT YOU ARE QUOTED CORRECTLY, BUT IF YOU WERE WE WANT THIS INFORMATION. . . .

I AM SURE THAT AS A GOOD CITIZEN AND AS A CANDIDATE FOR THE PRESIDENCY YOU WILL BE WILLING TO ASSIST US AND WOULD NOT MAKE THESE STATEMENTS WITHOUT EVIDENCE TO SUPPORT THEM. WE WOULD BE GLAD TO HAVE YOU FURNISH THE COMMITTEE WITH SUCH SOURCES OF INFORMATION AS WILL HELP THEM IN GETTING AT THESE FACTS, AND WE WOULD BE PLEASED TO HAVE YOU APPEAR BEFORE US PERSONALLY AT ANY TIME YOU MIGHT DESIRE, OR SEND A COMMUNICATION IF YOU PREFER, OR SEND SOMEONE WHO CAN GIVE THIS INFORMATION.

Senator Kenyon's telegram, however, was taken to indicate a certain deference to Mr. Cox as a presidential nominee, for he was not included in the list of those eventually subpoenaed. The sub-committee's action provoked plenty of gossip around both Republican and Democratic headquarters in Chicago, and it was freely predicted that the investigation was likely to show that both national committees were "flat broke and living from hand to mouth, week by week, in order to meet the payrolls for clerical help and the high prices that had to be paid for printed matter of all kinds."

According to information we received at Republican headquarters, no protests against Republican fund methods were considered in the Cox camp until after Democratic solicitors had been turned down by certain wealthy men in New York, Chicago, St. Louis, Detroit, and elsewhere who had contributed heavily to the Wilson campaign of 1916. The Wilson fund was $2,000,000, and the party was left with a deficit of $600,000. Up to August 1920, according to Chairman White, the Democrats had collected only $100,000 and were having a hard time borrowing money to keep the wheels turning. Unless their candidate made a better impression soon, their whole campaign was in danger of going on the financial rocks.

I had published the exact figures of the Republican budget—set at $3,076,000. Treasurer Upham reported that never in the party's history had campaign-fund quotas been so well distributed over the country. Approximately $900,000 already had been contributed, with only $216,-000 coming from New York. In former campaigns, New York State's share had been as high as 75 per cent.

Governor Cox continued his intemperate allegations, although he had revised his original charge of a $30,000,000 Republican slush fund to $15,000,000. In a speech at Pittsburgh he charged that the Republican National Committee had called upon fifty-one cities to contribute $8,145,000.

Flat denials, both specific and general, were made by Republican leaders in many parts of the country. It was shown that the amounts actually subscribed were far less than those given by Governor Cox from his "secret list."

When the Kenyon committee met on August 30 for its first hearing, Governor Cox was not present to substantiate his charges. After I had testified for several hours as to the falsity of the charges, I found an unexpected ally in Homer S. Cummings, keynoter of the Democratic convention and former national chairman, who followed me on the stand. He said that the expenses of both parties could be legitimately increased over the cost of 1916 and estimated the sum required to run a campaign in a year of high prices at about $2,800,000, not far below the $3,076,000 which I had set. He almost repeated the thought I had expressed earlier when he said:

"The real trouble with campaigns is not what the National Committee does, but what the independent, co-operating organizations which are not under proper control do. There the evil lies. The National Committee can't prevent it, but the government should. The law requires the National Committee to make a sworn statement before and after election, but does not require this of other organizations. I think Mr. Hays and I would not disagree on this subject at all."

To my original budget estimate I had added about $1,000,000 as the probable sum needed to be raised by the states for their own elections. This sum was to be handled by the National Committee under the centralized system then in operation, but the amounts raised by the state organizations were to be returned to them. These were no part of the National Committee's fund.

Before leaving the stand I took the offensive and delivered a few counterblows of my own, proving by documentary evidence that the liquor interests of New Jersey were being used by the Democrats to put over Cox as the savior of the wets and that New Jersey liquor men assumed that men of their trade in other states were acting with them. The salient points in the statement I read to the committee were these:

"We, of course, welcome the opportunity further to set forth the effort of the Republican National Committee to popularize the giving of money for campaign purposes by getting small contributions from a great many men and women rather than large contributions from a small number. This plan for the raising of money through small contributions grew out of two primary causes:

"1. The earnest desire to work a real reform in the elimination of any possible improper obligation. This purpose we believed would be advanced by getting the money from thousands of men and women in small amounts rather than from a few very large gifts.

"2. Out of the experience in connection with raising funds for war purposes these popular drives had become a familiar activity, and it seemed possible at this time to undertake that kind of action by a political organization. We particularly hoped that this activity would increase political interest.

"It was the purpose to endeavor to limit the contributions to a maximum of a thousand dollars before the nominating convention and a thousand after. We have all tried to adhere to that plan. It has been an innovation of recognized merit, but, being an innovation, it has been necessary to acquaint the public with the plan. . . .

"With the formation of the national ways and means committee came the effort to get a ways and means committee in every state . . . and then by such processes of organization as the localities might adopt to organize just as in a Red Cross or Liberty Loan campaign. The greatest publicity has been given to the movement because upon the acquainting of the party public with the purpose depends political interest.

"The budget estimate worked out—beginning as of July 1—of the total amount which would be needed for the actual campaign was $3,079,037.20."

Mr. Upham and I brought additional figures before the committee, showing that our funds since the convention had come from 12,389 individual contributors for an average of $88.11 each. Only eight contributions were for more than $1,000 and none over $2,500.

Governor Cox's slush-fund charges collapsed completely when Democratic Chairman White took the stand and Senator Kenyon asked: "Have you any evidence, one particle of evidence, to present to this committee to sustain the charges that Governor Cox has made in his speeches?"

Mr. White's reply was: "None whatever."

The Democratic candidate, however, continued to make his unsupported statements from the stump, but he never appeared before the Kenyon committee to substantiate them.

I have retold this story not only for its immediate bearing, but as an illustration of the common human tendency, in seeking to gain remote ends, to employ forms of exaggeration that so easily lead to outright falsification. Its final fruitage is that modern scourge of international relations, "The Big Lie."

CHAPTER 22

Humanizing the Postal Service

W H E N I entered the Post Office Department in the Harding administration, I did not "scrape the mud off my boots." That would have been impossible, for the habits of years don't change overnight. During 1919 and 1920 I had picked up soil from almost every state in the Union; mixed with the Hoosier topsoil, it made fertile ground for the growth of ideas planted during all the Indiana years.

I naturally carried with me into the department a reliance on co-operation; eagerness to improve the service; a belief in the essential goodness of human beings; a desire to better the lot of the employees; and a sensitivity to publicity.

I have earlier tried to show how large a part co-operation played in my Hoosier tradition. The sparsely settled "colonies" in our early western history compelled each man to trust his neighbor and stand as one against common enemies. The Hoosier character was the child of necessity. Continuous struggle made every man a past master at ways to lessen hardship, including harmoniously working together. Bearing such things in mind, one can understand in part why the following leftover sentiment appalled me when I heard it in Washington on my arrival as Postmaster General:

"You are going to have labor troubles, of course. You can make up your mind to that. Labor is a commodity, and you must treat it as such. If you have a job to do, and only one man can do it, he fixes the price; if a hundred men can do it, you fix the price. And if one man will do it at your price, that is all it is worth. Labor is a commodity the same as wheat."

That pronouncement of inhumane policy made a greater impression on me than anything that was said when I first went to the capital to investigate the workings of the Post Office Department. The idea of labor troubles was not unfamiliar, but the idea that a human being could be considered a "commodity," no matter what his station, was probably the best clue to the troubled workings of the postal service in 1920. I had given the job of the postmaster-generalship enough consideration to know that, to achieve results, the voluntary co-operation of the postal workers was absolutely necessary.

The Post Office Department job then entailed working with 326,000 persons. It is still the biggest distribution business in the world. In it I saw an opportunity to perform a public service, a chance to show the people that the new administration meant to do all the things that they had said in 1919 and 1920 they would do.

However, my decision to accept that Cabinet position had been by no means a foregone conclusion. After President Harding's election three prospects faced me in addition to the fact of the national chairmanship. First, I was strongly drawn to give my whole attention to the work of our family law firm. But the repeated opportunities to work with large groups of people have proved stronger impulses than the opportunity to argue at the Bar. I found more thrill in keeping people out of trouble by generating an atmosphere of co-operation than in getting them out of trouble through hours of expensive litigation.

The second course that I might have followed was connected with Senator Reed Smoot's desire that I come to Washington to work with a congressional committee on government reorganization. The mere suggestion then of such a full-time opportunity was almost as appealing to me as the job as Postmaster General.

The third avenue open foreshadowed by almost a year my later position with the movie industry, at more than seven times the salary of Postmaster General! William Fox of the Fox Film Corporation came to me in December of 1920 and invited me to go with his company. While the offer pleased me, I felt that it was not my field.

The national chairmanship in the early twenties was a full-time position, though carrying no salary, and I knew that I could not for long carry the work of Postmaster General and national chairman at the same time. I had willingly accepted a part of the Republican administration's responsibility in assuming the postmaster-generalship, and accordingly resigned the national chairmanship in June of 1921. John T. Adams succeeded me.

I could thereafter devote all my time to the postal service, unhampered by any outside responsibilities. Three months spent on labor relations, administration, and public relations had already gone by since my swearing-in as Postmaster General in March. Two days after being sworn into office I had decided to meet the Washington employees. My first purpose had been to tell them that, so far as we were concerned, labor was no commodity. The second had been to tell them how I meant to prove the theory. It took only a few days to see that the Post Office Department had been run for years, so far as the human element was concerned, on principles that went out of style more than nineteen hundred years ago that Easter. An illustration of the skepticism prevalent among the postal workers occurred one day at the General Post Office when I asked an employee a question. The worker shot back,

"Who the hell are you?" I answered, "I'm the Postmaster General." But that didn't satisfy the "man from Missouri." "How do you get that way? A lot of fellows say that." He had me cornered for a minute, but I finally found an Elks' identification card, and that was an "open sesame." The postal employee was an Elk too; we got along famously after that.

But words and Elks' identification cards were not enough to satisfy people who had become slightly callused in the treadmill. They wanted practical welfare measures, justified reinstatements, recognition of postal unions, changes in the retirement policy, grievance hearings, and a fairer interpretation of postal regulations to assure themselves that they were not falling victims to a political pied piper. And they got these things, not as gifts, but because they were deserved. Co-operation meant labor co-operation, which, in turn, meant that the employees would wait to respond until they knew what was on the employer's mind. Only by clear policy pronouncements could I get reaction from these people who had been victimized by war conditions and felt themselves cogs in a remorseless machine.

At the March sixth meeting the labor situation had been frankly discussed. Two thousand employees had been told that the government did not look upon them as automatons or regard their services as something to be paid for and forgotten. They had been told that they were part of a government which admired them for honest and loyal service under all kinds of difficulties, and that all must come to feel themselves partners in one great enterprise. To the people in the Post Office Department this must have sounded brand new, but to a Hoosier it was the only way to run a business. I had reminded them, too, that the spirit of the men was the most important consideration in this great public service. In an institution as large as the Post Office, touching every individual in the country, the regard for the human element was of paramount importance so far as the Postmaster General was concerned. The ideal of service was the only key that could transform general inertia into the most efficient postal service this country had ever seen. The spirit had to be complete within the department before it could be carried to the country. This meant that an era of kindness and consideration, "the very foundations of discipline," had to be inaugurated.

Humanizing the postal service meant a 1921 application of the Golden Rule, and business firms were ready with plenty of examples to demonstrate that it worked. Success under such a system was not tested by human idealism alone, but by common-sense experience which found it to work to the best advantage of employee and employer. Putting such a system—the application of the mutual-service principle—into operation in the Post Office Department not only meant getting better business methods into government, but it also meant getting personally acquainted with the employees, taking "private" signs off officials' doors, and actually bettering working conditions for everybody.

The quickest way to improve working conditions at that time was to answer the most crying needs of the employees by giving them something that every other large business institution had—a welfare department. Accordingly I had invited Dr. D. F. Garland and Dr. Lee K. Frankel to come to Washington in 1921. Both Dr. Garland of National Cash Register and Dr. Frankel, third vice-president of the Metropolitan Life Insurance Company, had had considerable experience in working out welfare plans in business. On the twenty-first of April these two men met with a postal employees' committee to consider details of welfare work and to discuss to what extent welfare measures could be adopted in the postal service. The committee, composed of representatives from seven postal organizations, took the job of collecting and disseminating ideas pertaining to welfare work among the employees. The discussions were destined to affect 21,000 railway postal clerks, 36,000 city letter carriers, and 100,000 Post Office Department clerks. In June I called for suggestions from local post offices. With the ground pretty well broken, on June 27 Dr. Frankel took charge of setting up and heading the new welfare department.

The presidents and secretaries of the postal unions and representatives of unorganized employees made up the membership in the first national council which functioned until a method of council selection by the employees themselves was worked out later. Each month the national council would meet in Washington with Dr. Frankel to discuss problems affecting working conditions, health, and general welfare of employees in post offices, mail trains, steamships, and other divisions. In addition to the national council, each city had a local council made up of the postmaster, or supervisory official appointed by the postmaster, and representatives of letter carriers, clerks, and other employees.

Activities of the welfare council began as soon as the local and national framework had been approved. First-aid classes and instruction in home nursing and care of the sick were begun with the co-operation of the Red Cross early in July. During the same month Dr. Frankel was investigating working conditions and holding conferences in Chicago, Omaha, Denver, Colorado Springs, Salt Lake City, Riverside, Los Angeles, San Diego, San Francisco, Portland, Seattle, Spokane, St. Paul, and St. Louis. The possibilities for local American Red Cross chapter and Public Health Service co-operation were also examined in each city. By November the city post office in Washington, D.C., could boast the initial first-aid hospital quarters with all first-aid appliances, a nurse on duty with two doctors subject to call, and a rest room for employees. Many minor improvements were effected in smaller post offices after conferences throughout the nation. But material improvements were often not so important as the establishment of local "forums" where basic employees' questions could be discussed and brought to the attention of the local welfare council, which could then heal many sore spots and thereby promote understanding and better feeling between the workers and the administration.

The establishment of a welfare department was the biggest project in the field of labor relations that the Post Office administration undertook in 1921. However, there were other measures and adjustments on a smaller scale which contributed toward "putting the heart back into the works," too. For instance, women postmasters were no longer penalized in their jobs for marriage. Following a decision by Post Office Solicitor John H. Edwards, a woman postmaster who married no longer had to seek a new appointment, execute a new bond, or pass another civil-service examination in competition with other candidates for an office that was already rightfully hers. This decision set a precedent in other fields regulated by civil-service rules, fields of activity where women's marriages had heretofore affected the status of their employment. Mrs. Helen H. Gardner, a member of the Civil Service Commission, brought the matter to the attention of the Post Office Department when such a case appeared among examination papers which she was handling.

Changes in seniority rules, methods of promoting clerks, scheme distribution, service-rating systems, public recognition of meritorious service, employee suggestion programs, recreation, and the elimination of objectionable features in civil-service examinations were all improvements which made it possible for Second Assistant Postmaster General Edward H. Shaughnessy to announce in August that efficiency had greatly increased, with a corresponding increase in better service—the bull's-eye on the target we were aiming for.

In addition to these things, public recognition was tendered to employees for improvement suggestions and for meritorious service. To alleviate the monotony of sorting mail, Postmaster Ed Purdy of Minneapolis approved the use of phonograph music in the workrooms, and even this small item gained recognition in October in the columns of the London *Illustrated News*. But working for improvement did not mean wantonly granting favors. Every measure was considered carefully, and the opinions of employees and supervisory officials were heard all the way down the line.

It was such things as Red Cross classes, after-hours recreation, concern over employees' eyesight as affected by lighting conditions, and the conferences where every postal employee could have his "day in court" —the genuine feeling was fostered that the employee was an indispensable human being with neighborly needs like anybody else.

It soon became clear that labor relations, administration, and public relations were inextricably bound up with each other. Good labor relations indicate good administrative policy, and the two together make for good public relations. No matter how I looked at it, it was still an equilateral triangle, and it was difficult to draw clean-cut lines between the three areas.

I felt as strongly about strengthening and broadening the civil service as I did about trying to make 326,000 employees feel themselves partners in one big enterprise. President Harding stated emphatically that all postmasters were to be appointed on a merit system and that the earlier Wilson Executive Order, which "froze" many postmasters in their offices who had never taken examinations, would be revoked. President Harding clarified his position by declaring further that Republicans and Democrats who had already passed the required examination would not be disturbed.

It was clear to me that the merit system was the only way to put the Post Office on an efficient basis, to give the employees some feeling of security, and to prevent all members of the department from being the constant shuttlecocks of politics. The idea of having open competitive examinations, with the top three men eligible for appointments as postmasters, was to get not only the most intelligent candidate but also the one with the highest executive ability, who would be most responsible to the business community. As a result of civil-service examinations held after the new Harding Executive Order, 760 new appointments were made.

Support for the new Executive Order and encouragement that the administration was on the right track were indicated when I found the Civil Service Commission itself entirely ready and willing to co-operate with the new order. They fully sympathized with and supported the directive discouraging personal recommendation on appointments until after the commission had drawn up its lists from examination ratings.

The new provisions naturally were met with skepticism as well as approval. Editorial comments sanctioned the idea of subjecting to examinations all who had not passed them and of seeking out fitness and efficiency. They expressed the opinion that the measure could do much toward removing the opinion that the wishes of the community were being ignored. A Philadelphia newspaper expressed qualified approval when it stated:

Mr. Hays is out to make politics his career, and would not likely antagonize powerful party leaders, but his obligation is to give good service, and in faithfully fulfilling that he commends the system which promotes efficiency instead of that which panders in politics. His determined attitude is a creditable reaction to the most shameless drive for offices Washington has ever seen.

One Washington editorial writer even made the suggestion that President Harding and Will Hays dreamed of the day when 300,000 workers in the postal service would be able to produce their own Postmaster General from the ranks—something that has since come to pass. The idea was not really so farfetched in view of the fact that I came from Indiana, where authority so often grows from the bottom up, not from the top down.

No matter what the consensus happened to be, the new postmasters themselves could testify that the department meant business. Early in 1922 every newly appointed postmaster was sent to school at the Central Accounting Post Office in each state. There he learned how to meet and to educate the public; his own place in the community; how to handle complaints and guard the mails; and his relationship with the department as a whole.

But the merit system was not the only field of action which fell under administration. Administrative economy was another objective to tackle. The country had recently been subjected to a wartime economy of a proportion which then seemed on a grand scale. But with the need for stringent measures past, the time to reduce wartime staffs and wartime budgets had come.

Some of our employees pointed out possible economies. One postal clerk suggested that a great deal of money could be saved on supply requisitions. Carriers' routes were inspected and equalized, and every residence and place of business was asked to install mail receptacles to eliminate lost time. Forces were shifted where needed in the interest of avoiding the hiring of temporary help. Through careful inspection and reorganization of the Sunday mail service $500,000 was saved on the railway mail service alone. This was the first time that a systematic survey of the Sunday service as a whole had ever been made. Fifty of the largest post offices were inspected under the direction of First Assistant Postmaster General Hubert Work to determine where peacetime reorganization might be effected to cut down wartime expenses. In one post office alone a saving of $101,000 resulted!

By the beginning of 1922, the Post Office Department had managed to save $15,000,000 out of an appropriation of approximately $575,000,-000. Three-per-cent saving does not sound like very much, but it beats a deficit all hollow. Actually it was accomplished in several ways. The co-operation of the employees was a main factor; I asked them to render a full day's work, and they did. A reorganization plan within the Post Office Department involved making the states units where central accounting offices could relieve Washington bookkeeping systems. By 1922, money orders were being cleared, listed, and filed within each state. As many claims as possible which could be settled locally were cleared at their sources. Innumerable forms were eliminated, and dead letters and packages were disposed of within the states. I suggested, too, that supplies could be contracted for in Washington and distributed through regional depots. Large post offices, already set up to some extent as miniature Post Office Departments, were equipped to relieve Washington and smaller post offices of congestion and delay.

While I had no responsibility for government reorganization beyond my own realm, I was fascinated by the possibilities—and by the need. In a speech to the American Newspaper Publishers Association in April, I suggested that the Coast Guard, the Supervisory Architect's Office, and the Public Health Service really bore little relation to the fiscal functions of the Treasury Department. The same anachronism appeared in the Interior Department, which guided the Bureau of Education, St. Elizabeth's Hospital, Howard University, the Patent Office, and the Bureau of Pensions, to cite a few quite unrelated activities. Duplicated activities under different department heads were all too frequent. For example, many times the Coast Guard under the Treasury Department had stations within two miles of lighthouses that were maintained by the Department of Commerce. In addition to activities carried out under departments which did not logically claim them, there were—even in 1921—at least forty bureaus which came directly under the supervision of the President and Congress. Duplication of work, overhead, plant equipment, and personnel defied classification.

Other activities under the Post Office administration of a more concrete nature than unofficial plans to overhaul the federal government included the "little cabinet" and the awarding of War Service Certificates. The former was made up of the four Assistant Postmasters General, the Chief Clerk, and the Post Office Department Solicitor. An innovation, the group met every Tuesday and Friday before the regular meetings of the President's Cabinet to consider all matters relating to the postal service itself. It was in the little cabinet that urgent matters were considered, to be taken up later in the President's Cabinet meeting, where all "XYZ" questions were discussed. "XYZ" became a kind of colloquialism in the department and at Cabinet meetings. During the presidential campaign, if a letter were sent out with "XYZ" on the back of it, the recipient knew immediately that it concerned a matter of urgency. That was the origin of the tag which became familiar in the new administration. The little cabinet was able to clear many problems at their source and to separate matters which seemed important enough to be brought up at the President's Cabinet sessions.

One such "XYZ" matter was the subject of War Service Certificates. During the war thousands of postal workers were "drafted" to serve with the AEF on postal communications, in many cases performing services for the Army similar to their peacetime duties with the Post Office Department. But I learned that these workers had no official veteran status or anything to indicate their share in the war effort. I brought the matter to President Harding's attention, with the result that 3,063 war certificates were issued to postal employees in December of 1921. Even as late as that year five postal workers were still serving with the Army of Occupation at Coblenz, Germany; one was in Paris; and in all, six had given their lives in foreign service. It seemed only fitting that these men who had served as soldiers should receive the recognition due a soldier.

SELLING THE POSTAL SERVICE

Better public relations—better understanding, co-operation, and approval—seemed to me the best proof of any improvement in labor relations and administration. Certainly both internal and external relations were involved.

Public relations begin at home, as my friend Paul Garrett of General Motors has said so often. In Washington I spent more than three hours on St. Patrick's Day being introduced to the heads of each bureau, clerks, engineers in overalls, elevator operators, and even retired employees. I tried to let them feel that they had a friend to whom they could come at any time. The far-reaching effects of trying to know the employees were humorously illustrated by an incident that happened four days after entering office, as reported in a Washington newspaper. A Negro messenger with a sheaf of official papers in his hand was going down an elevator in the Post Office Department building. He pulled a paper out to show it to the elevator operator. "See dar?" he said with a broad grin. "Dat's de signature of de new Pos' Marster General."

Occasionally small groups would be called together to discuss postal matters informally. At one such meeting I was talking about ancient postal history, telling how Darius was the first postmaster general and how, when he had done a good day's work capturing Babylon, he sent out a flock of news carriers in all directions bearing the message. I noticed that Special Assistant Joe Stewart apparently thought I had not done his story justice. Winking at me, he finished the tale: "And to ensure correctness in the message sent, and as a warrant against its being lost, he tattooed it on the backs of the messengers. It was rarely garbled in transmission."

KEEPING IN TOUCH WITH SCATTERED
POSTAL WORKERS

But the majority of postal workers were beyond the reaches of Washington and could not be contacted personally quite so frequently. However, the Post Office Department made use of its best facility at hand to keep in touch with them—the United States Mail. In addition to innumerable messages which went out daily, dealing strictly with business, I frequently wrote letters praising commendable effort, or of congratulation, or of condolence. One such letter was sent to the widow of a rural carrier who had died in service in the summer of 1921. He had served faithfully for sixteen years, and his death was a distinct loss to the service and to the community. In another case—one of extreme heroism—both President Harding and I wrote to the widow of a rural carrier who had lost his life trying to rescue a child from drowning. Postmasters were also encouraged to visit the sick in their communities in cases where persons were victims of mail-truck accidents, whether or not the accident had been the fault of the department. I urged them to join civic bodies, to take an interest in community affairs, and to use local meetings of the Chamber of Commerce and civic groups to disseminate postal information and to collect items of criticism from the public, things heard that would make a better postal service when they became things done. This, again, was getting down to the "grass roots."

In November I authorized postmasters to use the local facilities to help find missing persons. They were well equipped to help those who had lost track of loved ones. This new step in bringing the Post Office closer to the people bore fruit in many instances. One typical case was that of a woman in Claremont, New Hampshire, who was trying to locate a son she had not heard from since May of 1919. Logically enough, the son was located through his last known address in a Pennsylvania city.

Another instance of making postal facilities available for public use was the issuance of a directive permitting mothers on rural carriers' routes to use postal scales to weigh their babies! Perhaps I was suggesting the use by the public of postal facilities to too great an extent, to judge from the following letter that came from Los Angeles:

I have a subject to put before your eyes as there has never been a man sent by Reggersted Parcel post it will open the eyes of the people it will make the Govement Money. By the trance action through the mail it will make the Railroads money by the Excushen to Destanation to see man unpouched as I havent but 20 Dollars I would like to see my mother at Dallas, Tex, I would like to be sent by Parcel Post Reggersted to Miss ——, Dallas, Tex.

Mr. ——, your Honor, will you please grant me a permit to be sent from Los Angeles to Dallas, Tex. I only way one Hundred & Eaty pounds.

Thanking you in advance for the Future Favor for I haven't seen my Mother in a long time.

We not only encouraged service, but service with a smile. Postmasters were asked to make a concerted effort to sell the service to the public through courtesy and friendliness as well as through instructions. A touch of humor was added to this courtesy campaign when a fourth-class postmaster in Illinois resorted to a bit of doggerel:

> *I do wish that Mr. Hays*
> *Could see my sweet and charming ways*

And how polite and nice I am
When some guy comes to mail a ham.
How sweetly to those nuts I smile
When they are asking all the while
For stuff they've bought from Sears-Roebuck
To whom they sent one lonesome buck.
They're looking for a bale of tripe
A kiddie-kar or meerschaum pipe
And round the office they will stick
Till I get peeved and durn near sick.
But yet I have to smile and say—

"Your package has not come today."
And then they draw an ugly sigh
As if to say, "I think you lie."
I spread them one elastic grin
And say " 'Twill soon be comin' in."
If Mr. Hays would come and see
The way some folks are treating me,
I know, full well, that he would sob
And he would let me keep my job.
He'd say—"Dear Doc, if you'll stay here
I'll boost your pay two beans per year."

The June convention of the American Federation of Labor at Denver took time out to adopt resolutions approving the Post Office labor policy. The American Legion convention in July let it be known through similar resolutions that they sanctioned the civil-service policy of the Post Office Department regarding veterans' preference. This particular resolution, coming from the source that it did, was important in view of congressional accusations and National Civil Service Reform League skepticism in the matter of veterans' preference in appointments. The *American Legion Weekly* had a little fun with the new policy too. In November they suggested, "Postal employees, it is said, are enjoying their initiation into the mysteries of a 'humanized' postal service," and

A little Haysing now and then
Is relished by the best of men.

One postal aid set up for the benefit of the public was a Bureau of Information. This had its beginning in the Washington Post Office Department, where people could ask questions concerning the location of any government office or agency. Similar bureaus of information were eventually installed in the larger post offices all over the country. Further, names of towns were clearly displayed on local post offices, and smaller bureaus were supplied with information to help tourists passing through. H. I. Phillips facetiously urged all postmasters to help the flivvering classes: "I would suggest that the clerk who has charge of the special delivery letters be taken off this relatively unimportant task and detailed to stand in front of the Post Office with a roll of road maps under each arm." He also suggested replacing mailboxes with gasoline pumps.

The Philatelic Agency, like the Bureau of Information, was another means we used to bring the public and the postal service closer together. Immediate charge of the agency, located in the main post office in Washington, was under P. W. Gibbon, chief clerk, division of stamps. Service of this type had been demanded for thirty years, and the heavy requests from dealers and collectors justified the authorization of the new agency.

But by far the most important single public relations activity was the "mail early" campaign. This enveloped the whole country and involved an effort to eliminate the mountains of mail piling up all over the country from four to seven in the afternoon. In Washington, of 700,000 letters mailed daily, nearly 600,000 were mailed between the hours of four and seven. Advantages of "mail early" were preached as widely as possible, not merely to the postmasters. Businessmen and large mail-order houses were reached directly. Press conferences, local post office publicity, the co-operation of civic groups all over the country worked together to make the campaign a success. Postmasters kept the department in Washington informed on improvements. One reported that he was getting 52 per cent of the mail coming in faced, bundled, and sorted, which resulted in saving thirteen clerks' time and in connecting with early trains.

Another phase of the "mail early" campaign began in December, with special effort put forth to avert the worst features of a Christmas mailing peak. We enlisted the aid of twenty-five hundred women's organizations from coast to coast! A release for Monday, December 5, was sent to public schools all over the country, asking children to encourage their parents to wrap and tie parcels well, to address all mail plainly, not to send small cards which had to be hand-canceled and ran the risk of being lost, and to do their mailing for Christmas during that week. The Christmas "mail early" campaign reached as far north as Alaska, where the last load of Christmas mail reached the northernmost port, Una-laska, on Christmas Day. The feat was made possible by contracting for a new ship which could weather winter conditions in the North Pacific. The co-operation in the Christmas campaign was so excellent that no peak mailing resulted, although the volume of mail handled represented an increase over 1920 in almost every city.

The major aim of humanizing the postal service was only a recognition of the fact, perhaps too often forgotten, that the indispensable factor is the human one. Never has it been more dramatically expressed than in the motto on the façade of the General Post Office in New York:

Neither snow, nor rain, nor heat, nor gloom of night stays these couriers from the swift completion of their appointed rounds.

Again and again, I emphasized that the letter carrier himself was the one greatest humanizing agent. Horses have been replaced by motor vehicles, candles by electricity, sailboats by ocean liners—but no mechanism could replace humanity's main point of contact, the letter carrier. In telling this story to the nation, the press was by far our most important public relations agent.

My Post Office year was a busy one, with a single objective. Conferences, meetings, conventions, and bulletins within the department, campaigns conducted through women's clubs, school children, chambers of commerce, civic groups, and speeches made outside the department— all added up to public relations. Strengthening the civil service, awarding war certificates, and working for economy in government were administrative measures. Establishing a welfare department, setting up a new retirement policy, changing rural carriers' pay and working regulations, and permitting employees to have phonograph music in workrooms were labor policies. Each separate phase, each "policy," was all part of one objective, one triangle: humanizing the postal service. As I try to picture it in my own memory, the year was twelve months of constant planning and execution, of devising ways and means, on a very large scale, for bringing about better human relations—better health and happiness for everyone connected with the business, and consequently better service for everyone who used its product. The spirit of the 325,-000 associates in the department and the resulting better service to a nation of satisfied customers were the recognized results of a great wave of co-operation for which I have never ceased to be thankful.

CHAPTER 23

Trucks, Tubes, and Mail Robbers

I N addition to the human side of the postal service, there were the mechanical and technical sides. We had a thousand and one problems concerning such things as air mail, building facilities, communications, dead letters, foreign relations, postal savings, and postal rates—things of a functional nature. The institutions and mechanics of the Post Office Department comprised the "inhuman side."

An example of this side was the postal service's municipal "rolling stock." Trucks for city delivery and railroad-to-postal-station connections were a fairly recent innovation in 1921. The first suggestion that "old Dobbin" was to lose his time-honored place had come in 1899, when an advertisement appeared in a Chicago newspaper asking for bids on motor-vehicle service. A neigh of relief probably resounded through the livery stables when no answers were forthcoming. The old gray mare's obituary was finally signed in 1914, when a fleet of government-owned vehicles began to thread streets all over the country carrying the U.S. mail.

The inauguration of parcel post in 1913 also encouraged the increasing use of trucks for mail transportation. The effect of the automobile on the postal service can be seen by the fact that in 1915 Congress found it necessary to increase the rural carriers' salary to $1,800 per annum; authorized his route at not less than 50 miles; and superseded 928 horse routes with 491 motor-vehicle routes. These resulted in including 93,309 more families in the rural service. The increase in salary for rural carriers was necessitated by the fact that the rural carrier had to supply his own automobile, but extended service was ample compensation so far as the department was concerned.

In less than seventeen years the motor vehicle became a better medium of communication than the horse had ever been since its domestication in 1800 B.C. Out of 384,526 trips scheduled in one city for 1917, there were only 132 failures, or one in every 2,913 trips. The truck outdid the horse in economy of upkeep, distance covered, and speed in expedition of business.

This background may seem somewhat superfluous to the modern generation, but to me in 1921 the motor vehicle was still an innovation, and an unorganized innovation at that. Nearly 4,000 trucks were being used by the service at an annual operating cost of $15,000,000. Almost 25,000 tires per year were required to "keep 'em rolling." Overland, Reo, Lippard-Stewart, Selden, Denby, Riker, Federal, Gramm-Bernstein, Garford, Republic, Hurlburt and Peerless—these are not names of gas ranges or washing machines—were some of the many brands of automobiles used by the postal service then. Only names like "Ford," "GMC," and "White" saved the whole array from being dated close to the gaslight era. The problem facing the Post Office Department regarding its trucks was almost the same as that which faced the railroads nearly half a century before. Each make of truck called for special attention. Motor-vehicle items furnished by the department had increased from 70 to 279 by 1921. Something had to be done if the motor-vehicle service was to continue to be cheaper than the fairly recent horse-and-buggy, livery-stable arrangement.

In Ralph H. Matthiesen, I found a person who could do the something needed. President of the Motor Haulage Company of New York City, Mr. Matthiesen was selected as a special assistant to the Postmaster General because of his experience in the still new field of commercial trucking. He at once organized a Bureau of Motor Vehicle Transportation in the department of the Fourth Assistant Postmaster General. This new Bureau was to provide an "operations base" from which 5,000 supervisory officials, clerks, chauffeurs, and mechanics could be directed; and it established a central point from which purchase of vehicles and supplies, and their standardization, could be supervised.

Much of the rapid growth of the motor-vehicle service was directly due to the accompanying expansion of the parcel post service during the war years. Since its establishment in 1913, the growth of that service had been enormous: the number of parcels carried increased from 332,000,-000 in 1913 to nearly 2,000,000,000 by 1921! Not only the number, but also the size and weight of the parcels had increased. The Post Office Department was actually in the express business in a big way. Economy of shipping costs, reliability in delivery, scope of territory covered, and universality of service are probably the four main reasons why parcel post proved so popular with the public. The farmer and Sears, Roebuck might never have met had it not been for the mail-order catalogue and parcel post!

By 1921 the growth of parcel post began to cause some concern to the department and to Congress. No effort had been made to ascertain the actual costs involved, although it was a well-known fact that parcel post was considerably cheaper than private express companies' rates. So, with building facilities bursting and an allegedly huge deficit in the Post

Office Department because of parcel post, I called upon a firm of engineers to investigate conditions in one city. We picked St. Paul, where on July 1, 1920, an experiment in the use of parcel post for local delivery by merchants had been inaugurated. This service was costing the merchant an average of only nine cents per package. The most important conclusion in the engineers' report was the fact that merchants were saving money by using parcel post, but at the taxpayer's expense. Following this diagnosis, we cut off the large-scale parcel post local delivery service. This and certain new regulations appreciably cut down the national parcel post deficit.

Parcel post and war demands were two big factors which had made for outmoded postal facilities all over the country. Postal business in New York had increased 289 per cent from 1912 to 1920, but no changes in facilities during those years could be made because of the war. Two major changes were now effected in the policy on buildings: one designed to cut expenses; the other, to increase capacity. The former changed leasing arrangements; the latter called for new buildings. In cities like Chicago and New York we found it actually cheaper to own buildings than to rent them.

Another means of meeting the demands created during the war was to expand building facilities. In Washington we opened a branch office on the ground floor of the Post Office Department building, where for a long time previously a person could not even purchase a postage stamp.

In Chicago, after much investigation by the department, bids were finally opened for a large mail terminal at the new Union Station. A contract awarded in December called for an eight-story building with a floor capacity of 500,000 square feet. Equipment was to cost nearly $500,000. The building was designed with particular features to accommodate the large mail-order-house business. Conveying machinery calling for seven miles of belting alone, special loading and dumping platforms, and a sub-basement with railroad tracks running right into the building give some idea of the changes parcel post and trucks alone had necessitated in postal service.

The problem of facilities in New York was unique. New York was not just another big city; it was the gateway of the nation, where 15,000,000 pieces of mail were received and delivered daily by 12,000 employees. This represented a greater volume of mail service than the entire Dominion of Canada. In 1921, these employees worked daily to handle 50,000 pieces of registered mail, 650,000 pounds of newspapers and periodicals, and 350,000 pieces of misdirected mail! Adjusting postal facilities in New York could not be done without careful planning. The first change in New York was rerouting bank mail to avoid handling and delay at the General Post Office.

A second improvement was the New York harbor-boat service. A four-year contract awarded to the New York Central Railroad put two boats on twenty-four-hour harbor duty to handle incoming foreign mail starting August 1, 1921. New York Central also agreed to operate at cost a third ship turned over by the War Department, a surplus ship which had been laying up at Newark. The harbor-boat service picked up mail from incoming ships before they docked, delivered it directly to rail terminals and to postal stations in Brooklyn and all along the New Jersey shore. Having the mail sorted and placed in labeled sacks on shipboard and having it delivered directly to ports where it could leave for points south and west and north and east cut out as much as two days' delay in nationwide delivery. Sending the mail around the island vicinities saved time and money and relieved congestion in Manhattan.

Harbor boats provided one way to avoid street congestion. Underground tubes were another means to the same end. Both made for better service in the metropolitan area. Tube service in New York had been discontinued in 1918 on the plea that it was too expensive to operate. But by 1921 postal facilities were so inadequate that it became necessary to use every device at our disposal. Double tubes numbering 27.8 miles in length and connecting 26 main post office stations could be an invaluable adjunct to the postal service. Three thousand tube carriers were sitting idle, just waiting to make their thirty-mile-an-hour trips once more through these miniature subways eight inches in diameter. In 1921 businessmen and merchants in the metropolitan area were clamoring to have the tube service restored. In August I went to New York to get a bird's-eye view of the situation. The first move was the appointment of a citizen's advisory committee. With them I discussed the wisdom of revamping the City Hall post office or erecting new buildings and enlarging others. This big question was still unsettled when I resigned from the department in 1922. Postmaster General Hubert Work, my successor, recommended in his annual report for 1922 that the Post Office negotiate a purchase of the desired property, which in the long run would actually be cheaper than leasing. In 1921 we were paying annual rental of almost a million dollars for leased property in New York.

The postal business is the public's business, and whether it has its point of contact with a citizens' advisory committee or with the person receiving or sending a letter, the public is always conscious of its national postal communications network—particularly of any irregularities, interruptions, or variations in service. And mail robbery could be more than facetiously labeled an irregularity!

Almost everything common to civilization stages a "comeback"; and Wells-Fargo days were being revived in 1920 and 1921 with as much excitement as when the first stagecoach was robbed out West. A $6,000,-

ooo loss in 36 major robberies in those two years proved that the un-
gentle art of mail robbery was not dead.

While I was "humanizing" the mails in Washington on April 6, a
group of bandits were burglarizing them in Chicago. I was shocked by
the report that a $500,000 to $750,000 "haul" had been made at the
loading platform of the Dearborn Street Station. The story was that a
group of men started an ostensibly harmless baseball game shortly after
noon in a vacant lot across Federal Street from the station. At four-
thirty the game suddenly stopped, and the shooting started. They drew
their revolvers, made a dash for the loading platform, ordered an unarmed mail clerk to throw out the registered-mail sacks, and made their
getaway in an automobile. Whatever the details, the Post Office Department was suddenly running a huge deficit of more than half a million dollars. And as if that were not enough, the theft of one sack of
registered mail was reported from my home town on the same day!

I don't know whether the Chicago haul or the idea of somebody robbing my own back yard brought me to the boiling point the faster, but
something had to be done. Thirteen days after those two robberies we
announced a five-thousand-dollar reward for the capture and conviction
of any mail robber, and we also announced the arming of all postal
employees handling mail in places where robberies might occur. The
War Department released sixteen thousand .45-caliber pistols, hundreds
of repeating shotguns of the riot type, and a million rounds of ammunition for use by postal employees.

Issuing firearms may seem a drastic action, but it was needed to protect the lives of men performing their duties and public property
entrusted to the Post Office Department. Many postal employees had
been shot down in cold blood; others trained in the Army, Navy, and
Marine Corps were not to be denied the right to fight fire with fire if
other methods failed. At this same time I issued a report to the press,
inviting them to keep the public fully informed: "We do not care how
far the papers go in criticizing the Department. The public is entitled
to know if we are to blame and know just what we are doing to stop the
mail robbing."

Post office inspectors were called into immediate conference, and the
urgency of the situation was impressed upon them. The circumstances
surrounding all robberies for the past two years were reviewed, and the
whole department was briefed to be ready to handle our Public Enemy
No. 1.

Things quieted down to some extent after the April announcements,
and no more major robberies occurred until August, when a $60,000
theft occurred in Illinois. On the other side of the ledger, one of the
biggest mail-robbery rings had been cracked wide open. We picked up
a swindle king in Chicago who had coast-to-coast mail-robbery dealings;

in New York City this gang was responsible for a metropolitan theft of $3,000,000 in Sinclair Oil stock; in a Toledo robbery, the same group stole $1,000,000 early in February; they had conducted the Dearborn Street, Chicago, robbery and many other "jobs." Indictments were issued against eighteen men and one woman. The evidence against them had been accumulated over a six-month period. An agent running a "business school" on East Seventy-second Street in New York was also indicted on charges of trading in Liberty Bonds and savings stamps. A New York "real estate" dealer was picked up on similar charges. The group was responsible, too, for a "securities" outfit in the financial district of Chicago, an enterprise whose fraudulent dealings could be traced back to 1902! Their source of income in this association had come from dealings in stolen securities, illegally "washed" revenue stamps, and war savings securities. Judge Kenesaw M. Landis was the man who sentenced the group. During this same month we closed this case by picking up the remnants of the ring in Cleveland.

Another success involved our frustration of a mail-robbery attempt in Fort Worth. The robbers' plans were uncovered by FBI agents and postal inspectors working together, and were known also to an assistant chief clerk of the railway mail service in that district. He volunteered to act on the night of the proposed robbery as the messenger of mail car "X," accompanied by the regular clerks, who concealed themselves in the car. The train left Fort Worth at 11:40 P.M., ten minutes late. One minute later the expected robber entered mail car "X," covered the "messenger," and ordered him to open the door near the place where the mail was to be thrown off the train. At this point, according to plans, the robber was to kill the messenger—a thing that the assistant chief clerk knew. The mail was thrown off at the appointed place, where FBI agents and postal inspectors were ready to receive it. One robber who was waiting at the spot was killed trying to escape with the pouches. The one on the train was himself covered and disarmed before he could do more damage. The train backed up and picked up the mail, including a quantity of stage money, which had been substituted in registered-mail sacks. The reward was given shortly afterward to the clerk who, through his alertness, aroused the help of the FBI, the postal inspectors, and local police.

The department could announce in September that mail robberies had been greatly reduced. From April 8, 1920, to April 8, 1921, $6,346,407 had been stolen in 36 major robberies, of which $3,286,017 was recovered. But from April 9, 1921, to September 7 of that year, a total amount of only $88,580 had been stolen with a recovery of $78,555. The Inspection Department considered that the cut-down was due to the drastic measures taken in April, and newspapers were generous in their praise:

A few months ago, mail robberies were the breakfast dish of the country. In five months, they have netted only $10,025. Last year they were getting away with millions. This is good work, work of the sort that the country appreciates in a Post Office Department and by a Postmaster General.

However, the illusion of peace was rudely dashed in October, when an estimated $1,454,128 was quietly lifted from a mail truck going down the Canal Street grade on the way from the New York City Hall station to the General Post Office. The driver was carrying $27,104.82 in cash and coin, $74,306.09 in negotiable bonds, $1,054,977.83 in non-negotiable bonds, $223,545.89 in shares and stock, more than $11,000 worth of jewelry, coupons, notes and drafts, and letters. The driver, alone and unarmed, saw a green car pull up beside him. Two men leaped into the truck. Speeding off was impossible, because another car had simultaneously pulled across his path to prevent any escape. A laundry bag was pulled over his head and more than $1,000,000 changed hands.

The circumstances attending the robbery were full of ruthless irony. It was the third attempt: the first had been prevented by rain, the second by the chance appearance of a policeman, and the third, successful attempt was clearly witnessed by two men who thought that the truck had broken down and that the mail was being transferred. Another disconcerting thing was the fact that New York postal authorities had disregarded regulations which might have made the robbery impossible.

Chase National Bank had brought $453,000 worth of negotiable bonds to the City Hall Post Office that day under a seven-man guard, and yet a post office truck transferring more than $1,000,000 was being driven that night by one unarmed postal employee! Under postal regulations, any truck carrying more than $1,000,000 was to be accompanied by a motorcycle convoy and armed guards. These actual circumstances and the setup for the robbery were uncovered when we arrested a man in New York on entirely different charges. The post office delinquency came to light when I went to New York to conduct an investigation among metropolitan postal officials. Stricter regulations were put into effect immediately: all transfer trucks containing shipments of registered mail were to have motorcycle convoys; the driver was not to carry the key to the cage, which would be locked at the point of departure and remain locked until it reached its destination, where post office authorities would unload the shipment; and all trucks were to have guards who were to do nothing but keep their eyes open and their fingers on the trigger.

This robbery incident had another ironic twist when we re-enacted it late one night at Broadway and Leonard streets. A truck with a motorcycle guard passed by the scene, stopped the whole performance, thinking that it was another robbery, and refused to release us until we produced credentials! Following the investigation, three lesser officials of the New York Post Office were suspended for dereliction of duty in failing to carry out regulations.

Other robberies in Detroit, Paxton, and Kansas City made it evident that still more stringent measures had to be taken. In Detroit a horse-drawn wagon was robbed. In a Kansas City train-robbery attempt an express messenger was robbed and wounded by two bandits. In Paxton, Illinois, six train robbers equipped with everything from gas bombs to automobiles made good their escape after robbing the mail car on a trestle. The conduct of the mail clerks on that train presented a supreme example of loyalty: at the risk of their lives, they refused to open the locked doors of their mail car until they were literally blasted away. The robbers blew open the safe, removed the entire contents, burned about a ton of mail, and showed remarkably accurate knowledge in sorting out registered-mail sacks. The only trace left was a sack of registered mail containing $100,000 dropped by the bandits as they made their escape.

To discourage further attempts, one other drastic measure, which brought various reactions, was resorted to. On November 8, 1921, at my request, a thousand marines were called into the service of the Post Office Department. This action was taken after Cabinet consultation at a meeting where nothing but the robberies was discussed. The plan was supported by all the Cabinet members, who also agreed with my suggestion that we use the marines until the Post Office Department had trained its own armed guard. I then consulted with Major General John A. Lejeune, marine commander, and Secretary of the Navy Denby made a special address to the marine contingent being assigned to their new duties.

Three days later, sixty-five marines reported to Postmaster Morgan in New York. At the same time, the "leathernecks" were sent out all over the country, and armored cars were assigned to post offices in many cities. These were bulletproof and each was guarded by three marines, two stationed inside each truck to guard the registered mail, and a third with the driver. Each truck was equipped with sirens which could be heard for blocks; the driver could send an alarm by a foot control, while a marine in the truck could use a push button. Shipments of registered mail were segregated to ensure greater safety.

The reaction to enlisting the aid of marines was varied, but most newspapers considered it a necessary evil. A small western newspaper got the right idea when it editorialized:

Robbing the mails is not only an action against the government of this nation, but it is a direct violation of an important sort of security of every law-abiding citizen in the United States. More than any other institution, the post office is the property of all the people.

The mails are inviolate public property, and any type of tampering with them involved offenses far more serious than ordinary thieving. As a public servant at the head of the largest department having universal impact on the whole country, I felt it my duty to resort to any measure necessary to ensure protection of the mails.

The shooting by a marine of a suspect about to climb aboard a mail car in Wisconsin led to prolonged correspondence with the governor of the state, who wanted the marine turned over to him for trial. While the question raised by Governor Blaine was not new, it was nevertheless very important. The issues of federal authority superseding state authority in certain matters has been settled again and again by the Supreme Court. But for an off-the-record opinion, a New York newspaper rendered a succinct answer to the whole question, amplifying the point of view already set forth in my communications to Governor Blaine. The newspaper stated quite correctly that Governor Blaine was not responsible for the security of the mails; that the federal, not the state, government is; that soldiers cannot be trained "to expect that if they obey orders they will land in a county jail"; and that we could not afford to train outlaws to look for easy money every time they saw a mailbag.

Early in 1922 the marines were called off when our own force of postal guards was strong enough and sufficiently well trained to meet any crisis. On March 4, 1922, we released figures showing that, from May 1921 to March 1922, $300,000 was stolen, with the exception of the October New York mail robbery, which was the result of the failure of officials to carry out the orders of the department. The improvement we attributed to arming and training postal employees, offering the rewards, and using marines. One hundred and twenty-three persons were arrested over the year in connection with mail robberies; thirty-four were convicted, fifteen were discharged or acquitted, and the remainder awaited trial.

Before leaving this subject I can't help recalling the touch Will Rogers added to alleviate the gravity of the situation. One night when we were both attending the same dinner, Will came up to me and said:

"Suppose you noticed, speaking of what's happening up here, that we've had right smart of mail robberies?"

"Yes," I said. "Several people have spoken to me about that."

"I've been talkin' to people about it too," said Rogers. "Looks like they're tryin' t' git politics into it."

"No!"

"Yessir! The Democrats are claimin' there wasn't no robberies when they were runnin' the mails."

"They are?"

"Yessir. But the Republicans has got a good come-back. They say that when the Democrats was runnin' things the robbers never knew when the mails was goin' to arrive!"

Postal rates, in reference to certain classes of mail, may have important significance beyond mere costs. In 1921 the department had to cope with a situation involving a civil liberty which found its establishment in our American tradition when Andrew Hamilton courageously upheld the right of Peter Zenger to expose in print a corrupt New York governor. The situation in 1921 was far less spectacular, but important in preventing a precedent limiting freedom of the press. Certain "radical" newspapers had been denied the second-class privilege but were admitted to the mails at a higher rate of postage.

I granted second-class privileges to the New York *Call,* the New York *Liberator,* and the Milwaukee *Leader* on the theory that if these publications were permitted to use the mails at all they should be given the same privileges granted other similar publications. To deny second-class privileges to a publication would be, in effect, to declare that publication non-mailable. In the case of the *Liberator,* a monthly magazine published in New York, the application for the second-class privilege had been on file since the date of its founding, February 11, 1918. Every issue since that time had been accepted at third-class rates, considerably higher. As a result of admission to second-class, the Post Office refunded to the *Liberator* $11,277, the difference which the magazine had been charged over second-class rates.

In connection with the granting of these privileges, certain points in question were made clear. One was that applications for second class would be granted if found to comply with the law—that is, if they were mailable at all. Another was that if there were on foot a conspiracy to destroy our established government by force or violence, heretofore claimed by the department as a reason for not granting permits, the Department of Justice would deal with any conspirators as prescribed by law. We had no hesitancy in suppressing any publications that fell within the prohibitions of public law, including the Espionage Act of 1917, but there were laws in this country safeguarding the integrity of the freedom of the press, and these laws also had to be scrupulously observed.

Not directly related to press freedom, but involving a type of censorship, was H.R. 8508, to which I objected early in January 1922. The bill was primarily designed to prevent the transportation of lottery and betting devices through the mails, but Section 5 made it an abuse for newspapers to publish racing news. I was in favor of the bill but opposed to Section 5. The tendency toward curbing public morals through legislation was growing; but as witnessed by the failure of the prohibition amendment, a whole people cannot be legislated into a given pattern of behavior. This move to prohibit racing news seemed to me another step in the direction of regulating public conduct.

Ideas and money are two things which are no good if they are not kept in circulation. Safeguarding freedom of the press was one way of assuring continuous interchange of many shades of thought. Keeping money in circulation is sometimes a harder task. As a bank account is based on confidence, so the volume of postal savings indicates public confidence in the government. In some ways, too, postal savings provided a barometer of financial and industrial activities.

For that reason, getting into circulation an estimated billion dollars which had been sewn into mattresses and tied in stockings was a very important thing for business recovery in 1921. More than 70 per cent of the postal-savings depositors were foreign-born or of foreign extraction, trusting their savings to no institution but the United States Government. The government was in the banking business to facilitate national savings and to promote economy and thrift. But up to that time postal savings had not scratched the surface, notwithstanding the conception of public duty that had inspired its founding.

We were not in competition with banks, we did not want depositors who had already learned to trust private institutions, and the Post Office certainly was not making any money by maintaining a savings bank. Postal savings was the conduit through which money could be brought into circulation, and it acted as a training school of thrift that would ultimately make savers, investors, and private bank depositors out of countless thousands. Financial reform measures are taken up slowly at best, and while we could not accomplish some of the major changes we might have liked to see made, we did manage to arouse the interest of the public, bankers, and members of Congress in the advantages that would ultimately be reaped by the country as a whole in getting more money into circulation through the medium of postal savings.

One of the things that interested me most was the operations of the foreign mail, conducted through the Universal Postal Union, and based upon mutual agreement and mutual service. We sought to make the Postal Union the best possible agency in the promotion of international comity and understanding, since through it are concluded the agreements regulating rates for the exchange of foreign mails.

During 1921 parcel post conventions were concluded with Spain, Indo-China, Persia, the Straits Settlements, French Cameroons, Latvia, Finland, Kingdom of Serbs, Croats, Slovenes, and the Fiji Islands. Parcel post service was also resumed with Germany, Austria, and Hungary. In September, service to Russia via England was inaugurated.

Sea postal service, interrupted by the war, was resumed on June 26, 1921, when the steamship *America* departed from New York to Plymouth, Cherbourg, and Bremen. This service, established on nine vessels

by 1922, utilized the time of the voyage in the preparation of mail for
dispatch or delivery.

For the most part, foreign mail service in 1921 represented an adjustment to peacetime conditions. There were, however, two accomplishments of note which were not settled directly through the Universal
Postal Union. One of these was accomplished through the Pan-American Postal Congress, which met at Buenos Aires in July. The other was
an agreement with China to which the United States, along with other
foreign powers, became a party at the Washington Disarmament Conference, which opened in the fall of 1921.

The Pan-American Postal Congresses grew out of repeated complaints
from South American countries that business firms in the United States
were making a practice of sending postage-short letters to firms south
of the border and ultimately ruining good business relations between us
and them. The parcel post agreement, the second of the two concluded,
provided one uniform, simple system for all Pan-American countries in
place of nineteen separate and varying systems which had been in force
with the United States. Both agreements growing out of that Postal
Congress offered concrete evidence of the desire of the nineteen participating countries to bring about closer co-operation among themselves
and to improve their commercial relations through simplification and
improvement of their postal services. I saw by these concrete examples
that whatever improves the means of communication between peoples
and nations makes for the advancement of international commerce and
our common civilization.

Another agreement aimed at fostering a better basis for communications was signed at the Washington Disarmament Conference in 1921.
Four-power treaties, five-power treaties, nine-power agreements, naval
ratios, and other military conventions necessarily overshadowed an
agreement made with China regarding postal service. This resolution,
calling for the closing not later than January 1, 1923, of all foreign
postal agencies in China was another step in recognizing sovereignty
and receiving that country into the family of nations. In leased territory
and by special treaty, certain foreign postal services could be maintained
in the Far East, but as soon as the resolution was adopted the United
States commenced arrangements to close her postal station at Shanghai
by the appointed date. This agreement represented a definite step
toward China's achievement of territorial and administrative integrity.

The Washington Conference has already gone down in history as the
most successful disarmament conference of modern times, and while I
as Postmaster General had little to do with the actual arrangements, as a
Cabinet member I was an official host of my government to delegates
from foreign countries. The actual programming, developments, and
execution of the conference arrangements were done by the State De-

partment, but one detail in which I played a role was that of setting the date for the opening of the conferences. As President Harding and I were discussing the matter, it struck me that coincidence had blessed us with an occasion made to order. What could be more appropriate than to open a disarmament conference on Armistice Day, November 11, 1921? It was in the evening of that same day that the foreign delegates and official hosts from the United States gathered at Arlington Memorial Cemetery for the burial services of the Unknown Soldier.

Before leaving the city of Washington for the memorial ceremonies, the delegates attended a state dinner held to celebrate the opening of the Peace Conference. Each Cabinet member acted as official host to certain delegates. On my right sat the ranking Italian, chairman of his delegation, General Diaz, who during the war had been the top general in Italy's army. On my left was Admiral Tsai, who headed his delegation from China. Also seated nearby were Senator Pearce from Australia and Lord Lee from Great Britain. An interpreter who sat across from us may have seemed a superfluous fixture until I attempted to talk with General Diaz. I spoke no French or Italian; he, no English. The experience of realizing that I could not converse with him was one of the most mortifying things that has ever happened to me, making me realize more than ever the necessity for knowing more than one language.

Lord Lee, who had an American wife, took great interest in our air-mail development. My friend George Harvey, then Ambassador to Great Britain, had suggested separately to each of us that we get together at this conference, but that we should meet the first evening was a coincidence. Lord Lee later sent one of the British delegation, then in charge of air mail in that country, to talk with me. He was eager to know about our progress and explained regretfully that Britain could not do the same in developing air mail. The distances on the Isles were not great enough to make air mail a practical thing, and Britain was particularly sorry, because planes used by any government in commerce were not subject to restriction in type or quantity under international disarmament agreements.

I was delighted to find that Admiral Tsai spoke beautiful English. A Cornell graduate, he had been in charge of Chinese naval operations in World War I. Before the evening was over we were getting on so well together that he was calling me "Will." Among our topics of discussion was the movie industry. Admiral Tsai told me that he looked to the movies as the medium which could lift 400,000,000 honest people out of their lethargy. Not long after I resigned from the Post Office Department to assume my new duties as head of the Motion Picture Producers and Distributors of America, I learned that Admiral Tsai had taken a position on some movie board in China. I have not seen him now for many years, but I used to hear about him frequently through Louis

Chiang, son of H. H. Kung and nephew of Chiang Kai-shek through his mother's family. Louis knew Admiral Tsai, and through him I used to exchange verbal greetings with the admiral.

One other incident of personal note concerning the conference comes to mind. It concerns an automobile which did not belong to the government. On the day that the Cabinet met for the first time in March there was great joking about whether I had hitched my horse and buggy outside. I was the only Cabinet member who did not have an official car because, as former Postmaster General Burleson explained, he was the victim of a "Democratic kicker" who did not like him. The Hays & Hays law firm decided that I needed an automobile in Washington, though I think my friend Jim Connery of Chicago was at the bottom of the whole thing. Jim was like a second father to me, made some good investments for me, and was my frequent companion on later trips to California just because he wanted to keep me company. Anyway, the firm told me to pick out the best-looking car I could find, so I did. The car was so beautiful that the State Department "borrowed" it for second place in the procession which brought the delegates for the conference down Pennsylvania Avenue.

Secretary of Commerce Hoover was the first in the Harding administration to bring up the problem of unregulated radio communication, at a Cabinet meeting on April 5. He pointed out that there were no regulations in force to govern the sending and receiving of radio messages. A committee, consisting of Secretary of War Weeks, Secretary of the Navy Denby, Secretary of State Hughes, Mr. Hoover, and myself, was appointed to investigate the question of improving wireless conditions. Thus began, also, the interest of the Post Office Department in radio.

Seventeen days after this meeting we started a nationwide post office radio system. Fifteen large stations covering a belt from the capital to the Pacific coast comprised the network for the radio system which was *set up primarily as an important auxiliary of the air-mail service.* Market reports from the Bureau of Markets and weather reports were sent out several times a day. The first radio programs were strictly "shop talk" to help the farmer and the aviator. The inauguration of this service took place at ten-thirty on the morning of April 22 in the Washington radio station of the Post Office Department. Secretary of Agriculture Wallace, Dr. Charles F. Marvin, chief of the Weather Bureau; W. A. Wheeler, chief of the Bureau of Markets, Dr. Samuel Stratton, director of the Bureau of Standards, a number of government scientists and bureau heads were present when we made the first announcement to 6,000 licensed wireless operators that market and weather reports were on a daily schedule. Those who did not have this service and wanted it could get it by installing "simple receiving sets costing approximately $50 to $75."

As a result of setting up this nationwide service, many radio classes were started in agricultural colleges, where student farmers became intensely interested in the marketgram service. Another development was the decided increase in the number of wireless stations being erected and operated by amateurs.

By July it was evident that the service was proving of so great a value that Secretary Wallace and myself appointed a National Radio Service Commission to study further the broadcasting of livestock, grain, fruit, and vegetable market quotations and other information of interest to the farm communities. The National Radio Service Commission consisted of Mr. R. B. Howell of Omaha; William A. Wheeler, specialist on information in the Bureau of Markets; Courtland Smith; and J. C. Edgerton, radio expert of the Post Office Department. It was Mr. Howell who went to Europe in August at his own expense to investigate developments in radio abroad.

By July, too, daily reports were going out three or four times a day from air-mail stations covering radii of 300 to 500 miles each. It was then that we realized that, with the growing scale of radio communication, half a million dollars could be saved annually by consolidating all government radio, telegraph, and telephone communications in one bureau. The consolidation idea originated with Senator Townsend, who was chairman of the Joint Postal Commission. While the Federal Communications Commission did not come into being until the Communications Act of 1934, the need for such a bureau was already recognized in 1921. It is an interesting fact that at the same time we were working on radio improvements Britain was concerned with similar matters and appointed Winston Churchill, Colonial Secretary, as chairman of its commission.

In September a New York newspaper printed an interview with me which may have seemed anticipatory then but seems slightly bizarre now because of the terminology used. Knowing what the radio could do with weather reports and stock-market news, some of us in the government were getting enthusiastic over its possibilities. The interview read in part:

Get ready for a national radiophone newspaper, radiophone messages from the White House, radiophone ball scores and weather reports, and radiophone opera.

A national radiophone newspaper service, topped off at the end of the day with a bit of "Carmen" or "Il Pagliacci" . . . a hot weather breakfast menu and the newest dialogue from vaudeville was suggested as a possibility for radiophone developments. . . .

There was a notable fallacy in my predictions. I thought that radio would gain its zenith under government control since at that time the government was the only agency which maintained any stations and did any large-scale broadcasting. However, like the air-mail service, radio was later taken over by private industry, which has built it into one of our greatest institutions—an almost indispensable part of our daily lives. But it should be remembered that the first real broadcasting was done over radio stations set up as an auxiliary of the air-mail service.

By all odds the most noteworthy among postal developments of the past quarter century has been the building up of the air-mail service. That observation can now be made in a sentence, but it took volumes of testimony, hours of inquiry, and weeks of patience to make it true. The air-mail service in 1921 came very close to singing its Swan Song. One of the basic reasons that the air-mail service found itself in a precarious position was its tremendous cost, both in dollars and in human life. If the cost in dollars could be cut down, I thought the loss of human life might be eliminated through spending more money on technical improvements, better training facilities, and equipment. It was with the idea of improving the financial factors that I suggested that all flying services—Army, Navy, Department of Commerce, and Post Office Department—be consolidated under one head. This suggestion was made at a Cabinet meeting twenty-four days after I took office as Postmaster General, but I had to wait more than twenty-four years to see the consolidation not only of flying but of all defense departments. However, some of the groundwork was laid in 1921 with that end in mind.

Late in March I held a one-hour conference with Secretary of War Weeks to discuss possibilities for closer co-operation among the Army, Navy, Post Office, and other departments using aircraft. If consolidation was then beyond reach, possibly standardization of the machines in use was not entirely so. If money could be saved by standardizing postal service trucks, certainly a great deal could be saved by the use of planes suitable for both commercial and defense purposes. And it is far easier to convert an air-mail pilot into a fighter pilot than it is to make a fighter pilot out of a pedestrian. The Post Office Department was constantly training pilots for commercial purposes and using more aircraft in peacetime than any other department. Since peacetime commercial aircraft were unlimited by armaments agreements, the opportunity to develop aviation in the Post Office Department seemed to have unlimited possibilities. And if all departments of the government would buy similar aircraft on a unit-buying system, pilots trained by the Post Office Department could fly War Department planes in the event of a national emergency. At this same meeting with Secretary of War Weeks I suggested, too, that postal fliers be required to enter what was then the Army Aviation Reserve Corps.

When President Harding delivered a special report he anticipated by five years another report of a similar nature by the Morrow Commission of Inquiry.

President Harding, even in 1921, was concerned about the formulation of a national aviation policy, and the inquiry at this early date by the National Committee for Aeronautics was made at his specific request. The committee which made the inquiry recommended that Congress authorize new air-mail routes between Chicago, Minneapolis, and St. Paul, and between Chicago and St. Louis, and also suggested that a Bureau of Aeronautics be set up in the Commerce Department to provide national aviation regulations before the states set up their own regulatory laws. The Civil Aeronautics Authority was not established until 1938! It is significant, in this connection, that railroads were for more than seventy years a part of our lives before the need for national regulation was recognized, whereas in the case of commercial aviation, an insecure innovation in 1921, the need for national regulation was recognized almost immediately.

May 15 marked the third anniversary of the air-mail service inaugurated in 1918 and conducted for one year under Army supervision. During the preceding year more than 40,000,000 letters had been carried by air at a cost of $1.02 per mile! Four routes were being operated: the transcontinental—New York to San Francisco via Cleveland, Chicago, Omaha, Cheyenne, Salt Lake City, and Reno; another from Washington to New York; one from Chicago to Minneapolis; and a fourth from St. Louis to Chicago. But the upkeep of this service had cost the lives of thirteen pilots, five mechanics, and one official. The loss of nineteen lives represented an increase of almost 100 per cent over the first two years. Seven pilot fatalities had resulted from a defective mechanism in a type of plane later abandoned. Other factors which made flying the transcontinental route dangerous, with our inadequate planes and lack of flying aids, were the low ceilings over the Alleghenies and the blizzards in the Rocky Mountain areas. One pilot crashed in Jasper, Nevada, when the visibility was fifty yards! Another flying through blizzards and sleet between St. Louis and Chicago was so cold, sore, and stiff when he reached Chicago that he had to be helped out of his ship.

Will Rogers told me a story, too, that was typical of these early conditions. I never saw him more deeply affected. Just two nights previously he had come into Salt Lake City on a stormy night and was at the airport when the air-mail pilots were about to start out. All other planes were grounded, and he pleaded with them to wait. They insisted that they had received their orders and would go. He watched them take off against his strongest protests, only to learn that just out of Salt Lake City they crashed. Rogers was so deeply affected by the retelling of the incident that when he broadcast that night he could not do so in sight of his audience.

While these unfortunate things did sometimes occur, it was by no means the policy of the Post Office Department to require fliers to start on their trips under weather conditions that would endanger their lives. But accidents sometimes occurred because bad weather developed after a pilot had started his trip.

My May 12 annual report on the air-mail service was bound to be disturbing and provocative: either conditions for reasonably safe flying had to be developed or the service would have to be abandoned. In an effort to eliminate every possible disadvantage, we commenced an investigation on May 13, 1921. Among other things, we wanted to get to the bottom of these seven unexplained deaths.

Charges of "misconduct, inefficiency, criminal negligence, and gross mismanagement" provoked the investigation, which centered to a considerable extent around Checkerboard Field in Chicago. One of the chief witnesses, a pilot, testified that early in the year he had been discharged for bailing out near Minneapolis to save his life. But, maintained the pilot, the real reasons for his discharge were the complaints he had leveled against the literally drunken management of some of the airfields. This pilot's testimony was supported by an inspector of rigging at Minneapolis, who pointed out that planes left the fields with propellers so badly split that persons were warned to keep away from the landing fields lest a propeller fly off and injure someone. The same inspector testified that, under pain of discharge, the mechanics were forced to sign papers declaring the ships safe for flight whether or not parts to repair them were available.

There is a story told about Colonel Charles A. Lindbergh, whom I came to know first as an air-mail pilot. He had a reputation for being one of the safest and most reliable pilots in the service. Lindbergh reportedly never took a plane off the ground unless he was as sure of his flying conditions as he could be, and not until he had checked his whole plane himself from stem to stern. No matter how many "O.K.s" came out of the repair hangars, Lindbergh always checked his planes himself. More Charles Lindberghs might have made the road that air mail traveled less bumpy, but we had a bad situation and knew it. A New York newspaper, under the heading "No More Manslaughter," severely berated the air-mail service in its May condition and later publicly changed its mind when the air-mail arm was nearly amputated by Congress in February 1922.

I had been doing a lot of talking about how important I thought the air-mail service was, I had listened to testimony setting forth the difficulties of flying, but I had never flown myself! So after completing the necessary arrangements I flew the mail to New York with General Billy Mitchell late in May. I took a few other short hops around the country after that. Among newspapermen, Arthur Brisbane was one of the most ardent supporters of the air-mail service, but he was not gentle in his comments on my flying around in those "ash cans." Actually, flying a few air-mail routes gave me a closer feeling toward the men in the service, the service itself, and the importance of building up a trained force of pilots.

In spite of the fine record being established on the New York–Washington route, it was decided to discontinue it at the end of May and close the Newark airport. We were faced with a financial situation whereby the air-mail service was being largely supported through the railway-mail appropriation. Since the cost of maintenance was so great, we had to economize in every way possible. It may seem strange that the New York–Washington route, which was setting a good record, should fall under the butcher's cleaver in favor of the transcontinental route which had claimed nineteen lives. But it was the long run, not the short one, on which greater experimentation could be done and where the saving in time was greater.

In the meantime, changes were made in personnel and in conduct all along the line, stricter regulations were put in force on landing fields, and a safety-first campaign was begun. Planes were to be mechanically perfect before taking off, and pilots were forbidden to fly when bad weather conditions prevailed.

Late in June an opportunity was presented to me, through an interview, again to bring the air-mail service to the attention of the public. I held even then the conviction that our future, the future of the world, was in the air. I felt that how we developed or failed to develop aeronautics in the years following 1921 would determine whether we took first or a lesser place among the nations of the world.

It is hard to realize that in 1921 people were still not convinced of the value of human flight, and statistics showing 812 forced landings in 32 months did not strengthen the argument in favor of saving the remnants of aviation. The cost of operation for those 32 months showed an average close to $1.36 for each mile flown.

In July we combined business with a little recreation and staged a race to the West Coast with the Dempsey-Carpentier fight pictures—the air mail versus private planes and transcontinental fast mail trains. The air mail won by three hours, crossing the continent in 44½ hours. The fight pictures were on the streets in local newspapers less than 48 hours after the event had taken place. For those days, that was fast. In the meantime, Arthur Brisbane was shocking a lethargic public by telling them that we needed 5,000 planes *now*.

In midsummer we put into commission six planes taken over from the Army and remodeled at a cost of $3,000 each, as against an initial cost price of $15,000. The "new" planes carried 800 pounds of mail, or 32,000 letters, per trip. After much experiment the best type of plane was found to be a single-motored plane with a top speed of 115 mph, a landing speed of 50 mph, and a cruising endurance of four hours. Airplane No. 12, which had been the first to carry air mail between New York and Washington on May 15, 1918, was still in service after three years and five months! But it had only a carrying capacity of 200 pounds and a top speed of 75 mph. Such statistics, quoted today, seem unbelievable.

In October we released new statistics on the progress of the air mail. From July 1 to September 1 the performance record was 98 per cent, as against a record for the previous year of 78 per cent of the trips completed and 83 per cent of the miles. The cost of operation per mile was $73\frac{1}{3}$ cents as opposed to $1.02 per mile in May of 1921! And no fatalities had occurred on regular air-mail runs across the continent.

As a special tribute to Marshal Foch, a squadron of six air-mail planes flew in formation from Omaha to Kansas City, where the French leader was the honor guest of the American Legion's Third Annual Convention in Kansas City. During the three-day convention special air-mail service between the two cities was inaugurated.

A pending railway strike gave air mail another boost. One hundred members of the Aero Club in Omaha, under their club president, offered their services to recruit five hundred volunteer pilots to carry the mails in case of strike. The need to call out these fliers never arose, but recognition of the fact that planes could be an important commercial auxiliary was clearly indicated by this offer.

Making the air mail a part of the postal service had taken a tremendous amount of time, patience, money, and planning. During the year 1921 we had cut out almost every auxiliary route and devoted ourselves to making the transcontinental route a safe and indispensable time-saver. The performance record for the fiscal year 1921 was 85.96 per cent. The report in 1922, when the figure for performance was up to 94.39 per cent, was not at all apologetic. By the close of the fiscal year 1922 we could report that we had seventy planes in the air-mail service, a figure nearly doubling the thirty-six in service reported for 1921.

After the House of Representatives had clipped the wings of the Post Office Department, I picked up all the arguments I could muster and went flying over to the Senate Appropriations Committee, to give them ten good reasons why the air-mail appropriation should be restored in the Post Office Appropriations Bill for the fiscal year 1923. The one fatality in the last million miles flown, the economic resuscitation the service had undergone, the care which had been exercised in the operation of it, and the real need to preserve and build up air power for the sake of the country's defense were undoubtedly appealing arguments which helped to restore the $2,000,000 stricken from the bill.

In March 1922, after I had been Postmaster General exactly one year, I tendered my resignation from the Cabinet post to accept a new challenge in the field of motion pictures. The year had given me concentrated doses of working with thousands of people; managing the largest distribution business in the world; reorganizing men and materials, so that the optimum of output and efficiency might be achieved; and, most important of all, training in the highly specialized field of human relations. The experience, perforce, had taught me how to meet, greet, and treat my fellow man, if I had not known before. Cutting out $6,000,000 worth of highway robbery, building up the postal-savings system, installing better postal facilities in the interest of better service, standardizing equipment wherever we could—in short, tuning up the service in the most economical ways possible—gave me some confidence I did not have when William Fox approached me in December of 1920.

The year in the Post Office Department was a severe internship in human relations, public service, and business methods. My new job was made of the same ingredients but with somewhat different emphasis. Both the postal service and the later MPPDA involved jobs of public service. When through an incident in my own family I realized the tremendous influence of motion pictures on young and old, rich and poor—on everybody—I could no longer hesitate to accept the new responsibilities when a group of men felt that I could do the job. I was willing to accept the challenge and marched, though not fearlessly, into the most exciting, most eventful twenty-five years of my life.

CHAPTER 24

Live and Help Live

THIS chapter may at first strike one as unrelated, or out of place, but it is neither. As a matter of fact, it clearly looks both forward and back: back to my days in the Post Office Department and the struggles over the air mail that so sharpened my interest in commercial aviation, and forward to my days in motion pictures immediately following. It was our progress between 1922 and 1925 in bringing some degree of harmony into the competitive and undisciplined motion picture industry that led the commercial airplane people to ask me to sit in with their group as a sort of adviser on organization. It was an exciting and rewarding experience, one of the happiest bypaths in which I have ever found myself.

In no other field of activity did the doctrine of live and *help* live apply more literally than in the field of commercial aviation early in 1925. Looking back on the whole matter now, I believe that if we had not fought in 1922 to save the "mechanized carrier-pigeon" service of the Post Office Department not only air mail, but the whole development of commercial aviation as well would have been greatly—perhaps tragically—delayed.

Saving the air-mail service by congressional act was one way of assuring that the airplane would continue to play an important role in Americal life. The same solution could not be applied to save commercial aviation. Air-mail service was government business; commercial aviation was private enterprise. But aviation had fallen into a vicious pattern whereby manufacturers, in order to produce planes, had to depend on government contracts for their existence. The arrangement was quite one-sided. The aviation industry was the "sick man."

At this distance it is difficult to appreciate some of the factors that made commercial aviation almost wholly dependent on government contracts for survival immediately following World War I. First, the public mind failed to overcome quickly enough the idea that the airplane was only a weapon of war and to realize its peacetime value to commerce, industry, and national defense. But even in the midst of financial depression, political breakdown, and social chaos, Europe was building up commercial freight and passenger air-transport lines. In the second place, business, industry, and particularly Wall Street were slow in realizing that time had a dollar sign prefixing it. Bankers were just beginning to learn through the air-mail service that cutting out a day in financial transactions between New York and Chicago meant saving thousands of dollars in interest rates. The farmer, the forest ranger, the Coast Guard, and even immigration officials were only beginning to exploit the commercial value of the airplane. But a faster transformation in public thinking had to take place before such peacetime uses of the airplane could gain momentum and sustain the new industry.

Keystone of the arch, the air-mail service in this country alone provided the main liaison between the wartime use and the peacetime development of the airplane; it sustained the continual use of aviation until public confidence was strong enough to support aeronautical adventures by private industry. While aerial transport and passenger service, stimulated by continental governments' subsidies, grew by leaps and bounds among our European neighbors during the early twenties, the air-mail service, the Army and Navy flying services, and a few individual world records were the only testimony that America could produce. Expediting the mail became too conventional for continual public notice, but in 1923 the air mail met a challenge in which speed was the quintessence of a unique opportunity to perform a national public service. President Harding's sudden death on August 2, 1923, gave newsreel men a singular opportunity to record the funeral ceremonies so that the scenes might be presented quickly to thousands of sympathetic Americans throughout the country. The newsreel men could speed up production, but speed in distribution was the job of the airplane. When Edgar B. Patrick of International News Service learned that civilian planes would not be permitted to take off from Washington during the ceremonies, he immediately communicated with me at the MPPDA.

I got in touch with my old Indiana friend, Harry S. New, who was Postmaster General at that time. With enthusiastic sympathy for our plan of combining speed and public service, he immediately arranged for special air-mail planes to carry the films to New York, Chicago, and Boston. He also arranged for planes to leave New York the following morning to carry the newsreels west to Hollywood. On the evening of the morning Harding's death notice appeared in the newspapers, International had a "special" on the screen in New York, a film which covered every important phase of the President's career. The successful use of aviation at that time, with the entire country crisis-conscious and in deep mourning, put a feather in the cap of the air-mail service and gave the commercial use of aviation a striking boost in the public mind.

People in theaters from coast to coast were struck with amazement and gratitude at the opportunity to share in spirit, so close to the very hour, in the services laying President Harding away in his final rest.

Another step in the direction of slow but steady progress came when the air-mail service put night flying on a regular schedule on July 1, 1924.

While from my office at MPPDA I watched the development of the air-mail service with gratifying interest, I regretfully saw commercial aviation collapsing as if it had been a mere castle in the air. Even before I had any direct concern with commercial aviation, I had a sincere interest in its healthy growth, both from the point of view of the Post Office Department, and from an equally strong conviction that we needed the airplane as an instrument of national defense. The ultimate idea behind the whole mail-by-air scheme was that, as soon as it became feasible, the air-mail-carrying contracts would be let to private companies operating passenger or freight lines over the air-mail routes. Mail contracts, helping to support a vast network of private railroad and steamship lines, were a common part of our communications system. The U.S. Mail and commercial transportation have been good bedfellows for a long time! But in no case, until the airplane became a part of our civilization, had the Post Office Department actually operated a transportation system. A government flying service for commercial purposes was only temporary. While the government made a business of air mail, private business would supposedly be governing the growth of commercial aviation until such time as the new industry was strong enough to serve the government as the railroads do.

In 1925 the new Kelly Law, providing for the letting of air-mail contracts, showed healthy initiative on the part of the government, but the state of affairs in the commercial aviation field was discouraging, and I knew it. Of a $100,000,000 airplane investment in 1919, only one tenth remained. Fourteen thousand planes and 42,000 engines had become war casualties. Seven thousand trained pilots were scattered in almost as many walks of civilian life, and 250,000 operatives employed in 1919 had been forced for the most part to seek employment in other fields. In 1924 Curtiss confessed that it did not have the capital to produce one plane to compete for a world record! Suicidal methods within the shrinking industry itself were threatening to strangle it. I knew at the time I quoted these shocking facts in an address to the Economic Club in New York on January 16, 1925, how tragically accurate they were.

I first became familiar with the depression in the industry through a conversation with Lester D. Gardner, when he asked me to attend a luncheon of the aircraft interests at the University Club in New York on December 1, 1924. Major Gardner, at that time publisher of *Avia-*

tion, probably knew the prevailing situation among the manufacturers better than anyone else. His plan of calling together the aviation people was partially motivated by the interest stirred up over the investigation of the Congressional Select Committee of Inquiry into the Operations of the United States Air Services. In all, twenty-four persons attended that luncheon meeting, every one vitally interested in commercial aviation. Carl B. Fritsche, Inglis M. Uppercu, Lorillard Spencer, J. L. Callan, Edgar N. Gott, Reuben Fleet, Clement Keys, A. P. Loening, Glenn Martin, Raymond Ware, Chance Vought, Charles Lawrence, F. H. Russell, and Samuel S. Bradley were among those who had interests at stake.

Having Frank Schmitz, general manager of the Mahogany Association, and myself there was no accident. Both of us had already had experience at bringing conflicting industrial interests together under coordinated systems operating successfully. Because of my experience with the MPPDA, Major Gardner thought I could outline certain ideas and methods of trade co-operation that might be helpful to the aircraft industry in resolving some of its problems. A second reason for my presence was the fact that, as Postmaster General, I had taken a strong hand in encouraging aviation through the continuous development of the air-mail service. That my familiarity with Washington and my many friends there, including President Coolidge, might also aid us in untangling aircraft problems was perhaps a third reason for my invitation.

As intended, the luncheon turned into a conference on tactics to conquer the enemy on three fronts. Aviation had been fighting a losing battle in the public mind, in government circles, and even within itself, where there seemed to be a fifth column of saboteurs. Major Gardner sounded the keynote and then presented me to the group. The perplexities obstructing progress within the industry were not unlike those that had faced the MPPDA in 1922. I suggested that aviation, like motion pictures, railroads, and other forms of communication, had to be approached from a public-service point of view. If an industry can offer something of genuine use—something that the public will demand once it becomes familiar with a product or service—support will follow. The first thing that the industry had to do was to capture the public imagination; the second was to ascertain and produce what the government and the national economy needed, thereby becoming an essential industry; the third was to set its own house in order. Before the manufacturers could accomplish anything in the fields of engineering or production, they had to realize mutual confidence and esteem. With the full approval of the MPPDA, I told the group that I would be willing to work with any committee, whenever it was possible to help them in the accomplishment of their purposes.

In keeping with that commitment, I met with a committee at the

Yale Club in the early afternoon on December 6. This special committee of the aircraft industry was headed by Mr. Lawrence and included A. P. Loening, Glenn Martin, Chance Vought, Carl Fritsche, Frank Russell, and Sam Bradley as secretary. By that time they had already conducted two meetings among themselves and had formulated a brief, clear statement outlining the scope and purpose of their work. They had reached the conclusion that all aircraft manufacturers should be invited to the next open meeting. They also agreed on by-passing all detailed questions of a controversial nature. It was this decision which made progress possible. It is often the only basis on which any competitive group, not naturally drawn together, can accomplish anything of a lasting nature. By the time I met the committee they had prepared a statement of policies, together with their suggestions for best effecting them. By the close of that day, they had signed the resolution stating their purposes and had written letters of invitation to all the aircraft interests to attend an open meeting, enclosing a copy of their newly formulated resolution for all members in the industry to accept or reject.

The special committee met regularly thereafter, each Saturday at one in the Yale Club, well up to the end of June 1925. Together we worked out statements of policy, resolutions, arrangements for meetings with government officials, and various phases of co-operation within the industry, until all were reasonably sure that they had built up a framework in which manufacturers and government could work successfully to mutual advantage, and in which the industry itself could build a healthy expansion. Twenty-three competitive aircraft companies approved the resolution of co-operation, and later the industry endorsed the committee's statement of policy.

Several sections in the policy indicated the prevailing ills which the manufacturers were seeking to eliminate in order to avoid eliminating each other, as the movie interests had almost done during their early days. Section one was a pledge of mutual confidence and cordial relations; all differences were to be stated and settled among the aircraft interests themselves. In addition, the most annoying thorn was removed by the inviolate protection of "design rights," making healthy expansion possible. This operated to eliminate the bad features of the cross-license system which had been inaugurated as an emergency war measure in 1917, under which system Curtiss and Wright had been severely penalized, for airplane manufacturers without engineering staffs could take advantage of time and money put into engineering developments by other companies simply by paying an initiation fee of $1,000 to the government and a royalty—originally $200, later $100—for each plane built!

Another feature of the policy represented a move toward standardization of parts and equipment, with the purpose of being of greater value to the government. Twenty-three companies which had been suing each other and practicing the most destructive methods of competition agreed that the resolution and working policy should be presented to the President on behalf of all of them.

A second objective was realized December 18, when President Coolidge, sympathetic toward the industry's efforts, offered to arrange conferences between the special committee and the Secretaries of War and Navy. The President's suggestion was made during a conference I had with him the day we discussed commercial aviation conditions. On January 9, 1925, the committee met in the office of Secretary of War Weeks with the Secretary of the Navy Curtis D. Wilbur, General Mason M. Patrick, and Admiral Moffett, who were there to receive the committee's suggestions on a working policy for the government. Following this meeting, the group was received at the White House by President Coolidge, who discussed their plans at length. He told them that the actual need for planes was not nearly so great as the need for a sound industry which would be able to produce large quantities of planes in time of crisis.

In late February the special committee met in the office of the Assistant Secretary of War with Dwight Davis and General Patrick. Gaining the approval of the Army and the War Department of a policy suggested by a private industry and worked out carefully, with the interests of both involved, was a first-class accomplishment.

In July the Navy finally agreed to abandon trade practices objectionable to the industry. Specifically, they agreed with all the commitments made by the Army to respect the design-rights principle and to follow a more satisfactory and steady procurement plan. The Navy agreed to refrain from all aircraft construction and engineering experimentation.

The industry had set out to do two main jobs. It realized both of the objectives: The first was to formulate a working policy to rebuild the crumbling structure of the new aircraft industry and the second to gain government approval of certain principles which would guide both government and industry in their relations with each other.

In addition to laying a groundwork of harmony, the conferences early in 1925 directly resulted in the Morrow Commission of Inquiry in the latter half of that year. The Morrow Inquiry was made in keeping with the industry's purpose to ascertain how the aircraft might best serve the needs of the government. The Morrow Commission was largely motivated by the industry's interest in a government policy which would meet national needs without sacrificing industry's health and by the fact that the commission was essentially a public continuation of the private hearings held unofficially between the special committee and government administrators.

PUBLIC SERVICE: THE RIGHT MAN FOR THE RIGHT JOB

The drive to develop commercial aviation had many other ramifications, but certainly one of the most important was the appointment in September 1925 of the Morrow Commission of Inquiry. Morrow himself was an excellent choice for any type of public service. Through Colonel William Boyce Thompson, who had the greatest admiration for him, Dwight Morrow and I became close personal associates and very good friends when I was national chairman. I remember that he used to discuss his speeches with me. I still have the original manuscript of the speech he made in New Jersey when he came out for, the repeal of prohibition. It is one of those treasured mementos which I have always kept as a souvenir from an esteemed friend. Morrow's considerable public speaking was an indication that he had reached a time in his life when he was chiefly interested in rendering service.

He had turned down every offer of an administrative position under President Coolidge, his old Amherst College classmate, and his first opportunity to display his talents as a statesman did not come until he was later appointed Ambassador to Mexico. But he did tell Coolidge that he would do a "job" for him, and both President Coolidge and I were delighted that he was willing to head this commission on aeronautics. The commission had a clear purpose: to find the most satisfactory way for the aircraft industry to serve the government, in accordance with principles to which both had already agreed. It was encouraging to hear people like the Hon. Dwight F. Davis, Major General John L. Hines, Chief of Staff, United States Army; Brigadier General Hugh A. Drum, Major General Mason M. Patrick, the Hon. Curtis D. Wilbur, Secretary of Navy; Rear Admiral W. A. Moffett, Postmaster General New, Herbert Hoover, and others directly concerned with government interests in aviation take for granted that commercial aviation was here to stay and indicate in testimony their belief in its steady progress. By the time the inquiry was well under way, there were on record nineteen bids for air-mail-carrying contracts by commercial interests—another healthy indication of increasing assurance.

Differences of opinion over the wisdom of a united government air service were expressed, but the need and importance of a strong aviation industry were stressed again and again. Many suggestions already made by the special committee were reiterated with more optimism and assurance.

Another less direct outcome of bringing all the aviation interests together was the formal appointment in July 1925 of a public relations committee, established by the National Air Transport Corporation, itself an indirect outgrowth of the Saturday-afternoon conferences. This corporation was a commercial freight outfit rather than a manufacturing enterprise, but it included many directly concerned with aircraft manufacturing interests. Formed in Chicago with Howard E. Coffin as president, the corporation had as its purpose the expansion of commercial aviation on a scale hitherto unknown. It carried aircraft in interstate commerce, transported securities, freight, and merchandise of every description, contracted for air mail, bought, sold, and leased all types of aircraft engines and accessories. It was a real factor in the expansion.

The public relations committee had a single objective: to educate the public. It consisted of twenty-seven top newsmen. I was named chairman of the group, which functioned entirely without pay. We were actually no more than publicly designated apostles to preach man's conquest of the air and to help convert a terrestrially minded America to the commercial value of being able to have its head in the clouds, to mention nothing of the advantages of developing aviation as a measure of national defense.

Evidences that our promotion activities of 1925 had not been in vain came reassuringly on September 24, 1928, when the Aeronautical Chamber of Commerce was host at a dinner tendered to the motion picture industry. It was probably the first time in the history of the country that one industry had formally rendered such recognition to another. The dinner, given at the Waldorf, was in appreciation of the motion picture industry's contributions to the aircraft industry. Earl Rowland, winner of the Transcontinental Air Derby, Trubee Davison, Edward P. Warner, William P. MacCracken, Ray Hall, and Terry Ramsaye of Pathé; E. B. Patrick of International; Jack Darock, Michael Clofine, and Emanuel Cohen of Paramount; and Truman Talley of Fox were some of those represented in the group that evening. George Eastman, Judge William Young, John J. Pulleyn, Louis Wiley, Edward P. Grosvenor, T. G. Powell, W. J. Jackson, Adolph Zukor, William Fox, Nicholas Schenck, Albert and Harry Warner, Jesse Lasky, Carl Laemmle, Major Edward Bowes, and Sam Katz were others who attended.

After the dinner, a feature-length film of the air exploits of Colonel Lindbergh was shown for the first time. I later presented copies of the film to Major Gardner, representing the Aeronautical Chamber of Commerce, who in turn presented other copies to the kings of England and the Belgians, and to the President of France on a trip made to Europe the week following. I also presented a copy of the film to William R. Castle, Assistant Secretary of State. Similar copies were still later presented by Major Gardner to the heads of all the Central and South American countries which Lindbergh had visited on the trip sponsored by the Guggenheim Foundation. Millions of people had already seen newsreels of some of the Lindbergh flights, but many of the scenes presented that evening at the Waldorf had never been seen before. It was estimated that more than 477,000 feet of negative had been exposed in making the film.

It would be hard to overestimate the boost that American flying received in 1927 from the dramatic Paris flight of Colonel Lindbergh, and the transatlantic flights of Admiral Byrd and others that followed. They indicate how fast aviation was developing during that year. I shall want to tell a story about Lindbergh in connection with my motion picture experiences. He made a series of flights to seventy-five cities in this country and later the West Indies and many of the Central American countries. The trips were sponsored by the pioneer Daniel Guggenheim Foundation for the Promotion of Aeronautics, set up in 1926. Harry F. Guggenheim, president of the foundation from its inception in 1926 to its termination in 1930, was himself a member of the National Advisory Committee for Aeronautics from 1929 to 1938. So things worked together.

The film account of Lindbergh's exploits carried a greater meaning for me the night that it was presented at the dinner of the Aeronautical Chamber of Commerce to the MPPDA than anyone present suspected, I'm sure. There was not a single person there who knew the whole matter as completely as I knew it, and I am sure that nothing pleased Lindbergh more than Major Gardner's tribute to him, and the great compliment of having the longest documentary film, up to that time, in the archives of the State Department and in all the principal capitals of the world. The assembling of his experiences and the presentation of the films seemed to be the only fitting and dignified climax for one who had never lost his own sense of modesty and propriety in an atmosphere of great public acclaim.

Although I have never lost touch with many of those aviation people or lost interest in aeronautical development, that dinner and the circumstances surrounding it were the last formal connection I had with the aviation industry. Since 1928 I have eagerly watched a vast network of commercial airlines built up from coast to coast and from continent to continent. Shortly before the war, air-mail contracts were being let to commercial airlines employing a total of more than 15,000 people and flying at least 15,818,617,372 air-mail-pound miles annually. What a contrast with 1921, when less than 500 persons serviced and flew no more than 70 planes on coast-to-coast runs.

How far we have come from those days. I welcomed the final passage of the bill uniting the armed forces, "one great Department of National Defense under one head," a move which will probably prove a great boon to defense aviation, a common denominator of all branches.

Not long ago I took great pleasure in the long-overdue tribute accorded Major Gardner when he received the Daniel Guggenheim Medal for 1947, the highest aviation award, for "outstanding achievement in advancing aeronautics." And I look to the future with optimism, because we as a nation unquestionably realize the importance of aviation in national security and its contribution to peacetime commerce. If during those critical mid-twenties I had some small share in bringing the aviation industry closer together—and closer to the government—it was my good fortune. My long experience in politics and my experience in motion pictures, quite as individualistic and competitive and unpredictable a field as flying, had drilled into me some important lessons.

Just to recall those lessons will suggest their value to the men who were struggling with aviation in 1925. "Let's get together . . . Confidence and Co-operation . . . Seek Areas of Agreement, not of Discord . . . Advantages Are Mutual . . . The Public Can Be Trusted to Act if It Knows the Facts . . . Government and Industry Alike Are Forms of Public Service."

Because I believed these principles and had seen them work, I was able to help the men in aeronautics to apply them in their own marvelous field. Without a long schooling in patience and harmony, nothing that I could have said or done would have brought them closer to their goals of unity and strength. No suggestions I was able to make were based on technical knowledge, any more than they were in the film industry. It all boils down to what I believe is a rock-bottom principle of society: men must work together as harmoniously as possible if they are to achieve the greatest success in their endeavors.

In the dark months before the dawn of 1925, some of these troubled plane makers must have come close to saying to each other: "If we don't hang together, we'll hang separately." It was almost that bad.

PART FOUR...

...*Motion Pictures* 1922–1945

CHAPTER 25

The First Year in Hollywood, 1922–1923

H A D an Aladdin's genie appeared to me as I left New York on the fateful trip that was also to include a train accident, and had he told me that in a few days I would be offered the post of "czar" of the motion picture industry, I surely would have thought it a fairy tale. My astonishment was utter and complete when, on the eighth day of December, 1921, Saul Rogers and Lewis J. Selznick asked to see me in my suite at the Wardman Park Hotel.

I was still convalescing from injuries sustained in the train wreck, and I had never met either man before. My first impulse was to beg off the interview, which I thought vaguely must have to do with some motion picture problem of the Post Office Department. Surely this could wait. Yet, to be consistent with the "open door" policy I had already established, and since I did not think I was honestly too ill to receive visitors, I consented.

Mr. Rogers and Mr. Selznick came straight to the point. They handed me a round-robin letter signed by ten of the leading motion picture producers and by officers of two additional companies, asking me to become head of the Association they felt it urgently necessary to form. There had been a previous association under the presidency of the illustrious producer, William A. Brady, but this had become useless owing to lack of agreement among its members. In the face of pressing problems, a comprehensive and definite program was now being sought.

Beyond the fact that I had arranged for the newsreels to have proportionate coverage with the press during the campaign, I had never been identified with any phase of motion pictures. I was an Indiana lawyer who had become Republican national chairman, then Postmaster General. Just that. I was aware, of course, of a certain ferment going on in the industry and of increasing tension between the industry and some influential sections of the public. As happens in the history of every institution, human frailty had ushered in by degrees what appeared to many to be an era of scandal. This had even happened in our wholesome national game of baseball and had resulted in the selection of Judge Kenesaw M. Landis as an over-all commissioner, or "czar," as he was usually called. And recently in Hollywood there had occurred a series of unsavory incidents which had given the responsible-minded producers as much concern in their capacity as good citizens as in their professional status as picture-makers. I am sure these considerations influenced the producers and distributors in their decision to follow the lead of baseball.

The question still remained in my mind: why me?

Rogers and Selznick spoke sincerely and in a highly complimentary way, but I did not feel that their reasons for selecting me were justified. Since then I have read a number of rationalizations, in articles and books, setting forth what my qualifications might have been. These still strike me as more flattering than convincing. However, there it was. I promised to think it over during the Christmas holidays.

As it turned out, "thinking it over" proved to be a big job, at any rate subjectively. In this case I was not only trying to decide something but to weigh and analyze my own inner motive. I knew that if I accepted the offer I would be criticized for yielding to a mercenary object and renouncing, as it were, dignity for gain—as if being Postmaster General were something priestly, consecrated by vows which a man might not forsake with self-respect. I realized that such a view was simply dramatizing the matter; neither did it take into account my previously formed determination to return to private life as soon as I could, as I had told President Harding before his inauguration. It was understood that I would remain as Postmaster General only until the department was satisfactorily reorganized, and I felt that this had been accomplished.

I chuckle now at my fancy that the motion picture post would signify any kind of "private life."

There was another side to the problem I had to consider. I had been raised in a Christian home, and while I am not a reformer I hope that I have always been public-spirited. It required no great insight to see that the young movie giant might well grow up a Frankenstein. And precisely because I was not a reformer, I dreaded the blunders the reformers would make in dealing with this new and vital force. I was thinking of the parallel case of prohibition—which had by no means produced the era of national sobriety its proponents had contemplated.

For the moment I did not confide my problem to anyone. In a few days I would join my home folks in Sullivan. I had recovered sufficiently to attend to some routine matters preparatory to leaving when, to my dismay, the story of the offer broke in the press. Certainly I had given no indication of the business, even to intimate friends. I had wanted to think it out by myself. I knew, too, without having to be reassured, that neither Mr. Selznick, Mr. Rogers, nor any of their associates would wish to break the story prematurely. But it had leaked out, and it proved embarrassing. One newspaper went so far as to declare that I had flatly rejected the offer, which was news to me.

I was promptly beleaguered by callers and subjected to a barrage of messages from well-wishers, reporters, feature writers, and persons whom I had never met but who had free advice to give. There was also a lunatic fringe of those who wanted jobs in the movies, for themselves or for some talented brother-in-law, and who demanded that I use my mystic power to place them.

While I was still upset physically and mentally, Courtland Smith came to my rescue. He not only shielded me from the more importunate inquisitors but, perceiving that I was almost at the breaking point, forced me to take long walks with him through Rock Creek Park. It was December, and there was a wild and dismal beauty to many of its vistas which might have affected a more melancholy temperament adversely but which I found extremely relaxing. It seemed as if I were a million miles from the turmoil of telephone calls, questions, criticism, and flattery that the leak to the press had brought down about my ears.

Finally it was Courtland who decided I should get out of Washington earlier than planned and make what might be called, in a certain sense, a retreat. My hideaway for this purpose was the home of my great and good friend, Colonel William Boyce Thompson, at Yonkers, New York. I had sought his counsel on many previous occasions and valued it highly. This time he insisted that I take it easy, so literally that I spent the first few days in bed in a darkened room and was not even allowed to look at newspapers. I never knew a more kindly or solicitous host than Bill Thompson.

On Christmas Day in Sullivan I made up my mind. As I was sitting at breakfast, I overheard an argument in the next room. My boy Bill, who was six, and his two cousins, Charles and John, a little older and a little younger, were putting on the cowboy suits I had bought them.

"I want to be William S. Hart!" cried my boy.

"No, I'm going to be him!" contradicted one of my nephews.

"No, I am! You can be Doug, and Bill can be the bad guy," yelled the other.

The text from Scripture, "Out of the mouths of babes and sucklings Thou hast perfected praise" flashed through my mind. They wanted to be Bill Hart. Not Buffalo Bill. Not Daniel Boone. But William S. Hart! To these little boys and to thousands of others throughout our land, William S. Hart and Mary and Doug were real and important personages and, at least in their screen characters, models of character and behavior. And I may interject that if all of the pictures produced in Hollywood had been as wholesome as those in which Bill Hart, Mary Pickford, and Douglas Fairbanks appeared there would never have been such a storm of public protest as developed.

I realized on that Christmas morning that motion pictures had become as strong an influence on our children and on countless adults, too, as the daily press. The juvenile argument which I had overheard confirmed my feeling and my fears that the great motion picture industry might as easily become a corrupting as a beneficial influence on our future generations.

At any rate, this was the thing that crystallized my decision. And when some months later I related the incident to Bill Hart, he was deeply affected and the following Christmas sent my boy the bridle he had used in many pictures.

Now that I had made up my mind, it was up to me to think out my philosophy of the job I had been called upon to do. The Christmas respite came to an end all too quickly, and on January 2, 1922, I was in New York on my way back to Washington. Interviewed by the papers, I stated that I would meet the motion picture producers on January 14, which I subsequently did.

Meanwhile I had already become the target for the fusillade of criticism I had anticipated. My friend Senator Pat Harrison of Mississippi felt that a Cabinet officer had no business resigning his high office for an amusement-industry post. Henry Ford, who I am sure meant well, gave vent to his distress in his Dearborn *Independent*. Dr. Wilbur Crafts, an eminent divine, charged that I had been "bought."

The tenor of most of the criticism seemed to be that I was hiring myself out to the motion picture interests as a sort of "fixer," to shield them from public and possibly legislative wrath. This notion on the part of the champions of decency became especially articulate when they discovered that I was opposed, in principle, to censorship. That seemed to prove conclusively that my function would be that of a "mouthpiece" defending guilty clients.

For all I know, the idea of retaining a "mouthpiece," who would be something of a lobbyist, may have entered the minds of some of the motion picture men. They were sincere, but they were bewildered. Some producers genuinely desired to clean house but did not know how. Trade practices of the period were chaotic and savagely competitive. There were charges and countercharges of stealing and of cutthroat methods.

Ironically, many exhibitors also attacked me and the offer that the producers and distributors had made—on diametrically opposite grounds. In me they seemed to see a threat of blue-nosed regulation and political pressure.

Of course I had no intention of being a lobbyist, mouthpiece, or fixer. The cry of the children who idolized the movie stars was now the "Macedonian Call" as far as I was concerned, and I was not going to betray them by becoming a political front-runner for a contaminated product.

But I knew I was still opposed to censorship.

The processes of democracy are long and slow and often discouraging. But I have always believed that the principle of self-regulation, as contrasted with regulation from without, will take firm root if given a chance; that, if watered by patience and optimism (a patience that seems weakness to reformers, and an optimism beyond discernible reason), the principle will at length flourish and prove lasting. This is because *self-regulation educates and strengthens those who practice it.*

And I have always felt that in a democratic commonwealth each business, each industry, and each art has as much right to, and as much duty toward, self-regulation as has the general citizenry to self-government. This, I understand, was the fundamental idea behind the medieval trade guilds—the ancestors of our professional associations as well as of our labor unions.

Now the motion picture men had proposed an Association. That was their own idea, and they were kind enough to ask me to be the head of it. All these considerations made me determine that my office would not be a mere control tower, nor would I be a "czar," but that our Association would function *democratically.*

However, acting as missionary for the democratic concept of "home rule" and self-regulation was only half my job, as I envisioned it. The other half was to educate the movie-going public.

Right here someone is going to ask the question: "If the producers were not giving the public what it wanted, how could they stay in business?"

The answer to that is twofold: first, they were in some danger of not remaining in business, and not merely because of reform leagues and angry legislators. Gross receipts, so large during World War I and in the early post-war period, had begun to decline. At the time I became spokesman only one banker, Otto H. Kahn, would do business with the industry at all. This one exception may be explained by Mr. Kahn's well-known benevolence toward anything artistic or even potentially artistic. He had endowed the Metropolitan Opera Company of New York, had built the Century Theatre, and later, although not a Catholic, had become the philanthropic mainstay of the Catholic Writers' Guild.

The second part of the answer is that it cannot be moral or licit to supply an immoral or illicit demand. This is readily apparent in the case of the bootlegger, the smuggler, the narcotic peddler, and the pander. None of these things is legitimate. The motion picture industry was legitimate per se, and potentially a great force for good.

But self-regulation alone would not be enough. To make it worth while, *a demand had to be created for finer films.* There were co-operative services, too, which I felt the motion picture medium had an obligation to perform.

It was therefore my idea not only to try to compose the differences among the producing and distributing companies but also to urge the public, through women's clubs and various fine and influential groups, to encourage our growth—not with brickbats but with counsel and cooperation.

I knew it would not be easy, but I knew it could be done.

On January 14, 1922, I met with the producers in New York and gave them my answer.

In the days between my acceptance of the motion picture offer and the opening of the new office, it was interesting to watch the reactions—both in the press and in myself.

On the lighter side was a humorous cartoon of which the artist, Albert T. Reid, sent me an autographed print. It was titled "The Cynosure of Boyville." Two little urchins behind my back were discussing the reported salary when one broke in with, "Man! That ain't half of it. He gits to see all the movie shows for nothin'!" But in front of me, clasping my hand, another youngster is saying with a smile, "Gee, Mr. Hays—I congratulate you. I'd rather have your job than any job in the world."

That's about the way I felt myself.

Many people, however, either saw the industry as a frightful mess or thought I was going to march in like a dictator. But I remembered plenty of experiences in politics and in the Post Office Department which had proved that folks are willing and able to work together for a good end, if they can see it. I was sure that there were appeals in the movies capable of uniting industry and public in a joint program for better motion pictures.

That joint program was the keynote of my subsequent quarter century of effort. It never changed.

Of the industry leaders who were founding the Association, I said in my first press release of January 18, "I believe in the earnestness and integrity of their determination to carry out these purposes and am convinced of the possibilities of very large plans and successful consummation."

The statement of the founders' committee, professing similar faith in me, prophesied that the industry would move forward "to its predestined place of importance in the civilization of today and tomorrow." And I want to record, with gratitude and deep appreciation, that this "honeymoon" of January 1922 continued. As in all healthy human relations, there were often completely divergent points of view, once or twice so violently opposed that I broke the glass and cut my hand banging on the conference-table top. In so bitterly competitive an industry, it was often a struggle to find common ground, but in the end we usually got together and went ahead. Few men have been given a finer post-graduate course in the theory and practice of compromise, though I prefer to call it harmonization.

Sooner or later many appellations were bestowed on me. They included "Film-Master," "Movie-Man," "Landis of the Films," "Family Doctor of the Movies," "The Cat's Whiskers," "Film Co-ordinator," "Hoosier Crusader," "Doctor of Celluloid," "The Little White Father of the Cinema." In the years following, "Czar" was most often used. And that reminds me of Governor Milliken's observation that this common use may have been partly due to the fact that a single column of type has room for only four letters of the largest size used. If so, this was an unfortunate trick of fate, for if there was anything that I was *not*, as executive of the new and voluntary association, it was a "czar."

One reference to a trade-paper opinion may help to round out the picture. The *Exhibitors' Herald* of March 18 carried in its announcement the subtitle, "Former Cabinet Member Announces Purposes and Aims during First Day as President of New Producer-Distributor Alliance." The mere statement must have sounded a bit brash! They reported me correctly when they quoted: "I want to make it clear that I do not come into this industry to crusade or do any of the radical things that have been pointed out as part of my work. I realize that I am entering a gigantic field of which I know little. My sole work for some time will be to acquaint myself with affairs so that I can best aid the men with whom I am associated to do jointly those things they are mutually, but not competitively, interested in doing. It is a tremendous undertaking and I approach it with much concern, but with that confidence which springs from an earnest purpose, and with the conviction that we will have the generous help of everyone in accomplishing what must be recognized as an effort for the good of all."

When I said that "my sole work for some time" would be to acquaint myself with affairs, I hadn't met the affairs! When I did meet them they were not disposed to wait for me to conclude any deliberate, academic study. They were already lying there on my desk, marked "urgent." So, in the reverse slogan of one of our military services, it was a question of "learn while you earn."

Although I couldn't have known it when I entered the new office on Monday morning, March 6, 1922, there was what modern executives would call a "ten-point program" waiting for attention. Every item on the agenda had to be reached during the first year. At least the first five of them could be dignified by the now familiar term "emergency." They were:

> *Internal Disorders,* such as bad trade practices and scandals
> *Censorship* and other threatened restrictions
> *Mexican Diplomatic Crisis* over American films

Building a "more perfect *union*" in the industry, and one that would be
self-governing
  Improving the *Quality* of pictures quickly
  Improving the *Demand,* through organized public opinion
  Securing the *Practical Co-operation of Educators*
  Helping *Distributors* to overcome fraud and loss
  Helping *Exhibitors* adjust contract problems
  Improving the quality of *Advertising*

Although this listing of exactly ten major items is of course an oversimplification, it is close to the facts. From my brief summary of the ten
subjects hereafter, each can be seen to have been a project that couldn't
wait. And though most of the problems were continuous, the initial
approach to them was most important. In nearly every case circumstances forced me to take the bull by the horns and do something at
once. It was far better to attack than to defend.

From another viewpoint the analysis holds true that every one of the
ten projects was an attempt to carry out one or more of the Association's
basic objectives. I realized that there were so many active factors in the
industry that we had to take them all into account if we were to make
progress in solving the central problem, which was better pictures. And
in subdividing the work, we actually ended up with ten major departments.

INTERNAL DISORDERS

The industry had grown like a mushroom, more in scope and dollars
than in self-control. Tougher or more ruthless competition would have
been hard to find, or greater rewards for courage and resourcefulness. It
was that kind of business. And too often there was an apparent conflict
between making fine pictures and making more money.

The other side of it was that very few rules of the game—fair trade
practices—had yet been built up. Some that did exist were honored
more in the breach than in the observance. Our "industrial civilization"
was still in the future. In the early days jealousy and suspicion colored
the whole chaotic process of production, distribution, and exhibition.
Motion pictures were suffering from the rashness of youth and a bad
case of growing pains.

On the personal side, the industry was giving critics too many openings for attack. As Terry Ramsaye, the most thorough historian of the
art, wrote in his two-volume work, *A Million and One Nights:* "The
flow of scandals was telling at the box office. Censorship movements
were acquiring new strength. Professional enemies of the screen were
capitalizing opportunity." Plenty of people were only too willing to believe that stories like those of Fatty Arbuckle and Wally Reid were
typical. It seemed to make good copy for newspapers to connect all sorts

of irregularities in Los Angeles with the "screen" or "Hollywood." A veritable reader complex was built up—one that took us years to overcome.

As the success of a physician is often measured against the severity of the patient's sickness—and his friends' knowledge of it—so with the movies in 1922. The public pictured things as so dark that our organized attempts at improvement were heralded as "housecleaning," and I was hailed as "a prophet of peace and good will in the new moral order." People sensed that I was helping to crystallize an undercurrent of sound public opinion. Dr. George Chalmers Richmond, former rector of Old St. John's Episcopal Church, Philadelphia, said of me at the time, "He is a moral engineer." And Dr. Richmond was emphatically right when he added, "He will, of course, meet with stubborn opposition." Moral, social, and artistic implications were clear.

CENSORSHIP

As I went about the country talking with editors and others who knew what was going on, it was evident that the motion picture situation was bad. It was more than a question of mild censorship. *It was a case of self-regulation or prohibition.* Political censorship was again baring its teeth. Illogical and destructive as it has always proved to be, it stemmed from perfectly natural public resentment and distrust, which we had to recognize. Though it was the wrong cure, it looked attractive to reformers and bureaucrats who had little understanding of motion picture problems.

Before I had time to do more than get my bearings, I learned that a referendum on censorship was to confront the voters of Massachusetts in the fall election. A state-wide committee to remove the current law was already at work. Realizing the strategic value of defeating censorship legislation before it spread any farther, we decided to throw MPPDA's full weight into the fight. We never made a wiser decision nor won a more important test. Best of all, it was a victory for enlightened public opinion, which the press gave us tremendous help in informing. Every effort had to be made to present the case clearly. We had reason to believe that the Massachusetts citizens were not too happy about the law that had been enacted; an earlier statute had been vetoed by Calvin Coolidge when governor, and the legislature that passed the current statute seemed to have acted more from pressure than conviction.

Events in other quarters, however, indicated that censorship still had its supporters. In June of 1922 the Ohio Federation of Churches adopted a resolution declaring for state censorship. In July the Supreme Court of New York decided that newsreels were not exempt from supervision by the state's censorship board. Some form of censorship statute was in force in seven states—Ohio, New York, Pennsylvania, Maryland, Virginia, Kansas, and Florida. And the many specific protests reaching us, such as that ministers are "not foolish nor futile" as motion pictures too often portrayed them, showed clearly enough that people were demanding some kind of supervision.

In working with the Committee of Massachusetts Citizens against Censorship I again used the methods of practical politics: thorough publicity and personal organization. With our co-operation the Massachusetts committee issued a special edition of a report by Dean Charles N. Lathrop, executive secretary of the Department of Christian Social Service of the Protestant Episcopal Church, on "The Motion Picture Problem." The report called for some form of control which would place the responsibility "squarely on those who produce the pictures." This leaflet showed clearly how "the principles upon which the Better Movie Movement is based are self-determination and co-operation. Other movements have failed and all censorship plans have been ineffective and resented."

The whole case was put into the hands of the newspapers. Courtland Smith, a top newspaperman himself, president of the American Press Association from 1908 to 1921, and first secretary of MPPDA, talked to three hundred editors in every city and town of consequence in Massachusetts. The resulting attitude of the papers was a big factor in opening the eyes of the people.

Colonel Charles H. Cole, chairman of the Massachusetts committee, and I worked together closely in the matter of organization. I remember that in our first conference at the old Union League Club in New York, at that time still on Fifth Avenue, we worked out our general plan of campaign.

Knowing the chance we were taking in putting the good faith of the industry to the crucial test of a referendum in this first year, I asked two of the best men I knew to help organize the state-wide campaign. Harry Hogan, who earlier had successfully organized Wisconsin for Senator Lenroot's election when I was Republican national chairman, again turned in a grand job. Cal O'Laughlin also helped out in the final six weeks' effort.

When the vote was counted, the result created a sensation. It stood: No—553,173; Yes—208,252. Censorship had been thrown out by a majority of 344,921, defeated almost 3 to 1! The result gave us tremendous encouragement. It was just what the industry needed at that moment.

Certainly one interpretation of the vote was that it registered strong resentment against too much "thou shalt not." I came back from that experience surer than ever that the average American wants to run his own business—and thinks motion pictures are his business. The unpopular prohibition amendment had been in force less than three years. Various war-imposed restrictions were still fresh in people's minds. The slogan "Have you had enough?" brought a rousing Yes.

Never has the Association received a more gratifying vote of confidence. It had been in existence only from March of that year, and the only assurance Massachusetts citizens had of the industry's determination to clean itself up was my word. Willing to put the industry on its honor, they gave producers time to prove their good intentions. The result proved that Massachusetts shared our conviction that the people themselves should be the censors rather than some autocratic political commission.

Most important of all, the people's victory in Massachusetts turned the national tide—for all time, let us hope. Since March 1922, no state has passed a censorship law, though many have tried. In my opinion this is because the industry, whenever confronted with the censorship threat in any of the states, has been able to present convincing arguments against it. Bills were rejected in three states during 1922, and all bills introduced during the following three years were rejected: eighteen in 1923, two in 1924, and fourteen in 1925. Belief in censorship has been on a steady decline ever since. Backed up by the opinion of civic-minded groups, the industry has been able to maintain the position that censorship is unfair, unreasonable, and impossible of operation.

MEXICO AND THE FOREIGN PROBLEM

Another major question that struck us unexpectedly was the danger in offending the sensibilities of other nationals. The Mexican affair was on the agenda of the very first regular business meeting of our Board, April 13, 1922.

It came in the form of a bitter protest from the Mexican Government that American films were exploiting Mexicans as "bad men." At the time, our government had not even recognized the government of Mexico. Here was a diplomatic emergency to be met at once. Our directors saw it as I did. They instantly passed a resolution prohibiting the production of any picture derogatory to Mexico. By this formal statement producers pledged themselves to deal fairly with our neighbor and sought to overcome the unfortunate impression that had been created by some earlier films.

But this was not enough, and we knew it. Wounded national feelings need something more human than an official resolution. So that same day the Board authorized the sending of a personal representative to negotiate an understanding. By that decision the organized industry plunged into the sphere of foreign relations. Taking the initiative in this first instance, it assumed responsibilities that have made it almost an adjunct of our State Department.

This first mission was entrusted to Bernon T. Woodle, a capable and personable man. Those who have had experience in international dealings will not be surprised to learn that the negotiations consumed months. They were kept on the level of a diplomatic affair between equals, Mr. Woodle maintaining the attitude of an ambassador negotiating a bi-lateral "treaty" to preserve the honor and interests of both sides. It was neither an easy nor a simple task.

Meanwhile there were other indications that the question of national sensibilities was with us to stay. World War I had intensified national feeling everywhere. In May of 1922 we were informed that Honduras had established censorship regulations like those already in force in Costa Rica. In June, news columns carried a story headed "Spanish Make Protest." In November a letter came from a commercial attaché on German-American picture problems.

But a week before Christmas, while I was in California on my second trip, back came Bernon Woodle carrying a most imposing document. He had been in Mexico since September 28 and had succeeded in having their film ban lifted. He had negotiated a bona fide treaty between the government of Mexico and the Motion Picture Producers and Distributors of America, Inc.; on their side, entrance for American pictures was provided; on ours, promise was given to avoid putting Mexicans in an unfavorable light in any films produced by our members. Striking proof of the success of the understanding appeared in the announcement early in 1926, "Motion Pictures Gain Favor over Mexican Bullfighting."

This early success gave the industry added confidence in its new Association. To the public, it was fresh proof that films were something to be reckoned with. American motion pictures were in international business for good, although no one could have foreseen how deeply.

Nor could most people then see the full significance of something that had happened just the year before. Douglas Fairbanks and Mary Pickford, who had been married in 1920, toured Europe and Africa on the forerunner of all good-will tours by American film celebrities. They were acclaimed, literally, by millions of fans and intensified foreign demand for American films.

Thus the demand had been created; it was our responsibility to guard the quality of the supply. It was experiences like this first one with Mexico which later led to the inclusion in the Production Code of the provision that "the history, institutions, prominent people, and citizenry of all nations shall be presented fairly." Do what we could, however, national feelings continued to disturb the foreign market.

CREATING A SELF-GOVERNING ORGANIZATION

I believe that the new Association's members realized as well as I did that its success would depend on our concentrating at once on matters of agreement, not of disagreement. If we began by talking of competitive problems, trying to iron them out first, we might go on the rocks before we ever got out to sea. It was not easy to forget that an earlier attempt of the industry had dissolved for just this reason. In commenting on the Association's special character, Dr. Raymond Moley, in his book, *The Hays Office*, wrote: "The MPPDA turned out to be an association quite unlike any of the others, in fact an organization unique in American industrial life. . . . It was to be the expression and fulfillment of their co-operative impulses. It was to be the industry governing itself— in its own and in the public interest."

The next step was to draw up bylaws. Though allowing for latitude of action, they made responsibility for such action very definite. Stability was guarded by allowing a producer or distributor member to withdraw only upon written notice of his intention, given six months in advance. Wide industry representation in the Association was encouraged by providing unlimited membership in five classes.

Class A: Producers of motion pictures
Class B: Distributors of motion pictures
Class C: Individuals appointed by members of Class A
Class D: Individuals appointed by members of Class B
Class E: Other individuals

Place was even made through "Certificate of Affiliation" for participation by other groups, like chambers of commerce, directly interested in any branch of the motion picture industry.

From the beginning, most of the big companies were members, so that the Association comprised a large percentage of the industry. So far as general matters like censorship were concerned, the MPPDA was recognized as speaking for the whole industry, and we made it clear that all services of the Association were at the disposal of all motion picture companies, members and non-members alike. Thus, when the Association's Production Code seal later came to be the hallmark of an approved picture, all companies had exactly the same privileges in connection with securing and displaying it.

A beginning on trade practices was made in the bylaws. The Board of Directors was empowered to make provisions for the observation of "accepted standards of morality and good taste in the content of motion pictures," to register titles in order to avoid conflicting use by different producers, and to employ arbitration in cases of dispute.

Article IX of the bylaws concerned me most directly because it defined the "powers and duties of officers," including the president. The leaders of the industry gave me powers difficult for them to override. These men were shrewd enough to see that they needed an outsider, an "impartial chairman," to bind them into an effective group and to mediate between them and the public.

Since the provisions of this article are the actual charter under which I worked from 1922 to 1945, they are in a real sense autobiographical. Because of its importance to the understanding of an involved story, I beg the reader's indulgence to quote this section in full.

ARTICLE IX

Powers and Duties of Officers

Section 1. The President shall be the executive head of the Association and shall have general charge of its business and affairs. He shall be the Chairman of the Board of Directors and the Executive Committee, and shall preside at all meetings of the Association, the Board of Directors and the Executive Committee. He shall be the spokesman for the Association in all communications to the public.

The President shall have power to veto any action of the Board of Directors, the Executive Committee or the members. No action of the Board of Directors shall be valid or binding upon the Association over the veto of the President, unless and until such veto shall be overruled by the vote of two-thirds of all the directors; no action of the Executive Committee shall be valid or binding upon the Association over the veto of the President unless and until such veto shall be overruled by the vote of two-thirds of the members of the Executive Committee, and no action of the members shall be valid or binding upon the Association over the veto of the President unless and until such veto shall be overruled by the vote of two-thirds of the members of Class C and two-thirds of the members of Class D.

The President shall have the right and power to select and employ all executive officers, agents, and employees of the Association by whatsoever name or title denominated, and to enter into appropriate contracts of employment with them, except as otherwise provided by law, and he shall have the right and power to determine the kind and character of the work or service to be performed by them and the number to be employed, provided, however, that the President shall have no right or power to make contracts of employment for a term longer than one year and that the total compensation of all officers, agents and employees payable during any one month shall not exceed the amount of the membership dues payable during such month. The President shall have the right and power to control and direct the disbursement of all funds appropriated by the Board of Directors for carrying out the purposes of the Association.

It shall be the duty of the President to make an annual report showing the condition of the affairs of the Association and containing such recommendations as he thinks proper and submit the same to the Board of Directors at the meeting next preceding the annual meeting of the Association, and to bring before the Board or the Executive Committee from time to time such information as may be required touching the affairs and property of the Association. The President shall not, during his term of office, engage directly or indirectly in the motion picture business, nor in any branch or part thereof.

My first contract with the Association, dated April 15, 1922, was for three years. It was supplemented by a network of contracts by which the member companies bound themselves jointly and severally to guarantee the performance of the agreement. Even though there were times during that first year when some directors' meetings might have sounded through the keyhole like a street fight, we knew we were in this thing together, and we were going to see it through. In more than a quarter of a century I was never without a binding contract. And I never lost my belief that both the industry and the public would find, in better pictures, their common advantage.

The factors involved in the MPPDA relationships were carefully examined by Dr. Moley in preparation for his book, *The Hays Office*, the most thorough objective analysis yet made. At one point he says:

Hays was not being chosen as "Czar" of the Industry. But neither was he being employed merely to ward off the impending danger of Federal and State censorship legislation. There was an abundance of problems which the perturbed film men were finally willing to recognize as common—the protection of the interest of producers and distributors in foreign countries; the theft and piracy of films; the revenue, copyright and tariff laws affecting the Industry.

One very human aspect of the situation he puts thus:

Another feature of those preliminary discussions was the distrust some of the movie men felt for one another. . . . Each individual would have hotly denied that the thought of pulling out of this ambitious venture could ever cross his own mind. But each was reasonably certain that others in the group were quite capable of such conduct. The multiplication of contracts was the measure of this mutual distrust as much as it was the measure of the individual enthusiasm with which these men regarded Hays. Each had become genuinely convinced, for the moment at any rate, that Hays must be the captain of his own fate and master of his own soul in the three years that lay ahead.

My welcome into the great motion picture family came on March 16, only ten days after opening the office. In a life full of official dinners, I have rarely experienced such an occasion. The excitement was like that at the opening of a Rose Bowl game. A new team had been organized, a new coach engaged, and both team and fans were evidently hoping for victory.

The dinner, held at the Hotel Astor in New York under the auspices of the Motion Picture Directors Association, was attended by eleven hundred men and women, with every branch of the industry represented, as well as federal and city governments, finance, commerce, publishers, the stage, authors, and many other professions. It was an all-star cast!

At the guest table, in addition to motion picture executives, were such well-known persons as Arthur Brisbane, Paul Block, Anita Loos, Channing Pollock, Seward Prosser, Mae Murray, John Emerson, James J. Davis, then Secretary of Labor, John F. Hylan, mayor of New York, Constance Talmadge, Albert D. Lasker, William Randolph Hearst, Corinne Griffith, and Betty Blythe. Here and there at the tables were figures like Joseph Urban, Pedro de Cordoba, Nora Bayes, Conway Tearle, Elaine Hammerstein, Buster Collier, Henry King, and Dick Barthelmess sitting together, Edward Small, Otto Harbach, Nathan Burkan, Louella Parsons, Frank Gilmore, Matthew Woll, William Farnum, George Beban, Martin Quigley, Prince and Princess Rospigliosi, Mr. and Mrs. George J. Gould, Jr., J. W. Alicoate, and—what pleased me very much—three tables of "guests from the Post Office Department."

In the language of Indiana politics, this dinner was an old-fashioned "love feast." It was a tremendous boost in getting off to a good start. In more modern parlance, it was the jet propulsion that took us off the ground in a short run and helped us get altitude at once.

I tried in my speech to emphasize two things: first, that the new Association was created "to foster the common interests of all those engaged in the motion picture industry"; and second, that the "object" was not merely a pious wish nor a "vague gentlemen's agreement," but "the legal statement of a legal purpose by a legally organized body." We were committed to it completely! As to guarantees for the solution of our problem, I found them in two words: *confidence* and *co-operation*.

Back in the office after this rousing pledge of support, we set about organizing our tasks under various departments, of which there were eventually ten. With slight changes of name or function, these working divisions have continued through the years. I'll mention them briefly here:

Public Relations, after 1933 called Community Service Department. Its purpose was to stimulate co-operation with civic, welfare, and educational agencies, and to develop such demand for better pictures as would encourage producers to make them.

Public Information.

International Department, first called Foreign Relations. Its chief purpose was to keep foreign trade channels open. I shall later devote a chapter to this problem.

Legal Department. The detailed negotiations between exhibitors, distributors, and government, and other general matters were followed, but not directed, by this department.

Theatre Service lent its good offices to exhibitors in intra-industry relations.

Conservation—especially concerned with fire protection.

Title Registration, established in 1925.

Advertising Code Administration, fully developed after 1930.

Production Code Administration, an evolutionary process chiefly operating in Hollywood and reaching its final form in 1934.

Protective Department, which aimed to carry out the purpose of securing "freedom from unjust or unlawful exactions." Its general purpose was to keep informed about all proposals and acts of a legislative nature in cities, states, and in Washington, particularly those providing for political censorship or supervision.

Other related activities which were soon stimulated by the Association, though operating in Hollywood and not directly connected with the Hays Office, included the West Coast Association, the Central Casting Bureau and the Call Bureau, and the Labor Committee.

This gave us a well-rounded organization able to give attention to any problems that would normally come to us. From time to time temporary committees were formed for the technical working out of some specific problem like that of classroom films.

One peculiar feature of our setup was its "bi-location." Although the very term "movie" conjures up a picture of Hollywood, the home office of MPPDA has always been in New York City, where the major companies have their executive offices and their selling and distributing departments.

Production, on the other hand, had found its center of gravity in California years before our Association was founded. Our activities connected with the process of production and with the thousands of individual producers, directors, actors, extras, and technicians took place there.

IMPROVING THE SUPPLY

To make solid progress toward our primary goal of higher standards, I soon realized that two concurrent efforts were needed, one at the studios; the other with the public. These we called "improving the quality of the supply," and "improving the quality of the demand." This dual goal never changed.

I did my best to persuade the production heads that the improved supply should come first. As I kept pointing out, nothing educates public taste so well as watching motion pictures which are a little better in every way than the public expects. So the initial plea for better pictures was addressed to Hollywood, to which I journeyed in July of 1922.

I had been president of MPPDA for four months. It was a satisfaction to me that besides laying the foundation of what someone at the time called the "Pax Cinemana," bringing peace to the warring clans and the work of our preliminary meetings, we had also enlisted the sympathy of several fine civic and religious groups.

But now, with headquarters firmly established, plans mapped, and allies gained, I wanted to meet our front-line soldiers—the writers, directors, cameramen, actors, and actresses—who really made the pictures. These folks were the backbone of the industry, and without their understanding and support I knew that all of our fine resolutions "to achieve and maintain the highest possible moral and artistic standards" would be as sounding brass and tinkling cymbals.

I realized that there was only one place where any evil in motion picture production might be eliminated and its great and good advantages retained, and that was on the set, at the time and place the pictures were actually shot.

Finally, I was naturally curious. I trust I was never too much impressed by glamour. Had I been so, I would have been far too naïve to have been of any use. Nevertheless, I had a human hankering to see at first hand the remarkable Land of Make-Believe of which I had, four months previously, been elected Wizard.

Before I left New York, confidential friends who had recently returned from the West Coast told me that studio sentiment, like all Gaul, was divided into three parts: those who were enthusiastic, those willing to withhold judgment, and those who regarded the whole idea of hiring me, or anyone like me, as a tom-fool scheme born in the brains of their panic-stricken employers. It must be remembered that our organization was a producers' association, not an employees' guild. The distasteful appellation of "czar" had given some of the folks out there the notion that I was going to poke about the sets like a room inspector in a military school. By far the majority of actors and actresses were fine people whose lives, both private and professional, were above reproach. They were quite properly wondering whether to regard my advent as an expression of cordiality—which it was—or as an indignity.

Arriving on the California Limited late on Sunday afternoon, July 23, our party left the train at Pasadena, to be greeted by Jesse L. Lasky, Joseph M. Schenck, and Abraham Lehr, and taken to Mr. Lasky's home at Hillside and LaBrea Avenue for tea. Afterward I was asked by an interviewer if I felt nervous as I alighted from the train to begin this new adventure. I replied that our party included my boyhood chum Max Puett, Jim Connery, Maurice McKenzie, Fred Beetson, and Joe O'Neill. I am sure that had I gotten stage fright these good friends would have seen me through. As it happened, however, I was far too engrossed in our problems and in the work that lay ahead of us. It may be that

Hoosiers do not faze easily, or perhaps I felt a sort of pre-kickoff elation.

In 1922, Hollywood proper was chiefly a residential district with spacious grounds and gracious homes, and I am sure that if some of the earlier inhabitants who have passed on or moved elsewhere were to return to Hollywood Boulevard and Vine Street today they would feel like Rip Van Winkle coming back to Times Square. And most of the studios were still centered there. Jesse Lasky's "lot" was a block south of the now famous Hollywood and Vine corner, standing on a site that had been an orange grove not many years before. The term "Hollywood" has gradually become a geographical misnomer, so far as the location of the motion picture industry is concerned. It is, of course, a section of Los Angeles, as Harlem or Greenwich Village is a section of New York. But of the major studios today, only Paramount, RKO, and Columbia are situated in Hollywood, while Twentieth Century-Fox maintains the old "Fox lot" at Western Avenue and Sunset Boulevard, as an annex to its main location in Beverly Hills, and some independent studios remain in the Hollywood area. The other major production centers are now in San Fernando Valley, north of the city, or in Culver City to the southwest.

This situation has given rise to the witticism that Hollywood, like Boston, is not so much a place as a state of mind. I have often thought of it as a great university. And no animosity has ever existed between "town and gown," between the home folk of Hollywood and the motion picture industry. It has always seemed to me significant that the prestige of the industry and of its people increases, rather than decreases, the nearer one gets to the city where pictures are made; in that city, most familiar with picture personalities and production, there is less resentment and criticism than anywhere else. This struck me forcibly on my first visit. That evening, as we walked about the grounds of my friend Max Puett's home, bareheaded and in shirt sleeves, Hollywood seemed for all the world like any normal American community on any summer Sunday night.

Not that I was deceived by superficial appearances. I realized our "university" would need a lot of cleaning up if its almost terrifying influence was to be beneficial and not baneful. But I was going to disappoint those who expected me to behave like a house detective. At my first press conference that evening I declared that threats of censorship would be removed only when its causes were removed, and that removing those causes was part of my job.

In the next five days I was to meet so many people and to see so many new faces that my memories of the tour are somewhat kaleidoscopic. The two chief impressions I formed were of the vastness of the enterprise and the earnestness of all those participating in it. On my trip to Hollywood during World War I in behalf of the 1918 Liberty Loan drive, I had addressed open-air lunch-hour groups at several studios. But

I had not particularly noticed the mammoth scale of production, which had grown by leaps and bounds in the intervening years. As to the earnestness of the stars, production heads, and employees, I felt sure that if all the stories of Hollywood debauchery had been true there would have been no time to make motion pictures. I found "motion pictures" to be almost a monomania with motion picture folk, almost to the exclusion of other interests. I had been warned in advance that directors and actors especially were given to "talking shop." This was all right with me; I had not come to Hollywood to talk about the price of eggs. But I quickly realized that few people in our country were as diligent or as interested in their profession as the film folk.

Every day of the week was crowded, the ride on the whirligig beginning Monday morning. We left Max's home shortly after eight o'clock, traveling downtown in a motorcade of a dozen automobiles preceded by motorcycles with their sirens screaming. The streets were decorated with bunting and flags and big signs reading WELCOME WILL HAYS! In the caravan were Jesse Lasky, Abraham Lehr, Irving Thalberg, Hal Roach, Thomas H. Ince, Charles Christie, Joseph Schenck, and others. Although the day was hot, Mayor George E. Cryer and a number of city officials were standing in the sun outside the Chamber of Commerce Building (the old location at Second Street and Broadway) and extended to me a welcome which, although it lasted only a few minutes, was so genuine and sincere that for once I was at a loss for words. Then we began our flying visits to a number of studios, starting with Fox, whose great lot now situated between Beverly Hills and Westwood had not yet been built. Mr. Fox and his able lieutenant, Sol Wurtzel, were presiding over the studio now used as an annex. Not for a moment did I forget that I had come to Hollywood to learn. And I had quite a faculty of tutors; somebody humorously estimated that it consisted of twelve general managers, thirteen attorneys, twenty-six director generals, and the Los Angeles Chamber of Commerce!

At the Fox lot I was genuinely affected by the warmth of the greeting accorded me, which I took as homage to the Association. Flattery is a heady wine, easy to dispense but difficult to withstand. I knew that my reception here as at the other studios was sincere—the closing down of the sets, celebrities and assistants swarming out to the specially rigged platform in the sunshine, smiling as warmly as the sun itself—but to have taken it as a tribute to my own ego would have been wholly misleading. Show folk are proverbially hospitable, but I reminded myself that I was here to do a job and to try to "sell" something. The fact that the folks were smiling was no surety that they were prepared to buy my brand of goods, still less that they had already bought it.

I was in a curious position. Opposed though I was to censorship, my name in Hollywood had nevertheless become a symbol of censorship.

The very thing I was endeavoring to fight seemed, to many, the issue that I stood for. It was a strange anomaly, reminiscent of the fable of the frogs. To save themselves from powerful enemies, they elected a frog-eating stork to be their king. To quite a lot of folks, I was not only a "czar" but a stork in a fable.

Others on the Coast were more understanding. Milton Sills and Conrad Nagel, both stars, and Fred Niblo, the director, were among those who supported me from the first; but I will not deny that there was much initial hostility and even more misunderstanding.

I addressed a group at all the studios that day and the next. Despite the skepticism of some, it was a day of making new friends. At the Ince Studio I met Rupert Hughes for the first time. He jumped on the running board of my automobile and introduced himself just as we were swinging into the circular driveway in front of the colonial mansion that was the main building of the lot. I told him that we had a mutual friend, Ralph Hayes, in Washington, who had asked me to say hello for him. Then Rupert bent over and whispered in my ear:

"I'm supposed to deliver a eulogy about you. What do you know that's any good about yourself?"

"Not a thing!" I replied.

That was the beginning of a continuing and very warm friendship. I recall how Rupert broke down the barriers of constraint when introducing me to the crowd by pointing to me, speaking as if none of them had ever heard of me until this moment, and telling them who I was and what I hoped to do. This started everyone laughing and got the group in a receptive mood.

Another friend I made that day is Cecil B. De Mille. It was he who introduced me at the Lasky lot. In all, I made five speeches that morning to the personnel of as many studios. I remember that at Lasky's, ancestor of the present Paramount Studios, there was a small boy—not a child actor but a "water boy." In those days a few such youngsters were lucky enough to get jobs during their school vacations as errand boys for the stars and the director on the set, and one of their duties was to fetch water. I was warming up to my subject, telling the folks that I was not a dictator with a new broom but that we were all partners with similar responsibilities, all for one and one for all, share and share alike. At this point the small boy, who was in the front row looking up at me, sang out:

"Does that mean you and me split salaries?"

I believe I was the first to guffaw, and there was a tremendous roar of laughter. The interruption did my cause more good than harm, I think, and I feel this was largely due to the witty way in which De Mille handled the situation.

Following my address at Lasky's, I was whisked to Universal City, and before being introduced I was taken on a set. The picture had just started that morning. I met the cast, including Mary Philbin, the ingenue star and an extremely lovely girl, George Hackathorne, Norman Kerry, and George Seigmann, the big menacing villain who was anything but that off the screen. He was a veteran of stage, screen, and the Army; he had played Silas Lynch, the scoundrelly carpetbagger in *The Birth of a Nation* and had served as an officer in World War I. Another memory of the war came back to me in meeting the director of *Merry-Go-Round*, Erich von Stroheim, for he told me that in 1918 when I had addressed the Universal employees in behalf of the Liberty Loan drive he had stood in the crowd as an "extra." Now, four years later, on the same lot, he was one of the most important directors. I have always been fond of Von Stroheim, who is a great artist, not without a strain of Rabelais. And in spite of his horrifying "Prussian-officer" appearance when he himself was acting on the screen, he is one of Hollywood's most genial souls.

I was guest of honor that day at a luncheon given by the Chamber of Commerce at the Hotel Alexandria in downtown Los Angeles. On the way I was greeted by the band of Branch No. 24 of the National Association of Letter Carriers, an organization of which I am a proud life member. In my speech there I told them quite sincerely that I was approaching motion pictures not merely with the viewpoint of the men who had millions of dollars invested in the business, but with that of the parents who had millions of children interested in it. Nobody applauded that statement more heartily, or shook my hand more cordially when I had finished, than the motion picture executives at the table with me.

It had been a strenuous morning and I had been promised a quiet afternoon. I wonder now if that, too, was a prank, for the afternoon was devoted exclusively to a visit to the Douglas Fairbanks studio. I would hardly call an afternoon with that dynamic popular favorite, as he was in his heyday, quiet or restful. He was shooting *Robin Hood,* with Allan Dwan directing and Enid Bennett playing opposite him as Maid Marian. I climbed about the sets and saw everything. Although he was not to make *The Thief of Bagdad* for a year, he spoke to me earnestly of the project, of which he was already dreaming. I found Doug and Mary an extremely gracious host and hostess.

There was one experience on the Fairbanks lot I was fortunate enough to escape. Doug, a great practical joker, had an "electric chair" rigged up in the parlor of his bungalow on the lot. Visitors were always urged to sit in the chair, which appeared the most comfortable in the room, whereupon Doug would push a button and the visitor would get a shock. Since I had heard something about it, I managed to side-step the chair, despite Doug's earnest entreaties, and we had a good laugh when I finally admitted that I knew all about it.

That night it was my turn to see Doug get a bit of hazing, for he was one of a hundred candidates initiated into the Loyal Order of Moose. As a member of the Indianapolis lodge, I was invited to attend. Sidney Chaplin and his famous brother Charlie "went through" that night. The Moose is an order of loyal American principles. I do not know whether Charlie still belongs.

On the following day I visited Warner Brothers Studios at its old Hollywood location, the Christie Studios, and Metro. The last-named was not yet Metro-Goldwyn-Mayer, and the lot was situated on Santa Monica Boulevard, near Cahuenga.

At United Studios I was the guest of Joe Schenck and his wife, Norma Talmadge. Endeavoring, as one must occasionally in setting down memoirs, to pin-point exactly what happened on that particular day, I have had recourse to the back numbers of two newspapers. One states I had lunch with Mr. Schenck and Miss Talmadge in their private bungalow, the other that I had lunch with a thousand people! Maybe I just thought I was lunching with a thousand people; they were an exciting couple.

At any rate, Miss Talmadge was making a picture called *A Voice from the Minaret*, of which Mr. Schenck was the producer and Frank Lloyd the director. On the set, I found the actual operations of picture-making to be fascinating. This was my second day and I was beginning to feel like an old-timer. But a couple of days later I got my come-uppance at Metro, when I walked onto a set that was supposed to be the office of a rural justice of the peace. I was greatly impressed by its realism; it looked for all the world like a hundred such offices I had seen back home. I remembered having a telephone call to make, and I walked over to the wall and picked up the receiver while the folks on the set watched me, suppressing their smiles. The telephone, of course, was a "prop" and, after clicking the receiver several times and getting no response, I turned around and everybody burst out laughing.

At least I had not been sent, as many newcomers were, for the "key to the camera" or a "box of smiles."

Another incident proved to me that I was still a tenderfoot, although I hope that when it comes to a matter of sentiment I shall always remain one. Little Jackie Coogan, who was to become a husky Air Force pilot and who will probably not relish the appellation, was making one of his appealing "kid" pictures on the set next to Miss Talmadge. I believe the name of the picture was *Fiddle and I*, although the title may subsequently have been changed. E. Mason Hopper was directing, and producer Sol Lesser was present with Jack Coogan, Sr. As we entered the set the forlorn little figure of Jackie, with his wistful face and ragged clothes, was stealing from what was supposed to be his home and bidding a silent good-by to his sleeping grandparents because he realized that they were so poor that they could no longer support him. "The

Kid" was a masterly little actor and he was putting his whole heart and soul into the touching farewell scene, blinking at the sleeping old couple and brushing away the tears with his ragged little sleeve.

I broke down and started to cry myself. Then I remembered where I was and turned to hurry off the set. Joe Schenck grinned and called out, "Will! You forgot your hat!"

But I was not thinking about my hat. What the world needed—and I believe I said so at the time—was more human and heart-warming pictures like that. And if we got them, the agitation for censorship would become an unnecessary impertinence.

On that day I also visited Robertson-Cole Studios, where RKO now stands, and there met Jane Novak, Carter DeHaven, and Ethel Clayton. Later I was introduced to Buster Keaton, Conway Tearle, Baby Peggy, Ruth Roland, Tom Mix (another of my son's boyhood heroes), Clyde Cook, and Marie Prevost. The same day, at Metro, I met Lon Chaney for the first time. He was something of a predecessor of Boris Karloff as the man with a thousand horrific faces, and his appearances were always masterpieces of his own and the make-up artist's skill. I asked him humorously which face he was wearing that afternoon.

"Just my everyday one, Mr. Hays," he grinned.

The next evening I was happy to see Jackie Coogan, no longer wistful or in tatters, at the banquet which the studios gave at the Hotel Ambassador in my honor or, as I prefer to think, in honor of the Association.

I have attended many testimonial dinners, and a few of them, if I may brag a little, were tendered to me. But I think there were never so many celebrities gathered in one dining room as on this brilliant occasion. I remember that crowds of curiosity seekers and fans gathered, hours ahead of time, on Wilshire Boulevard in front of the Ambassador and pressed up to the very doors, so that it was with difficulty that the traffic policemen were able to keep the approach to the hotel open.

These fans had not gathered to get a peek at me. There were in all some fifteen hundred people in the banquet room—this was a year before the famous Coconut Grove had opened—and just about all the stars in the industry were present, among hundreds of other prominent people.

Prior to the banquet, in an anteroom which at the time I thought must have been the size of Grand Central Station, there was a reception at which I was introduced to representatives of the Motion Picture Directors' Association, the American Society of Cinematographers, Actors' Equity, the Los Angeles Film Exchange, the Board of Trade, the Screen Writers' Guild, Western Motion Picture Advertisers, Theatre Owners' Association, the Assistance League, Assistant Directors' Association, the Motion Picture Producers' Association, and perhaps a few others.

Following the reception, we entered the banquet room and took our places at table. Practically all of the stars present were brilliantly arrayed, some of the ladies wearing jewels that a ranee might have envied. I was delighted to find that the toastmaster was none other than my newly found friend, Rupert Hughes. The invocation was delivered by the Reverend Neal Dodd—and the event was on!

As I looked over the gathering of fifteen hundred, I came nearer to feeling a touch of stage fright than ever before or since. To be quite frank, there was good reason. Many of these people were already on my side, but I knew that others had come as an act of civility, or for purely social reasons. Some of these, quite properly from their point of view, were indifferent to me and to my program. And some resented the idea of Will Hays, whose name they still confounded with the word "censorship."

This was only natural, and I blamed nobody. Had I been touchy about it, I would not have undertaken the job in the first place. There is no use accepting an executive office and imagining that everyone is going to become your friend and follower overnight.

Rupert Hughes kiddingly complimented the guests on how nicely they had behaved and how well they looked in their evening clothes, furnished (he professed to believe) by the Western Costume Company. Everybody laughed. Benignly he said he felt sure that they had made a good impression on the guest of honor. The guest of honor himself, looking at the people, wondered how many of them gave a continental what kind of impression they had made on him. What was more to the point was what sort of impression I would be able to make on them.

My friend Jesse Lasky, who had been my guardian angel ever since I arrived, was called upon to introduce me. It was a tense moment, and the air was like ice. I knew I would be courteously listened to, but it was not at all improbable that if I said the wrong thing someone would rise at the conclusion of my remarks and challenge my position.

Apparently I did not say the wrong thing.

Several times in the course of my address various groups began to applaud. I will not pretend that I was reluctant to employ showmanship, especially facing showmen, and there is no insincerity in a public speaker striving to make the strongest impression possible; but on this occasion I was so wound up that I kept right on talking through the applause, thus forcing it to subside. I told them of my disagreement with the whole principle of censorship and of my faith in the more manly and democratic process of *self-control* and *self-regulation;* but I said that such self-regulation had become a necessity, not only because of outside threats, but because the industry—the folks sitting before me—had become very important. They were important to their country, as trade no longer followed the flag, it now followed the films. If American pictures, shown everywhere, were to reflect credit on and not contempt of the

American way of life, the ladies and gentlemen of Hollywood must
henceforth regard themselves as ambassadors of Hollywood and of
America. They had become important, too, I said, to the youth of our
land, to the children who admired them, in some cases indiscriminately,
even to the point of frank emulation. I had not come, I added, as one
seeking to impose pressure, but in order to study the problem jointly
with them.

I was gratified at the ovation. Jesse Lasky, mopping his brow, came
over to me and shook my hand and told me he was proud of me. That
was the greatest accolade of all.

I was under no illusion that my words had completely broken down
all resistance. That was to be the work of months, if not of years, but I
do think that that dinner, brilliant on its social side, marked the beginning of the process. In that hour the skepticism and hostility with which
the Association was regarded began to dissolve. And I am still grateful,
even after all these years, to the members of all the committees who
made the affair possible, and to all the distinguished people—many of
them now passed on—who did me the honor of attending and listening
to my plea.

Thursday, the day following the banquet, was almost as busy as the
preceding ones. At the Hal Roach Studio, I remember, we were taken
on a set and seated near an arena to watch a performing lion being
photographed. He was a big devil with a great black mane, and evidently
a temperamental artist in his own right, for after a few moments he suddenly bounded to the top of a platform and then leaped over the screening that separated us from the arena. For the second time that week I
left a set hurriedly, without bothering about my hat.

That night I was again the guest of honor, this time at a dinner of the
Chamber of Commerce at the Los Angeles Women's Club. Walter
Long, a distinguished actor and also, at that time, Commander of the
Hollywood American Legion Post, spoke at the dinner and said some
very complimentary things. It indicated, at least, that a large section of
the actors were for me, and Walter remained one of the stalwarts upon
whom I knew I could depend. Amusingly enough, Walter Long, like
George Seigmann and Lon Chaney, generally played villains. Most of
the prominent screen "heavies" whom I have met seem, in real life, to be
the antithesis of their dramatic roles.

By now my week at the "front" was speeding to its close. On Friday
I had lunch at the Little Club with Elmer Harris, Arch Reeve, Frank
Lloyd, Maurice Campbell, Frank E. Woods, and others. Woods was
then president of the Screen Writers' Guild; I believe there has been a
break in the continuity of the organization and that it was not the same
Guild which made headlines not so long ago because of alleged Communist involvement of some of its members. In those days we were at

least spared the presence of a "Communist problem" in Hollywood.

On the same day, I met with a large group of writers, directors, publicists, and advertising men—I think about one hundred and fifty in all. It was an especially favorable occasion, for this was the most articulate section of the industry. I sometimes think that writers, even more than actors, are individualists; while their external conduct is more repressed, their attitude is more apt to be cynical. Hence at this, as at every other opportunity, I emphasized the fact that I carried no arbitrary power and was in no sense a dictator. Speaking to the directors, I appealed to their ingenuity and artistic pride, hinting that it takes vastly more artistry to be interesting while observing decent limits than when being risqué. I told them, for example, that instead of seeing how far they could get an actress to lift her skirt and still stay within the law they might try seeing how low she could leave her skirts and still maintain audience interest. They laughed heartily and got the point. It was a very candid group; but somehow that made them easier to convince.

The week ended in a blaze of glory with a mammoth all-industry rally at the Hollywood Bowl. This great outdoor amphitheatre, built in the hills above Hollywood and now nationally famous, was at that time just a huge excavation with a temporary stage; the granite tiers had not yet been installed. I am told that on Saturday afternoon, at the time of the rally, there were fifty thousand people present, and from where I sat on the rostrum I could see that the place was not only jammed to overflowing but that crowds had taken positions of vantage on the surrounding hillsides. It was gratifying, too, to see that a large block of seats—I think about four hundred—had been reserved for the postal workers of the Los Angeles area.

The committee on arrangements included William S. Hart, chairman, Irving Thalberg, Mike Levee, B. F. Rosenberg, Glenn Harper, Jesse Lasky, Frank Woods, Sol Lesser, Bert Lytell, Joseph W. Engel, and John McCormick. Thanks to these gentlemen, everything went like clockwork. All the studios shut down at noon, and the personnel of each marched in a body to the great Bowl, many of the players in the costumes of the productions they were currently making. It was a riot of color, yet it all blended into a harmonious pattern on that glorious, cloudless summer day.

The gates of the Bowl were thrown open at half-past two, although in obedience to the decree of the committee I did not arrive until later. At the appointed hour I was escorted from Max Puett's home by a police detail, which preceded my car. At Hollywood Boulevard and Cahuenga Pass I joined the "big shots" and, as we turned off the boulevard to Highland Avenue, the American Legion band met us and marched ahead of us to the Bowl. Crowds lined the sidewalks, and everywhere I looked cameras were clicking.

The Legion band retired as we reached the gates of the Bowl, and my old friends—the band of Branch No. 24 of the National Association of Letter Carriers—played as I was escorted to the platform. There were more bands that day! Sid Grauman had his own theatre orchestra there and also a number of variety acts to entertain the folks prior to calling the rally to order.

The first thing I was asked to do was to call the roll of the studios. The response was most impressive. An interesting feature of the proceedings was the greeting broadcast to the rally by radio station KHJ and picked up by a radio car furnished by Harry Chandler of the Los Angeles *Times*. That was new and hot stuff in those days, and the *Times* reported that it was the first time such a radio stunt had ever taken place.

I did not make the only speech that afternoon, but I was determined to make the speech of my life. It was my opportunity to address the public and the industry jointly—with nearly the whole personnel of the industry there. We live in a critical age, and reading of the unanimity of the occasion, it may occur to some that there was a certain amount of "management pressure" involved. Well, if on the Great Day of Judgment we learn that this was partly true, I for one do not care. I was not a candidate seeking office—I already had the office—and this was their business as much as mine.

Hitherto I had spoken to individuals or to selected groups. I had spoken to the companies actually shooting on the days I had happened to visit the studios. Even at the banquet, the preceding Wednesday night, I had spoken mainly to the "elite." This time I had before me the entire fellowship of the "university," practically the whole population of filmdom.

Jesse Lasky was chairman of the historic occasion. I was introduced, however, by Dr. Allen Shore, president of the Hollywood (not Los Angeles) Chamber of Commerce, for this was Hollywood's day.

It was my day too. Tears came to my eyes as, spontaneously, the people of Hollywood rose and cheered. And while it took another ten years to evolve the Production Code which is now practically constitutional in the industry, the wedge had been driven. It was the first step to be judged not by its length but by the direction it took. The folks of Hollywood had bought the goods.

That night I entrained for San Francisco. I had had one of the busiest and certainly one of the most delightful and informative weeks of my life. I had made a number of friendships which were destined to last over a quarter of a century, and had won a personal hearing from many who previously had been hostile.

I am pleased to state, to the honor of the industry, that there were at least five thousand columns of favorable publicity covering the events of the week, the credit being due to the publicity committee, of which Pete Smith was chairman.

It was with real regret that I bade good-by to Hollywood that evening. On the train I met two fellow passengers—Rudolph Valentino and King Baggot. It was the first time I had shaken hands with either of them. It seemed another touch of welcome.

IMPROVING THE DEMAND

Even as early as July of 1922, when I first visited Hollywood, my plea for a public demand for better movies was already backed by millions of Americans who had authorized me to present their requests. I had discussed the whole problem before the convention of the General Federation of Women's Clubs and the National Education Association, and with the representatives of more than eighty civic, welfare, and religious organizations in a conference held in New York. Figuratively, I carried their proxies in my pocket. The organized development of public relations sentiment, via an active committee, consumed a good deal of my time for the next few years.

I considered the movies to be an activity which should be judged in the light of its total impact on great numbers of people. It should be responsive to public demand, and although the Association was organized and financed by motion picture companies to promote their common interests and interpret those to the public, I personally felt an equal obligation to interpret the wishes of the public to the industry. I saw my task, again, as one of *mediation,* and I took my stand on the threshold of a two-way "open door." At once we set out to make our customers our friends and advisers. Booster and knocker must alike be heard. As to the most violent critics, I recalled my father's advice to "get so close to the mule he can't kick you"; and the well-wishers must be shown ways to make their good will bring practical results. I question whether any other industry has ever made such a record of organizing active good will in its support on so large a scale. So great became this volunteer force of co-operators, affiliated with the industry through our Public Relations Department, that as many as 600,000 men and women at one time were doing something on an organized basis for better pictures. And we made it an affirmative force: "What kind of pictures do you want?" was calculated to do producers more good than "What kind do you not want?" Here was a chance—indeed, a necessity—for a public relations job on a really grand scale.

Who had the right to insist that motion pictures be held to a stricter standard of taste and morality and merit than other media of entertainment and information and communication? The only answer was "the enlightened public." We could not presume to do it by ourselves; but we could enlist the public to help us, and thereby to share our huge problem. In obviation of externally imposed legal censorship, we could and did bring the public in on "our side." The screen had become, as we lawyers say, "public domain"; it had outgrown the right or the power of any narrow interest to control. And it was a little surprising to find that the public held motion pictures to a higher moral standard than any other form of general entertainment or of writing. Perhaps this was because we made the standard partly the public's responsibility. To me, this gradual development of a unique attitude toward movies was a fascinating thing to watch during the 1920s—and a reassuring thing.

Everybody agreed that the movies needed "something," and the best way I knew to answer public criticism was to welcome it. This meant setting up a genuine, conscientious complaints department and a workable procedure for taking the complaints to Hollywood. "Everybody has two businesses: his own and motion pictures" soon became a by-word around the Association offices. This was our "open door" policy, and it reflected in earnest operation the lessons I had learned from more than twenty years of political activity that "politics is people" and that the *enlightened* people show irrefutable common sense in choosing the right policies and in seeing that they are carried out. When the most popular after-dinner speech in America became "Let's go to the movies," the public was fully aware of its "half interest" in the business.

The co-operation of newspapers has played a big part in every public cause with which I have been connected. You can count on the American newspapers to be on the right side "when the chips are down." And they know news when they see it. They realized that anything affecting the standards of motion pictures or the theatre-going habits of 80,000,000 people was news, so they gave an enormous total amount of space to our activities, and their interest in turn enabled us to acquaint the public fully with our program. For instance, Harry Chandler, publisher of the Los Angeles *Times,* who previously had not shown special interest in motion pictures, listened to my description of the serious efforts being made to improve movies and arranged a pilgrimage for representatives of something like 150 of the country's leading newspapers to Hollywood so they could really see what the motion picture colony was doing. From that day on there was a fairer attitude toward the industry on the part of prominent newspapers.

In announcing our "open door" policy toward the general public, we uncovered voluntary interest that had already taken form in various places. The Indiana Indorsers of Photoplays had been active since 1915, and in 1922 the Southeastern Conference for Better Films was held in Atlanta, at which was adopted the principle of "selection rather than

censorship." The General Federation of Women's Clubs had been trying for eight years to do something for better films. We considered such
groups as partners in our program. In 1922 I invited more than a hundred representatives of civic, welfare, religious, and educational groups
to New York to discuss "ways and means for public co-operation," and
the response was enthusiastic and selfless. As soon as they were convinced that their counsel not only would be welcomed continually but
would play a definite part in creating the kind of pictures they wanted,
it became merely a question of "How?" We urged their active participation in "creating a demand for better pictures" through a permanent
committee of their own. As a result, an Executive Committee of Twenty
was formed among them to represent all such groups, with the capable
Jason S. Joy as its executive secretary. The General Federation of
Women's Clubs hailed the move as the "logical outcome" of the federation's eight-year work for better movies. One of the most continuous
activities of the committee, carried on quietly by smaller units located in
many towns and cities, was the encouragement of better pictures in their
local theatres. This was education at the grass roots. To almost 100 per
cent of these conscientious people, censorship was always an anathema, a
bungling, destructive thing; it was no moral cure. They set about telling
the producers in advance what they wanted, not afterward what they
didn't want. I have always been proud of this method of creating new
standards in a commercial industry through the quiet expression of enlightened, organized public opinion. The late C. C. Pettijohn, MPPDA
counsel, said to the 1929 Public Relations Conference: "This industry
has always been spoken of as a three-legged stool: production, distribution, exhibition. Mr. Hays made it a four-legged one, as it is now regarded. The fourth leg is the public."

By 1925 the committee felt that its work had grown beyond the
original concept and needed a more permanent form of organization; its
members considered a union with the MPPDA to be desirable, in order
to make its requests an intrinsic part of the industry instead of an ex-
trinsic influence. Thus the Association formed a Public Relations Department, into which the committee merged its activities, with Jason
Joy as the department's director. In 1926, Joy moved to California as
head of a Joint Department of Public Relations and Industrial Relations
in the California Association, to bring these activities closer to the
"source" of production. I must admit it took some effort to persuade the
producers to accept a public relations representative in Hollywood, but
this move was the forerunner of the subsequent Production Code Administration. We were then fairly embarked on the sea of *self-regulation,*
before the wind of public good will, and we had avoided the wrecking
storm of censorship.

EDUCATIONAL CO-OPERATION

On the subject of public relations, it is worth noting that Jean Benoit-Levy, prominent French producer, divides his whole book, *The Art of the Motion Picture,* into two equal sections: "The Motion Picture in Education" and "The Motion Picture in the Art of Entertainment." The adaptation of films to education has always been a hobby with me.

That first summer we made real progress. We soon discovered that most so-called "educational pictures" were pretty poor. Since they could not compare with good commercial pictures, they did not command serious attention from school people. Seeing a real problem to be solved, I thought it best to go direct to the most influential educational body, the National Education Association.

I accepted that association's invitation to address its annual meeting in Boston on July 6, 1922. In bringing the industry's offer of assistance, I called attention to the fact that the United States Commissioner of Education had recently said: "Within the celluloid film lies the most powerful weapon for the attack against ignorance that the world has ever known." Emphasizing the screen's responsibility to children, I said: "Above everything else, perhaps, is our duty to youth." I pointed out that crusade for better pictures was not a one-man job, nor a one-group job, but "the multitude's job," in which I asked their co-operation. I recalled recent experiments proving that pupils, with the aid of films, made much more progress than pupils without such aid. I made a prophecy, which took years to fulfill, that "there will be series of motion pictures adopted soon by boards of education, just as now series of textbooks are adopted. They must be, of course, scientifically, psychologically, and pedagogically sound." On behalf of our organization I promised all the facilities of the industry in the necessary process of experimentation, and proposed that we jointly study the growing demand and jointly find ways and means of supplying it. I suggested that "it would be just as silly to use language exclusively for writing novels as it would be to use motion pictures exclusively for theatrical entertainment."

It was readily admitted that picture-makers were not educators and that educators were not technical picture-makers, but, beginning with that day, the two extremes began to meet. We all saw that the educational theory would have to come from one side and the technical resources from the other. At my request, the Association at once appointed a small committee of able educators, headed by Dr. Charles H. Judd of the University of Chicago, and together we went to work.

HELPING DISTRIBUTORS

That first year we attacked four chief distribution problems: unethical practices of exhibitors, by which distributors were robbed of legitimate income; film thefts; an improved Railway Express plan for transportation of films; and regional boards of trade to assist in common problems of selling and distributing.

Distribution then involved the unbelievably complicated process of making contracts with over fifteen thousand theatres to cover their whole year's supply, seeing that prints reached the theatres on time, from once or twice to several times a week, and then getting them back safely and quickly for their next run. The chances for slip-up were endless. One of the dishonest schemes practiced by some exhibitors was "bicycling"— running a film over to a second theatre which was not paying rental on it, and getting it back in time to ship out on schedule.

Theft was a major problem that had to be tackled at once, and we held an important meeting on that subject just before Christmas of 1922. A general film-theft committee agreed upon a plan by which the Burns Detective Agency was to extend to all exchange centers the service that had operated so well in the New York territory: recovering strayed or stolen prints and prosecuting thieves. Sherman Burns also promised that his local branches would arrange with the public carriers in each exchange center to notify them of any film undelivered because of mislabeling, so that it would promptly be returned to the owner rather than discarded or sold for shipping charges. MPPDA agreed to keep the agency supplied with lists of missing prints owned by company members. The remedy worked. Here was effective co-operation in a "common interest."

Other matters discussed included an improved film-delivery system, worked out by R. E. M. Cowie, vice-president of the American Railway Express Company; a practical method of identifying prints; and a proposal for junking film at one central point where all companies could work together to ensure the destruction of prints no longer fit for showing.

In midsummer William Marston Seabury, brother of Judge Samuel Seabury, had prepared a plan for the formation of Film Boards of Trade to operate in the thirty-odd distribution centers. These Boards had no organic connection with the Hays Office.

HELPING EXHIBITORS

Though it was several years before our Theatre Service Department was formally organized under David Palfreyman, we at once began to render services. The most important matters that first year were a uniform exhibition contract and a method of arbitrating disputes connected with contracts.

MPPDA was composed of producers and distributors only; exhibitors were not included in it. In trying to explain this situation, I want to quote from Raymond Moley's introduction to his chapter on "Intra-Industry Relations." He writes:

In that vastly complex field of industry relations—the wholesale market place—in which producers and distributors dealt with exhibitors, the role of Hays is only that of an individual who serves as a detached mediatory advocate of harmony and co-operation. I have likened this function to that of a *catalyst* in the realm of chemistry—an agent which, by its presence, is capable of inducing change in another compound, while itself remaining unchanged. Throughout the long years in which he gave a large part of his time to the seeking of means to stabilize Producer-Distributor-Exhibitor relations, Hays has been scrupulous in avoiding specific responsibility for any decisions in that field.

In a business as big and complicated as was this, there were many ways in which unscrupulous men, either distributors or exhibitors, could cut corners. By 1922 there were annually more than half a million separate contracts for the exhibition of pictures. Eleven million deliveries were being made each year. Each of these transactions was a possible source of confusion or argument. Every contract had at least ten provisions. Most amazing of all, no two contracts in those days were alike. In 1922 at least four thousand lawsuits arose!

The idea of devising a uniform contract came from the exhibitors themselves. We then held a series of talks with exhibitor groups, both in our office and elsewhere, and later brought such distributors as the late Sidney Kent, a man universally admired, into the discussions. After months of work a uniform contract was adopted and put into effect in April 1923.

The most constructive feature of this new contract was an agreement to submit disputes to arbitration, out of which grew one of the most notable features of those early efforts, the Film Boards of Trade. So complete was this arbitration provision that the decision of arbitrators was made enforcible in any court of competent jurisdiction. Faith in the impartial counsel and good offices of the Association undoubtedly hastened these processes. By July 1923 the uniform contract was in fairly general use, and eighteen hundred disputes were settled by arbitration that first year.

To me it is particularly gratifying to recall that in November of 1921, at a conference of association executives with Secretary of Commerce Hoover, resolutions had been adopted urging business organizations to create their own arbitration, mediation, and conciliation committees for handling business disputes. At that time we were serving together in the President's Cabinet.

Another vivid recollection concerns Jimmy Walker. In April of 1922, when I spoke at a meeting of the Motion Picture Theatre Owners of New York, I was enthusiastically introduced by Jimmy, who was then general counsel of the Motion Picture Theatre Owners of America. He was eloquent in urging the advantages of co-operation. By fall, exhibitors at a distance were beginning to use the good offices of the Association, and groups like the Nebraska Theatre Owners were passing strong resolutions of support.

IMPROVING ADVERTISING

It took little time to discover that sensational and suggestive advertising was a menace. Although protests were strong, the temper of the times encouraged some movie men to skate near the edge of the ice. Within the first year we began definite efforts. For one thing, we sought the understanding and support of the international association of advertising men. I made a direct appeal to newspapers not to lower their general standards of advertising when dealing with motion pictures. And I appealed to the promotion departments of all our member companies. As the public can guess, this proved to be one of our toughest problems, but we made a beginning.

I arrived in Hollywood for my second official visit on December 13, 1922, and if the week was less gala than my first one, back in July, there were more specific and businesslike problems to be solved. The opening of a Hollywood office of the MPPDA had been authorized by a meeting of the Board held on September 20; to head that office I chose Thomas G. Patten of New York, a man of wide acquaintance and a happy knack of getting along with theatrical people, and himself a student of the drama. He had been a member of the House of Representatives from 1912 to 1916 and had subsequently been postmaster of New York.

The existence of this West Coast office side by side with the "West Coast Association" (now known as the MPPA and incorporated since 1924) has always been a source of confusion to the uninitiate. The last-named—the Motion Picture Producers' Association—is, and was, a fine group, not to be confused with the MPPDA of which I was the head. For some years there had been an association on the West Coast, organized to take care of local matters. The producers and studio heads who made up its membership had not judged, in the crises precipitated by the Arbuckle case and the William Desmond Taylor murder, that it was equipped either to handle public relations on a national scale or to secure the unified effort needed toward industry self-regulation. Hence the MPPDA was founded; but the West Coast group continued to function, and still functions, very effectually in its sphere.

However, while its membership has always been almost identical with that of the Motion Picture Producers and Distributors group, I have never held office in it. This gave rise to some confusion and caused people to ask me many times why I did not set up my own office in Hollywood. The answer is that, while Hollywood is the production center, the motion picture industry is national and even international, with many foreign problems and ramifications. The Motion Picture Producers and Distributors of America, Inc. (today simply called the Motion Picture Association of America, Inc.), the national organization with which my duties were concerned, established its headquarters in New York, where the large companies maintained their offices.

One of the striking phenomena of our truly phenomenal business, as I've said, is its bi-location. There are two centers, Hollywood and New York, and there is a certain sense in which Hollywood, in so far as picture production and even manners, customs, and points of view are concerned, is an annex or suburb of New York. The people of Hollywood are not "Westerners," although California is the farthest western state. Many of the picture folk are transplanted New Yorkers or came to Hollywood by way of the New York stage. And, with the exception of the cowboys, even those who are native to the West seem like New Yorkers after they have been around in pictures for a while.

The origin of this duocentricity was the early migration of production to the Pacific seaboard, with its climate, its sunshine, mountains, deserts, and plains. For the director, California was a dream come true. Every studio location department knows that within a few hours' journey of Hollywood the characteristic scenery of almost any country or clime in the world, except that of the arctic regions, may be found—at least in plausible facsimile. At the same time, the financial and distribution center of the industry has always been New York.

This system, which is less a system than a happenstance, has both advantages and disadvantages. It seems to have bred a curious tendency to insularity on the part of many motion picture folks, especially among those who "commute" between the two cities. There is a tendency among them to regard the rest of the United States as a hinterland with a railroad connecting the two great entertainment capitals. Although there is no friction between "town and gown" in Hollywood, there may be a certain amount of it between what has been called the "New York-Hollywood Axis" and other sections of our country.

It is, of course, a situation over which neither I nor any other man has any control; but I have sometimes thought that a part of the value I may have had to the industry was the fact, despite my long residence in New York, that I have somehow remained an unreconstructed Middle Westerner from "the sticks."

With Jesse Lasky, on my December trip to Hollywood, I had the pleasure of visiting De Mille at his Paradise Ranch on the far side of the beautiful San Fernando Mountains, and I also attended a private showing of *The Covered Wagon* in Jesse's home. This great, wholesome outdoor spectacle, reflecting the heroism of American pioneer life, had not yet been released. A fellow guest at the showing was the author, Zane Grey. It was the first time I had ever met him, and we hit it off like old pals.

Lasky and I had an amusing experience—I forget whether it was on this trip or a later one—when he was filming *The Rough Riders*. It was a fine production, for which Hermann Hagedorn, the noted biographer, had done research and also contributed to the scenario. The difficulty was finding an actor who looked enough like Teddy Roosevelt to play the lead. After some experimentation one of the Lasky exchanges in a distant city telegraphed that they had found a man, not a professional actor but a perfect double for T.R. They sent him on and Jesse signed him up.

There is more to being an actor, however, than looking the part, and after a few days of shooting, Jesse realized he had not only put himself in an embarrassing position but was faced with the necessity of firing, and thus humiliating, the innocent amateur whom he had engaged. The trouble was a terrific case of stage fright; although Victor Fleming, the director, had tried to encourage the poor man, he suffered from such timidity that neither director nor producer could do anything with him.

I happened to visit Jesse at his office and he told me the problem. Perhaps we both got the same idea at the same time. Jesse sent for the man, and I ducked out of the office with the understanding that I would return in ten minutes.

I was amazed when I got back. The actor, in his Rough Rider uniform, was startlingly like Teddy in appearance. But only in appearance. In manner he might better have been cast in the title role of *Broken Blossoms*, so lacking was he in self-confidence. Then Jesse winked at me, which was the signal. I stepped up to the actor.

"Colonel!" I said. "This is indeed a great honor!"

I shook his hand heartily, yet maintained the deference that one would when meeting the President of the United States. The change in the man was as prompt as it was astounding. All at once he *became* the character he was to portray, and before the interview had ended he was talking and laughing, not really imitating Teddy consciously, but with his own confidence restored. Jesse gave orders to all the people on the picture that henceforth the chap was to be called "Colonel" and treated with the respect due the role, off the set as well as on. As a result, he gave a brilliant performance, finishing the picture with flying colors.

During that December week I saw Tom Patten and helped him get installed in our Hollywood office, and when I left, Joseph J. O'Neill stayed behind to assist in getting it organized. For a time Tom and Joe comprised our entire office staff. With the West Coast Association I conferred on the Monroe Doctrine Centennial Commemoration, scheduled for the following summer and in which the industry took a notable part. We were getting closer together all the time, and a few weeks later I received a fine tribute from Carl Laemmle, the founder and Grand Old Man of Universal, in the form of a New Year greeting in which he said: "You proved to us that our interests were nearer identical than we imagined." Since "Uncle Carl," as he was called throughout the industry, had been one of the signers of the round-robin letter of a year before, I was gratified that his faith in the Association he had helped to launch, and in me, was being justified.

It was not all business that week. Christmas was approaching and I had to take at least one afternoon off, for my son had wired me that he expected Santa Claus to bring him a railroad train, complete with caboose, and an airplane with no less than two wings, and the order had to be filled in triplicate because, he added, "This goes for Harry and Frank, too."

On December 20 I left for home, and my last official act of 1922 was one destined to cause more discussion than anything I had done in my new job. I removed the official employment ban against Roscoe ("Fatty") Arbuckle.

In doing this, I was not acting without long deliberation. Of the criminal charge against him, Arbuckle had been acquitted; he had been leading an orderly life ever since. I happened to know that he was well-nigh bankrupt. It was not my wish that he again become a movie actor, as many at the time professed to believe, nor was I exuding sentimentality for a comedian whom I had never met. I merely refused to stand in the man's way of earning a living in the only business he knew.

It had been decided by the producers of some unreleased Arbuckle films that those pictures would never be seen in any theatre, although they were not outmoded—for that type of slapstick comedy is hardly topical—nor unsavory. The two men who deserve the credit for that decision are Joseph M. Schenck, who had Arbuckle under contract, and Adolph Zukor of Paramount, who had been producing the latest Arbuckle comedies. With hundreds of thousands of dollars tied up in completed but unreleased films, Zukor decided to make a sacrifice rather than bring further discredit on the industry or give the slightest added impetus to public outrage. So far as he was concerned, the outrage was very real. Arbuckle had let him down—he had let the whole industry down no less than his fans—and Zukor was prepared to take the loss. I wish to reveal here, too, that although the Association promulgated the ban on these pictures, it was Zukor who first thought of it and decided on it and then insisted that the Association take the credit. As a matter of fact, I wanted Zukor to issue the statement for Paramount, but he had replied: "No, Will, let the Association give it out. That will show that the Association means business." Even that early in the game Adolph Zukor had passed the stage in which profit was the primary concern of his activity. If any man ever had the "alma mater" spirit for the industry which had made him, and which he had largely made, that man was he.

The ban on the Arbuckle pictures was not affected by what some people called my "pardon" of Arbuckle himself. But it did seem to me that if work could be found for the man as a comedy director, perhaps, or as a technician, it was not my job to bar him from such a chance. In a spirit of American fair play, and I hope of Christian charity, I proposed that he be given that chance.

It seemed a relatively commonplace decision to me, and I anticipated no such excitement as ensued. But I had no sooner made the statement than "Help!", "Murder!", "Police!", "Hays Brings Arbuckle Back to Nation's Screens!" seized the headlines.

To this day I do not know whether Arbuckle, in the short remainder of his life, made another picture, but I do not think he did. It is my impression that he earned his livelihood as a gag-man or director of custard-pie two-reelers. But for the next three months it became a *cause célèbre,* sort of a Dreyfus case in reverse, as newspaper editorials and civic leagues presented me with every public building in the country, brick by brick. Dr. Willsie Martin, pastor of the First Methodist Church of Hollywood, declared that I had betrayed the innocent childhood of America. From Providence, Rhode Island, to Seattle, I was attacked as a promoter of Arbuckle and a condoner of his previous dissipations. Many newspapers called for my resignation or ignominious dismissal. At best, these critics termed me a sentimentalist who had been duped by the all-grasping producers!

To make matters worse, two days after my departure from Hollywood a story broke in the press disclosing a very real narcotic scandal involving a highly paid and hitherto popular star. This man made a magnificent fight against the weakness he had fallen into and he died shortly thereafter, but at the time it seemed to the Anvil Chorus that I should have been detective enough to have known about, and stopped, his tragic course. I was not the industry's house detective, however, and the news of his trouble was as great a surprise and shock to me as it was to everyone else. Coming on the heels of the Arbuckle statement, it was an unfortunate coincidence, and for a dark moment it looked as if all our good work for a year past, and all the fine relationships we had built and the confidence we had gained, might be smashed beyond hope of salvage.

Others, of course, commended my stand. The Toledo *Blade*, the Troy *Observer*, *The New Republic* (issue of January 1, 1923), The Springfield (Mass.) *Union*, the Muncie *Star*, the Columbus (Ga.) *Sun*, and the Atlanta *Constitution* were among the newspapers which approved.

The controversy, however, had not left me unmoved. It had seemed to me an obvious, even a somewhat negative, act. But there are times when, if everyone is shouting loudly enough, a man may begin to doubt the rightness of his own decisions. Upon arriving home, I hesitated to face my aunt Sally, who was always somewhat strait-laced. The one thing I felt I could not stand at the moment was the disapproval of my home folks. Duty, however, as well as affection—and maybe a desire to "get it over with"—impelled me to seek her out at once.

Aunt Sally was at home. As I entered the parlor she turned and looked at me. Then she threw her arms around me.

"Will! I'm proud of you!" she exclaimed.

That Christmas, in spite of the storm of protest and of the snowstorm outside, I was kind of proud of myself.

That first year was such a fast-moving panorama that any such review as I have here made must miss many touches of color and drama. One I don't want to miss occurred when George Eastman came to our office, said he was much interested in the success of the Association and wanted to join. In the spring it was also my pleasure to welcome David Belasco, the veteran producer, to the motion picture industry. He was joining Warner Brothers staff to aid in producing some of his notable stage successes.

In the fall a dinner was given to the "three czars": Judge Landis of baseball, introduced by DeWolf Hopper; Augustus Thomas of the theatre, introduced by Irvin S. Cobb; and myself, of the movies, introduced by Will Rogers, who was to become one of my closest friends. "Absolute Kings Now Rule Baseball, Movies, Drama," appeared in the headlines. And in one paper, under photographs and cartoons of the three of us, was the interesting legend: "Here we have three men that are kings in the three greatest fields of recreation in America. They're the ones that are saying what is to go and what is not to go."

That first year, seeking to tell our story quickly to as many organizations as possible, I traveled thousands of miles and addressed scores of gatherings. Things kept popping! In Washington, plans were perfected for the construction of model buildings to house film exchanges. The U. S. Shipping Board prohibited film service on Pacific liners until fireproof booths were installed, but later granted an extension so that there might be no interruption in the showings. In Ohio, our representative elicited from the president of the exhibitors' organization an enthusiastic promise to work with us to keep all partisan politics off the screen.

From editorial comments and public reactions it seemed that the country viewed hopefully the ambitious program of MPPDA. Freedom of the films was beginning to be a popular cause. Censorship had been scotched. There were signs of improvement in public taste. Pictures were seen to have value not only as entertainment but as a force in education.

It was a year of tremendous growth, with plenty of growing pains thrown in! We had had to face nearly every major problem, and we could fairly feel that to some, at least, we were beginning to find a solution.

The whole year was a year of beginnings. As Medill McCormick, the great publisher, said: "You can't start any proposition like a newspaper at the top. You have to build slowly from the ground up."

And I can still remember the symbolic line from Kipling which opened the foreword to the program of the dinner dance that welcomed me into the movie family:

> Begin at the beginning and
> go on to the end.

CHAPTER 26

The "Silent" Reaches Its Zenith
(March 1923–August 1926)

W H E N the silver screen found its voice, in August of 1926, it sounded the knell of an era in the evolution of the motion picture. The single-minded devotion which had brought the silent movie to the height of its art and its influence, and which had created such classics as *The Big Parade* and *The Ten Commandments* was no longer enough.

Similarly, the provisions which our Association had quietly built up for the self-regulation of themes and stories and which had guided producers into a golden era of heightened quality and public acclaim, were to break down under the onrush of sound. But before that time arrived, the industry and the Association had both learned some lessons in confidence and co-operation that helped to guide them through the "big switch." They had also learned that they must make good as a great new service to the public.

Perhaps one can picture this second period in MPPDA development like this: first, as a constant, optimistic effort to create a strong esprit de corps within the Association; and second, as the gradual building of machinery for putting good resolutions into practice. Without the spirit, the machinery would have ground to a standstill; without machinery, the spirit would have evaporated in pious sentiment. Since the members and I had both had experience with projects in which policy and means were equally necessary, we could generally agree on the kinds of steps needed.

The mere size of the motion picture industry was bound to command growing attention. There were no longer any "little" questions. So swift was the growth during this period that by 1926 our industry was reckoned the fourth largest in the United States. The strong men who had built up this giant industry were not the kind to be legislated into a new course, however desirable theoretically. It was necessary to propose new standards a step at a time, in line with the expressed wishes of the intelligent public. The MPPDA members had to see the desirability of a new idea or a new principle, and accept it voluntarily. Any other course would have busted us up! This creative art industry was no place for any rule but self-rule; for any regulation but self-regulation. That was my story and I stuck to it!

The appearance of better pictures, year by year, and popular appreciation of them, accompanied by rising national prosperity and a steady growth in the industry, strengthened the feeling among the members that we were on the right road. That in turn gave a lift to their will to do. Skill in the art of making silent pictures was nearing the zenith. New arts and techniques were being brought into play. Our pictures were going abroad in increasing numbers, and the resources of other nations were being drawn into Hollywood. The late Marcus Loew, when interviewed in London in 1923, was quoted as expressing the opinion that the big production activity of the season was "due, to a large extent, to an increased confidence engendered by the organization of the whole industry under Hays, who had raised the standard of pictures." It would be a truer way of stating it to say that I was able to serve as an instrument for unifying an industry which had infinite possibilities within itself.

At the very same time, pictures and picture people did not escape violent criticism. Part of this was deserved, for some very bad pictures were put out, a few of them inexcusably senational in titles and advertising. Flash headlines had their innings as a device for casting doubt on the movies. "What's Wrong with the Motion Pictures?", "Hokum: The Tarnish on the Silver Screen," and so on. There was also the perennial question of the effect of movies on conduct.

One of the memorable experiences of this period—and it sheds light on the status of American pictures—was my 1923 trip to England.

Although I had visited London as a young attorney intrigued by the swift processes of English law, this second visit, as "Czar of the American Cinema"—so said the British press—had quite a different scenario. Our Ambassador to England, George Harvey, who had invited me to go as his guest, directed the story, and we went "on location" as far out of the city as romantic Warwick Castle. The group scenes were luncheons and dinners of Britain's cinema industry.

Coming after eighteen months of intense uphill activity in my new job, this trip served as a wonderful vacation. The ocean voyage on the *Leviathan*, over and back, furnished an ideal rest, and Colonel Harvey was a perfect host and fine friend. He was far more than formally interested in motion pictures. As a top-flight newspaperman and publicist, he fully appreciated the influence of the screen; he believed in American films; he wanted them to have free world-wide circulation. Realizing that the British Empire was naturally our largest market, he wanted to help us win and hold that market, beginning with the United Kingdom. It was the first of many times when I was to receive from our State Department the most generous co-operation.

Not only was George Harvey a distinguished ambassador and a great American, but he was a very good friend. My relations with him had been close through years of political activity, and he had assured me that if I would come over to London he would undertake to help bring about a more favorable attitude toward American pictures. He had been Ambassador since April of 1921, was highly regarded for his wit and for his all-round intellectual capacities—T. P. O'Connor called him "far and away the wittiest ambassador America has sent us for many years" —and had made many friends.

I had first met him in Indianapolis years before when he came to speak at a testimonial dinner to our best-loved Hoosier poet, James Whitcomb Riley. Being young at the time, I felt much complimented that I had been invited. The dinner seemed almost a memorial occasion, for Riley was far from well. I remember that he sat, with white gloves on, as he received his guests, but his mind was alert and his presence a benediction.

Harvey was the most famous of the speakers, and his address was magnificent. I was close enough to see that he spoke merely from some penciled notes on Pullman-car stationery made on his trip out. And I still remember a story he told about a friend who had recently come over from Philadelphia to New York to see him. Taking the friend to lunch at a place which he thought would be pleasing, Harvey asked him what he would like, and the guest replied, "Do they have snails here?" Harvey said, "Yes, surely; and what else?" "Just let me have some snails now," the friend said. When he had finished them Harvey asked what he would like next, and his guest said, "Well, if it's all right, I'd just like to have some more snails." His curiosity aroused, Harvey asked, "Don't you have snails in Philadelphia?" And the friend replied, "Oh yes, we have snails in Philadelphia, but we can't catch them."

On this London trip I was accompanied by my wife's brother, Colonel Frederick L. Herron of our Foreign Relations Department. We were guests of Colonel Harvey at the Hyde Park Hotel. He made himself familiar with our problem and aided us in presenting our case to the British authorities. He anticipated no great future obstacles to the circulation of American pictures unless their content should be such as to cause resentment on nationalistic or moral grounds. He knew that our pictures were immensely popular with the English people. But American pictures were already occupying such a large percentage of English playing time that British producers were not too happy about it.

However, no critical problems had yet developed, and the contacts we made in London were largely for the sake of public relations and mutual understanding. We had private discussions with the heads of the three branches of the British industry, but one of the newspaper articles was headed, "Hays Disappoints London by Maintaining Silence"

—a thing of which I have rarely been accused. They had a right to believe I was on a holiday. One London paper commented: "No one seems to know exactly what his visit to London portends, but I presume he is observing the trend of the trade in this country." At several luncheons and dinners, however, we did meet most of the British industry's leaders, as well as a number of leaders in other fields.

Scenically and historically, my most interesting experience was a weekend at Warwick Castle. We had arrived on the *Leviathan* on September 14. On the twentieth the papers announced that we were leaving for Warwick Castle—to which they referred as "the Ambassador's favorite country retreat." To me, the scene is unforgettable. We went out on a Thursday and stayed until Monday—which I gathered was a usual weekend over there! And what seemed most strange was that this magnificent English landmark, in all its beautiful and romantic setting, should be under a ten-year lease to an American, Harry Marsh, whom I had known for years. The insurance firm of Marsh and McLennan of Chicago had long been a client of our Indiana law firm, and it never ceased to intrigue me that an American business rooted in the great Middle West was keeping up this grand old castle.

Among the other guests was the Duke of Marlborough, who turned out to be most likable and companionable. I also recall a good deal of talk about arranging a hunt. But the only hunt Colonel Herron and I carried on, with Hoosier curiosity, was for new and strange features in the myriad furnishings of the castle—from the armor in the great hall to the carving on the imposing bedsteads in the still more imposing guest rooms. I wondered what my grandmother Cain, used to stiff furniture in a boxlike frame house, would have thought.

The item in the weekend program which I had arranged was the showing of a recent feature picture, *Little Old New York,* starring Marion Davies. We had brought all the projection equipment with us, and it was set up in the great hall, which was filled with guests, neighbors, and servants. What with our own little group and the picture itself, there was a good deal of American atmosphere. The film made a great impression. Just released, it became one of the hits of the season. I'll admit to a feeling of some pride at the result of the showing and of great joy in the sense of common heritage that it aroused. Afterward George Harvey said: "I never was so thrilled in my life as when Old Glory broke out in the breeze over Fulton's *Clermont.*"

One of our events was a luncheon given by the American Society of London to Lloyd George. He made a splendid speech and naturally referred to the fact that he planned to go to the United States soon afterward. About the same time, as it happened, the famous English race horse Papyrus was scheduled for a match race with that year's American champion, Zev, winner of the 1923 Derby. When my turn came to speak, I said I hoped Lloyd George would have a most successful trip, and that I knew he was as sure to win the good will of America as Papyrus was certain to lose the race. And so it happened!

Lord Beaverbrook gave a dinner for me at the Embassy Club that same day. It was quite a day!

The distinguished wit, T. P. O'Connor, known to all his friends as "Tay Pay," was celebrating his seventy-fifth birthday, and much was made of it by his friends. At the time he was still serving as the president of the Board of Film Censors. The following week he wrote of the American Society luncheon most graciously, if extravagantly, in the London *Telegraph,* telling of his delight at being present and saying that I "looked a mere boy" but "made a speech of such compelling eloquence, sometimes of such exalted emotion, that the company was stunned into silent admiration." That's probably a fair sample of the blarney of an Irish journalist and national leader who twice had successfully toured the United States to gather funds for the nationalist movement. He was a unique character—often affectionately referred to as "the Father of the House of Commons"—and it was a thrill to meet him. I remember some significant things he said about motion pictures. He was clear that "the cinema industry could not be conducted on the lines of a Sunday-school entertainment. It must be primarily for amusement; but it must be clean amusement."

The incident which topped all others in impressiveness was my visit to a meeting of the Imperial Conference, where the prime ministers of all the commonwealths were in active session when Harvey took me over.

I remember how they looked as we entered. There sat the distinguished Balfour, whom I had met as chairman of the British group at the Limitation of Arms Conference in Washington in 1921. Stanley Baldwin, then Chancellor of the Exchequer, I had just met in connection with George Harvey's visits to him, as together they worked out the debt settlement. General Smuts of South Africa impressed me more strongly than any man at the conference, and Mackenzie King, representing Canada, also created a splendid impression. Stanley Baldwin made the introductions. When we were leaving, Baldwin went out with us and graciously expressed his pleasure at meeting me. But in farewell he could not restrain himself from saying, "Mussolini went to Corfu and put England out of the League, and you fellows put out the United States." Needless to say, I could hardly agree, but we parted cordially. Seeing this august conference in action—history's most striking example of far-flung commonwealths united by kindred bonds in a common purpose—was a fitting climax to my London visit.

We were all amused by the facetious welcome given us by one of the London papers: "Cabinets crash and thrones totter all the world over when an American movie boss winks an eyelid." According to most press comments, percentage—the proportion of playing time occupied by American films—was still the absorbing topic.

On my return home, trying to summarize my impressions, I said to our staff, "The most striking realization is that 90 per cent of all pictures shown in England are American-made pictures and that they so please the great number of Britons who go to see them." In my report to the industry I assured it that its efforts toward improvement were of as much interest over there as here. In particular, my experience had emphasized the importance of the motion picture as an instrument of international amity. I brought back renewed conviction that "the international understanding by the peoples of the world, each of the other, which will be brought about by the right kind of American pictures all over the world, will move us very far indeed in the direction of world peace." It is no fault of motion pictures that world peace does not look nearer.

Even before I actually entered the movie industry I must have sensed that our basic problem went far deeper than the screen itself. It involved the tastes and attitudes of the great majority of our people. Granted that our goal frankly included establishing and maintaining the highest possible moral standards, our court of last resort was the moral sense of Americans. And bound up with "moral standards" was a whole network of manners and customs and traditions. I knew that the changes had been tremendous since I graduated from college and began to practice law at the turn of the century, and especially in the years following World War I.

Undoubtedly the war accelerated many domestic changes already being felt. Mark Sullivan, in his monumental and brilliant *Our Times,* notes that "in 1914 that early Puritan spirit lingered in spots and among some religious denominations." Billy Sunday, the most striking of American evangelists, was still a power. On the other hand, "growing patronage of public amusements, Sunday and weekday, was the rule." By the end of the war, motion picture competition had proved too much for the legitimate theatre in all but a handful of American cities and had sounded the death knell of the "road shows" that used to play every "opera house" in the land. The "movies" had taken their place! Sullivan points out also that other changes, quite apart from the war, were taking place. The energy and "ferment" characteristic of the time were favorable to a new art form like the motion picture. "Dynamic materialism and dynamic humanitarianism" were growing side by side, illustrated so strikingly in Andrew Carnegie. Larger production, less human effort, and the now-famous "assembly line" were creating more income and more leisure—ideal conditions for the growth of a popular form of entertainment which could be brought to the people, anywhere.

Among the "new influences on the American mind," Sullivan makes much of Sigmund Freud, whose ideas were being heavily imported between 1909 and 1914; and though to the average man these were "disgusting and wild interpretations," overemphasizing sex, acceptance of them seemed to make earlier literature old-fashioned, so far as it dealt with love or religion. George Bernard Shaw was also adjudged the interpreter if not the instigator of many of the new ideas, and the creator of a pose which was widely imitated. "The whole of his unhappy cosmos," writes Sullivan, "led him to take on insolence, and incredible impudence, as an armor of defense against a world which, whatever way he turned, wounded his ego. . . . He reasoned that by standing any familiar idea or accepted convention on its head, the world can be shocked into paying attention." There was even the "dance craze." The formal grace and beauty of the waltz had given way before the rhythm, speed, and noise of the "Ragtime Revolution." Sullivan mentions also "the increasing decrease of women's raiment," talk of eugenic marriage, increasing divorce, the progressive migration from farmhouse to flat, accompanying progressive industrialization, and such phenomena as the Montessori system of self-activity in education, bottle babies, and both profusion and diffusion of wealth.

When, in addition to all these minor changes, one weighs the major changes wrought by the Great War and all the importation of different ideas and standards that followed it, one appreciates the battle of standards that was inevitable on the screen. Quite frankly, it was often a case of inherited American standards—products of a Christian civilization—against alien customs variously considered "modern," "liberal," or "pagan." Hosts of Americans clung firmly to their own ideals and strongly resisted the alien invasion.

If I needed any excuse for stressing this point of a conservative American tradition, let me borrow it from Edward G. Lowry, who, in a magazine sketch written in the early twenties, proposed me as "the 100 per cent American" who "belonged in the Bureau of Standards rather than in the Post Office Department." From this point of view I want to make one or two comments.

Going back for a moment to the Chicago World's Fair of 1893, with its fascinating "national buildings" displaying the cultures of the whole world, let's says that America became acutely conscious of many lacks in its own culture. We suddenly developed an appreciation for many things that were "foreign" and a preference for things "imported." Many of these things, like Old World architecture, paintings, and products of science, appealed to us as "beautiful, true, and good."

The point is, as I see it, that we perhaps became overeager, overreceptive to many things just because they were foreign and different. In the decades that followed we not only sent thousands of students abroad to study but we began to import and to have foisted upon us a stream of ideas containing, along with the good, much that was decadent in art, literature, economics, and politics. I wonder whether subsequent troubles in Europe may not be traced, in part, to the very trends that many of our generation considered it "smart" to imitate.

But now I turn to something more cheerful, to one of the most brilliant chapters ever written by American pioneers.

Edison and Eastman are two of the greatest names in American invention and industry. They were two of the creative geniuses in the development of that modern miracle, the moving picture, which reached its "silent" flowering during this period. Both of them I am proud to have counted as my good friends. Their memories are bound up not only with the most significant events in the creation of the movies but with the early growth of our Association and with the expanding use of the film which we were striving so vigorously to bring about. Both men lived long, rich lives of prodigious service. Both were great Americans. Both were striking examples of personal achievement and tireless work. In a unique way their work was complementary: one invented the machine, the other the film which made the machine work. Between them they contributed more to this modern art-industry, beyond any possible question, than any other two men. Truly, in the words of Old Testament scripture, "there were giants in those days."

But I find an interesting contrast between them, too—one which I could observe in my personal associations with them as well as in the written records. Edison, said to have been interested in creating moving pictures chiefly as an accompaniment to his earlier phonograph, was so little concerned over the future of his new projection machine that he neglected to take out patents in foreign countries. And in May of 1926, when commercial talking pictures were almost ready for the screen, the great inventor, then seventy-nine years old, doubted whether the new product would "come into general use as long as the American public continues to display its present attitude."

George Eastman, on the other hand, though an inventor of consequence, was primarily a manufacturer, organizer, and philanthropist. His faith in the uses of motion pictures was boundless, and he repeatedly backed his faith by princely gifts. He was one of the great humanitarians of our age, and education, music, and motion pictures were the media through which he gave most largely, in the hope of bringing satisfaction and pleasure to great numbers of his fellow citizens.

I remember a visit with Mr. Edison at the opening of the Paramount Theatre in New York on November 19, 1926. I still have a picture taken that night showing Edison, Adolph Zukor, Jesse Lasky, and myself, which recalls a crack Mr. Edison made about me. I had gone out to the curb to meet him, and as we entered the great lobby we were greeted by Zukor and Lasky, prime factors in the growth of the Paramount enterprises. News photographers were waiting for us, but they didn't use flash bulbs. Instead, we were grouped in the middle of the lobby, with that enormous chandelier—a huge cluster of Edison's own incandescent lights—giving almost the brightness of day. There we stood for a series of pictures, all time exposures. As we finished and moved toward the entrance Edison leaned over to me, his hand on my arm, and said: "I'll warrant that's the longest you ever stood still in your life."

I remember also the Golden Jubilee Anniversary of Edison's incandescent light, staged by Henry Ford at Dearborn, Michigan, October 21, 1929. Unexpectedly I had received a letter from Mr. Eastman inviting me to attend the celebration with him. Men and women had gathered from all over the world to honor the occasion. I joined Mr. Eastman on the train and we literally spent the day together at Dearborn. We saw the same sights, heard the same discussions, talked to the same people. Thus I shared the most intimate conversations of Mr. Edison, Mr. Ford, Mr. Eastman, and Owen Young. After the inspiring banquet that evening, we went together to the train, talking over the impressions of the day as we waited in the station. Few occasions have ever seemed to me more symbolic both of the simplicity and of the greatness of America and its builders.

On November 5, 1930, in his eighty-third year, Mr. Edison delivered a memorable valedictory to the leaders of the motion picture industry. That night the third annual dinner of the Motion Picture Academy of Arts and Sciences gave rapt attention, by eye and ear, to a talking screen set up in their banquet hall. Gazing at his face and listening to his voice, they received the last personal message from the man who had brought both their art and their profession into being.

Though in this story I am thinking primarily of George Eastman's connection with motion picture film, that remained a small fraction of his business for a great many years after 1889. As the whole world knows, when we think of Eastman we think of "Kodak," for he was to the camera what Ford was to the automobile—but more so. His flexible film was originally developed for his "roll" camera, which had to be sent to the Eastman plant for development and reloading, and today the millions of Kodaks in the hands of amateurs are still the company's greatest market. According to one estimate, motion picture film constitutes only 12 per cent of the entire business, though that 12 per cent is enormous in total footage.

Mr. Eastman's personal interest in the motion picture sharpened his eagerness to see its use extended to many fields. He became far more interested in educational pioneering than in selling film.

Two or three personal experiences with him—cases in which almost singlehanded he carried the motion picture ahead to a desired goal—I remember most vividly. The year 1926 happened to be the one in which two of these projects were launched. The fact that he was seventy-two years old at the time shows the ceaseless vigor and imagination of the man.

The first project was the development of educational films specifically planned for the classroom—what we knew as "teaching films." Of more than $75,000,000 given to various philanthropic objects during his lifetime, a considerable proportion went to education. I doubt if he considered anything more important, and I took pains to keep him informed about the joint efforts to develop useful films for schools. Another project that interested him was medical films.

In October of 1926 I had definitely offered the industry's co-operation to the American College of Surgeons meeting in annual convention at Montreal. To them I had said: "Today a new scroll is handed the doctor upon which he may write in terms so simple that none may be dismayed and in scenes so clear that none may misunderstand. Today he has the moving picture upon which to record his knowledge." Small beginnings, made both here and in Europe, were enough to show that surgical operations could be successfully recorded on motion picture film. After promising to serve the science of medicine in any way possible, I had to make good! The college, warmly welcoming the offer, appointed a committee of distinguished members to suggest working plans. We knew that money would be needed, and wondered who would underwrite this new venture. Mr. Eastman naturally came to mind. On a Saturday afternoon in mid-December I wrote him saying that there was something I should like to discuss with him, and offering to come to Rochester to see him. Mr. Eastman's recent gift of $5,000,000, matching a similar gift by the Rockefeller Foundation, for a medical center in Rochester seemed to prove his tremendous interest in medicine.

On the following Monday he telephoned me that he was interested and asked me to come up. Taking the night train from New York, I saw him in his office Tuesday morning and told him about the Montreal meeting, reporting that a scientific study of surgical films was being carried on by a very strong committee including such men as Dr. Charles H. Mayo of Rochester, Minnesota, Dr. George W. Crile of Cleveland, Dr. J. Bentley Squier of New York, chairman, Dr. Allen B. Kanavel of Chicago, and Dr. Franklin Martin, director general of the American College of Surgeons. I explained that this committee had concluded that thorough experimentation would be needed before the best methods could be discovered, and that they had hoped some money could be raised.

Mr. Eastman was keenly interested and at once asked, "How much will it take?" I said, "We believe that the committee should have $500,000." Without a moment's hesitation he said that he would give it and asked how we should proceed. We agreed that he should invite the committee of surgeons and myself to come to his home to discuss the entire project, and we were able to set the meeting for one week from that night. Mr. Eastman never saw any use in delay. These busy doctors all rearranged their schedules—how, I don't know—and we met at Rochester as agreed.

Arriving in the morning, we were greeted by Eugene Chrystal, whom I had acquainted with our progress to date, and taken to Mr. Eastman's office. After a cordial welcome we got down to business, Mr. Eastman having assured the gentlemen that $500,000 was at their disposal, to be furnished as required. After discussing the plan in general terms and agreeing on procedure, we were shown through the tremendous plant and had lunch together. We found more to see in the afternoon, noticing especially anything that would bear on our own project. Then we dined with Mr. Eastman at his home that evening.

The dinner was a most delightful affair. His beautiful residence was a wonderful setting for such a conference. The pipe organ, one of the finest in the country, was played for us as we dined. After dinner we went into a room where a projection machine and screen had been set up. During the evening he had told us quite a little about the Martin and Osa Johnson camera hunts of wild game in Africa, explaining how they set up decoys and blinds and how they were able to get remarkable pictures without too much personal risk. In particular, he explained how he himself had been provided with a white hunter who would never leave his side while he was taking pictures, and whose duty it was to shoot any beast that might start to charge the cameraman—Mr. Eastman.

We were absorbed in watching these pictures when a shot that shocked us all flashed on the screen. A rhinoceros charged straight at us and seemed to fall at our very feet. The moment the reel was finished we all turned to Mr. Eastman, exclaiming about the risk he had run. One of the surgeons—I think it was Dr. Mayo—said, "George, that was a terrible thing to do! Anything might have happened. That white hunter might have dropped dead." Then I asked, "Mr. Eastman, how far was that rhinoceros from the camera when he was shot?" He answered, "Six paces. Two paces when he fell."

There sat this modest, white-haired little gentleman, taking all our consternation calmly, saying nothing. When the equally distinguished circle of surgeons, all his juniors, had exhausted their vocabularies pouring out their concern, George Eastman said in his quiet voice: "Well, you've got to trust your organization." It was a simple but striking observation, well epitomizing the key to his success. This belief in cooperation was one of his great contributions to our industry as well as to the life of the nation. His aid in the field of medical and surgical films brought quick results. An extensive series produced by his company was shown to the American College of Surgeons at Detroit in October. Thus, in less than the interval between successive annual meetings, our plan had borne fruit—thanks to George Eastman!

As already mentioned, the three years from 1923 to 1926 formed a period of significant growth. The silent film was reaching its zenith, the services of the screen were being proved in new fields, and the screen's two great allies—color and sound—were almost ready for the miraculous merger which today we take for granted. But having lived through the subsequent revolutions involved, I can testify that some of the events were no calmer than those of any other revolution. The three years before 1926 were like the lull before the storm, and they were fruitful days. Even in my first Christmas card I had called our business "a great service to mankind," and each year brought out some new service.

I liked to think that the early inventors and pioneers had visioned many of these possibilities of motion pictures. I can honestly say that it was such vision that continued to give my work its endless fascination. To me, the screen was a magical medium of expression which could be used in countless ways. I called it a mechanism for the distribution of intelligence, a source of amusement, a new language that leaps the barriers of Babel, and the most popular art in all history.

Church people were quick to feel the emotional and spiritual appeal of fine motion pictures. The perennial response to *King of Kings*, which has been seen by more people than any other film, is a classic example: the power of a reverent portrayal of Christ on the screen is unanswerable. De Mille's later epic, *The Crusades*, had a similar spiritual appeal. It did not surprise me, therefore, to see early use of religious pictures both in church and Sunday school. Much of our later work in educational pictures had the church school also in mind.

In September of 1923, Dr. Carl S. Patton, pastor of the First Congregational Church of Los Angeles, strongly championed the use of photoplays in churches. By 1926 there were many cases of direct co-operation between local churches and motion picture theatres, in which church committees helped to choose programs. As a practical gesture, the Harmon Foundation of New York City, always interested in education, offered to supply motion pictures to churches at cost.

The film as an aid in character training was early recognized by many people dealing with youth, and of course that includes judges and clergy. Judge Ben Lindsey, famous juvenile court head of Denver, who said in a speech in Chicago that "religion and education are all that youth needs," was a stout defender of motion pictures. As a matter of fact, there never before had been a time when the organized church could influence any organized business as it could then help to guide motion pictures.

In 1926 the industry was able to render a unique service to world-wide religion. That year the great Eucharistic Congress, the biggest religious event ever witnessed in the New World, was held in Chicago. As I said at the première of the documentary Eucharistic Congress film, "Nationalism was forgotten. Everything was forgotten except the one central act of worship. The world was united in the adoration of God. . . . Now comes to the service of this magnificent purpose this great new instrument; with the motion picture, the Eucharistic Congress will go to the farthest corners of the earth, carrying the message of faith, the voice of religion. Men of all languages, of all races, may draw from it inspiration and understanding. Where thousands saw, now millions will see—hundreds of millions."

Another substantial project was under way at Yale University. Late in 1923 appeared the first of a projected series of thirty-three photoplays covering the dramatic highlights in four hundred years of American history and called *Chronicles of America.*

It was one of the many functions of the Association to encourage and to lead the participation of the industry, as a great popular force, in projects of national and international philanthropy. One of my first requests to the members was that they help raise funds for the Japanese earthquake sufferers of 1923. We always worked with the Red Cross. Another typical instance was our co-operation with the American Child Health Association and the General Federation of Women's Clubs in their Child Health Plan; our Association itself prepared slides and distributed them to any motion picture theatre in the country desiring them. At our request, producers and distributors were sending an increasing supply of films to more than five hundred public and private institutions—such as orphanages, hospitals, and old people's homes—bringing pleasure to shut-ins of all types. Among these gratis films were those shown every Friday night to immigrants detained on Ellis Island, as well as those shown to immigrants coming over on ocean liners.

Not forgetting the members of our own profession, the Motion Picture Relief Fund of America, Inc., was organized in 1925. Needless to say, it has been a boon to many.

Although we fought successfully to keep paid advertising and propaganda pressure off the screen, I never hesitated to encourage our people to boost any worth-while movement for national welfare. Many of the commercial newsreels played a big part in relief work by arousing sympathy. In this work we could greatly supplement the press.

Instances of non-commercial exhibition could be multiplied indefinitely, whether considered as philanthropy or just plain convenience. One of the best illustrations was the lumber camps of Maine, where, according to a story in the New York *Herald Tribune,* "the men keep up an intense interest in stars and in pictures which makes them look forward eagerly to the coming of movie night. Phonographs provide the musical accompaniment." I stimulated many such non-theatrical show-ings as part of the industry's social responsibility.

These early years were years of building, of organizing, of intense nationwide activity in a multitude of fields. Frankly, it was a terrific grind. I had been fortunate in finding for our staff a number of men of varied talents who saw this thing much as I did, who put into it long hours and contagious enthusiasm, and who made strong team play pos-sible. I want to pay tribute not only to the loyal support these men gave me but to the imagination and initiative they contributed in their own special departments.

Though many people doubtless considered me devoted to organization as such, I knew that in this business only one thing would win, and that was the right spirit, the voluntary desire on the part of the leaders to make the industry responsible and self-regulating. This desire, which I felt it my number-one responsibility to strengthen, no matter how long it took, I always thought of as the "will-to-do."

Probably the commonest public criticism of the Hays Office in those early days was that I did not crack down. People wanted to see me swing the ax. But they had a complete misconception of the process. From the first I had known that no kind of external orders, laws, or regimentation would create good pictures, though it might cut scenes out of a so-called bad picture or take it off the market.

To me, it was axiomatic that the producers who had succeeded in the business knew most about making good pictures. Some of the amateur-ish attempts to make "educational" pictures without adequate experience or budget drove that lesson home. It seemed to me that the first thing to do was to convince these men that they were all sitting on the same side of the table. The second was to weld them into something like the editorial board of a great national newspaper capable of forming and observing policies good both for themselves and for the right-thinking public.

This method of responsible self-direction, considerate of the public good as well as of the box office, I sometimes called "policyship." More often I thought of it as the will-to-do. It was a flower of slow growth. I did my best to encourage the flower, but any forcing would have killed it. You can't tell creators how to create; Hitler tried it and killed the German film industry.

The co-operative attitude had been partially recognized by some of the newspapers even during the first year. Commenting on the Landis-Thomas-Hays dinner given to three alleged "czars of recreation," the Boston *Globe* had said:

The gold rush days of the movies are over. Team play between companies is coming in without so much of the reckless competition of pioneer days. Producers are saying quietly, "Let's sit down and talk it over. Perhaps we can work for each other's good as well as our own." This adjustment is what Mr. Hays is working for. He's going to weld them together, just like a Board of Trade or Chamber of Commerce.

I took every occasion to show that the Association was working for the good of the whole industry, and no one could doubt that the Association was busy. Hard work and co-operative methods were now paying off in growing prestige for MPPDA. The Public Relations Committee enlisted thousands of helpers. Our MPPDA membership within this period grew from an original nine companies to twenty-two, and these included not only most of the large companies, but several of the smaller ones. When our members, after wrestling with a problem, found a solution, it was tantamount to a solution for everyone.

The beauty of this process was that every time the directors took such action it strengthened their confidence in their own ability, through self-government, to ensure both the freedom of the art and the prosperity of the business. After the industry's violent past, the new confidence in each other could not be born in a minute. But at the very least, the organized program of their Association, which I never allowed to lose its tone of optimism, provided a way to do right. The greatest figures in the industry had put their faith in this venture, and against the background of those earlier days it *was* an act of faith, as was mine in accepting the invitation. I was determined not to let them down, nor the public that so earnestly hoped for better things.

Incidentally, there was one thing I had to be careful about. Because widely advertised as a Presbyterian elder and incorrectly called a czar, I sometimes bent over backward to erase any impression of being a "blue-nose" censor. I didn't mind a prominent cartoon of me in the latter role, but I didn't want it taken seriously. In Hollywood I saw to it that I danced with some of the stars and attended many of the social events. Since I've always enjoyed dancing, this part of my job was not difficult.

Before leaving this period I want to mention briefly some matters handled by various departments of the Association as early steps in our program.

In the field of public relations and information, I sought frequent occasion to "report to the public," as in effect their representative. Close relations were maintained with the press, and our Speakers' Bureau kept busy. Activity in foreign countries was steadily promoted as it was increasingly realized that pictures constitute a universal language. Exhibitors and distributors were aided by the introduction of a standard exhibition contract, with its arbitration clause. Only 17 cases out of 5,450 in the first year were taken to the courts after an arbitration board had made its award. In the field of conservation, better protection against both fire and theft was developed. Better copyright legislation and title registration saved money and headaches, and helped to kill the "sex film title." Similar progress was made in preventing "salacious, misleading, and dishonest advertising."

In progress toward a production code, ninety-one stories in a year were barred from the movies, and twenty-four companies were using the new MPPDA emblem. We measurably prevented the then prevalent types of books and plays from invading our pictures.

With the co-operation of editors, tremendous sentiment was marshaled against censorship. Aid was given in cases where unreasonable admission taxes had been slapped on. Connecticut was the best example. Here, in 1925, a tax of twenty dollars per reel was levied on every reel brought into the state. With the co-operation of distributors and exhibitors, a method of splitting and taking care of the tax was worked out, until the law was repealed the next year.

These were the years when our new departments and activities were beginning to be organized in California. Finding that it was necessary to spend considerable time out there, I soon adopted a regular schedule of trips to the Coast. The Association of Motion Picture Producers, an independent California group but closely affiliated with the MPPDA, planned its meetings to coincide with my trips. And there were always matters waiting for me in the Hollywood office of our Association.

During this period the most important West Coast development, under the aegis of our Association, was the Central Casting Corporation. In January 1926, the industry's free employment bureau for extra people was created. It was founded as a subsidiary to the West Coast Association. It is with the facts behind these bare facts—the wistful longings, the vain ambitions, and the power of Hollywood that attracts thousands annually to seek their fame and fortune by trying to crash the movies, only to be disillusioned—that I was primarily concerned in this connection. This problem had been in my mind since my first official visit to Hollywood in July 1922. I knew that we paid our labor well and that working conditions were ideal. But the lot of the "extras," as the supers are called in the movies, had bothered me for a long time.

It was first flashed to me by dramatic incident following the great Hollywood Bowl rally on the last day of my first visit. As we were leaving the Bowl a gaunt, emaciated man with a beard leaped on the running board of my automobile and asked me to give him a job in a studio. He said he had been an extra but had not been employed for a long time and was desperate. Of course I had no authority to give such jobs to anybody. I handed the man what change I had in my pocket, and that was the last I saw of him. But I never forgot the incident, and I determined to find out as soon as I could why so many folks should choose such a precarious occupation, especially in the early twenties, when national employment was high.

The first thing I learned was that two types of persons, for the most part, composed the vast corps of casual, hand-to-mouth workers who appeared in the "mob scenes" or in the society sequences of our movies. These were the old-timers—actors, actresses, and performers whose years of professional usefulness were over, yet who knew no other trade—and the people who arrived in Hollywood on every train and bus, eager for a glamorous career.

At that time the studios made no particular effort to discourage this influx, although they had not sought it. It just happened. Young girls in small towns, whose friends told them that they had talent or that they resembled some famous star of the moment, would leave home, sometimes with gala farewells and brass bands. Upon failing not only to reach stardom but even to make a living in the film capital, they would grow desperate. Hence, while Hollywood was a city of fame and fortune for some, it shared with Broadway the distinction of being a valley of broken hearts and broken hopes. Nor were all of the aspirants girls. It will surprise many to learn that an even greater number of these hopefuls were men, sometimes perfectly dignified middle-aged men who had always been stage-struck and now believed the motion picture industry might use their talents.

Fundamentally it was a labor problem—a vital, human problem. Every human being, I have always believed, has an intrinsic worth of his own as an individual. That is the Christian concept and, in so far as democracy has any validity as a way of life and not a mere shibboleth, it is the democratic concept. If the extra players, despite the fact that many of them might more wisely have chosen other occupations, found themselves in the category of a mere commodity, I wanted to know about it and I wanted to do something about it. Accordingly, I asked the Russell Sage Foundation to make a survey of the industry, especially with regard to the extra player. The Foundation sent one of its most brilliant and experienced investigators, Miss Mary Van Kleeck, to Hollywood.

Meanwhile, our two allied associations—MPPDA and MPPA—had been concerning themselves with other types of welfare for the industry's employees. In February of 1925 we had effected a permanent organization for a Y.W.C.A. "Studio Club" for young women in motion picture work, and this included not only established actresses and starlets, but office clerks, readers, and secretaries. This fine residence is located in the very heart of Hollywood, on a quiet street in a respectable neighborhood.

At the same time, in concert with the Board of Education, we made plans for the schooling of children employed in studios. No one in pictures works all the time, and for the most part these children have always attended their own district or parochial school, but up to that time there had been an interruption in their education whenever they were called on the sets. We solved this by providing for a schoolroom in every studio with a full-time teacher, appointed by the Board of Education but paid by the studio. There is one particular rule from which we expected trouble, and that is that no child whose grades do not come up to a certain standard may appear on the set, even of his current production. It may seem incredible, but in the quarter of a century since the establishment of these schools (which John Ford persists in calling "hedge schools") there have been very few such disputes, and none of them serious. The penalty for the child actor who gets low marks is exclusion from the set. It has worked like a charm!

Miss Van Kleeck's investigations were made in co-operation with the State Industrial Welfare Commission, which generously appointed Dr. Louis Bloch to co-operate with her. The gist of her report, submitted through State Labor Commissioner Walter G. Mathewson, was that the extra player was being exploited shamefully, not so much by the studios as by the employment agencies which furnished this live "commodity" to the sets. For this service, which in many cases amounted to no service at all, since the extra hustled his own job anyhow, the agency would charge a commission, generally 7 or 8 per cent. The agency was able to do this because the extra was not paid in cash at the end of the day, but by a voucher at the agency. The best remedy seemed to be the establishment of some kind of free employment facility, eliminating the agents altogether.

At precisely the same time, another factor appeared which determined us to "decasualize," as Miss Van Kleeck had put it, our extra help. This was the bad publicity the industry was beginning to derive from irresponsible persons and even criminals who, upon being apprehended, claimed to be actors and actresses, even if only extras. It was impossible to prove that they were not. I think that one of the many good incidental features of the Central Casting Bureau was the establishment, long before Social Security, of records of employment.

A little later, too, Fred Beetson, first president of the Central Casting Corporation, arranged with the Los Angeles police to notify his office whenever thieves, pickpockets, or ladies of easy virtue claimed to be extras. By that time it had become possible to find out in a very few minutes if the miscreants were really registrants. Generally, they were not—or if they were, they soon ceased permanently to be registrants. And there were other abuses which the investigation brought to light, including at least half a dozen methods of graft.

Although we became aware of many evils, applying the obvious remedy was more difficult than might be supposed. Unlike most industries confronted with simpler problems of "decasualization," we were up against a vast multitude of people who had daydreamed and wish-thought themselves into believing that they were potential stars. It was like trying to "decasualize" a gold rush. And there could be no such thing as seniority, for example, among people who were hired on a basis of appearance or type. So in 1925 there were at least thirty thousand extras, or persons who called themselves such, for maybe a thousand jobs. Incidentally, that is a liberal average for daily extras' jobs, even in boom times.

In August of 1925 the Board of Directors of the West Coast Association unanimously approved forming a non-profit corporation with capital stock of $30,000. Of this sum, I believe 60 per cent was subscribed by First National, Metro-Goldwyn-Mayer, Universal, and Fox, and the remaining 40 per cent by the other studio corporations. I have estimated that in the early days it cost the producers $110,000 per year to run Central Casting; but it saved the extra people $1,000,000 in commissions. This meant something when one considers that the daily earning of an extra in those days was $3.20, plus a box lunch, and I fear that some of the agencies would have taken part of the lunch, had there been a way to do it.

On January 19, 1926, I had the pleasure of being present at the foundation of the corporation: Central Casting Corporation. Fred Beetson, whom I had sent out earlier as my personal representative and who was at this time a vice-president of the MPPA, became the first president of Central Casting. I wish to emphasize that although the Central Casting Corporation was created as a result of investigations I had suggested, it has never been a part of our Association. It is more closely related to the MPPA, or West Coast Association. I was at most a kind of godfather. The corporation operates through and controls the Central Casting Bureau, which has a general manager and bureau personnel.

At about that time I took the opportunity to warn the public against various and sundry fake "movie schools" and "scenario-writing schools" which pretended to be able to secure jobs in studios for their successful "graduates." The industry has always refused to endorse any school pretending to train people to be extras. This is not to say that there are not a number of reputable talent schools, or that the producers do not wish the extras to attend them. But schools purporting to train extras, as such, are manifestly rackets, for the simple reason that an extra needs no preliminary training. And right here the distinction should be pointed out between an extra and an actor. The extra is not an apprentice or a kind of junior-grade actor who may, simply because he is an extra, aspire to better roles. Unlike Napoleon's recruit, he carries no marshal's baton in his knapsack. It is notable that of the seventy thousand or so people who have been extras at one time or another, not more than a dozen have risen to stardom. This tiny group—composed of the exceptions which prove the rule—deserves the greatest credit. It includes Erich von Stroheim, Jean Arthur, the late Jean Harlow, Charles Farrell, Janet

Gaynor, Dennis O'Keefe, Richard Arlen, and Gilbert Roland. A few others served as extras for a brief time early in their careers—such as Clark Gable, Joel McCrea, Walter Brennan, and Gary Cooper. Gary, I believe, was a "Western" extra and, as such, belonged to a category of which a certain amount of experience and skill is required. For special talents, such as horsemanship or chorus singing and dancing, there are special rates of pay and a slightly better chance of advancement.

The functioning of the Central Casting Bureau began on March 27, 1926, a year to the day from our receipt of Commissioner Mathewson's report based on Miss Van Kleeck's survey. The chief feature of the Bureau's operation was the method of paying the extra in cash, or with a negotiable check, in exchange for a Bureau voucher—and this regardless of whether the extra had been hired through the Bureau or directly by the studio. All placements were free. The studios, in effect, paid the commissions. We were glad to find that nearly all opportunities for graft had been automatically eliminated.

The one thing we could not eliminate, and have never been able to, was the problem of too many people for too few jobs.

The first general manager and chief casting director of the Bureau was Dave Allen, later to become head of the Special Effects Department at Columbia Studios. Allen had founded the Screen Service Bureau, which had been one of the more reputable of the employment agencies for extras. Because of this and because he had been an extra himself, he understood and sympathized with the extra player's problem. He was given charge of the office and helped to install the first system of really fair and equitable employment that this class of labor had ever known. First he sold his own agency to the corporation for one dollar.

No doubt many instances of favoritism, nepotism, and outright impropriety had occurred in the early days, but the operational methods of the Bureau rendered such practices all but archaic. From the very beginning the Bureau has employed two trained interviewers of impeccable reputation, a man for the male registrants and a woman for the distaff side. As far as Central Casting is concerned, therefore, the uglier possibilities of employment exploitation were early eliminated.

But Allen was accused falsely of favoring his friends. In those days, and even since, the extra legions have contained not only steady and dependable troupers, but many irrepressible and irresponsible characters who have never learned to discipline their emotions. Some years before, during the filming of The Sea-Hawk, starring Milton Sills, Allen had had all his teeth knocked out by a disgruntled extra who had appeared as a pirate in the picture. On another occasion a cowboy extra, standing six feet four inches and weighing about two hundred and fifty pounds, broke into the inner sanctum and menaced Fred Beetson, Dave Allen, and their assistant, Gus Dembling, with a .44. By dint of fast talking, they succeeded in getting the gun away from him. When the man broke down, it was discovered that he was literally starving. The boys kept his gun but loaned him enough money to get a fresh start. In a few weeks he had paid back the money, and I am happy to say that he is working today as an extra and is a respected member of the community.

Such incidents were part of the daily routine of the early casting directors at Central, and during Fred Beetson's term as president there occurred one bomb plot, revealed by an extra named Major Cavell, who notified both Beetson and the police; the planting on the premises of another homemade bomb; one attempted extortion, when an eastern gangster appeared in Beetson's office and offered to protect for a price "all the stars in Hollywood" from kidnaping (he was arrested while in the office); and one major case of malicious mischief, when an anonymous extra sent a hearse from an estimable local firm of undertakers to pick up the body of a casting director, who was in the men's room when the attendants arrived. This, of course, does not include the thousands of threatening notes and "nut letters," nor the many occasions when extras, with real or fancied grievances, suddenly hauled off and punched the Bureau's executives in the jaw. Allen continued with the Bureau for about ten years, giving fine if hazardous service, and was succeeded by Campbell MacCulloch, who had formerly been an executive at the Metro-Goldwyn-Mayer Studios. Since 1940 the Bureau has been in the capable hands of Mr. Howard R. Philbrick.

The Bureau offices open at six o'clock each weekday morning and stay open until far into the night. Registered extras desirous of work are advised to telephone once an hour during the day until about 3 P.M., after which they may call every fifteen minutes to see if there will be a job available the following day. The reason for the increased activity in the late afternoon is that this is the time, as a rule, when directors and unit managers determine their next day's requirements. In the early days the great volume of telephone calls swamped and all but wrecked the Hollywood Central Exchange. The telephone company thereupon assigned the Bureau an exchange all its own. Today the Bureau's switchboard is equipped to handle four thousand calls per hour, and this is second only to the capacity of the switchboard in the Pentagon Building in Washington.

Provision is made for the studios to engage some extras by request, but this must now be done through the Bureau. When a job aspirant calls in, he or she is given one of six replies by the operators. The first is, "Hold the line." The operator then calls the applicant's name over a loud-speaker to the casting directors, who know just what the studios' requirements are for that particular day. It might be supposed that valuable minutes would be consumed while the casting directors consult the files to see if the caller is the kind of extra needed. But that would be to underestimate the trained memories of these experts. They actually manage to carry the identities and descriptions of four thousand registered people in their minds. Not only do they know if "Joe Doakes," waiting on the line, is the type, but in most cases they can tell you off-hand his hat size.

The second signal is, "Try later," which indicates that a job may break. The third is, "No work," which is all too frequent and all too clear. The other responses are "Men only," if, for example, the sole requirement that day is for a Civil War battle scene, or "Women only," if the location is a beauty parlor or a girls' college. The fifth is, "Call Station M," and this means that the studio has requested that particular extra, but he must now call back to a special station in order to have his hiring confirmed.

The wage scales for extras have varied and, in the course of time, greatly increased. In conformity with increased living costs, the latest daily wage scale I noted was as follows:

Atmosphere people	$ 9.45
"Stand-ins"	13.90
Ordinary extras	15.56
Dress extras	22.23

Once again, it appears, the "soup-and-fish" has come into its own!

There is one service that Central Casting renders actors higher in the scheme of things than extras; it is the Call Bureau. This department keeps a record, for ready consultation by prospective employers, of all players, whether under contract or not, whether currently working or not. In this way any actor, or at least his personal agent, can be located by any producer who may wish to offer him a part—or, if he is under contract or is working at the time, the Call Bureau furnishes this information. This is a boon to players and producers alike, and an actor need never miss a job because the producer does not know where to find him. Established in 1929, the Call Bureau is an example of inter-studio co-operation that would not have been dreamed of in the anarchic, warring-clan period when I first entered the industry.

The extra's livelihood is still precarious. In a recent year the total number of registrants was 3,853. These earned $1,031,784 for that year. A little long division will show that the average annual income for the extras was about $267.78. Few earned more than $1,000.

Problems still remain, and I suppose they will as long as the human race inhabits the earth. I am satisfied that the industry has done every conceivable thing to protect the extra and to make his lot in life more agreeable, but the economic law that motion picture leaders call the "cockeyed equation"—too many people for too few jobs—is still in full force.

Next to the evolution of the Production Code, I believe I am prouder of the Central Casting Bureau than of anything else that was accomplished in my quarter-century administration as director general, or democratic "czar," or "cat's whiskers" of the industry. While I helped to create it, however, I did not build it brick by brock, nor schematize its operations day by day; and the credit for this belongs to the men who devoted days and nights, labor and ingenuity, to doing so. To them, and to the studios which have maintained the Bureau, I doff my Sunday hat.

I am proud, too, that our industry entered this field so early, thus anticipating the national trend of putting security into occupations. Past the experimental stage—by a good two decades—the Central Casting Bureau is a Hollywood institution and a monument to the enlightened sentiments of the industry as a whole.

The many-phased expanding service of the films in the early years of the Association was of course due as much to improved quality as to greater recognition of possible uses. Aiding this quality improvement was the fact that much valuable European experience became ours through the importation of able directors, actors, and technicians. I always encouraged this trend, because it made our films still more international.

Although steady progress was being made, and although American films had already won the highest awards at the International Exhibition of Optical and Cinematographical Photography, complaints about the character of current pictures continued to bombard my office—and not all from reformers or crackpots. Though we had a long way to go, I thought that overemphasis on destructive criticism was doing no good. It seemed to me that we had had enough talk, for the moment, of the "who-put-the-sin-in-cinema" variety. So before press associations and chambers of commerce and women's clubs—wherever good opportunity offered—I began to take the theme, "What's RIGHT with the Movies?" I reported what I firmly believed to be true: that the movie industry was in splendid condition, with sound business methods prevailing, harmony in the ranks of the Association, and ever-increasing artistry in the pictures themselves. I assured my hearers that any really fine motion picture, no matter by whom produced, was bound to have proper distribution, exhibition, and appreciation. I argued for the freedom of the screen, censored only by the good taste of the American public, and I explained the methods that producers had begun to set up in recognition of standards of decency and good taste. In appealing for constructive co-operation rather than destructive criticism, I always said in effect, "This is not the job of one group, it is the multitude's job. In doing it, there is work for all—for you as definitely as for the producers." The response to this appeal was a big factor in getting better pictures.

Recognition of this progress on the part of outsiders again confirmed me in the belief that we were on the right road. The *Exhibitors' Daily Review,* in an issue of March 20, 1926, giving its whole issue to the Association and its whole back page to pictures of eighteen of our leading staff members, ran as a banner headline—INDUSTRIAL HARMONY GREETS FOURTH MILESTONE OF HAYS ASSOCIATION—and a full-page editorial under the caption, "Picture Business Has Made Real Progress." The editor echoed my own appeal in his words: "A mighty change has taken place in four years. Don't hold back in your co-operation with Will Hays in the next four years, for far greater progress must be made."

On the excellent theory that the proof of the pudding is in the eating, I want to mention a few of the great pictures and fine actors that made these last years of the silent era notable. Some of these pictures have never been surpassed in appeal and quality.

Taking the years 1923 to 1926, and analyzing the "Ten Best Pictures" of each year, I find that of the thirty-six stars listed, the names of Douglas Fairbanks and John Gilbert appear four times each; Lon Chaney and Harold Lloyd, three times; John Barrymore, Monte Blue, Rene Adoree, and Emil Jannings, twice. The list is studded with memorable names. With many of these fine actors, like Milton Sills, for whose child I served as godfather, I formed deep and sincere friendships. The same can be said of directors like Cecil B. De Mille, D. W. Griffith, Rupert Hughes, and Fred Niblo. And this was the era of the first big budgets—*The Covered Wagon* at $800,000, and *The Ten Commandments* at $1,600,000.

Of the pictures themselves, it would be easy to rhapsodize. It is an astounding list, considering that color was in its infancy and sound not yet born. But these products of the true dramatic techniques of the silent film, devoted in many cases to themes of imperishable value, demonstrate better than any words of mine the inspiring progress our industry was making. It is only fair to say of the Association—whose members produced the majority of these pictures—that its ideals and its efforts contributed substantially to the excellence of the results reflected in the following list.

TEN BEST PICTURES OF THE YEARS 1923 TO 1926

1923
The Covered Wagon
Merry-Go-Round
The Hunchback of Notre Dame
Robin Hood
The Green Goddess
Scaramouche
Safety Last
Rosita
Down to the Sea in Ships
Little Old New York

1924
The Thief of Bagdad
The Sea-Hawk
Monsieur Beaucaire
Beau Brummell
Secrets

1924

The Marriage Circle
The Ten Commandments
Girl Shy
Abraham Lincoln
America

1925

The Gold Rush
The Unholy Three
Don Q, Son of Zorro
Merry Widow
The Last Laugh
The Freshman
The Phantom of the Opera

Lost World
The Big Parade
Kiss Me Again

1926

Variety
Ben Hur
The Big Parade
Black Pirate
Beau Geste
Stella Dallas
The Volga Boatman
What Price Glory
The Sea Beast
La Boheme

CHAPTER 27

Sound Arrives (August 6, 1926–June 6, 1930)

I N the span of just a little over three years the motion picture felt the impact of two major revolutions: the coming of sound in 1926 and the Great Depression in 1929. Well-nigh punch-drunk by this smashing "one-two," the industry began to find its balance in the NRA codes of 1930, weathered the lean years, cleared its head through its own Production Code Administration set up in 1934, and went on to unparalleled achievement. I had been elected the industry's number one "trouble-shooter," and for troubles per day, this period took the prize.

The spring of 1926 found the American motion picture industry happily absorbed in its world mission of entertainment and mass education. Its films, though silent, were full of action, humor, appeal. Then came the world-shaking discovery: motion pictures could also speak, if equipped with the newfangled electrical mechanisms. It was like a ship in need of drastic overhauling which could not take even one day off to go into port; it must stay at sea, on active duty, yet somehow install a new set of engines and an entirely new communication system while keeping under full steam. It was an almost impossible prospect.

Worst of all, there were no blueprints for the overhauling and no guarantee of results. How could anyone be sure that the public would permanently prefer the "talkie" to the "silent"? Some of the most experienced men, such as Edison, did not believe people would like the new product as well as they evidently liked the old. Silent motion pictures had reached an unchallenged peak in popularity. A hundred million people each week crowded into twenty thousand American theatres. Eight hundred feature pictures a year were being produced for a public that seemed insatiable.

On the warm summer night of August 6, 1926, when the screen first spoke to a public audience, all marveled; but we were still unsure. The four Warner brothers, who had brought this new wonder to the screen, were holding their breaths. And I knew that for the electric companies which had spent heavily on experimentation, even facing stockholders' suits because of it, this night was a showdown too. Earlier attempts had fizzled. Had a new art form finally come into being?

I want to pay my tribute to Sam Warner, the first producer to act on the reports coming out of the Western Electric Company's Bell Laboratories. Others waited to see. But to Sam, sound with pictures made an instant appeal. He had always liked mechanical devices. To the Bell Laboratories he came, saw, and was conquered by the new synchronized talking device. He went to work on his brothers. It was not easy, because sad stories were told about producers who had dabbled in sound. But he succeeded in persuading Harry, the president of their company, to attend a demonstration. That did it. Convinced, Harry was ready to put all their resources behind the improved talking device, staking everything on one high throw. In April of 1926 the Western Electric Company licensed Warner Brothers to produce talking pictures under its patents. Of the two available methods, disk and sound track, the Warners chose the disk, giving it the name "Vitaphone," and making their first experiments in the old Vitagraph Studio in Flatbush, Brooklyn.

About this time Harry telephoned me concerning plans for the première to be held at their own theatre at Broadway and Fifty-second Street in New York City, the only theatre in the world then equipped for Vitaphone. As the feature they were to present John Barrymore's latest picture, *Don Juan,* which they were just completing. Though not a "talking picture," the New York Philharmonic Orchestra, under the direction of Henry Hadley, had made a synchronized musical accompaniment. In addition, Harry told me, they had decided to present half a dozen Vitaphone short subjects as a prelude to the feature picture, and he wanted me to speak from the screen on behalf of the industry. A few days later I went with Mr. Warner to the Manhattan Opera House, where recording equipment was set up. Because it was not only my first experience but the first speech ever recorded for talking pictures, I remember every detail.

My 325-word speech was ready by afternoon and sent over for okay. At dinnertime I rehearsed it. Wanting to guard against any possible slip-up, I telephoned Kirk Russell of our own staff and asked him if within two hours he could copy the speech in inch-high letters on big cards so that it could stand on two easels where I could see it while speaking. This he did. In the recording room that evening I stood in front of a microphone and camera and said my piece—with gestures. Just twenty years later, in 1946, that same record was replayed in Warner Brothers' theatres as a reminder of the talkies' birth!

The Vitaphone première passed off without accident, but it didn't set the world on fire. I went over to the theatre with Walter Gifford of Western Electric, who was as concerned as I because, as president of the A.T. & T., he had approved putting money into the venture.

The invited guests included, among numerous others, Otto Kahn, the first financier to recognize movies as a safe field of investment; Mme.

Galli-Curci, Anna Case, Marion Talley, Elsie Janis, Hope Hampton and her husband Jules Brulatour, Mischa Elman, Efrem Zimbalist and Alma Gluck, his wife, Harold Bauer, and Henry W. Savage, who had done so much for grand opera in English. Adolph Zukor was down in front, and afterward we heard that he said: "It's a fad, it won't last." This naturally disturbed Walter Gifford, because Mr. Zukor's judgment carried such weight.

The orchestral accompaniment of the feature picture was surprisingly effective; and the singing of Martinelli, Anna Case, and Marion Talley, as well as the playing of Elman, Zimbalist, and Bauer, aroused genuine enthusiasm in the audience. As Earl Sponable, familiar with the development of sound pictures, described the performance: "It received favorable comment from some papers, enthusiastic comment from others, and grave doubts from the industry that talking pictures would ever be commercial." The invention which "synchronized voice and music with screen actors' actions" was reported as the "latest scientific wonder," and the significant statement was made in a UP dispatch that "the world's great singers, musicians, symphony orchestras, and speakers have been brought within reach of every town in the United States where there is a movie house." But it took years and a lot of headaches to fulfill that promise.

In my screen talk, which served as a tribute to the industry's influence and to the Warners' achievement, I hailed the occasion as the beginning of a new era in music and motion pictures, adding that "the motion picture is a most potent factor in the development of national appreciation of good music. Now neither the artist nor his art will ever wholly die." This meaning for the whole country caught the attention of the press. Within two weeks a Dallas newspaper, in a long story headed "Talking Moving Pictures Arouse Interest Throughout Country," commented prophetically, "Nothing has happened in New York this summer which is more important for Dallas than the opening of the New Warner Motion Picture Theatre. It means that before long the greatest artists will be available to the remotest village, in a form so lifelike that the very personality of the artist seems to be present, and it is easier than not to believe he is actually before you."

Today such comments are now much less interesting than those of the contemporary prophets of doom who saw neither virtue nor reason in combining words and moving pictures. "Synchronization of Voices with Screen Pantomime Will Harm Them" was the heading of an article by George Jean Nathan a few days after the first Vitaphone showing. Of it, he wrote, "It will bring to the motion picture exactly the thing that the motion picture should have no use for, to wit, the human voice; and further, once it brings it, the motion picture will have a tough time holding its own." Mr. Nathan, as a dramatic critic, considered that the actors who appeared in the movies, even the best of them, were "pantomimists rather than dramatic performers," and that "any effort to make them articulate would be not only paradoxical and absurd but utterly futile. To expect a pantomimist, talented though he be, to be the possessor of a vocal organ capable of expressing all the shadings of dramatic speech is surely expecting a lot."

Strange as this may sound today when numbers of the finest actors move easily back and forth from stage to screen, starring in both roles, many people felt the same way. One of the trade papers had stated only a few weeks before the Vitaphone première, "Americans require a restful quiet in the motion picture theatre, and for them talking from the lips of the figures on the screen destroys the illusion." At first there was probably more curiosity than genuine enjoyment.

We watched eagerly for signs. Technical problems had to be solved and actors had to learn the ropes before smooth results were secured. That took from two to three years. During the change-over many plans and notions had to be amended, many hearts were broken, and many pocketbooks went flat. Beloved stars faded out. Such stories came to me constantly, and I was often besought to do something about it. But with national prosperity at its height, the huge added costs were somehow absorbed and the change was accomplished.

Meanwhile I knew that William Fox had been encouraging two young inventors, Theodore W. Case and Earl J. Sponable, who for years had been working on a sound-on-film method. Interrupted by the war, their efforts in infra-red light rays had helped our convoys control their ship positions. By 1926 they were sure enough of their sound-film process to show the results to Mr. Fox, who gladly financed further experiments. In August the Fox Case Corporation was organized and my helpful colleague, Courtland Smith, MPPDA secretary, was made head of the organization. The name they chose for their device was "Movietone." The company first turned its attention to the development of talking newsreels and then to Movietone short subjects.

Movietone was first publicly demonstrated in January 1927 at the première of the Fox feature, *What Price Glory*. The first all-Movietone program was presented in May and included *Seventh Heaven*, a silent film with synchronized music, Raquel Meller, the Spanish singer, Chic Sale, Ben Bernie's orchestra, and Gertrude Lawrence in a song she had introduced with great success in the first *Charlot's Revue*.

Still more striking, because destined to go down in aviation history, was the newsreel showing the take-off of a tall young man named Lindbergh on his Paris flight. New York audiences heard the whir and roar of the airplane's motor, listened to the shouts of farewell, to the gasps of the onlookers as the plane hesitated, skipped, and then leaped from the ground into the mist of that early morning. Within twenty-four hours millions wanted to see and hear his daring take-off. The Movietone record was a sensation.

The big questions kept repeating themselves, each bearing on the others. How good would the reproduction of sound be? Would people prefer it, or even want it? Would films for abroad have to be done in the various foreign languages? Would the present stars last? Would talkies be entitled to the same degree of free speech as the stage and the novel? What kinds of subjects and stories would be best for the talkies? Would it be hard to control the language used, and how much trouble might actors cause by ad libbing? How much more would talkies cost to produce, and would audiences pay the higher admissions? How long would it take electrical manufacturers to supply equipment, and could the smaller theatres afford to install it? Could silents and talkies thrive side by side? No one of these was merely an academic question; every one of them had to be answered. They were so well answered that the "Ten Best" pictures of 1929 were all talkies, which was a great tribute to the nerve and resourcefulness of the men who pioneered sound movies.

And now these developments threw into the lap of the MPPDA some of the knottiest problems we ever faced. Most of all, would talking pictures be entitled to the same degree of "free speech" as the stage and the novel? If not, could they be self-regulated? As to American pictures shipped abroad: would they have to be done all over again in various foreign languages? All these became, and still remain, major questions.

The Association served as a busy clearinghouse on all such matters. For instance, early in 1927 the so-called "Big Five" companies agreed to stand together for the purpose of determining the best sound system, using the facilities of the Hays Office for this investigation.

The turning point in the coming of sound was the release of the Warner Brothers' picture, *The Jazz Singer*, starring Al Jolson. This had been set for October 6, 1927, fourteen months after the appearance of Vitaphone, but was postponed by the illness of Sam Warner. The story was based on the theme "The Show Must Go On," tragically fitting the fact that the brothers were all in California and that Sam had just died when the première took place. It was a startling success; the industry was convinced. From that evening, sound became the imperative element in production. By the end of 1927 one hundred and fifty-seven theatres were equipped for sound, of which fifty-five included film units rather than the disk device. When the "Big Five" signed contracts with Electrical Research Products, Inc., the Western Electric Company's unit formed to develop sound pictures, their general use was ensured. Our new goal was set, and our program had to be re-formed accordingly.

During this development period the industry gained a growing sense of cohesion. By the fall of 1929—the year of the first general production of successful "talkies"—sixty studios had recording apparatus and more than five thousand theatres in this country had reproducing equipment. Late in 1928 the Los Angeles première of Paramount's first all-talking picture, *Interference,* starring Doris Kenyon, Evelyn Brent, William Powell, and Clive Brook, was greeted with tremendous enthusiasm. I remember it particularly because not long before I had stood up as god-father to a fine baby boy, Kenyon Clarence, son of Mr. and Mrs. Milton Sills.

With the technical problems pretty well solved and a form of standard release print which was satisfactory, competition became keener than ever. Sound was estimated to have added ten million weekly patrons during 1929. We were glad of that; but the new fields of dramatic material opened up for the screen made the job of self-regulation in Hollywood much harder. The effect of the spoken word was so much more pointed than mere screen action that an entirely new problem arose. Earlier regulations proved inadequate. It was this new factor which gave censors new arguments and made the Production Code of 1930 so necessary.

Early in 1929 Max Reinhardt, while engaged in making his first motion picture, came out with the dictum that "the talking picture is a new art form in itself and will replace neither the stage nor the silent picture." He believed that the talking picture had brought to the drama that "absolute silence" that is the dream of every true actor, and that it "makes possible concentration that is unattainable in any other medium of stagecraft." It was this conviction of the screen's extraordinary power that drove me constantly to see that its power was not misused, but poured into every proper channel.

Nineteen twenty-nine was certainly the "change-over" year. I remember that early that year Universal made a statistical test by running a picture entitled *Broadway,* in both silent and sound versions, at two different theatres on Broadway at the same time. It was already evident that the public had made its decision—never reversed. They wanted pictures to talk.

I know that what concerned me most was the danger of a new wave of censorship. I told the producers that the industry must stoutly resist any attempts to censor speech from the screen, and that the best defense was the renewed determination to make pictures of such quality that no reasonable person could claim any need for censorship. And I emphasized that this attitude should be maintained not only for the good of the industry itself but in defense of the whole right of free speech.

The high cost of installing sound equipment, added to film rentals, worked a terrible hardship on managers and owners of at least fourteen hundred small theatres. We all recognized this essential injustice. After considerable discussion twelve producing companies agreed to reduce film rental prices to small independent exhibitors wherever the exhibitor could show justifiable reason, even though this meant a readjustment of existing contracts. An exhibitors' committee had appealed to me for help, and I was able to arrange conferences in New York between exhibitors and producers which received such newspaper headlines as "Hays Intervention Saves Independent Exhibitors from Sound Film Troubles." It was a good example of the way our Association could mediate. One leading New York paper commented: "It is probably the first time in the history of business that vendors have afforded so great a group of purchasers the opportunity of negotiating the payment for merchandise in proportion to the capacity to pay rather than in strict adherence to the agreed price. The legality of the contracts was unquestioned, but it was disregarded."

Compared with the revolution caused by sound, the adding of color was gradual and relatively simple. Flowering at almost the same time, however, color played its part in giving the talking film its tremendous appeal. Many producers did not at first believe in color. In the Association office we came to the conclusion that this question, like others, would be decided by the public: if they demanded it and were willing to pay for it, more and more pictures would be in color. We kept channeling public opinion to the industry.

Although the first Academy Award for color photography was not given until 1939, for *Gone with the Wind*, the public interest was considerable by 1926, keenly aroused by Douglas Fairbanks' picture, *The Black Pirate*, photographed off Catalina Island.

From 1926 to 1930, our chief problems seemed to fall into three divisions: moral; artistic and technical; financial and legal.

The fight against filth kept us busy. The sensationalism of the printed page was bound to work its way into movie scripts. It was "the style." The technique of the talkie made it easy to slip in things that parents wanted kept out. Better ways of checking on both production and advertising, soon to be represented by the Codes of 1930, had to be worked out. The dozens of ways of injecting sex into films led to a veritable game of hide-and-seek, in which we tried our best to keep producers advised on the cutting out of unfit words or scenes before they reached the screen. Some billboards displayed copy and pictures that would not for a moment pass today. One of the most amazing of the many demands directed at the industry, reported by *Variety* in 1927, was by atheists, who requested that God be kept out of films! I replied, "God is everywhere."

The influence of movies on conduct, particularly the question of their effect on juvenile delinquency and crime, was debated endlessly. It has always seemed to me a question of interpretation rather than of statistics. Nineteen twenty-nine happened to be the year in which an unusually definite charge was made by a statistician of national prominence, Roger W. Babson, who said: "Such studies as I have made lead directly to the movies as the basic cause of the crime wave of today." One interesting statement in his report was based on answers to a questionnaire sent to the school principals of New England. Asked whether the school, the church, or the home "had the greatest influence in molding the character of our young people today," 70 per cent scratched off all three and wrote in, "The movies."

This charge received so much notice that I felt we ought to answer it. As a result, Governor Milliken, secretary of the Association, replied to Mr. Babson in a long letter illustrated by statistics and judgments of others and also by a cartoon. This drawing showed an angry father, with a double-barreled shotgun, dashing out of his front door and saying, "I'm going to track down the real cause of my children's ill conduct." In the second scene, after a wandering course through the nearby woods, the tracks bring the astounded father back to his own house, marked with the legend, "Neglected Home Training." From opinions in the press, our reply seemed to carry considerable conviction and to clear the movies of any primary responsibility for crime. But we kept our eyes and ears open.

The new production problems connected with sound were keeping me on the jump. Two striking evidences of the expansion were the big new theatres rising across the country and the almost incredible statement, resulting from a survey, that "one in every four persons attends movies daily." The movies were already carrying most of the amusement load. Recognizing these growing needs, the Association had established a Theatre Service Department to assist exhibitors.

The mention of producers and exhibitors reminds me of my long-time friend, Joseph P. Kennedy, and his article of 1927 entitled "Why Blame the Producer?" Explaining the intangible factors which enter into every production, he concluded: "There is no formula for success in motion pictures. They do not lend themselves to standardization. They are produced by human beings whose ideas of humor, tragedy, and drama vary." And he showed that public taste is just as hard to gauge. Paying a compliment to Cecil B. De Mille for harmonizing so well the advice of Catholics, Protestants, and Jews in the production of The King of Kings, he stated the producer's goal quite simply: "We must make pictures that have appeal to all."

This was the period when showmanship in the motion picture theatre rose to new heights under S. L. Rothafel—the one and only "Roxy"—and those who followed in his footsteps. I remember his saying, "Good will and good pictures are our two great assets." Exhibitors of his type were among our strongest supporters. At our national Public Relations Conference of 1929, Roxy said to the luncheon guests: "I believe the greatest thing any exhibitor can do in his community is to make and keep his theatre clean physically and morally."

Realizing that motion picture audiences have all sorts of tastes, I always urged making pictures of many types. Sound and color both helped. Fantasy, epic, true drama, comedy, musical extravaganza, travelogue with narrative, documentary, historical biography, all now developed more distinctive characteristics. This trend brought other developments which interested me. Internationally famous authors, like W. J. Locke and P. G. Wodehouse, settled in Hollywood for periods to write original stories for the screen. The competition for good stories, of which there were never enough, further boosted production costs.

This was also the period when great public institutions woke up to the importance of establishing motion picture archives—a recognition that certain films are documents of permanent value. It was my privilege to discuss this repeatedly with President Coolidge and President Hoover. In May of 1930 we reported that President Hoover and the industry were appointing committees to assure "permanent preservation of the motion picture records of historical events." In addition to private collections and newsreel files, important archives were established by Harvard University, the New York Museum of Modern Art, the D.A.R., the great New York City Library, and a number of state libraries. In many cases I was able to arrange for more generous, practical co-operation by the member companies than the public ever discovered.

The artistic ideals and achievements of professional motion picture people had, in 1927, voluntarily crystallized in the Academy of Motion Picture Arts and Sciences. While this organization remained independent of our Association, I watched its development with the keenest interest, and I always felt that the Academy Awards Dinner—in which I have often participated—was a dramatic demonstration of industry goals.

The industry was able to solve financial problems, between itself and the public, even through the depression, because people kept flocking to the theatres. The added equipment and production costs were absorbed, and the companies continued to supply films gratis where needed. And the American motion picture was aiding American business in general. In addressing groups like the New York Board of Trade, I emphasized motion pictures as a business of vast proportions and influence, as in fact "a world salesman," which was another reason why the character of the product should present America favorably. Repeatedly I pointed out that there was an increased spiral of demand, at home and abroad, for American-manufactured products, and motion pictures were a major factor in creating that demand. Trade followed the film. A well-known writer had said that "American pictures abroad are doing for American business the work of 100,000 salesmen," and I supplemented this by quoting a British authority as saying: "The cinema is the greatest advertising power in the world. . . . Motion pictures are influencing fashions, behavior, dress, housing. People everywhere are deliberately going to the cinema as to an animated catalogue to get ideas."

But the legal questions were not so easily solved, for government sought to take things into its own hands and interpret the industry in its own terms. When we began to realize where censorship might lead if boards presumed to censor speech, even in newsreels, we had a new problem.

With the improvement in the quality of pictures, with increased motion picture attendance, and with the clearer distinction between first-run and later-run theatres, more complicated problems of distribution and exhibition developed.

As I have already noted, two legal provisions recently adopted by the industry amply justified themselves: the uniform exhibition contract, and arbitration. As Gabriel Hess, MPPDA counsel, explained to the Public Relations Conference of 1929, the exhibition contract, which I had encouraged in 1923, was a mutual one both in origin and operation. "For the first time to my knowledge," he said, "an industry in this country—buyer and seller—sat down and agreed upon the terms of future contracts." Endless misunderstandings between distributor and exhibitor were thus avoided.

Where a difference of opinion persisted, there was a provision that the dispute be settled by arbitration. The American Arbitration Association, which co-operated with us fully, gives the motion picture industry credit for having made real contributions in this field. In her volume, *American Arbitration,* Miss Frances Kellor, first vice-president of the association, noted that our industry was the first to adopt arbitration. Chronologically, she begins with the 1920 enactment of the first modern arbitration law by New York State, and she records that "in 1923 Will H. Hays, soon to become a Director of the Society, established an arbitration system in the Film Boards of Trade for the motion picture industry"; and not until 1926 was the organization of the American Arbitration Association accomplished. Miss Kellor also devotes a whole chapter to "Practice under the Motion Picture Consent Decree" of 1940, which she notes "made arbitration history."

Our methods of arbitration, which in 1926 had been praised by the Department of Justice, had been fully discussed and approved at the Trade Practice Conference held in October 1927, and we continued to urge their use. In November we sent out a memorandum of recommendations for procedure based on suggestions of the American Arbitration Association.

In the spring of 1928 the best legal opinion we could secure—from Cadwalader, Wickersham & Taft—welcomed the opportunity to test the legality of the arbitration plan administered through the Film Boards of Trade scattered throughout the country. On April 27 a "friendly suit" was filed in Federal Court by the Department of Justice, charging the ten leading film distributors and thirty-two Film Boards of Trade with conspiracy to violate the Sherman Anti-Trust Act.

Ironically, 1928 was our best year. In my annual report I said: "The arbitration system in our industry, which rather serves as a model for business groups, reached its maximum usefulness in 1928. During the year 23,869 controversies, involving $6,503,474.75, arose between exhibitors and distributors. Fifty-two per cent of these claims were settled between the time of filing and actual hearing by the arbitration boards. Only 28 claims required a seventh arbiter, and not a single claim was litigated before arbitration. In the five years since the institution of this system, 73,652 controversies, involving $17,724,380, have been disposed of. This achievement, unprecedented in the annals of [any other] industry, has more than an economic importance. It breathes the very spirit of ethical conduct in business."

In the fall of 1929 Judge Thomas D. Thacher, in the U. S. District Court of the Southern District of New York, rendered a paradoxical decision. In effect, he said that arbitration had been fairly administered for the benefit of every element in the industry and that it did not lessen competition, but that "competition between the distributors has been promoted by the adoption of the Standard Exhibition Contract and that in many ways general trade conditions have been vastly improved." As counsel commented: ". . . Judge Thacher in concluding his opinion suggests that the Government and the Industry indicate provisions to be incorporated in the *Decree* under which the use of a uniform contract containing an arbitration clause may be continued. Therefore, the Industry will undoubtedly proceed immediately to try to agree with the Government upon such practical changes as may be necessary to accomplish this result."

When on November 24, 1930, our case was finally reviewed in Washington, the Supreme Court rendered its decision declaring the arbitration provision invalid. Miss Kellor, in seeking to explain this decision, states that "in an endeavor to secure standard trade practices," exhibitors were required to accept the uniform contract, and that to facilitate arbitration the companies exchanged information on the credit position of the exhibitors. This concerted action, as she puts it, was considered by the Supreme Court to be "compulsory arbitration" and hence a violation of the anti-trust laws. The arbitration system of the Film Boards of Trade thus ended, and it took ten years to arrive at the 1940 Consent Decree. One cannot help reflecting on the extent to which the federal government itself, in various fields, had imposed "compulsory" action upon all its citizens before that year.

After the Supreme Court decision we felt as if a truck had run over us. It was the more surprising because of the solid feeling resulting from the Trade Practice Conference of October 1927, convoked by the Federal Trade Commission itself. At that conference, which had been called to air grievances and adopt some fair practices, the industry—including producers, distributors, and exhibitors—was fully represented. Of thirty-seven resolutions offered and discussed, twenty-six were unanimously adopted. So great was the sense of common interest that it was agreed that we should hold such conferences annually. The chief matter of radical disagreement was "block-booking." This common practice of selling in bulk, by which an exhibitor contracts to take certain "blocks," or groups, of pictures, was the distributor's method of doing business wholesale and thus greatly reducing the number of separate contracts needed.

Several things looking toward a "voluntary code of ethics" were accomplished in the conference. The "Don'ts" and "Be Carefuls" were adopted as Rule 21 of the Code of the Motion Picture Industry. This was a partial code of prohibitions, preceding the complete Code of 1930. A joint committee was formed to revise the uniform contract, which the commissioner stated to be a private agreement not concerning the FTC, and which was unanimously agreed to be a fair trade practice. I felt that material progress had been made in clearing up the industry's position on several matters not previously understood. The insertion of commercial advertising in motion picture productions leased to exhibitors as entertainment was ruled unfair, as I had consistently urged. The distributors announced the policy, in reference to block-booking, that any pictures which might be offensive locally by reason of any racial or religious content need not be shown.

Commenting afterward on the conference, Mr. R. H. Cochrane, chairman of the distributors' group, said: "We found out that real progress could be made. . . . We all found that we could work out some of the difficulties that most of us believed to be insurmountable." Thus we all felt, "So far, so good," and were encouraged both by the evidence of greater co-operation within the industry and by the attitude of general approval by the government.

As long as it was left to work out its own problems, our complex industry was making excellent progress: all three sides came out of the 1927 conference feeling good, and in this mood the industry worked ahead to perfect sound pictures. Our policies were shaping toward constructive working codes, and there were plenty of signs that we were making headway.

Motion pictures were doing another service by making our citizens more conscious of beauty and encouraging them to beautify their homes. They were proving an asset to community health, a means of recreation of benefit to millions of workers and their families. The Westinghouse "salute" of March 4, 1930, was given to the motion picture industry, "whose romance, whose activity, whose magic, has woven itself into the fabric of our lives and happiness, bringing us the blessings of truth and imagination."

One illustration of the way our self-governing Association was expanding was the addition in 1929 of new members representing the electrical industries. RCA Photophone, Inc., and John E. Otterson, president of Electrical Research Products, Inc., were both elected to membership. This meant that the leading forces in the sound picture field would be guided by the same co-operative, self-regulating policies developing within MPPDA since 1922.

I want to mention one other typical example of important progress. One of our members, Universal Pictures Corporation, put on its staff a professional psychologist, Dr. William M. Marston, as adviser in improving the psychological effects of their pictures.

During these growing years the industry began to reach out more vigorously toward far lands as well as toward new techniques. And I like to remember that the story of American films abroad, from 1926 to 1930, was highlighted by some of the most distinguished names of our generation—G. K. Chesterton, H. G. Wells, Myron T. Herrick, Charles Lindbergh, Herriot, Kellogg, Briand, George Eastman, and Admiral Byrd. I must mention a few of the incidents that will show the way things were moving.

In 1926, G. K. Chesterton was defending the moral aspect of films and H. G. Wells was beginning to write scenarios. Later I had interesting meetings with Mr. Wells when he came over to this country. This same year saw motion pictures protected against international piracy by an article of the Berne Convention.

In 1927 the lines of development began to diverge more sharply. On the one hand, as Governor Milliken told the World Federation of Education Associations meeting in Toronto, "the 51,066 motion picture theatres in the world today are serving as schoolrooms in which the children of all nations are being taught tolerance of others." On the other hand, trade barriers with the purpose of limiting the importation of our pictures began to appear. At a luncheon which we gave that summer in New York to Ludwig Klitzsch, president of the Association of the German Film Industry, I said, "Trade barriers against motion pictures are no more proper than would be trade barriers against books or music."

This gave me a good chance to refer to the position just taken by the World Economic Conference meeting at Geneva under the auspices of the League of Nations. The conference had agreed that "each nation's commerce is today being hampered by barriers established by other nations, resulting in a situation, especially in Europe, that is highly detrimental to the general welfare." I particularly pointed out that this conference, in which all nations took part, decreed against the fixing of *quotas,* the very practice to which we objected so strenuously.

Mr. Klitzsch said in reply—and his words are significant in the light of the 1930 German-American Trade Conference in Paris: "Our film industry is in a period of transition. Neither do we have as complete an organization for the distribution of German films in the world market as you have in America. Therefore, we believe that for the time being we cannot forgo a certain protection of our industry." How often we were to hear this story! Things were not normal—"for the time being." But we never saw why we should be penalized either for their failures or for our successes.

Two of my most important foreign trips were to France, though matters discussed there concerned other European countries as well. That is especially true of the 1930 conference.

The 1928 trip was taken with the hope of easing sharp restrictions which France had just imposed on the entry of our films. But one of my happiest memories of those spring days in Paris is of a personal telephone call, via London, to my son Bill, Jr., then thirteen years old, in Sullivan, Indiana. I was told that it was the first such non-commercial call put through. I expected Bill to be impressed by that fact, and I had jotted down a few profound notes from which to address him, but the instant I got him he shouted excitedly, "Is that you, Dad? Dad, I'm a First-Class Boy Scout now; I got my badge last night!" I tore up my notes. At that moment, quite logically, successful scouting was the biggest fact in his life.

One other story made a lasting impression on me. It was the retelling of Lindbergh's descent on Paris on May 21, 1927. My host, Ambassador Myron T. Herrick, who had taken the young flyer under his wing with pride and almost paternal affection, told me something of those historic days, as Lindbergh himself had done modestly when he flew to New York to talk with me about a movie offer that had been wired to him just after his Paris landing, which he refused. I was immensely impressed by Lindbergh.

During my Paris visit of 1928 Ambassador Herrick more than once referred to the splendid way in which Lindbergh had carried himself through the hectic days of Gallic welcome. Everyone wanted to entertain him, and Herrick had his hands full protecting him from over-zealous attentions. The one incident that sticks in my mind is the story of the flyer's speech at a formal affair tendered him by the leading figures in French aviation. This being almost a "court appearance," the Ambassador felt responsibility for what the young man should say. At

Lindbergh's request, Mr. Herrick drafted the points which he thought should be covered.

When the event arrived and it came Lindbergh's turn to speak, he rose with complete self-possession. Suddenly the Ambassador realized with a twinge of alarm that Lindbergh was not following the prearranged outline. With the innate deference which endeared him to the French, the flyer was telling the group that this event should not have been held to honor him, who had made his flight when aviation was already far advanced and when conditions were right; those most deserving of such honor were men sitting all about him, Frenchmen who had pioneered, and most of all Blériot, who had flown the English Channel so many years before. The reaction of the French was instantaneous. They cheered wildly. When quiet had been restored, Lindbergh swung into his prepared speech without a note in hand, and Ambassador Herrick said he did not miss a single point. Herrick could not compliment too highly the young man's ability, poise, and tact. He was a splendid example of American manhood.

The new regulations which the French Cinema Control Commission had issued early in 1928 would practically have kept American motion pictures out of France if put into effect literally. MPPDA directors and foreign managers agreed with me that quick action was necessary, and I sailed on the *Leviathan* late in March. Earl Bright accompanied me as secretary and assistant. He was another Hoosier, had been a court reporter, and was quite an executive as well. Maurice McKenzie, an amazing secretary who had been with me in politics and who came with me to the Association, had found Earl. Both men were invaluable. Bright was to become secretary to General Eisenhower in World War II and to fill other trusted assignments for the national government. He had been my representative in Hollywood for some time before going into the Army—a thing he was set on doing, although forty years old at the time. General Eisenhower thought so much of him that, as Allied Commander, he sent a request for Bright to follow him to London, but the General Staff felt that he was needed here.

And right here I want to say that among all the forms of loyalty in the world, I should have to hunt hard to find anything exceeding that of a real "secretary." No man could be more fortunate than I have been in the devotion, ability, and resourcefulness of such men and women who have stood by me through thick and thin, through years of almost endless detail, at what I know was often heavy cost to themselves in time and effort. They have made it possible for me to carry out countless projects. Besides Earl Bright, there have been Julia Kelly, Frances Kelly, Maurice McKenzie, Milton Hodenfield, and Mildred Grant—a list that reminds me of the famous New Testament roster of men and women of faith, and at times, I fear, somewhat of the "blessed company of martyrs." I want to pay them the warmest possible tribute of appreciation and gratitude. Never was the famous prefacing phrase, "without whose help," more appropriate.

In addition to Bright, I persuaded my good friend Dr. George W. Riley, an osteopath upon whom I had relied ever since the Chicago convention of 1920, to go with me to France because I was in the midst of a heavy case of flu—which Dr. Riley always insisted. was pneumonia—and he was helping to take care of me. With the treatments and the rest on the boat, I felt better when we landed. Harold Smith, formerly a vice-consul at the Paris Embassy and at that time our European representative, had things ready. I reported first to the American Embassy, as I always maintained that the film industry could not successfully carry on a contest with a foreign government, but that our government could quite properly negotiate or contest with a foreign government in behalf of the entire industry. In this case, as in others, our State Department both advised my trip and gave me the strongest kind of co-operation.

Ambassador Herrick generously made the whole affair a personal matter. He suggested I stay at the Embassy, although we remained at the Hotel Crillon, and went to great lengths to further my mission. By personal request he got me one of the best interpreters in France, one M. Camerlynck, whom the government used only for major international affairs. I could depend on him absolutely, and he made things much easier. The Ambassador also gave me stenographers and other assistants and made himself available at any time, both at his office and at his house. It wasn't hard to see why he was so beloved by the French and treated like one of their own heroes. He was a man of impressive appearance and great charm, and he carried the wisdom of seventy-four years with commanding dignity. In every French office I entered, introduction by Ambassador Herrick was almost as good as a request from the French Government itself. Myron Herrick has always seemed to me an example of what a foreign representative of our government should be—a man who understands both America and the nation to which he is accredited, and who can persuasively bring them together.

Conferences arranged by the Ambassador soon made clear to both of us that the question could be settled only at the highest level. Since motion pictures came under the ministry headed by Édouard Herriot, Herrick said he would write the minister, making it an official matter, and he asked me to prepare a draft embodying the points that needed covering. I dictated such a letter to Earl Bright, who transcribed it on Embassy stationery. The next morning I gave it to the Ambassador, who used it verbatim, with one addition which he alone could make: "While this request is informal, it nevertheless represents the reasoned judgment of my Government—Herrick, Ambassador."

Herriot acted promptly, calling a meeting of the commission for four o'clock the next afternoon, and letting us know that he would cause action to be taken then. Since he requested that I see him in advance, I called and explained what the American film companies needed if they were to continue business in France. He was cordial, said he understood, and promised to come into the meeting, which he said would be presided over by M. Lumière, the Edison of France, who had the respect of both film industry and government.

The meeting went off exactly as planned. M. Lumière, after remarks of welcome, called on me. I presented our needs as pointedly as possible, but with appreciation of the French position and with confidence that they would in fairness meet our necessities. As I finished—and on the minute agreed upon, as if by cue—Herriot made a dramatic entrance. He at once took control of the meeting, outlined the suggested alteration, and asked that it be adopted. This was done by proper vote of the body; and then, suggesting that I accompany him, Herriot left as abruptly as he had entered. Afterward I learned from Harold Smith that the meeting was quickly concluded and that a good deal of diplomacy had been exercised in bringing in representatives of all the different branches of the industry and a good number of officials from the ministry.

Even so, there was still much to do in preparing detailed statements and in conferring with French officials before the tracks were cleared under the new regulations. This was done as rapidly as possible, and we made ready to leave. It had been necessary to decline almost all personal invitations from French industry members and others, sticking to our story that we were there simply to aid our government in negotiating with theirs. It had been quite an experience to see the wheels of government at such close range.

A high point of that Paris trip was a memorable day I spent with General Pershing. Knowing that he was staying at the Crillon, I had sent him a message of good wishes and had received a cordial reply. I believe he was there in his capacity of chairman of the American Battle Monuments Commission, a responsibility which he took seriously, as was his nature.

On a Friday soon after our arrival the general telephoned to ask how I would like to drive out with him to visit the battlefields. I told him that I would rather do that than anything I could think of; all he had to do was to name the day and my plans would be made accordingly. He suggested that we go the following Saturday, starting at seven o'clock —an early hour for Paris.

We went in a car driven by an officer who had been his chauffeur during the war. Pershing took along an elaborate book of maps which listed pertinent facts about the areas and the events of the war. We spent the whole day on tour, and it was one of the most revealing experiences I have ever had. At important spots we would stop and get out of the car, and the general would explain what had happened there ten years before, using the maps to clarify the geography.

It was during this trip that he went into detail about the difficulties he had met in the course of making our Army an independent force. "I really had to fight two wars," he said, "one against the Germans and one to preserve the integrity of the American Army as a separate unit." But he paid sincere compliments to Secretary Baker and President Wilson, both of whom had strongly backed him up.

At one point he described vividly, as if he could recall every word, an important tactical conference held there between Marshal Joffre, General Haig, General Pétain, Marshal Foch, and himself. The question was one of immediate maneuver and redisposal of forces. In the sharp difference of opinion that developed, Haig suggested one plan, Pétain another, and General Pershing conceived something different. But Marshal Foch said, clearly and positively, "We will do thus-and-so," which was an entirely different plan. In a flash every other man saw the soundness of the idea. "See that point of land?" General Pershing asked me, identifying it on the map. "We moved a million men over there." We motored some distance to the area Foch had designated. As I stood there, trying to re-create the scene, I realized I had just heard from our number-one American soldier the frankest possible acknowledgment of the military genius and personal power of the man who rightly became Supreme Allied Commander.

When we got back to the hotel about midnight, the general inscribed the book of maps and gave it to me as a cherished personal reminder of the day.

Not long after I returned to America, General Pershing let me know of his own return, as I had asked him to do, and I saw him several times that year. His son Warren was a student at Yale, and I was glad of the chance to lend him my car to simplify his trips to New Haven. At this time, although it was well set for Hoover to be nominated, there was some talk of Pershing for President—a most natural tribute to his great services and character.

And that vividly recalls a scene on the day the Republican National Convention of 1928 opened, when Pershing had invited me to lunch with him in his suite at the old Waldorf. His friend General Harbord, then president of RCA, had sent over the best radio that could be obtained. In front of that radio our luncheon table was spread, at twelve o'clock New York time, since the convention opened at eleven in Kansas City.

We were quietly eating when the convention was finally called to order by the temporary chairman, Senator Simeon D. Fess. The invocation was impressive, even over the radio. We sat very still, listening. Then the audience was asked to rise while Schumann-Heink sang "The Star-Spangled Banner." A moment later the first tones of that magnificent voice came thrillingly over the airways: "O say! can you see . . ." Instantly the equally magnificent John J. Pershing, General of the Armies of the United States, jumped to his feet and stood rigidly at attention, his hand at salute. He did it as unconsciously as he would have said "Thank you," or opened the door for a lady. The singer and the convention were twelve hundred miles away, but for Pershing the song was with us in that room. Schumann-Heink was there, the flag was there, America was there—and the general stood at attention. What a moment! I jumped up faster than I ever jumped in all my life!

The general had many distinguished traits. I remember a Cabinet meeting when Secretary of War Weeks, coming in a little late, leaned over to me and whispered, "I've just been with Pershing and I'll have to do some apologizing to the President. I'm sorry I'm late, but, Will Hays, you know Pershing is a great soldier."

"I agree with you, Mr. Secretary," I said. "He certainly is. In fact, he's general of all the armies."

"No," said Weeks, "I don't mean that. Of course he's a great general, but I mean more than that. I mean he's a great *soldier.* I outrank him and I make suggestions, but I have to be careful what I say because he's likely to take it as an order and go out and do it. What do I mean by a soldier? He can take orders, can Pershing, better than any man I ever knew. He's not only a great general; he's a great soldier."

The National Conference on Motion Pictures, held at the Hotel Montclair, New York City, September 24–27, 1929—similar to our 1922 conference—was as stimulating a gathering as I ever attended. Coming at the height of a period of fabulous growth, it registered a pitch of enthusiasm and co-operation that I find hard to express. Ironically, it occurred just a month before the stock-market crash!

The words of my greeting sound as true to me today as they did that morning when I said:

"You are opening today a meeting wholly unprecedented in business. You, a group of intelligent men and women representing the leading social, religious, civic, and educational forces in this country, have come together to tell us what we can do to give you good motion pictures. You have planned the program yourselves; you have listed the subjects you wanted to discuss and the subjects you wanted the leading men in this industry to discuss.

"Some of the men here are pioneers in this business. When they tell you of the trails they have blazed, the hardships they have undergone, the rivers they have bridged, and the failures they have turned into successes, they will be telling you their own stories. . . .

"Most of those who entered the motion picture industry were men without wealth or fame. They have achieved their present positions through ability and perseverance. As you hear the details of this business you will realize that men of courage and worth and, frequently, of genius have brought this industry to its present position. . . ."

Referring to the improvement of relations between the public and the industry—the need of which had called the Association into being— I said: "In undertaking it, we grappled with new forces, with the mastering of human associations and an understanding of co-operation, with problems of living together and working together under complex conditions. I believe it is the greatest single contribution of this age to the science of human relations. It is a complete reversal of the old idea that the public had no voice in the conduct of any business."

Twenty-one states and Canada were represented at the conference. One hundred and sixty men and women were in regular attendance. Though invited as individuals rather than as official delegates, the majority were members of groups participating in motion picture work, either in their own communities or in national organizations of wide influence. In all, since forty-six public groups were represented, a tremendous body of sentiment was voiced. At the same time, more heads of motion picture companies were present at the Thursday luncheon than were ever brought together at one public function in the history of the industry.

The conference was a prime example of the "open door" operating on a national scale, at the "top level." The people who could speak for the most influential groups on both sides were there to meet each other, and they spoke freely. As the story of motion pictures was told, much was learned in both directions, and the biggest questions were aired, whether an immediate answer could be found or not.

The sessions were also a sort of "normal course" in which the laymen could learn enough about the inner workings of the industry to make them more effective co-operators. Finding out something about techniques and finances, they learned how to be practical in criticism. For one thing, they all saw that the general public which supports the entire motion picture structure could never be expected to take a steady diet of "high-brow" films. As Sidney Kent, one of the most articulate producers, put it, "Art must have crutches." He explained: "This business is a form of art. It has to have a combination of pictures that we know will be successful at the box office, and of 'prestige' pictures that are made to push the industry ahead." We really gave a "refresher course" to the whole public relations movement, to bring it up to date with the development of the talkie and to work out better ways for it to make itself felt for the good of all concerned.

Perhaps the most paradoxical question we discussed involved superior films that had lost money. Among those were *Old Ironsides, Range*

Riders, Nanook of the North, Siam Wild Life, and Commander Byrd's *South Pole Expedition.* When the facts were presented by film men, Mrs. N. D. Chapman, former national chairman of Better Films, D.A.R., said, "We, as a public relations group, are responsible for the success of such pictures." I pointed out that even as great a picture as *Disraeli,* with George Arliss, took active pump-priming before it became a box-office success. We all agreed that this was one place where the shoe pinched, since these were just the kinds of pictures for which thoughtful groups had been asking.

SOME RESULTS

The by-products of this conference seemed to me as important as the direct actions taken. These latter, which developed as the delegates worked over the leading questions, were four in number:

1. *Request for a direct representative of organized women in the motion picture industry,* to "interpret to the makers of motion pictures the feeling and wishes of womanhood in regard to the medium's development to its greatest usefulness." A committee of eleven women nominated for this post Mrs. Thomas G. Winter, a past president of the General Federation of Women's Clubs, and Mrs. Winter accepted.

2. Suggestion that a textbook, or *handbook*—to contain actual experiences of communities which were achieving success in motion picture work—be prepared for wide distribution. This book came out in 1930 under the title *The Neighborhood and Its Motion Pictures,* and I felt that it proved its usefulness.

3. Suggestion that pictures especially desirable for *children's matinees* be listed and that those films be made available for such purposes. This was soon done, with good results.

4. Appointment by the conference of a committee to study and help develop the use of films in *religious education.* Also done.

It was agreed that resolutions and programs were all right but that *continuous work was needed if much was to be accomplished.* My staunch friend James West, head of the Boy Scouts, who had first suggested this conference, well summed up the situation when he said: "There is every reason to believe that we are headed in the right direction. But at the same time we cannot avoid the realization that conditions still existing put upon us the major part of the responsibility as to what progress will yet be made."

When the sessions were over I felt that our purpose had been accomplished. A new level of mutual understanding and respect had been reached. Producers had seen a surprising demonstration of intelligent public interest and support. They admitted as much to me. The public had been given a helpful view of inner workings. All in all, I felt that it was the climax of the Association activities for the first seven years.

And it was certainly a satisfaction to me to see this healthy sentiment find another effective way to influence Hollywood: Mrs. Winter was chosen to represent the organized women of the country in their relations with the industry. Mrs. John F. Sippel, then president of the General Federation of Women's Clubs, put it picturesquely when she said, following Mrs. Winter's acceptance, "We all knew there was an open doorway, but we wanted a woman within the portals to whom we could go."

Alice Ames Winter, now deceased, was one of the most remarkable women I have ever known. Her spirit was contagious; her ideals were high; her judgment was sound; her loyalty and courage boundless. In the intricate process of building higher motion picture standards she was a substantial factor. To tell how she worked in Hollywood from 1929 to 1942 would be too long a story. But here I must try at least to set down something of her amazing personality, her background, her wide interests, and the "drive" she gave to anything she did. My memory was refreshed when I recently had a visit with her daughter, Mrs. Paul McGinnis, whose husband has made quite a study of her mother's life. They gave me some glimpses of Mrs. Winter's earlier days that shed light on her character.

As I would have expected, her roots went deep into a rich American heritage. Her father, Charles Gordon Ames, pastor of a Unitarian church in Boston, moved to Minnesota in the early days. Visitors to his home never failed to notice, in almost every room, copies of his favorite motto: "Always Leave Things Better Than You Find Them," which evidently made a lasting impression on the daughter. Her father had been a friend of Emerson, Longfellow, and the other "Transcendentalists," among whose distinguishing beliefs was a lively hope for "a better world."

Mrs. Winter's middle years were full of activity centered in Minneapolis and, as national president of the GFWC, reaching out into the whole country. She was only a little over five feet in height and "very broad" (her daughter's words), and her vitality and energy seemed unlimited. Everyone liked her; all felt her charm. In almost any group she was apt to become the center of attention. Her civic record, especially her influence in the "Better Homes in America" movement, is memorialized in the Alice Ames Winter Cottage in Minneapolis. She was a member of Herbert Hoover's Food-Saving Committee for Minnesota, a part of the State Council of Defense. On the advisory committee of the Washington Disarmament Conference of 1921, she was the only woman delegate representing an organization —the General Federation. Still earlier, I had met her in connection with the Harding campaign. I could see that she was a born organizer, with enormous influence among women.

Most important for the Association, she had been president of the General Federation in 1922 when I made my first appeal to their convention and they agreed to co-operate actively with our program for better pictures. To me, it was thus a happy choice that brought her, after seven years, actively into our organization.

She was the American "clubwoman" at her best. One single example of her popularity is that she was asked to be the principal speaker at the Triennial National Council of Jewish Women held at Washington in 1926. About that time she had moved to California because of her husband's health and had settled in Pasadena. Being so near Hollywood, she had naturally become more interested in the practical problems of motion picture production. She often told me how providential this all seemed.

When she was unanimously chosen to represent the women, we all realized that her unconscious preparation for the work had been extraordinarily fortunate. She knew public relations, and she knew what the more conscientious segments of the public would support. We gave her the full facilities of the Hollywood office, to make her contact with producers easy, and I felt that she should have the privilege of working to a large degree independently. The fact that she was willing to undertake such a task in her middle sixties and that she carried on for longer than she should have done in view of her health is a wonderful tribute. Her daughter told me that Mrs. Winter was never free from a headache during all her latter years!

This amazing woman knew what she was trying to do—"to reflect the wishes and reactions of organized women throughout the world in regard to the content and theme treatment of motion pictures." She was extremely resourceful in getting their suggestions, and as persuasive in urging them to patronize good pictures. She kept on trying to help the women of the world to understand some of the problems that confront motion picture producers. With all her problems, she never lost her patience and she never got mad.

No one of us could ever doubt her sincerity. She once wrote:

No wonder the Movies become everybody's business. No wonder, particularly, that we women care. While men build the great fabric of the outer world, we are still at our ancient job of concerning ourselves with the happiness and onward moving of our children and our homes. We want these forces that play on them to be of the best and most inspiring kind.

She always struck me as the most practical kind of optimist; her whole life was affirmative. And she had a great sense of humor too. She always laughed about the fact that the first actor she met in Hollywood was Bull Montana! And when she was thinking of the movies' responsibility to children, emphasizing the fact that they often composed 40 per cent of the audience, she would say that "they didn't need Mae West as a teacher." She felt how ridiculous it was to be referred to as the "czarina" but was perfectly willing to act as a "lightning rod," to take the attacks and kicks and drain off the danger.

As the days went by, we could see Mrs. Winter's influence, and that of the millions of women behind her, reflected on the daily flow of pictures. She had a keen, objective mind, and she believed that she remained impartial. The producers frequently sought her opinion and took it.

She completely agreed with my philosophy of cultivating the industry's "will-to-do." She believed that steady persuasion brought results. She thought she helped to prove that good pictures pay. She was as opposed as the rest of us to censorship, recognizing that it was confused and terribly wasteful in practice. She felt the utter difference between compulsion and voluntary action.

On these basic policies and objectives, there was never the slightest disagreement between us. I felt her support and the wisdom of her judgment. Through the years I often consulted her on the reinterpretation of the Code as it applied to some specific case with which she had occasion to be familiar, and I came to have great respect for her viewpoint. The confidence of others in what we were doing may sometimes have wavered, but not hers. In fact, from Alice Ames Winter we all drew fresh courage and confidence.

Though the MPPDA and the U.S.A. don't have the same election system, the four years covered by this chapter—1926 to 1930—could be called my "second term." And there were four more terms still to come.

This second term I always think of as a period of invention and acceleration, connected chiefly with sound. Not until 1928 did I have reason to speak of screen and drama as "blood brothers in art." Not until 1929 could my little book, *See and Hear,* a brief history of motion pictures and the development of sound, have been written. One could actually feel the screen growing, both in form and stature.

During these years I was both attacked and defended with increasing warmth. There was almost as violent complaint about too much morality on the screen as there was about too little—so perhaps we were steering a sane middle course. Extremists objected equally to "soot" and to "Puritanism," and, as if I could turn them on or off at will, in both cases I was the target. But people were coming to see that what we were aiming at was "judicious self-control." I knew that our standards were not yet well enough defined, but we were inching along.

Some deep personal associations are bound up with these years. My function in the movies was still an enigma to folks on the outside, but serious attempts began to be made to explain the mystery. One that attracted some attention was a magazine story by my close friend, columnist O. O. McIntyre, which appeared in *The New Movie Magazine* for March 1930. It was entitled "The Truth about the Czar of the Movies," and with all his banter about such things as early rising and bow ties, he pretty well demolished the idea that I was a czar of any kind at all.

Perhaps he put his finger on one key to my attitude toward the Association and the industry when he quoted Meredith Nicholson as saying of me, "He can impersonate the impersonal." But from my own point of view, there could have been nothing more personal than the motion picture as an art, as an industry, or as a group of people. Again, when McIntyre wrote, "He is a prestidigitator with the commonplace; he can make the mediocre things of the world take on an astounding importance," he was only paraphrasing the simple truth I first learned in the form, "There are no little things in politics," and found equally true of the movies. Bearing out the position I had tried to take in this breeziest of professions, McIntyre said, "He is a strict Presbyterian, yet manages to escape being a prude. . . . Somehow gay parties like to have Hays around. They respect him, and he does not preach. . . . He likes all sorts of people."

But enough of that.

Two of my lifelong hobbies are autographed books and miscellaneous mementos. Of the latter, two of the most prized are gifts from Dick Byrd, who as Commander and later Admiral Richard E. Byrd began during these years to write thrilling chapters in the history of American aviation and exploration. He would come to the office to talk things over, and I was able to be of some help in his interim activities, especially after his flight over the North Pole in 1926. A tiny American flag that he carried with him on that flight, then across the Atlantic in June of 1927, and finally over the South Pole in November of 1929, is one of my proudest possessions.

I remember that when he came in just before he left for the South Pole the second time and I had lunch sent over from the Algonquin, he specially ordered tea, doubling the order. He drank it and drank it—and very strong. When I remarked about it he told me that in Little America they kept tea brewing constantly, because they had found that it gave them something they needed. I thought of that again when William Odom reported years later on his record-breaking flight around the world, on which he experimented for the Air Force on the best beverages for long-range flights. It was stated that as a result of his findings air crews from now on would drink tea, with sugar and lemon, instead of coffee and cream. This struck me as an interesting confirmation of what Admiral Byrd had told me twenty years before.

Along with the little silk flag, I prize a piece of rock—dark in color and irregular in shape—that Dick brought back from a spot in one of the five new Antarctic mountain ranges he discovered, which he did me the honor of naming "Mount Will H. Hays." So it's easy to imagine my interest in the extensive film record that was being made of the first Antarctic expedition and of the reports that reached us from time to time of the unusual camera material they were obtaining, like the pictures of Scott Island. Later the commander told me that motion picture men went along on all the flights, photographing great stretches of newly discovered land, human-interest scenes of the explorers at work and play, and animal life in those frozen regions. The edited picture became one of the most valuable documentary films of our time, and under the title, *With Byrd at the South Pole,* was ranked as one of the "Ten Best" of 1930. In this case my satisfaction in the achievements of the industry was all mixed up with personal pride in the work of the explorer and with affection for the friend.

Few visitors ever enjoyed a brief stay in Hollywood more, or made a finer impression on that lively community, than President and Mrs. Coolidge when they visited it during the first week in March 1930.

In California at the time, I received a telegram one day from Dade, Florida, signed "Calvin Coolidge," which I took at first to be a hoax, since I neither knew the President was in Florida nor had ever heard of Dade. It simply read: "How long will you be there?" As soon as I could verify the facts, I wired I would be in California until he arrived. He had told no one else but the Los Angeles postmaster, intending to slip into town very quietly.

The Coolidges' arrival was about as quiet as Lindbergh's in Paris! After a session at the famous Breakfast Club, a committee of motion picture people took them in tow. At Warner Brothers' studio Lubitsch was directing an elaborate Venetian café scene. The Coolidges and the committee were seated on a platform about three feet high so they could watch everything. In the front row, I remember, Coolidge sat at the end, Mrs. Coolidge next to him, and then Mrs. Winter and Mary Pickford. I sat just behind the President. In the midst of the shooting Joe Scott, an outstanding Catholic layman who was voted Los Angeles' Most Useful Citizen in 1931, eased up beside me and said, "You've heard the story about Coolidge coming back from church and being asked by his wife what the preacher talked about, and he said, 'Sin,' and Mrs. Coolidge asked, 'What did he say?' and Coolidge answered, 'He was against it.'" I told Joe I'd heard it, and then he said, "Ask the President if it really happened." When I said, "No, you ask him," Joe moved up beside Coolidge, and with his head close to the President's recited the story and asked his question. Coolidge didn't say a word. He didn't seem to notice Joe. I began to be embarrassed, wondering whether our guest was knocking the man's ears down. However, after what seemed like a painfully long wait, Coolidge said, "Well, that's probably the attitude the preacher would have taken under the circumstances." The reply struck me as being fully as good as the original story.

At the end of this full day, as we were driving back to the hotel, Mrs. Coolidge said, "Calvin and I hate to leave. When we get back to New England it will be New England, and this is so very pleasant." After a pause Coolidge quietly said, looking out of the window—and I sensed that he was thinking of more than the weather—"Well, it will be spring when you get there."

Thinking of Coolidge recalls an amusing incident at a White House luncheon when he had been more taciturn than usual—and that was taciturn *cum laude!* An Amherst classmate and his wife were the special guests, but the President had not said a word to this lady, sitting at his right, all through the meal. Others who were there began to notice it, so resounding was the quiet. Finally, in the midst of one of those long, dead silences that sometimes come, Coolidge, picking up a dish of olives and, holding it out toward his very nice guest, who had been fairly talking her head off in the effort to get him started, said, "Will you have an olive?" The lady instantly replied in a gay tone that could be heard by everyone, "Oh, you little chatterbox!" And Coolidge burst out laughing. He understood.

I think my interest in Coolidge first grew out of Dwight Morrow's, which dated from their days as classmates at Amherst. Morrow was for years my most intimate friend in New York. I was with him when his partner and close friend, Tom Cochran, was trying to dissuade him from accepting Coolidge's appointment as Ambassador to Mexico. Morrow had earlier told Coolidge that he couldn't "accept a position" but he would "take a job." He had reached the place where he was interested only in doing something useful. Cochran finally said, "What can you do down there? You can't do anything. If you could, it would be all right." Quietly Dwight replied with a smile, "Well, Tom, I can like 'em."

William Boyce Thompson had been my introduction to the industrial, financial, and civic leaders of New York. I met him first when I came on as national chairman and was immediately struck by his cordiality and his readiness to pitch in when there was any good thing to do. He stays in my mind as a symbol of native American strength, common sense, daring imagination, courage, and prodigious accomplishment. He is one of the men who added brilliantly to the resources and the spirit of our nation.

It was through him that I met Dwight Morrow and—directly or indirectly—Coleman duPont, George Perkins, Andrew W. Mellon, Henry Clay Frick, and George F. Baker, Sr. I soon found myself thinking of these men and others like them as "finalists" in the great national game of American business. The "finals" in this game, as in so many athletic contests, are oftenest played in New York, and those who win have had to show the qualities of all true champions—skill, self-control, coolness under pressure. As I worked with these men and others like them, they struck me as having a great deal in common. They shared a sort of camaraderie that stood out above their individual characteristics. It embraced a vital patriotism, a common honesty, great ability, and deep loyalty. In my early days in New York the lengths to which these top men downtown would trust each other in responsible financial dealings struck me as almost fantastic.

In Colonel Thompson these qualities fairly shone. He was a polar bear among chipmunks. One could have stopped his force about as easily as one could dam up Niagara Falls. But he was as kindly and thoughtful a friend as I have ever had, and his lovely home at Yonkers was a haven to me. He was a thoroughbred, homespun and simple. Our typical summer supper on the screened-in porch in Yonkers usually consisted— in addition to a bowl of fruit—of mush and milk. But when he started to drive for anything—like the great horticultural institute for plant research which he established by an initial gift of $5,000,000, just across the road from his home—he drove like today's big Diesel locomotives.

When he finally had the stroke from which he died, he had me come to see him at Picket's Post—his place out at the Magma Copper Company, near Superior, Arizona. His home was a sort of eagle's nest, built up in the crags. Below it, stretching out into the desert, he had developed a unique arboretum containing more than sixteen hundred varieties of cactus, which he had already given to the State of Arizona. This idea had probably grown out of the Yonkers institute.

Here in the desert this great fighter, following the stroke, was convalescing. He was in bad shape. It was spring, 1930, and the desert in bloom was one of the most beautiful sights I have ever seen.

One could visit with the colonel for only an hour once a day. On the day I recall so vividly he was in a wheel chair—with his trusted manservant pushing him, and a nurse carrying an umbrella on the other side. I was walking by his side through a labyrinth of paths, marveling at the strange wonders of the desert garden. Finally we came, at the end of a path, close to the fence separating us from the transcontinental Roosevelt Highway.

At that point we stopped, watching and listening to the automobiles tearing by. There they streaked—exhausts open, seventy-five miles an hour, filled with people—one after another, rending the air with their roar. Pausing, the colonel motioned with the hand that he could use, asking me to bend down so that he could make himself heard. I leaned over, and Colonel Thompson, talking slowly—his finger moving right and left as the cars roared by—said in a low, intense voice, "Everybody—everybody—damn big hurry. Bad business." There the broken fighter sat, sixty-one years old, with over $100,000,000 that he had made—and a fatal stroke. He was trying to tell me something.

Was it the same thing I had tried to tell in the story, "Why Do We Kill All Our Presidents?" They had all died too young: T.R. at sixty; Harding at fifty-eight; Coolidge at sixty. And the seven "finalists" I have named, if their average age had not been brought up by Mellon at eighty-two and Baker at ninety-one, would have averaged only sixty-one! Must leadership and great responsibility pay so heavy a price?

The Film Conference of 1930, held in Paris, between leading German and American representatives was the inevitable result of the revolution set off in 1926 by the coming of sound. After four years of scientific development, Germany and America had outdistanced all competitors. Between them they held nearly all the basic patents controlling the new recording and reproducing processes. Both had developed the know-how of building, installing, and servicing the complicated apparatus. But by the summer of 1930 only a fraction of the fifty-eight thousand theatres in the world had been wired for sound.

Competition in the manufacture and selling of sound equipment was world-wide and deadly keen. Quantity and quality of product were both involved. Although the United States was by far the largest national market for sound apparatus, our electrical manufacturers were by no means in complete control of it. They had spent far more money in research, probably held a preponderance of valuable patents, and believed their equipment superior to that of the Germans; yet they could not avoid the danger of infringing on German patents. By the summer of 1930 no less than seventeen German patent suits, for a total of a billion dollars, had been instituted in various countries. While we were on shipboard, bound for Paris, we heard that one of those suits, then being tried in Delaware, had gone against the American companies. Later in the conference, when the Germans were rather protesting at the way our companies were invading some world markets which they considered in the German orbit, an American representative said, in effect, "We have been busy selling, while you have been busy in litigation."

The whole thing had come on us fast. The use of sound was the big issue. Some general understanding on patents and on licenses to motion picture producers who wanted to use the various processes had to be reached. The future was tremendous; all the money that has been made in sound pictures ever since was at stake. Both German and American firms wanted an end to litigation so that they could give their attention to world-wide development.

Leaders in both the electrical and the picture-producing fields had seen the problem grow. A year earlier—in July of 1929—a representative of the German "electrics" had come to New York, at the invitation of our apparatus manufacturers, to seek a solution for some of their mutual differences. There was much discussion, and the Americans made certain proposals and suggestions. But little solution came out of this meeting. A thorough discussion, at the highest level, was necessary if serious trouble was to be avoided. The conference being mutually agreed upon by both groups of electrical manufacturers, and the Americans offering to go abroad, Paris was chosen as a neutral meeting place, and the conference opened on June 19, 1930. Since the whole question of patents and licenses directly concerned the producers of sound pictures, especially the eight large companies that did the bulk of the foreign business, they too were invited. They had chosen as their spokesman Mr. J. C. Graham, Paramount's London representative, and were fortunate in their choice. Because of this large interest on the part of MPPDA's members, and because it was already apparent that the income from a substantial foreign trade was essential to the quality of American pictures, the Association was asked to participate in the conference, and I was delegated by our Board to attend. It was a tribute to the impartial position of the MPPDA, in reference to this highly technical and legal matter, that on nomination of the German delegation, and by unanimous consent, I was elected chairman of the conference.

The five weeks I spent in Paris and in Berlin, from June 17 to July 23, 1930, were as fascinating and exciting to me as they were significant in the international development of the industry. And if anyone had had any doubts that the new marvel was here to stay, he would have been jolted by one of the first acts of the conference: the agreement that "the territory under consideration is the world." But to reach agreement on how to handle patent and license rights throughout the world was a job! There seemed to be no end to the discussion, nor to the absolute differences of opinion. The ninety-three pages of official minutes are well sprinkled with the reply: "We find your proposal totally unacceptable." But in each case a reasonably satisfactory solution was finally found or the topic was eliminated from the immediate agenda. Looking back through the years of World War II and the totalitarian tides, one wonders that so many solutions *were* found. But German science and industry were still under the guidance of some of the finest and ablest men I have ever worked with, and the black shadow of Hitler's fanatical rule was still three years away.

The details of the conference discussions have no place in this account, but some of the points most often emphasized throw light on the international questions we faced, and possibly on some subsequent economic developments in Europe. The three chief subjects on the agenda were: manufacturing and distribution of apparatus, production and distribution of sound pictures, and legislation and other governmental matters. Though the third lay outside the immediate work of the conference, it had to be reckoned with. And the German delegation agreed to do anything within their power to prevent unfavorable orders by their Minister of the Interior. They didn't want cramping legislation any more than we did.

Early in the conference Dr. Lüschen stated clearly that "the aim of the discussions is to give a new stimulus to the film industry by freeing the way of obstacles. That means (1) the Germans have in mind an exchange of patents to abolish the difficulties which have arisen from this element, and (2) they want to influence the legislation toward free trade in films."

The hope of both German and American representatives was that they could come to agreement on enough major questions so that they could drop all patent litigation and use each other's patent processes freely. It was not by chance that the memorandum coming out of the conference and signed by all official delegates, was called simply "Agreement." That's what we came together for, and that's what we got, though many of our daily sessions had closed with the storm signals flying over one or both camps. On several of these occasions, when negotiations had broken down, I had to spend half the night going back and forth between the groups until a new basis had been found on which talks could reopen in the morning. More than once it was a close squeak; but one side or the other would find a new approach, or both would agree to some compromise measure which I, more nearly neutral, could propose as being in the interest of the international industry.

I vividly recall the conference room at the Hotel Royal Monceau. The chairman's place was in the center, like the moderator of a forum. On my left were the members of the German delegation—Dr. Fritz Lüschen, the chairman, president of Siemens und Halske, which was similar in position to our American Tel and Tel; Dr. Emil Mayer, head of the great Allgemeine Elektrisitats Gesellschaft, corresponding to our General Electric; and Milton Diamond, representing the influential TOBIS group, which included both German and Dutch corporations producing sound films. Back of them were ranged the forty members of the technical and advisory group, men familiar with every phase of talking pictures, as well as with German and Dutch legal, commercial, and financial affairs in general.

To my right were the American delegates: Mr. Otterson, representing Electrical Research Products, Inc., which held the majority of our patents; Mr. C. J. Ross, executive vice-president of RCA Photophone, Inc., which held the remaining American patents; and Mr. J. C. Graham, representing the chief American film producers and distributors interested in international business and then operating under licenses from the American electric companies. The advisory and technical staff of twelve—including such men as George R. Canty, American Trade Commissioner for Motion Pictures, Douglas Miller, then Assistant Commercial Attaché at Berlin and later author of the significant book, *You Can't Do Business with Hitler,* and several European representatives of American electric or motion picture companies—looked small in comparison with their "opposite numbers."

PATENTS

One of the most delicate topics before the conference was the relative value of German and American patents, on which our delegates had strong convictions. These seemed to be backed up by the overwhelming position that American talking pictures had already secured in the cinemas of the world. Mr. Otterson pointed out that the Western Electric had contributed largely to the adoption of talking pictures, and hence that whatever business had resulted for the Germans was due largely to Western Electric's pioneer commercial work. The German delegates, acknowledging that fact, stated in rebuttal that a large proportion of American equipment infringed on German patents and that they believed that part of this business, therefore, belonged to them. Or, in other words, a large part of this business had been done because German patents were disregarded. In reply, the Americans held that the Germans could not operate on a large scale and make quality apparatus without infringing on the Western Electric patents. There was doubtless much to be said on both sides, although the quantity and probably the quality of the American patents and equipment were superior.

As I look back on those days I believe that both sides realized the seriousness of the situation to be solved. I recall that one of the Germans, in acknowledging some remarks that I had made, said that "the replacement of the silent film by the talking picture has caused a critical period for the film industry in all countries." The fact that American films had captured so large a portion of the world's screens gave point to American Delegate Otterson's remarks when he said it was his understanding that the conference "was now trying to bring about conditions which would permit American producers to go into Germany to make pictures in four or five languages and build up the business which would help the Germans to sell their machines." Obviously, the thing that held the delegates together was the realization that their interests were inescapably connected.

As chairman, I had an opportunity early in the conference to help increase this sense of mutual co-operation. My election doubtless recognized the fact that the Americans had taken the initiative in promoting the conference and had done the Germans the courtesy of going to Europe to meet them. In the circumstances, it seemed to me that the best thing I could do was to tender a dinner to the delegates at the very opening of our proceedings. This dinner was arranged for June 20, the second day of the conference, at the Château de Madrid in the Bois de Boulogne. The affair was planned in the best French style and gave a perfect opportunity for the delegates to get acquainted with each other on a friendly basis. The thing I can never forget was the almost hysterical joy of the Germans, who had been through years of national hardship following World War I, when they saw on the menu, and later in their glasses, one of the finest and rarest of all German wines, the Liebfraumilch Cabinet Auslese 1911!

The business philosophy of the Germans was sharply different from ours. Repeatedly they made it clear that agreements must be "on a basis which would not jeopardize our position." More than once they came back to the thesis that "the conference must find some way to assure us of a fair share of the business in the non-exclusive territories." The Americans, on the other hand, being already strong in the field and aggressive in selling, were willing to leave the results to their own efforts without seeking any such guarantees.

Political and ideological elements did not enter our discussions as often as would have been the case a few years later. But patents and the infringement of patents were a constant problem, though we found common ground in the desire of both sides to reach a position where mutual exchange of manufacturing processes could become a reality. Both sides were anxious to get away from the fear of infringement and ruinous lawsuits. Both were willing to help each other as against any "bootleg" apparatus. Hence it was not too difficult to reach an agreement that brought an end to litigation. During the discussion on England, Dr. Fritz Lüschen, chairman of the Germans, suggested that if the Americans and Germans would pool their patents they could drive out all competition. At this point, our Mr. Otterson, as I recall, remarked that Western Electric and RCA together would have installed eighteen hundred theatres by the end of the current year. He did not think it worth while bringing patent suits for the small block of possibilities remaining, especially as he thought he would eventually get the business anyway. To this, one of the German delegates replied that through no fault of theirs, in his opinion, the Americans had obtained an unusual commercial position. Hence their one chance was to get compensation for past business to compensate them for their patent position, especially in that their chance of competing in that country was small. At another point in the discussion they said that they wished to be compensated in some way for the possibility they had lost. It was evident that the Germans felt they were being deprived of business they had hoped to get, while the Americans were perfectly willing to trust to their luck.

It was a good thing for everybody that the conference took a breathing spell in the middle of July. We had been in session almost every day since June 19, and patience was wearing thin. Then, fortunately, along came Bastille Day, July 14. No one in Paris wanted to work. The Germans wanted to go back home for a visit and to look after their business. So we recessed.

Invited by the German leaders to go to Berlin with them, I jumped at the chance. There were things to be learned from the other side. Dr. Lüschen took me to his home for dinner, along with Dr. Mayer. It was an excellent, dignified home, and the doctor had a fine family. He brought in his son and daughter and introduced them. I congratulated him on having so fine a son to follow him in his profession. To my great surprise, the father said that the boy wanted to go to America. Dr. Lüschen said quite frankly that he didn't like the prospect of the revolution that seemed to be in the making and he wanted his son to get out before it came. He also talked earnestly about the infiltration of Communism which was then going on in Germany. But I am sure none of us that night could have guessed at a fraction of the tragic consequences that were to follow.

Returning to Paris along with the German delegates, we entered the final stages of the conference. A joint committee had been appointed to work on a draft of an agreement which should incorporate all the basic terms on which the two parties had been able to unite. And despite the fact that in some respects these viewpoints were diametrically opposed, it was a triumph of good sense and co-operation that such a satisfactory agreement was reached.

The thinking of the Americans was based chiefly on the two concepts of free trade and open competition. Free trade was not only the policy of the industry at large but a specific objective of the MPPDA. As a Republican, supposedly favoring protective tariffs, I had to take a lot of joshing for my defense of free trade in the motion picture field. When sound pictures came in, my position was unchanged, and this viewpoint held in the minds of the official delegates at the Paris 1930 conference. America has never put any tariff on foreign motion pictures. And this attitude was basic to our discussions in the conference.

Our managers and producers were more than willing to accept the principle of free competition; in fact, they welcomed it. The Americans never considered a market saturated. They were confident that good pictures would always find an audience.

Though little was said about it, our men undoubtedly believed firmly in the superior quality of their product. The vast financial resources behind our great corporations and their splendid research departments were constantly improving American apparatus, and they were willing to stand on the matter of quality and take their chances on the future. The German representatives, on the other hand, came into the conference with a strong sense of defending their "patent position," which they felt was sufficient to give them a certain guaranteed security in the business and the markets of the future. They wished some sort of assurance that adequate revenues would be continued.

It is still hard to estimate what would have been the action of the German manufacturers if they had been as free as were the Americans to dictate the terms of motion picture business in their own country. But they were not free; there was no escaping their severe government regulations.

The virtue of long and thorough negotiations was proved by the clearness and definiteness with which the terms for the final agreement were formulated. This agreement gave any contracting manufacturer or producer the basic terms to be incorporated in legal contracts entered into thereafter. An interesting sidelight is thrown on international relations by the fact that it was agreed "that the contracts shall be construed under the English laws and that the usual arbitration clause is to be incorporated." In order that the atmosphere of harmony might continue to surround the conference in the minds of the public, a joint statement of the German and the American representatives was given to the press from time to time, of which one of the later statements was as follows: "Understandings were reached which, it is believed, will result in an agreement providing for complete interchangeability of motion picture sound recording and sound reproducing apparatus between the interests involved. The purpose of the understandings is to aid in the full development of the art and in the freeing of the industry from any handicaps under which it may have labored because of conflicting patent interests." We were careful in every case to avoid any statement implying that one side had gained any "victory" over the other.

Most important of all, litigation between parties, which at the moment included suits for upward of a billion dollars, was to be at once dropped. Both parties were released from any and all charges or claims by reason of past infringement of patents or other claims involved in such litigation.

To me, the most interesting personal sequel to the conference was the story of Dr. Emil Mayer, head of the great German company corresponding to our General Electric, and a man of extraordinary wisdom and force. Throughout our difficult Paris negotiations, when a critical deadlock threatened, it was he who came forward with a new proposal which opened the door to a solution. My admiration for the man's mind and spirit has never ceased. Being a Jew, he had to be removed from his tremendously influential position when Hitler came into power and instituted the Aryan regulations. Because of Dr. Mayer's tremendous value to Germany, the authorities urged him to take the opportunity to remain in his position by changing his name and concealing his race. In fact, they begged him to do so. He gave them a complete refusal. Not long after, he arrived in America and came to call on me. A refugee from his own country, he set himself up here as a consulting engineer—an inspiring example of the unquenchable love for freedom which his German masters had been unable to kill.

In 1931—the year following the German-American Film Conference —one of our most interesting international contacts was made through the work of Mrs. Ambrose N. Diehl at Rome, in connection with the League of Nations. Mrs. Diehl, wife of a vice-president of the United States Steel Corporation who was later put in charge of building the Golden Gate Bridge, had been one of our most powerful co-operators from the earliest days of the Association. She and I became very good friends, and I developed a great admiration for her understanding, executive ability, and keen appreciation of what motion pictures can mean in the life of the world.

She went to Rome that year as—take a deep breath—chairman of the Motion Picture Committee of the National Council of Women, U.S.A., to the International Council of Women at the International Educational Cinematographic Institute of the League of Nations. Although its connection with the League was never strong, this institute had held its first big powwow in Rome in 1924. I realized that such an organization needed watching, and saw to it that Governor Milliken, as secretary of our Association, was a delegate. I believe there were some six hundred delegates from forty-five countries in attendance. It was quite a show.

When the governor returned and told me what had gone on, it looked pretty much as if the whole idea of the institute was based on Mussolini's ambition to move the European motion picture center from Paris to Rome. Partly because of this nationalistic bias, the institute achieved little importance as an international force. We did give it credit, however, for the Geneva Convention by which pictures authenticated by their governments as educational were allowed to pass customs-free; and I wanted to co-operate with any movement looking to such an end.

I know from my own later Rome visit of 1936 that the institute stayed alive and that Mussolini continued to magnify it. Before talking with him then I took pains to visit the institute—which was practically in his back yard—and in pleading with him for freer admission of American films I emphasized Rome's historic role as a world center of art. That ideal was always in his mind, and it doubtless helped persuade him to lighten the restrictions which his Cinema Commission had imposed.

The institute continued to be the international center of a certain

amount of women's interest in films. Mrs. Diehl was a logical chairman
of the Motion Picture Committee of the National Council of Women
because, as she told the delegates at Rome, her election "derives from
work done for many years in two groups: as motion picture chairman of
the General Federation of Women's Clubs in the United States, which
has a membership of three million women; also as chairman of the
Motion Picture Department of the League of American Pen Women."
She reported to them on the processes which organized American women
had found to work best for the improvement of films. Reflecting the aim
of all our public relations efforts, she emphasized that the women of
America advocated constructive action instead of denunciation. Illus-
trating her disbelief in motion picture censorship by referring to America's "painful experiment" in trying to enforce prohibition, she said with
finality, "The results have not encouraged us to believe that laws make
good men." She explained the "policy of co-operation" between the
industry and the American public on which the program of our association was based; and I can imagine the amazement with which this truly
democratic story was heard by some of the delegates from countries
accustomed to authoritarian edicts.

My mention of Mussolini recalls to my mind a couple of experiences
our Association had with Huey Long, evidencing the latter's dictatorial
attitude—to put it mildly.

The first was in 1928, when the American Arbitration Association
was active in securing the adoption of "the first comprehensive commercial arbitration law in the South"—Act 262—by the State of Louisiana, with the approval of Governor Long. The Arbitration Association
credited the MPPDA's support and co-operation with being a decisive
factor in this accomplishment. Our general counsel, Charles Pettijohn,
had asked Illinois Congressman Frank Reid to phone Governor Long
and explain the proven advantages of arbitration laws in settling motion
picture disputes. In signing the bill, Governor Long had written to
Congressman Reid: "I approve the arbitration bill which you requested,
and just take your word for the matter. I do not have time to investigate
very much."

Our second experience with Huey Long was in 1935, the year of his
death, when he was a United States senator. In July, quite without
warning, a confiscatory motion picture censorship law was passed by
the Louisiana legislature. It provided heavy fees and penalties, the tax
alone being four dollars per thousand feet of film. It created a State
Board of Censors, with power to approve or disapprove all pictures, to
impose the heavy taxes and inspection fees, and to assess penalties for
violation, up to five hundred dollars. If enforced, it would have squeezed
distributors and exhibitors out of business in Louisiana.

Mr. Pettijohn, himself a good Democrat, was not long in discovering what lay behind the law. We persuaded Senator Long to come to New York and sit down to lunch with leading distributors and sales agents. They must have done a good job of "harmonizing," because the distributors were told that it would be sufficient if they merely submitted a script for review, rather than the completed film, and that no fees of any sort would be imposed. As a matter of subsequent fact, no producer was ever asked to submit even an outline of any film. By phone, Long later advised Pettijohn that "the matter for the time being is in status quo." But to make things doubly sure, Long promised to phone me from New Orleans to California, and he did so. I had no phone then in my residence in Hidden Valley, thirty-five miles north of Hollywood, and I had to drive eight miles to a store to find a booth from which I could talk to him. I sat in that sweltering cubicle—it was on the porch in the blazing sun—for over an hour, getting hotter and hotter in more ways than one as I listened to Huey Long's harangue. Incidentally, it was right afterward that I arranged for phone wires to be strung into my ranch.

Huey said he didn't really have it in for the motion picture industry and he didn't want to have a fight with me, since he had nothing against me personally, but what he was doing he simply had to do in self-respect. This sounded a little strange, coming from him. Then he repeated to me what he had agreed to do: to see that the censorship law was *not enforced!* When I asked him why he had got the law passed in the first place, he said he was going to get even with the Rockefellers, because they owned RKO, and RKO had put out a "March of Time" film falsely representing him in a very unfair light in an alleged fight at a Long Island country club; he said further that he had run the insurance companies out of Louisiana and was going to fix the motion picture industry, and that although he liked the movies he couldn't let such a personal affront get by. He explained his great power, his great anger, and his great magnanimity, and the fact that he could pass a law and could nullify it by ordering that it go unenforced. He then said that he would repeal the law in question—he would be proud to show us that he could—but he wanted the industry to understand that he ran Louisiana and that he couldn't be kicked around! All this in a loud voice. It was a shocking, almost unbelievable piece of exhibitionism, as frightening in its implications as it was shameful in performance. The "Kingfish" had simply caused the bill to be passed, then caused it to lie unenforced, and was now preparing to introduce a bill in the Louisiana legislature for its repeal. The later, dramatic fact was that he actually had that bill in his pocket, on his way to the State House to have it passed, when he was assassinated. After his death, his own people did carry out that purpose.

CHAPTER 28

The Production Code

T H I S may prove to be both the easiest and the hardest chapter of my story to write. The *easiest*, because there is so much material and so much has already been written and said. And the *hardest* for at least two reasons: first, because the Code has often been such a storm center—with every important question hotly debated; and second, because it is the spirit behind and beneath the document which I must try to reveal. And *spirit* is not easy to define in words. I know this particular spirit because I lived with it for a quarter of a century and saw it develop. Fortunately, it was invested with a name. Since that term will appear frequently in this chapter, as it has already appeared elsewhere, it should be revealed at once. Its name is the *will-to-do*.

At the very outset one should think of the Production Code as a dual problem: rule adoption and rule enforcement. Those are two separate matters, but they are closely related. The Articles of Incorporation of the MPPDA defined its primary purpose as "to foster the common interests of those engaged in the motion picture industry in the United States by establishing and maintaining the highest possible moral and artistic standards in motion picture production." There was revealed this dual nature of the problem: "establishing and maintaining"—setting standards and gaining adherence to them.

Since January 1922, when I told the producers that I would tackle the Association job, I had been mulling over in my mind how best to do it. As I saw things, my initial functions were, on one hand, to stave off the rising tide of public disapprobation that threatened the industry's freedom, if not its very existence, and on the other, to influence the industry away from the themes, tastes, and practices that had provoked the peril. That posed two problems, much akin and yet separate, and I hunted for a connecting link between them. As often happens, the solution came as the result of a simple incident as I was giving a farewell dinner to my fellow Cabinet officers at the New Willard Hotel in Washington. In the elevator I heard two men talking about the progress in school of their respective sons, and one remarked that his boy was getting low marks in algebra, so he guessed he would have to "take time out to help him." I sullenly realized that the various uplift groups, dedicated to civic betterment, had fallen into the habit of berating, or at best ignoring, a great and potent art industry, but had never thought to "take time out" to help it. Accordingly, I set out at once to bring about a friendly, co-operative relationship between such groups and the industry. And through the doubtful months and years of slow building, I had an anchor to windward: it was my faith in the American people, whom I consider to be the "heroes" of this story. It was their confidence and support, both in encouraging and in disciplining moviemakers, that again and again kept the industry from getting off the track and kept it free to develop.

Meanwhile I did not forget the urgent problem of raising the standards of motion pictures from within. It was no singlehanded task, and I can never render a sufficiently high tribute to the heads of our member companies for their co-operation, not infrequently at heavy financial loss, without which the Hays Office—with or without Hays—would have been doomed from the start.

There was a perfectly natural skepticism on the part of some producers at first. After all, I was urging them not only to change their product in certain particulars but to help change the demands of the box office— to do the immeasurably difficult thing of changing people's thinking. This had hitherto been regarded as none of the business of a showman, for it had always been taken for granted that his only function was to supply whatever the demand might be. It took time for many people to realize that the motion picture was not just a circus passing through town but an institution with a potential influence comparable to that of a great university.

The difficulties of discovering or fashioning proper screen standards stemmed from several deep sources, and perhaps the most profound was a widespread disagreement as to exactly what constituted right and wrong. I firmly believe that a sense of right and wrong is implanted in the heart of every human being not an imbecile and over the age of six, but if this sense is ill nourished and unguided, it is not likely to produce archangels in our busy marts of trade. The Ten Commandments, though most people approve of them, are not exempt from differences of opinion in particular applications. What was required, I could clearly see—though it was still some years away—was a precise code of particular applications with a uniform interpretation.

Another difficulty was the mutual distrust among the motion picture companies themselves. It was thankless work to persuade one company to abandon plans for making a sensational picture, only to have its less docile competitor cash in on the same theme. It was hardly encouraging to the rightly disposed producer, and we were still some distance from the unanimity that made later advances possible.

Still another difficulty is inherent in the medium itself. It seems that the larger the audience, the lower the moral mass resistance to suggestion. And the movies, unlike stage plays and books, are universal entertainment. That is why I believed it so necessary to correct, as far as possible and without such violence as might have spoiled everything, the demand as well as the supply.

My plea to the producers was simply this: our case stood between legislative censorship, with all its attendant evils, and the more manly and democratic process of self-regulation; and self-regulation was needed because the industry had become important to our country and to civilization. For "martial law" we would substitute the organized will of public-spirited citizens; to educate public appreciation we would produce some superior pictures. It was my creed that good pictures would outdraw bad pictures. And we already knew, whenever we faced it honestly, that unless offensive pictures were eliminated the whole freedom of the screen was threatened.

But I was neither so optimistic nor naïve as to believe that the industry of 1922 would instantly embrace my faith. Current advertising, even of wholesome productions, tended to make them appear unwholesome. This practice was rooted in the belief, by no means yet dead, that patrons in the mass will pay more for what is euphemistically called "spice" than for good clean entertainment. Although this has time and again been shown up as a fallacy, the idea lives on.

There is just enough truth in that belief to appeal to the penny-wise, pound-foolish operator concerned with a hit-and-run profit rather than with the durability of an industry. Even if one admits a margin of truth in the assumption, there is no more excuse for such indecency than for participation in the smuggling of narcotics simply because it happens to be momentarily profitable. And in most cases deceit was involved. The picture did not come up to the risqué standards promised by the billboards, which probably created still more ill will.

I felt that cleaning up that style of advertising was a job for the West Coast Association. At the same time, I realized that it would be futile to bear down on the advertising until the goods being advertised were brought to a suitable norm. It is notable that we succeeded in securing an Advertising Code in the same year as the adoption of the Production Code.

During the 1920s the licentious mood of current books and stage plays was another important factor. After analyzing the problem over a long period I was forced to conclude that we could not assume responsibility for anything connected with a movie story except what was actually in that film version. Often that was headache enough. Our industry has always been dependent on published works for much of its raw material, and if it became less "raw"—in a salacious sense—when presented in our medium, we decided that our responsibility had been fulfilled. Incidentally, it has often seemed to me that a little self-regulation would do no harm in the book industry.

As a move toward the solution of the book-movie problem we devised what came to be known as the "Hays Formula," and while I feel that this exclusive allocation of "screen credit" is exaggerated, since I was not the whole Association, I am delighted to have participated in the first real step toward the goal of motion picture jurisprudence. In February of 1934 our Board of Directors unanimously resolved to call upon each studio to have its reading department send us a synopsis of every book, play, and story submitted to it. We then undertook to advise our members if any such property might prove unacceptable and, if so, to recommend that it not be purchased. The various reading departments in the Hollywood area promptly complied with instructions. A trifle less promptly, some of the producers complied with our requests. The results, however, were on the whole good and, in some instances, singularly fortunate. The Formula may not have been a law, but it was a dike.

In 1924, before the "itch" to write had infected so many, everything went through the reading departments—hence their co-operation was essential to our first historic step. It should be noted that, so far, we had no corrective power beyond that of giving advice; and even this did not apply to most of the scripts made into pictures—such as original stories from the desks of studio writers—but only to books and plays.

Frequently giving advice was about as far as we got. Fred Beetson was my representative in Hollywood. The producers liked him and appreciated his unflagging efforts, but he was still just the remote proconsul of an authority which, even at its center, possessed no sanctions to enforce its suggestions. What was needed, I could see, was a separate functionary in Hollywood whose sole job, and not just his incidental one, would be to keep his eye on that aspect.

The formula which we had devised, in spite of its inadequacy *qua nunc*, had represented not one but two steps forward in the right direction. In May of 1924 I pointed out as strongly as I could the need of preventing what was then the prevalent type of book and play from becoming the prevalent type of movie. This was in perfect accord with the spirit of the Formula, and I think anyone who is old enough to remember the crop of fiction current at the time, and especially the 1924–25 New York theatrical season, will agree that if what had prevailed in other media had been allowed to predominate on the screen, federal censorship would have been a mild result.

In June of 1924 we reaffirmed the Formula and amplified it. The Association members agreed not to produce or distribute any picture which, by reason of its title, story, exploitation requirements, or general theme, failed to measure up to our preamble. It is obvious now—and I would only make myself ridiculous to claim otherwise—that some members forgot the agreement after a while. They were sincere; but so are those who make New Year's resolutions. We cannot find fault if a highly complex subject is not learned overnight.

The reason we were so concerned was that we knew the immense influence that motion pictures were exerting, especially on young people. Excessive drinking on the screen during the prohibition era was certain to weaken respect for *all* law; and the glamorizing of certain modes of conduct or of brittle, vulgar speech—at that time indicated in subtitles— was sure to inspire imitation. This was especially true of movies because of the star-fan relationship, which existed also in the legitimate theatre but to a far lesser degree.

In the matter of illicit or immoral sex themes, the possibilities became even more sinister. This is because sex is a normal instinct, beautiful in its proper scope, but one which cannot rightly be compared with any other instinct, being special and singular. As such, it is TNT, which is also proper to its scope; but we cannot compare high explosives with custard pies. Accordingly, I have never believed that themes based on such an instinct were to be bandied around lightly by playwrights and comedians to garner a few more dollars at the box office. Hence I concluded that this element, of all those that might be badly handled on the screen, could well prove the most dangerous if left unregulated. I say this lest it seem in this chronicle that I, or any of my associates, was overweening or at any time overscrupulous on the subject.

To be sure, not all of our troubles stemmed from scandals, censors, and sin. We were also different from the stage in that we were supposed to please everybody and offend no one. I remember one particular message I was obliged to bring to the directors of the West Coast Association. It was a request from the Yellow Cab Company that henceforth we cease showing taxicabs as a means of transportation in "cops-and-robbers" movies, lest the public get the idea that criminals always escaped in taxis. This was not an isolated case. In the next few years we were to receive communications from the National Billiard Association, which objected to showing low-grade poolrooms on the screen; still another from the American Hotel Association, which objected to movies showing people smoking in bed. School authorities asked us to discourage the use of comedy characters who stammered; a number of youngsters, it seems, were beginning to imitate such characters and might form a stammering habit. Finally, following the repeal of the Eighteenth Amendment, an organization of glass blowers objected to movies showing canned beer. Thus, not all of the complaints that reached us were from groups concerned with morality. By far the greater number came from professional organizations, unions, and individuals who felt that their trades and professions were being shown, however unintentionally, in an unfavorable light. Many such matters also had to be considered in the future Code—especially as concerned the nationals of other countries.

The foundation of our "industrial civilization"—of which I regard the Code and some of the finer pictures later made as the highest expressions—*had been laid,* and that foundation was solid.

Perhaps a good subtitle for the Code story would be "Inching Along." The next two or three years, when the "silent" was reaching its zenith, were marked by several forward steps. Taken together, they indicated both the growing influence of public opinion and a larger recognition by the industry that there was a body of rules founded on something besides arbitrary personal opinion. When the Formula proved inadequate, other forces moved in to support or replace it.

Though the Formula was mild, it was often opposed or at least treated with skepticism. Inadequate and without teeth, it was still regarded on occasion as too restrictive. But it did succeed that first year in preventing the screening of sixty-seven literary properties that had been successful as plays or novels.

Meanwhile, previewing groups in their reports and recommendations were helping gradually to "improve the demand"—one of our two constant goals, the other being to improve the supply.

In 1925 we also established our Title Registration Bureau, mainly to stop the too frequent arguments between two producing companies who happened to hit on the same title for projects which they had planned. I soon saw that the Bureau might perform a still more important function: it could eliminate suggestive titles altogether.

Another step more directly affecting production was the setting up in Hollywood of the Studio Relations Committee, which was the immediate ancestor of the present Production Code Administration. That the studios co-operated, even eagerly, with Colonel Joy at that stage is proved by the fact that in the first nine months of 1927 his Studio Relations Committee was consulted on 162 feature pictures. Among the men who helped him in this work was the late Lamar Trotti, who became one of Hollywood's brilliant writer-producers. Plucked from the newspaper field, he had begun his motion picture work in our New York office.

In the same year that Joy set up Studio Relations, our Association concluded an agreement with the Authors League of America, which for the preceding three years had been the most vociferous group-critic of the Formula. This was natural, inasmuch as rejections of stories by our Association prevented the authors from realizing handsome profits from screen rights. The new agreement provided that if we rejected a work the dramatist or novelist himself might appear before our Board to plead his case. If the Board persisted in the rejection, the author might still rewrite his story, eliminating what we objected to and using a new title.

By this time the function which I had hoped the Title Registration Bureau might perform was flourishing well under the direction of Governor Carl E. Milliken, secretary of our Association and one of the highest-minded gentlemen it has ever been my privilege to meet. He was also a shrewd New Englander, having been governor of Maine and having served in the state House and Senate for a decade.

The Formula, thus modified, worked out surprisingly well. Producers seldom or never contested a decision of the Board regarding a rejection. When one company which might have desired to buy a certain story refrained from doing so, all the other member companies similarly refused to consider it.

One of our unforeseen and most fortunate developments grew out of Colonel Joy's visits to censors. Out of these grass-roots experiences came a group of generalizations that seemed to indicate fairly accurately the prevailing moral sense of the United States and Canada. These were composite judgments founded on scores of opinions. Though censor boards differed widely in some of the specific rulings—in one state it was held immoral for a young wife to indicate, even by knitting booties, that she expected a baby—yet Colonel Joy and his assistants managed to work out a rough common denominator.

I happened to be in Hollywood in May of 1927 and spoke to the West Coast Association about things which *must not* be done on the screen, and other things which *should not* be done. Of course my point of view, though strongly expressed, was merely a recommendation, for I had no direct authority in the West Coast group. To their great credit, my talk resulted in the appointment of a committee consisting of Irving G. Thalberg, E. H. Allen, and Sol Wurtzel to co-operate with Joy in devising a system of rules. This system, which came to be known as the "Don'ts and Be Carefuls," was officially adopted by the West Coast Association in June of that year.

Despite its arbitrary rules and absence of philosophy, the adoption of this pre-Code was gratifying, especially as it included several subjects that I had always wanted to declare taboo and had earlier considered listing as such. However, the making by our group of such a list prior to the adoption of a practical production policy by the West Coast group might well have constituted a case of restraint of trade. I am lawyer enough to know that there is sometimes a distinction between what is morally right and what is legally defensible. It was another example of why a West Coast Association, separate from our own, was a valuable organization.

As concrete evidence on the subjects that had to be considered, the reader might like to see the eleven Don'ts as adopted in the original draft. They follow:

Pointed profanity—by either title or lip: this includes the words *God, Lord, Jesus, Christ* (unless they be used reverently in connection with proper religious ceremonies), *hell, damn, gawd,* and every other profane and vulgar expression however it may be spelled.

Any licentious or suggestive nudity—in fact or in silhouette; and any lecherous or licentious notice thereof by other characters in the picture.

The illegal traffic in drugs.

Any inference of sex perversion.

White slavery.

Miscegenation (sex relationships between the white and black races).

Sex hygiene and venereal diseases.

Scenes of actual childbirth—in fact or in silhouette.

Children's sex organs.

Ridicule of the clergy.

Willful offense to any nation, race, or creed.

For all the merits of the "Don'ts" and "Be Carefuls," their observance was still optional. And it is a commentary on human nature that while the studio heads and directors hung on Joy's words when he was merely the advance scout for possible censorship hurdles, many of them began ignoring his admonitions when he was backed by a body of rules. Essentially they were nothing more or less than the sum of his experiences, with a tiny grain of theory added by me. But now those experiences were codified, so some of the old "Red Gulch" opposition to formal law was rekindled. It was one thing to refrain from selling whisky to savages because it might start a massacre, but a totally different thing to refrain because the law commanded it.

Individual producers had the choice of submitting or declining to submit scenarios to Joy's committee in advance of shooting. In a few cases the scripts were submitted; but even then the associate producers, or "supervisors" as they were then called, might disagree with the authority. Some of these supervisors were relatives of the boss, some were writers, and some merely promoters who had been actors' agents or Broadway characters. It was not until after the adoption of the Code that studios were required to show all advance scripts to the Studio Relations Committee.

Figures bear out that a greater compliance with the committee would have been more economical, for it was found that while censor boards deleted a total of only 1.9 per cent from pictures which Joy had passed, they cut almost 6 per cent on the average from films about which he had not been consulted. Out of 176 amputations from pictures which he had been permitted to judge, he had failed to foresee and warn the producers about only seven. Personally, I consider this an almost clair-voyant power on Joy's part, and I think if I had been a producer I would have welcomed his suggestions.

To give a semblance of compulsion to the observance of the "Don'ts" and "Be Carefuls," the Hollywood Jury was established. This was a panel of West Coast producers from which an arbitration group of three was chosen whenever a dispute arose. It was an effort at self-censorship which might have worked better had the jurors been objective in their findings, but in most cases they were not. Perhaps that was too much to expect. Plagued by the same problems that confronted their fellow producer, or expecting to use the same device themselves the next week, they hesitated to be impartial and in most instances decided in favor of the producer and against Colonel Joy. Even in the case of an adverse decision, the studio producer had the right to appeal to the Board of Directors of our Association, a privilege that Joy's committee did not enjoy until a later period.

Five years' work had at least given us a solid foundation on which to build a reasonable code. Public demand and popular protest had helped fashion an imposing group of "Don'ts" and "Be Carefuls," and these were recognized as so sound that the Trade Practice Conference for the industry, meeting in October of 1927, adopted them as fair trade practices, as the original West Coast resolution of adoption had recognized them.

Mention of that fact may remind the reader that improving the pictures themselves was not the whole task. A body of trade practices covering a network of producer-distributor-exhibitor-public relationships had also to be constantly studied and clarified. It was in this field that litigation so often occurred. It was here that anti-trust suits were brought against the big companies and even against the Association. Our efforts to strengthen our system of industry self-government were aimed to free the industry from "unjust or unlawful exactions," as well as from censorship that would limit the freedom of the screen itself.

With out first set of "rules" we had made considerable headway in at least defining our production problems. And it must never be forgotten that they were adopted voluntarily by the West Coast group—the Motion Picture Producers' Association. But the questions of interpretation and observance were something else! And two developments of the late 1920s—the coming of sound, and the depression that hit the nation in 1929—came tragically close to wrecking our efforts. For the depression, we certainly were not responsible. For the invention and development of talking pictures we were ultimately to be more than grateful. But along the way both gave the industry some bad times.

When spoken words were added to moving pictures our whole job took on a new dimension. A new and more powerful art form had come.

But quite as surely, the new medium brought us headaches in the way of unwholesome trends. The so-called Hays formula, as well as the "Don'ts" and "Be Carefuls," groaned under the strain of the next three years, until we got a code. Not since the Gold Rush of '49 had there been such a mass movement westward as the influx of Broadway people —playwrights, actors, song writers, vaudevillians, and burlesque comedians—in 1927 and particularly in 1928, which is still called in Hollywood "The Year of the Big Trek." There were many fine artists among the newcomers, but some others tended to misunderstand the purpose of the rules and to ridicule and ignore all warnings. At that time we had no sanctions, only advisory powers. And the new recruits lacked some of the grim experience we had gained since 1922.

Nor were some studios themselves of too much help. As they succumbed to the magic of dialogue, their established producers and stars scrambled to acquire New York stage successes, while many literary properties, hitherto considered inappropriate for the screen, were dusted off, disinfected slightly, photographed, and released.

As an illustration of the problems created by the talkie, let us take the case of profanity. I had to give a warning about the new possibilities of giving offense and cited a fairly surface example in a Warner Brothers short subject, in which the word "damn" had occurred three or four times. Personally, I believe that this word, unattended by any prefix invoking the Almighty, represents the mildest of "cuss words," and I cannot see that "darn" means anything different. Still, I declared that as a matter of policy we ought to avoid expressions that would rub any notable section of the public the wrong way. And it is amusing to record that when we were ready for the Code and the Producers Committee went to work in 1930, this subject received more attention than any other. The use or non-use of profanity was discussed—incidentally, with plenty of profanity—at many meetings and until far into many a night. I believe a record of those meetings would convince the most skeptical that the Code was not something imposed upon the producers, ready-made and without their co-operation, but a document that they largely hammered out themselves with serious purpose and sleeves rolled up.

Early in 1929, however, when talking pictures had gotten into full swing, the clouds of protest were again piling up. As I had feared, occasional excesses and the all too common injections of vulgarity into films had met with an indignant reaction. A bare ten months earlier "Red" Kann had declared that censorship was no longer a threat, but I had been far from optimistic. Now I had to warn the West Coast Association that too many objectionable things were creeping into some of the pictures.

To be sure, those in authority were in the habit of looking at the dailies, or "rushes" as they used to be called, which are quick prints made of each day's work and viewed and criticized by the executives the following morning. So far as moral values were concerned, however, those were piecemeal and apart from context, and a busy studio head could hardly be blamed if under pressure he was more engrossed with acting, lighting, and composition than with matters affecting potential moral values. Furthermore, once a scene was shot—particularly if it was a big one on a costly set, using large numbers of people—it was next to impossible to induce anyone to reshoot it.

Accordingly, I also cautioned the rank and file of directors and lesser studio executives, the men on the sets who had immediate control of the details that could make or mar a picture from a public relations standpoint. It may be supposed that I was concerned only with the public relations aspect, whereas they were interested only in "box office," but that would be a mistake. I knew that the mere negative approval of reform groups could never make our industry prosperous, and that our pictures had to be entertaining; but I did not think there was a necessary incongruity between decency and success. Except for hit-and-run money, decent entertainment is immeasurably more profitable than the risqué—and I am talking of dollars and cents, not of merit in heaven. Regarding this, the late Brock Pemberton once declared: "Most dirty plays are dull. They are dirty because they are dull. The playwright just fills up the cracks with dirt to give piquancy. Art and genius do not need dirt as a filler."

At that time, however, it was considered gay to add spice to scripts, scenes, and sequences. Hollywood Boulevard abounded with colorful characters, some of whom managed to clutch at the fringes of the industry. Such "wits" and their "witticisms" were quoted at smart dinner parties and in popular restaurants alike. The town was full of middle-aged pranksters and professional "screwballs." Mere eccentricity was often mistaken for genius, and it was the foible of the era to regard this kind of nonsense as cute and to seek to inject it into pictures which were being made.

Accordingly, I warned the executives of their responsibility to keep offensive ad libs out of their productions and to see that the scripts themselves conformed, even more strictly than before the advent of sound, to the provisions of the "Don'ts" and "Be Carefuls." I told them that the dark clouds of a storm were gathering. But it was occasionally a strain both on diplomacy and Christian charity to deal with those pseudo-sophisticates in our midst. Had they been allowed to dominate the industry's thinking, they would have put the movies right back into the peep-show class, something fit only for Skid Row theatres and amusement parks. The censor-minded groups, on the other hand, would have vitiated the motion picture and turned the whole business into a political football. Either eventuality would have been a calamity for art, as well as for a major American industry.

It was just at this time that I received a candid report from Colonel Joy. It was not a complaint, but he wanted me to understand his position. I not only understood it, but marveled at the patience of a man who would continue to shoulder such responsibilities with no sort of authority. It was an inspiration to me, for I had often felt in exactly the same position. In his discussion, Joy revealed that less than half the member companies of the West Coast Association were making any effort at co-operation, and that only about one out of five feature films were being submitted to him or his staff for opinion.

I refused to be disheartened and I begged Colonel Joy to hang on. After all, in seven years we had advanced from competitive anarchy to a fair measure of co-operative trade practice. The average of films was less sensational and many were culturally finer. Much remained to be done, but we had progressed from chaos to the Formula, which on the whole was being observed, and from the Formula to the rules, which were not. The over-all progress looked as good as the immediate problem seemed desperate.

Finally, in November of 1929, came the financial crash that swept away fortunes and made everybody frantic. It hit movie people as hard as it did everyone else, and the studios tried to save themselves, it seemed, at any cost to standards. Endeavoring to preach morality in that cataclysm was like a voice crying in the wilderness.

Still we were not licked! Out of this very storm and apparent setback came the greatest forward stride of all: the formulation of the principles underlying the Production Code, named a "Code to Govern the Making of Talking, Synchronized and Silent Motion Pictures."

But let no one imagine that the Code, like Athena, the goddess of wisdom, "sprang full-blown from the head of Zeus." It was a very human instrument taking shape slowly in the heads and hearts of many men, forged in the fires of experience, hammered out on the anvils of long debate. Nothing ready-made or handed down from on high would have worked or would even have been accepted. It grew out of honest and original thinking, which is something quite different from external legislation or fiat!

Actually we had been getting closer to our goal than we knew. This goal was the formulation of a production ethic, capable of uniform interpretation and based not on arbitrary do's and don'ts, but on principles. Mere rules, however adequate for the moment, are pragmatic; the time will come when they will not be observed unless rooted in immutable laws. There is no such thing as a traffic "law." There are laws of gravity and laws of God, but traffic is governed by regulations.

Hence a morality was necessary, a philosophy of right and wrong.

The industry was growing up, and the list of "Don'ts" and "Be Carefuls" had served its day.

Prior to 1929 neither industry nor public was psychologically ready to accept a philosophy, as distinguished from mere prudent rules. It was a question of timing. I am sure that if the Code had been adopted a year—or an hour—before it was, it would have fallen of its own weight. One does not teach a beginner at the piano the intricacies of Chopin. We do not expect an arithmetic class to comprehend calculus. The patriarchs of old reached a fair level of justice in the law of "an eye for an eye," with the concept of mercy awaiting later development.

Now every sign indicated that the time had come. Sound had combined with the motion picture to produce a dynamic art that was here to stay. The movies had become as cosmopolitan as journalism or international diplomacy. Great areas of public opinion had been prepared, owing to our persistent policy of creating the demand, and this public expected the industry to take its place among the great institutions of mankind. The exhibitor, who had feared these groups, was now dining and sharing seminars with them. The very fact that the "Don'ts" and "Be Carefuls" were too often flouted proved to me that the child had grown and had a right to know the reasons for the rules.

On a summer day in 1929 I was alone in my New York headquarters thinking about these matters—brooding, in fact, about them—when I received a phone call from Martin Quigley in Chicago. He said he would be in New York the next day and wanted to see me. Although it is much too coincidental to be believed were it written in a movie script, I had wanted to see Martin. He was a friend of many years, a trade-magazine publisher of outstanding success and exceptional moral and intellectual quality, who had demonstrated his devotion to our industry while more than once administering an editorial "spanking" when in his judgment that was needed. He had repeatedly championed both the Association and me. And when I met him for lunch the day after his phone call, we were two minds with a single thought. *The hour had struck.*

I say that I had been yearning for a *corpus* of philosophy; but it was Martin who had committed its premises to paper, and he showed me a rough draft. My eyes nearly popped out when I read it. This was the very thing I had been looking for! Martin said he had been giving the matter serious attention all summer; that ever since the sound picture had become permanent he had felt the need for something more comprehensive than the current "rules." So he had attempted to crystallize the principles upon which the rules were based—in fact, on which all moral laws are based. Fundamentally, he explained, these are the Ten Commandments and the Natural Law which is written into the heart of every human being of sound reason and morals. However, feeling that he was a newspaperman and a film man, but not primarily a moralist, he had had some preliminary talks with a friend whom he respected, the Reverend Daniel A. Lord, S.J., of the faculty of St. Louis University.

As far as I was concerned, both men were supremely qualified for the studies which they had undertaken voluntarily in the public's interest. I knew Father Lord, having met him when he had served with Dr. George Reid Andrews and Rabbi Edgar F. Magnin as a technical adviser to Cecil De Mille during the filming of *The King of Kings*. He was not only a theologian but a professor of English and dramatic literature and an author of note, particularly of one-act plays.

For the remainder of the summer we three were in constant communication. Father Lord visited Martin in Chicago and, at my earnest invitation, came to see me in New York. Meanwhile, I broached the matter to some of our members and made a quick trip West to sound out Hollywood sentiment. There I talked to numerous individuals about the project and in nearly every case got a favorable reaction. It was surprising how strongly the idea of a code with dimension and depth appealed to everyone.

Encouraged by what I had discovered, I returned East. The Code was nearly ready, and when I saw it I was delighted. What made it distinctive was that emphasis was placed upon rational considerations, with a minimum of prohibitive don'ts. It was affirmative rather than negative, constructive and not inhibiting. Some years after its adoption it was remarked by hostile critics that since its original authors had both been Catholics—and one a Jesuit priest—the Code must necessarily be considered a Catholic instrument designed to force Catholic theology on the screen. Nothing could be more absurd. Even before I read their joint draft I knew my men well enough to realize that matters of dogma would have no bearing. They had merely assumed that, while motion pictures are primarily entertainment, without any implied mission to preach or teach, they cannot escape the responsibility of affecting the thought of those who see them. A movie about a technical operation, such as an Army training film, may be an indifferent thing; but theatrical motion pictures, dealing as they must with human emotions, are in the wider sense moral, whether they like it or not. They may be immoral. But they cannot ever be morally neutral in effect.

Again I might have supposed, had I not known better, that since Father Lord was a clergyman his views would have been too rigorous and that he would have tried to forbid us from presenting on the screen any wrongdoing, so necessary to dramatic conflict. But their Code prohibited nothing of the kind, nor did they merely allow for "black-and-white" characters, so ingrained in the formulas of action picture plots and so far removed from life. All characters need not be good. All bad characters need not kick dogs or rob blind men. Our first consideration was the audience, and in our philosophical discussions we never forgot for an instant that we were serving an entertainment medium and that the Code must embody not so much a schoolman's philosophy as a showman's philosophy.

I had already acquainted the Board of Directors of our Association with my hopes and perhaps infected them with my enthusiasm; they not only seemed to share it but, in one or two instances, outdid me. Early in January of 1930 it was decided that I should go to the Coast at once, taking with me the Code upon which Martin and Father Lord had worked so tirelessly. By the twenty-third of that month I was in Holly-wood discussing the matter with the producers and directors on the front line. Now I had something in writing, I was "peddling a script," and I anticipated a certain amount of opposition. Instead, folks out there, with a western exuberance that was becoming native to them, exceeded the New York group in their eagerness to get at it. The West Coast Association at once designated a committee to study the matter with me: Irving Thalberg, chairman, Carl Laemmle, Jr., B. P. Schulberg, Sol Wurtzel, C. E. Sullivan, Charles Chrisdle, J. L. Warner, and Joseph M. Schenck. It was the hardest-working committee that De Mille, president that year, ever appointed.

This was no ready-made constitution. There was plenty of room for discussion and change. Like profanity, vulgarity was also proscribed, but now that we were getting down to definitions it was necessary to get a uniform interpretation. Just what is vulgarity? Discussion brought out that while there may be an identity between what is vulgar and what is immoral there may in other cases be a distinction. What is immoral is always immoral, in the twelfth century or in the twentieth, in China or in Hollywood. But what is vulgar may vary from age to age, or from country to country. Every person on the committee brought his own dictionary to the meetings. As finally hammered out in the Code, vulgarity was defined as "the treatment of low, disgusting, unpleasant, though not necessarily evil, subjects." The article then specified that these shall always be subject to the dictates of good taste, with due regard for the sensibilities of audiences. To close any gap that might lurk in the phrase "good taste," vulgarity was clearly distinguished from obscenity and also from scenes of carnal passion, immodest costumes, and improper dances. These are all defined and forbidden under separate headings.

Early in the discussions Martin Quigley came to Hollywood. So far we had been working on the second part of the Code—"Particular Applications"—which was the part containing the specific "Do's" and "Don'ts," and which bore a resemblance to the "Don'ts" and "Be Carefuls." These needed to be defined and modified according to the philosophy of the first part of the Code, which is straight moral philosophy. Movie-wise, we had been shooting the last scene first and concentrating on practical provisions. This does not mean we had been neglecting the more important part, now called "Reasons Underlying the Code," and regarded as an integral part of the document. But when the time came to check the committee's conclusions with the "Reasons," we needed both Martin Quigley and Father Lord. Through three lively and sleepless sessions Martin propounded the theory and answered questions to the satisfaction of all concerned.

A matter that came in for a lot of discussion was the definition of "realism" and the distinction between realism and romance. We all agreed that as far as possible life should not be presented in such a way as to place in the minds of youth false values of life. From this premise it was brought out clearly by Martin and by Father Lord—whom I had managed to pry away from his classroom long enough to make a quick trip to Hollywood—that what had hitherto passed for realism had actually been "literalism," an entirely different thing. Realism, meaning fidelity to life, is desirable, but the term had been corrupted by the literalists.

Romance sins by the opposite error. Too often romance, no less than literalism, presents life as it is not. In evaluating tendencies, however, we agreed that it is the lesser of two evils. There is a sense in which the movies, as a product of our century and civilization, are certain to be saddled with one or the other and must make a choice. We analyzed all these things. But we were concerned, after all, in getting out a code. We were not missionaries whose job was to found a new civilization, but movie men bent on making our art conform to the best of this cilivization. I believe we succeeded.

At last we were ready, on February 17, 1930, to present the Code to a full-dress meeting of the West Coast Board of Directors. The finished product was acclaimed and unanimously adopted. I am sure that, despite lapses and periods of backsliding, the industry has never been the same since. A giant which might have become a Frankenstein was that night endowed with a conscience. And while the light of conscience has burned dimly at times, it has been there ever since.

On March 31, 1930, five weeks to the day from the action of the West Coast producers, the Code was similarly adopted by our Association in New York, the Motion Picture Producers and Distributors of America, Inc.

The finished product was a pamphlet of nineteen pages. It is interesting to note that very few changes have been made during the passing years, because fundamental morality does not change. The administration of the Code made the job of the Studio Relations Committee easier in one way but more complex in another. Foreseeing this, I had suggested to the West Coast Association the need of increasing the appropriation for the Studio Relations Committee, urging them to consider such costs part of the production budgets. The West Coast producers had agreed and, from the first, the authority administering the Codes had been maintained by a fee system, paid by the studios in the form of a stated sum for each production passed upon. Thus neither the Studio Relations Committee nor the Production Code Administration has ever been supported financially by the Association.

Owing to the deepening depression, there was subsequently a tendency to forget the Code. But it must not be imagined that it was forgotten all at once or that it failed to produce improvement. For the moment, at least, the new broom was sweeping clean—or, at any rate, cleaner.

From the wiseacres there was plenty of criticism. A comment of *Variety* of that period was headlined "Warming Up Film Cinderellas," and it shook its head gloomily over the fact that what it called the "Hays Edict" and the public demand did not harmonize.

The "Hays Edict," indeed!

More optimistic was one of the sponsors of the Code and one of the greatest of producers, Irving Thalberg. While the trade paper was moaning, Irving was telling a group that he was an ardent believer in the Code and regarded it as his motion picture "bible." In that same group were such leaders as Winfield Sheehan, Darryl Zanuck, Jesse Lasky, B. P. Schulberg, and Walter Wanger, all of them Code cooperators in one way or another.

It was gratifying to see that the best sections of the press and the public hailed the arrival of a set of principles, as distinguished from regulations, with real appreciation. One of the most thoughtful comments came from Dr. Robert A. Millikan, who said:

I regard this as one of the most significant exhibitions I have ever seen of the possibility of our typical American method of private initiative bringing about the most beneficent development of our modern civilization. The motion picture has in it the possibility of becoming one of the most stupendous forces of modern life, and this looks as though it had appreciated this possibility and set about to realize it. It has chosen the right method. No government censorship could be one thousandth part as effective.

The thing that delighted me was that, although others had prepared the philosophical ground, the producers themselves had done the planting; and after the long winter of the depression, they were destined to reap a finer reward, materially and morally, than could have been dreamed of in 1922.

In this movie saga, nothing is harder than "to make a long story short." Nothing happened that way. Nor can the Code story be neatly dissected out of its network of ramifications. After the Code was adopted, and as the depression got worse, the industry went through rough sailing. At the height of the storm the directors even debated abandoning ship—scrapping the Code. Instead, they reaffirmed it in an all-night session that tested the faith—and the guts—of every man on the Board of Directors. As champions do under pressure, they came through. They held to their faith in the motion picture, I held to my faith in them, and we both held to our faith in the public. Audiences continued to flock to picture theatres during the first years of the depression. The boom brought about by the arrival of excellent talkies carried on.

Of all reactions, I was probably most gratified by those of picture-makers themselves. One of the keenest judgments was given in a press interview by my friend Alfred E. Green, who had directed the notable picture *Disraeli:*

> The only real bugbears to the modern director are those who would hack and cut and denounce in order to force their own narrow ideals on the screen. The director welcomes the constructive criticism which helps, not hinders, motion picture progress. There are few relationships in life that cannot be made beautiful by really artistic treatment, and there are none that cannot be ruined by arrant vulgarities. And I may say that the progressive director welcomes this latest challenge to his profession, if for no other reason than merely because it demands elimination of hackneyed and time-worn situations and calls for the creation of new effects.

One important studio writer privately told Fred Beetson that the Code was no hindrance to the scenario art, but that all writers needed to do was to think a little harder along finer lines. This seems to have been typical of the early consensus in Hollywood. A full year later B. P. Schulberg, then production chief at Paramount and one of the original signers, summed up what the producers had learned. According to Ben, they had discovered that the public wanted family entertainment with real characters and down-to-earth themes, and that the trend was away from "sophistication" because the old type of post-war thought, which had found its life in sex and frankness, was dying. Incidentally, they found that many character actors, as well as glamorized stars, had become drawing cards.

One of the most significant public reactions to the Code was that of the Parliament of the Province of Quebec, which adopted it, almost verbatim, as a law for the guidance of its official censor board.

In spite of the auspicious beginning, the next four years were destined to be hectic. Our "shakedown cruise" was inevitably to take us deeper into the uncharted sea of the depression, and it is true that we all but foundered before the storm abated and we returned to port. It was inevitable that mistakes should have been made. Factors apparently beyond anyone's control played directly upon whatever human weakness there may have been. Hence it would be oversimplification to say that the industry adopted a moral code and then promptly forgot it until a rearoused public threatened a boycott. The aberrations of a man or of an industry struggling with economic depression cannot fairly be judged years later amid the comfortable surroundings of prosperity.

Of all dramatic elements hard to keep within bounds, sex and gangsterism proved the most difficult. The biggest factor bringing obloquy upon the industry was sex. There were other causes of public displeasure, such as the flaunting of drinking scenes, but when the chips were down—as they were finally laid down in 1934—sex pictures were the prime cause. It was the studios' preoccupation with sex, in a manner contrary to the spirit of the Code, that let loose the barrage.

Gangster stories created another type of problem that might have run the sex picture a close second had we not gotten it under control fairly early. The gangster cycle was natural because the gangster cult had been a main theme of journalism for a decade. But there was no tendency in these crime stories to say to the audience, "Go thou and do likewise." On the whole, penologists acquitted the industry of any incitement to crime and sometimes even praised it as a deterrent to crime.

Another question naturally arose: Did the Code cancel and supersede all previous agreements and formulas? The answer, of course, was no. Title Registration and the Authors Agreement both stood, and both were outside the jurisdiction of the Code. To settle all doubts, the Board of Directors of MPPDA and the heads of the member companies drew up and issued late in 1930 a clear "Declaration of Clarification." There was something refreshingly peremptory about the language of the Declaration, as if I or somebody else had actually been granted power to enforce its provisions, which was not so. We only had an agreement.

Although Colonel Joy, watching over the observance of the Code, was generally encouraged, the year 1931 brought faint rumblings of what might lie ahead. Dwindling box-office receipts gave some folks an excuse to lay the blame on the strictures of the Code. But it was only a coincidence that the Code and the depression had come in almost together. Some elements of the public, too, may have objected to the changes influenced by the Code. But I had listened to civic groups, mothers, teachers, responsible citizens. And those were the people who at length prevailed. In the last analysis, they became the enforcement agency.

Some unfortunate pictures still reached the screen when the advice of Colonel Joy's committee was disregarded. A social-problem type of picture, using the "mistress" theme, was tightening censorship restrictions. And the net result added up to a growing restlessness.

On the brighter side, and indicating the generosity of motion picture people, the industry did more than its share to relieve the ills of the depression. The philanthropic activities as a whole, both by groups and individuals, would make a long list, confirming and enhancing the charitable tradition of "show business."

There were other signs of progress, one being that people still trusted the good intentions of producers and gave them the benefit of the doubt. The Code received encouraging praise from the Vatican. Submission of scripts to the Studio Relations Department was made mandatory. New producers—non-members—were using the Code and applying for the services of Colonel Joy's department. A motion to liberalize the Code's prohibition of profanity was defeated. Late in 1931 Joy was able to express at least tentative satisfaction with the way producers were co-operating. Though liquor and sex pictures continued to be damaging, we had one more concrete evidence of improvement: our "batting average"—the percentage of films passed as "good" by the influential pre-viewing groups—rose from 77 per cent for features and 72 per cent for shorts to 82 per cent for features and 84.8 per cent for shorts. And this was in the midst of the depression.

But as the steady down-pull of external forces went on, things gradually took a turn for the worse. In 1932 Merlin Aylesworth, then president of RKO, admitted that unless drastic economies were effected the industry would be bankrupt within ninety days. As it turned out, his prophecy was not far from wrong. Everybody was anxious and un-happy. It was pardonable that folks were thinking of other things more than of the Code. In desperation, and without consulting with anyone, some of the companies announced a series of flaming pictures. I was able to persuade the companies to give up those particular projects, and in other cases to use less suggestive titles. We were wrong enough as it was.

The strain of trying to "hold the line" had told on Jason Joy, and he was showing the effects. When in September of 1932 he told me that Fox studios had offered him the post of director of public relations, which was not only more lucrative but far less controversial, I advised him to accept. I did this with regret, for he had given the industry nearly a decade of devoted service, most of it on the firing line. He had earned a respite. An unusual tribute could be inferred from an estimate published by *Variety*, hitherto often critical, that the Studio Relations Committee had saved the studios $4,000,000 and 40 per cent in deletions.

To take Colonel Joy's place, we induced Dr. James Wingate, formerly head of the New York State Board of Censors, to come to Hollywood. He was a man who fully understood and sympathized with our prob-lems and, as an ex-censor, he was not likely to overlook anything. But coming in at a time of critical tensions, with morale under such pressure, the situation was probably too much for any man. Many executives were desperate and many producers willing to take a chance. In the vernacu-lar, Dr. Wingate was "pushed around," and there were no sanctions to be invoked.

Thus it was that 1932 moved to its close in a cloud of fear and gloom. And early in 1933, in the gathering shadows of financial chaos and economic night, some voices called for repudiation of the Code and all prior restrictive agreements. Some felt that if the industry was to save itself and keep its thousands of people in their jobs it had to "Let 'er go, Gallagher," with anything permitted so long as it brought in the money. This clamor was not widespread, but it was loud enough to be heard in New York. Our response took us through the most dramatic hours in the life of the Association.

On March 4, 1933, Franklin D. Roosevelt was inaugurated. Two days later the emergency bank holiday was declared. That night of March 6 we in our Association held a meeting in New York that lasted until seven o'clock the following morning. Much of what transpired must be left to the imagination and to the memory of those who passed through it. We had come together to discuss the financial situation and the grave problems it posed for the whole industry. But out of that meeting, as out of what the Bible calls "the refiner's fire," came the answer to those who were advocating retreat from our original purposes, and in particular from the forthright moral position of the Code. Instead of abandoning anything, the heads of our member companies reaffirmed their entire pledge. This meant that all of the member companies of the Association, represented that night by their presidents or other officers, bound themselves anew to even stricter observance of all policies previously adopted. And I believe that this reaffirmation would have been well kept but for the staggering economic problems that soon faced the whole country. I say that the reaffirmation was sincere, because that night there was no particular fear of public displeasure. That was to come later.

The reaffirmation of March 7 applied specifically to the Production Code. Three weeks later, on March 27, the members added a renewal of dedication to our original objectives, as set forth back in 1922, "to establish and maintain the highest possible moral and artistic standards of motion picture production." The statement further recalled our agreement of June 1927, in which certain things had been listed as improper screen material; as well as the Authors' League agreements and the Production and Advertising Codes. The leaders again acknowledged their responsibility to the public for strict maintenance of the standards and purposes that had been adopted.

Following these twin reaffirmations, I communicated the Association's decisions to the West Coast, and the Association of Motion Picture Producers thoroughly endorsed the action we had taken in New York. This was not merely lip service. Any forthright acknowledgment that right is right and wrong is wrong cannot be mere lip service even though mistakes may subsequently be made.

Upon the inauguration of Franklin D. Roosevelt, I had at once pledged the support of the industry to the new administration. During the following years he and I were to have many conferences, some of them of deep consequence to motion pictures both here and abroad. More than once, when the going got tough, I found him a real friend at court. The industry co-operated to the full extent of its power with the government in connection with the National Recovery Act, enacted June 16, 1933; but a Motion Picture Code under NRA was no new problem. We had been operating for three years under comprehensive production and advertising codes; our trade practices had been examined and commended by the Federal Trade Commission; our wages and working conditions were sometimes referred to as "the best in the world." Nevertheless, advisers close to the President, ambitious to extend federal control over the media of communication, looked at the screen with longing eyes. They went so far as to draw up an elaborate scheme for a super-organization to oversee the entire industry, and even suggested Owen D. Young, I believe, as the co-ordinator. When the scheme reached the President he said that "any plan will have to be okayed by Hays, he will have to favor it," and he sent for me. Before the end of our conversation he assured me that neither this plan nor any similar one would be contemplated further, in view of my representations concerning the industry's self-regulation and the fact that our plan was working as well as any plan could work. No more was heard of a federal co-ordinator. Our Association's original resolve, and our reaffirmations thereof, to discipline ourselves for the mutual benefit of the industry and the public, together with our past actions in that direction, satisfied this remarkable man fully.

Though the "batting average" of New Year's resolutions completely carried out is probably negligible, who shall say that they are cynical or valueless? Reaffirmation of good intent could not do away with all temptations and backsliding. Human nature being what it is, something more would be needed. That meant some form of enforcement, though from my viewpoint it must be self-adopted, whatever the circumstances that might bring it about. That last step in the evolution of the Code was still to come. And it had to come the same way as each earlier step: through the democratic processes of self-regulation. The leaders must see the need, frame a plan, and voluntarily adopt it—but it was my duty to help. Perhaps I thought again of what my father once wrote his brother: "I give Providence the glory; but I did the engineering."

There were unmistakable signs that a change had to come. Some American pictures were barred in nearly all foreign countries. Both the Studio Relations Committee and I were roundly upbraided by press and public. The review of *Baby Face* in *Liberty* magazine was headed: "Three Cheers for Sin!" One newspaper columnist asked if the Studio

Relations Department had "been out to lunch all year." And this, in spite of the fact that the industry had turned out more high-grade pictures than in any similar period in its history.

Then in Hollywood, in August of 1933, came a momentous meeting that brought home to the West Coast Association how badly the guilty minority had besmirched the standing of the screen. I had asked two laymen to address the group. I thought it would carry more weight if a couple of our friends outside the industry were to tell their story face to face. One was Dr. A. H. Giannini, whose financial aid to the studios had often been indispensable but who was now badly worried about the low moral tone of some recent films. The other was Joseph Scott, one of the leading attorneys of Los Angeles, and, like Dr. Giannini, a prominent Catholic layman.

They both pulled no punches. And as they spoke it was evident that they had gone deeper into the subject than I had guessed, for they had already conferred with Bishop John J. Cantwell, later to become Archbishop of Los Angeles. And it may be that as an elder in my own denomination I was quick to feel the significance of Giannini's and Scott's remarks. Since the movie colony was located in Bishop Cantwell's territory, his words would be listened to by every ecclesiastic of his church; in fact, they were waiting for those very words.

All this flashed through my mind as I listened to Joe Scott. I realized, too, that the Catholic groups had been the most patient and least belligerent up to now; indeed, certain Protestant Church organizations had complained that they would have "cracked down" long ago had their Roman Catholic brethren not counseled moderation. Too, their method would have been federal censorship. But now, as Scott told us, these same groups were reproaching the Catholic bishops and putting it squarely up to them. Practically, they had challenged the Catholics to act. Something like the Legion of Decency was indicated.

Dr. Giannini went still further, reminding us that Pope Pius had taken enthusiastic personal note of the Code when promulgated in 1930 and had exhorted its observance. But he reported that disappointment, not to say disillusionment, had replaced the former hopes entertained in Vatican circles. Hollywood, the cinema leader of the world, had become as famous for its sex pictures as for its cultural and artistic achievements, to the detriment of civilization. Nor did Dr. Giannini fail to hint that any convenience the Bank of America might extend the studios would thereafter become a moot problem of conscience in his own personal case, unless a change of policy were quickly effected.

Had all this merely been a Catholic Church matter, it would have augured ill enough. Even at that time, communicants of that faith numbered about 20 per cent of our total population and were concentrated chiefly in the great urban centers which sent the industry most of its revenue. In our foreign market, the percentage was much higher. But it was not exclusively a Catholic reaction. These people, as a religious group, had been the last to lose patience and had even interceded for us with the others. We were in for a storm. Approaching the end of its shakedown cruise, the industry was in for still another shaking. Something was due to happen!

The Legion of Decency soon supplied the answer, and one long invited. It was not merely that too many bad pictures had "asked for it." Our whole open-door policy had always sought honest reaction and advice from high-minded organizations. Humanly speaking, it was the moral force of the Catholic Church that gave the *coup de grâce* to Code-breakers. And it was the concrete program of the Legion of Decency, quickly taken up by other groups, that spearheaded the public demand for Code enforcement.

Far from considering the Legion an enemy, I welcomed its co-operation with open arms. Here was one of the most striking examples of "Let's get together" I ever experienced. To this day, the majority of people probably consider the Legion's work an "attack." I saw it as a "defense" of the moral standards we had ourselves adopted. We actually created a "mutual defense pact" that finally made the Code a working reality. Letters that passed between the bishops and myself give ample evidence of that fact.

But the story of the Legion—its formation, its program, and its decisive influence—is too long for these pages. I can try only to suggest its spirit, its tolerance, and its practical wisdom.

In October of 1933 Archbishop A. G. Cicognani, apostolic delegate to the United States, addressing the National Conference of Catholic Charities at the Metropolitan Opera House in New York, fired the opening gun. Among other things, he declared: "What a massacre of innocent youth is taking place hour by hour! How shall the crimes that have their direct source in motion pictures be measured?" There had been times in the last several years when I had wished I might have spoken as bluntly myself.

Some studio folks continued to live in a fool's paradise, "buying and selling and lampooning marriage"—if I may paraphrase the Scriptures— and these, ironically, were the ones who became the most resentful and "righteously indignant" when the storm broke. Early in November, Bishop Cantwell, speaking at a Knights of Columbus banquet in Los Angeles, urged that group to make a movement in behalf of clean films one of its projects. At almost the same moment Bishop Michael J. Gallagher, in Detroit, attacked indecency on the screen, in books, and in periodicals, and formed the Detroit Council of Catholic Organizations to combat those forces.

Later in the month the Catholic bishops of the United States gathered at Washington for their annual meeting. The motion picture situation was the subject of a careful report and a warning by Bishop Cantwell—his words making a deep impression. Speaking of the Production Code, he stated:

> "Steadily during the past two or three years the regulations of the Code have been 'honored more in the breach than in the observance,' with the result that a new and complete overhauling is imperative *if the motion picture industry is to survive unhampered by additional state censorship bodies or a federal censorship law.*"

But it is a pleasure to record that he concluded by saying that, despite the offensive pictures, most of the outstanding successes were "clean as a hound's tooth." As a result of that address, the bishops appointed a motion picture committee to study the situation. In December, Cardinal O'Connell, Archbishop of Boston, appealed to the League of Catholic Women, which resolved to boycott offensive films.

Apparently Hollywood was not greatly alarmed at the action indicated by the church leaders. I have always been an optimist, but nobody is as optimistic as a self-kidder. The sentiment seemed to be that this threat, like so many others, would blow over. But I sensed that it was something different.

On April 28, 1934, the formation of the Legion of Decency was officially announced in Washington by the Bishops' Committee. A pledge to remain away from all offensive motion pictures, and all theatres where such pictures were shown as a matter of policy, was published, and it was proposed to enroll the 103 Catholic dioceses of the United States in the Legion. Non-Catholic churches were invited to join the campaign—and needed no urging.

The whistle had blown! Immediately protests against salacious films and offensive advertising swept across the country in a rising tide. From Hollywood, where I was, it sounded like a roar. Clear across the nation, especially in cities, folks of all denominations eagerly signed pledges, and the first 300,000 printed went in a couple of days. The movement was like an avenging fire, seeking to clean as it burned. For the most part, it took the form of a popular movement, in some cases the clergy being obliged to restrain their people from boycotting even decent shows and condemning all movies!

Will Rogers, following his attendance at the convention of the Motion Picture Theatre Owners in May, wrote:

> Their convention informed the producers that as about everything in the way of sex had been produced, and the audience didn't care to see it over again, they suggested that for a change they thought the audience would like

to see just an old-fashioned movie. And they also want to eliminate the sensational and suggestive advertising used for pictures. You can't make a picture as bad as the ads lead you to believe it is.

That was about the size of it.

By this time nearly everyone in the industry was convinced that we could not sit in the cyclone cellar and wait for the storm to pass. The whole protest proved the need of overhauling our machinery and revising procedures so that no such provocation could be given again. It had become clear to me that a thorough house cleaning could not be done without something resembling police power. Our industry metropolis had grown too large for good behavior by mutual agreement only. The motion picture community itself, to say nothing of the public, would have to be protected from those within its gates who might be tempted too easily to cut corners.

Accordingly, in June of 1934, the Association concluded the final steps of an arrangement we had been working on for some time: requiring the same standards in the distribution and exploitation of motion pictures as had been prescribed for their production. It should be explained that while the studios and distributors were responsible for much of the advertising, some of it was left to the theatre circuits or the individual theatre managers. By the arrangements effected at the June 13 meeting, theatres were thenceforth required to conform to the same Code and advertising standards as the producers.

The most important resolution passed on that occasion, however, was one which strengthened our Code enforcement machinery and changed the whole nature of the Studio Relations Department, which had always been a branch of the West Coast Association. It later became a department of our New York Association, with plenipotentiary power to order changes in any picture which it might consider to have violated the Code, the changes to be made before release. The plenipotentiary feature automatically abolished the "Hollywood Jury." Therefore, it was provided that the producer of a film rejected by the department might appeal to the Board of Directors of our Association in New York, whose decision would be final.

Some of the producers asked if there was never going to be an end to this thing. Their guess was as good as mine, but I had a glimmer of hope when I heard that the Bishops' Committee on Motion Pictures, which had started the ball rolling, was scheduled to meet in Cincinnati for three days in June. I was doubly interested when I learned that Martin Quigley, as co-author of the Code, had been invited to attend the sessions as a guest of the chairman, Archbishop McNicholas. I asked him to lunch with me and a few of our company heads at the Harvard Club, and we there asked him if he would act as the official representative of the organized industry at the conference. We pointed to the overhauling of the machinery that had been effected at our meeting on the thirteenth and told him we would take any measures that seemed reasonable and proper to secure the good will of the committee and establish a peace that would leave us some dignity, as well as the freedom of the screen.

Martin consented to represent us and to make an agreement if possible, on condition that we give him full power to act. Whatever he agreed that the organized industry should do, we would do, without his needing to interrupt the sessions to consult us.

That seemed fair. One or two of our fellow lunchers were reluctant, but we were the parties seeking the truce. The meeting had not been called for the purpose of treating with a representative of the industry; that was our addition. It was a private party, and we were crashing the gate. On the other hand, I knew that we could trust Martin's judgment; he knew industry problems almost as well as we, and Catholic bishops much better. Hence, before the luncheon was over, we were all in accord.

It was agreed that Joe Breen would accompany Martin in order to explain to the committee the Code enforcement machinery and the new powers we had invested it with. Telephoning Joe in Hollywood, I asked him how he would like to preach to his clergy instead of vice versa. Joe said that he would meet Martin in Cincinnati.

Martin and Joe had naturally intended to go to a hotel, but with true monastic hospitality, Archbishop McNicholas insisted that they be his house guests, together with the dignitaries of the Church. These two representatives of the industry were the only laymen present, and we might have searched the world and not found two men better qualified for the distinction or the job.

The meeting lasted three days. None of us in the Association knew what was going on in Cincinnati. There was nothing to do but wait. At length we received a telegram from Joe saying that the meeting was over and that he and Martin would be back in New York the next day. The following morning everyone was in my office at half-past eight—and the train was late! About noon our two ambassadors arrived at the office, having come straight from the station. I knew that everything was all right when I saw the cat-ate-the-canary expressions on their faces. Everyone crowded around them anxiously, but they, being Irish, could not resist having a little fun with us and keeping us guessing. Then they told their news: the war had been called off.

However, it had been called off only conditionally. The bishops confirmed rather than dissolved the Legion of Decency, and announced that it would continue to solicit pledges but that theatres showing decent films had nothing to fear. The films had to be decent. The yardstick was nothing new—just the Code that we had had for four years. All they asked was that the industry live up to it.

Practically by acclamation, Breen was confirmed as head of the Studio Relations Department, which was then rechristened the Production Code Administration and taken over by our New York Association. At last we had a police department, or at least a civilian-defense force, and the best part of it was that this was acceptable to the producers, which it would never have been until recent months.

On that same day, June 22, I publicly announced the resolutions taken by our Board of Directors on the thirteenth and the appointment of Joe Breen as Code administrator. Furthermore, our Association strengthened his hand by prescribing a fine of twenty-five thousand dollars to be imposed on any member company which should ever release a picture without the certificate and seal of approval of the PCA. Here, at last, was authority. This was the sanction, owing to the growth and importance of the industry, that was required. I am glad to record that in all the years since the prescription of the fine the Association has never had to invoke it. I might add that the PCA has never lost an appeal regarding a script, and only three or four altogether with respect to finished films.

We had finally reached our goal: a reasonable code that could be enforced by the will of the majority. What followed through the years is to the eternal credit of Joe Breen, the man who made it go.

If I may moralize a moment on this strange pilgrimage, with its almost rhythmic succession of mountains and valleys, fair skies and threatening clouds, it might be thus:

Is there an honest man or woman alive who has failed to experience the endless problem of self-discipline? The motion picture industry has had the same experience—always will. At least it has acknowledged the fact, defined the difficulties, and drawn up a clear set of moral principles to guide it— with a seal as the reward, public obloquy and a fine as penalty. This it has done of its own free will, supported by the interest of the public. Is that a bad record?

CHAPTER 29

Full Steam Ahead (July 6, 1934–March 29, 1937)

THE industry's buffeted ship reached open water on the Fourth of July, 1934, with the firm establishment of the Production Code Administration. The skies were clearing, and we were free to go full steam ahead.

Not forgetting the lessons of warning, and determined to prove what could be done when placed on their honor, the motion picture companies proceeded to make a record of good pictures that has perhaps never been surpassed within a similar period of time. From that moment until the first clouds of World War II appeared on the eastern horizon, motion pictures wrote an amazing story upon the screens of the world. Producers vied with each other from 1934 to 1937 to turn out the best pictures that could be made, both to demonstrate their good faith and to help lift the morale of a nation only beginning to recover from the depression. This boosting of spirits is one of the greatest things the movie has ever done.

Themes of many sorts were presented on the screen. In the reproduction of literary classics, and in the screen portrayal of historical characters and varied dramatic types, the record is striking. The best minds in the industry were working at top speed. And some of the very best— Will Rogers, Irving Thalberg, Martin Johnson—were taken away from us at just this time. Meanwhile, other prominent figures, like Joseph P. Kennedy, Dr. A. H. Giannini, M. H. Aylesworth, as well as J. Arthur Rank and H. G. Wells of England, began to play important roles in the industry. The seed time had been long, but a rich harvest was now being reaped.

In thinking of this period, which the industry recognizes as a definite era in the development of pictures, I find myself hunting for figures of speech to express the sudden outburst of creative energy. Producers acted like students who have been taken off probation and are going to show the administration they know how to earn A's.

For the MPPDA and for myself it was an equally stirring time. Our machinery of self-government had been strengthened by the new Production Code Administration. Now the question was: How well would it work? As president, I found myself in a new position, finally wielding a measure of the "power" that had been wrongly attributed to me as alleged "czar." But we were still on the spot. It was up to all of us to heed the biblical admonition, "Show me thy faith by thy works." The pictures of these three years were our showing.

I suggested that one answer to depression-family budgets was to reduce prices; and at one time the average admission charge was estimated to be only twenty cents, with the companies having the satisfaction of knowing that they were supplying the best tonic in the country.

As we talked over the common problems, it was not hard to point out incentives to good performance: the best way to avoid censorship was to produce pictures that did not need censorship; the best way to avoid other legalities was to follow sound trade practices. So well were these policies followed that the popularity of motion pictures increased decidedly and audiences widened; though the quality of pictures went up, the admission price went down, and the "batting average" of pictures rose to an all-time high—in at least one case to 97 per cent. We even saw such voluntary ads published as that by the Kansas City Council of Churches: "Let's Go to the Movies." In the midst of such world scenes as the rise of Hitler, the Ethiopian and Spanish wars, and major strikes here and abroad, the flowering went on, nurtured by the dozen departments of MPPDA. Technical advances were great. Artistic skills reached new heights. Moral standards and social values went up. The screen found new uses. In the international field, American films attained near domination.

In all this process the American people again came out the winner and, to my mind, the *hero*. While the Germans were ousting *It Can't Happen Here*, and the French were claiming the right to exclude any films they wished on political grounds; while the Japanese were barring *Mary of Scotland* in deference to the throne and *Mutiny on the Bounty* because it was too revolutionary, our people exercised their humor and good sense by welcoming pictures of every sort for whatever they were worth. It was hard for them to understand the touchiness of other nations whenever they thought one of their race was being presented unfavorably. Our people once more proved that they know good and evil exist alongside each other, that the struggle between them is essential to drama, and that it is the business of human beings to learn how to distinguish between the two.

Audiences supported our policy that commercial—theatrical—motion pictures were properly used for entertainment, news, and popular education, but improperly used if twisted to serve the interests of propaganda, pressure groups, or commercial advertising. We watched to keep this young giant of the talking shadows free from such malformations or abuse.

I am not at all sure but that another excellent argument for the wholesomeness of American taste in pictures could be built around the striking popularity of child actors and actresses—not so much the babies as the children of six to ten or twelve. Jackie Coogan, Shirley Temple, and Freddie Bartholomew are good examples.

It is doubtless one more proof of the spirit of this golden period that Shirley Temple, a box-office favorite from *Little Miss Marker* on, was designated by the nation's showmen as leading the "First Ten Money-Making Stars of 1937." The same year another child actress—Jane Withers—stood number six. The preceding year the reviewing committee of the G.F.W.C. had chosen Bonita Granville, Freddie Bartholomew, and Shirley Temple as the best in the classification "Children"; they were great favorites with nearly everyone. All this seems to me still, as it seemed then, to refute any charge that popular movies have to be built on the sensational, on crime, and on sex. For here, in its purest form, was the unsophisticated, the natural, and the humanly appealing.

One of the most interesting national conferences during this period was held in Washington for four days in December of 1934. Governors of all the states and delegates representing legal, medical, sociological, religious, scientific, educational, civic, criminological, patriotic, welfare, and other organizations, with representatives of the press, radio, and motion pictures, were invited to this Attorney General's Conference on Crime. The latter inclusions were significant. The delegates representing our Association included Governor Carl E. Milliken, secretary; Charles C. Pettijohn, general counsel; and Gabriel L. Hess, general attorney.

Because of the many loose charges that had been flung at the movies as a stimulation to crime, I welcomed this opportunity to present our case and studied it from every angle. Our delegates told the conference how the processes of self-censorship worked in the making of pictures which used crime as a dramatic theme. Films were shown to indicate specific lessons in character training already found in many feature pictures.

Every phase of crime and many methods of dealing with it were discussed. Press, radio, and screen—in the persons of Fulton Oursler, H. V. Kaltenborn, and Carl E. Milliken—took similar positions, all discussing their role in the war against crime. The puzzling thing, however, continued to be the sharp differences of opinion as to crime's causes, and as to the effects of various screen portrayals of criminals.

This whole subject had recently been under such intense study by congressional committees, with the proportions of crime in America hailed as "gigantic," that I felt the serious charges against the movies demanded examination. We got together a sheaf of statements, reviews, and editorials, under the title "Authoritative Statements Concerning the Screen and Behavior." The study touched the heart of the Association's problem of self-regulation: Were pictures succeeding in making crime repulsive rather than attractive? This question was hotly debated. There were those who loosely claimed that movies had substantially increased crime in this country by stimulating criminal tendencies in potential delinquents. Every time the question was raised, I tried my best to estimate the relative value of the alleged facts advanced, the interpretations put on them, and the widely different conclusions drawn.

As I look back on those middle years, I can't help wondering whether there were not factors involved that made it unusually hard to draw sound conclusions. Upsetting changes in home life had followed World War I. Many family roots had been torn up. Schools were crowded. Cities were growing. Exciting commercial amusements were increasing. The depression brought phenomena we had never seen before. And in addition to everything else, I believe, an intensifying of sheer publicity, notoriety, and organized pressures tended to throw the truth out of focus and to turn opinion into violent attack.

At this point Dr. Raymond Moley stepped into the picture. Knowing that for several years he had been studying criminal law administration and related research on the causes of crime and delinquency, I called on him for advice. I learned that most earlier researches had "modestly suggested the possible influence of certain factors upon human conduct, while they made it perfectly clear that their findings were limited in scope and significance by the inadequacy of our present methods," but that Dr. Moley had grave misgivings about other people presently engaged in "the use of what is called the 'scientific method,' making careless demonstrations and drawing reckless conclusions from the most inadequate and deceptive materials." He felt that it would be a service to point out the "errors and prejudices" embedded in such findings. This task was undertaken by Dr. Mortimer Adler of the University of Chicago. Dr. Adler was well fitted for the job because a few years previously, collaborating with Professor Jerome Michael of the Columbia Law School in a study of research methods in the field of crime and delinquency, he had punctured several pseudo-scientific studies. Better still, he was already engaged in an analysis of the role which motion pictures play in contemporary life.

In the resulting book, *Art and Prudence* (1937), Dr. Adler discussed "the moral, political and esthetic aspects of the motion picture." The author showed that the moral questions we were debating so hectically in the early 1930s had been a perennial problem of art from the earliest classical period, and capable of no easy solution.

Among the questions discussed were whether the movies actually have come to exist as an art or are merely an amusement, like a circus or a prize fight, and what are the moral and social obligations of an art as popular as motion pictures. Dr. Adler and I discussed these questions at great length, and I explained that my personal convictions about the social responsibility of the movies had had much to do with my entering the field.

As Dr. Adler pointed out, the questions involved go deeper than the legal problems of censorship and prohibition. They led him to consider all types of criticism, the relation of art to the moralist, the relation of church, state, and family in achieving the welfare of the community and the integrity of the individual. Painstakingly he discussed the relation of moral and aesthetic standards in criticism. This work put a scholarly, philosophical foundation under the self-regulating structure which the Association had built up within the industry.

When he examined the findings of earlier studies on the influence of movies on conduct, he found many of them inconsistent and by no means proven. He kept on the lookout to distinguish between knowledge and opinion, statistics and interpretation. The latter he found uncertain, affected by personal bias, and often based on erroneous facts. He found no accurate way to measure the relative influence on children of movies as compared with home, school, church, friends, books. To quote him on only one important point, juvenile delinquency, "In the matter of moral influence, the relevance of the scientific data is questionable. To whatever extent they can be considered as reliable, the findings are inconsistent and tend to be negative. . . . If all this has significance after unreliability of methods and data have been taken into account and inconsistencies nullify each other, *it tends to cast some doubt upon the popular concern about the moral influence of motion pictures upon the immature.*"

That's a pretty strong statement and goes farther than I ever cared to go. But it was a body blow to the theory that movies were primarily or even largely responsible for juvenile delinquency. Similarly, Moley concluded that children were not "movie-made."

The discussion of movies and morals, pro and con, went on endlessly in the press, reflecting people's thinking. I was glad that it did, and I always felt that it was one of my jobs to see that editors were kept informed. They were quick to scent bias in pressure reports, and just as quick to pass on interesting facts to the public. They stood almost 100 per cent against censorship, which was the usual goal of the "movie-menace" decriers. They remained among my staunchest allies in the cultivation of a constructive attitude on the part of the rank and file. Here is one out of the hundreds of illuminating current newspaper comments of 1933 and 1934:

St. Paul, Minn., Dispatch: It is just a little amusing to see the investigators trotting up and dumping at the studio door all the ills of society from crime to vanity that have at other times been blamed upon co-education, the bunny-hug, jazz music, French novels, high heels, the split skirt, one-piece bathing suits, and so many other things. Anyone who has lived 30 years or more could make an impressive list of menaces which we have somehow managed to survive.

Many social scientists were equally unwilling to accept findings in conflict with their own observation. One of the best objective opinions was found in the concise statement of Dr. George W. Kirchwey, formerly warden of Sing Sing Prison: "In so far as motion pictures have any direct effect, they do not encourage crime, they discourage it." And an even more striking bit of evidence was given by Mr. Joseph F. Fishman, formerly United States Inspector of Prisons, writing in *Harper's* magazine for July 1933: "To these films belongs entirely the credit for the public understanding of, and revulsion against, gang rule today." This was the sort of public education I had always believed the screen could render.

Though I never believed that either the public or the industry had to be "lawed" into line, there were plenty of people, both in and out of courts, who continued to take the opposite view. Their endless activities added to our problems. The doctrine of "government regulation" was growing. NRA was with us until its demise in May of 1935. The New Deal weather was developing some aspects that seemed to me, as applied to our industry, hardly healthful. But my personal relations with the administration sometimes aided the consideration of our special problems.

Though legislative matters were the concern of the companies rather than of the Association, they did determine the "climate" in which we lived and worked: one of the trade papers reported over 50 "anti-pix" bills under consideration early in 1935. Owing to changing concepts of government, it was a period of legislative uncertainties, and the law at times took a rather dim view of certain forms of co-operation which had grown up quite naturally. Such customs as block-booking and clearance (the time elapsing between the first and second run of a picture), though admitted to be advantageous, were declared to be technically illegal, according to existing statutes. To me, this was an illogical situation; it was the reason I so often pleaded for the revision of outdated laws, many of which had been passed before motion pictures had ever reached the screen.

The year 1936 gave the industry some relief. The final report on NRA had urged federal control of our industry, but we saw no immediate effects. Soon afterward, the Sabbath film probe was halted by the plea of Joseph P. Kennedy. And in June we were informed that no film bills had been passed by the Seventy-fourth Congress. Within our own industry the process of "conciliation"—somewhat different from arbitration—was beginning to operate in all key centers.

But during the following year—1937—pressure increased again, in spite of undeniably improved picture production! Since the Association's Articles of Incorporation had stated one of the ways of fostering "the common interests of those engaged in the motion picture industry in the United States" to be "by securing freedom from unjust or unlawful exactions," we tried to use our good offices in helping to answer unjust attacks and to avoid unlawful exactions. Among the measures contemplated in various states in 1937 were a 2 per cent admissions tax, the raising of censoring fees from $18 to $120 a feature, "control of sponsored commercial films in theatres," the "exclusion of newsreel cameramen from courtrooms," and the requiring of "a toilet for every 150 theatre seats." Our industry was a happy hunting ground!

That hardy perennial, bureaucratic censorship, naturally had a much harder time to keep alive in the face of improved Code administration. As *Variety* picturesquely put it in the autumn of 1936, "Picture Censors Jittery. *Joebreening* to K.O. their jobs." (Joe Breen was the efficient head of the Production Code Administration.) "Self-Regulation by Hollywood Leaves Little or Nothing for Sundry Censors to Do."

Both press and public were overwhelmingly with the industry in resisting the arbitrary, illogical, or humorless decisions of official censors. Both believed in self-censorship by the industry and were sporting enough to say, "Give 'em a fair chance." Langdon Post came out with the crisp statement, "Censors are incompetent." And the Committee of Catholic Bishops, as eager as anyone to see moral standards preserved, had no use for political censorship. As part of our educational publicity program, a wealth of humorous press comment was published by the Association in June of 1936 under the title *Concience by Proxy—America's Indictment of Censorship.*

Right here I want to take my hat off to that great American institution, the cartoon, and the artist-philosopher-satirists who have made this medium of expression such a force in American life. In my own public activities the cartoon seems to have played quite a role. Plenty of times I was the subject, with my big ears as the favorite trademark. Once when Ring Lardner wrote a piece about me, it was illustrated by a drawing showing me as a traffic cop, with the legend: "Traffic had to detour around his ears." It was in the same vein that Irene Dunne, at an Indiana Society dinner in Chicago, pulling my ear, referred to me as "the Clark Gable of Indiana." The great cartoonists have stood right alongside the great editors as molders of public opinion. Two of the most distinguished—both good friends of mine—whose work began in 1896, come to mind. Our grand Hoosier, John T. McCutcheon, born in Tippecanoe County in 1870, was one of the great figures on the Chicago *Tribune* for almost half a century. Indiana was always proud of him. I remember when I was a sophomore in Wabash College how we followed in the papers his trip around the world on a U.S. dispatch boat. It was through his eyes and his drawings, made on board during our war against Spain—including the battle of Manila Bay—that many of us saw these events. Clifford Berryman, on the other hand, was born in Kentucky and came to cartooning from the field of general illustration. It was his drawing of me in the Washington *Star*, as someone being kidnaped from the Post Office Department by movie bandits, that drew attention to a transition that seemed to many people inexplicable.

Both the editorial comments and cartoons were sprightly, to say the least, with censorship taking quite a beating. By the mid-thirties we had made real gains. The Charlottesville (Va.) *Progress* commented: "The activities of the Board are completely useless inasmuch as they merely duplicate the strict code of the Hays Office, and they cost the people some $25,000 every year." So it looked as if, by sticking to our objectives, we were at least making progress, and the "Joebreening" had reached a point where many people felt that the situation was getting fairly well in hand by 1936 or 1937.

Among the interesting events of this period, illustrative of a type of attack which often threatened and which I had to try to forestall, was my meeting with Father Charles Edward Coughlin at his Shrine of the Little Flower at Royal Oak, near Detroit, in August of 1934. This was shortly after the Production Code Administration had gotten under way.

For some time Father Coughlin's had been a voice of wide influence. His broadcasts were listened to in many homes. His pronouncements on any subject were accepted by thousands, possibly millions, of people. He had built up a great army of loyal followers, as well as a conscientious opposition. Here was a public relations factor of consequences: if he were publicly to take any strong position on the movies, it must be reckoned with.

In midsummer of 1934 a report did reach me to the effect that Father Coughlin planned to make a speech in the Chicago Coliseum in the near future in which he was going to attack motion pictures. It was further reported that he was likely to use motion pictures as the means of an attack on the Jews, claiming that they dominated the business, and blaming its evils on them. There seemed to be too much substance to the report to overlook it. From my viewpoint, any such pronouncement would be not only intolerance but intolerable. Such a thing must not happen if it could be avoided. Under the circumstances a face-to-face talk was the only thing. Having already planned to go up to Leland, Michigan, to spend a few days with my brother and his family, I decided to stop off at Detroit and call on Father Coughlin. He had the reputation of being a tough opponent in a fight, but politics had introduced me to a number of tough opponents, and I had found that the right side of a question could usually stand up. But I believed this should be handled as a confidential mission.

Seeking in advance whatever information I could get as to Father

Coughlin's daily habits, and habits of mind, I decided to make my call on a Saturday morning, when he would probably be at home preparing for the Sabbath. This I did, at about ten o'clock in the morning of a beautiful summer day.

I found his cottage on a corner, next door to the church. In answer to my knock the door was opened by a young priest, evidently a member of the parish staff. In reply to my inquiry I was told that the pastor was over in the "Tower" preparing his sermon and that he received no callers on Saturday. I remained undiscouraged. I said, nevertheless, that I was having a good deal to do with the Catholic Church at the time and that I thought it important for me to talk over the motion picture situation with Father Coughlin.

The young man said then that he had recently come to Royal Oak from Cincinnati, where he had worked under Archbishop McNicholas of the Bishops' Committee on Motion Pictures. He knew what had gone on in connection with the Legion of Decency and was kind enough to add that Archbishop McNicholas had a high regard for me. He even told me that he had seen some of the correspondence between us, and became very cordial. When I told him I had in my pocket a letter bearing significantly on the relationship between the industry and the Legion, he said, "I think you'd better wait while I go over to the Tower and tell Father Coughlin you're here. He wouldn't like it if I didn't." Returning almost immediately, he said that I was to go right over myself.

Father Coughlin greeted me cordially and asked me to come upstairs. Under his cassock I could see that he was as rugged as a truck driver. On the way up to his study we passed a room where there were perhaps fifty girls opening letters and making records. I was told that the letters, most of them containing currency or checks, came from all over the country to support his activities and those of the shrine. When we entered his study on the upper floor the clock, resembling the circular clock in a captain's cabin, registered exactly ten minutes after ten. We sat there until twelve.

As we talked I told him that the reason for my coming was that I wanted to discuss with him the whole matter of motion pictures, in which I understood he had great concern, and to tell him what the organized industry was trying to do. He expressed interest, and I told him the story. At half-past eleven he asked me if I had any engagement for "dinner," meaning the noon meal. I told him I had no other engagement than to see him. It seems that each Saturday he had dinner with his mother, that they both looked forward to these visits, and that he wanted to take me with him. I accepted gladly, and he telephoned that he was bringing a friend.

In this two-hour morning conversation we covered a lot of ground, though our chief topic was motion pictures, and I didn't by any means do all the talking. Father Coughlin made some vigorous interpolations as I spoke of films, and expressed his views on many other things. He said that he was sympathetically interested in pictures, that he by no means "had it in" for them, and that he felt that the producers, although they made mistakes, had made great headway. He thought motion pictures had the greatest popular influence of any medium of expression —perhaps even greater than the churches! When he referred specifically to pictures in schools, I told him what we were doing in that field. And as he spoke of what he considered good pictures and bad pictures, he seemed to me to express some distinctly good judgments. As to the basic spirit and attitude behind these statements, however, I somehow still felt in the dark. Something seemed out of key. The strength of the man, his clarity and even brilliance of expression were undeniable, but I could not feel quite so sure that in every case, as the Scripture puts it, "out of the heart the mouth speaketh."

At noon we drove over to his mother's home and I met a white-haired lady, cordial and gracious, who was a real benediction. She already knew my business and talked appreciatively about pictures. It was evident that she was very proud of her boy. We sat down to a dinner of fried chicken and mashed potatoes, cream gravy, baking-powder biscuits, jellies, and jams that was pure joy. There was the feeling of a fine Christian household.

Our dinner conversation, in which the mother joined fully, touched many subjects—religion, politics, and public affairs, as well as motion pictures. No reference of any kind was made to any speech under consideration.

Soon after we had finished dinner Father Coughlin suggested I go downtown with him while he did some errands. It seemed he was having a men's supper at his house that evening for which he had to lay in provisions. The occasion was a telephone session he was going to have with Mickey Cochrane and the Detroit Tigers, who were playing that day in Boston. He had invited quite a group of his Detroit friends to sit in—and eat in—on it. I can testify they must have had plenty to eat; when we got back from the grocery store it was all Father Coughlin and the young man and I could do to carry the food from the car to the kitchen.

After the supplies were disposed of, we went back into the living room and talked further; we seemed to be on most comfortable terms, and I was enjoying it all. As a matter of fact, my pleasure was equaled only by my surprise. As I reported on the industry's plans and progress in self-regulation and expressed my belief that we would succeed in this purpose, Father Coughlin's reaction was distinctly favorable.

When it came time later for me to leave, he insisted on driving me to the station, where we parted most cordially. A few days later he made the Chicago speech and advocated repudiation of $20,000,000,000 of this country's gold obligation. He did not mention motion pictures. Afterward I wrote him a letter of appreciation, expressing hope that the industry would continue to deserve the confidence of all who were generous enough to repose their confidence in its program.

The vitality of this mid-thirties period is also shown by important new names, already well known in other fields, that were being added to the growing motion picture roster. This was not only a personal satisfaction to me, but proof that more and more people were finding motion pictures an important enterprise. I must mention only a few of these men, with all of whom I had close association.

Raymond Moley I have already spoken of as a first-class scholar and publicist, who early began to write with discernment on the influence of pictures. Will Irwin, a popular writer, contributed one of the most interpretive series of articles ever to appear in a movie magazine, *The New Movie*. Joseph P. Kennedy, with a broad background in finance and organization, who had earlier been president of the Film Booking Offices of America and of Pathé Exchange, again came into our field as adviser to Paramount. Dr. A. H. Giannini was elected president of United Artists. He was a brother, and for a long time a partner, of A. P. Giannini, who founded the Bank of America, and these two were the first national bankers of prominence to make big loans to motion picture companies. Dr. Giannini had long been a good friend and had helped convince producers that they must put out decent, moral pictures "or else." About the same time M. H. Aylesworth quit NBC for a post with RKO.

The English scene began to change with the growing influence of J. Arthur Rank, who in 1936 was reportedly seeking four or five hundred motion picture theatres in Great Britain. I welcomed his vigorous entrance into the field, with the prospect of increasing competition from abroad. H. G. Wells first came to Hollywood in 1935, adding another interesting personality and delightful companion to our Coast community.

But these same years also saw the too early close of some of the most distinguished careers ever involved with the American screen. We lost Irving Thalberg, one of the true creative geniuses of the motion picture; Martin Johnson, the distinguished maker of wild animal pictures; Jeff McCarthy, the real founder of the Advertising Code Administration; and Will Rogers—that true gentleman of America.

As to Irving Thalberg, it is hard even after this lapse of years to speak with moderation. He was an outstanding human being and a great artist. His unexpected death at the age of thirty-seven stunned the industry. The early work of the "boy wonder" had blossomed into such productions as *Mutiny on the Bounty*. On the purely personal side, the home life of Irving and his lovely wife, Norma Shearer, a fine artist in her own right, was an example of the finest kind. Mrs. Hays and I were very fond of them both.

So strongly did I feel Irving's significance that I wrote in my Annual Report for 1936:

> None can consider the artistic stature of the motion picture today without pausing to pay tribute to the memory of Irving Thalberg, whose creative leadership was lost to the Industry in 1936. . . . His work, his devotion, his artistic integrity and his social consciousness contributed vastly to bringing about an era of motion picture entertainment in which distingushed works of literature, drama and music were transferred to the screen.

Speaking of him immediately after his death, I said: "Brilliant, courageous, a careful workman, who always gave his best, he had the vision and the genius which made him a leader in the Industry's constant progress toward the highest levels of art and entertainment. Such productions as *The Big Parade, The Barretts of Wimpole Street,* and *Romeo and Juliet* will stand as monuments to Irving Thalberg, but he was destined for even finer things." He belonged to that little group who might be thought of as super-producers, men who compass the whole range of possibilities in the creation of a picture, and who thus secure deeper, finer, and more perfectly integrated results. It is these men who best show us the role which the screen is capable of filling.

Another industry milestone was passed early in 1937 when we paid our tribute to the pioneering, wise, courageous Adolph Zukor on the twenty-fifth anniversary of his entrance into the business. Industry leaders had expressed their personal appreciation in letters bound into a big memorial volume. In presenting it to Mr. Zukor in their behalf at a dinner at the Paramount studios, I tried to put our feeling into words like these—words which in a sense might be applied to many a motion picture pioneer:

> "You are a great leader because you have had the mind to dream and the heart to make your dreams come true. Your willingness to study and learn has been equaled only by your courage in pursuing new ideas which an almost uncanny sense of public reaction told you were sound. Fear has never been a part of your make-up.
>
> "You are a pioneer in an effort to satisfy the growing desire for better motion picture entertainment. You made feature pictures at a time when such an innovation was considered financial suicide. You recognized and met the problem of distribution. In an ever-widening circle, you made it possible for the best artists, directors and technicians to give to the tired world the tonic of youth, beauty and romance.
>
> "And throughout, you have proved the truth of the adage—'The secret of success is constancy of purpose.' "

This event in honor of Mr. Zukor was reinforced by the appearance in the New York *Times Magazine,* the following month, of a history of his twenty-five years, under the excellent title "From the Nickelodeon to the Picture Palace"—a journey of which this daring pioneer knew every step. Much of my feeling for the early days and their difficulties I have gotten in long hours of conversation with Mr. Zukor. The way in which he and others had solved their problems was always an encouragement to me and a cause for increased belief in the potentialities of the motion picture. It gave me a similar thrill, early in 1947, to send congratulations on the Zukors' golden wedding anniversary—another symbol of the wide span of this able leader's life.

Martin Johnson also meant much both to me and to the industry. He has been well called a "moving picture explorer." He married Osa years before my connection with pictures, and the courageous couple had traveled around the world half a dozen years in the South Seas and five years in Africa. Their work interested me keenly because it was in the best sense educational as well as entertaining. We talked things over considerably before they undertook the making of their five-year film record of the vanishing wild life of Africa. Begun in 1924, this ambitious project, which wrote film history, had one unfortunate result: it so aroused popular interest in wild life that unscrupulous producers were too often tempted into "nature faking." In films like *Ingagi* this sometimes became more than a worry. We've had since to insist that education and entertainment, romance and natural science, must not masquerade in each other's garb.

For Jeff McCarthy, the man who first made the Advertising Code work, I had both admiration and affection. His death in 1937 at the age of fifty-eight was a heavy blow. Jeff could wear with honor and humor the appellation bestowed on the Notre Dame football team: he was one of the "fighting Irish." And because he knew from the ground up the game of motion picture advertising, the publicity men of the various companies found him a hard man to fool.

In still another way McCarthy was a symbol. He was one of the first successful showmen of the legitimate theatre to recognize the motion picture as a serious competitor. He was the man who, in 1915, had presented D. W. Griffith's *Birth of a Nation* at the Liberty Theatre in New York, with orchestral accompaniment, sound effects, and reserved seats, at the unheard-of admission price of two dollars. It was the vision and daring of this man McCarthy which almost overnight gained recognition for Griffith's genius and new dignity for the screen. And it is marvels like this—most of them performed within three decades by a relatively small group of men—that have made me say over and over, *"No story ever written for the screen is as dramatic as the story of the screen itself."*

Jeff McCarthy also personified another tenet in our Association creed: the freedom of the screen, the principle which I believed most basic of all. Because of his many clashes with censors, Jeff found himself in the forefront of the fight for freedom. He joined the Hays organization in 1933, with a broad background of showmanship, a prodigious knowledge of the country, and keen understanding of American audiences. He recognized that sensational advertising was causing the industry embarrassment to the point of serious danger. His own particular contribution as chairman of the Advertising Advisory Council from November 17, 1933, to the time of his death on February 25, 1937, was unique. I want to pay tribute to the force of a personality that enabled him to hold out for standards of taste and ethics. His success was so great that the system of self-regulation which he set up received widespread commendation. As *Printers' Ink,* the advertisers' weekly journal, said: "The truly cooperative attitude by all parties concerned has made this first large-scale experiment of a major industry to regulate its advertising from within really practical and successful." What more could be said!

I come now to a story quite beyond my power to tell as I would like. Will Rogers meant too much to me; we were too close. Born only one day apart, our lives ran strangely parallel, especially from November 9, 1922—the night of the Friars Club dinner, when Will introduced me as one of the "Three Czars"—to the day of his tragic death, August 15, 1935. And Betty Rogers is very much a part of that whole story. From that day to this it has been one of my deepest interests to help keep his spirit alive in the industry and in the nation through the activities of the Rogers Memorial Commission.

Some of our earliest relations, beginning long before 1922, were in connection with national politics. In his talks Will used to say that I had introduced him to three presidents: Theodore Roosevelt, Harding, and Coolidge. Going back still farther, Betty loved to tell how, when Will had gotten a pony to use in his roping act at the St. Louis World's Fair in 1904, he had named him Teddy for Colonel Roosevelt. I know that among Will's most prized possessions—and he had a lot of them— were two notes written in the hand of Colonel Roosevelt and sent to him during the old vaudeville days when, with jokes about the colonel and others, he was making his first humorous comments on national affairs.

I remember as clearly as if it were yesterday introducing Rogers to Harding in the President's office. The two men hit it off like a couple of collie pups. Harding's nature instinctively reached out to take Rogers into his circle, and anyone who did that was in turn absorbed by Rogers. After a characteristic dialogue, Will told a very good story and Harding said, "Oh, Rogers, I've heard that story of yours before," and Rogers said, "No, that one you haven't heard, Mr. President; I don't tell that except for pay, and I've only told it on the Amsterdam Roof." Smiling, Harding said, "Well?"

About the inhuman burdens put on our presidents, Will and I felt exactly alike. For the same reason that I wrote the magazine article called "Shall We Kill All Our Presidents?" he wrote a chapter in his delightful *Illiterate Digest* under the heading "Let's Treat Our Presidents Like Human Beings." For the light it throws on these two good friends of mine, so different and yet in plain human qualities so alike, I must quote some paragraphs written just after the death of President Harding:

I am writing this away out here in California days before you read it; it's Sunday and everybody's thoughts and sympathies are with a train rushing clear across our country passing sorrowfully through little towns with Just Folks standing bareheaded paying their respects to Just Folks going back to Marion to stay with Just Folks.

He goes to his resting place a martyr, a martyr to the Boneheadedness of Reception Committees. You wouldn't ask your hired man to do in one week the amount of real physical work that each Committee asked him to do in one day. Imagine three long speeches in one day, and a parade for two hours in the hot sun with his hat off most of the time. . . .

So when the next Congress meets they should pass a law to shoot all Reception Committees or teach them consideration for other people. . . .

You may have read in the papers last year that the Diplomatic Relations were strained between President Harding and some of my jokes on the Administration. Now, I want to say that nothing was farther from the truth. Why, he could stand all the jokes ever told about him or his policies. The first time I met him Will Hays introduced me to him in the White House and he repeated to me a lot of jokes that I had told away before.

And I told him then: "Now, Mr. Harding, I don't want you to think that I am hard on you at all. You know I told some pretty hard ones on the Democrats when they were in; in fact, I think I told funnier ones on the Democrats because they were doing funnier things." I explained to him that it would not be fair to the Democrats to kid them while they were down, but the minute they got their head above water again, I would take a whack at them. . . .

I liked President Harding. You see I had met him, and I don't believe any man could meet him and talk to him and not like him. I thought I would be scared when they took me in, but he made me feel just like talking to some good old prosperous ranchman out home.

I only hope our future presidents can be gifted with his sense of humor and justice. . . . He was a good friend to all kinds of people. For he had the right dope after all. Everybody is Just Folks. HE WAS A REAL HONEST-TO-GOD MAN.

Rogers liked Calvin Coolidge, too, and his particular brand of dry Yankee humor. He called him "one of the wisest little birds that was ever in there." Once he said, "Mr. Coolidge, I have told many jokes about you, and this don't mean I am going to quit, for we love jokes about those we like."

It was during Coolidge's presidency that Will's "Letters of a Self-Made Diplomat to His President" appeared, written originally for *The Saturday Evening Post,* and he often referred to him in other writings. In kidding about his own operation for gallstones, under the title *Ether and Me,* Rogers related the preliminary conference between surgeons:

" 'What do you advise?' the first doctor asked.

" 'I advise an operation,' said the second.

" 'That's what I advised,' said the first.

"Imagine asking a surgeon what he advises! It would be like asking Coolidge, 'Do you advise economy?' "

A few pages farther on in *Ether and Me,* Will wrote: "We got to wondering what had brought on this severe attack at this time. We laid it to everything we could think of. Will Hays had just been out here and spent the day with us. Now, I don't lay the illness directly on to him, but a continual listening to the merits of the movies and the Republican Party will sometimes react disastrously on a previously ailing stomach."

The simple fact that we were both "in the movies" from 1922 to 1935, and neighbors in California, would naturally have brought Will Rogers and me together. But that alone could never have accounted for the kind of friendship that developed. As the years passed, we realized how much we had in common. In recalling some of the things Will said and did, I find it hard to draw a sharp line between his feelings and mine—they were so much alike.

Even the time and place of our major moves were strangely related. Though we grew up in states that were much unlike, we both loved the country—horses most of all—and liked to have plenty of room. In California we loved to talk about our "ranches."

Without stretching it too far, we might be said to have entered "national politics" about the same time, Will as a commentator from the stage of the *Ziegfeld Follies,* and I as chairman of the Indiana State Council of Defense. He beat me into the movies with his screen debut on Long Island in 1918, just after I had established headquarters in New York as Republican national chairman. He had rented Fred Stone's home at Amityville for the summer, and I visited him there. After he had made his first picture he accepted a two-year offer from Sam Goldwyn to make pictures in California.

As Betty often told me, Will liked the work at the studio from the very beginning. And the studios certainly liked him. He was a hard worker: nothing was ever too much bother, and no hours too long. He had a hand in his scripts and wrote all the running titles in his silent pictures. Playing opposite Irene Rich in *The Strange Border, Jes' Call*

Me Jim, and many other films, Will loved to tell me how good-natured and wonderful to work with he always found her. The Rich and Rogers families were soon fast friends, and later the Hays family was glad to be a member of that circle.

Although he was one of the few who submitted to no censorship on the air, Will never enjoyed the radio as much as he did making movies, which he called "the grandest show business I know anything about, and the only place where an actor can act and at the same time sit down in front and clap for himself."

In 1922, the year I left Washington to enter the Association, Will became a columnist, his first weekly article appearing in the New York *Times,* and soon syndicated all over the country. We both had to shuttle back and forth between New York and Los Angeles, our two stamping grounds. In California, Will got a lot of pleasure out of his Sunday polo games—his usual mates including Ed Borein, the cowboy artist, Leo Carrillo, Vernon Castle, Jim Minnick, Fred Stone, and occasionally Frank Tinney. It was great fun to see them play. "The people who watched us play on Sunday games," Will once said, "soon learned that in a spill, if the falling rider lit on his feet, it was Fred Stone. If he lit on his head, it was me. We were both equally safe."

In 1924, my third year with the Association, Rogers was back in New York again and working in the *Follies.* That was the year the Prince of Wales came over here to see the international polo matches. Will couldn't miss the chance to make jokes about the Prince falling off his horse. Once he asked the audience: "Are the Prince and I supposed to fall with the horses or are we supposed to stay up in the air until the horse gets up and comes back under us?"

It would be easy to fill many pages with recollections of Will Rogers, of what his spirit did for his friends, of his restless energy and tireless activities, of our visits back and forth, of his innate kindness and understanding, of his generous giving of time and money. He probably appeared in more benefit performances than any entertainer of his time. During the latter part of World War I he wrote William Fox, head of the Red Cross Committee for the Amusement Industry: "I pray to God that this terrible war will be over in less than a year, but if not, I hereby pledge myself to continue my subscription of $100 a week for the duration of the war."

After sound was established on the screen, the Rogers family returned to California, settling there for good. When Will signed with William Fox to make talking pictures and Winfield Sheehan showed him a ponderous document purporting to be a contract, he groaned at even the thought of struggling through it. Merely turning the document over, he wrote on the back, "I haven't read this thing, but if Winnie Sheehan says it's all right, that's good enough for me." Then he signed his name.

From this time on our paths crossed often. In 1927, when Will made his first visit to Mexico as a guest of Dwight Morrow and toured that country, he began a great friendship with the man who had been the best friend of my early New York days. In common, too, we had a deep concern for commercial aviation, though Will was keener to fly than I was, and we both had close associations with Lindbergh. Will had met him the first time in San Diego soon after his transatlantic flight, and Lindbergh flew Mr. and Mrs. Rogers back to Los Angeles the next day. Will told me that he had liked the boy at once. From the very beginning there was an understanding between them that developed into a lasting friendship.

There is no call for me either to eulogize Will Rogers or try to analyze his humor. His place is fixed. He thought of himself as an entertainer but never took himself too seriously. As Betty often said, he seemed casual, even skeptical, about his professional work; he reckoned they would eventually "catch on to him." I think this traced back to his innate modesty and absolute honesty. He didn't like buncombe in himself or in anybody else. He refused to consider himself a "public figure." In the same way he hated to see men who were running for office, or in office, get a blown-up idea of their own importance. I remember his saying during one of the national campaigns: "And when I said that they both were taking themselves too serious, that the United States was bigger than any two men or any two Parties, why that's the way I feel about it."

After watching political actviities for over fifty years, I would say without question that Will Rogers' relation to politics was unique. Politics had always fascinated him, but as a student, not as a participant. While he regretted that he had taken so little advantage of his opportunities to get a good education, few men were better educated in the true values of politics. He seldom read books, saying he didn't have time, but few men knew better the facts of current events as recorded in the newspapers. And I know that none were more welcome visitors at the White House or on Capitol Hill.

When Will was about to "retire" from the air, Vice-President Garner and a group of senators sent this message:

Dear Will: What is this we hear about your radio retirement? Does that mean that you will not preside over the Senate again? We have enjoyed your recent talks on the air and want your assurance that you will soon return with your humorous and wholesome comment on national affairs.

Deeply moved by the message, he replied over the air:

"This is one of the most wonderful things that I have had happen to me in many a day. It shows that you can tell jokes about people and still retain their friendship. I am very proud of that."

Will's humor was never bitter or synthetic. It was almost always in the form of comment on current events, often introduced by his famous "All I know is what I read in the papers." He always claimed that he could get all the comedy he needed by reporting the facts, with perhaps just a little exaggeration. But there wasn't an unworthy motive in anything he did. He never aimed at notoriety, or at making more money, or at getting back at anybody. He never said a mean thing and he refused to gossip. His only natural reaction was to lend a hand when anyone was in difficulty, whether private citizen or public figure. So it gave me a thrill when the Post Office Department recently came out with the three-cent stamp carrying his picture and his words: "I never met a man I didn't like."

During World War II, when movie companies were having so much difficulty getting out of England the money impounded there, I used to think of a passage in "The Letters of a Self-Made Diplomat": "My trip came at a time [1926] when foreign relations are at their most perilous peak; that is, when we were trying to collect money. Any man can fight a war, but it takes a smart man to jar loose change out of any part of Europe. Especially when they already eat up the money that was loaned them." Another time he said: "The United States never lost a war or won a conference."

Will and I more than once talked about another taste we had in common—we both liked to get to the "grass roots" on any important question and find out how "the people" were thinking. That's the way I was raised in politics, and I found the policy just as good in the movies. Will once said to a New York audience: "I'm getting tired of talking to Broadway. I want to get away and talk to America." Of all his jokes, he liked best the ones that rang true to everybody.

He always scouted the idea that people of different groups or of different sections of the country were any different at heart. We often talked about this. One of his finest tributes came when he was speaking of the great jockey, Earl Sande, just after he had been badly hurt in a race:

Some Westerners who don't know are always saying that Easterners have no heart. Everything is for themselves and the dough. Say, don't tell me that! *Geography don't change human nature.* If you are right, people are for you whether it's in Africa or Siberia. A wire was sent by Mr. Widener, a millionaire racing official, to Dr. Russell, the great specialist of Roosevelt Hospital, New York: "Come at once. Spare no expense. Sande is hurt!" That's all Secretary Slemp could do if President Coolidge was hurt.

I seem to remember best some of the things that happened during the last year of Will's life. In January of 1935 I made a talk at a Los Angeles Realty Board banquet at which he was presented with a watch in token of his selection as the city's "Most Valuable Citizen for 1934." He had already become the popular honorary mayor of Beverly Hills.

And I particularly remember a Sunday in mid-July when I went over to his house. He had just returned from a hectic week's trip during which he had helped in some Oklahoma harvesting, attended a family reunion in Texas, flown to Washington to confer with the Russian Ambassador preparatory to flying into Russia with Wiley Post, visited Fred Stone in New York and his own daughter Mary, who was playing in stock somewhere in New England, chartered a private plane to get back to New York—commercial planes being grounded by bad weather—and finally caught a transcontinental plane to California. What a man! I rode a horse and roped some calves, with a generous assist from Rogers, the rancher. I have some humorous snapshots of the doings.

On the Saturday before the Monday when he set out on his last flight we spent the whole day together. About eight o'clock in the morning he came by and picked me up at the house in Bel Air Bay, where we were living while our ranch house in Hidden Valley was being built. He arrived in a little jalopy that didn't look as if it could possibly stand the rugged trip we had planned. We drove out the Roosevelt Highway from Santa Monica to look at corral fences and other improvements on some ranches quite a distance out. After grabbing a noon lunch of hot dogs at a wayside stand, Rogers struck out through Sycamore Canyon. It was not easy to get through in an automobile, but he knew the way, and even where to find the keys to the gates that were locked. He was interested in the possibility of buying the canyon, later purchased by my friend, the late Carl Beal, the petroleum geologist and engineer.

After looking over Sycamore Canyon as carefully as we wanted to, we came out on the Hidden Valley side, drifted down into the valley, and came to our place where the men were at work clearing the ground on the side of the hill that slopes up from the road. It was about three o'clock. Rogers was at home with the workmen in a jiffy. He just stood around and talked, and then sat around and spat and kidded. The twenty men stopped work, gathered around him, and just listened and laughed with Will. It was a scene I'll never forget. It lasted so long that it was already late when we started back to town. I couldn't help talking with him about the danger of these airplane trips of his, in which he seemed to relish taking chances. I did this frequently, partly because of my own feeling about it and partly at the suggestion of Betty. But now he said: "This is one time, Bill, you don't have to worry, this is a cinch. Why, Wiley can set that boat down on a millpond."

We drove in slowly—much more so than usual—and we talked about everything, and especially about our boys. His son Jimmy was to return Monday from a roundup on a friend's ranch in Texas, and the father was happy about it, recalling his own ranching as a boy in Oklahoma. And then, right out of the blue, he broke in, "Bill, doggone it, Bill, I'm going to give you two horses." I tried to refuse. "Yes, I am," he said.

"I'm going to give you two horses, and I know just which ones." I again objected, but let it drop because there wasn't any use arguing with him. Anyway, I was sure he would forget all about it. We got in and had a bite to eat, and the next day—Sunday—I went with him to Westwood to the preview of his last picture, *Steamboat Round the Bend*, with Irvin Cobb.

Then on Monday morning, I remember, I stopped at his house on the way in for just a minute or two before he left on the flight that ended in Alaska on August 15.

When the word of his death was flashed to us, NBC asked me to say something about him over the air that evening. It was not an easy thing to do, but I am sure that whatever I may have said was simply the expression of what was in the hearts of those who were listening. Based on a transcript made that night, the press carried the following message:

Will and I spent the last Saturday together before he flew North, puttering about in an old car in the hills. That was one day in a friendship extending unbroken and unmarred, since years ago when I brought him to another Roosevelt who loved him—Theodore Roosevelt.

It is very difficult for anyone who knew this lovable friend to feel or express any emotion tonight except shocking personal loss. Yet, he was the world's. In kindliness, humor, faith, his was a universal spirit. All doors opened to him; every family circle has an empty place.

Belonging to the world, Will belonged to his own country as homespun belongs to a wearer. He knew these States, inside out, more intimately than any contemporary. Good deeds, foibles, weaknesses—all were tied and branded when he swung his rope of common sense, humor and philosophy. The crime of sham was never his.

He would want to leave a message of confidence and faith. Knowing his own people as he knew them, Will never once doubted. He was a *convinced* American.

Will never cared for flowery talk. He had no gift for it; no use for it. He was kindly and simple. He said: "I never kidded a man unless I liked him."

In the plain American language which he loved—a *man* has gone West.

The millions who had learned to know and love Will Rogers on the screen, over the radio, or in his newspaper column had a chance to pay their tribute the following week. Throughout the nation the motion picture screens were darkened for two minutes—timed so far as possible to coincide with the funeral services held in Hollywood. In many theatres other brief ceremonies were held. Studios where Will was best known suspended all activities for the afternoon, and every studio paused in the day's work to do him honor. Our industry never felt a greater personal loss nor paid a greater tribute of personal affection.

But for me there was still another message, the fulfillment of a promise, yet to come. Five or six weeks later, while in New York, I had a telephone call from Roger Miller, who was supervising the building of our new home in Hidden Valley. "The Rogers ranch truck just brought over two of the prettiest horses you ever saw and I don't know what to do with them," Miller said. "Well," I told him, "take the very best care of them you know how, for to me they are the most prized horses in the whole world."

There could now be no doubt that Will Rogers, when he got home from our jaunt that last Saturday evening, had told Betty of his promise and had named the horses. And they were beauties! One was Golden Breeze, rated the fastest polo pony in all that section and a great ranch horse as well; the other was a crack rodeo and stock horse which Jimmy had ridden for years. We rode those horses for a long time, and never without thinking of Will. Here was a man whose whole life proved that he knew "it is more blessed to give than to receive." As Betty wrote of him, after recounting many such acts of which the public never knew: "It was of such things and of the spirit that prompted them that Will's natural, living philosophy of helpfulness, honesty, and tolerance was composed."

Late that fall Twentieth Century-Fox Studios, where Will had worked so long, dedicated a magnificent new sound stage to his memory. The leaders of the industry were there, with Rupert Hughes presiding. Gladys Swarthout sang "The Parting of Friends." When Irvin Cobb, visibly affected, spoke reverently of his old friend, there was no holding back the tears. Fred Stone, Will's closest friend, faltered as he told of his love for "my pal who has gone." Finally, when little Shirley Temple unveiled the memorial bronze plaque, she said it all most simply, "I loved Mr. Rogers too."

In the midst of talking about pictures and working for pictures, I have time and again paused to ask myself, as has many another fan, what about the pictures themselves? What do they mean to me? What do they mean to other people? What do they do to us, or for us? What more could they do if they were better? So much has been taken for granted that it is hard to get down to bedrock in one's thinking. Estimating the net result of pictures is so puzzling that many a person has at one time or another been brought to the point of wondering whether he would rather "kiss 'em or kill 'em."

As I think back to the day when I decided to accept the movie offer—after seeing Bill, Jr., and my nephews vying with each other to be Bill Hart—it was the sheer influence of the movies that got me. And on that score I've never changed my mind. Though techniques have improved a thousand per cent, and though the field of the movie is world-wide, it is its tremendous impact on the eye and the ear, the mind and the heart, that still gets me.

Executives and producers have worked out a vocabulary for the various aspects of the motion picture and its effects on audiences; but the simple fact is that its influence is hard to explain. That is why I was always concerned about how the influence was used. And between 1934 and 1937, when developments were so swift, these questions kept crowding on us. I felt a little bit the way people feel today about atomic power: it was wonderful—but it could be so easily misused!

For the motion picture, like the written word or the painted picture, is both a medium of expression and a form of art. The medium itself determines neither content nor taste. As a matter of fact, its range of expression is so wide and its possibilities of error so great that the moviemaker must be on guard. There are always explosive possibilities, often as fleeting as a "shot," a word, or a facial expression. There is a touch of the Frankenstein in the movie. That is why intelligent self-regulation during production is the only guarantee of right results.

Although the reader already has a pretty good idea of what I think about pictures, I want to try to put it here in black and white, for my own sake, perhaps, as much as for his. Being a lawyer, I shall try to present my case.

In doing this, I am making no *nunc pro tunc* argument. Way back in 1922 I told the National Education Association that it was "as sensible to limit the use of the motion picture to amusement as it would be to limit the use of language to novels." I saw an open door leading into unknown fields. These first impressions, supplemented by fifteen years' work, had by 1937 developed into a set of convictions that became a sort of motion picture creed. In current parlance, they seemed to shape up into a sort of "seven-point program," which can perhaps be stated somewhat as follows:

1. The motion picture is *the entertainment of the people,* with almost universal appeal. This entertainment possesses in itself and of itself a moral value and is a vital necessity to the millions whom we serve.

This theme I made the subject of an address before the alumni of Wabash, my college, during the Commencement season of 1934. Trying to appraise the motion picture in the light of the history of popular entertainment, I pointed out that mass entertainment, as such, never even existed until the rise of the motion picture. Further, the talking picture had succeeded in "democratizing" all the other arts.

2. *Information* and, in the broadest sense, *"educational values"* are carried by the majority of pictures. Especially when one thinks of newsreels, documentaries, and films based on history or popular science, the place of the screen in "general education" is clear. Watching the effects of newsreels led me to the conclusion that they were probably the most universally enjoyed part of the theatre program. Here we saw current events and history, popular sport and tragedy, war and disarmament,

religion and the Easter Parade, African jungle and North Pole. Here was general education in a form that no previous generation had enjoyed. The film continues to be eagerly sought as an ally of home, church, and school. Its aid is used by every great national philanthropy or public cause. The screen serves as a national voice and messenger, but not as a biased propagandist or commercial advertiser.

3. Motion pictures produce in their audiences *emotional effects of definable nature socially as well as individually.* The entire setting of a motion picture theatre—the comfort, darkness, and quiet, which induce relaxation, and the absorbing concentration on the screen—puts the audience in an ideal state to receive forcible impressions. It has become axiomatic that the screen has exerted enormous influence in setting style in dress, manners, language, attitudes, and even popular modes of thought. This power can be put to good use. Good pictures have a genuine therapeutic effect. They can be a morale builder, a re-creator, an energizer. They give exercise to the spirit of fun. They are the visible and audible embodiment of the grander hopes that arise, in individual shapes, in all of us.

4. It is through the process which we have come to call *maximization* that this amazing influence of the screen has been built up. In its simplest sense, we use the word to represent the combination of arts and media that have given us the finished talking picture. Each medium gains something from its blending with the others. In another sense "maximization" indicates the propulsive power of the movie, the power with which it "gets over" to its immense audience. It is literally the only form in which so much art is brought to so many.

5. Another conviction which kept growing through the years is that we should distinguish clearly between *different types* of pictures. The category "motion picture" is scarcely more definitive than the category "literature."

6. As a direct corollary of the above, I urged not only the better adaptation of various films to different uses and different tastes, but also constant *education of the public in discrimination and appreciation.* Most films, of course, like most sermons, have to be prepared for a mixed audience. But producers, as well as parents and previewing committees, must sometimes recognize the difference between children and adults, between tragedy and comedy, between entertainment and education.

One of the interesting questions that kept popping up is one that I talked over with Mortimer Adler as he was writing his *Art and Prudence.* He there reminds the reader that "two general questions remain for discussion: (1) what is a good motion picture, and (2) what is a likable motion picture? The first states the problem of criticism; the second, the problem of taste."

As in questions of books, or travel, or clothes, or friends, I have always believed that personal taste should be considered, but that it is also worth while learning to distinguish between types of films. "To each his own."

7. Finally—and in a sense this is most important of all—I stand with those who consider the motion picture, in its own right, a *new art form*. Generally recognized as "the people's art," it is strengthened in its place by the fact that "alone among the arts it was handed upward from the masses and not downward from the intelligentsia," as Martin Quigley puts it. It is a "democratic art," and from that fact derives a certain sort of authority. It is a living and lively art, in step with its times and with the various national cultures from which it springs. As an art, it must plead its own case with good films, not with words of defense. There is no stock defense of the screen. Each film must stand or fall on its own merit, subject to the general laws common to all arts and to civilized society itself.

In November of 1934 the citizens of California re-elected Governor Frank F. Merriam. His opponent had been Upton Sinclair, whose forces for a time had seemed in the ascendancy. Because of his tax theories, it had been considered probable that a Sinclair victory would have compelled the shutdown of every Hollywood studio and the transference of production to some other state.

On November 8 the Los Angeles *Times* carried a headline reading: "Defeated Candidate Says He 'Concedes That Election Was Stolen.' " Later in the article Mr. Sinclair is quoted as saying of his "Epic" movement, "By 1936 we shall be the Democratic party of the entire West."

When the studio heads, thumping the tub for Merriam and donating to his campaign fund, solicited support from higher-paid studio personnel, Communist agitators were quick to exploit the resentment in some artists. Now, for the first time, Communism appeared openly and identifiably in Hollywood.

At the same time, films were gaining, both from the moral point of view and widening mass appeal. The Catholic magazine *America* published a generous tribute from the Reverend Gerard B. Donnelly, beginning with the words: "Catholics are just beginning to realize how much they owe to Mr. Will Hays." Well, I could stand hearing a little of that.

Ironically, if humorously, rumors continued to imply that I was soon to be succeeded by someone else. Almost any prominent name seemed to do. Among my rumored successors, to mention only a few, were Edward J. Flynn, Jim Farley, and Frank Walker—on the assumption, perhaps, that the postmaster generalship was a kind of training ground for the presidency of MPPDA—Alfred E. Smith, General Hugh Johnson, Harry Hopkins, James J. Walker, Nelson Rockefeller, Herbert

Bayard Swope, and George Ackerson, a former secretary to President Hoover. And all the time I had mutually binding contracts with the Association.

My family and I spent that Christmas in Hollywood. Will, Jr., and I wound up the year on a mountain-lion hunt in the San Benito Mountains with Jay Bruce, the famous California lion hunter. And I will go on record as stating that, after the events of 1934, that lion hunt was the most idyllically restful thing that could be imagined.

During the thirties our activities in the field of education were proceeding apace. During 1929 we had made a survey of the potential use of talkies in education and had convened a conference of several hundred college presidents and other educators on the subject. As a result, the Committee on Social Values in Motion Pictures was appointed to investigate the possibilities further—its expenses paid by the MPPDA—and I obtained the generous permission of producers for the committee to review a number of films and to make twenty prints each of excerpts from eight selected pictures. In 1933 the committee chose the name "Secrets of Success" for this clip of films, which were used experimentally by teachers and others for a couple of years, and the success of which caused the committee to want more such pictures. The producers were agreeable, accepting the idea of educational pictures as a noncompetitive public service.

The Human Relations Department of the General Education Board (Rockefeller Foundation) got wind of the "Secrets of Success" films, and offered to help on the project. With the Association representing the industry, a working arrangement was set up by which the Commission on Human Relations of the Progressive Education Association, already at work in this field and now aided by a grant of $75,000 from the General Education Board, conducted a thoroughgoing, three-year study and period of experimentation. The Commission created new "Human Relations" films, brought out in the form of 16-millimeter excerpts from non-current feature pictures which we made available to it. By January 1939, seventy-five of these had been prepared, tested under experimental conditions in classrooms, and pronounced ready for proving in general school use. To the delight of the MPPDA, it developed that pictures made for commercial theatre use were better for the study of human relations than those produced for the specific purpose. At the conclusion of this successful study the Human Relations Commission was liquidated and the films made available for educational distribution through the Advisory Committee on the use of Motion Pictures in Education, which had been organized by Dr. Mark A. May of Yale University—whom I had invited to recommend our next step in the program—and which was incorporated in 1938 as a non-profit educational agency renamed Teaching Film Custodians, Inc. In 1937 the MPPDA had appropriated $50,000 to share the cost of reviewing and selecting useful short subjects for the Advisory Committee—subsequently the TFCI—and in 1939 the results of this job were published in a comprehensive "Catalog of Films for Classroom Use," which contained descriptions of more than 400 films already available. This process of review, selection, and distribution has continued steadily ever since, with the demand increasing all the time.

In 1939 I reported to the annual convention of the National Education Association our progress in this field, estimating that the program had reached 6,000 schools and perhaps 6,000,000 students by that time.

Since 1946, under more liberal contracts with producing companies, excerpting from feature pictures, instead of merely from short subjects, has been granted; distribution has been extended to all agencies having educational programs, as well as to schools; and foreign distribution has been permitted when not in conflict with the contracting company.

Teaching Film Custodians, Inc., has 50,000 reels of film, and each is booked ten times a year (500,000 bookings in 1951), with each booking averaging four showings (2,000,000 showings altogether that year), and with each showing seen by an average of fifty pupils (making 100,-000,000 pupil showings in 1951). By special licensing agreements, TFCI is linked to nearly 900 educational film libraries throughout America. Because the companies accept no fees or royalties, and committee members no salaries, the volume of the rental fees to users, though moderate in scale, supplies a substantial balance which can be devoted to various educational services. In making the program work, TFCI staff members have traveled a total of nearly 700,000 miles. The companies have practically thrown their vaults open to the directors of TFCI for educational purposes. As Barney Balaban, president of Paramount, once said, "We must never make any money out of this." This non-profit giving by the producers, as a service to education, is doubtless the most distinctive characteristic of the whole program; in that respect, it stands alone.

Surely no better evidence of the motion picture's place in the world today need be found than its recognized status in the education of our sons and daughters.

As I look back, it seems ironical that during the thirties the world supply of films was coming into such a "golden age" on the very eve of world conflict. In our newsreels, world events were receiving such a neutral and unbiased treatment and such a prodigious distribution as would have been unthinkable a few years before. Snow White and the Seven Dwarfs was just around the corner.

At last I could draw a long breath.

But for how long?

CHAPTER 30

Before the Storm (1937–1941)

LOOKING back to the immediate pre-war years may not change the record already written, but it may help us to improve what we are yet to write. Perhaps some things can be learned from the story of the motion picture industry in those years that may have significance far beyond the industry itself.

Developments of the years 1937 to 1941 were confusing, but we could see that some of the things at which we had been working for nearly twenty years were now paying off. With our industry, as with most of the world, the war was the great test we were soon to face.

As I have so often said of the movies, it is a hardy young industry that could go through two world wars and a depression and still thrive as it has done. I like to think that the "rules of health" adopted at the incorporation of MPPDA in 1922 had something to do with this vigorous growth.

I know they had much to do with our ability to fight off the two most serious diseases that were always threatening the industry—censorship and governmental restrictions. Again and again it was my business, as a sort of consulting physician, to warn the patient when I saw dangerous symptoms developing and to urge a stricter diet of self-regulation. To me, self-regulation was nothing more nor less than application to responsible industry of the self-government on which our nation was founded. I always went on the theory that the way to avoid illness is to stay well—consciously, methodically, continuously.

Fortunately the industry seemed to have been in training for the tough game that it faced in 1941. It had learned the plays, it had developed skill and resourcefulness, it had mastered techniques, and it had stored up energy, capital, and experience. Altogether it had gained the poise of a well-drilled football team. Not only did it have competence and the consciousness of self-discipline, but it had a large and sympathetic following, both here and abroad—a tremendous body of fans.

Some of the problems we faced were of a most serious sort. Our foreign markets were shrinking. In our own country, legislators seemed to think it was open season: a new wave of restrictive and "control" legislation seemed to be making headway.

This was also the period when suddenly expanding demands by labor, supported by the favoring Wagner Act and the opportunistic, unsolicited, stepped-up activities of Communists, became increasingly important factors in American life. Hollywood was a prime target of both these forces.

I want to try to recall the people and events that were most important during this four-year period, and the chief issues in the complicated international enterprise into which the American motion picture had developed. They seem to group themselves around familiar themes: freedom of the screen; education; foreign relations; the legal aspect of trade practices; politics; defense; and memorable personalities.

I always felt that no single issue held the key to more of our vital problems than did freedom of the screen. This issue was tangled in the ideological controversies confusing the world as World War II loomed on the horizon.

The freedom of the movies was part and parcel of the daring which had sparked the industry. I remember Joe Schenck saying early in 1938 over a nationwide hookup, as he told some of the things the industry had done to advance prosperity: "Optimism has always been the guiding force of the motion picture business." Men of that type could think and work in no other terms than those of freedom—freedom to experiment, to build, to express.

When we recall how steadily freedom was being lost elsewhere, I am glad our industry played a definite part in preserving it here. Within the limits of good taste and common morality, we sought to assure creative genius the opportunity to function freely in any field, for the purpose of entertainment—not propaganda.

With the enlarging scope of the screen, new interpretations of code principles were constantly needed; but the principles were solid enough to carry the added weight without cracking. One interesting illustration of the process of amendment took place at a meeting of the West Coast Association which I attended late in 1938, when I called attention to the importance of dealing promptly with the cycle of pictures in which boys' gangs were portrayed. Joe Breen and I had just been discussing it. Called on to elaborate, he said that the details of crime itself could be dealt with under sections of the existing Code but that it was the generally offensive behavior of members of these youthful gangs, their uncouth spitting and obnoxious mannerisms, which at the moment constituted the crux of the problem.

At this point Louis B. Mayer of M-G-M stated that because of the respect for Mr. Breen on the part of the producers, Mr. Breen should not hesitate to insist upon deletions which his experience indicated were for the good of the industry. After thorough discussion of gang pictures, the following section was added to the Production Code provisions on crime:

Pictures dealing with criminal activities in which minors participate or to which minors are related shall not be approved if they incite demoralizing imitation on the part of youth.

Nor was the code process any longer merely a matter of "don'ts." We had gratifying experiences on the constructive side. Because I sat in on it in Hollywood, I remember a case in which a Charles Boyer film was being considered by the PCA. Boyer and the film's director had a long and tense argument with Joe Breen. Over loud protests Joe's side won out. Later Boyer wrote me from Paris a gracious letter in which he apologized over the rumpus they had caused, generously admitting that the final version of the picture, made in accordance with Breen's suggestions, was far better than the other would have been.

One of the best proofs that the Code's seal had become a *sine qua non* was given when in 1938 a member company put the Code in its exhibition contract, as reported in the *Motion Picture Herald* story of April 9:

Showmen of intelligence and good intent must view with special approval the provision of the new season's exhibition contracts of 20th Century-Fox Film Corporation prohibiting the showing of its pictures on double bills with films not approved by the Production Code Administration. . . .

The fact of an accepted code, however, did not put an end to current requests or complaints. Take the gangster picture, for example, which had sprung into popularity years before with the release of Paramount's *Underworld,* dealing with gang life in Chicago. One of the best comments I ever saw on this sort of thing came from the late Will Irwin, who wrote: "The history of the motion picture is a story of fashions, popular crazes, waves. . . . The gangster appeal to that streak in human nature which has made the Robin Hood story a classic of English tradition—the fascination of the outlaw."

Of all the complaints, protests from pacifists were among the strongest. In 1937 the National Council for the Prevention of War objected to the use of United States military forces in the filming of Universal's picture, *Wings over Honolulu.* At the same time the Council commended four newsreel services for the "peace sentiment" displayed in their pictures of the Army Day celebration.

Only a year later the following news story appeared, marked "Special to the New York *Times*":

Government pressure on Paramount Pictures to eliminate all pacifist preachment in *Men with Wings,* a history of aviation, has brought a re-writing of the final twenty pages of dialogue. . . . It was asserted by a thoroughly reliable source that "the Army, the State Department and the Executive Division" had protested the pacifist quality of the film and that, because the studio had a number of films which depend on Washington co-operation, it was decided to eliminate the offending sequences rather than raise an issue.

In 1941 the industry was called to Washington for a Senate committee investigation on charges of "propaganda purposes designed to influence the public mind in the direction of participation in the European war"! No matter which way you looked, we were in the middle!

Another line that often proved hard to draw—as hard as that between pacifism and warmongering—was that between the "educational" and the salacious. It was often a matter of interpretation. That often left the question: Whose interpretation was correct? We had a good example in the case of two pictures telling a story of dope, or "reefers," made by "independents," which were banned by the New York State authorities. In this case the Board of Regents of New York upheld Mr. Esmond, the director of the Motion Picture Division of the State Education Department, in denying licenses to *The Pace That Kills* and *Assassin of Youth,* as well as to a third feature, *Souls for Sale,* described by the director as "the story of an immoral life throughout, with suicide at the end." The owner of *Assassin of Youth* described it as an "educational picture carrying a message"—a warning to youth not to use marijuana in any of its forms.

The Board of Regents, on the other hand, held that the picture portrays "the sex exhilaration alleged to be due to marijuana, and the sources of supply." In the opinion of Mr. Esmond, "the picture arouses curiosity, which is never satisfied on the part of some youngsters until they have felt the effect of marijuana itself, believing as they invariably do that they themselves will never become the victims of the habit."

At the same time, this picture was approved by Delaware, Maryland, and New Jersey; and a group of representative clubwomen campaigned to force the Pennsylvania Censor Board to reverse its ruling so that the picture could be shown there.

The apparent need of some sort of censorship was probably kept alive by an infinitesimal fraction of offenders. I was delighted to get the report which the top executive of the Pennsylvania Censor Board gave to *Variety* early in 1938, when he said that "all censoring in this state is made necessary by only 2 per cent of the entire output of the film industry." These films were rarely exhibited in standard theatres. He expressed the belief that "if all films went through the Hays Office, need for the Censor Board would be abolished. We breathe a sigh of relief when we note the Hays Office seal on a film, for we know that most of our work is eliminated."

Probably reflecting trade sentiment, *Variety* had already expressed its opinion in the following headline: "Any New Censorial Measures Are Seen as Spite Work against Film Business Already Self-Purged at the Source." I am sure that's the way it looked to most people on the inside. *Variety* waxed a bit caustic in proclaiming "Censoring a Sweet Racket" and saying, "Solons ofttimes lured by revenue. Political patronage another angle, but costly to pix biz." The two sides of this matter looked completely different to different people!

Perhaps no piece about the movies better showed the importance of the subject in the public mind than the notable illustrated story in *Fortune* for December of 1938. In essence, it was the story of how our self-regulation had met the attacks of critics and had thus preserved the freedom of the films. This was its striking heading: "The Hays Office Cuts Cuss Words, Navels, Attractive Adultery, and Irrelevant Drunks. In so doing it has saved the screen for entertainment by warding off political censorship." Calling me a "mediator between the extremes—Broadway and Main Street," the article rightly commented: "Will Hays has always tried to find the golden mean."

Two main problems were still with us: keeping the advertising of motion pictures in line with the principles of our Advertising Code, and guarding the entertainment screen from encroachments by commercial advertising—that is, the advertising of various commercial concerns or products in entertainment pictures.

Should our advertising policy be similar to that of radio? Was there room on the theatrical screen for "sponsored" films produced and paid for by industrial or commercial firms? We knew that they were welcome in schools. And how about subtle mention of commercial products in pure entertainment films? If an automobile appeared in a picture and the brand could be identified, had anyone paid to have his product shown? For years I had been telling chambers of commerce that American motion pictures were proving a marvelous international salesman, but was it fair to plug "Singers" or only "sewing machines"?

Those who favored commercial screen advertising on a national scale naturally included producers of industrial films, advertising companies, commercial and industrial firms, and small exhibitors who welcomed an occasional free film to cut down their budget and, as some claimed, "keep them out of the red." Those opposed included the large majority of major producers, distributors, and exhibitors—and, it appeared, most patrons of picture theatres. The general manager of one theatre circuit, for instance, told his sales convention that no commercially sponsored film would be shown in any theatre controlled by the company. The opposition also included newspapers, the great American advertising medium.

The whole question looked a good deal like getting a bear by the tail: if the industry took hold, where could it let go? Hollywood was bothered. And I remember receiving from a top industrial concern a sharp complaint that its competitors were being played up in screen productions, and alleging that one of them had spent more than twenty-five thousand dollars to plant his product in a certain picture. When our investigators checked recent films, they did uncover several examples of apparent "plants." Advertising agencies saw in sponsored films and two-minute advertising trailers an important exploitation medium. But this expansion held such a threat that both picture producers and newspapers seriously considered plans to curb it. The question was thrown squarely into my lap, and I realized that here again the interests of audiences should be the deciding factor. Just at this moment one colorful bit of evidence reached us in a report from Arkansas: a "Society of Boo-ers" had been organized to greet all advertising films on the screen! This looked like the answer, and it was in line with the Association's aim to guard the screen's independence. It has remained an accepted policy.

I wanted the screen to be free to render service in any legitimate field, and especially in education. By 1939 I was glad to see that interest in educational motion pictures was really spreading. The *Journal of Educational Sociology* devoted a whole issue to the subject. The screen was variously hailed as an agency of British-American understanding; as of interest to the League of Nations in the field of child welfare; as valuable in physical education.

In their enthusiasm, educators saw school films as eventually aiding exhibitors too. This feeling was evident as early as 1937, when the National Conference on Visual Education felt that the critical study of films was making boys and girls "more avid movie fans." In many towns and cities high school students were beginning to make newsreels of their athletic and other activities. This worked well, for the exhibitor who often supplied the equipment for production got the privilege of the first showing. Such activities both made students movie-minded and built up healthy relationships between schools and exhibitors. As demand for pictures and equipment increased, we tried to remedy the lack. By 1938 twenty-six states had visual education departments, with which we kept in touch.

Few Association activities gave me more satisfaction than our part in the publication and distribution of Study Guides—aids to the better appreciation of feature pictures. Each of these well-illustrated brochures, published like a magazine in a monthly series, was devoted to one significant picture. These Study Guides were widely used in other discussion groups as well as in school classes. No single project in our program did more to raise a generation of discriminating fans.

One of the perplexing experiences of this period was the variety of viewpoints on the moral and educational responsibility of theatrical motion pictures. I had always held that the primary function of theatrical feature pictures was to furnish entertainment. The producers held the same view, considering themselves showmen rather than teachers or preachers. But there was an increasing demand for films of "social insight"—a term being used especially by groups considered progressive or ultra liberal. It was interesting to note that this was another trend which took more definite shape about 1938.

I found myself again "in the middle." Many groups urged us to ride their particular hobby. Such folks often lost sight of the simple fact that the commercial motion picture is entertainment that people pay for.

It is plain fact to report that the years 1937 to 1941 witnessed a rich crop of pictures. Profiting by years of pathfinding and of public education, they were reaching one of the high points in their evolution. How well I remember talking over with the Paramount heads their plans to produce *Madame Butterfly* with Gladys Swarthout and John Boles. The Association constantly took part in publicizing pictures of special significance, such as De Mille's *The Buccaneer*, the story of the famous privateer, Jean Lafitte, who helped to beat the British in 1812. The New York première of *Snow White and the Seven Dwarfs* was unforgettable. As *Snow White* spread like wildfire across the screens of the nation it hung up records that were as fantastic as the picture itself. Railroads ran special excursions; early daily openings in city theatres were ordered; police had to be called to prevent stampedes; in Tennessee, the governor led a parade from the State House to the theatre. This response was perhaps as great a tribute to the spirit of the American people as to the genius of Walt Disney. The Atlanta première of *Gone with the Wind* in December of 1939 was one of the red-letter days of Movieland, opening a perennial "run" that as early as 1943 had passed $32,000,000, more than three times the then record of any other picture. Of "The Great Hundred" feature pictures down through the years, as chosen by the *International Motion Picture Almanac*, fifteen were produced between 1937 and 1941.

Progress was being made in many fields almost unknown to the layman but of which I tried to keep abreast on my visits to Hollywood: ultra-violet recording; multiple-channel recording; a new and more feasible snow machine; a device by which outdoor night shots could be taken in the daytime; a composite shot process by which as many as a dozen exposures could be made on the same shot; highly sensitized microphones which could record perfectly without being moved around; Jack Dawn's "facial inlay" system, first used in *The Good Earth*, which made it possible to put almost any face on any player; and even a new device which nullifies the effect of sub-zero temperatures on camera work and film.

No wonder that the gamut of the screen was being so greatly expanded. Never before had an art form acquired such a range of techniques in one man's lifetime.

With the invasion of Poland in 1939, the Foreign Department suddenly claimed my closest attention. When I think back, I can feel
again the gradually mounting tension. Every month brought news of
some fresh difficulty abroad or a new crisis to face. But few things have
ever done more to bind the industry into a co-operating unit or to force
it to greater resourcefulness.

I have already noted that the United States put practically no obstacles in the way of foreign films entering our country. In 1938 we
figured out that our domestic market for foreign films had trebled in
three years: there were upward of two hundred theatres in eighty-four
cities showing the pictures of other countries. One Newark theatre was
proud to tell us in 1938 that in a recent four-week period it had played
films of eight different nations! Of course there were instances in which
a state or a city banned the showing of a particular foreign picture. Such
cases usually remained local affairs and not our direct concern, though
undoubtedly the Association was often blamed. About this time both
Spanish and German "political" films were attacked in New York, New
Jersey, Pennsylvania, and Ohio. Early in 1937, New Brunswick, New
Jersey, had barred the showing of Spain in Flames as Red propaganda.
In Pennsylvania, where Spain in Flames was banned by the State
Censor Board, the North American Committee for Spanish Democracy
threatened to carry the fight to the courts.

A case which at this distance looks slightly ironical, though at the
time serious enough, was one in which the Police Censor Board of
Chicago barred a March of Time film entitled Inside Nazi Germany.
The Board explained that they imposed the ban because of the film's
"propaganda opposing the policies of the Nazi Government in Germany," further explaining: "We rejected it because this country is on
friendly diplomatic terms with Germany." The Police Board had certainly not had our experiences in dealing with Hitler and the Nazis
since 1933! And they seemed to make no distinction between reporting
and "propaganda." A few days later, however, the Chicago ban was
lifted.

Even before the war brought serious physical problems, international
politics and two major streams of ideology were confusing censors and
exhibitors. Red Russia was not sending out as many films as was Germany, but they raised serious issues. Our people saw things on the screen
they had certainly never seen in America, and they wondered how the
"ideologies" of nations could differ so violently. They gradually became
aware of the menace of Communism, as they were already aware of the
mad dictatorship of Hitler.

Motion picture people noted that Germany was the third nation to establish a state-controlled film structure. Russia took over after the early Red revolution, and Mussolini acquired "supervision" for his Fascist state not long after his Black Shirts marched on Rome in 1922. None of these iron-fisted dictators was anxious to have his own people or his satellites see the better, freer way of life pictured so naturally in American films.

The Nazis took offense even with films produced within their own circle. In the case of *Condottieri*—a pretentious Italian film intended to occupy the first-run houses—Nazi censors ran into a scene they couldn't possibly pass. The story, laid in the Italian Renaissance period, was full of rough soldiers of fortune. The film was also filled with religious scenes, since the Catholic faith was portrayed as a major factor in the story's events. But when the warlike chief was shown kneeling to the Pope in a picture supposed to exalt the "Fuehrer principle"—that was too much! The Propaganda Ministry hustled the film back to the studios for a recutting.

I remember that American producing companies had some difficulties with Chinese censors because of scenes considered derogatory to Chinese custom. Our script writers and directors, accustomed to the American sense of humor, occasionally gave offense to the "ancient dignity" which American missionaries and observant travelers had always noted in oriental peoples. Our producers naturally felt that an occasional character from a "foreign" nation added contrast and color to a story filled with Americans. But as charming and gay a picture as *Theodora Goes Wild*, with Irene Dunne and Cary Grant, was held up by Chinese censors for six weeks simply because it showed a servant of apparently Chinese lineage.

The foreign situation became so serious that early in 1938 the United States Government sent us an explicit warning: "The problems of rising nationalism, of quotas, discrimination, exchange restrictions and tariff barriers must be adjusted if the American motion picture is to operate on as wide a scale as heretofore in the markets of the world."

One of the most pedantic and laborious measures we encountered was a Danish bill presented to the House of Commons in 1938 by the Minister of Justice, limiting imports and profits and barring block-booking. It showed the old tendency to fall back on officialdom for results which can be achieved only by individual imagination and free creative effort. A government official was to set up a cultural and artistic standard! Some of the proposed licenses were to be used as political favors or as remuneration from the government "for outstanding achievement in the world of art." Limited Danish imports were to be distributed only through the state distributing company, an entirely new institution. A Film Board was to be created to co-operate with the Minister of

Justice. The Film Board was to "heighten the standards of the industry by giving advice to the newly instituted Film Central, which was to obtain and distribute films of educational value." Finally, "a heavy impost" was to be "laid upon all exhibitors showing a net profit of over $2,200 a year"! Presumably, the bill originated in an effort to keep large trusts, especially foreign ones, out of the business. It actually paved the way for the destruction of private initiative. I have quoted from it to highlight the complete contrast with our own system. Since there were only 358 Danish theatres at the time, our American companies considered that it was easier to write them off than to struggle against such obstacles.

In France, the left-wing Cinema Workers Syndicate, seeking a nationalization of the industry, proposed the making of 450 pictures, although the 120 then being made annually were scarcely recovering their cost. A Paris report stated: "It is obvious that the French trade unions would like to make the French cinema a means of propaganda, as already done in Russia."

As German attendance slumped badly in 1938, it was suggested there that more extensive promotion be undertaken to encourage film attendance during the summer months. At the same time, the German Film Chamber was reporting that the public preferred non-German films and that the three longest runs went to two American and one French film. The revival hoped for with government control failed to appear. And it was bluntly reported in a New York *Times* story that "since the Nazi Government came to power, there has been virtually no foreign demand for German films."

Italy was making a determined effort to become a leading European producer. In one of these years she spent $5,000,000 in the production of 38 features, which was an average cost of $131,580—about like our Class-B pictures. But Italy's annual requirement was nearly 300 pictures; and more than 75 per cent of the 245 films imported were from our studios!

In Mexico, two congressmen proposed "strict prohibition of the importation and exhibition of any picture in English or other foreign language" as a means of compelling alien producers to enter Mexico on a large scale and employ Mexican players and technicians.

More startling reports reached us from Russia. Early in 1938, Stalin's "purge" apparently reached the state-owned motion picture industry. Moscow newspapers reported that the general director, Boris Z. Shumiatsky, was condemned for allegedly permitting a steep decline in production of Russian pictures. Nor did the Soviet cinema apparently do any better as a business enterprise than as a means of popular entertainment. Early in 1938 a New York *Times* correspondent, Harold Denny, cabled: "The Soviet cinema has been a heavy drain on the state's purse because wasteful and extravagant practices created huge deficits." He told the story of one film company, taking sequences in a pleasant Black Sea resort, which turned the job into a long-drawn-out vacation at state expense. Half a million rubles had been allotted for 50 days' stay; the comrades remained 167 days, only 54 of which were devoted to work, and spent 1,400,000 rubles. Even a reduced Soviet schedule of 62 films was being only 40 per cent met. It was reported that many films, after completion, were scrapped as worthless.

All these dictatorial and bureaucratic methods I have touched on were of course completely "foreign" to the spirit of our American motion picture industry. Our only guarantee of success lay in continuing to make the best possible pictures. And in spite of all the difficulties, American films did an amazing job of holding their own up to 1938. Six million more feet of film were shipped to foreign countries in 1937 than in 1936.

Throughout this period of spectacular growth, the industry withstood a wave of restrictive domestic legislation and anti-trust suits that made for constant uncertainties. If every one of these moves had gone through, the industry as we know it would have been decimated.

As I try to get a bird's-eye view of these trends it is hard to see why an alien philosophy of statism, which in other countries had already proved harmful both to creative art and financial success, should have gained credence here. The country experienced a series of new invasions into fields of private initiative such as the film industry. We witnessed a growing conception that a politically appointed commission or bureau, by some strange infusion of official wisdom, could show creators how to create and executives how to execute. The words "regulation" and "control" were increasingly used to express a new relation of government to business.

The whole philosophy of our Association was built on the belief that the industry could so govern itself as to justify both freedom of expression and freedom of operation. We had developed moral and artistic principles, trade practices and traditions that seemed to fit our needs and give results. The screens of the nation were kept supplied, and the audiences, generally speaking, satisfied.

A tremendous industry had grown up without losing the personal touch in creating or the popular touch in exhibiting. The American section of the industry was the most ruggedly healthy in the world. That seemed to me pretty good proof that it was on the right track, that it knew how to take care of itself as well as its patrons.

But motion pictures frequently had far more than their "day in court." In one case which I followed with interest, the New York Federal Circuit Court of Appeals denied the right of a trial by a statutory court to compel the state authorities to lift their ban against *Ecstasy*, a European film. The attorneys for the producing company claimed that because the film had passed federal customs, no state could bar it. But the court decided that "the state authorities and the individual state laws predominated."

At this time I had much to do with John Lord O'Brien and Thurman Arnold, seeking a better understanding of the Department of Justice's attitude toward certain trade practices, a thing often difficult to ascertain in advance of a suit. And in the spring of 1937 four anti-trust suits were in progress all at once, some instigated by claims of exhibitors that major distributors were "oppressing" independents.

In state legislatures, every session saw the introduction of adverse bills, most of them calculated to increase tax burdens of exhibitors. Almost all died in committee or were killed on the floor. One bill proposed to prohibit the sale of a seat in a public assembly without having one actually available, and imposing a fine of not less than $24 or more than $100! Edward Kuykendall, president of the Motion Picture Theatre Owners of America, criticized the tactics of resorting to legislation for remedies, "as it tends only to invite state and federal regulation and interference in this business."

Certain other trends were reflected in decisions that were helpful. A Supreme Court ruling strengthened the copyright laws on motion pictures, thus indicating the increased value attached to original films. In the case of one amateur film, *Shooting Big Game with a Camera*, which had been taken by my friend Frederick B. Patterson, president of the National Cash Register Company, and shown non-commercially to employees and others, it was held that such exhibition constituted publication and was sufficient to justify infringement proceedings.

When "Bank Nights" were ruled a lottery and had to be discontinued, many exhibitors found this a real blow to their attendance.

The most important single decision during this period was that handed down in the now famous Consent Decree late in 1940. This compromise measure brought to a conclusion a long process of anti-trust litigation by the federal government against a group of major motion picture distributing companies as defendants. This was the concern of the companies themselves, and MPPDA tried to keep out of these legal affairs as much as we could. But in this particular case I was put on the stand for several days. In summing up, a judge in Oklahoma expressed the opinion that the affairs of the industry had been handled in a manner fair to all the different groups and interests involved; but the Consent Decree was issued just the same.

In the decree which they signed as a settlement of the case the defendants "consented" to conduct their business according to certain stipulated rules embodied in the decree. Unfortunately, it seemed to me, the Department of Justice repeatedly took the view that the actions and understandings among the major companies, considered by them to be fair trade practices, resulted in "monopoly." Against this legalistic view it should be remembered that in the very founding of the Association we set ourselves to build up co-operative methods in the areas of common interest, like foreign markets, while preserving open competition among companies. I repeatedly urged re-interpretation of the anti-trust laws in the light of complex modern business methods.

Several times during these negotiations I was called to Washington to confer with members of the Department of Justice on the nature and operation of our trade practices, the experience back of them, and their relation to current anti-trust interpretations. But it must be remembered that new philosophies of government were developing within the federal departments, changes and shifts of personnel were common, and policies were not always predictable.

One very important item in the federal recommendations—the divorcement of production from distribution—continued to be appealed and debated until 1949, when the Supreme Court handed down a decision that divorcement must take place. Some companies at once accepted the decision and proceeded to separate their distribution from production, setting up two distinct corporations. Others considered further appeal.

Early in 1941 the American Arbitration Association, which had been of such value to us and in which I had long taken an active interest, began to handle the first cases referred to them under the Consent Decree. The distributors had consented to be bound to arbitrate when exhibitors exercised their voluntary right to do so. The earliest requests were in debatable questions of "clearance"—the provision under which a first-run theatre, paying top rental for a new film, is protected within a given geographical radius from other showings before a specified time has elapsed. This has always been a two-sided question, with the automobile very much enlarging the natural territory of a given theatre.

Labor questions assumed new importance after the Supreme Court validated the Wagner Act, with new demands coming thick and fast. This was true in spite of the fact that wages and salaries in Hollywood were already probably higher than anywhere else in the country. Although direct labor relations were the affair of each company, both MPPDA and the West Coast Association had done a great deal, as by the service of the Central Casting Bureau, to improve all-round conditions.

If one were able to appraise all the personal work going on in the studios, he might well wonder how all such varying special talents and creative abilities of thousands of men and women could ever be reduced to union formulas.

In the spring of 1937 the Screen Actors' Guild, backed by five other unions, was again seeking recognition. Among its five thousand members were both stars and extras. Among the other union presidents attending the conference which framed the new demand were Daniel J. Tobin of the International Teamsters, Dan W. Tracy of the Electrical Workers, and William L. Hutcheson, representing the United Carpenters and Joiners.

It was probably true that labor contests were precipitated partly by the rivalry for union supremacy between the AFL and John L. Lewis' Committee for Industrial Organization. It was at this time that the CIO called a Hollywood workers' mass meeting for unionization. One news report commented: "Hollywood has apparently been unaware of the possibility that the CIO might precipitate at least the production branch into the same position as the automobile, coal, and textile fields."

Pat Casey, placed in charge of labor relations by a group of West Coast studios, set April 5 as the time and New York as the place for a meeting between producers and five studio crafts to draft a new basic contract. These developments attracted national attention.

In May the New York *Times* carried a story, "Boycott Is Called on Five Movie Actors," all officers of the Screen Actors' Guild, and reported: "The striking Federated Motion Picture Crafts today formally requested labor unions throughout the nation to boycott all films in which five well-known actors appear, and threatened also to extend the strike to independent studios." Interestingly enough, on the following day the Executive Committee for the Federated Crafts repudiated the above request, which had been telegraphed to labor organizations by its publicity committee. But the incident illustrates the hectic activity within the labor organizations.

During its unusual growth, Hollywood had probably felt itself a unique and favored community, as it actually was. Now aggressive action on the international labor front sought to draw it into the main stream. The dictatorial tone was heard more often. In May, George E. Browne, international president of the International Alliance of Theatrical Stage Employees, said he might call a strike if his organization did not approve any agreement reached by the striking Federation of Motion Picture Crafts and the film producers. He was reported as having added: "There will be peace in Hollywood soon, but it will be a peace of our dictation." That was far from the spirit in which our Association carried on its work.

A similar viewpoint was expressed at the IATSE convention of 1938: that all theatrical workers, especially film and stage actors, should be included in the one Alliance. Their committee believed "that leadership over performers should be ours because, since we are the parent of theatrical organizations and the strongest, these people quite properly belong with us." One could philosophize at length over that proposal and what it suggests.

I must mention one more extension of the organized labor theory under the Wagner Act. In the early summer of 1938 the National Labor Relations Board ordered an election by screen writers, in spite of the fact that only a year before five-year contracts had been signed by Screen Playwrights with seven major studios! The Board ruled that film writers are employees under the Wagner Act, although the companies contended that they are usually employed under individual contracts, render services that are "creative and professional" in character, and receive higher salaries than average. The election was to determine whether Screen Playwrights, Inc., or the Screen Writers' Guild, Inc., often considered ultra-liberal in complexion, or neither, should represent them in collective bargaining.

Any reader of this story who has a legal turn of mind will appreciate something of the atmosphere in which the industry lived at this period when he reads the following commentary of the Labor Board on its ruling: ". . . We do not believe that, under the policies and provisions of the Act, employees should be precluded from having the opportunity to select new representatives for collective bargaining for a period of as long as five years because of a contract running for that length of time." One might be pardoned for wondering why the contract already in force was to be considered invalid.

So much for the legal trends of these years.

The fact that I had served in the Cabinet of one President made it seem wholly natural to be discussing motion pictures with Washington departments functioning under another. My work took me to the capital oftener than usual those days.

As I have already noted, changes in national policies seemed more evident after Franklin Roosevelt's second term got well under way. The developing New Deal philosophy was again being applied to industry, as it had been under NRA. We were often completely puzzled by adverse government reaction to practices that had long proved sound. It reminded me of a crack currently made by a sports writer: "I don't understand the game of politics as the New Deal plays it. They choose their own umpires and make the rules as they go along."

In addition to being a regulator, the federal government also became a competitor. It must be admitted that the competition was not too severe, because few of the films were of the entertainment variety. But it can well be imagined that motion picture people looked askance at such competition. Late in 1939, 87 films were reported already put out by the New Deal administration, and a few months later the government had 373 pictures in circulation.

It must be remembered that after Germany entered Poland on September 1, 1939, we were living under the shadow of war. After President

Roosevelt proclaimed a "limited national emergency" on the eighth, the situation seemed to encourage controls. At the same time, the Golden Gate International Exposition, which had opened in San Francisco in February and the New York World's Fair in April gave an industrial and patriotic boost that was of definite benefit to pictures.

Just as the period ended, in May of 1941, the President proclaimed "an unlimited state of national emergency." The situation tightened up in many directions, both abroad and at home. Not only were the industry, its executives and stars hit hard by increased federal and state taxes, but at one time Secretary of the Interior Ickes proposed to tax even film "locations." Prosperity made pictures a target.

Two examples will show the extent to which government watchfulness went: at one point sixty-eight interrogatories were propounded, and the industry even had to maintain annotated geographical "weather" maps showing where the major companies were facing government suits.

Lest all this account seem too grim and mechanical, let me hasten to say that on the personal side my contacts with the President were on a plane of extreme cordiality and friendliness. The same applies to Secretary Cordell Hull, with whom I repeatedly conferred on foreign problems of vital importance to the industry's markets. I am sure government leaders recognized the value of keeping American films on the screens of the world.

The trade papers, like the sports pages, use a good deal of slang. Their favorite word for my Washington conferences was "huddle." Late in 1937 I was reported as having gone into one of these huddles with President Roosevelt on foreign film quotas. From my first visit I had found him sympathetic to our foreign plans and of course well posted on general conditions in the major European countries, which formed our chief concern too. He was decidedly fond of pictures himself, and about this time the Association office was able to see that modern motion picture equipment was installed in the White House to take the place of some that had become outmoded.

In the fall of '38, when things abroad were definitely tightening, I had a most satisfactory conference with Cordell Hull. His strong convictions about reciprocal trade agreements and his skill in negotiating them were of great value. Motion pictures were a product in which we were eager to trade freely, and the Secretary's good offices were invoked many times on difficult foreign matters. I shall never forget the courtly manner in which Secretary Hull always received me, and his patience in working out solutions to the problems which he recognized as his government's problems too.

A little later that fall I again saw the President, this time to discuss our plans for making a great composite film that would reveal to World's

Fair visitors the glory and romance of American history. The concept appealed to him at once. The resulting film, *Land of Liberty*, was a unique achievement. It was authorized by MPPDA in the summer, and its production supervised by the Association as a joint enterprise. The translation of the story into pictures was an eye-opener, even to the industry, for it was found that every sequence needed in the epic had already been filmed for some earlier picture and lay waiting in the vault of one or another company. The only problem was one of selection and of editing. The première at the New York World's Fair on June 14, 1939, made a profound impression. Here was a document of such sweep and patriotic fervor as had never before been conceived. So great was the effect created that we at once began to lay plans for general release. In our minutes is a significant resolution that all income from the later commercial showings be devoted to charitable purposes. The total reached a substantial figure.

At the beginning of 1941 the *Wall Street Journal* reported the industry in better shape than a year ago "as a result of the adjustments it has made." The report continued: "At the opening of 1940 Hollywood was faced with two major uncertainties, one of which—the war abroad—had cut heavily into income; the other, Thurman Arnold's anti-trust suit, held unknown terrors but threatened possible disruption of the industry. Now that both have taken concrete form, the industry has found itself able to cope with them a great deal better than had been hoped." Exhibitors grossed 73 per cent of the total U.S. amusement income, employed 59 per cent of all employed in the amusement field, and carried 64 per cent of the entire pay roll. The Census Bureau was already recognizing pictures as "the backbone of American amusements," a claim we had long made. Because people were increasingly budget-minded, I thought it was fair to explain over the radio how their admission dollar was spent. I pointed out that only an average of 30 per cent went for film rentals and that 70 per cent was expended locally for maintenance of the theatres, salaries, and a variety of sustaining and exploitation expenses.

A perplexing question for us during this period was how far Communistic ideas were finding their way into our own entertainment pictures. Opinions differed widely. As early as February of 1937, Archbishop John Timothy McNicholas of Cincinnati made the statement that Communism was using the screen, and he instructed his pastors to deliver sermons to that effect. I was of course sharply reminded of what the Pope had told me in Rome only three months before when he showed me copies of orders sent out from Moscow to "capture the cinema of the world." During the summer of 1938 charges and denials of Communistic coloring in films multiplied. I fear it must be admitted that some court decisions during the mid-thirties were such as to make it easier for Communist sympathizers to gain influence in Hollywood, as they were apparently ordered to do. I knew where I stood: the program of Communism had no place in American life anywhere, at any time!

The stock in trade of the motion picture art industry, from the germ of a story to the picture on the screen, is always *people*. Hundreds of these people I have been proud to call my friends. Since in 1939 we were celebrating the motion picture's Golden Anniversary, my thoughts turned often to the pioneers, most of whom were still active.

The majority of our Board of Directors—the men with whom I had so much to do—were among the pioneers. Others who meant much to the industry were particularly close friends: such figures as Major Edward Bowes, a man of great vision who, with his wife Margaret Illington, was always a welcome guest at our home in California; Admiral Dick Byrd, who welcomed motion picture films as an important part of his exploration record and credited the entertainment pictures freely supplied him by the producers with "keeping the tempers of men on an even keel when books, games and conversation had been exhausted as entertainment mediums in the icy solitude of Little America"; William Randolph Hearst, so influential in the development of the newsreel; Winfield Sheehan, another man with a newspaper background, long a power in Fox Films and Twentieth Century-Fox, whose death in 1945 was a great loss; Wendell Willkie, who took part in 1941 in the defense of the industry before a Senate committee charging it with propaganda for war.

These same years were marked by the passing of a dozen or more figures, nearly all identified with the screen, with whom I had enjoyed associations of a most interesting sort. Their going seemed to mark a real break with the early days.

Amelia Earhart, whose plane was reported lost over the Pacific in July of 1937, will always be associated in my mind with the memory of Will Rogers. Not only did they meet death in the same guise, but they had something of the same bold spirit. And Amelia spent hours in the Rogers home, discussing the future, just before her last flight. Mrs. Hays and I were there with Mrs. Rogers. I will never forget her telling us about flying the Atlantic in 1928. When she was a third of the way across, with all her lights out, her exhaust suddenly began to shoot out fire. She knew something might explode. The immediate decision to be made was whether to go on or turn back. She went on rather than give up her goal! As to the problem of flying, she said to us: "There are a hundred gadgets on my dashboard. We'll never be safe until they get it more simple." She was a vivid personality.

Only a few weeks before had come the tragic death of another young woman of equally striking personality, one of the most popular of all screen stars—Jean Harlow. She was a distinctive "type" and left a definite mark on screen traditions.

The year 1938 also saw the passing of a group of stars whose names bring back to millions, as they do to me, poignant memories of many a picture. Pearl White—heroine of hair-raising serials like *The Perils of Pauline,* which practically pulled the audiences into picture theatres—died in Paris.

Warner Oland, actually of Swedish descent but indelibly stamped as an oriental detective called "Charlie Chan," left a vacant place in the hearts of his audiences.

Pauline Frederick and Conway Tearle, legitimate actors of high ability who brought a true dramatic sense to the screen, were both missed.

Of the losses in 1939 of Carl Laemmle and Douglas Fairbanks, it would be hard to speak with moderation. "Papa" Laemmle was one of that little group who started from scratch, had great visions, and realized them. Douglas Fairbanks, to generations of movie fans, was "Mr. Movie." It would be hard to measure the verve, the wild romance, the sheer sense of daring that Douglas injected into the literature of the screen. He has already become a legend. And as the first president of the Academy of Motion Picture Arts and Sciences, his contributions to picture progress were real.

Having been raised in the old Hoosier tradition that "politics is people," I was quite at home in the realization that the whole motion picture enterprise is *people,* and I did what I could to keep it so. As Nicholas Schenck once said: "It is my firm opinion that the determining factor in the success of a motion picture enterprise is the man power which operates it." I am moved to remark that, so far at least as motion pictures are concerned, there is no such thing as purchasing so much "average" or "standard" ability, loyalty, or effort. In many industries materials, factories, formulas, patents, trade-marks, and other elements give a corporation a measure of stability. In pictures there is no such backlog to guarantee next year's success. There is no insuring the springs of genius or getting seven hours of creative writing out of a seven-hour day.

And, speaking of creative personalities, my home state of Indiana has furnished its quota of screen actors, including Richard Bennett of Deacon's Mills; Monte Blue of Indianapolis, who started with Griffith; Charles Butterworth of South Bend; Louise Fazenda, Lafayette; Norman Foster, Richmond; Buck Jones, Vincennes; and Carole Lombard, Fort Wayne—whose last service to the Indiana war effort ended in her tragic death in a plane crash. Cole Porter of Peru should of course be remembered for his great screen contributions as lyricist and composer.

Even the briefest glance at my letter files for those days shows how our motion picture enterprise was reaching out into many fields of national life and personally touching many people.

I notice a letter of inquiry from the biographer of Arthur Brisbane, with whom I had much to do in the earlier days. Charles Evans Hughes thanked me in connection with a newsreel early in 1940. There is a sheaf of correspondence with two notable Texans, Amon Carter and Jesse Jones. Artur Rodzinski wrote me both on an immigration matter and about a newsreel. There was a letter from Winnie Sheehan about his buying a ranch, and not long afterward he became a ranch neighbor of ours in Hidden Valley, north of Los Angeles; letters from Doris Kenyon, a star of early talkies, about her son, Kenyon Sills, my godchild; and correspondence with Catholic bishops about the continuing work of the Legion of Decency, one of our staunchest allies in maintaining moral standards.

Among others with whom I had close contacts were Henry L. Stoddard, Republican stalwart and author; Edward Arnold, always a popular actor; Senator James J. Davis; Roy Howard of the Scripps-Howard newspapers; Booth Tarkington, for whom we Hoosiers planned a big testimonial dinner in 1937; Frank C. Walker, whom I congratulated on becoming Postmaster General. Senator Styles Bridges and Governor Raymond E. Baldwin, both of whom visited Hollywood in 1939; General Robert E. Wood, who invited me to join the America First Committee; Patrick J. Hurley; Senators Vandenberg and Taft, the latter of whom called on L. B. Mayer in Hollywood. One of the pleasant contacts I was able to make between Hollywood and Indiana was in helping to arrange for Jeanette MacDonald to visit Muncie, for which my old friend George A. Ball was very grateful.

It was during this period, of course, that my Hoosier neighbor, the late Wendell Willkie, was nominated for President, and I took a great deal of pleasure in that occasion and in congratulating Senator Homer Capehart on the arrangements for the notification meeting at Elwood—the hot weather notwithstanding.

Other friends whose names light up the events of these years include Jasper Crane of the du Pont Company, who gave a dinner for me at the University of New York; Charles G. Dawes, who sent me his book, *Journal as Ambassador to Great Britain;* and Dwight H. Green, an Indiana boy whom I congratulated on his election to the governorship of Illinois. With James A. Farley I had a considerable correspondence, for we were able to be of service to each other on a number of occasions.

It was during this period that Edward R. Stettinius, Jr., and his family visited Hollywood and gave me the pleasure of showing them the studio sights. He also sent me a set of economic studies of great interest. Not long after, Mr. and Mrs. Richard Mellon also looked in on us in Hollywood. About the same time I had the pleasure of congratulating Mr. and Mrs. Fred Stone on the marriage of Carol, and Billie Burke on the birth of her granddaughter. Time was marching on, even in this infant industry.

Other names I can only mention, though every one of them recalls pleasant relations of one sort or another. There were Dr. Max Mason, Mark Sullivan, Walter Chrysler, Count René de Chambrun, who sent me his book, *I Saw France Fall*; Henry L. Doherty, General L. R. Gignilliat of Culver Military Academy, Dr. Robert A. Millikan, head of the California Institute of Technology, a strong supporter of our Production Code; Senator Tom Connally, Otis Skinner, and Senator Burton K. Wheeler.

In 1937 we lost by death three great Republican leaders, all men of conspicuous ability and large services to the country: Elihu Root, Andrew W. Mellon, and Ogden L. Mills.

I like to think that the spirit of these men and of many others who hold the same ideals was symbolized in that splendid painting, "The Signing of the Constitution," by Howard Chandler Christy. The unveiling of the painting in 1937 was an inspiring occasion, of which I have a constant reminder in the form of a copy of the picture bearing an inscription of warm friendship from Howard Christy, whom death recently took away from us. The copy hung in my office, where I could almost reach out and touch it.

During these same years, too, there seemed to be an unusual number of significant occasions on which I was asked to speak, either as a representative of the industry or simply as a citizen interested in public affairs. Three occasions that stand out in my mind most clearly are the dinner of the Poor Richard Club in Philadelphia, when I spoke on "What's Right with America"; the Atlantic City Radio program of messages on the freedom of press, radio, and movies, when I broadcast "Voices of a Free People"; and Lincoln's Birthday at Los Angeles in 1941, when, under the title "He Belongs to Us," I quoted some of Lincoln's little-known words and tried to show how they applied to the country of our own day.

As an indication of the varied interests that filled these days I took part in a Department of Commerce broadcast; an American Red Cross luncheon in Washington; a testimonial dinner to Louis B. Mayer at Los Angeles; the dedication of a tablet on the site of the old Koster & Bial music hall, where moving pictures were first projected; the New York *Herald Tribune* Forum, where I spoke on motion pictures; a broadcast with Sir John Simon and Joe Kennedy on newsreels; a meeting of civic, religious, and educational youth leaders.

I spoke at the World's Fair on Indiana Day; to the Phi Delta Theta convention at Indianapolis; at Princeton University, on "Science and the Motion Picture," on the Cyrus Fogg Brackett Lectureship in Applied Engineering and Technology; to sales and advertising executives on picture problems; to a D.A.R. convention at French Lick on "Patriotism and Security"; to the N.E.A. convention on "The Motion Picture in Education"; at the 150th anniversary of Lafayette's visit to Gallipolis, Ohio.

On this latter day, August 11, 1940, when a great civic ceremony was held at twilight on the banks of the Ohio River, with five thousand citizens crowded in as close as they could get, there was rendered a violin composition written for that service by my good friend Charles G. Dawes, former Vice-President. Each of three speakers delivered a eulogy on a deceased citizen of the town. Senator John W. Bricker, then governor of Ohio, spoke about a judge, Mr. Dawes about a newspaper editor, and I about my old friend O. O. McIntyre, the beloved columnist. It was a patriotic and moving occasion. After the ceremony a number of guests, some of them from quite a distance, gathered at Mrs. McIntyre's home, where a reception was held. Later in the evening the talk that I had made was rebroadcast there—much to my embarrassment, for I had spoken from the heart.

I want to mention briefly some other events that marked progress in the development either of pictures or of other matters of interest to me. At the twenty-fifth anniversary luncheon to Cecil De Mille, where I had the privilege of serving as toastmaster, we were all impressed by what our host, Dr. Nicholas Murray Butler, president of Columbia University, said in praising the role of motion pictures in adult education. He felt strongly that they could be made "important instruments in the molding of public opinion." It was gratifying to me that the luncheon was given by the Division of Film Study of Columbia.

"The adult does not want to go back to school," Dr. Butler said, "but he does want something in his leisure hours which stimulates thought. The motion picture has shown amazing progress in that field. Therefore, its administration should be on the high plane it has assumed." In replying, De Mille said it was "thrilling" that the great universities were becoming interested in the study of motion pictures. Thinking out loud among his friends, he said that he was not certain whether the film should "entertain, instruct, or reflect the life of a period it depicts. Perhaps," he concluded, "the real function would be a combination of the three."

It was at just this time, in June of 1938, that we again sought light on the probable future relations between movies and television, when the first full-length film was televised in this country by NBC. Listeners and lookers-in over a radius of more than forty miles from mid-Manhattan followed the dramatic action of Alexander Korda's *The Return of the Scarlet Pimpernel*. After discussing similar questions so long in our own field, it was of special interest to me to learn that the production had been selected in order to find out whether pictures of this type would hold the attention of the television audience for an hour and a half.

The Roosevelt Memorial Association continued to find new ways in which T.R.'s influence might make itself felt. During this period Roosevelt Medals were given, among others, to Helen Keller and her teacher, Anne Sullivan Macy; to George Washington Carver, Frank Ross McCoy, and Carl Sandburg. I was able to be of some service in interesting the Hearst press in the observance of Rededication Day, the papers taking an active part in publishing editorials and in organizing mass meetings. We had a notable Rededication broadcast in December of 1938.

Among the events at my own college, Wabash, we trustees took considerable satisfaction in the dedication of Goodrich Hall, our new science building, at which the address was delivered by Dr. Arthur H. Compton. I have always felt strongly about the role of our Christian liberal arts colleges and the faith in which they were founded.

The year 1939 was highlighted by two golden jubilees, with both of which I was concerned. One was the fiftieth anniversary of the founding of the Y.M.C.A., for which I served as one of the sponsors. This probably struck me with double force because we were also celebrating the fiftieth anniversary of the motion picture, commemorating the day in 1889 when Thomas Edison placed the first picture in motion on his new Kinetoscope in West Orange, New Jersey. We naturally made the most of this event as an occasion for national promotion, with the distribution of nineteen thousand press books to be used by exhibitors all over the country in local campaigns.

It was a notable anniversary, for at the end of fifty years' journeying the American Motion Picture Industry stood on a mountaintop from which the beacon of its silver screen was sending rays of light and color and joy into every corner of the earth.

CHAPTER 31

Foreign Relations

AMERICAN films have not always entered other countries through the wide, unguarded "open door" by which the films of other nations have come to us. Too often we have had to knock at doors on which someone—usually a government film commission of one sort or another—had tacked up a sign reading "Not Welcome—Unless," the warning usually being followed by various terms and taxes. It was one of my most interesting responsibilities to find out the reasons for those conditions, to carry on negotiations to lighten or remove them, and, with the active co-operation of our own State Department, to get new signs put up reading "Welcome, If"—with the "ifs" as few as possible.

But this was no one-man job, as I realized within a few days after taking office. Mexico's sharp complaint of April 1922, amounting to a virtual ban on all American pictures, was a dramatic warning that we would need to maintain an active Foreign Department that would keep producers and distributors in touch with conditions in other countries. This we proceeded to do without delay, and we were fortunate in finding as its director Lieutenant Colonel Frederick L. Herron, a man of wide experience in both civil and military affairs, who remained in this helpful position until 1941, when he returned to military service. Before long, regional offices were established in Paris and London.

An amazing volume and variety of business passed through this department during the years that I was so vitally interested in it. And even the later change in its name meant something. In 1943 we changed the name from Foreign to International Department. The world was moving fast during these years, and we wanted to emphasize the fact that we considered that motion pictures had become a vital, almost universal, international medium of communication, and that no nation was "foreign" to their sphere of influence.

The interest of the MPPDA in international relations was simply a continuation of an interest already keenly felt in the industry before 1922. Among most of America's industrial enterprises, the "foreign" or export side is a comparatively minor factor in relation to gross income; export often becomes merely an added "department." But not so with motion pictures. Aside from the amazing fact that from 35 to 40 per cent of the industry's income is normally derived from foreign sources, the global ramifications of the screen make foreign relations a vital and integral part of the business.

The long-dominant position of American films on the world screen is due to many factors; but the one to which I attribute the most importance is the extraordinary freedom, both in the making and showing of films, which is enjoyed in this country. The proof seems to be that in no foreign nation have bureaucratic control and restrictive laws been able to create a strong film industry, while American films, in the face of a strong competitive market and in spite of severe handicaps imposed by foreign governments, have steadily forged ahead to pre-eminent position throughout the world.

Although the technical and artistic development of the motion picture has been an international enterprise, American inventiveness and technical ingenuity have played a very large role in our supremacy. The epoch-making contributions of Thomas Edison have proved incalculable American assets.

Even before World War I, American pictures were making a strong bid for world supremacy. It has been pointed out on historical grounds that the first producers and exhibitors of films in the United States were largely of the Jewish race, often called the most internationally minded of all peoples. It is perhaps natural that their product should have been successfully slanted toward a global appeal. Also, American films of the earliest silent picture era had to be designed to appeal to the less educated groups and to the large foreign-language sections of our own population. It was essential that the viewer should be able to follow the story whether understanding English or not. Hence our silent pictures early developed a style and form that commended them to all races and groups of people, without the aid of words. Our film writers and directors acquired a universal human touch that ever since has kept American pictures paramount on the international screen.

The wide co-operation which the American motion picture has received at home has been, I am sure, another great factor in its ability to win and hold world markets. The instances of that co-operation—the projects that were carried out only through the group "will-to-do"—fill a good part of my memory.

As a result of all these factors, and in particular because promising European progress was so sharply cut off in 1914 by World War I, just when our silent picture was finding its wings, the American motion picture industry was the first to reach maturity. It was the first to supply quality in quantity. It was the first to be able to offer to world markets anything like an adequate supply. So we gained a near monopoly of the early market. Because of the inherent strength of the industry's economic structure, its position became almost unassailable.

This very success, however, created an endless string of problems and rivalries. Our elaborate and costly production policy and program came to depend on receiving at least 35 per cent of the gross income from abroad. While this comfortingly proved the popularity of American films, it made it absolutely necessary to hold our foreign markets, in order to maintain both quality and quantity in production. This was the sword of Damocles always hanging over our heads.

So far as my own views were concerned, there was another factor that counted. I am sure that one thing that impelled me to accept the Association presidency was the vision of the motion pictures as a universal language! I believed that we were building not only for the United States but for the United Nations. That's why I always urged free trade in pictures. That's why we sought an amicable exchange of patent rights. That's why the companies were willing to forgo full payments during the World War II years to help keep up morale. And I'm glad to say that the leading producers and distributors thought very much as I did. Anything that would increase the usefulness of motion pictures anywhere in the world was our common concern.

The greatest difference between the industry's situation at home and abroad was the kind of opposition it encountered. Here at home the difficulties were largely connected with official or unofficial censorship, complaints about the moral or artistic lapses in pictures, and repeated threats of government control. But as long as there was an honest effort at progress, things rarely came to a crippling showdown.

Abroad it was different. There, producers and distributors were competing not only with each other but with a "foreign power." Though the people of every nation wanted to see our pictures, their governments could find sixteen ways to make the importation of them difficult. It was the rising tide of nationalism that swept all these measures into execution. At times American pictures were all but overwhelmed by that tide.

Whatever the alleged grounds for foreign objection or opposition, our negotiations usually discovered a perfectly natural economic rivalry at the bottom of them. This fear of competition from the United States increased as our hold on the screens of the world assumed larger proportions. When American films occupied as much as 80 per cent of the playing time in a given country, as often happened, and when a considerable amount of money flowed back to the United States, a foreign government could hardly be blamed for trying to do something about it. American companies, never subsidized and depending on their own resources alone, were willing to leave the matter to open competition and let the audience choose; but foreign governmental efforts to bar as many

American films as possible from their screens were usually in the hope that the resultant entertainment hunger in their own countries might in some mysterious way create a domestic industry and a financial asset comparable to that possessed by the United States. Too often this has been but vain and wishful thinking.

It is a tribute both to the appeal of our pictures and to the resourcefulness of our picture men that this "stop America" problem has been solved sufficiently to keep our films in circulation.

Censorship on the grounds of national objection to something offensive to their sense of morals or manners, or to their pride or traditions in matters like dress or language, was something our producers always had to watch.

Political or ideological censorship, increasing during the thirties, was a more serious matter. It became an "affair of state." The battle of international propaganda was raging in Europe, and American pictures were targets for all kinds of accusations.

The old protest of "unfair representation of nationals" was still heard —and doubtless deserved to be, at times.

Language was bound to be a constant problem. It had been a fairly simple operation, as long as pictures were silent, to translate the titles, though it was something of a chore to add titles in five different languages, as sometimes had to be done for pictures exhibited in some Balkan regions. Then the advent of sound had two opposite effects: curiosity made people eager to "see and hear" the new marvel, but difference of language was a bar to understanding. Here again national consciousness asserted itself, and by 1933 the pressure for compulsory translation into the different languages, by the process called "dubbing in" the substitute dialogue, was very heavy. This was a difficult and expensive task at best, since it meant synchronizing an entirely different language with the lip movements of the original American actor. Beyond that, some nations took advantage of the situation to add heavy dubbing taxes and to lay down rules that made the work even more difficult.

As a matter of record, the variety of taxes devised was amazing. There were tariffs, import license fees, fees for censorship, for visa, for dubbing, for exhibition, and so on. The result was at times so discriminatory and burdensome that distribution became impossible.

Unfavorable foreign exchange was another facet of the problem. Germany was the first nation to set up exchange barriers as early as 1925. By 1933, more than thirty countries were forbidding the exit of any foreign exchange.

The most burdensome measures specifically devised to restrict the importation of American pictures were the "quota" or "contingent" laws in various forms. Their simple purpose was to limit the number of American pictures imported to a certain fraction of the total pictures exhibited. In extreme cases these laws resulted in making American companies practically pay for the production of a foreign nation's own pictures.

Government subsidies, which contributed substantially toward the domestic production of pictures in several countries, would strike most Americans, raised on free enterprise, as "unfair competition." Yet they never succeeded in building up a strong industry, because money alone, if tied to regimentation, is powerless to create.

Shipment and transportation presented almost insuperable difficulties during World War II. Thousands of films had to be flown to regions which could not be reached quickly in any other way.

"Frozen funds," owing primarily to war and exchange, became our last and toughest problem. At one time more than a hundred million dollars, already earned, was withheld.

Such problems could be met, if at all, only by joint efforts of producers, distributors, the Association, and the State Department. It was a splendid example of the ability of teamwork to win victories against heavy odds.

The policy of our team was to support the American picture position in every practicable way: by making the best possible pictures; by maintaining free trade; by inviting co-operation from every quarter; by keeping well informed on foreign problems of all sorts; by seeking solutions in person, on the basis of mutual advantage; by drawing into the American art industry the talent of other nations in order to make it more truly universal; and, finally, by a confident and resourceful sales policy.

The American industry, which had cut its teeth on the toughest kind of competition, had learned that there is no substitute for quality. Abroad, too, it welcomed and stimulated competition, especially along technical and artistic lines. Companies didn't make one set of pictures for home consumption and an inferior brand to ship abroad. In fact, the necessity of making pictures that would sell throughout the world kept prodding our companies to produce good pictures with universal appeal. The pictures that did best here were apt to do best abroad. They were entertainment pictures—fiction on the screen—and essentially free from propaganda.

Our natural attitude toward motion pictures logically led us to urge free trade back and forth. I felt very strongly on the matter and, as a Republican, had to take some ribbing on my position. But I found no reason to change my conviction that the screen was the nearest approach to a world language and hence should transcend national barriers.

Repeatedly I went to Washington, conferring with the President, the Secretary of State, or members of the Department of Commerce, with the double purpose of keeping films on our own free list and of getting our government's help in surmounting obstacles abroad.

I'm sure the Association played a vital part in maintaining the free-trade position. For example, as early as 1923, after my first trip to England, I suggested to some of our distributor members that their position abroad would be strengthened if they imported a few good foreign pictures, and I recall how quickly Marcus Loew, for one, took up the idea. With the growth in our importation, the total number of foreign films released here reached 174 in 1934, 241 in 1935, 235 in 1936, and 216—from 15 countries—in 1937. To indicate the world growth, 1937 saw a total of 1,809 feature pictures produced outside the United States, of which, strange to say, Japan produced 500 and India 350.

The American industry never relinquished its position: we were always ready to grant to others the same right we asked for ourselves. We wished the privilege of supplying good pictures; we were always ready to leave the choice to the public. In the exchange of information, education, and entertainment recorded on silent or talking films, we recognized no frontiers.

If in our Foreign Department we developed any "secret weapon," it was patient and personal co-operation at every level. Colonel Herron, the first director of the department, spent the first three years chiefly in getting acquainted. He steadily built up close working relations with the foreign managers of the large picture companies that did overseas business, with their representatives abroad, with officials in our Departments of State and Commerce, and with key officials of foreign governments in the United States and abroad. In making many of these contacts Colonel Herron and I worked together closely. And when it is recalled that I came to the MPPDA direct from the Cabinet, it will be seen as wholly natural that we should appreciate the help that government departments could render. Harding, Coolidge, Hoover, and Roosevelt—all showed genuine interest in pictures, and each did the industry a definite service: Harding gave us strong support on the educational program; Coolidge on freedom from censorship and on permanent archives; Hoover on voluntary self-regulation; Roosevelt on the influence of American pictures abroad.

One of our most gratifying international contacts concerned our Production Code. In April of 1935 I received a request from England to come over and explain its workings. Unable to get away, I asked Martin Quigley, publisher of the *Motion Picture Herald,* who had been a prime force in the creation of the Code five years before, and Governor Milliken, secretary of the Association, to go as our representatives. They brought back reports of a most cordial reception and a fruitful conference. They were there eleven days, conferring with the leading British producers. Some newspapers at first lampooned them as "Purity Ambassadors." But they won their way. Governor Milliken suggested to the British producers that they would be wise to send us pictures that complied with our Code, and that it would be best for them to send over their scripts, for advance review, in order to obviate later trouble. As an immediate result, and at the request of Great Britain, we set up in New York a branch office of the Production Code Administration to expedite questions affecting Europe. They soon thanked us for saving them from trouble. Within two years we had established practical co-operation with the British in the matter of title registry, and they were submitting to us scripts of pictures which they hoped to exhibit in the United States.

Of my own several motion picture trips abroad, that of 1936 to Italy, France, and England was certainly the most dramatic.

The foreign problems of our industry always showed up in sharper outline when I discussed them in Rome, Berlin, Paris, or London. The tremendous advantages that pictures enjoyed in America, our almost unlimited possibilities, our creed on freedom of the screen, all loomed larger the farther from home I got.

As we have all come to realize, even the most important of "international relations" have to be carried on by individuals. These individuals cannot be expected to shed their human frailties or personal idiosyncrasies just because they are conducting affairs of state. Often it is quite the reverse. And always it took longer to solve one of these international picture problems than the layman would imagine. One of the biggest reasons is that importing or exporting is necessarily a complex operation. The interests of producer, distributor, exhibitor, and government are by no means the same.

The Italian situation, through the latter half of 1936, is a good illustration. Under Mussolini, their government could be as dictatorial as it pleased. But Il Duce was a smart man; he knew the advantage of doing favors, and he basked in the reputation of doing much for his people. His little bureaucrats, however, wanted to put almost anything over in order to try to justify their efforts before the Big Boss; and in the Motion Picture Bureau they were trying to make an impression by pushing for decrees and restrictions which would keep American pictures out and build up the Italian industry. Italian producers sided with them. But Italian exhibitors, whose success depended upon the public pouring into their theatres, were on the other side; they knew they couldn't hold their audiences without American pictures.

In the five months before I sailed for Rome in November of 1936, a steady stream of reports on Italy had poured in on new difficulties that were brewing. In June, Harold Smith wrote Colonel Herron that "pressure is being brought to bear on Warners in Italy to force them to produce a film there"; that, in fact, "the proposed Italian film decree . . . includes compulsory production of one Italian for seven imported films, and the retention of the dubbing tax." During those critical days the American commercial attaché in Rome, Charles A. Livengood, was keeping his eye on the Italian decree developments and keeping us informed.

So dire were the rumors that our European representative was repeatedly under pressure from American film-company men abroad to send emergency cables based on reports that sometimes turned out to be false. It took diplomacy to handle such requests. Sometimes it was enough to tell the company representative that our Foreign Department in New York was in constant contact with the State Department, whose commercial attachés were watching developments just as closely as we were.

Certainly no American film company in Italy, in the summer of 1936, could have been anything but apprehensive. We were informed that it was proposed to issue a decree, ironically on the Fourth of July, which would empower the Italian Government to take over the distribution of all films. Member-company representatives did their best to oppose these changes in the Federazione de Spectacle. It was all too clear that any such decree would make the importer-distributors the first and most direct victims. Foreign distribution at the time was close to a total of fifty million lire annually, and Italy had been seeing something like two hundred American feature pictures a year.

This looked like a genuine emergency. We were told by company representatives that it was "absolutely necessary" that Washington, through our Embassy in Rome, protest in the strongest possible terms, and that American producers issue a joint statement that any further restrictions on their activities in Italy would entail cessation of their business there. We asked the State Department to check.

The last day in June our continental managers met to discuss the situation. One of them expressed the opinion that "the Italians are going to propose these measures to see how we react, and that the truth is that they have no foreign exchange to let us take out our money." In New York we had difficulty in believing that the Italian Government would take the radical step reported, because only the preceding winter they had assured our Embassy that they "had no intention whatsoever of taking over the motion picture business of the country then or at any time." Il Duce had indicated that he knew the picture industry must be self-supporting and competitive, and that it did not require political interference or control.

Suffice it to say that something apparently quieted down the Italian Government in July and no decree was enacted. But on October 8, and again on October 11, decrees were promulgated that were all but confiscatory. Our Ambassador in Rome at once lodged protests with the Foreign Office there, each one stronger than the last.

It was now clear to everyone concerned that we were facing a major issue.

I was convinced that the solution could be worked out only on the highest level. No negotiations between American and Italian film interests would be sufficient. But I believed that if direct negotiations, fostered by our government, could be had with the Italian Government, our chances of success would be far greater. So with our State Department in Washington we worked out a joint plan of action.

The Italian decree of October limited the annual import of American films into Italy to forty-two and forbade our companies to take out more than eight million lire per year—cuts of at least 80 per cent. Nor could there be any camouflaged exchange—that is, they could not take out dollar value in some other commodity. It was the judgment of the State Department that I go over as soon as possible and seek to negotiate personally with the Italian Government. Because of the department's active support, I became a quasi-government representative. Although I had no official or formal recognition, an outsider would have thought I had, from the help given at every stage, both by Washington and by our Embassy in Rome. My visit was approved and encouraged by William Phillips, our Ambassador, and those in his Embassy who had long been working on the affair.

With preliminary plans completed, Mrs. Hays and I sailed on the *Conte di Savoia* on November 7. It was most fortunate for us that on the same passenger list we found Cardinal Pacelli—the present Pope Pius XII—and Count Enrico Galleazzi. The cardinal, then Papal Secretary of State, had been in America on a significant mission. Count Galleazzi, who had accompanied him throughout the trip, was a leading Catholic layman, a distinguished engineer, and one of the most intelligent, cultured, and companionable men I have ever known.

Our trip was the pleasanter for finding a number of old friends on board and, then and there, several of us made our plans to return together a month later on the *Normandie*. Melville Eaton, whom I had known as Republican state chairman of New York, and his delightful wife were of this group, as were George Kline and Rodney Sharpe. We spent much time with Mr. and Mrs. Edmond Coblentz, of whom we had seen a great deal in New York. At the time, Mr. Coblentz was editor of the New York *American* and later moved to San Francisco as publisher of the *Call-Bulletin*. He recently celebrated the completion of fifty years in journalism. The most serious quandary I can recall was the proper disposal of a quart of famous vintage champagne that had been sent to the boat by our good friend Herbert Kaufman, the late editorial writer. Neither Mr. Coblentz nor myself drank. Friends, however, came to our rescue.

The most significant experiences of the trip, especially in the light of later events, were my visits with Cardinal Pacelli and Count Galleazzi, which the latter graciously arranged. In two pleasant social calls Mrs. Hays and I found the cardinal most sympathetic and surprisingly well informed about America. He spoke excellent English. I also had another visit of at least two hours, during which he told me quite frankly the purpose of his visit to the United States—it had to do with the Pro Deo movement—noting that it was the first such official visit of a papal secretary of state. It was during these visits that I learned that a private audience with Pope Pius XI would be arranged for me soon after we reached Rome.

All in all, the trip over was one of the most delightful I have ever made. When we cast anchor on the morning of November 14 in the startlingly beautiful harbor of Naples, the experience was complete. The sun was breaking through the mist and smoke from Vesuvius floated in the distance and the water all about us was blue as indigo. I had never seen Naples, and I shall never forget it.

On the dock Harold Smith, our Paris representative, was waiting to welcome us, accompanied by Signor Luperino, the Rome representative of United Artists. Both men were to prove indispensable, contributing much to the pleasure and the practical results of our visit.

Being so near Pompeii, the Eatons and ourselves drove over there for lunch and took time to see the most famous of the landmarks. We reached Rome at ten o'clock and settled ourselves at the Excelsior Hotel, which was to be our home for ten days. The following day being Sunday, we had time to visit some of the great historic monuments, including the Colosseum. Even familiarity with grandiose movie sets had hardly prepared me for the realization that this great amphitheatre of the first century held 87,000 people—a few hundred more than saw the fifth game of the 1948 World Series, then the biggest baseball crowd of all time. We also examined modern developments like the imposing Mussolini Forum, which we found to be down below the Villa Madonna, Dorothy di Frasso's house. It was there we had another reminder that American motion pictures girdle the globe when we saw on her backgammon table a photograph of one of our familiar movie stars.

Monday morning I went to work like any American businessman; but unlike most of them, I was given an office in the Embassy and the fullest co-operation from the whole staff. Our Ambassador, William Phillips, was an example of the best that a career in our State Department could produce. He thoroughly understood our industry problem and its importance. He took pains to explain fully all that had been done and to outline what, in his opinion, would still need to be done. This included my personally presenting the whole case to the Foreign Minister, Count Galeazzo Ciano, Il Duce's son-in-law, who, we hoped, would take a personal interest in it and see that something was done.

Mr. Phillips was able to arrange an appointment with Ciano for the following Wednesday. After a lunch at the Embassy he and I made our official call at the Foreign Office, where our conference lasted almost two hours.

After hearing the whole story, with plenty of supporting facts, Count Ciano said that he recognized our needs, that he certainly favored reaching an understanding, and that he would "do anything he could." He was friendly and impressive and showed a lively interest in motion pictures. Though he was logically interested in the development of the Italian industry, he felt that American films should have a fair chance in Italy. He impressed me as being considerably more capable than his general reputation would indicate. He felt strongly that we must win the support of the Finance Minister, Guanari, and the Minister of Propaganda, Alfieri.

I never met Guanari, although he sent his card over immediately upon my arrival. Alfieri I met several times. One other quasi-government man, Luigi Freddi, became a bit of a problem because he kept trying to get into the negotiations, in which he had no official part. His title was Direttore Generale per la Cinematografia. This Freddi, known as the film director of the Italian Propaganda Ministry, was the man who only five months later signed for Italy a pact with Germany and Japan creating an anti-Hollywood bloc.

When we left Ciano, we questioned just how zealously he would pursue the matter with the other two ministers. The Ambassador thought he would try. We had told Ciano that we did not plan any conferences with Italian movie men but that we had thought it proper to discuss the matter with Alfieri on a plane of common interest, without seeking to work out any program. This appealed to Ciano, and the actual negotiations were left in his hands. But when we had heard nothing from him by Saturday we felt that something needed to be done to hurry things up. It was decided that I should try to get President Roosevelt to send some sort of communication direct to Mussolini. This was a bold suggestion, but I thought it feasible in view of the President's interest. I called up our New York office by telephone and explained the situation to Colonel Herron. President Roosevelt, sensing the emergency, cabled Mussolini on Sunday, and we were informed that the cable had been sent. So on Monday morning we knew that our project had become "top-drawer."

We had not been idle over the weekend. And we didn't miss church either, attending the ten o'clock service at St. Peter's, where the cardinal officiated. Then while Mrs. Hays went out to the Villa d'Este, Harold Smith and I worked at the Embassy. Our informal discussions with the Minister of Propaganda had indicated the advisability of drawing up some additional data and figures, although we thought we had come to

Italy sufficiently prepared. Meanwhile, on Saturday and again on Monday morning, the Ambassador could get no word from Ciano except that he "had not yet heard from the other ministries." The real opposition came from Guanari, the Minister of Finance.

The break came just before noon on Monday. While I was at the Ambassador's desk the telephone rang. Through his English-speaking secretary, Alfieri invited me to go with him that afternoon at five to call upon Il Duce. I asked the secretary to wait a moment and I repeated the message to Mr. Phillips. Although I was a bit concerned about what Ciano would think if we went over his head, the Ambassador advised that I instantly accept the invitation. "You have to go," he added. "Il Duce asked you to come, and I am quite sure it won't offend Ciano. In any event, I'll tell him about it beforehand." I accepted.

Two days later we learned just what had brought about the invitation when Alfieri, with some ceremony, gave me the original letter in which he had requested Mussolini to invite me to come and see him or to let Alfieri take me there. In large letters, in blue pencil, Mussolini had written at the top of the page "Si," and at the bottom simply a big "M."

This Alfieri turned out to be quite a boy. He looked like a Peoria whisky salesman and jumped around just as lively. He was undoubtedly ambitious and apparently close to Il Duce. He is the same Alfieri who later became Fascist Ambassador to Nazi Berlin, and during his term as Ambassador there was shot by a Nazi officer who came home and found him with his wife.

With Ambassador Phillips' aid we planned thoroughly for this conference which might hold the key to our problem. I prepared as carefully as a student for a final exam and was ready when the Minister and his secretary, a likable young man, called for me in their car and whisked me over to the government building. The imposing Palazzo Venezia had appeared so often in newsreels, usually with Il Duce orating from the balcony, that it seemed strangely familiar. But I was hardly prepared for the labyrinth of halls and rooms inside. Mussolini's waiting room, cold and austere, looked more like a museum of medieval armor than a modern reception room. But the next room we entered was warm, friendly, and comfortable. A pleasant Italian gentleman was in charge, and a younger man deferentially took our coats and helped to make us feel welcome, saying quickly, "I will let Il Duce know you are here."

Alfieri, not waiting for word from the Chief, preceded the receptionist into an inner room. Within three minutes General Italo Balbo emerged and came straight over to me, smiling. I easily recognized him, having seen him in New York following the famous group flight to America not long before. He was as gracious and amiable there in the government offices as he had been when entertained in New York. It flashed through my mind that he must be a very popular man. When I later learned how summarily he had been disposed of, it was a terrific shock.

There was time for only a word of greeting before Alfieri came to the door and motioned for me to enter. Never shall I forget the room, or the experience, that lay beyond that door. The room seemed to be at least fifty feet wide and two hundred feet long! We started to walk east down the length of this football field—almost—at the far end of which, in front of a great mantelpiece and a little to the right of it, stood Mussolini's massive desk. I had time only to realize that we were advancing over a tiled or mosaic floor, that the indirect lighting was coming from the level of the picture molding, that there was a large light over the desk, guest chairs in front and at the left, and no other furniture. Il Duce himself was standing—as a matter of fact, pacing back and forth—behind his desk, his arms behind him and his hands clasped, shoulders hunched up and chin on chest, as if he had taken over from Atlas and Caesar combined and now had the world as well as the empire on his shoulders.

Click-click went our heels as we advanced toward the goal line of his desk, Alfieri a step or two behind me. A moment later Mussolini stepped around the right end of the desk toward me. As he approached I stopped short, clicking my heels in a manner which would have done credit to any reporting officer. He smiled, cordially extended his hand, and greeted me in first-rate English, with appropriate felicitations. I sat down opposite him and he asked me to tell my story. I will say he gave me plenty of time. Without interruption, for a full half hour I told him of our necessities.

Nine days in Rome had given me time to see and hear plenty of evidence of constructive things that Mussolini had done for Italy. For one thing, he seemed to be especially interested in the youth, both in their morale and in their training. This proved to be a sympathetic approach from which I could naturally move into my interest in youth, what we were doing in motion pictures, and some of the objectives of our organized American industry, including education.

This caught his ear and he seemed quite ready to hear our story. Incidentally, I had also referred to my relations with our former Ambassador to Italy, Richard Washburn Child, and to the fact that Child had sent me the second copy, he had said, of his *Life of Mussolini*. And since Ambassador Phillips had assured me that one could talk plainly to Mussolini without pulling any punches, I did just that.

First I pointed out that the total Italian receipts from motion pictures was a vast amount, with many families supported by the earnings of American motion pictures, from which same source the Italian Government also received 100,000,000 lire in taxes. I think the theatre receipts on American pictures totaled about 600,000,000 lire.

As to the position of American producers and distributors, I told him that the recent Italian decree was confiscatory and that we should have to move out of Italy unless some compromise were reached. We should have to close our exchanges and abandon all business. On the other hand, I assured him that we were as much interested in international amity as he was; that we stood ready to do anything possible; that in my opinion Rome was the "cradle of all art," and that under his guidance there was no question about the success of the Italian motion picture industry. Since it would soon be branching out from Rome all over the world, I knew that he was as much interested as I in maintaining a free flow of pictures across international boundaries. I told him that I had gone out to see the Cinematographic Institute establishment, with all its fine equipment—practically in Mussolini's back yard—and I explained to him how our industry had helped to finance it.

By now our conversation had become a joint exchange, and at this point Il Duce suddenly asked, "What do you want?" It was as direct as that. I answered as directly: "We want to bring into Italy all the American motion pictures that the traffic will stand, and we want to take out enough money to enable us to live."

Mussolini said at once, "That seems fair," and picked up his telephone. Though I did not know it at the time, he was talking to Ciano—in Italian, of course. In a moment he turned to me. "All right," he said, "we'll give you twenty million lire." (That was a rise from the edict's eight million.) "You can bring in all the American pictures you want and there will be no fraud in the exchange."

I replied, "All right, we'll do that, and the American motion picture will not move out of Italy." Perhaps I had no actual authority to make that definite agreement on behalf of the producers and distributors, but his offer was probably a better one than they had expected, and I was sure they would want it accepted.

Throughout the entire conference Alfieri had sat there not saying a word, but I think he understood English well enough to get the drift. And now, since somewhere in the conversation it had been mentioned that Il Duce was planning to make a trip to Tripoli within a few days and that his famous white horse was to be there as a part of the trappings of some ceremonial occasion, I said, "Further, Your Excellency, the American newsreels will be at Tripoli." He acknowledged this courtesy with obvious pride. And our serious business having been concluded in an atmosphere of cordial understanding, we went on to talk about other things, chiefly of the future. Early in our talk I had become convinced that Mussolini was not interested in Fascism as an export product, as we Americans were in pictures. This feeling colored my later discussions with him. I know he didn't want Communists active in Barcelona because the Mediterranean made contact so easy, but he wasn't trying to take Fascism to anybody, anywhere, so far as I could gather. He thought Fascism a good thing for Italy, but there his interest seemed to end.

Nor did anti-Semitism seem to have any place in his thought. I understood that there were not more than thirty thousand Jewish people in Italy at the time, and there was no evidence that he had any feeling on the subject. In discussing American motion pictures, the fact that there were many Jews in the business, if it came up at all, was incidental.

I then brought the conference to a close. Mussolini was talking on with great animation, but I felt that our work was done. As we stood up he came around the desk to say good-by. When he reached me he put out his right hand and clasped mine warmly; he did not release my hand but held it as we slowly retraced the length of the room, chatting with great friendliness. Just as we reached the door he released my hand and opened the door, pulling it back. He then squared away, saluted, and put his right hand on my shoulder as he said with a proud blend of joviality and authority, "Well, Hays, we fixed it!" And with a laugh he said good-by.

I went at once to our Embassy and saw Ambassador Phillips. He had already learned from Count Ciano the result of the interview. Further, Mussolini had directed Ciano to advise me that they were giving me the highest decoration that Italy could present to a foreigner. Ciano was personally to advise me of this that same evening at a dinner being given in his honor at the Ambassador's residence. I at once told Mr. Phillips that I had grave doubts about the propriety of accepting the decoration, and he felt that that was a matter for me to decide. As to the results of my meeting with Il Duce, he was decidedly pleased and rightly had the satisfaction of feeling that all our joint efforts through the weeks had contributed to the solution.

The Ambassador's dinner that last Monday evening was enjoyable and memorable, the whole affair beautifully handled. It happened to be the first formal dinner that Mr. Phillips had given as our new Ambassador since his arrival in August. In addition to Count and Countess Ciano (Edda Mussolini), there were more than a score of guests. Alfieri was one of a dozen Italians present. The Americans included Mrs. Henry Rogers; Captain Thaddeus Thompson, Jr., naval attaché at the Embassy; Samuel Reber, second secretary, a relative of General Nelson Miles; and Robert McGregor, Jr., third secretary. I sat between Countess Edda Ciano and the Countess Vitetti—an American who had married Count Vitetti when he was military attaché in the Italian Embassy in Washington. The two girls were chums and kept up a gay conversation, only part of which I could follow.

As the dinner progressed they were obviously discussing some intriguing secret which they were trying to keep from me, although it must have passed back and forth over my plate several times. Finally I discovered that they were talking about what they wanted to do first when they got to Hollywood. I said the answer was easy: it was to meet Clark Gable. They insisted that wasn't it at all. Finally I wormed it out of them: the very first thing they wanted was "to be made up by Max Factor"! Thus the influence of movie stars!

After the Mussolini conference and the Ambassador's dinner our affairs could be wound up quickly as far as personal conferences on the revised understanding were concerned, and we made ready to leave on Wednesday. But it must be recorded that in the course of drawing up the new decree to replace the confiscatory decree of October there was a hitch.

It seems Mussolini later discovered that an unlimited import privilege was illegal and hence that a definite number had to be fixed. This word, relayed to us via the Embassy and the State Department after our return, was disturbing. During a subsequent Board meeting, a telephone message came through from Washington that Mussolini was willing for me to fix the number. I turned from the phone, reported this to the Board members, and suggested that we say 250. This was instantly approved, and I asked the State Department to advise the Italian Government that we understood the difficulties and would be perfectly satisfied to have the terms limit the imported films to 250 and the revenue to be taken out to 20,000,000 lire, with no camouflaged exchange. Thus was our mission completed.

But I must go back to Rome to recount the other most significant experience of that 1936 trip. That experience was our private audience with Pope Pius XI, then nearing the end of his life but spiritually and mentally vigorous. The audience was arranged by Count Galleazzi for noon on Tuesday, November 17. The day before, we were told that Mrs. Hays might also go if she wished, which pleased us both. We were given essential information as to apparel and custom, the count bringing Mrs. Hays the mantilla which she would wear.

On the way to the Vatican, Count Galleazzi told us that he would interpret, since the Holy Father did not speak English, though he could understand it. What was more important, he told me that, contrary to usual custom, I was free to ask questions as well as to answer them and to carry on the interview in a perfectly natural manner. This pleased me greatly.

The approach to the Vatican, its courts and halls, the Swiss guards, the various officials and functionaries in impressive dress, the many rooms through which we passed, the great group of people in an outer room—this, to an American who grew up in an Indiana village and attended a simple little Presbyterian church, was all most impressive, clothed with the stately dignity of a great spiritual tradition.

Finally reaching the secretary's room adjoining the private office of the Holy Father, we were greeted most cordially in scholarly English of a distinctly New England flavor by a man who seemed like an old friend. He repeated Count Galleazzi's suggestion about speaking freely and said he would see us when we came out. This was none other than our own Cardinal Spellman! A moment later we found ourselves in the presence of the Pope, seated at his broad desk placed in the middle of a small platform raised perhaps a foot above the floor. He was in the familiar white raiment, with the white cap; and his calm presence was a benediction. I was shown to a chair at the Holy Father's right, with Count Galleazzi at my right and Mrs. Hays still farther to the right, opposite the Holy Father.

In opening the conversation, with the count interpreting, the Pope said: "Mr. Hays, we have asked you to come here in order that we might express to you the appreciation of the Church for the improvement in the moral content of American motion pictures." That positive statement by the Holy Father I was privileged to give to the official who interviewed me on the way out, and also to the lay press. When I met this publicity official later he suggested that he would be glad if in my subsequent private conversations I emphasized the apparent good health of the Pope, when it seemed fitting to do so, because of some recent talk about his being ill. This report was shortly to appear in thousands of American newspapers.

The interview lasted nearly an hour. I was amazed at the detail in his own observations about motion pictures and in his pointed inquiries as to just how we conducted the Production Code Administration. He wanted me to clarify its origin and certain of its methods, though he already seemed familiar with the general story.

He then said—and I have quoted his words scores of times because of their significance: "You sit at the valve in the conduit through which flows the principal amusement of the great majority of all the people in the world. Your impress is upon the quality of this entertainment and you are very important to us. We are deeply interested, of course, in the success of your efforts."

I had hoped there might be opportunity to discuss with the Pope our organized effort to improve the quality of the demand as well as the quality of the supply, and to explain how we were finding in actual practice that these twin necessities were interrelated; how we had proved without question that support and patronage of good pictures helped to assure the continuous flow of good pictures. To my satisfaction and surprise, though I need not have been surprised, the Holy Father brought up this very point himself. He said that he had no doubt that the organized American industry would continue to guard the moral content of motion pictures, but that his primary concern was that the people would want to see the good and would support the good. He had picked up in substance, and almost in the very words, what I my-self had hoped to express to him.

Nor did he drop the thought there. He went on to explain how vital it was that there grow in the minds and hearts of the people the desire to see the realization of the good. On that theme he preached a wonderful sermon that made me profoundly happy. I thought then, and I have thought many times since, that it was worth all the worries and the travail of the Italian picture problem to have had such a heartening experience with this holy man.

One particular incident of this meeting was indelibly etched in my memory. In the midst of the conversation the Pope picked up a big loose-leaf book, two or three inches thick, lying on his table, and pushed it toward me. He explained that this volume of reports contained the series of original communiqués sent out from the Comintern in Moscow to comrades and fellow travelers all over the world, and that one of the most emphatic orders was to "go out and get hold of the cinema of the world." This was a shocking revelation, backed as it was by such irrefutable evidence, and it sheds clear light on Communist efforts in subsequent years.

When we had finished discussing motion pictures, the Holy Father went at once into the Pro Deo movement, of which Cardinal Pacelli had given me some account on our trip over. I was again impressed by the unity and the world sweep of the organized idea: that the Church was leading a movement of religionists everywhere, a united movement for God and the good in a concerted drive to oppose the spread of Communism.

Before we left his presence—and I left with reluctance and deep reverence—the Holy Father blessed us. It was an inspiring experience, for which I shall never cease to be thankful.

Although my visits with the Pope and with Mussolini and the Ambassador's dinner were the high spots of my ten days in Rome, many other activities fitted into the intricate web of our foreign relations in this Old World capital. We took time to see the points of greatest interest, old and new, from churches to restaurants; various friends in Rome were always ready to accompany us on such jaunts. Both the members of our Embassy staff and Italian film men, including representatives of our American companies, were helpful. Harold Smith always knew what could be done there to advantage, to further good relations. Signor Roncoroni—perhaps the leading figure in the Italian film industry—took me to lunch and showed me through the great motion picture studios recently completed at the Quadaro, near Rome. I remember watching the filming of a scene from a historical Roman picture and unconsciously comparing it with Hollywood. I met all our film men and the representatives of the press, who were extremely useful in seeing that the newspapers were kept advised of progress in negotiations, which was quite as good for the Italians as for us. Then on Wednesday, November 25, we finished up and, accompanied by Harold Smith, took the noon train for Paris.

It was good to reach Paris on Thanksgiving morning, for we seemed a long step nearer home. It was our wedding anniversary. We got settled at the Hotel Crillon and then went to a genuine Thanksgiving service at the American Church, of which Dr. Beekman was rector. We had lunch with some film men, and I spent the afternoon working with them. But in the evening Mrs. Hays and I had our Thanksgiving and anniversary dinner, all in one, at La Rue's.

On Friday I again met with our Paris film men, discussing their problems, some of which were similar to those in Italy, and trying to anticipate points of possible danger. Mrs. Hays had lunch with Michel Clemenceau, son of "The Tiger," whom we had known previously. On Saturday we happened to run into Admiral Cary Grayson and another top man in the Red Cross, whom we were to see again as we came back on the *Normandie* together.

Leaving for London the night of the twenty-eighth, we arrived there the next day, stopping at the Savoy and having luncheon with James Beck. We kept running into old friends, like Zazu Pitts and H. B. Warner; and Mrs. Hays had lunch with Claire Hampton, widow of Ben Hampton, who had played a big part in the development of motion pictures.

Monday noon I was the guest, as president of the MPPDA, at a luncheon given by the Cinematograph Exhibitors' Association of Great Britain and Ireland, at the Trocadero Restaurant. It greatly interested me to hear the president of this association say of themselves, in referring to the recent report of the Lord Moyne Committee, that he "wondered whether we required a state commission or, to give it its proper name, a cinema control board to solve the trade's many problems." He felt, as he had always felt and always advocated, that they "should solve their problems within the trade." To this idea, on the basis of our experience in America, I could add a hearty "Amen." And in replying to the president's greeting, I once more voiced my unchanging belief that co-operation was the one essential for the final success of an industry so complicated as that of the cinema.

On Tuesday, the last day of our brief stay, I was given a formal dinner by the Film Group of the Federation of British Industries. The guests were chiefly heads of British production units belonging to the Film Group and managing directors of renting companies with American affiliations. The friendly discussion of our common problems—from Mickey Mouse, Shirley Temple, and George Arliss to film rentals and the threat of censorship if film producers became careless—made the dinner a splendid windup of the London visit, leaving a vivid impression of our mutual interests and our common goal.

The following day, after a luncheon at the Carlisle House, we took the boat train to Southampton and boarded the *Normandie,* along with a big group of our old friends and with Mistinguette and a company of French dancers who, we all admitted, considerably enlivened the homeward crossing.

Because our films so well depict the life of a free people under democratic government, the Axis nations virtually declared war on them long before Pearl Harbor. This film war had begun in Germany soon after the Nazis came to power in 1933. The Nuremberg laws imposed Nazi supervision upon all the German branches of our American film companies. Censorship by the Nazi Propaganda Bureau also was included among these elaborate devices to prevent the showing of outstanding American pictures.

The Nazis not only feared the effects of American films on their own people, but they also feared their influence on world opinion. They took all the measures they could to combat the release of our pictures in Latin America and the Far East as well. Their activities in the International Film Chamber, which they formed with representatives of other countries in Europe, but which was essentially an Axis instrument, were aimed primarily at reducing the markets for American pictures on the European continent. With the growing tension there as the war clouds darkened, political censorship became particularly severe.

An interesting bit of honest evidence on the other side came from pre-war Germany, where with characteristic German thoroughness Dr. Franz Loelsch, industrial physician to the Bavarian Government, reported on tests made there. Said Dr. Koelsch:

We find in Germany that the increasing popularity of motion pictures leads more and more to the whole family taking its recreation as a unit. That is great progress from a sociological standpoint. Tests which we made of the psychological effect of American motion pictures brought us to the conclusion that the inevitability of punishment, as portrayed in plots under the safeguards voluntarily adopted by the producers in the United States, tend to make the screen a positive deterrent from crime.

Foreign governments have always found difficulty in objecting to American films on ideological or propaganda grounds. The scrupulous care observed by American producers in following the Production Code has barred such charges from any serious basis of truth. It is their natural, healthful, ingenuous freedom from propaganda that has made our films not only palatable but refreshing to people living under widely differing civilizations.

I can think of no more ironical illustration than the strange case of Hitler himself, the number-one enemy of the American motion picture industry—officially! In 1937, Sinclair Lewis' story, *It Can't Happen Here,* was absolutely banned in Germany because it was a bitter portrayal of how a dictator can rob a people of their freedom. But a dispatch to the New York *Times* by its Stockholm representative on November 14, 1943, presented the following interesting revelation:

Hitler is a great film fan and is disinclined to forgo this pleasure while traveling—hence a moving picture theatre on wheels. He likes especially American films, and wherever his army or navy is able to seize any late American releases, the reels are speeded to him for a showing.

Last week a nice windfall reached him this way when the Germans confiscated a large number of copies of the more recent American films aboard the Swedish liner *Drottningholm,* returning from Scotland after a voyage with exchanged prisoners of war.

The Germans took off the films at their Kristiansand control port in Norway. So this week Hitler has been able to see Walt Disney's *Bambi,* and *Crash Dive,* starring Tyrone Power, *Cairo,* starring von Stroheim, and *Coney Island* featuring Betty Grable.

The Fuehrer thus betrayed, quite without intention, the essential reason why American pictures have a future. Everybody likes them.

One grimly humorous side light on the influence of American pictures, as symbolized by the "stars," appeared in an item carried by *Newsweek* in January of 1948. The story told how in Russia the pictures of Clark Gable, Dorothy Lamour, and others were found over and over in beauty parlors, barbershops, and wherever people were apt to gather informally. Then came the crushing order: "This unique advertising of American cinema trash . . . the output of trashy displays with portraits of Hollywood cinema actors, is categorically forbidden."

Maybe the Russians knew what they were doing! Maybe there is more explosive democracy in our pictures than we realize. In my annual report for 1944 I wrote: "The vitality of all our democratic processes depends upon the freedom of communication among free men." That's just what Russia fears!

I want to close this attempt at defining the international impact of American motion pictures by quoting a statement I have heard Governor Milliken repeatedly make at the headquarters of the Association in New York:

"From this office, through the channels of the industry we represent, go out more currents of thought, world-wide, than from any other single source."

That's something worth mulling over!

CHAPTER 32

Motion Pictures and the War (1941–1945)

I T is impossible to review motion pictures during the critical World War II years without amazement at the contributions which the industry made toward sustaining morale and winning the War. Yet all the special war projects were carried on without skimping the job of keeping a hundred million people supplied with weekly entertainment. It was a superb job of industry-wide co-operation.

I have never been timid when praising the motion picture as a constructive force, and I am not alone in this feeling. The judgment has often been expressed that motion pictures did more for the war effort than any other industry except those directly producing war material. If this is so, it is because motion pictures reached the most people, both here and abroad. The record made was a striking example of patriotism in action. Demands of every kind were made on the industry, and most of them were met with a speed and effectiveness that often surprised both public officials and the people. These demands also hastened technical and educational developments that might otherwise have taken years.

It would be idle to say that those of us who had been wrapped up for more than twenty years in the work of the Association were not gratified. It certainly looked like a justification of the Association's policies. Personally, I was thrilled to find myself once more heading an organization capable of rendering so many needed services on so many fronts. And never have I seen a more wholehearted response. In my 1945 report I called it a "Protean role" which the industry was playing, going on to say, "By actual demonstration during these war years the screen has shown not only how significant are its functions as a medium of entertainment and communication, but also how important a weapon of training and education films have become."

Like the early American pioneers who in hardship had learned courage and resourcefulness, so this pioneering industry had learned the daring and inventiveness that now enabled it to solve problems never before presented. I remember thinking how fortunate it was that our industry had so many facilities for helping: boundless imagination, originality and individual initiative, scientific resources and technical skills, and a talent pool of personnel such as had never before been assembled "under one top." In brief, *the industry was ready*. Many of the individual skills, to say nothing of the strength of a closely knit organization, could now be transferred bodily to one or another war project. From long acquaintance I knew that both by spirit and experience motion picture men were singularly adapted to meeting such an emergency. In temperament they were bold and venturesome. They had built up their enterprises under conditions of vigorous American freedom. The influential leaders were men of intense enthusiasm and high patriotism. They were gratified to be asked to put their immense resources at the disposal of Uncle Sam and to find themselves and their companies so useful. Since the studios needed no "retooling," they sprang into war production in one leap, with total results almost beyond computation.

Great as were its tasks in producing films for the training of recruits and in sending pictures and stars all over the world to entertain war-weary, lonely troops, there was a deeper though less conspicuous thing that the motion picture industry accomplished. It presented an actual picturization of the war to the great mass of our people; and by transporting them in imagination to the very scenes of conflict, it made them participants as nothing else could have done. The motion picture thus created a community of feeling throughout the civilian population that was one of the most powerful bulwarks of morale and incentives to sacrifice. Few examples of "let's get together" have ever equaled it.

My 1941 report had been titled: "Motion Pictures and Total Defense." When the storm of world conflict broke over our heads, I was thankful to be connected with an enterprise able to jump into the thick of the struggle.

Glad I was, too, that the industry had developed such strength that it was able, without stumbling, to carry the huge extra burdens imposed alike on personnel and purses.

A tremendous amount of our service, especially to fighting men, was an outright gift running into many millions of dollars. Only "big business" could have delivered the goods and made such gifts. And only a very big industry, "drawing its materials from the far reaches of the world" and having a world-wide distribution service, could have carried its offerings around the globe under the doubled difficulties of war.

But financial and material advantages alone would not have been enough; the only true explanation could be found in the American spirit of freedom. Comparing our situation with that of dictator-controlled nations, I later said: "Fantastically as the enemy may have fought, the morale secured among free peoples by free media of information, education, and entertainment was vastly more durable than the morale which tyranny and dictatorship could impose by terror and training."

Long before Pearl Harbor the patriotic help of the screen had won high praise. President Roosevelt's tribute, radioed to an annual dinner of the Academy of Motion Picture Arts and Sciences, received wide notice. The President warmly thanked the film industry for its "splendid co-operation with all those who are directing the expansion of defense forces." He acknowledged the part already played by the industry in its "sincere effort to help the people of this hemisphere to come to know each other," and asked further aid from films in creating inter-American solidarity. Emphasizing the screen's educational influence, he noted as an example the "great service which the newsreels have performed in acquainting the public with all the implications of lend-lease as it takes its way through the various legislative stages."

In a story headed "Another Posy for Pix," *Variety* reported a tribute from another source: "Motion pictures took another bow last Thursday as the U. S. Department of Commerce described the industry as offering 'an invaluable opportunity for massed training of students in high schools and colleges in specialized crafts essential to the national defense.'"

As to entertainment value, the strongest kind of testimony was given early in 1941 by Admiral Chester W. Nimitz, then chief of the U. S. Bureau of Navigation. In hearings on the Navy appropriations bill, Admiral Nimitz said: "Motion pictures have become the most important element contributing to maintenance of naval morale."

As soon as the Association had realized the size of the national defense tasks facing the industry, we organized the National Co-ordinating Committee, with George J. Schaefer, an executive connected with pictures for three decades, as chairman, and my assistant, Francis S. Harmon, as co-ordinator. By early 1941, activities were being stepped up. Comprehensive releasing jobs on government-made films were well under way, two of the earliest films having been on recruiting and on "Power for Defense." The Co-ordinating Committee nudged the newsreel producers and editors, and as a result of their zeal, the factual reporting by the five American newsreels was soon recognized as the outstanding treatment of the defense problem. It gave an actual visualization of the government effort.

Such results, however, were not secured without constant study, co-operation, and effort. One specific instance of helpful negotiations carried on by the Association at this stage was with the Office of Production Management. As one news story stated: "It is to be noted that a number of defense projects now in progress, both for internal official purposes and for presentation to the public, are dependent on motion pictures. This more than implies that the motion picture is an essential industry." Pressing needs—metals, plant facilities, and labor—were given full consideration.

As with other industries and organizations, it is important to remember that the government, including the military establishment, was having to find new paths to new goals. Misunderstandings and mistakes were bound to occur in this complicated process of conversion, and our industry was not exempt. In the uncertainties of getting started, a remarkable, and for a time a decidedly critical, situation developed. To refer to it may shed light on one particular kind of problem I encountered during this period.

One day late in 1941 two generals turned up unexpectedly in Hollywood. They went there, just as many other persons would have gone, because they thought it was the place to negotiate terms of co-operation with the industry. They had already seen the need of some training films and at once thought of Hollywood as the center of production. Sidney R. Kent, when he met them, at once brought them to New York, for only there could the heads of the major companies, represented on the Association's Board of Directors, be quickly gotten together for "top-drawer" consultation.

Here was a perfect situation for MPPDA. As "catalyst" for the industry (a term conferred on my office by Ray Moley), I brought the company leaders together to meet the generals and receive their requests. The time was ripe for the formation of an official co-ordinating agency to supervise all industry efforts, and fortunately such an agency was already at hand, its machinery ready to be thrown into high gear. Our directors promptly came to a decision. Just as our Motion Picture Committee Co-ordinating for National Defense had been formed within a week after Dunkirk, so now our over-all War Activities Committee—Motion Picture Industry was formed within a week after Pearl Harbor.

In streamlining the earlier committee for the bigger tasks, its main outlines were continued: George Schaefer carried on as chairman; Francis Harmon was now drafted as full-time executive vice-chairman and industry co-ordinator. The company heads, who had already been working with him, asked MPPDA to loan Francis to the committee for the duration. To close the gaps, our industry leaders at once requested President Roosevelt to designate a co-ordinator of government films through whom all of Washington's requests would be channeled to the industry. Needless to say, they pledged all-out co-operation to the Commander in Chief in the fight for freedom.

The new War Activities Committee became a striking reflection of the whole industry, both in spirit and organization. It operated through its seven departmental divisions and thirty-one exchange area organizations, seeking to stimulate and co-ordinate every kind of motion picture activity that might aid the government, the military, or the people

themselves in the prosecution of the war effort. The spread of the com-
mittee's work is suggested by merely naming its seven divisions:
Theatres, Distributors, Hollywood, Newsreels, Trade Press, Foreign
Managers, and Public Relations.

What seemed to many the industry's most striking gift was the
prodigious number of personal appearances by motion picture stars.
According to the Third Annual Report of the Hollywood Victory Committee, organized three days after Pearl Harbor as a vehicle for talent
participation, 3,671 individual artists made 41,463 personal appearances
in 6,070 different events. Screen personnel traveled more than 4,000,000
miles, spent 1,430 weeks on the "fox-hole circuit" overseas, and made
more than 18,000 personal appearances in hospitals and camps in the
United States!

To me it was equally gratifying that even by the end of 1943 the
War Activities Committee was receiving help from 200,000 volunteers,
representing motion picture theatres, production, distribution, and associated agencies! It came as near being a "100 per cent effort" as you
could find.

I can never think of those strenuous years without seeing again the
tremendous enthusiasm and the superb workmanship that Francis
Harmon put into this great enterprise. It was the kind of task for which
his talents and experience had admirably prepared him. Both a lawyer
and an editor, he had held significant posts as president of the National
Council of Y.M.C.A.s of the United States and general secretary of the
International Committee of Y.M.C.A.s of the United States and Canada
before joining the executive staff of MPPDA in 1937. In World War I
he had had front-line experience as a lieutenant of field artillery, seeing
action at St. Mihiel and the Meuse-Argonne, so that he knew the life
of a fighting man in a foreign country.

Though the bulk of the detailed work was done in and out of Hollywood, the headquarters of the War Activities Committee remained in
New York, with its own separate office at 1501 Broadway. This office
remained the nerve center of a world-wide network of pictures and
persons bringing information and inspiration beyond all measure.

Though films and special services for soldiers and civilians were often
the same, it makes it easier to understand the whole project if we think
of the two groups separately, putting the soldiers first. The industry's
contributions to the military and naval services, as they group themselves in my mind, were particularly: educational and training films,
entertainment films, personal appearances of stars, and miscellaneous
technical equipment.

In the early stages we found the problems of co-ordination very real.
The President had appointed Lowell Mellett as government co-ordinator,
a channel through whom all Washington requests might come to us.

As our industry's co-ordinator, it was Francis Harmon's task to arrange necessary clearances with government war agencies, to help various branches of the industry to work together effectively, and to supply information and inspiration at industry rallies and public gatherings. Liaison between these two men was of the greatest importance, and it was my privilege to confer with them, both separately and jointly, and with top military leaders like General Marshall on vital questions of policy and procedure.

And before going any further I want to pay personal tribute to the spirit of the industry leaders who worked so splendidly on the War Activities Committee. Those men clearly saw the world conflict as a struggle between the forces of freedom, represented by the democracies, and the forces of compulsion. While Russia was our ally, our country gave little attention to her inner nature—though men like Admiral Standley, our Ambassador there, sought to alert us.

In taking up its work, the committee drew encouragement from a statement issued by President Roosevelt eleven days after Pearl Harbor, when he said: "I want no censorship of the motion picture; I want no restrictions placed thereon which will impair the usefulness of the film other than those very necessary restrictions which the dictates of safety make imperative."

The minute we entered the war, an old act of 1917 automatically came back into force, making it necessary that every picture entering, and especially leaving, the country be approved and given a visa. This at first threw the overworked industry into confusion, because an otherwise harmless feature picture of "boy meets girl" might have them saying good-by on a strip of coast line which had suddenly become of military importance. We quickly had to work out methods of double-checking the contents of films on this count, of getting them promptly reviewed and officially approved, and then passed through customs with a minimum of red tape.

On this problem Governor Milliken, Association secretary, was once more of invaluable help. Having earlier been in the customs service in Maine, he knew the ropes. We asked him to go to Hollywood to find a solution. As one minor illustration of the difficulties, customs men thought they had to review every print that passed through their hands, even though a dozen might be identical. In this case a special ruling was secured by which all duplicates might receive a blanket okay.

The major question of reviewing and approving was similarly solved. Through direct negotiations with the Treasury Department, machinery was set up whereby films were reviewed as much as possible at the source in Hollywood, to relieve border customs offices of a job out of their sphere. These reviewing boards, properly appointed by the government, could then act officially and smoothly. In addition, Joe Breen's office would notify the companies, while films were in production, of any possibly dangerous items, so that they could be corrected before official review. This close co-operation saved the companies both time and money, and the Customs Department a lot of headaches.

The Office of War Information, with which we dealt primarily through Lowell Mellett (who was also known as an administrative assistant to the President), was a natural and necessary organization. At first it seemed a little bothersome, especially to an industry raised on self-censorship, but the relationships in the main were smoothed out. Nelson Poynter, sent as government representative to the Coast, created some added complications and was later relieved of his duties there. He was probably unwise in demanding too early, and with too little justification, that he see all films being produced in Hollywood. Experienced movie producers could hardly be expected to take kindly to "advice," much less supervision, from an inexperienced layman—government or no.

In the field of educational and training films, the record stands as a monument to imagination, ingenuity, and co-operation. It was one of Lowell Mellett's functions to co-operate with the War Activities Committee in the preparation of documentaries and training films. Some were produced by the government itself and some by the film companies as regular output.

Many effective films were produced and shown to millions of recruits, on the "Causes of War," the "Principles at Stake," "Sex Hygiene," and "Personal Hygiene," which every new inductee was required to see and which drew high praise from the Chief of Staff and the surgeon general's office. These were often referred to as "indoctrination" films. Under any name, they were a great achievement in group education. Frank Capra, who headed a unit of his own, was engaged chiefly in making such indoctrination films—the "Why We Fight" series. His "Prelude to War" was so good that the Army wanted it released in theatres for the general public to see. Another group of films, about "Foreign Peoples, Places and Customs," gave troops in advance an amazing amount of information about countries where they were soon to find themselves.

The films on the techniques of war and the use of various weapons and instruments, usually called "training films," were really something new under the sun. They were an amazing achievement and a big contribution to the theory of educational films. They convincingly demonstrated that complicated equipment and processes could be made clear when the trainees saw the thing correctly done in pictures and that a thousand could be instructed at once by film as easily as a handful standing around a gun and listening to the explanation of an instructor. Our men testified that training films were hard to make: they had a definite technique, they had to be accurate, yet they had to hold interest without resort to gags or witticisms.

In a broadcast of January 4, 1944, I tried to estimate the value of this work, quoting the experience of educators: "It has long been a matter of general recognition that group instruction can be most rapidly accomplished through visual methods, but recent experiments in some of our Army centers appear to indicate that, out of what we learn and remember by use of the five senses, as much as 83 per cent is attributable to sight.

"It is thus that our Hollywood studios have been an important aid in training our suddenly and enormously expanded American Army.

"The success of our training films, now being made exclusively by motion picture units of the Army and Navy, undoubtedly foretells a far wider employment of visual education in future classrooms."

Entertainment films, supplied to the armed services at home and abroad, early proved to be one of the fundamental "services of supply."

To show how quickly and completely our motion picture companies met this emergency, let me quote two paragraphs from my twentieth annual report, published March 30, 1942:

The eleven national distributors of theatrical motion pictures, upon learning that the War Department this year would need four prints each of 300 current feature pictures together with prints of more than 400 current short subjects for gratis showing to our expeditionary forces in combat areas, presented the entire 1200 programs to the War Department without cost. Companies which had never before agreed to reduce current product to 16 mm. width reversed their policies in order that soldiers overseas might see latest releases at the same time these pictures were playing in their home theatres. Film manufacturers, upon learning of the project, generously agreed to supply the millions of feet of raw stock needed for this service.

Distributors and exhibitors cooperated in working out procedures here at home under which the entire current product of our studios is made available to the U. S. Army Motion Picture Service, on mutually acceptable terms, for exhibition in post theatres which exceeded 450 in number when we entered the war and will exceed 650 in number by mid-year. Ten thousand showings per week at 277 army posts in the United States and on the Atlantic bases from Trinidad to Newfoundland are required to provide this popular and inexpensive form of wholesome entertainment to our greatly expanded army. Similar arrangements provide current films for navy and coast guard on ship and shore. For men in uniform on leave, exhibitor committees in many cities provide free admissions for thousands each week, while reduced admissions for all men in uniform are in effect in hundreds of communities across the country.

Within two years, Eastman and du Pont contributed 32,277,489 feet of 16-mm film toward the gift of motion pictures from the entire industry to the Army for free showing in combat areas to persons in uniform. Early in 1944 General Somervell accepted the ten thousandth motion picture program given by the industry.

And as I pointed out the previous year in a speech at Rochester, films were paving a two-way avenue of constant communication between homes in the United States and our boys scattered abroad:

"In packages no bigger than a suitcase go many hours of entertainment, of relaxation, for our armed forces. In those hours they re-live the experiences of home, they get the thrill of a new story, with all its realism of color and sound, as they sit or stand in jungle or desert night, watching the story unfold.

"The newsreels and the pictures taken at the fighting front enable us to take a vicarious part in the history now being made in the world. In free countries it is most important that all the people be educated and informed in order that they may effectively participate in their self-government."

There were interesting and humorous angles to this huge project. On the G.I. transports movies were going on night and day; on the *Queen Elizabeth* and *Queen Mary* there were five theatres with seven shows a day! In the Pacific area the Japs sometimes forgot the war to slip into an outdoor American movie show; an American officer once found eleven of a gun crew in a U.S. movie audience, their guns unmanned. One returned soldier, when offered the choice of the latest movies showing in a West Coast city, said he had already seen them all. An officer on General MacArthur's staff called movies a "two-hour furlough home." One returned soldier called movies, mail, and beer the "three cheerer-uppers." And the champion movie-goer of the Army, when he got back home, reported, if I remember correctly, that he had seen 332 movies while in the service.

As I see it in retrospect, the service of motion pictures to our civilians was quite as essential as—though less dramatic than—the services they rendered our armed forces. It was varied, continuous, and almost universal in coverage. There was no interruption of regular programs; indeed, these were expanded to meet special needs. Though the theatres increased the richness of their table d'hôte offering, they did their best to preserve a balanced diet. And they tried to make Americans better informed and more ready to help. Comments generally indicated that they succeeded.

From England's experience, we had earlier found out that it was absolutely necessary for motion picture theatres to stay open and that they were crowded as never before, even when war had reached their own shores. English theatres stayed open even during the period of the heaviest air raids. Demand similarly increased here, and both producers and exhibitors vied with each other to give audiences the best programs possible, for entertainment was more needed than ever.

In 1943 President Roosevelt again congratulated the industry on the way it had freely served America at war "without the slightest resort to the totalitarian methods of our enemies." The job was getting done in our own way. We continued to follow the watchwords, *recreation, education,* and *inspiration,* which had guided us well through an era of peaceful development.

Nor was it simply our own notion that pictures continued to be an "essential industry." As the President of the United States told us: "Entertainment is invaluable in times of peace; it is indispensable in time of war." And the Vice-President, stressing the amount of information coming through the films, said: "The American people will never fully appreciate the debt of gratitude they owe the motion picture."

My good friend Earl Warren, speaking in the mid-war period as governor of California, spoke quite as significantly when he said to one of our Hollywood gatherings: "Your contribution to the war effort is a paramount sector of the production line. You provide our armed forces with films for their visual education with the greatest possible speed. Indeed, I am proud to be the governor of a state with such a farsighted and patriotically minded industry. And I believe you will have a foremost part in the reconstruction of the shattered world after the war is over."

Under the anxieties of war, we soon found that men and women needed movies that would give a real boost to their morale. The list of fine feature pictures of 1941 to 1945 shows how producers rose to the occasion. I am thinking of such pictures as *How Green Was My Valley, Sergeant York, The Philadelphia Story, Mrs. Miniver, Pride of the Yankees, In Which We Serve, Holiday Inn, Yankee Doodle Dandy, Random Harvest, This Is the Army, My Friend Flicka, Phantom of the Opera, Claudia, Dixie, Going My Way, Song of Bernadette, Madame Curie, White Cliffs of Dover, Lassie Come Home, Guadalcanal Diary.* Such a list tells its own story. In the big industrial centers, where men were working three shifts a day, theatres were scarcely able to meet the demands on their space and time. And comedies proved more important than ever. In my 1942 report I said:

Comedies do not merely wash away fatigue and worry by the magic metabolism of laughter. They also keep alive in us what is *one of our most precious national traits—our irrepressible sense of humor,* enjoying the joke at our own expense, finding nothing so grim and dour that it cannot be relieved by lightness and farce. *Laughter and liberty are reciprocally invigorating* factors in the American way of life.

Therein lies our strength, our resiliency in even the darkest hour, and our avoidance of the blind fanaticism which the totalitarian tyrant demands. *The tyrant not only banishes freedom from the world, but with it comedy.* Laughter which is the restorative of sanity, and the comic sense which preserves man's humanity by reminding him of his weakness, are alien to the world which breeds typical Nazis of every creed and color.

Probably no bigger job of "adult education" was ever done than our screen's job in keeping America abreast of the issues and progress of World War II. As far as global news-gathering was concerned, the result was amazing. In company, library, and archive vaults lies such a historical record as never before could have been made. From week to week people waited for the next edition of the newsreels as they would wait for the five-star finals to hit the street. But the vividness of the motion pictures gave them an advantage over every form of communication. People felt that they had actually witnessed these stirring scenes all over the world, that they had shared these experiences, that they began to understand.

It is to the everlasting credit of the industry that its members gave such huge amounts of free service and free films. Suggesting the wide spread of this service, I noted in my 1944 report, among the highlights: "The outstanding fact is that throughout 1943 Hollywood supplied film entertainment needed throughout the free world to a vast civilian audience in 16,793 American theatres, to more than 6,000 Latin-American theatres and to many thousand theatres in other Allied and neutral nations." Even a Disney short, *Food for Thought*, helped educate people as to what constitutes a good diet, and hence did its bit in the cause.

It is only in our lifetime that men have first discussed peace in world terms. It is also in our lifetime that an art has achieved world dimensions as a medium of expression and as a source of entertainment to all men everywhere.

These two facts are not unconnected. *An international community in the art of motion pictures already exists.* In it men of every race, creed, and nationality have found a common denominator.

So I wrote in my annual report for 1942, reflecting on the actual record, and so I firmly believe. When the earth's peoples enter their movie theatres they are moved by common emotions, participate in a common experience. Not in the contentious area of political negotiations or economic planning, but through promoting mutual understanding and human sympathy can motion pictures best contribute to the peace we are all seeking. This the motion picture men recognize, never losing their consciousness of the duty to preserve the only international community in existence. As the role of the United States in world affairs broadens, and as the position of American films continues pre-eminent, we should be grossly negligent if we did not see to it that the screen remains an effective good-will ambassador. I don't know where we can find a more persuasive means of honestly presenting the glories of freedom.

As the war progressed and occupied territories were freed, I was interested to learn how American films followed in the wake of our victorious forces. Firsthand reports indicated that our pictures again and again reawakened in downtrodden people faith in an aroused democracy. If the industry lives up to its opportunities, it may well prove one of the few cohesive forces in a world torn by doubt, discord, and fear.

Just as I had helped to throw the Republican organizations of the forty-eight states into bond drives and other war activities in 1918, so now it was my privilege to help mobilize the theatres and the personnel of the industry for a more prolonged series of fund-raising and conservation efforts. Sixteen thousand theatres were open to war messages, bond sales, and a long list of special appeals. In fact, many of our men became extremely professional and skillful at these special war tasks.

To show how widespread were these efforts, our Association had word of more than fifteen thousand "bond premières" in the one year of 1944. For these premières the distributors furnished the films and the exhibitors waived cash receipts in favor of free admissions for bond purchasers. I was proud of the way thousands of theatres kept on selling E Bonds to millions of patrons, serving as the only sales outlet available to war workers during nights, Sundays, and holidays. Ted Gamble, one of our prominent exhibitors, who served as national director of the War Finance Division of the United States Treasury Department, told me that motion picture theatres, although representing less than 10 per cent of the issuing agents throughout the country, were directly or indirectly responsible for the sale of more than 20 per cent of individual E Bonds. The motion picture industry thus gave away the only commodities it had for sale: its films and its theatre seats. The value of these premières alone during 1944 exceeded fifteen million dollars, to which should be added millions more spent in advertising campaigns, rearrangement of production schedules to permit participation of stars, and millions of hours of salaried employees' service spent in selling and promoting the purchase of bonds.

Show business, always generous, set new records for contributions from the industry and its patrons during 1944. A total of $6,793,060 was delivered to the American Red Cross, representing theatre collections of $5,501,450 from patrons, contributions of $657,379 from Hollywood, and corporate contributions of $634,231 from the industry. Close to $5,000,000 was secured in the March of Dimes, more than doubling the 1943 collection for infantile paralysis victims, and representing 42.8 per cent of the entire amount received by the National Foundation for Infantile Paralysis that year. The theatres, with a total of 9,000,000 seats, collected an average of 54 cents a seat from 55,000,000 patrons.

The industry also participated vigorously in the drive for the National War Fund, with a total war-chest contribution from Hollywood alone of $1,170,400, one seventh of the entire Los Angeles total and representing contributions by 24,740 men and women.

And war demands gave a great boost to movie theatres as community centers. That was where people rallied for the latest news and the latest appeal. On a hundred and forty occasions the screens of almost seventeen thousand theatres were used by the government to transmit war information to the people of the country, while the stream of newsreels and shorts never ceased. But we of the Industry well knew that it was the perennial pull of enjoyable entertainment pictures that had built the movie habit and had made the theatre such a popular community center.

My friend Damon Runyon, whose heroic battle for life so stirred us all, and who knew well the problems of the screen, paid it one of the clearest tributes I can recall. Writing in the New York *Daily Mirror* in 1941, he said: "We sometimes wonder how we ever got along without the motion picture. . . . It is a boon to humanity. No other medium affords as much mental and even physical relaxation to as many people. . . . It makes dreams come true, if only for a few minutes. The person who derides the motion picture or views it with condescension is a fool. Nothing more important has ever been devised, and it is still in its infancy. . . ."

It was unavoidable that the war period should put severe strains on the screen's freedom of expression, even in America. In many other countries it had quite disappeared. Government, from the President down, disclaimed any desire to censor, except for national security. But we did run into some ticklish situations with the OWI and with Congress, for example. More than once films were accused of injuring the feelings of a "minority," or of "propaganda."

In the course of reporting world events it was inevitable that this latter charge arise, sometimes from both sides. The judgments often depended much upon the critic's initial viewpoint and upon interpretation of "intent," as in law. It was something to be reckoned with, however, when the industry was called before a Senate sub-committee for a formal inquiry into charges of "warmongering." This was in 1941, a few months before Pearl Harbor. The accusation was embodied in Senate Resolution 152, introduced August 1, 1941, which set up a sub-committee of the Committee on Interstate Commerce to conduct an investigation of any "propaganda disseminated by motion pictures" inciting the public toward war. It was supplemented by an amendment on September 5, authorizing investigation of any monopoly within the industry.

The matter had been brewing in the minds of one or more senators for several months. Early that year Senator Burton K. Wheeler of Montana repeatedly accused the films of stirring up a demand for war. On one occasion he was reported in the New York *Times* to have told the America First group in Utah that movies were "designed to incite the public" and that they were the "Benedict Arnold of '41." In the light of the facts, the statements were generally recognized as being extreme. In justice it must be said that the burden of the speech, as reported, was isolationism. Specifically, the senator was quoted at one point as saying: "They [motion pictures] are cleverly directed for passion-rousing effect, and to bring an overwhelming call for convoys. And convoys, as any clear-thinking American will know, means entrance of the United States into the European conflict."

I lost no time in answering Senator Wheeler's charges. In a letter dated January 14, 1941, I emphatically denied that our films could be called "warmongering" or "inciting." I wrote him that "the facts utterly deny the merit of such charges," and that at least half the protests currently reaching our office "asserted with equal fervor that screen portrayal of the horrors of war gave aid to pacifist groups." I reminded him that the industry continued to believe that "our primary service to our nation at this time can be rendered through the provision of wholesome entertainment, a service more important than ever in a period of great stress and strain." To give the senator a quick glimpse into the facts, I briefly analyzed the three classes of films currently being shown in the theatres: newsreels, short subjects, and feature pictures. Of newsreel subjects, 16 per cent were factual reports of our country's efforts to make freedom secure through adequate preparations for national defense. Only 2.4 per cent of the short subjects and 5 per cent of the features had any relation to European politics or the European war.

It was interesting to note the reaction of the press to my categorical denial of Senator Wheeler's charges. Of the editorials and signed columns, 87 per cent supported my position advocating continued freedom of the screen.

In spite of these facts, the demand of a small sector of Congress continued, and the Senate resolution introduced on August 1 by D. Worth Clark of Idaho, for himself and Gerald P. Nye of North Dakota, was approved. To me the issue seemed of strategic importance, coming up in a period when democracy was being challenged to defend, even from encroachments on its own governments, the institutions of a free society.

The sub-committee held public hearings from September 9 to 26, 1941. Several senators testified, and other witnesses were summoned and heard, including prominent motion picture men.

On September 1, in anticipation of the hearings and to make our position clear in advance, I had written Senator D. Worth Clark, chairman of the sub-committee, emphatically denouncing the charges as false and shameful, and, in answer to the chairman's invitation to appear before the committee, welcoming an opportunity to present the facts. On September 8, Wendell Willkie, whose law firm had been asked to represent the industry, wrote Senator Clark, stating in some detail our position on the leading questions and saying at once that the industry's attitude toward Hitler was no different from that of other average citizens.

After the hearing got under way I planned to complete the testimony for the industry by a comprehensive summary statement covering our philosophy and the analysis of recent pictures. That statement, with detailed factual appendices, was ready by September 22. But "more urgent" congressional business interrupted the work of the Senate sub-committee. In October the hearings were temporarily discontinued, and on *December 8, 1941,* Senator Clark publicly announced their abandonment. On January 12, 1942, the Senate itself officially recognized the termination of the inquiry without receiving any formal report.

Probably the attitude of the public remains the best guarantee of continued freedom for the screen. Americans don't like to be pushed around by anybody, and they wouldn't like the motion picture, which they feel they practically own, pushed around either. Personally, I have always believed that the freedom of the films and radio are fully covered, in spirit, by the first article in the Bill of Rights. There has been real progress in this recognition. I was gratified when Congress recognized newsreels on a par with other methods of gathering and distributing the news, by Senate Concurrent Resolution 53, September 21, 1944. Who can say how much the actual wartime accomplishments of the American newsreels, often filmed in "the valley of the shadow of death," had earned for them this deserved recognition? Perhaps it was a diploma "after the fact." The American people, by unanimous vote, had already bestowed the honorary degree.

Motion picture men and women, by hundreds and thousands, gave themselves to the service of America in the war. So keen were many of them to get into "active service" that it was often a tough question how certain pictures were to be completed on schedule and obligations met.

One of the first questions I had to discuss with government authorities was how far film workers should be considered "essential" and, hence, deferred or exempted. At one period it seemed to be the impression that only men at work on government films would be deferred. But the question was not so simple, because practically all films were needed if the Army was to be kept supplied with entertainment. And it was hard to keep our men out of service; early in 1943 it was estimated that 29 per cent of them were in the armed forces.

Early in the war I had a significant conference with General Marshall on this difficult question, about which he had already done some specific thinking. As one possible solution he suggested that inducted men who were essential to current picture-making be stationed as near production centers as possible, so that they could be used at the studios when necessary. Our discussion had especially to do with male stars, and particularly with one star who, though no longer a young man, was determined to go into military service and who did so, taking the tough training in stride.

Our industry is one that never had to turn to the government for subsidy or loan. Quite the reverse: during the war it was able to give to the government and the military services, in goods and services, an estimated total of more than $40,000,000.

In an art industry built so largely on people, both as producers and consumers, statistics are anything but impersonal—especially to me, since I have known so many of these "statistics" as friends! In the most complete checkup ever made by government quizzers in the census, a "breath-taking comeback" had been made between 1937 and 1939: the dollar volume of our output went up 9 per cent to $215,000,000, from a 1937 total which had already gained 22 per cent over 1935. The number of separate establishments had doubled to a 1939 figure of 178.

The 1939 production budget had more than doubled since 1925, the year before sound appeared. And the total number of workers employed in the Los Angeles industrial area rose from 23,000 in 1935 to 30,000 in 1939, while the annual salary bill was rising from $98,000,000 to $130,000,000—with California accounting for 86 per cent of production. It is easy to see why "Hollywood" bulked so large in all our calculations and why I spent so many weeks there several times a year. With my "ranch" in Hidden Valley, California had become my second home.

As the world situation tightened up, we heard the phrase "subversive activities" more often, and sometimes the accusation was directed at pictures. The answer was rarely easy; the question continued to be one of the most difficult ones of this period. This was particularly so when the critic was one of the Association's long-time friends, like the International Federation of Catholic Alumnae.

I continued to receive objections, too, from organized groups who felt that their professional honor had been disregarded by one or another movie. Some of these cases would have been funny if they had not been so serious. And the newspapers could usually be counted on to see the ridiculous side. The Dayton (Ohio) News came out with an editorial to which Joe Breen and I could add a hearty "Amen!"—and I am a lawyer myself. It ran in part: "The American Bar Association, we hear, has notified Will Hays that the movies must be kind, hereafter, to the lawyers. No longer must they be pictured in any unpleasant light. . . . When the movies have thus been divested of everything anybody can take exception to, they'll be as interesting and significant as a glass of water, the multiplication table or the sighing of the breeze. Who'll go? Poor movies! Poor Will Hays!"

Those days were full of highlights, and many of them were bright. One of them, a mere seven words spoken by Nicholas Schenck, made an indelible impression on me. The Board of Directors of MPPDA were deep in discussion of their relations with exhibitors, always a field for sharp competition. In the early days of the Association there had been distributor-exhibitor damage suits galore. Now some broad-gauge policies were developing. Mr. Schenck had just outlined a proposal for a very liberal treatment of exhibitors which he believed fair and profitable to both sides. When one of the other heads broke in: "But, Nick, you can't do that! It would be giving the exhibitors too much," Nick quietly replied: "I never found that it didn't pay."

At about the same time I had another very heart-warming experience in hearing the kind of appreciation of Joe Breen that was voiced in the press. Much to my regret, Joe felt that he must resign from the Production Code Administration, though we were greatly relieved when he later was able to return to us. I can't resist quoting from an editorial in the Kansas City *Star,* whose managing editor, Roy Roberts, was one of our staunch supporters. In his turn he had attacked the movies for making a travesty of newspapermen, but he was no bigot and he stood squarely with us on freedom of expression. The editorial gives an excellent estimate of the personality and accomplishment of the man who first made the Code work:

By all accounts, Joe Breen has done a remarkable job. . . .

When he was called in . . . there was some fear that in cleaning the movies up he might largely destroy their entertainment value.

Nothing of the sort happened. Joe Breen proved to be a new kind of censor. He was jovial, tactful and, above all, intelligent. Instead of sniping at minor details, he concentrated on such fundamental complaints as that the crime pictures actually were tending to teach criminal procedure to the younger generation of theatre-goers.

Soon even the skeptics were forced to admit that in many respects the influence of Joe Breen helped to improve the quality of the industry's product. A situation that had seemed to be getting out of hand was brought back under control, and, despite inevitable differences of opinion on matters of detail, general satisfaction was reported all around. Now Joe Breen is retiring at his own request. He says he needs a change, that he is "punch-drunk" and wants to get acquainted with his family. The industry he leaves may have a hard time finding his successor.

Another of my happy associations through the years with two of our most inspiring religious leaders is suggested by a tribute that appeared at this time in *The Christian Herald.* Dr. Dan Poling, the editor, had long been one of my close and valued friends. His son was one of the "Four Chaplains" whose voluntary self-sacrifice at sea was not only commemorated by a special postage stamp but is to be permanently memorialized in an interfaith chapel at Temple University, of which Dr. Poling was made honorary chaplain.

The writer of *The Christian Herald* article was Dr. Norman Vincent Peale, pastor of the Marble Collegiate Church, New York, who through pulpit and page is constantly communicating to others the inspiring uplift in Christian faith.

In this article Dr. Peale called motion pictures, along with the church and radio, the three greatest "personality-molding agencies," and pleaded for an understanding and sympathetic relationship between the three. He knew whereof he spoke in saying that the church should welcome the opportunity to influence the movies, for he had served effectively as technical adviser on pictures in which the church was prominently portrayed. He knew that the motion picture could give the church "another powerful ally in emphasizing the decent, upright ideals of American living," and he believed that this helpful relationship was being achieved:

It has been my observation that within recent years there has been an increasing number of truly notable pictures built around the lives of great and inspiring characters. Moreover, the production of historical films is making a profound contribution to the development of a fine patriotism. In all these pictures honor, idealism and religion are elements of outstanding emphasis.

In the autumn of 1944, fifty years after the first public exhibition of motion pictures, we had a great "roundup" of the people who had helped us most to create higher standards. This Public Relations Conference gave our friendly critics opportunity to tell us what they would most like to see films do if they were better to discharge their responsibility to a growing public. It was one of the friendliest and frankest discussions I have ever heard. The horizon was broad, for its war record already proved what the industry could do, and the approaching end of the war suggested some of the problems shared. As I said in opening the conference, we asked for no resolutions but we wanted all the advice we could get.

I promised the seventy delegates, meeting in the Waldorf-Astoria in New York City, an account of our stewardship. Joe Breen carefully explained the exact way in which the Production Code Administration operated; Governor Milliken discussed the wide network of activities carried on by the Community Service Department, with its thousands of volunteer "branches"; and Francis Harmon told about the work of the War Activities Committee.

The late Dr. James Rowland Angell, president emeritus of Yale University and educational director of RCA, one of our wisest advisers, emphasized that the entertainment picture can quite fairly be held to consistency with the prevailing mores of the day, with the ethical standards generally current. He agreed that, if it offends those, it justly brings down on itself the disapproval of at least the thoughtful people in the community, and eventually financial disadvantage as well.

N. Peter Rathvon, speaking as president of RKO, emphasized two points that were related to nearly all our discussions. The first was the potency of a medium "that can for three hours keep people more or less spellbound." The second was that people, including children, judge all films by the criteria of the motion picture theatre, and hence that professionally produced pictures are necessary in almost any case.

Other interests only partly connected with motion pictures crowded into these busy years. In 1941 I was invited to attend a summer meeting at the late George Ade's farm near Brook, Indiana, which brought back in memory the unique ceremony at the same spot when Taft was officially notified of his nomination as President.

Later that same summer, in Los Angeles, we had a most delightful dinner for Lord Halifax, the British Ambassador to the United States from 1941 to 1946, at which I was asked to introduce the guest of honor. Because of our continuous efforts to keep England supplied with films at the urgent request of the Ambassador, our associations had been frequent. No one who knew Lord Halifax could fail to admire his ability, dignity, and vision. And he was a truly spiritual man. I could recall nothing that better illustrated this quality than the impression he had made on India. I told how he was Knight Grand Commander of the Indian Empire, but that to Mahatma Gandhi he was "my friend Irwin," that "noblest of Englishmen," whose word could always be trusted and who once, after driving all night, walked alone through an Indian village to pray with the Indian leader at dawn.

In January of 1942 Eugene Pulliam, the chairman of the War Bond Campaign in Indiana, and Governor Henry F. Schricker invited me to come out to Indianapolis for a great War Bond rally and to speak at some of the ceremonies. Never did I accept an invitation more gladly. And I have rarely seen a great civic function carried through with such finish and such enthusiasm.

One of the vividly memorable features of the occasion was the presence of Indiana's charming Carole Lombard, in private life Mrs. Clark Gable. The committee had been eager to have her there, because she had been a Fort Wayne girl and was very popular throughout the state; and she had been as happy to come, though it meant a special trip from Hollywood. With her mother, Mrs. Elizabeth Peters, she threw herself joyously into every event of the crowded day. During those twelve hours of January 15—almost her last twelve on earth, though none could have know it—she fulfilled, in the midst of wildly cheering crowds, the greatest moments of her fine life.

When I arrived in Indianapolis that morning it was a clear, beautiful winter day that by midafternoon had almost an autumn warmth. The events had been well planned. And the hearty patriotism native to the great Midwest, with its memories of national struggle, had drawn the crowd together. I felt the same tides of deep feeling that had made the work of our State Council of Defense in the earlier war such a thrilling experience.

It was a full day, beginning with an early luncheon attended by Mayor Reginald H. Sullivan, city and state officials, leaders in the bond-selling campaign, and other representative citizens. From the luncheon the mayor, Mr. Pulliam, and I went directly to the Union Station to meet Miss Lombard and her mother, whom we drove at once to the east lawn of the State House for the flag raising. There must have been ten thousand people there, packed in as close as they could get. Waiting for us on the platform at the foot of the flagpole were the governor; Dr. Christopher B. Coleman, director of the Indiana Historical Bureau; Sergeant Alex Ardi of South Bend, the Indiana soldier who had fired the first shot marking the entrance of the American Expeditionary Force into World War I; and Lieutenant Arthur P. Braxton, who had been in command of the gun that fired that shot.

It was a brilliant occasion. The military guard was composed of the crack Culver Rifles, the precision drill group from the infantry battalion of Culver Military Academy, and music was furnished by the Culver drum-and-bugle corps. As the climax of the ceremony, the governor presented to the Indiana Historical Bureau the flag which had flown over the national Capitol the day Congress declared war on Japan, and which our congressman, Louis Ludlow, with customary Hoosier political modesty, had managed to acquire. Carole Lombard herself attached it to the halyard, and as it rose against the clear winter sky she brought rousing cheers from the crowd as she impulsively threw up her hand in the sign of V for Victory. Applause rose again as Sergeant Ardi was presented to the crowd, carrying the shell from which the famous shot had been fired, and which was then autographed by Miss Lombard, the governor, the mayor, Mr. Pulliam, and myself—all with brief speeches.

It was clear from the first moment that Miss Lombard, beautiful and talented Hoosier girl back home on a glad mission, the vitality of her spirit equaled only by the obvious sincerity of every word and gesture, had completely won the hearts of the crowd. She was living the role that she was that day playing—the supreme role of her career. As we were riding through the crowds that evening on the way to the mass meeting, I saw a homely example of her quick response. Noticing on the curb a family from her home town, who had evidently come to Indianapolis hoping to see her, I said quickly, "Those people are from

Fort Wayne." Instantly she stretched out both arms to them, crying, "Hello, folks! Hello, folks from home! Glad to see you from Fort Wayne! Hello! Hello!"

After the flag-raising ceremonies we went into the main-floor lobby of the State House, where some three thousand people were waiting. Following brief remarks by Governor Schricker and myself, Miss Lombard plunged into the actual selling of bonds. And what a sale! The committee had set the day's quota at $500,000, but it was soon apparent that they had far undershot the mark. I stood and marveled at the speed and ease with which Carole passed out the receipts—receipts that, as long as the supply lasted, carried her autograph and her picture. And never did customers respond more eagerly. As a star of the screen, Carole Lombard never made a greater impression, and never did she herself get more from any experience, as she repeatedly told me that day.

From the State House corridor she was taken to the Claypool Hotel, where there was another brief flag-raising in the center of the lobby, to the music of a United States Army band. It was Miss Lombard who raised the flag as "The Star-Spangled Banner" echoed through the hotel.

From the Claypool the celebration moved to the Governor's Mansion for tea and a reception for the Hollywood guests of honor. This had been planned as a social affair only, but by that time everyone was thinking and talking bonds. The report had reached us downtown, where we stopped to catch our breath, that the guests were actually selling bonds to each other, with Carole again the spark that ignited the flame.

As soon as it was possible to whisk the guests away and give them a few minutes to rest and dress, it was time for them to join us at dinner. Both Miss Lombard and her mother were utterly gracious and delightful. It was here that I first learned from Mrs. Peters that her daughter had decided they must fly back to California late that night, as Carole felt she should get right back to the studio for some retakes she knew had to be made.

As soon as we could get through dinner it was time to drive over to the Tabernacle for the big mass meeting. A crowd banked the curbs all the way from the hotel to the hall—and this in Indianapolis, not New York or Los Angeles! It felt like an old-time political rally, and I thought what a joy it would be to any campaign manager to have such a candidate as this evening's star. She was the first principal I had ever seen go through such an occasion with never a single mistake; every time there was anything to be said or done, she said or did exactly the right thing. Her observations were all appropriate and at times absolutely brilliant. It was ad libbing at its best. At no time was there the slightest tinge of acting.

As we neared the hall the crowd increased, and it seemed like a great Hollywood première awaiting the arrival of the star. As we entered the packed auditorium there was a great flare-up of greeting. Music had been playing for some time; the Indiana University and Purdue University bands and the Culver Military Academy drum-and-bugle corps were all there in full-dress uniform. With a blare of bugles the show was on.

The program was a moving one. The colors were presented in a spectacular pageant. The Lord's Prayer was sung by a fine chorus of Negro men and women. Then the chairman presented Governor Schricker, who made a vigorous appeal. Mr. Pulliam's remarks as chairman, and the entire program of the day, showed how well he deserved the Treasury Department decoration he later received for his conduct of the entire series of bond drives in Indiana, second to none in the nation.

When it came my turn to speak, I realized once more that I had never sensed a deeper consecration to the national cause than was burning in everyone's heart. This was only a month after Pearl Harbor!

Following a number by the Purdue University symphonic choir, the governor presented Miss Lombard. She was dressed in exquisite taste, her natural beauty and charm heightened by the uplift of the occasion, and her presence created a profound impression. What she said was equally moving, coming straight from her heart. At the conclusion the audience joined her in singing "The Star-Spangled Banner," with the powerful support of two university bands and the Tabernacle pipe organ. In my souvenir file I treasure no picture more than one taken at that moment.

Summing up the tangible results of the day's bond sales, the chairman announced that as against a quota of $500,000 set by the committee, there had actually been raised a grand total of $2,017,513!

On our way back from the meeting Carole spoke with great feeling of the joy that the day had given her. I tried to express our appreciation, but she insisted the debt was all the other way. As she talked I realized anew, more deeply than in days of easy peace, that under the entire surface of this Land of Liberty lies a great reservoir of patriotism at tremendous pressure. When the need comes we tap it, and it leaps high into the free air of heaven with a mighty and irresistible force.

Back in the hotel, the governor, Gene Pulliam, and I stopped for a few minutes of final visit with the two ladies. They had to pack, but Carole still wanted to talk. She was full of the day's events. I doubt if she had ever been happier in her life. Seeing her at that moment, no one in his right senses could have questioned that "it is more blessed to give than to receive." And largely through her inspiration Indiana's whole fund-raising effort got off to a phenomenal start.

As I got up to leave I told her I was going to wire Clark how well she had carried out her mission, and as we walked to the elevator she said, "Good! Give the old boy a shot, it'll do him good." A few minutes later I sent him the following telegram:

GREAT DAY HERE. CAROLE WAS PERFECT. REALLY SHE WAS MAGNIFICENT, AND THEY SOLD IN THIS ONE DAY $2,017,513 WORTH OF BONDS, WITH A QUOTA OF ONLY $500,000. EVERYONE DEEPLY GRATEFUL. I FEEL I MUST SEND YOU THIS EXPRESSION OF MY PERSONAL APPRECIATION.

When I left, though she was gay and radiant, tears came to her eyes as she once more voiced her gratitude for the reception the people of her native state had given her. The plain fact is, Carole Lombard wanted to serve her country with all that she had. And she did just that.

In that service she gave her life.

That night I took the sleeper to Chicago, arriving just in time for a Board meeting of the C.&E.I. Railroad, with its entirely different atmosphere, and I worked there all day until I took a midafternoon train to New York. During these same daylight hours, our two friends had been flying toward Hollywood, and that evening about seven o'clock came the sudden tragedy in Nevada, when their plane crashed into the side of a mountain. Of this I had no word that night. Saturday morning, arriving in New York, Mrs. Hays met me at the station and rode with me to the office. She had the news but, thinking I also knew, waited for me to speak. Before we reached the office she said, "That is a terrible, terrible thing about Carole." That was the first word I had received, and I found it impossible to reconcile with the vivid experiences of two days before, which I had been reciting to Mrs. Hays with such enthusiasm.

Carole Lombard's tragic death made a profound impression on the country, as on me. But that impression is surpassed by the radiance of her life, which lives on in the hearts of all her friends and in the memory of the loyal "public" for whom she had such a spontaneous and warm affection.

Under the intriguing title, *The Film That Was Lost*, the Museum of Modern Art in New York dramatically pictured on the screen the function of its growing Film Library as "primarily to recover, revive, and preserve outstanding movies of the past." An interesting meeting was held at the Museum in the fall of 1942 to publicize this program. I was impressed with their vigorous plans, with which our Association had from the first co-operated closely, and gratified by what had already been accomplished. As a matter of fact, this unique Film Library had apparently come into existence only just in time to save much of the historic screen material of the cinema's first thirty years from becoming "film that was lost."

Other notable short films were shown, and the "short subject," which had been almost a hobby with me, was emphasized as an important form of historical record. The Museum officials told us how they were collecting "documentaries" from other nations also, to illustrate more widely the power of the film to inform, to persuade, to exhort, or to incite. They had been especially hard at work on the "non-fiction film," including films of opinion and orientation of all kinds, stressing the freedom of the screen as essential to the development.

Whatever my generation has done or left undone, it has certainly developed both the promotional and the testimonal dinner to a fine art. Eating together seems to make it easier to "get together" on any proposal. Looking back over half a century of such dinners—political, cinematical, philanthropic, and otherwise—I am reminded of something my long-time friend, the late James Rowland Angell, said at a dinner of his Yale alumni. The toastmaster in his introduction had given Dr. Angell high praise for all sorts of notable things he had done for the university. When the Yale president rose to speak, and in a flash of memory pictured all the similar dinners he had attended through the years, he turned and said, "Mr. Toastmaster, you omitted one thing; you forgot to tell how many fried chickens I've eaten for Yale."

Well, my souvenir file, too, contains a long chain of dinners, and among them are many of my happiest memories of people and events. One of the most delightful was a Variety Club dinner given to Cordell Hull during the Thanksgiving season of 1944, three days before his resignation took effect, at which the Honorable James F. Byrnes, then Director of War Mobilization and Reconversion, made the chief address, paying his tribute to the retiring Secretary of State, whose office he was to fill only eight months later. That evening I had the double privilege of paying my personal tribute to the guest of honor and of introducing the main speaker. For years the Secretary of State had worked with us like a Trojan to keep the foreign channels open for American films. He had been a tough fighter when American rights were unfairly restricted. Though the disruptions of war made it an unequal battle, he never stopped fighting.

One day in the autumn of 1944 I was lunching in Hollywood with Cecil De Mille when the now-famous "dollar incident" had its beginning. As we were eating, a messenger boy handed him a telegram. When he had read and re-read it, he silently handed it across the table to me, his face flushed, his expression set and stern. It was from the American Federation of Radio Artists, AFL, giving notice that an assessment of one dollar each had been levied on its three thousand members, of whom he was one of the most prominent. The fund was to be used to defeat an anti-closed-shop amendment about to appear on the California ballot, an amendment for which De Mille intended to vote. Few demands for a dollar have ever stirred up such strong reactions. Mr. De Mille saw that noon—and increasing numbers of people see today—two vital questions involved: first, the right of a labor union to dictate the political thinking of its members; and second, the "right to work."

As De Mille said to his wife the night before the deadline for paying: "I believe in unions, but this assessment is the destruction of a man's right to work. It is a disastrous thing. Tomorrow I must pay—or else." The "or else" was the giving up of $125,000 a year, and all that went with it, as director of one of the most popular programs on the air. "You have no choice," said Mrs. De Mille without hesitation. "If you pay that dollar you will know positively that you put money above principle." De Mille sat down and wrote a formal letter to AFRA, declaring he would not pay the assessment. He was suspended in December of 1944 and has been off the air ever since.

It was as a direct result of this "incident" that Cecil B. De Mille became the national leader of a movement urging "right-to-work" legislation on Congress. With the help of public contributions, he established the De Mille Foundation for Political Freedom, to promote thinking and action in this direction.

He took his own case to the California courts, seeking, as he said, a decision as to "whether the constitution of a union supersedes the Constitution of the United States." Two lower courts have ruled—quite wrongly, I think—that the union had the right to make the assessment, including the penalty of suspension for non-payment. It seems to me that a voluntary contribution to a union fund from those who believe in its objective is one thing, but that wielding the power of professional life or death to enforce the political "party line" of the union's officers is wrong. With my Hoosier political traditions, it looks to me like a confession that the union's case, in such an instance, is not good enough to be left to the judgment and conscience of the members but must be enforced at the sword's point of financial loss.

From another point of view, according to a more recent news story sent out from Hollywood by John M. Carlisle for the North American Newspaper Alliance, there seems to be a similarity between the union's attitude in this case and that of some federal bureaus discussed in the Hoover report. Mr. Carlisle writes:

Now, Claude L. McCue, executive secretary of A.F.R.A., says that "I believe De Mille was sincere on principle."
I wish we could have avoided this. He had a principle and we had a

principle, and they could not be reconciled. We felt we had to defeat the proposal and it was defeated.

In the fifteen states where there is "right-to-work" legislation, A.F.R.A. has been put out of business. Right to work legislation will either destroy us or seriously impair our union's activities.

Of the "freedoms" and "human rights" of which we are hearing such vocal defense these days, one would expect that the "right to work" would be accepted as axiomatic. It seems to me a complete anomaly that a group of workers should be so organized and so controlled that it can take away from one of its members, because he exercises the right to express a political opinion, the very right to work which the union was presumably organized to safeguard. Is not his right to express political opinion exactly equal to that of any or all members of the union's governing board to express theirs? By whose authority can the constitution of a labor union supersede the Bill of Rights of the Constitution of the United States of America? When was a part greater than the whole?

But to end these personal reflections on a happier note, the last year of this period saw me in the same setting as the first. Again I was "back home in Indiana," this time for the Eighth Bond Drive, still in the capable hands of Eugene Pulliam. This time the governor was Ralph E. Gates, a man whose sincerity and force I greatly admire; the movie star was Ann Sothern; the scene was the State Fair Grounds, with bands, music, skating, and generally high spirits. We drove out in sleighs, the governor and Ann Sothern in the first, Mrs. Gates and I in the second. We were pushed around the ice by skaters in great glee. But no amount of ice could chill the warm hearts of these good folks.

Some questions are perennial because inherent in human nature, or the constitution of the universe, or the relation between the two. Jesus said, for instance, "The poor ye have always with you." So, apparently, with some international problems. One of my last official conferences before resigning the presidency of MPPDA in September of 1945 was with Donald Nelson, then president of the Independent Motion Picture Producers' Association, and President Truman, just five months after he took office. Foreign distribution was the thing we discussed. Earlier that year our Association had formed the new Export Association, to get more effective united action in handling all overseas matters. This was another definite chapter in industry co-operation, of which our earlier wartime financial dealings with Great Britain had proved perhaps the most striking example.

Now that it is past and over, we can look back with a wry smile on the tug-of-war that resulted in bringing back to America more than

$130,000,000 in impounded funds owed to our industry by Great Britain, Australia, and New Zealand.

Difficulties, negotiations, delays seemed endless. Now there remain chiefly the memory of a tough problem, two groups of men seeking earnestly to solve it, and the sense of relief when the solution was found. Judged both by the importance of the international factors concerned and by the amount of money involved, it was the biggest financial problem of my Association days. And in no other case was the co-operation of our State Department more brilliantly illustrated.

At best, when war struck England, her domestic picture production had to give way to more urgent needs. In the reaction to the blow, theatres in England closed. But they remained so for only seventy hours. By popular demand they were forced to reopen, because otherwise "people had no place to go, and they had to find relief somewhere." As Lord Halifax said to us with utmost urgency, "We've got to have pictures—a lot of them—to keep up the people's morale!" We sent them over, fast, even by air. And we kept it up.

Like any doctor or pharmaceutical laboratory answering an emergency call, we sent the pictures and much later worried about the bill. But we did begin worrying by the autumn of 1940, when I had long conferences with Joe Kennedy about the possibility of British payments. Our normal income from England had passed $30,000,000 by 1936, and now that the British were almost solely dependent on us, the figure was naturally mounting. Within another year our companies were to be giving millions in free films and service to the government and to our men in training, but they had to have income. It was particularly hard for the smaller companies.

Both sides recognizing that full cash payments for films were at present out of the question, a special arrangement was made, implemented by a series of three annual agreements with Great Britain, Australia, and New Zealand. These agreements provided for the retention or "freezing" of a substantial part of the revenues currently due to American producers.

By 1941 our British problem, beginning to be acute as well as chronic, had to receive attention. Over there war had been going on for two years. Losses had been heavy; resistance magnificent. We were told that we were doing a lot to hold up the morale of the people. The destruction of the "Hays Office" in London by Nazi bombs in February of 1941 made us feel that much closer.

But by contract agreement we were restricted to $12,000,000 payment out of $35,000,000 or more. When it appeared that American companies would have nearly $50,000,000 frozen in England, Australia, and New Zealand by November 1, when the current financial pact with Britain was to expire, and that $40,000,000 of this was in the British Isles, various proposals were considered. But hope was still held that reasonable money transfers might soon be made.

It had been the British claim that they were making as large payments as their amount of exchange warranted. But without more income from abroad our companies could not keep up both quality and quantity. The British were getting their percentage of earnings from our pictures, but we were not.

Fortunately we had put in the contract that if credit conditions changed, the terms could be reconsidered. When the Lend-Lease Bill was before Congress, I thought the moment had arrived. I called on Cordell Hull; he called the President the very day Congress was voting on the bill. They passed it, the President signed it that night, and I saw him the next noon. After I explained the situation to President Roosevelt, he said, "What do you want me to do?" He called Lord Halifax, the British Ambassador, and said, "I think Mr. Hays has something important to talk over."

I was with Lord Halifax from four to six in the afternoon. He fully appreciated our position and the practical difficulties as well. He arranged for me to see the proper British officials. One of them—Gerald H. S. Pinsent, financial adviser to the Embassy—proved a very tough gentleman, and I talked with him all evening. At this first meeting I could get little out of him beyond "I don't think you can do anything." Probably it was his function, like that of football linemen on defense, to "hold the line."

Looking back at it, I don't see that they could be blamed for trying. Through years of empire development, Great Britain and her far-flung representatives had learned how to protect and conserve her interests. Nearly every major nation but ours had followed pretty much the same policy. Now Britain, led by the indomitable Winston Churchill, was fighting for her life and, side by side, we were both fighting to keep freedom alive in the world. Money to buy the sinews of war was part of her lifeblood. She didn't want to see tens of millions leave her shores unless it had to, even though that particular money had been paid in to see our pictures. As I recall it, one of the top officials said to me, "I suppose you want your pay for pictures we had to have."

Well, we did; we wanted it and needed it. So we kept on negotiating back and forth. It was not the kind of matter to display on the front pages of newspapers. It would have been unfair and harmful to spread an impression that there was "trouble" between us. In these early stages Lord Halifax quite properly asked that no American film company officials discuss the matter in public. And these company officials early agreed that this, of all matters, was the very one to be handled strictly by the officers of their Association, working through the State Department. One thing that gave our cause added weight was that I "held the umbrella" over all the independents in exactly the same way as over the companies that were MPPDA members.

I am perfectly sure that it was the steady and patient work of the preceding dozen years that had put us in so strong a position with the Department of State. I had always kept them informed on our foreign problems, especially the major ones dealing with Britain, Germany, France, and Italy. Mr. Hull thoroughly understood the difference between this matter and the ordinary commercial transaction. We had succeeded in convincing Washington that the free circulation of our films was an international necessity, in time of war more than ever. So both Mr. Hull and the President were ready to go to bat for us.

But there lay ahead of us two more years of hard work before things were cleared up in 1943. That work was of many kinds. The viewpoint of all the companies, members and non-members, had to be kept united so there would be no pulling in different directions. We had to keep our contacts in London alive and fully informed. Fayette W. Allport, our Association representative there, did a grand job; he not only had to keep us up to date on the exact financial status of all the company film accounts in Britain and on any other matters of importance, but also to keep the American Ambassador—Joe Kennedy and then the late John G. Winant—constantly briefed. My telephone calls to London were many and long, but they kept our case solid. At any minute we knew exactly what Britain's bill was, and we could talk facts and figures in Washington.

In several respects we were fortunate. Our larger companies were strong enough financially to carry the extra burden in 1942 and 1943, until relief could be secured, and their overseas distributing organizations were so good that they could keep films in maximum use. Perhaps no other industry could afford to do what ours did. And the Association office had the personnel and experience to keep the most detailed reports and negotiations going, though I remember the weekend and Sunday overtime office burden with some feeling of apology to the people who always "stood by."

Gradually the thaw set in and the westward flow of funds increased. Came a day when Cordell Hull got to the end of his patience and put his foot down—or maybe it was his fist—saying, "It's high time to settle this thing." It was done. In a release of early November, 1942, I stated: "The Treasury announces that as a result of conversations which have recently taken place in Washington it has been agreed with the American film companies concerned that the whole of the sterling balances accumulated by them at October 24, 1942, as a result of the special restrictions imposed upon the film agreements of the previous three years will now be released. . . . The amount which has been transferred this week is approximately forty-two and one-half million dollars."

There was great relief and rejoicing on the part of the Association and all the American companies. At one time they received $52,000,000 in gold. During this period a total of $134,000,000 of unfrozen funds came back to our shores. In May of 1943 I was able to release another statement that in effect wrote "finis" to this problem.

By the end of this period "The Americas," the "Good Neighbor Policy," and "Hemispheric Solidarity" had become familiar slogans. To use one of the favorite words of government bureaus, many of them sought to "implement" these ideals in various ways. So important was this considered that a Co-Ordinator of Inter-American Affairs became an essential official, and Nelson Rockefeller rendered valuable service in this post through the war years. We had much to do with him and found him extremely helpful in furthering constructive film projects. This was also true of John Hay Whitney, appointed by the Department of State as a special adviser and consultant on public affairs, who served as chairman of the film division of the Rockefeller Committee on Inter-American Relations.

The war did not violently disturb South American trade, but many readjustments were necessary. Countries like Brazil, where in 1940 our American films occupied 90 per cent of the screen time, had more trouble with their own production, worrying particularly about putting out anything considered objectionable to the nations at war. Yet the 1,350 picture theatres in Brazil, with an average weekly attendance of 2,000,000, meant a considerable demand.

Naturally it was both good business and good diplomacy to give redoubled attention to our inter-American trade. By 1941 the *Motion Picture Herald* was able to report "Films on Way to Latins for Hollywood and U.S. Good Will," and to note how both production and distribution efforts, directed southward in a definite program to stimulate cultural exchange, were already taking effect. The whole industry, heartily participating in the "Good Neighbor Policy," gave another example of its adaptability. A big committee of producers, directors, writers, and other creative artists, working with Mr. Whitney, gave practical guidance to this project. It was a good illustration of the inevitable fact that, whatever "policy" the government might announce and encourage, it was the folks in the "front-line trenches" of professional production and distribution who knew how to carry it out.

In at least three of the motion picture's regular functions we now gave special attention to our southern neighbors. Extra effort was put into finding story themes for feature pictures which could draw effectively on the history, music, and settings of the leading Pan-American republics; newsreel coverage similarly was extended as far as possible to the whole Western Hemisphere; and an increased number of short subjects and travelogues on Latin America appeared. This often meant adding further experts to studio staffs, to check details of Latin-American customs, settings, and costumes before filming in the Hollywood studios. This helped avoid offense, and it made better pictures.

The added burden which this put on the Production Code Administration prompted me to add to our Hollywood staff a specialist in Spanish-American customs, language, and history. I appointed Addison Durland, who had had wide experience in newspaper and radio work. Born in Cuba, Mr. Durland had received his education both there and in the United States, had served as associate editor of the Latin American Wireless Service of the New York *Herald Tribune,* had acted as New York correspondent for a number of Cuban publications, and had edited a literary magazine in Havana. He came to us from a position as chief of the Spanish section of NBC, where he had been conducting programs that included a weekly review. Our PCA was thus able to give producers many helpful suggestions on the acceptability of pictures south of the border.

There was still another program in which movie stars figured in much the same way as in entertaining troops and selling bonds. Under the aegis of the Rockefeller committee a "good-will trek" to South America was organized on a grand scale. The studios became so interested that they not only sent two or more of their best-known actors but volunteered to pay the cost. The Whitney office acted as a clearinghouse to prevent too many players on these personal appearance tours from landing in the same spot at the same time. At the request of President Roosevelt, Douglas Fairbanks, Jr., acted as a sort of good-will film ambassador-at-large.

Reactions that reached us were of interest as again showing the uncertainties of popular response. The New York *Times* reported the banning of a U.S. film, *Argentine Nights,* because, in the words of an Argentine film editor, "Hollywood insists on seeing Argentina as an incredibly ridiculous tropical country." In stories laid in a foreign country, American picture audiences particularly enjoy backgrounds, scenery, and customs as different from our own as possible, and the differences are easy to exaggerate. Mexico, particularly, preferred that we use American locales in our films, feeling that we were liable to make mistakes in using theirs, even with the best of intentions. Perhaps one reason was that Mexico, leading the Spanish-speaking lands in production, was soon producing upward of a hundred films a year.

By 1944 the effective work of the Motion Picture Society for the Americas, the industry's own organization, working for three years without publicity fanfare—in itself quite an achievement!—had reached a position of recognized importance, in which I took considerable satisfaction. The president, Joe Breen, summed up the new trend as "a recognition of Latin-American cultural achievements and the depicting of the Latin-American scene as it really is, and not as Hollywood used to think it should be."

I have called foreign difficulties a perennial problem. But the American industry showed itself a still hardier perennial. Enemy nations had declared war on our industry long before they declared war on our nation; but both won. And before Victory Day I think we had all realized that Hollywood must help do an international public relations job for the United States and the American way of life after the war. And we saw that every effort would have to be made to present America fairly.

In this planning the State Department, like ourselves, saw the need of seeking free trade for the screen. We all tried to formulate the most practical programs for international post-war distribution. An old bogey again popped up, however, for the Department of Justice suggested that full participation in official meetings "might not be in conformity with the anti-trust statutes," and it was considered safer to let the industry men comprise a consulting and advisory committee having no official connection with the conferences. In these conferences films were treated both as a commercial commodity and as a medium of culture.

One of the episodes in this public relations program was the series of broadcasts from America to France, in French, by Harold Smith, who had been our effective Association representative in Paris right up to the invasion, barely getting out in time. The message was rebroadcast to all French colonies. Harold began by identifying himself as one of Pershing's soldiers who had fought at St. Mihiel and who had served seven years in the American consular service before becoming Paris representative of the American motion picture industry. After saying, "I think of you every day, of your cruel sufferings under the heel of the invader," he went on to tell them of the tremendous services of the American films to the Allied cause all over the world, and of the work of the War Activities Committee.

In many such ways we sought to keep alive the ties which had been so long in building. Around the world encouraging and discouraging signs were both evident. We knew that before the war the American film had reached an eighth of the human race. Our pictures were popular even in faraway China. The Commerce Department reported our lead threatened in Finland, and it looked as if Finland might prove a good testing ground for the post-war competition with Great Britain and Russia. In 1944 our pictures were still playing in three hundred commercial theatres in Italy and Sicily, although any income had to be deposited in a special account for American companies, to be divided among them later. Italian audiences particularly enjoyed our musicals, but the OWI reported that they had been fed so much propaganda for twenty-odd years that they could "smell it a mile off."

One of the most interesting reports came from New Zealand. With mobs of American servicemen in the towns, young New Zealanders were fast becoming "Americanized," their taste swinging to the kinds of stars popular with the youngsters who had come down to their region to help fight the Pacific war. As a dispatch to the New York *Times* put it, "The more fervidly American a film is, the stronger is its appeal, for in the South Seas the United States has become what the marines call 'the mainland.' "

One of the most dramatic statements ever made about the world influence of American films was made by Francis Harmon as executive vice-chairman of the War Activities Committee. Speaking on the subject, "The Motion Picture and the World Community," on a radio forum broadcast nationally by NBC on July 31, 1943, he said: "Yes, American films have world casts and appear on world screens to a world audience. . . . In a world torn asunder by unparalleled economic and political disorder, the talking picture achieved its present international influence and world-wide usefulness during a period when other types of international relationships were breaking down. Hollywood succeeded even if Geneva failed." Such was our Association goal.

And finally, two other memories from 1945 show the unshaken faith that we had in the screen's world role. As I was about to conclude my service as MPPDA president, eager to see our international activities go forward strongly, I invited former Justice James F. Byrnes to become general counsel and foreign representative of the Association. Mr. Byrnes held off, saying that there was only one thing that would keep him from accepting, something that might embarrass Ed Stettinius if mentioned. In July, Byrnes became Secretary of State!

At the United Nations Conference for World Organization held in San Francisco, the motion picture had a definite role. Through the courtesy of the industry, a special entertainment movie theatre was set up, rededicated the "United Nations Theatre," with the marquee reading: "This Theatre Exclusively for Those Holding Credentials to the World Security Conference." Here each day were shown feature productions chosen from the product of the various countries. In the St. Francis Hotel the industry also operated a small theatre where documentary films from the United Nations were exhibited. A special newsreel crew made pictures of the conference and the delegations. These were shown in the United Nations Theatre. After the conference the Motion Picture Committee presented delegations with a film story record of the conference, featuring the delegates' activities, with the commentary in the language selected by the country receiving the gift.

Thus did the motion picture, witnessing the birth of the UN, record for all time another of the mileposts along history's strife-strewn road toward that "better world" that all men of good will are seeking.

CHAPTER 33

The Presbyterian Pension Fund

B E F O R E I come to the final chapter of this book, I should like to go back in time for a moment to the years 1923 to 1927, and in subject to an endeavor, unrelated to motion pictures, which gives me deep satisfaction to recall. It involved one of the biggest projects ever undertaken by our national Presbyterian Church.

As a boy growing up in Sullivan, it never occurred to me that our Presbyterian church, our fraternal orders, and our many civic interests were any less Father's "business" than his law practice. I must have grown up with the idea that these things were a man's responsibility as truly as his own profession. So I have always tried to do my part in such projects, starting with my church and my college, and going on through Red Cross, Y.M.C.A., and Boy Scouts, to such specialized institutions as the Theodore Roosevelt Association and the Institute for the Crippled and Disabled, built up so splendidly by my friend Jeremiah Milbank.

During my lifetime I have seen these educational and philanthropic programs multiply manifold in number, scope, and effectiveness. They constitute one of the great glories of America. The particular one into which I personally put the most time and effort was the Presbyterian Pension Fund, which between 1923 and 1927 raised fifteen million dollars to establish a sound retirement plan for Presbyterian ministers. It was an inspiring experience.

The reader who has scanned the earlier chapters of this story will understand why such a thing as a pension plan for ministers appealed to me so strongly. I remembered my grandfather as a wonderful man and a wonderful preacher. I grew up in a Christian home. From my father and my mother I learned to look up to our own minister, and church activities were always a part of my life.

While I was still a young lawyer the Young People's Club of our church became quite active. We helped "put over" the idea of Sunday-evening union services in our town, and the idea of churches working together got hold of me for keeps. Just at that time, by a chance coincidence, I developed a strange interest in ministers' salaries. I had always thought it was poor policy to have all the churches open Sunday evening, often with few people in them; it seemed a waste of fuel, janitor service, and light—to say the least. So I made a survey of the state to find out how many Protestant churches there were in each town or city, the total seating capacity, and the average attendance on Sunday evenings. Then I figured out that if all would agree to hold union services, "they could pay their preachers four or five times as much." Many ministers at that time, especially in the smaller places, were receiving less than a thousand dollars a year, even with "donations"! I am sure that my readiness to pitch into the Presbyterian Pension Fund, when the call came, traces back to my getting worked up over this question so young.

Three other factors may have helped. As an elder in our little Sullivan church I learned that church finances should be the job of laymen and that they should make decent provision for their pastors. Politics had taught me that you need national organization to bring about changes. Working with the movie industry was emphasizing that continual education of the public brought results and that the priests and ministers of the country are a tremendous force.

I'll never forget how the Pension Fund was first put up to me, right out of the blue. The Reverend George Francis Greene, D.D., long-time president of the Presbyterian Board which had to do with "ministerial relief," asked me to meet him. We had lunch at the old Union League Club in New York.

Dr. Greene was a great old boy and, as I soon came to know, a real man of God. It was his spirit that first fired the project. It is a joy to have served with him! He explained to me that the General Assembly— the national governing body of our church—had authorized his Board to form a Laymen's Committee to study the possibilities of a better pension plan and to develop it. He said they were going to enlist a group of laymen suitable for the task, and asked me if I would be willing to be a member. I remember I told him at the time that I would do it, provided I could "raise a little hell." He said that was just what they would like to have done!

I know I felt the downright outrage of inadequate pay to preachers— the men who baptize our babies and bury our mothers—many of whom, to this day, we pay far less than a "living wage." Some of these convictions, which I had put into a piece written for our Young People's Club thirty years earlier, were to form the core of a speech in behalf of the Pension Fund appeal which went all over the country.

So I tackled the job.

In talking for three years to groups of men up and down the country, I found no better way to open the story than to say, as at Indianapolis in 1927: "Two hundred and ten years ago today, somewhere, Presbyterians were meeting to discuss this same subject. For more than two centuries our church has had a pension system. It has been as much the policy of the Presbyterian Church to try to care for its disabled and aged servants as it has been to hold Sunday services." And it was even more of a surprise for many of our people to hear that "the Presbyterian Church was the first pension-paying agency on the North American continent. Several generations before a soldier of the Revolutionary War received the first pension from the government, the Presbyterian Church created its 'Fund for Pious Uses.' "

By 1923 it was felt that the time was ripe to push toward what was hoped would be a "final solution" to the problem—placing the fund on a sound actuarial basis. Times and costs had changed enormously. The Laymen's Committee was instructed to "devise and launch a pension system which would be adequate and in keeping, to some degree at least, with the power and wealth of the Presbyterian Church and with the worthiness of the objective." The wisdom of this strategy grew more and more apparent as the movement developed, for it made the matter a laymen's undertaking for the purpose of doing justice to the ministers, rather than a movement in which ministers would be obliged to take aggressive leadership in behalf of their own future welfare.

The General Assembly lost no time in seeing that a Laymen's Committee of thirteen was appointed. At the first meeting, in my absence, I was elected chairman. I soon realized that no man could have conceived a finer, abler, or more devoted group of men.

Without question, the movement owed an incalculable debt to the influence and generosity of the Honorable Andrew W. Mellon, Secretary of the Treasury and the foremost fiscal figure in the world, who served throughout, with the utmost faithfulness, as treasurer of our fund.

I remember clearly my first visit with Mr. Mellon to talk about the plan. I knew that he was a Presbyterian and that his whole family were very liberal supporters of a strong Presbyterian church in Pittsburgh. When I went to see him it was with a very firm hope that he would consent to be treasurer. I explained that we wanted him to serve in that capacity so that every check, whether for fifty cents or fifty thousand dollars, would be made out to him; I said that this would give a sense of stability to the fund and of assurance to every donor.

He immediately said: "I cannot do that. You know as well as anybody how busy I am. Just yesterday I declined, under a good deal of pressure, to act as treasurer, at the request of General Pershing and others who personally asked me to do it, in the raising of the money to finish the Episcopal Cathedral here in Washington, and I just can't do it."

However, we continued to discuss the whole matter at some length. The result was that before I left him that afternoon he agreed to be treasurer of the fund, and he further promised me two checks, each for two hundred thousand dollars—one from himself and one from his brother Richard—to go toward the expenses of raising the fifteen million dollars we had to have. He was a remarkable man, meek and mild in manner, but strong in character, strong in mind, and strong in his loyalties. The other committee members, each of distinguished ability, brought influence from their various fields of experience and various sections of the country.

With especial attention to our distinguished treasurer, here is what my very dear old friend Will Rogers said about the fund in a letter to me:

DEAR WILLIE HAYS:

Say, I got your letter about raising 15 Millions for the Presbyterians. My Lord! Since you went into the Movies you got the Churches talking in Millions. 15 Millions! Say, all the Presbyterians I ever knew couldn't even SAY 15 MILLIONS. Who's going to count it if you do get it? You'll have to get an Episcopal to explain to you how much it is.

15 Millions! What are you trying to make out of them? A Feature Church? They are nothing but an ordinary program church, along in the class with the Baptists and Camelites and the Holy Rollers. Their sales quota in the entire United States and Europe and Australia couldn't gross over two million. . . .

I see by your advance publicity that Andy Mellon is mixed up with you. That Guy is mixed up in every business in the world, and now he's in the Church business—Treasurer as usual. I will help you on one condition and that is, if you Presbyterians get your 15 Millions, you will help us Methodists get $483.27. That's this year's quota and we feel that we shot a little high on it. . . .

Enclosed find check for $100. to compensate you for your ambition. You notice the check is made out to Andy. I don't want you to think I didn't trust you, because I do. In fact, I trust you just as much as I do him. It should have been made out to "Hays and Mellon—Probable Beneficiaries, the Presbyterians." Please don't allow Mellon to apply this on the National Debt; I'd just as soon it would reach the Foreign Missions as that.

You may raise this, Bill; anything is possible in politics. Look what Vare and Smith raised. When you do get it, save the heathen and the Movies first.

I am praying that justice won't be done in your case, William.

An Amateur Highbinder—
Yours—WILL.

Obviously, a plan was the first thing to develop. So in close co-operation between the Board of Ministerial Relief and the Laymen's Committee, and with the invaluable help of actuaries from two of the great insurance companies, there was drawn up a modern, self-perpetuating, contributory pension system. It was based on a wealth of actuarial experience, including data on our own ministers, and it made use of all the knowledge of pension funds that could be found. The basic elements were simple, and because people could understand them, it proved an easy plan to sell. The most important features were these: the pension plan was based on length of service and average salary; it was available to ministers, missionaries, and other employed workers of the church, and also to their widows and minor children; it was operative normally at the age of sixty-five, even without requiring retirement, but it could be invoked earlier in case of disability. An extremely fair and considerate feature of the plan was that for those of sixty-five or more years of age, still in active service, it provided a minimum retirement pension of six hundred dollars, provided they registered within one year—this latter provision to be financed out of the Laymen's Committee fund of fifteen million dollars.

We made our first announcement in 1923 at the General Assembly held that year at Indianapolis. Representing the laymen, I opened my address with the slogan used so often during the campaign: "Religion is the one essential industry in the world," and went on: "The management of that industry is in the hands of ministers. Though its genesis is divine and its revelations are eternal, its usefulness and, indeed, its survival are in the hands of these administrators. For this life of service their average material compensation is less than that paid our garbage collectors. This situation, long endured, is an economic and moral crime." And I closed my statement thus: "Our so-called soulless corporations, with more conscience than most of our churches in this regard, all find it good business to pension their faithful employees; the Army and Navy set splendid examples; the City of New York extends the same benevolence even to the horses of the fire department when they are worn out, and sends them to the upstate farm to be cared for during the rest of their lives.

"It is grotesque to be caring for the old age of firemen, policemen, soldiers, workmen in all other lines—just and wise as all this is—yet leaving the leaders of our really indispensable work to the tender mercies of a frigid world! We will raise what is needed, of course—without question, without hesitation, without apprehension."

It sometimes seems as if the rhythm of my life had been marked by a long series of national conventions beginning way back in 1896; but the General Assembly of 1924, which unanimously adopted the perfected pension plan, was one of the most satisfying. It authorized the Board of Ministerial Relief to proceed with the enrolling of the four thousand churches and the four thousand ministers needed to initiate it.

For the next two years, while churches and ministers were joining, the Laymen's Committee came gradually to realize the necessity of building up a broad national organization. In the early stages too many people, merely by wishful thinking, hoped the money could be secured from a small number of wealthy families. This was only an unwise hope.

Small efforts were not going to earn big results. So we worked ahead in two directions: in drawing up the story and telling it to selected groups of individuals, through both inspirational meetings and booklets, and in building carefully toward a "National Committee of 100."

Early in 1926, convinced that we needed the best professional advice and counsel on our plan of campaign, we were fortunate in securing the services of Mr. Arnaud C. Marts, president of Marts & Lundy, Inc., who had directed some large fund-raising projects. He brought to the undertaking the judgment of an experienced campaign director and, as such, he guided the work of our Laymen's Committee in completing its job. His ability and wisdom, his understanding and Christian character, his indefatigable industry and deep devotion were large factors in the conduct and ultimate success of the campaign.

In April of 1926 two hundred men—members of the National Committee, other laymen and representative ministers—in an all-day conference at the Bankers Club in New York, discussed the whole project and agreed on a line of march. It was emphasized that pensions are not charity but a form of "profit sharing," after the service which made the profit possible has been rendered, or a form of withheld pay, given back in an equitable and businesslike way. Although it was primarily a laymen's job, it was agreed that a tremendous amount of help from the ministers would be needed if we were to carry the message to the whole church.

By this time the logic of the program was so clear that, as chairman, I was able to go before the 1926 General Assembly in Baltimore on May 29 and announce that we were ready to launch the intensive campaign, since enough churches and ministers were ready to go into the plan, and tell them that "we were very certain that it must be made the major purpose of the church and be taken to the whole membership." It was no small satisfaction to be able to say that "all the money collected will go to the fund itself," as the money for the necessary work entailed had been contributed by a handful of men. Many a time during the following year, when ministers and workers from far and wide were invited into the larger centers to attend inspirational or report meetings, someone would ask: "Who's paying the expenses?" When he heard the answer—"Andy Mellon"—he would say, "Okay! I'll come."

And that reminds me of the last gift made toward the expense fund, and the inspiration that came from the response of that fine old gentleman, Captain Robert Dollar of the steamship line, and from his splendid wife.

I came to Los Angeles to meet them when they were down from San Francisco, and asked them if they would be willing to give thirty thousand dollars needed, in addition to what we had, to pay for the expenses of the drive. I told them of Mr. Mellon's gifts. I remember the morning so well when these fine old people, both over eighty, heard my story and old Captain Dollar said to his gray-haired, lovely wife, "What do you think about it, Mother?" And Mrs. Dollar said, "I think we should do it, Robert." And their smiles and their blessings meant as much to me personally as their reputation and endorsement meant to the cause.

At this 1926 General Assembly meeting in Baltimore, the General Assembly unanimously adopted a resolution "calling on every pastor and church and individual member to co-operate in the campaign."

Now our forward march began in earnest. We aimed to span the country with our appeal in exactly one year! By dint of continued efforts, we had built our National Committee up to 210, choosing one or more outstanding laymen from each of the presbyteries. These men pledged themselves to lead the intensive phase of the campaign—the personal solicitation of gifts—in their respective territories. The country was divided into four regions, which were campaigned from East to West with all the forces we could muster. It was our aim to reach down through many channels into the life of every local church and into the heart of every individual Presbyterian.

The first region, composed of the Pennsylvania, Baltimore, and West Virginia synods, we covered during September and October, opening an office in each presbytery: the presbytery chairman appointed an executive committee of laymen, and he asked each local church to appoint a committee which would solicit their prospective contributors. From the presbytery headquarters Pension Fund literature was mailed out. A series of inspirational meetings was held at the central point of the territory for pastors and representative laymen engaged in the effort. On a designated "Pension Sunday" pastors were asked to preach on the project. But no public appeal for funds was made. The committee in each church personally solicited their own possible contributors and gathered for two or three report meetings to maintain unity of endeavor and to receive inspiration to complete their job. Never have I seen more efficient campaign meetings nor a better spirit among campaign workers.

After this first region was completed, we moved to the New York, New Jersey, and New England synods, where we followed the same plan through November and December. During January and February our forces worked in Ohio, Michigan, Indiana, and Kentucky, with the tide of interest steadily rising.

"On March 15," as the director of the campaign summarized it, "the Laymen's Committee commended the organization of the last region in their spectacular westward march, and set for themselves the task of organizing the intensive appeal in the fourteen Synods of the Central and Far West, from Illinois to California, with the announced intention of completing the entire campaign in time for Mr. Hays to make his final report to the General Assembly on May 28, 1927, at San Francisco." By that time millions of dollars had accumulated and such momentum had been gained that it was possible to achieve this imposing undertaking; and when I stepped upon the platform of the General Assembly I was able to report $15,045,000 in hand, with many other thousands reported on the way, and was able to announce that the Pension Plan could go into operation at once.

As I look back to that morning in San Francisco, the significant thing was the number of people who had served unselfishly in that campaign, and the sum total of their personal loyalties! More than 110,000 families had subscribed to the Pension Fund. The individual gifts ranged all the way from twenty-five cents to $300,000. Over thirty thousand men and women had worked actively and earnestly on the numberless committees! And better still, as I reported that day, "never in my experience have I known giving with such grace and with so little necessity of argument."

The newspapers of the nation were of the greatest service. Clippings on the Pension Fund campaign fill scores of scrapbooks. I here confess that I have kept them. I suppose they are one of the many reasons why my family and every secretary I have ever had call me sometimes, with a deep sigh, a "saver." But this particular record of the Pension Plan is testimony which I have no wish to destroy. An editorial in the Chicago *Tribune* closed with this thought: "Ministers cannot live by religion only. They need bread. And man needs both religion and good ministers."

As I look back through the years, it would be hard for me to pick out any single endeavor that has given me more satisfaction, both in the doing and in reflection, than the Pension Fund. And it would be hard to find a finer body of folks than the thousands of men and women who responded when the laymen and the ministers both called, "Let's get together and do this thing."

Another proof of the rightness of this enterprise is the richness of its "by-products," which our final report gave occasion to point out. The cause was so appealing that it leaped across denominational boundaries: the first substantial gift was five thousand dollars from a Baptist in Washington, and the last was fifty thousand dollars from a Catholic in California. This is America!

One result that came as a welcome surprise to some who had been fearful about it was that the generous and widespread giving to the Pension Fund stimulated, rather than decreased, giving to other regular and special causes. Giving, like so many other good things in life, seems to be a habit that has to be learned and that, once learned, gives a lot of pleasure. One elder in a little village church wrote us: "Since the Pension Fund campaign, we have had our annual budget campaign, and we raised 65 per cent more than we raised a year ago."

Another constructive by-product was that our project stimulated the pension cause in other communions. Leaders of at least six other denominations told us that our results encouraged their own pension boards to undertake more complete plans.

I firmly believe that this great group gift by more than a hundred thousand Christian families not only brought joy to the homes of ten thousand devoted ministers and missionaries but bore striking witness to our common faith in the Fatherhood of God and in the brotherhood of man.

One of the most treasured recollections of my life is of that moment on the platform during the General Assembly of 1927 when the Reverend Andrew Mutch, D.D., of Bryn Mawr turned to me and said: "Mr. Hays, it is a great honor and a high privilege that falls to me, as president of the Board of Pensions, to hand to you and ask you to accept this watch from the ministers of your church. You and your committee undertook a colossal task . . . and you have reported the task accomplished."

The inscription on the watch reads:

Presented to

WILL H. HAYS

by the Ministers of the Presbyterian Church
U. S. A.
in Appreciation of His Leadership
in Establishment of the

SERVICE PENSION FUND

San Francisco, May 28th, 1927

But let one of those faithful servants, for whose relief the church united to create the new Pension Fund, say the last word. His letter came to me from a little town in Iowa only a few days after the completion of our effort:

The Hon. Will H. Hays,
Most honored and dear Sir:
My heart thrilled over the results of that which you and your splendid committee has accomplished for the beloved ministers of our church.
I wrote to my boys—four of them—and signed cards, and told them, they who knew my life of sacrifice, that they should honor that which I signed for them and myself. . . .
Myself—$25. per year
My doctor son—$25. per year

Aubrey—Ralph—Arthur—and another adopted son, each $10. per year—and I told them if they could not meet it, I should manage to somehow.

Their loving replies, proudly responding, thrilled my heart. I am facing sixty-eight years old—have served only in our beloved church for forty-two years—have raised those dear boys—and this year am told "that this church needs a younger man," and so am leaving to supply a small country church—at about half my salary.

My pension will be a boon, for I have not been able to save anything, scarcely enough to move with to the country place—and so you see what a blessing this has brought to me for so long a service.

I cannot but lovingly thank you for your inspired heart, and thoughts, and your splendid ability in being able to do this for me—us—and I do most sincerely thank you.

I shall always have a thrill when your name comes to me, for it will always remind me that I petition the adorable throne, to thank God for your gracious work truly heaven-inspired.

Believe me—very truly yours, in Him.

CHAPTER 34

In the Fullness of Time

LATE in 1947 the Columbia Broadcasting System instituted a new feature program under the general title of "What Ever Happened To ——?"—which E. H. Gammons, a vice-president of CBS, told me was proving very popular. The broadcast of November 26 was titled, "What Ever Happened to Will Hays?" Commenting on the public's response, Mr. Gammons said that "even in this busy world, sometimes your friends remember you, which I am sure would be the case among the many who know you." In writing to him about the program when he suggested it to me, I had said that that was a question I ask myself when things go so fast that one can't see the fence posts.

The CBS broadcast was introduced with these words: "Here is a story out of the past. News of yesterday, against a background of today. A reminder that good news stories do not grow old." Let's hope not!

We have all discovered how the past lives on in the present and how it keeps repeating itself in different forms. But how much depends upon the way we read it and what we ourselves bring to that reading! Especially by our convictions about the things that do not change. So I want to turn over the pages of these last few years, in the light of all that has gone before. I find that my fundamental convictions have changed little.

When in the autumn of 1945 I resigned the presidency of the Motion Picture Association, to be followed by Eric Johnston, my interest by no means ended. I was made adviser to the organized industry for a period of five years, to render such services as might be requested either in New York or Hollywood. During this period one very big job was handed me.

Along the way came many experiences to keep me in touch with the expanding and constantly debated influence of the screen. One of the first was the formal acceptance, on behalf of the motion picture industry, of a citation for its contribution to American unity and tolerance, awarded by the National Conference of Christians and Jews. Referring especially to its magnificent war service, I told them that because my role was now impersonal I had no inhibitions in declaring the tribute well deserved.

The Association's principles of self-government and its form of organization continued to serve as a model for other groups. In replying to one request for information from a big industry on the Pacific coast, I explained that we had tried to demonstrate that a highly competitive business can still regulate itself and thereby obtain the freedom of operation necessary for the maintenance of the American system.

The biggest job that came to me, and one of the most difficult I ever encountered in connection with our foreign trade, was what we called the "Arbitration of French Remittances." Millions of dollars due American motion picture companies on wartime film rentals, and still held up, were about to be transferred to America. Owing to war and post-war conditions and to extremely complicated problems of foreign distribution and exchange, the exact division of the money among the several companies seemed to defy solution. No formula for procedure of settlement could be found. It was a perfect illustration of the difficulties that could arise in conducting such large operations abroad.

Finally, all the company presidents asked me to arbitrate the case and mutually agreed to accept any decision that I rendered. We set up a court of arbitration, heard evidence, argument, and counterargument for months on end. Scores of exhibits were involved, as well as many delays for reciprocal examination of figures and other evidence. With many points of law and trade custom involved, the records ran into volumes. After more than a year of hearings, my decision was rendered and accepted. I confess it was a load off my mind. But I was honored that they should have called on me to handle such a problem.

During these same days came a sharp recollection of a wartime experience touching Russia. It was brought back one day in 1950 when Commander John S. Young, an aide to Admiral William H. Standley when he was our Ambassador to Russia, called on me in New York. Our conversation revolved around the admiral's historic statement of March 8, 1943, exposing Russian attitudes now only too well confirmed, and a subsequent personal request that resulted in a large shipment of our films to Russia early that summer, in the personal charge of Commander Young.

It is an amazing story, amply documented in the files of the Association and of the newspapers, but too long to be detailed here. As Ambassador to Russia in 1942 and 1943, the admiral bore a distinguished record of service to the Navy and to our country in other capacities. He was independent, realistic, and fearless. As a member of the Beaverbrook-Harriman mission to Moscow in 1941, he had seen enough to keep his eyes and ears open. The first-page story in the New York *Times* of March 9, 1943, with a dateline "Moscow, Mar. 8," began: "Admiral William H. Standley, United States Ambassador, said today that news of important American aid was being kept from the Russian people, and he suggested that Russian authorities sought to give the impression that Russia was fighting the war entirely alone."

The industry's experience with its shipment of films proved equally unsatisfactory, and far more protracted. Though they were ready within two weeks, and though we had a complete understanding with our State Department and our Embassy in Moscow, Russia put unbelievable obstacles in the way of the films' arrival. Ready to start in July, they did not reach Russia until mid-December—long after Admiral Standley had been recalled. And through the OWI we were soon to receive word of the inability of the Russian Government to live up to the letter of the "gentleman's agreement" made with our industry about the pre-viewing, exhibition, and control of the films. At one point Admiral Standley's successor cabled the OWI: "The Soviet Government cannot [he meant should not] be treated with mistrust and suspicion by the motion picture industry. . . ."

Suffice it to say that for three years the motion picture companies repeatedly had to seek the aid of the Association and of the State Department in regaining possession of their properties—it must be remembered that theatrical films are rented, not sold—and that as late as 1950 the Association could not be sure that all the films had come back.

Some of us found it hard to understand how Admiral Standley's statement should have caused any reaction here. But we appreciated his belief that our motion pictures could at least help convey the spirit of America to the Russian people, however difficult this continues to prove.

During these last years both the industry and its pioneers have been celebrating some important anniversaries. On the personal side, the most notable was Adolph Zukor's completion of fifty years in motion pictures, a record of vision and achievement hard to match.

Opportunity to pay my personal tribute to Mr. Zukor came when he received the Grand Lodge 50-Year Service Medal on the anniversary of his entrance into the Masonic Order. Because of our long association, I had been asked to serve as master of ceremonies and to speak in behalf of the motion picture industry. Without reservation I bore testimony to our old friend as a great co-operator, leader, citizen, and friend.

The maturity of the industry was brought home to me in other ways. In September of 1948 appeared a notable anniversary volume of the *Motion Picture Herald* entitled "Martin Quigley's Third of a Century." Terry Ramsaye, in his editing, threw a mellow spotlight on notable motion picture events and personalities as recorded in thirty-three years of Quigley publications. Glancing through the pages of this bird's-eye review—with its interpretive narration, its pictures from the old files, its excerpts from editorials on questions that had held us through the years, its striking glimpses of then and now—brought the long story into perspective. It made me glad I had been a part of the procession!

Five years later a similar record appeared. Under the title "35 Years Is a Long Time in Pictures," the *Film Daily* published it thirty-fifth anniversary volume, again chock-full of reminiscences. In a section called "The Film Daily Family Album" I found scores of early pictures of the men I had later known as they hammered away at the big thing they had in common—the motion picture.

And to remind me once more of the way I had spent the last thirty years myself, I was asked to write the Foreword for a book which came out in 1952, entitled *Hollywood, U.S.A.—From Script to Screen.* I was glad to do it because the book, by Alice Evans Field, was the outgrowth of the steady educational work the Association had done in building up popular taste and appreciation.

The fast-moving years since 1945 have continued to bring home the fact that the motion picture is always the child of its own generation. Though it helps to shape popular thought, it is itself a storm center for the interplay of forces, mechanisms, and demands that are constantly changing.

No one knows this better than the men who make the pictures. Knowing an emergency when they see it coming, they try to meet it in advance. Though I always felt the universal appeal of the screen, no one longer imagines that it has any exclusive hold on that universality. The tremendous growth of television—the motion picture technique brought into the home—has made the whole picture industry re-examine itself. The only proper result should be better techniques and better service in both fields.

Within the motion picture's own field, as we know better every day, tremendous efforts are being made to give the public the "bigger and better" pictures believed capable of holding their own against any competition. Thus 3-D, CinemaScope, wide screen, and all the rest! The motion picture is still on the march!

In the autumn of 1950 there appeared in the *Motion Picture Herald* a story with the title, "Will Hays Takes to Private Life and Goes Back Home to Vote." No twelve words could say it better. And Terry Ramsaye, the author, was generous enough to begin his story: "The Industry of the Motion Picture passed a tall milestone in its history the other day—the end of three decades of Will H. Hays. It began March 5, 1922, when the industry was just filling out its stature and maturity as a world institution, signalized by a pox of problems coming with recognition of responsibility." Recounting a recent visit in my study, technically a journalistic interview, Terry quoted me as saying: "I have come at last to what I set out for when I left Washington—private life."

When it finally came—as much as it ever came—it meant, for one thing, a little more time to think of Indiana and politics. Neither had ever been "out of sight, out of mind." As Terry had an imaginary Sullivan neighbor explaining: "He's got plenty to attend to if he wants to —a lot of farm and law offices, big one here and 'nother in Indianapolis. . . . Anybody want to guess how he voted?"

There had never been any long period when I had not gotten back home. One of the most important occasions was the 1945 Indianapolis mass meeting of the Indiana Committee for Victory, when I spoke on "World Peace and the San Francisco Conference." Ed Stettinius and I had talked about how I might help to influence the public's attitude toward the approaching conference. He felt it could best be done if I were to speak as an individual rather than from any official connection with our American delegation. So it was arranged that I speak over a national hookup from Indianapolis, making the theme American cooperation in international relations. Twenty-five of the strongest civic groups of Indiana jointly sponsored the occasion on which I pleaded as strongly as I could for unity within our own country and between nations. I felt that the purposes at stake represented a sharp challenge to the core of reason and tolerance in the American character. I could not help thinking back to the days when we were seeking unity at Versailles.

The most important Republican gathering in which I participated during this period occurred in Washington in 1949. It was a dinner at the Mayflower Hotel on August 4, given by the Republican membership of the House and the Senate for the members of the Republican National Committee. Asked to make the principal speech, I felt deeply the significance of the occasion and the honor paid me as one of the alleged "elder statesmen." At least I had been a working party member for almost fifty years. For wider circulation the talk was reprinted from the *Congressional Record* under the title, "The Central Issue of These Times Is between Government OF the People and Government OVER the People."

In October I was again back home for "Republican Day in Indiana" —and making another speech! It was a real old-time home-coming, reminding me of the years I had been so immersed in the politics of my state. The luncheon, reception, and dinner brought together past state chairmen and vice-chairmen; past national committeemen; Republican U.S. senators and congressmen; the ninety-two county chairmen and vice-chairmen, with their committeemen and party workers; and other specially invited guests. The meetings, under the leadership of Cale J. Holder, state chairman, sought to point up the crusade of 1950, to demonstrate party interest in victory at the next election, and to reawaken party workers to the job ahead. Here was really something special that prompted me to exclaim:

"It's good to be home!

"In the last three decades I have spent much time in areas like New York and Hollywood and Washington, but my heart has always remained right here as a pledge. It is, I suppose, the comfort of having body and heart in the same place that accounts for the warm glow that fills me tonight, as always on Indiana soil."

A striking headline in the *News Sentinel* of Fort Wayne, commenting editorially on my talk, read, "Hays Says GOP Can Save Americans' Fate." Well, I won't deny it.

One of the quieter activities of these days came in counseling an occasional graduate student on his thesis in the field of political science. These requests for help were spontaneous and purely personal, but I was delighted that such a subject as "The National Chairmanship" should have become a matter of historic and academic interest. And to show how youngsters are being awakened to civic interest, I received a delightful request from the fifth grade of the Branciforte Elementary School of Santa Cruz, California. They said they were "eager to form good habits of citizenship" and asked for suggestions. I sent a copy of a talk on citizenship, and I mentioned some of the lessons I had learned as a boy, such as that friendship is the natural feeling between fellow citizens, and that good will—not hate—makes it possible for people to live and work together for their mutual benefit.

Like so many of my fellow citizens, I have continued to be deeply concerned over the evil power of Communism, in any form or degree. More than once I have recalled a prophetic article that appeared way back in the March 1919 issue of the *North American Review* by the editor, the brilliant George Harvey, later our Ambassador to Great Britain and my host there in 1923. It was entitled, "The Political Situation. The Issue: Socialism vs. Americanism."

Here I find another instance of the almost fantastic analogy between the years following the two world wars. In those earlier years the danger of Socialism was a new thing, hardly to be considered seriously, but men like Harvey saw the issue. At one point he put the question in terms of what he called Mr. Wilson's "programme," saying, in words that raise many questions:

He has forsaken nationalism and espoused internationalism. His proposed League or Association of Nations is wide as the world itself and, so far from conferring benefits on this country, it not only violates all the traditions of the Fathers of the Republic but, under any one of the plans yet suggested, could not fail to add greatly to our own burdens, to the enormous advantage of Germany and, in a lesser degree, of England, France and Italy, as well as of the smaller states. . . .

The extent to which Mr. Wilson will attract our own people to his stand-ard of socialistic government, hidden within the Society of Nations, has yet to be measured. . . .

For ourselves, we welcome the test. It must come sometime; it might as well come now. And we have no question of the result. . . .

And this was written in 1919!

On the question of Communism in the United States today, I have relied much upon my good friend of many years, J. Edgar Hoover, one of America's great public servants. To me, it is stark atheism and stark treason if, in the words of William Z. Foster, quoted in one of Hoover's informative articles, "the workers of this country and the workers of every country have only one flag, and that is the red flag."

This political phase of my story found its "happy ending" in the re-sounding election of General Dwight D. Eisenhower in November of 1952. I would not minimize my satisfaction over this event. And I believe it was the culmination of many forces and the will of many Americans. One concrete expression of this will, it seems to me, came in Raymond Moley's book, *How to Keep Our Liberty,* published in 1952. There he sought not only to describe the current trend toward Socialism in the United States, but to present an alternative series of policies and to show the citizen exactly how he could help put them into effect.

When President Eisenhower took office, it would have been difficult for me to refrain from adding my personal word of support. In my letter I again voiced my faith that "the heart of America is sound," continuing:

That heart spoke in the November election, calling for a return to principles that have made America strong. I am sure that no man believes in those prin-ciples more strongly than do you. How to make them prevail in a vastly complicated government and how to make them influential in a confused, threatened world is the greatest responsibility to which a man could be called. I can assure you that you enter upon this high duty with an uplifting tide of support from the men and women of America.

My belief in the influence of the church on the life of the world has only grown stronger with the years. I have tried to express this belief in any way I could. For instance, in "A Tribute to Ministers," which I was asked to contribute to a pamphlet series called *Selected Sermon Briefs,* I stated my conviction quite simply: "They insure the perpetuity of the Church, without which the Republic would die."

A most practical project in line with this conviction presented itself in 1946: the Presbyterian Restoration Fund, with a goal of twenty-seven million dollars. Here was another analogy, for twenty years before I had been chairman of the Laymen's Committee that raised fifteen million dollars for the Presbyterian Pension Fund—of which, in a broader sense, this was an extension. Now the appeal reached out to other lands where war had wrought havoc with churches, clergy, and people. In one talk I raised the question as to whether we were "concerned that the Christian Gospel be preached and taught to people who are valiantly fighting to keep Christianity alive against the growing pressure of atheistic Communism." Again, with a splendid response, the goal was reached.

Various other forms of philanthropic effort, especially in education and health, had increasing appeal as a lessening of routine duties made it possible for me to give them more attention.

The work of the Institute for the Crippled and Disabled, which I was happy to serve as a trustee, has been an inspiring thing to watch. The vision and hard work of my friend Jeremiah Milbank have resulted in rehabilitation achievements that are equally to the credit of science and the patients and, in end result, almost miraculous.

The Will Rogers Memorial Hospital at Saranac Lake has always been close to my heart. It is one of his truest memorials. Here is a unique institution, "owned" by everybody in the amusement industry Will loved so well. There, anyone in the industry needing tuberculosis treatment can have it freely. Naturally, the motion picture industry has always been a strong financial supporter.

It goes without saying that my Alma Mater, Wabash College, has never long been out of mind. And lately I have been particularly happy about two growing trends: the increasing appreciation by professional and business leaders of what the small liberal arts college contributes to the making of valuable citizens, and a parallel increase in the financial support that industrial corporations are giving the colleges. This rising tide of practical interest in what educators call the "humanities," including spiritual values, is a good sign.

A civic testimonial to another great American, brought to completion during these years, involved men of every faith. I was glad to accept Cardinal Spellman's invitation to serve on the executive group of the National Memorial Committee of the Alfred E. Smith Memorial-St. Vincent Hospital Campaign. As the Cardinal wrote: "No one American in our time was ever more beloved than Alfred Emanuel Smith. . . . And we know that of the treasury of Al Smith's many graces, one of the most memorable and lovable was his grace to give—to give freely of all he had, to give fully of all he was." A great wing of the hospital now carries on this unselfish giving. Here is another perfect example of philanthropy.

One more instance—and this is unique and individual too—is Flanner House, situated in the heart of a Negro section of Indianapolis. Late in 1948 I had the pleasure of helping to celebrate its fiftieth anniversary as an effective community center. In its editorial following the celebration, the Indianapolis *Star* rightly quoted me as having said at the anniversary luncheon: "Flanner House is not concerned with a class, or even a race, but with individual men, women and children. . . . Here is an institution, here are a group of men and women, whose efforts transcend charity, for they dispense not only help, but a commodity vastly more valuable. They dispense opportunity. . . . Flanner House does not believe in handing out gifts, but in enabling people to discover and make full use of the gifts that God gave them." And the editorial continued: "Thus Flanner House is a peculiarly American type of charity. Its principles come straight out of the Constitution of our country. Like American democracy itself, it regards the individual as the center of the universe. . . . The American ideal, after all, is not security as a gift, but security as a personal achievement."

One's own life, like that of his country, grows more complicated with the years. New interests develop, but it is hard to drop old ones. I have often found myself saying, in response to a request for participation in some new project: "My frontier is already extended from New York to California, with an important home base in Indiana; I mustn't spread out too thin."

Many earlier interests have continued undiminished, though the activity has taken new forms. The Roosevelt Memorial Association, which we founded in January of 1919 immediately after the colonel's death, and recently renamed the Theodore Roosevelt Association, continues a vital force. Its headquarters continue to be in his former town house on Twentieth Street in New York City, but we were all gratified when his big rambling house at Oyster Bay, where so many people visited him, was made a national shrine. This typical American home, full of the mementos of the colonel's amazing life and breathing the spirit of the vigorous American family, was impressively dedicated by President Eisenhower on June 14, 1953. As a former Postmaster General, I was particularly interested in the fact that the Post Office Department issued a commemorative stamp showing the house just as I had first seen it.

Many Indiana civic projects continued to interest me. One was a banquet honoring John M. Budd, president of the C. & E.I. Railroad, when he left us to go with another line. Another was called the "Save the Shades" campaign, carried on by the Indiana Department of Conservation. I was glad to contribute toward the purchase of this beautiful tract of land so that it might be preserved and added to our Indiana system of state parks. My very good friend Ralph Gates, then governor, was pushing this matter splendidly.

In 1947, in quite another area, I was asked to write a brief statement, which I called "The Supreme Ideal," for the annual observation of

Brotherhood Week. Here came memories stretching way back to high school and college days when I had tried to formulate the same conviction: that it would be hard to find a truer measure of greatness for individual or nation than the extent to which the brotherhood of man is made the final test of action. As far as I know myself, that conviction has never changed.

But ways of daily life have changed mightily, and it is a satisfaction to realize that, like so many of my fellow citizens, I had a little share in some of these changes. For instance, I always kept up my interest in commercial aviation. But it was a real surprise, not long after the plans for this book were known, to receive a letter from one of the aviation leaders, saying: "When you come to the years 1924 and 1925 don't forget to let the world know that you were among the leading crusaders for American aviation. I don't think you know, or ever did know, exactly how much the industry at that time needed the kind of support you gave it." But how vivid is my memory of the vision, initiative, and perseverance of the men who built this colossal American industry. It again came back forcibly when Major Lester D. Gardner, one of these old friends, received the well-deserved Daniel Guggenheim Medal in 1947. We all owe a debt to him and to other pioneers like Charles Lawrence, Sam Bradley, Glenn Martin, Chance Vought, and A. P. Loening—those friends of the middle twenties.

A free and responsible press has always seemed to me one of our strongest civic bulwarks. I have always counted on the press as an ally and have seldom been disappointed. Two things recently brought this home to me once more.

In 1947, Frank B. Noyes, the then eighty-three-year-old president of the Washington *Evening Star,* received a notable tribute that reflected credit on the press as a whole. The members of the Associated Press adopted a resolution praising his fifty-four years of service on its Board of Directors and its predecessor, the old Illinois Corporation. Mr. Noyes was honored as the last surviving founder of AP and its first president— from 1900 to 1938—to whom the Association and the public owed a great debt. The event interested me all the more because the man elected to succeed him as a director was my friend Norman Chandler of the Los Angeles *Times,* whose father, Harry Chandler, had helped to correct an early wave of unjustified press attacks on Hollywood.

About the same time another bit of evidence came to me in an exchange of letters with Seymour Berkson, managing editor of INS, who sent me a copy of his article which had appeared in *Editor and Publisher* —"A Working Program for Freedom of the Press." Copies of the article had been sent to the State Department and to the chairman of the U.S. delegation to the U.N.O. I welcomed this opportunity to discuss once more a topic which, both in its original form and as "Freedom of the Screen," was so long my daily companion.

Glancing back across more than half a century of adult life—and what a half century in the world's life!—one must ask himself: "*How do things look?*" Never were contrasts sharper: between peace and war; between our national prosperity and great regions of poverty; between order and chaos; between West and East. But it seems to me that a striking thing is happening. In the midst of blatant confusion and atheism, a quiet undercurrent of faith seems to be left. Among the best-selling books, more than once the majority recently have been books with a clear spiritual message. Several could have shared the title that had such an appeal—*This I Believe*. On every side thoughtful men have been voicing the same conviction: what the world needs is a return to God.

In this conviction one of our strong Indiana newspapers, the Indianapolis *Star,* ran a series of articles in its Sunday magazine under the general heading "I Believe." Eugene Pulliam, the editor, asked me to contribute a statement which appeared in April of 1951 under the title "Faith Is the Key." Because it was so truly autobiographical I want to quote a few words of the opening:

I am grateful that I always believed in God. It has seemed perfectly natural. At any time in my life—as I look back through the years—it would have been a struggle to give up that belief. Trying to live in a world without God would have been unthinkable.

In the autumn of that year there occurred a journalistic event that seemed to me significant. In an editorial in the *Star* on Sunday, November 4, 1951, it was announced that the paper had changed its motto from "Fair and First" to "Where the Spirit of the Lord is, There is Liberty."

Lately I encountered another statement of the American ideal that struck me as so eloquent and so true that I asked Dr. Francis Pendleton Gaines, president of Washington and Lee University, for a copy. I want the privilege of quoting a few sentences, since they express my own creed too:

In the perspective of the centuries, the contribution of America is to be not cloud-piercing architecture, not unprecedented gadgets for the comfortableness of life, not military prowess diverting the current of history. The contribution of our country is an idea—the American idea. . . .

The essence of the idea is the substitution of an inner aspiration for outer authority. An educator might define it as "the incentive philosophy of a free people. . . ."

This freedom translated into the great world is the promise of the American idea—freedom boldly to dream, mightily to struggle, richly to achieve. . . .

Some personal ties seem more precious as the activities in which they were formed fade into the distance. One such is my memory of the late Bill Hart—the two-gun William S. Hart of the "silent." His last letter to me was full of nostalgia as he wrote:

DEAR PARDNER BILL HAYS:

You write of the times we had together—being always fresh in your mind. It is the same here, Bill Hays. It is a vivid remembrance to me, too! A one hundred per cent exemplification of real men's enjoyment. Not forgetting it was just about tops in personnel too! Cecil deMille, Jesse Lasky, Bill Hays and Bill Hart. The rustic cabin and the mountain streams . . .

Yes! I gave my old home to Los Angeles.

When I kick off I intend this my present home shall travel the same trail. The public will get it—one of the finest homes in California. I love every foot of its acres, and my dumb animals that roam over these hills.

When you drift this way—don't forget me.

I have never wavered in my liking for you, although at times the trail has been full of rough stones and sharp daggers.

Almost at the same moment, but from the other side of the country, came similar friendly words from a stalwart in the academic world who was perhaps almost as fond of the political arena. After I had congratulated Dr. Nicholas Murray Butler on his retirement after forty-four years in office as head of Columbia and sixty-seven years' association with it, I received an immediate reply with words pleasant to hear. In particular he spoke of a week of campaigning he had given us in Indiana in 1916, saying: "I well recall the fact that owing to your foresight and method of organization we carried the State of Indiana in splendid fashion. All this is now a happy memory and I shall never forget it."

One of the strongest ties that has held through the years is that with Herbert Hoover, from the days when he helped to guide our Council of Defense in Indiana, and our year together in President Harding's Cabinet, to our recent years as neighbors in the Waldorf Towers in New York. And surely nothing in these later years has given me deeper satisfaction than to feel our citizens' growing appreciation of this great man's services to America, now spanning four decades—national and international services of the highest value. Where can we find his like! In his 1949 book, 27 *Masters of Politics*, Raymond Moley included Hoover among five "party choices," but with the poetic title "A Stone Rejected." He was referring particularly to the fact that the following administration declined his offered co-operation. But in these late years, in connection with two great Hoover commissions dealing with the complex problems of governmental administration, that "stone" has been given its due place in our national arch. Jim Farley and I were included in the book as "Party Managers." Again on the closer personal side, as in day-to-day associations, Herbert Hoover's friendship, counsel, and understanding have been something beyond words to describe. As to his great seventy-fifth birthday party, it made on all of us a deep impression.

This long story must be brought to a close in the spot where it opened —in my home town of Sullivan, in the southwest corner of Indiana, in the Wabash River valley.

First and last, I have taken a lot of joshing about things back home in Indiana—including my story of catfish. I had told Terry Ramsaye about a time when two catfish, weighing respectively 90 and 110 pounds, were caught at the same time on the same trotline. I also told him that this unprecedented event was a fine thing for the law firm of Hays & Hays, for Father was in the boat with the Wabash River fishermen when the line was taken up and was able to substantiate the authenticity of the miracle. Nothing ever excelled for local publicity the attention the name of Hays received that time in our region! Commenting humorously on my story in the columns of the *Motion Picture Herald*, Terry wrote: "The pursuit of the catfish is the perfect pastime of the philosopher. One drops the bait to the bottom and awaits results. They may be had immediately—or never. There is no hurry." Well, I don't know whether I learned that lesson from catfishing, but there have been plenty of times in politics and in the motion picture cavalcade when I had to wait years for something to come about. But it didn't just happen; I was doing my best to help it along.

From generation to generation our country, and the families in it, daily weave the fabric of history, whether we sense it or not. Every family is a thread woven into the fabric. For more than three quarters of a century the office of Hays and Hays has been known in Sullivan. Just as I was taken into partnership with my father, so my son joined me—and my nephew joined his father. But Bill, Jr., developed an even stronger urge to write. Following one of my other paths, he went to Hollywood and co-operated with the late Lamar Trotti on some of the latter's last productions. And then came the event toward which every writer works—the acceptance of his first book. Many a time during the writing we had talked about it. The setting is our own Indiana—but the story is Bill's. It would be a strange father who would not feel justified happiness and pride.

And so I say—God bless the next generation, and the next, and the next. May they have more wisdom and a deeper understanding of the world than we have been able to develop. I hope they may learn something from what we have done. And I hope that the faith of the fathers, woven into the life of our America, may guide them.

Index